THE BLESSINGS OF
ABRAHAM

BECOMING A ZION PEOPLE

Great Sea
(*Mediterranean*)

• Ur
Haran •

• Aleppo

Euphrates R.

• Damascus
• Dan

*Sea of
Galilee*

Shechem
& Salem •
Bethel • • Ai   • Jershon (*Jerash*)
Mount Moriah ▲ (*Jerusalem*)
Hebron •   *Dead Sea*
Beersheba •

Sodom &
Gomorrah

EGYPT

• Memphis

Nile R.

SINAI

N

THE WORLD OF
ABRAHAM

Map © Andy Livingston 2005

Thebes •

Red Sea

0 |▮|▮|▮|▮| 100 miles

THE BLESSINGS OF
ABRAHAM

BECOMING A ZION PEOPLE

E. Douglas Clark

Covenant

Covenant Communications, Inc.

Published by Covenant Communications, Inc.
American Fork, Utah

Printed in Canada
First Printing: October 2005

11 10 09 08 07 06 05   10 9 8 7 6 5 4 3 2 1

ISBN 1-59156-919-2

For my children, Christine, Joseph, and John,

with the hope and confidence that they will prove themselves

true children of Abraham and Sarah

As the seed of Abraham, we . . . are commanded to
come to Christ by doing "the works of Abraham" . . .
to [receive] the blessings of the covenant of Abraham—
"the blessings of salvation, even of life eternal."
—President James E. Faust

Only by "doing the works of Abraham"
can we hope to establish. . . . Zion.
—Hugh Nibley

Do the works of Abraham.
—Doctrine and Covenants 132:32

TABLE OF CONTENTS

FOREWORD

When the BYU Jerusalem Center for Near Eastern Studies was near completion, a discussion was held on what to name it. One proposal was *Beit Abraham*, meaning "house of Abraham."

Why so?

Because in Jerusalem all three monotheistic religions, Judaism, Christianity and Islam—and more inclusively still, the Latter-day Saints—identify with Abraham. Members of each tradition trace crucial elements of their faith, their sense of mission, their aspirations, their mode of life, and even their rituals to him.

The name, it was thought, would suggest that the Center was focused on reconciling the family of Abraham. At the core would be the Messiah. We soon found that many segments of the religious world tend to claim Abraham unto themselves and only themselves. And those divisions run deep. So the name idea was dropped.

Yet common roots go deeper. DNA analysis suggests that 95 percent of the present population of the earth have a genetic connection to Abraham. He has become not only the father of nations but the father of virtually all nations. For these and other reasons, Abraham has been described as the most pivotal man in human history.[1]

In the *Encyclopedia of Mormonism*, Douglas Clark has written a concise and coherent summary of all this. Now in lively detail he has distilled decades of exhaustive study into this book.

The task required that he become adept in Hebrew and related languages, compass the entire spectrum of documents, some only recently recovered, including canonical books, legends, inscriptions, iconography, and apocryphal and pseudepigraphal works. And much else. At the heart of his study are much-neglected insights in the Book of Abraham, the Doctrine and Covenants, and the teachings of the Prophet Joseph Smith.

There is a Biblical and Talmudic admonition never to speak of God as "the God of Abraham, Isaac, and Jacob." But rather as "the God of Abraham, the God of Isaac, and the God of Jacob"—thus to underline that each patriarch and matriarch came directly to God. Each found him in the same way and at the same sacrificial cost.

Our own Book of Abraham describes how Abraham's eyes were opened to wondrous visions of the cosmos and his place in it. He was touched by the hand of God. And then he began to see.

Then what superlative promises and fulfillments came to him and to his? And how do they relate to our destiny in the cause of Christ, which will culminate in the redemption of Zion?

This book is a definitive answer. It enables one to see, with 20/20 clarity, the legacy of Abraham and Sarah and what it means—or can mean—to all the human family. Read on.

Truman G. Madsen

PREFACE

One cannot grow up in the Church, attending seminary and Sunday school, without learning something about the greatness of Abraham. For me, however, he seemed merely one of many such prophets and patriarchs of ages past—until one day as a senior in high school I opened our monthly Church magazine and began to read an article by Dr. Hugh Nibley. The subject was Abraham, whose life was depicted from numerous ancient traditions and sources of which I had never heard. I still cannot adequately express what I experienced, except to say that as I read, I felt irresistibly drawn to this uniquely remarkable man and felt utterly compelled to find out everything possible about him. This book, completed some thirty-five years later, is the result.

The years following high school afforded me increasing opportunities to learn of the great Patriarch. As a student at Brigham Young University, I sat on the front row of Dr. Nibley's Pearl of Great Price class, attended all his lectures on campus, collected all his publications, asked him questions about Abraham, and bought his book *Abraham in Egypt* the day it first appeared in the campus bookstore. Years later I felt honored to be asked to write the foreword to the expanded edition of that book.

Other BYU professors also taught me about Abraham, men like Dr. Truman Madsen, whose stories in our Book of Mormon class about his tour of the Holy Land with President Hugh B. Brown remain vivid in my memory. But it was a research paper assignment in an Old Testament class that allowed me to discover for myself some of the sources that Nibley had quoted. For a week I practically lived in the library, missing all my classes while mining newly found treasures telling of Abraham. So why hadn't someone, I began to ask myself, woven all this information into a comprehensive biography? I was sure that such a book must have been written, and I continued to search for it long after I completed my research paper. Only when I concluded that the book did not exist did I determine to try and write it myself.

Doors seemed to open as I pursued the project. During law school at BYU, Professor John ("Jack") Welch's biblical law seminar afforded me an opportunity to plumb the depths of the story of Isaac's offering in ways I had not done before. Since then I have been a beneficiary of Jack's friendship and significant scholarly contributions.

It was also during law school that I came to feel stymied because I could not read the Genesis story of Abraham in its original Hebrew. Weeks later in a casual conversation with a friend, I happened to learn of a beginning Hebrew seminar to be taught on campus the following summer by David Noel Freedman, renowned biblical scholar and editor-in-chief of Doubleday's prestigious Anchor Bible series. I immediately registered for one of the few remaining slots. On the first day of class, Dr. Freedman announced that he had chosen Genesis 22, the story of Abraham's offering of Isaac, as the text from which to teach us Hebrew.

Our daily classes lasted all morning, and in the afternoons Dr. Freedman kept visiting hours, of which I took full advantage. To my surprise, I was usually the only one there, asking question after question in what turned into personal tutoring sessions on Abraham by Dr. Freedman. The next summer I was fortunate to be a part of his follow-up course.

From Dr. Freedman I learned of the Society of Biblical Literature and its annual meeting, a four-day event held every November that attracts thousands of biblical scholars who present papers, exchange ideas, and discuss research. My attendance at these meetings over the next two decades provided significant opportunities to learn from numerous scholars.

Those same years saw an unprecedented emergence of ancient Abrahamic texts that had been lost or forgotten for many centuries. Much of this material is part of that body of Bible-related literature known as the *pseudepigrapha*—the word literally means "false writings" or "writings with false superscriptions"—so called because it is generally assumed that these texts could not possibly have been written by the purported authors, namely prophets and patriarchs going all the way back to Abraham and Enoch and even Adam. We Latter-day Saints, with our restored scriptures containing actual words of those very men, have a different view of what is possible.

While some of those recently emerged ancient texts have been available for a century or more, many more became available for the first time in the 1980s, with the publication of a massive two-volume set edited by James H. Charlesworth of Princeton. A few years later, thanks to an aggressive media campaign waged by Hershel Shanks, editor of *Biblical Archeology Review*, the remaining unreleased Dead Sea Scrolls, first discovered in the late 1940s, were finally made available. Meanwhile, other ancient documents and traditions have continued to come to light in what might well be called an explosion of biblical texts, greatly expanding our knowledge of the Abraham story. It was an unusually propitious time to be seeking information about him.

During my initial years of law practice in Salt Lake City, I was fortunate to take an evening Hebrew class from John Tvedtnes, and then arranged for private tutoring by him in the Abraham portion of the Hebrew Bible. In the ensuing years, John has magnanimously shared from his extensive knowledge, answering numerous questions I have posed to him about Abraham and other subjects. I was also fortunate to be part of a guest seminar taught at BYU by visiting lecturer Rabbi Aron Siegman, who read the book of Genesis with us in Hebrew and shared with us his lifetime of rabbinical learning. He kindly discussed with me various aspects of the Abraham story and deepened my understanding of the rich rabbinical heritage that preserved so much of that story.

As a young lawyer, I participated in a two-week legal study tour of the Soviet Union. There I saw what I still believe to be the greatest work of Abrahamic art ever produced. It is Rembrandt's immortal masterpiece of Abraham's sacrifice of Isaac, and it hangs in the Hermitage in St. Petersburg (called Leningrad when I was there). The cover of this book is adorned by Abraham's face from that painting, which is fully replicated in black and white in chapter ten. On the day I first saw the painting, I wrote the following in my journal.

> In late afternoon I went into the Hermitage and, after a long and brisk walk, guided by the responses to my repeated question "Where's Rembrandt?," my own eyes beheld Rembrandt's beautiful original canvas *The Sacrifice of Abraham*. I was awed, and remained there for approximately an hour as I studied the painting intensely and reflected on this most graphic and moving depiction. The areas of greatest light on the canvas are Abraham's face and Isaac's youthful body. The knife is in midair, just dropped from Abraham's strong hand. Abraham's face, and particularly the eyes, tell the real story. His brow is wrinkled with intensity. Tears are visible. But the eyes show a resolute submission, a look of having already made the sacrifice. They represent resignation to and trust in the wisdom of Him who ordered the deed; they show a total lack of under-standing of why the deed is necessary, combined with a total resolve to do it; they reveal ultimate obedience, submission; and startled by the voice from heaven, Abraham appears almost in a trance, but ever ready to hear and obey. My eyes were fixed on his eyes for a long while as I tried to contemplate the greatness of the soul of Abraham. My soul was touched, as I realized that I am a descendant of these men, inheritor, through faithfulness, of the blessings of Abraham. I also contemplated the fact that as Abraham did not withhold his son, so God did not withhold a later Son of

both Abraham and God so that all of God's children might be blessed. Standing before that work of art, I vowed to God to finish my book.

Back home as I worked toward my goal, I came to believe that there were important things about Abraham I would not understand until I walked where he had walked. After substantial planning, I traveled for a month to the Mediterranean and the Middle East, where I retraced Abraham's route in the spring of 1987, fortuitously just months before the Intifada closed much of the West Bank that contains key Abrahamic sites. My journey began with a flight from Salt Lake to New York, and then to Rome, where I walked through the Christian catacombs and saw the frescoes of the Bible stories, including the sacrifice of Isaac. Athens was my next stop, where I visited the Agora, where the Apostle Paul had preached the gospel, as he said, in fulfillment of God's covenant to Abraham.

Continuing to Istanbul, I encountered a gracious university professor who liberally imparted from his wealth of knowledge about the area of Urfa (or SanliUrfa, "famous Urfa"), Turkey—my destination as the probable place of Abraham's birth—and then generously shared a disproportionate share of his family's evening meal. From Istanbul I flew west to Ankara, and from there still west to Diyarbakir, where I hired a taxi for the long ride to Urfa. When I explained to the Kurdish driver that I was there to explore the route of Abraham, or Ibrahim, he corrected me with a smile: "Ibrahim Khalil," he emphasized— "Abraham the Friend." The ancient Patriarch's friendship with the Almighty is still a living reality for many of his descendants.

In fact, their friendship seemed to shelter me as I traveled through the land of our mutual forefather, the land "whose hills and valleys echo with the footsteps of the Patriarchs."[1] For two days in Urfa and Haran a young Turkish guide cheerfully guided me with no expectation of reward, recounting the local traditions about the birth and early life of the prophet Abraham. When I left Turkey for Syria, a fellow traveler from Lybia took it upon himself to watch over me and assure my safety as he included me in his small circle of travelers, which included a student from Lebanon and a sheik from Saudi Arabia. Not long before, the United States had bombed Libya, but my Libyan friend assured me earnestly: "Reagan, Qaddafi—enemies. You, me—friends." It seemed remarkable that traveling in Arab lands, where many Americans feared to tread, I felt shielded by the legendary Muslim hospitality that remains part of the living heritage of Abraham.

In Egypt I joined a BYU travel study group for an unforgettable tour of Giza, Luxor, and the Valley of the Kings, where our Book of Abraham, as Parley Pratt described, "slumbered in the bosom of the dead" for over three millennia, "in the sacred archives of Egypt's moldering ruins."[2] Slumbering with it in the Valley of the Kings were many of the once mighty pharaohs who had falsely claimed the patriarchal authority possessed by Abraham.

And as Abraham came out of Egypt to Canaan, so did we. Dann and Shirley Hone graciously put me up in their Jerusalem home and made sure that I got to see every place I desired. I walked around one of Abraham's wells near Beersheba; stood between Bethel and Ai, where Abraham had camped; visited Nablus near where Abraham may have met Melchizedek; looked with wonder on the great stone in Jerusalem's Dome of the Rock, where Abraham nearly offered his son; and went to Hebron, where Abraham entertained the three mysterious strangers and where he was later buried. Even more memorable were my visits to the places where Abraham's preeminent Descendant, the Son of God himself, walked in the flesh, worked his miracles, wrought the Atonement, and rose from the dead—all in fulfillment of the Abrahamic covenant.

Not long after returning home, I was asked to write the article on Abraham for the *Encyclopedia of Mormonism*, a task that required me to stop and crystallize what I had learned about the great Patriarch so far. My expert editor, Dr. Kent Brown of BYU, helped immensely in compressing what I wanted to say into the short space allotted.

As I had left Israel, I was told that visiting Jerusalem would change my life forever. It did, for I soon met the wonderful woman who would become my wife, Mila. We were married in the Salt Lake Temple, where I heard the same phrase that had been spoken many years earlier by an inspired patriarch: "the blessings of Abraham."

Within a couple of years, our growing family moved to Mesa, Arizona, settling in a family neighborhood that at first seemed nothing out of the ordinary. We soon discovered, however, that we had landed among a group of extraordinary saints whose lives were Abrahamic in every important way. They were building Zion by raising a righteous posterity, magnifying their callings, serving in the temple, teaching the gospel, and graciously reaching out in love to bless mankind. I found that I was learning things about Abraham and Sarah that I could not learn in books.

Perhaps it was this experiential convergence of the themes of Zion and Abraham that prepared me to discover a new dimension to the Abraham story that I had somehow missed. One day I was reading for the first time a New Testament apocryphal text called the Revelation of Stephen, which included Stephen's description of the Savior's Second Coming. It was as if I were hearing a familiar melody, but one that I could not quite recognize, and my mind raced to grasp it. It took a few minutes before it dawned on me that I was hearing echoes of the Book of Abraham passage (which is much more detailed than the corresponding biblical account) in which the Lord covenants with Abraham and calls him to go forth to bless the world (Abr. 2:6–11). The parallels between the Abraham and Stephen passages seemed so striking as to defy coincidence. For the first time, I considered the possibility that the

Lord's covenant to Abraham to begin his momentous mission may have been intentionally couched in language looking forward to the latter-day fulfillment of that
covenant. The beginning of the process encompassed the end.

"I thought I knew this story"[3] admitted one modern writer of his "aha" experience with the Abraham story, and so it happened with me as I began to see things
I had never noticed in the story I thought I knew so well. What I came to see was
not only a closer connection between Abraham and the latter-day Zion than I had
imagined, but also that Abraham's mission and accomplishments were in fact all
about Zion. More than merely one additional fact or source among so many, this
was proving to be a key to understanding Abraham, the unifying theme running
throughout his long and eventful life. It is not for nothing that Isaiah's words—
"great words," the Savior called them—urging the righteous to look to Abraham,
also tell why we should do so: "For the Lord shall comfort Zion." Abraham
provides the pattern for his posterity to build Zion.

The global significance of the Abrahamic covenant in our day has come home
to me in an expanded way in the last several years in my work for a pro-family
organization accredited in the United Nations. Attending meetings in New York
and various parts of the world, I have felt continually awed to see the Kingdom of
God rolling forth in direct fulfillment of God's covenant with Abraham to bless all
nations. This is the day to which Abraham and numerous other prophets looked
forward with joy, explained the Prophet Joseph, and it is our privilege to participate in the fulfillment of the covenant to Abraham as we extend his blessings to
our brothers and sisters across the globe.

In reconstructing the life of Abraham and its significance, I begin with the certain-
ties known to us through the Restoration, with its revelations and restored scripture
about Abraham. "Rich treasures"[4] is what Wilford Woodruff called these, and with
good reason, for besides their striking corroboration by the voluminous ancient texts
that have come to light since, their most important information and insights remain
unmatched among any of those additional texts. What these texts do offer is rich
supporting detail consistent with the Restoration's portrait of Abraham. That these texts
hail from such a diversity of places and times is, I have come to believe, a stunning
reflection of the promise made to Abraham that through him and his posterity, all
nations would be blessed. His admiring descendants through the ages and around the
globe carefully preserved their traditions about him. And despite the inevitable speculations and embellishments that accrued along the way, the common core remains a
remarkable witness to the antiquity and authenticity of those traditions. It was Nibley
who observed that "after viewing many texts from many times and places, all telling the
same story, one emerges with the conviction that there was indeed one Abraham story."[5]

And what a story! Studying the life of Abraham is eye-opening, exhilarating, and
ultimately transforming. One begins to see what matters and what the Lord cares

about. One begins also to appreciate as never before the majesty and wisdom of God's great plan, at the center of which is the life and atoning sacrifice of Jesus the Christ.

I am grateful to the many people who have helped me with this project, including the ones mentioned above, plus Abrahamic friends who have blessed my life. They are too numerous to mention all, but include many in the Vineyard Ward in Mesa—like Wilford Andersen, Dea Montague, Terry Chapman, and Reece McNeil—and many others, like George Durrant, Brad Perkinson, Johhn Infanger, Spencer Hatch, Winn Mitchell, Shawn Mitchell, Larry Bluth, David Gates, Mr. Sharon Clark, Steve Lund, Greg Miles, Charlie Davis, Scott Gillette, Bruce Whiting, David Glass, Tom Tipton, Craig Cardon, and especially my brother Rob, whose life is a sermon on Abraham.

I am indebted also to the talented people at Covenant Communications who believed in this book and helped make it better, including Shauna Humphreys, designers Margaret Weber and Kyle Iman, and especially my editors Kirk Shaw and Peter Jasinski, who have cheerfully devoted their expertise and zeal in an effort above and beyond the call of duty. I wish to thank Andy Livingston for his production of the map. Most of all, I am eternally grateful to my wife, Mila, and to our children, Christine, Joseph, and John, and to my parents, Bob and Verna Clark.

The conclusions reached in the book are mine, and do not necessarily reflect the position or belief of any other person or of the publisher or of The Church of Jesus Christ of Latter-day Saints. I alone accept full responsibility for any errors. I also look forward to what I am convinced will be a continuing crescendo of yet additional Abrahamic texts brought forth from antiquity to tell us more about the man whose works we are commanded to do.

Meanwhile, as his descendants and heirs to his blessings, we can indeed rise up and bless him as our forefather as we follow his lead in seeking to bring forth and establish the cause of Zion, offering to all the blessings of Abraham made available through his Descendant Jesus the Christ.

Chronology of Abraham's Life

0	Abram born in Ur of the Chaldees
14	Observes creations, seeks Creator
	Remains pure, prays for guidance, receives answers
	Opposes idolatry and its evils; endures persecution and prison
	Delivered from death on the altar in Ur
	Marries Sarai
	Migrates to Haran, where they live for years
	Studies the patriarchal records and preaches
62	Receives gospel, patriarchal priesthood, call, and promise of posterity
62	Leaves Haran, seeks Enoch's Zion, building Zion as he goes
	Travels to and through the promised land, preaching the gospel
	Forced by famine to travel to Egypt
	On border of Egypt, is taught astronomy by the Creator
	Sarai taken to palace; God protects her, plagues Pharaoh
	Abram heals Pharaoh, sits on throne of Egypt
	Returns to promised land
	Gives Lot the land of his choice
	Wages military rescue of Lot and the people of Sodom
	Pays tithing, receives Melchizedek Priesthood
	Performs covenant ceremony, ascends to heaven
86	Marries Hagar, who bears Ishmael
99	Abram circumcised; name changed to Abraham
99	Visited by three messengers
99	Pleads for Sodom
100	Sarah gives birth to Isaac
	Abraham builds temples, offers hospitality
125	Offers Isaac on Mount Moriah
137	Sarah dies, is buried at Hebron
	Abraham remarries, has additional children
	Teaches posterity, leaves records, continues to serve
175	Dies and is buried in Hebron

INTRODUCTION

A New Abrahamic Drama of Zion

In the spring of 1820 in upstate New York, when a fourteen-year-old farm boy knelt in a secluded grove of trees to pray, the scene was one of history's most dramatic reenactments. Some three and a half millennia earlier another fourteen-year-old had similarly sought the Creator in the solitude of prayer. His name was Abram, and the blessings that ensued from that prayer would change his life, his name, and the very course of history. The later prayer of Joseph Smith, a descendant of Abraham, turned the key to restore the blessings of Abraham and fulfill God's promises to the ancient Patriarch, opening the curtain on the great Abrahamic drama of the latter days.

As the prophet Joseph Smith received revelation after revelation, one theme repeatedly stood out in what God told his people: their mission was to build Zion,[1] a task, the Prophet would say, that should be "our greatest object."[2] And just what is Zion? As the revelations make clear, it is a condition of heart that we are commanded to live now, as well as an order of things that we are commanded to create and that will someday prevail on the earth—again.[3] For as only Latter-day Saints know,[4] there was once on this planet in the days of Enoch a society of such beauty, harmony, and goodness that the Lord deigned literally to dwell there, and then actually removed it from this world to a place of paradisiacal glory.[5] There it remains pristine and preserved to this day, awaiting its literal return to earth in the last days.[6]

The last days are now, say the revelations,[7] and we are the people God has chosen to build Zion here below in preparation for the return of the ancient Zion. As we "move the cause of Zion" (D&C 21:7) foreward to fulfill our mission, we find ourselves in common cause with the Saints and prophets of ages past, who, as the Prophet Joseph explained, looked ahead longingly to the glorious events of our day.

The building up of Zion is a cause that has interested the people of God in every age; it is a theme upon which prophets, priests and kings have dwelt with peculiar delight; they have looked forward with joyful anticipation to the day in which we live; and fired with heavenly and joyful anticipations they have sung and written and prophesied of this our day; but they died without the sight; we are the favored people that God has made choice of to bring about the Latter-day glory; it is left for us to see, participate in and help to roll forward the Latter-day glory, "the dispensation of the fulness of times, when God will gather together all things that are in heaven, and all things that are upon the earth," "even in one," when the Saints of God will be gathered in one from every nation, and kindred, and people, and tongue, when the Jews will be gathered together into one, the wicked will also be gathered together to be destroyed, as spoken of by the prophets; the Spirit of God will also dwell with His people, and be withdrawn from the rest of the nations, and all things whether in heaven or on earth will be in one, even in Christ. The heavenly Priesthood will unite with the earthly, to bring about those great purposes; and whilst we are thus united in one common cause, to roll forth the kingdom of God, the heavenly Priesthood are not idle spectators, the Spirit of God will be showered down from above, and it will dwell in our midst. The blessings of the Most High will rest upon our tabernacles, and our name will be handed down to future ages; our children will rise up and call us blessed; and generations yet unborn will dwell with peculiar delight upon the scenes that we have passed through, the privations that we have endured; the untiring zeal that we have manifested; the all but insurmountable difficulties that we have overcome in laying the foundation of a work that brought about the glory and blessing which they will realize; a work that God and angels have contemplated with delight for generations past; that fired the souls of the ancient patriarchs and prophets; a work that is destined to bring about the destruction of the powers of darkness, the renovation of the earth, the glory of God, and the salvation of the human family.[8]

A Pattern to Build Zion

So how are we to go about such a great work? Unfortunately, the view of Enoch's Zion that we are granted even in restored scripture is merely a distant glimpse in a few captivating but short verses. "What happened," asks Hugh Nibley, "in th[at] earthly city of Zion, between the lines of those . . . brief verses?"9 We are not told, and are left craving to know what the inhabitants of Enoch's Zion did to attain such glory.

But at least we *know of* Zion in restored scripture, whereas the traditional version of Genesis fails so much as to mention that it ever existed. In fact, the history in Genesis for that early age of the world is like a wide-angle lens quickly panning the landscape. Then suddenly the story undergoes a dramatic change of focus. With the entrance of Abraham at the end of chapter 11, the camera zooms in for a close-up of this one man and his wife, the first woman to be named in the Bible after Mother Eve. The lens will never leave Abraham and Sarah,10 showing the particulars of their lives through some twelve chapters, and providing us with far more personal detail than for any other Old Testament character or couple either before or after them. Then without missing a beat, the biblical camera lens turns to their chosen line, Isaac and then Jacob, and their posterity, for whom ever afterward the God of heaven is called the God of Abraham, the God of Isaac, and the God of Jacob.

But it is Abraham and Sarah who continue to hold the most prominent place of honor in the biblical record, as seen in the record of Isaiah. The value of Isaiah's prophetic words to Saints of old is indicated by the fact that he is the most quoted prophet in the Old and New Testaments, the Book of Mormon, and the Dead Sea Scrolls, and the prophet emphatically endorsed by the resurrected Lord Himself when he commanded the Nephites to "search" Isaiah's prophecies "diligently; for great are the words of Isaiah" (3 Ne. 23:1). Great not only for providing divine principles to live by, but great for what they foretell of the future: "For surely he spake as touching all things concerning my people which are of the house of Israel," continued the Savior, "and all things that he spake have been and shall be, even according to the words which he spake" (3 Ne. 23:3). The last Book of Mormon author, the solitary survivor Moroni, likewise urged his future readers to "search the prophecies of Isaiah," adding that "as the Lord liveth, he will remember the covenant" (Morm. 8:23).

Searching Isaiah's great words we find that God repeatedly singles out Abraham for unusual distinction, calling him "my friend" (Isa. 41:8)11—or, as better translated, "my beloved friend,"12 and referring to him by the same metaphor elsewhere used for God Himself—"the rock." From the rock of Abraham, God says, Israel has been quarried, and must look to their origin to understand their destiny: Zion. Isaiah writes,

> Hearken to me, ye that follow after righteousness, ye that seek the
> LORD: look unto the rock whence ye are hewn, and to the hole of

the pit whence ye are digged. Look unto Abraham your father, and unto Sarah that bare you: for I called him alone, and blessed him, and increased him. For the LORD shall comfort Zion. (Isa. 51:1–3.)[13]

Restoration of Knowledge about Abraham

The early Latter-day Saints, charged with the mission of building Zion, had good reason to believe that the Lord was about to provide them with additional information about their forefather Abraham. The Book of Mormon, published just weeks before the organization of the Church in 1830, not only emphasized the pivotal role of Abraham and his covenant in the last days (3 Ne. 16:4–7), but prophesied that the great latter-day Restoration would be of "great worth" to a branch of Abraham's posterity in "bringing them to the knowledge of their fathers" and "the knowledge of the covenants" made to those ancient fathers (2 Ne. 3:7, 12).[14]

Such information was not long in coming. Within a year after the organization of the Church,[15] Joseph Smith had completed the Abrahamic portion of Genesis in his inspired translation of the Bible, which added significant passages to the biblical story of Abraham.[16] Just four years later, in 1835, the Prophet Joseph felt impressed to purchase some Egyptian scrolls that turned out to include a unique treasure: an autobiographical account of Abraham. Time pressures and priorities delayed work on the translation,[17] which was finally completed in 1842 and was received with unbounded enthusiasm. Wilford Woodruff, who helped set the type for its publication in the Nauvoo paper *Times and Seasons* beginning in March 1842, rejoiced in the book's "great and glorious" truths, "which are among the rich treasures that are revealed unto us in the last days."[18]

With certain knowledge that authentic Abrahamic traditions had survived outside of the corpus of the biblical text, Latter-day Saint leaders eagerly took notice of yet additional ancient sources that began to emerge about Abraham. In September of that same year, the Prophet Joseph Smith penned an article for *Times and Seasons* mentioning Abraham's story as told not only in the Book of Abraham but also in another nonbiblical source published just two years earlier[19] in New York, namely the Book of Jasher—"which has not been disproved as a bad author," the Prophet noted.[20]

His open-minded attitude to this type of noncanonical material appears to have been shaped by the revelation he had received years earlier concerning the Apocrypha, the fourteen quasi-canonical books translated by the King James translators. The Prophet was not required, the Lord had said, to translate this material with the rest of the Bible, for the Apocrypha contained "many things . . . that are not true, which are interpolations by the hands of men." However, it also contained "many things . . . that are true, and it is mostly translated correctly," so that "whoso readeth it, let him understand, for the Spirit manifesteth truth; and whoso is enlightened by the Spirit shall obtain benefit therefrom" (D&C 91:1–5).

Among those seeking benefit from the Jasher account of Abraham were Brigham Young, John Taylor, and Wilford Woodruff, all of whom repeated in their public sermons to the Saints the Jasher story of young Abraham smashing his father's idols.[21] The 1840 edition of Jasher was even reprinted in Salt Lake City beginning in 1887, making it widely available to the Saints.

In the 1892 Church general conference, Apostle Franklin D. Richards, complier of the Pearl of Great Price, spoke with enthusiasm about their ancestor Abraham and emerging sources about him: "How singular it was that you and I got the spirit of gathering in the way that we did! When we came to hear the Gospel we became as strangers right in the lands in which we were born. . . . It was so with father Abraham. The Bible tells us very little about him. Other histories inform us further. . . ." He then summarized several legends from Jasher and mentioned the Qur'an as a source of Abrahamic material.[22]

Just six years later, the Latter-day Saints were treated to one of the most important ancient Abrahamic texts ever to emerge. In 1898 a Church member noticed an article in a San Francisco newspaper by a German Professor Bonwetsch about a text called the Apocalypse of Abraham, with a partial translation. The previous year Bonwetsch had published a German translation of the entire work. Obtaining his permission, the *Improvement Era,* the official Church publication, translated the German to English and published it—the first full English translation, and the only one for some twenty years.

The Apocalypse of Abraham, like the Book of Abraham, is written in first person, and tells not only of Abraham's fight against idolatry but also of his remarkable heavenly visions. The *Improvement Era's* introduction included the disclaimer that "how much of this story . . . is tinged with fable" versus "how much represents the true visions of the patriarch Abraham . . . we cannot pretend to say," but from the first it had been seen to contain "many things of a character both as to incidents and doctrines that [are] parallel with what is recorded in the Book of Abraham." Such parallels included "especially . . . the idolatrous character of Abraham's immediate forefathers, his call to depart from them, the future promise of a special inheritance, the fact of his receiving a special revelation from God, making known great things concerning the structure of the heavens and the earth, the pre-existence of the spirits of men, and the choice of certain of them to be God's rulers in the earth, Abraham being among them. All these corroborating facts . . . [are] intensely interesting and important."[23]

Had the Saints then had access to the Joseph Smith Translation (JST) of Genesis, they would have seen yet another remarkable corroboration in that both the JST and the Apocalypse of Abraham, referring to the same event in Abraham's life, assert that he saw in vision the ministry of the mortal Messiah.[24] And if the Saints had scoured the record of the *Journal of Discourses,* they would have discovered intriguing statements by two of their most prominent leaders, statements about Abraham that were now corroborated by the Apocalypse of Abraham. In the Church's 1874 semiannual general conference, Elder Wilford Woodruff stated that Abraham had seen in vision the last days and "the dispensation of the fulness of times" and the building up of "the great Zion of God," as well as the millennial "reign of righteousness."[25] A few years later, in 1881, President John Taylor declared that "through the spirit of prophecy" Abraham "had gazed upon his posterity as they should exist through the various ages of time."[26]

The amazing thing about both these statements is that when made they were entirely unsupported by any known ancient text, either scriptural or apocryphal. To this day, these statements remain without parallel in any scriptural text, but they are now in fact paralleled by several passages in apocryphal texts, the first of which to emerge was (and the most important of which still is) the Apocalypse of Abraham. It describes Abraham's vision of his posterity through the generations, including his latter-day posterity, and the glorious coming of the Messiah to bless that posterity.[27] It remains remarkable that the Apocalypse of Abraham, an extremely ancient and important text, would come forth in English translation first among the Latter-day Saints, corroborating what their leaders had stated by inspiration and providing further information about their exemplary forefather. (For further background on this and other key sources and commentators cited in this work, please see the glossary included in this volume.)

An Astonishing Outpouring of Forgotten Texts

Yet other texts continued to appear, slowly at first. A few were published by R. H. Charles in the first part of the twentieth century.[28] But the pace began to accelerate with the 1947 discovery of the Dead Sea Scrolls, including the Genesis Apocryphon—yet another autobiographical account of the Patriarch. In the ensuing decades, the emergence of yet other ancient biblical-related texts grew rapidly. Many of these claimed to have been composed originally by early biblical figures like Abraham and Enoch and even Adam, and although once used as authentic texts in early Jewish and Christian communities, they had long since been set aside, lost, or otherwise forgotten. Their sudden recovery from oblivion after many centuries is hailed as something of a miracle even by secular scholars. "By the strangest quirk of fate respecting literature that I know of," wrote Samuel Sandmel in 1983, "large numbers of writings by Jews were completely lost from the transmitted Jewish heritage. . . . Now . . . a door is being opened anew to treasures that are very old."[29]

Hugh Nibley's assessment is similar, referring to that "astonishing outpouring of ancient writings that is the peculiar blessing of our generation."[30] Part of the blessing is the remarkable corroboration that these newly emerged writings offer to the prior latter-day revelations and texts, a phenomenon noted even by no less a figure than Harold Bloom. In one of his widely read books, the prominent Bloom, not a Latter-day Saint, called attention to Joseph Smith's "uncanny recovery of elements in ancient Jewish theurgy that had ceased to be available either to normative Judaism or to Christianity, and that had survived only in esoteric traditions unlikely to have touched Smith directly."[31]

Bloom further called Joseph Smith "an authentic religious genius, unique in our national history," with "insight [that] could have come only from a remarkably apt reading of the Bible. . . . So strong was this act of reading that it broke through all the orthodoxies—Protestant, Catholic, Judaic—and found its way back to elements that Smith rightly intuited had been censored out of the stories of the archaic Jewish religion."[32] Such vindication of the Prophet Joseph's work was prophesied by himself: "The world will prove Joseph Smith a true prophet by circumstantial evidence,"[33] he foretold.

The corroboration provided by the emerging Abrahamic texts may also possibly be part of what the Lord foretold in the Book of Mormon regarding the coming forth of sacred records in the latter days from various nations: the newly emerged records will corroborate each other in dramatic evidence of their authenticity (2 Ne. 29:8) at the same time the Lord will prove to the world that he covenanted with Abraham that he would remember his posterity forever (2 Ne. 29:14).

Hence while some scholars today question whether Abraham ever really existed, Latter-day Saints know better. The authentic scriptural Abraham texts given to them as part of the great Restoration have now been dramatically corroborated by the emergence of additional long-forgotten ancient texts.

But these texts do even more than corroborate. They also give much additional detail about the life of Abraham, consistent with the foundational Abrahamic sources already provided by the Restoration. Such detail is a welcome source of information to Latter-day Saints, who have been expressly commanded by the Savior: "Do the works of Abraham" (D&C 132:32).

Look to Abraham

The Savior's commandment echoes what He had declared anciently through the prophet Isaiah, that the righteous are to look to Abraham. But that the commandment was repeated after the Savior's mortal ministry may appear remarkable. The Savior came, as President Harold B. Lee taught, not only to atone for our sins, but also to set the perfect example for us. Indeed, only He as the Son of God was capable of perfection, said Joseph Smith.[34] Only Jesus the Christ can and does invite all to follow Him (2 Ne. 31:10; D&C 38:22; 56:2) and to be as He is (3 Ne. 27:27). "I have set an example for you," he invitingly informs us (3 Ne.

18:16). Why, then, has He, the only Perfect One, selected from the ranks of the rest of us one additional examplar?

Maybe because Abraham's life demonstrates how closely it is possible to emulate that of the Savior. "In the aspect of his character," wrote W. F. P. Noble, "Abraham was more like Jesus Christ, stood nearer the most illustrious of his descendants, than perhaps any man."[35] Ancient sources uniformly attest to the godly character of Abraham, who "feared . . . God from his youth," says the book of Jasher, "and . . . served the Lord . . . from childhood to the day of his death."[36] The fourth-century Christian writer Epiphanius called Abraham "perfection itself in godliness,"[37] while the ancient book of Jubilees records he was "perfect in all of his actions with the LORD and was pleasing through righteousness all the days of his life."[38] In the words of Josephus, Abraham was "a man outstanding in every virtue,"[39] while the Muslim scholar al-Thalabi insisted that the great Patriarch "combined many qualities of goodness and virtue, such as is usually gathered in a nation."[40] Abraham's earliest biographer, Philo of Alexandria, said of him that he was "one who obeyed the law, some will say, but rather . . . [was] himself a law and an unwritten statute."[41] Laws later given to Israel were, according to Philo, nothing more than reminders of their distinguished forefather, "whose love for God and, especially, whose faith or trust in God qualifies him as 'the law itself.'"[42]

Such statements are borne out by the expanded picture we now have of the great Patriarch, whose life shines with the striking brilliance of a rare and flawless jewel of many facets. The laws of obedience, sacrifice, living the gospel, purity, and consecration are all perfectly illustrated by Abraham, who is is the epitome also of faith, hope, and charity, and every godly trait. And if charity, or the pure love of Christ, is the greatest of all, then Abraham's qualification stands supreme, being forever remembered in Judaism as "the man of kindness"[43] and the very incarnation of love.

In short, his life leads us surely and powerfully to the Savior Himself and the blessings He offers all mankind. "As we follow Abraham's example," explained President Kimball, "we will grow from grace to grace, we will find greater happiness and peace and rest, we will find favor with God and with man. As we follow his example, we will confirm upon ourselves and our families joy and fulfillment in this life and for all eternity."[44] The transformative power of Abraham's example was known anciently, as expressed by the medieval Jewish sage Maimonides: whoever follows the path of Abraham "brings benefit and blessing to himself."[45] And not just to oneself, for the collective work of building Zion can be accomplished only by following the blueprint of Abraham's life. "Only by 'doing the works of Abraham,'" says Hugh Nibley, "can we hope to establish . . . that order of Zion" long lost from the earth.[46]

But if Abraham demonstrated how to build Zion, he also foreshadowed it in remarkable ways. His life is "a lesson of the future,"[47] according to Jewish tradition, which holds that everything Abraham did prefigured what would happen to his posterity. This is particularly the case, as we shall see, regarding the lives of his descendants Jesus and Joseph Smith, but it is no less so for latter-day Zion collectively, whose destiny is Abraham's life writ large. At the same time, his life is a reflection of the heroes of Zion past, making him a uniquely central figure. "Abraham is squarely in the middle," explains Hugh Nibley. "All things seem to zero in on him. He has been called 'the most pivotal and strategic figure in all of human history.' In his position he binds all things together and gives meaning and purpose to everything that happened."[48]

But even more than prefiguring the destiny of his descendants, Abraham actually secured it by the covenants God made to him. For as the Book of Mormon emphasizes, those covenants speak directly to the ultimate victory of latter-day Zion. "I will show unto them that fight against my . . . people," the Lord declares, "that I am God, and that I covenanted with Abraham that I would remember his seed forever" (2 Ne. 29:14). And as with the final destiny of Zion, so with its founding and rolling forth, all secured by the Abrahamic covenant, whose fulfillment includes the opening of the heavens to Joseph Smith and the Restoration and establishment of God's latter-day kingdom as Israel is gathered and all nations and families are blessed through Abraham's seed.

Abraham's covenant is equally efficacious for Latter-day Saints individually and as couples, who, being of Abraham, are heir to the same promise made to him that his seed would be as the sand of the seashore and the stars of heaven. The promise includes the blessing of endless increase of posterity for those who achieve exaltation in Celestial glory, where, we are told, Abraham already sits on his throne as a god and a model of that eternal life awaiting those who become his seed by accepting the gospel, magnifying the priesthood, and making and keeping the same temple covenants that Abraham made and kept.

As we follow the Lord's counsel to look to Abraham, we will also discover that his life is a story of high drama set in a dark and decadent world uncannily like our own. It is a tale of grave danger and divine deliverance, of deep anguish and overwhelming joy, of difficult trials and signal triumphs, and of some unusual encounters and events the likes of which the world has not seen since. Stranger and more exciting than fiction, the account of Abraham is certainly one of the most intriguing on record, revealing a man of such unusual faith and love and compassion as to demonstrate the heights that mortals can reach in becoming truly Christlike.

For Latter-day Saints, then, Abraham is more than just another interesting figure from scriptural history whose life might be studied casually or occasionally. He looms large in latter-day revelation, as well as in the teachings of latter-day prophets, as simply indispensable to our work in qualifying for the blessings of coming unto Christ and building Zion.

The life of Abraham also happens to be one of the world's greatest love stories. To refer to Abraham or tell his story is necessarily to include Sarah. They were a team working in perfect harmony, mutually dependent and wholly committed to each other and the greater good of the marriage and the mission God had given them. If she is mentioned less in this book than he, she was no less important, nor, I am convinced, would she feel slighted in the least. Jewish tradition emphasizes not only that her life was a tapestry of perfection,[49] but that her prophetic power and spiritual capacity in certain ways actually exceeded that of her husband.[50] Despite her superlative talent, she never sought the limelight, operating in perfect partnership with her husband—whom she loved totally and followed in some of the most difficult trials imaginable. Together Abraham and Sarah built Zion, and together they are to be remembered by their righteous posterity who aspire to build Zion. Together they teach us how to build Zion and qualify for the very blessings once bestowed on them for their faithfulness.

"Come," invites a rabbinic text, "and learn from Abraham."[51] Or, as the early Christian writer Ephrem the Syrian urged, "See the works of Abraham."[52] And see, thereby, the blessings of Abraham and how they may be attained. For as Elder Franklin D. Richards declared, "They that would inherit the blessings of Abraham, must do the works of Abraham."[53]

Abraham's Birthplace

CHAPTER 1

Alone with God in a World without Zion:
Young Abraham in Ur

Draw near unto me and I will draw near unto you;
seek me diligently and ye shall find me; ask, and ye shall receive;
knock, and it shall be opened unto you.
—DOCTRINE AND COVENANTS 88:63

In the Beginning

The biblical story of Abraham begins in Ur of the Chaldees, where we are first introduced to Abraham only as an adult; not a word is spared for his formative years of youth and preparation. Not so in other ancient sources, which take us back to his boyhood and birth and even before, all the way back to the creation of the world, during which, as Genesis relates, God used the word "good" to describe the result of each successive creative period (Gen. 1:10, 12, 18, 21, 25).

With the creation of man, however, and with God's blessing pronounced upon them, God saw that his creation was "very good" (Gen. 1:31). As to why it was now so, Genesis itself offers no explanation, but ancient rabbinic texts do: the Genesis passage "teaches that . . . the Holy One . . . brought out all the souls of the righteous—the souls of Abraham, Isaac and Jacob" and their future descendants, "the souls of Israel," all they who would keep God's law.[1] In this sense, the world was created "for the sake of Abraham"[2] and his wife Sarah,[3] which "is tantamount to saying that it was created for the sake of Israel since they are the parents of the people of Israel."[4] And more than a mere beneficiary, Abraham was actually a participant with God in the creation, according to the rabbis.[5] "God created the world 'with Abraham,'" says rabbinic tradition.[6]

What motivated God to undertake the grand enterprise? Tradition insists that he acted out of *hesed*, a Hebrew word whose meaning includes loving-kindness and mercy. The Psalmist declared that "the world is built on *hesed*,"[7] while the medieval Jewish scholar Moses Maimonides taught that "all being is an act of divine *hesed*, for the universe has come into existence only by virtue of God's abundant grace or loving-kindness."[8] But another essential element of God's *hesed* is his loyalty to the covenant,[9] which apparently was a factor even in the Creation, for tradition indicates it was then when God first made a covenant with Abraham.[10]

Such traditions bear conspicuous resemblance to Abraham's own writings as restored in the Book of Abraham, in which the Patriarch reports being shown in vision a vast host of premortal spirits among whom "were many of the noble and great ones; and God saw these souls that they were good, and he stood in the midst of them, and he said: These I will make my rulers; for he stood among those that were spirits, and he saw that they were good; and he said unto me: Abraham, thou art one of them; thou wast chosen before thou wast born" (Abr. 3:22–23). Abraham then beheld how he and the other noble spirits, called "gods" in the Book of Abraham, participated with the Lord in the creation for the benefit of the future righteous (Abr. 3:24; 4:1). Latter-day prophets have further explained that Abraham and others were not only appointed and foreordained to their early missions,[11] but trained and prepared to perform them (D&C 138:56).

That Genesis may well have originally contained such information was indicated by Joseph Smith, who said that the very first word of Genesis, altered long ago, originally spoke of a council of the gods called forth by the head god before the creation of the world.[12] Likewise, the prominent biblical scholar Nahum Sarna has emphasized that Genesis as it has come down to us is unique among all other ancient Near Eastern creation dramas in its failure to mention a gathering of the gods before creation—indicating, says Sarna, that anciently an account of that gathering was had in ancient Israel also.[13] But in Genesis as we have it, Abraham is not mentioned until his due time in human history.

The beginning of that human history took place in the most ideal and idyllic setting, the beautiful Garden of Eden planted for Adam and Eve by God, who then actually walked and talked with them there (see Gen. 2–3). A wealth of ancient tradition adds that the garden was what would later be symbolically re-created on Jerusalem's Temple Mount: Zion, a place of supreme holiness, beauty, and perfection, a venue where gods and human beings associate.[14] As one scholar explains, "The notion of Zion as the first of God's creations, which is not explicit in the Bible, is reflected in rabbinic literature." [15] Human history began, in a word, with Zion.

But Zion's pristine glory was soon lost when Adam and Eve ate the forbidden fruit and were expelled, an event that turned out to be but the first in a series of escalating acts of mankind's disobedience. As the story unfolds in those earthly chapters of Genesis, an era called "primeval history," the errant human race seems bent on distancing itself ever further from its Creator.[16] An apparent exception is the brief mention of Enoch, who walked with God and then was not, for God took him (Gen. 5:24), but there is no explanation in Genesis of what that cryptic passage might mean beyond some kind of unique fellowship between Enoch and God. Nor did Enoch's experience turn the tide of further rebellions by the human race, with each new breach bringing its consequent punishment. Fortunately, each time there followed a divine manifestation of mercy. Even after the Flood, God spoke again in mercy to man.

Pivotal Time, Pivotal Man

Ominously, however, the pattern is broken with the Tower of Babel, whose builders set out to "make a name for ourselves" (NRSV Gen. 11:4) in their rebellion against the Almighty.[17] Again there was punishment, but no word of divine mercy. As pointed out by German scholar Gerhard von Rad, it was a time of cosmic crisis.

> The whole primeval history . . . seems to break off in shrill dissonance, and the question . . . arises . . . urgently: Is God's relationship to the nations now finally broken; is God's gracious forbearance now exhausted; has God rejected the nations in wrath forever? That is the burdensome question which no thoughtful reader of ch[apter] 11 can avoid; indeed, one can say that our narrator intended by means of his whole plan of primeval history to raise precisely this question and to pose it in all its severity.[18]

The implication is that the world again seems to be ripe for destruction, which is precisely what the Apostle Peter, according to an early Christian source, reported about the world of Abraham: "The whole world was again overspread with errors, and . . . for the hideousness of its crimes destruction was ready for it, this time not by water, but fire, and . . . already the scourge was hanging over the whole earth."[19] Never in the troubled history of mankind had there been greater darkness and depravity. It was a world as far from Zion as possible.

A more detailed description is given in the book of Jubilees, an ancient Jewish source, which speaks in terms reminiscent of several Book of Mormon passages recounting the wickedness of that people and the hold that Satan had on their hearts.[20] According to Jubilees,

> Noah's children began to fight one another, to take captive, and to kill one another; to shed human blood on the earth, to consume

blood; to build fortified cities, walls, and towers; men to elevate
themselves over peoples, to set up the first kingdoms; to go to
war—people against people, nations against nations, city against
city; and everyone to do evil, to acquire weapons, and to teach
warfare to their sons. City began to capture city and to sell male
and female slaves. . . . They made molten images for themselves.
Each one would worship the idol which he had made as his own
molten image. They began to make statues, images, and unclean
things; the spirits of the savage ones were helping and misleading
them so that they would commit sins, impurities, and transgression. Prince Mastema [Satan] was exerting his power in effecting
all these actions and, by means of the spirits, he was sending to
those who were placed in his control the ability to commit every
kind of error and sin and every kind of transgression; to corrupt,
to destroy, and to shed blood on the earth.[21]

So expert did they become at fighting that, according to Israeli archaeologist
Yigael Yadin, it was during this era that the art of warfare reached its "highest standard," thanks in large measure to the chariot, one of the most important instruments
on the field of battle and "assuredly a formidable and decisive instrument of
warfare."[22] The image of the chariot struck terror into the hearts of people everywhere. "There was worldwide cruelty, inhospitality, insecurity, suspicion," making for
"a world of desperate wickedness."[23] Who in that violent and cruel age could ever
have guessed that generations earlier there had existed on this earth a society of perfect
righteousness, peace, and love? It was Enoch's city of Zion (see Moses 7:12–21),
known to us in the latter days thanks to the scriptures restored through Joseph Smith.

Those scriptures speak also of the light that had once visibly emanated from
the city (see Moses 7:17), in contrast to the darkness that had settled over the
planet by Abraham's day, when, according to the Book of the Rolls, mankind
"wandered in error and rebelled," and "Satan certainly blinded their hearts and left
them in darkness without light."[24] As with so much of Abraham's life and times,
the condition of his world looks both backward and forward—backward to the
time of the Flood, when "Satan had a great chain in his hand, and it veiled the
whole face of the earth with darkness; and he looked up and laughed, and his
angels rejoiced" (Moses 7:26). And forward to the latter-days, when, as Enoch had
foretold, "a veil of darkness shall cover the earth" (Moses 7:61).

As for Enoch himself, who had been known as a seer because of his visions
(see Moses 6:36), he had been taken up with the rest of his righteous city (7:69),
leaving behind a line of mortals with the patriarchal priesthood authority to establish Zion again on the earth (8:2).[25] By Abraham's day, however, that authority

had apparently disappeared due to generations of apostasy. "They cast off the Kingdom of Heaven from themselves," reports the Pirke de Rabbi Eliezer.[26] Even so, Zion had also left precious scriptural records prophesying that righteousness would again be established on the earth. Where these records were before Abraham came on the scene—whether they were hidden away in the earth or locked away in some treasury or perhaps even enshrined in some temple or palace as a now-unreadable relic of an earlier age—we do not know.

We do know of ancient prophecies about Abraham, which may well have been contained in those records, prophecies such as that found in a text called 1 Enoch. There the patriarch Enoch foretold—in a passage whose context unquestionably refers to Abraham[27]—that one of Enoch's descendants "shall be chosen as a plant of righteous judgement; and his posterity shall come forth as a plant of eternal righteousness."[28]

Enoch's great-grandson Noah, according to a recently restored column of the Genesis Apocryphon, similarly saw in vision and recorded that from his posterity "will spring a righteous plant" that "will stand forever"—another prophecy whose context seems necessarily to refer to Abraham.[29]

And according to Pseudo Philo, on the day that Abraham's great-great-grand-mother gave birth to her son Serug, she foretold: "From this one there will be born in the fourth generation one who will set his dwelling on high and will be called perfect and blameless; and he will be the father of nations, and his covenant will not be broken, and his seed will be multiplied forever."[30] Abraham was the hope of Zion, a Zion long since fled from the world.

Ur of the Chaldees

Thus had the world become at the time when, in the words of John Taylor, "a singular kind of personage appeared on the stage of action, named Abraham."[31] The particular stage on which he appeared—as attested in the Bible, Book of Abraham, and numerous ancient sources—was *Ur of the Chaldees*. Most Bible maps equate Abraham's Ur with the great Ur in southern Mesopotamia, in present-day Iraq. After lying buried and in ruins for millennia, the city began to be excavated in the 1850s, the results convincing some that it was Abraham's native city.[32]

But it was Sir Leonard Woolley's celebrated excavations in the 1920s that stirred public imagination. Among the artifacts Woolley unearthed was a gold and lapis lazuli figure of a ram standing with its forefeet and head in the branches of a tree. Now on display in the British Museum, the figure calls to mind Abraham's ram in a thicket, and left no doubt in Woolley's mind that he was digging in Abraham's birth-place. His dispatches to London created widespread excitement, and when he later published a book describing his excavations—Ur of the Chaldees—it was full of references to Abraham, who later became the subject of another book by Woolley called *Abraham: Recent Discoveries and Hebrew Origins*. Public opinion since has generally followed Woolley in his location of Abraham's Ur.

But in 1982 when Cornell University Press published a revised and updated version of Woolley's book on Ur, the reviser made a monumental alteration, which he explained in the preface: "Ur's fame as the birthplace of Abraham has given it a special position in the literary legacy of Judaism and Islam. Contrary to the view consistently argued by Woolley, there is no actual proof that Tell el-Mukayyar, the Ur of this book, was identical with 'Ur of the Chaldees' in Genesis 11:29–32." Therefore, "it seemed best to write of the excavations of Ur at this time without mention of Abraham."[33]

It was a wise decision, for as scholars of the Bible had long recognized, the great Ur of the south was not Ur of the Chaldees until long after Abraham's day, making it an anachronism. So where was Abraham's Ur? According to Genesis, when the aged Abraham sends his servant back to his "country and kindred" to find a wife for Isaac, it is to the city of Nahor, in northern Mesopotamia. It was this region, insisted the assiduous biblical scholar Nachmanides in the thirteenth century, that was always the habitat of Abraham's ancestors, and where he himself was born.[34] A similar conclusion is reached by the modern eminent biblical scholar Claus Westermann, who insists that "upper Mesopotamia in the region of Haran was the place of origin of the patriarchs. There is no trace of any connection with Ur in the south; there is only the name."[35]

Not everyone agrees with Westermann—the issue of a northern versus the southern Ur continues to be disputed, as it has been in the pages of *Biblical Archeology Review*[36]—but a majority of scholars now favor a northern Ur,[37] and for compelling reasons. Abraham and his family follow customs from the area of northern Mesopotamia, which contains various places that in antiquity bore or contained the name "Ur" or a close variation. The name Nimrod (Abraham's rival) also occurs as a place name in a number of locations in the region.

Latter-day Saints have an additional reason for locating Abraham's Ur somewhere in northern Mesopotamia. As we will see, the Book of Abraham depicts heavy Egyptian influence there during Abraham's day, making the southern location impossible: ancient Egypt never exercised control over the southern Ur, but it did in upper Palestine and in the region of Urfa.

Even without the Book of Abraham, however, a number of eminent biblical scholars assert that Abraham's Ur of the Chaldees has to have been in northern Mesopotamia, and point to the most likely location as the modern Turkish city of Urfa.[38] Urfa is not the only place in the northern region that claims the distinction of being Abraham's birthplace,[39] but its claim is particularly compelling. Urfa was previously called Edessa, but before that was known as Erekh or Orhay,[40] both names appearing to contain the name Ur. Founded by Abraham's nemesis Nimrod as the city where he ruled,[41] landmarks of the city memorialize both men: "the names of Nimrod and Abraham cling to this city and its environs to the present time."[42] Located in southeastern Turkey some twenty-five miles north of Haran, Urfa happens also to be in the region of other sites that have been identified as ancient cities bearing the names of several of Abraham's immediate ancestors.[43] In Urfa is a cave that was thought to be Abraham's birthplace long before the city of Urfa came under Islamic control.[44] It is now a Muslim shrine located just a stone's throw away from where Abraham is said to have been saved by divine intervention when Nimrod tried to take his life.[45]

But as neatly as the evidence seems to point to Urfa, does it really matter where Abraham was born? In Gianni Granzotto's masterful biography of Columbus, whose birthplace is claimed by various countries, the chapter analyzing the explorer's native land is titled "The Irrelevant Country." Would history have been different, Granzotto asks, if Columbus had not been born in Genoa? After all, wherever Columbus's birthplace, he left it early to pursue his dreams. "And dreams have no native country."[46] So it is with Abraham's Ur. Wherever it was, he would eventually leave it behind to go forth and "be a blessing" (Gen. 12:2) to the world. And blessings have no native country.

A Remarkable and Portentous Birth

As there were ten generations from Adam to Noah, so likewise according to Jewish sources, were there ten from Noah to Abraham[47] (although some sources say eleven[48]). And "it was indeed high time that the 'friend of God' should make his appearance upon the earth,"[49] for already there had arisen a pretender who audaciously claimed the patriarchal authority of Zion to rule over the human race and all living things: the proud and powerful King Nimrod.[50]

He is mentioned in both the Bible and the Book of Mormon as a mighty hunter,[51] and echoes of his name survive yet today in several ancient places, including in the region of Turkey that contains the city of Urfa.[52] The name Nimrod appears to derive from the Hebrew word "to rebel,"[53] while tradition held him to be "a deceiver."[54] According to Jewish sources, his claim of divine authority to rule the world was based on the patriarchal garment he had in his possession, the garment handed down from Adam through Noah and then stolen from him.[55] Donning the garment of Zion, he sought mightily to create a facade of Zion and the harmony by which it is known. "Having gathered mankind in a monumental building project, Nimrod could turn the resulting sense of unity to his own ends."[56] He would conveniently take all the glory—even as Satan had attempted in the Grand Council in heaven. Nimrod was indeed the very "antithesis of Zion."[57]

But despite the outward trappings of Zion, what Nimrod had established was not the peaceable earthly kingdom of God but the military earthly dominion of

Satan. Nimrod had subdued nations and extended his kingdom far and wide, and is remembered in legend as one of the most ruthlessly effective conquerors ever. He "held sway over the entire world," says a Turkish Islamic source.[58]

The profile of Nimrod the conqueror as painted by tradition seems to correspond closely to what historical sources say about the ideal of kingship in the ancient Hittite empire, the likely location for the scene.[59] According to such sources, "the Hittite king was the supreme military commander of his people," while "the ideology of kingship demanded that he demonstrate his fitness to rule by doing great military deeds, comparable with and where possible surpassing the achievements of his predecessors. 'Military expansion became an ideology in its own right, a true sport of kings.'" Indeed, one of the Hittite kings from this same era recorded his military exploits in terms of "a lion pouncing upon his prey and destroying it without mercy—an image of ruthless savagery" that "was to become a regular symbol of Hittite power."[60]

Legend further remembers Nimrod as the most wicked of any man since the Flood, imposing idolatry and all manner of evil practices on his subjects, and forcing them to worship him as a god.[61] "Nimrod made men forget the love and worship of the true God, the Creator of the Universe, and led them on the path of sin and transgression."[62] Thus, Nimrod the hunter hunted not only great beasts but also the souls of men, seeking to turn them away from God.[63] We are reminded of the Book of Mormon's exclamation: "How much iniquity doth one wicked king cause to be committed . . . !" (Mosiah 29:17.)

Among those led astray was the man who would be Abraham's father, Terah, who is depicted in legend as extremely talented and successful, occupying a high position of power in Nimrod's court. As "the prince of Nimrod's host," Terah was "very great in the sight of the king and his subjects, and the king and princes loved him, and they elevated him very high."[64]

In that violent age of conflict and conquest, the world no doubt seemed to be determined by battles, not unlike a later age about which one writer observed: "Nobody thought of babies, everyone was thinking of battles. We fancy God can manage His world only with great battalions, when all the time he is doing it with beautiful babies. When a wrong wants righting, or a truth wants preaching, . . . God sends a baby into the world to do it."[65] And so it happened at that dark time of the world when, as Maimonides explained, the turning point came with the appearance of Abraham.[66]

Despite Nimrod's increasing power and arrogance, he lived in constant fear of losing his throne.[67] His concern heightened, says a Samaritan source, upon being advised by his wise men that "they had seen in the Book of Signs which had been handed down to them, that there would arise a man" destined to overthrow the idols and smite the idol worshipers. When his wise men pinpointed the projected date of birth, Nimrod imprisoned temporarily the men of his kingdom, to prevent the conception of this dangerous infant. But an unusual sign in the heavens created a panic that allowed Terah, in response to a vision that came to him, to escape unnoticed and be with his wife, and then slip back to the prison. Meanwhile, when Nimrod's wizards saw that the sign had been lifted, they exclaimed: "The child has reached the womb of his mother." Nimrod released the prisoners, himself still a captive to an ever deepening anxiety.[68]

Portents of trouble continued to appear. According to a Turkish account from early Islamic tradition, Nimrod had a dream in which he saw his throne overturned by a charging ram. Nimrod's soothsayers interpreted the dream to mean that a boy would be born who would ruin Nimrod's empire.[69] In the Jewish version of the story, one night Nimrod's astrologers witnessed an amazing phenomenon in the sky as a star rose in the east and seemed to swallow up the four stars in the four corners of the heavens. Hastening to their king, the astrologers reported the event as a sign that an infant was born that day who was destined to rule the world and overthrow Nimrod's kingdom.

Various ancient sources report a heinous crime by the arrogant and cruel Nimrod as he ordered a terrible slaughter.

> He had a proclamation published throughout his whole kingdom, summoning all the architects to build a great house for him. . . . After it was completed, he issued a second proclamation, summoning all pregnant women thither, and there they were to remain until their confinement. Officers were appointed to take the women to the house, and guards were stationed in it and about it, to prevent the women from escaping thence. He furthermore sent midwives to the house, and commanded them to slay the men children at their mothers' breasts. But if a woman bore a girl, she was to be arrayed in [linen,] silk, and embroidered garments, and led forth from the house of detention amid great honors. No less than seventy thousand children were slaughtered thus.[70]

If such a thing sounds too evil to be real, one need only remember the tragic slaughter of the infants that would threaten the life of both Moses and Jesus as each of them entered mortality. Satan was waiting for these particular infants and determined to thwart their foreordained missions.

The infant Abraham was saved only by being born in a cave and hidden away there for a time. "Let there be light" is how one modern Jewish writer describes Abraham's entrance into history,[71] and the phrase is aptly descriptive of the signal birth that began to disperse the spiritual darkness of that age. At Abraham's birth, the cave to which his mother had fled "was filled with the light of the child's countenance as with the splendor of the sun."[72]

Describing Abraham's birth, an Ethiopic source adds that the bright light so astonished those present that they fell to the ground, whereupon there was heard "an outcry in a mighty voice, which said, 'Woe is me! Woe is me! There has just been born him that shall crush my kingdom to dust.' And the voice wept."[73] Thus were the powers of both heaven and hell stirred when this infant, "trailing clouds of glory," to borrow William Wordsworth's poetic language, came from realms of light into the spiritually dark world of that day. Abraham was "a prince in the heavens," noted John Taylor, "and by right came to the earth in his time to accomplish the things given him to do."[74] With Abraham's birth, according to Jewish tradition, "desolation was over and a new light began to shine upon humanity."[75] Even so, it was an extremely dangerous place to be born, a culture of death in which many infants did not survive.

The name he was given, "Abram"—meaning "the father is exalted"[76] or "the father is high" or "the father lifts himself on high"[77]—refers, says one legend, to Terah's high status in Nimrod's court: "Terah called the name of his son that was born to him Abram, because the king had raised him in those days, and dignified him above all his princes that were with him."[78]

As would be the case with so much in the life of Abraham, even his entrance into mortality echoed the past and foreshadowed the future. The brilliant light at his birth echoed that at Creation, when Christ the Creator, the Light of the world, had formed the great celestial luminary that would shine in the darkness and bring light to the earth. The light at Abraham's birth also foreshadowed the time when the Creator would be born in the flesh as a light shining in a spiritually dark world (see John 1:1–5; D&C 93:8–11). Early Christian sources further describe a "brilliant light" that surrounded the newborn infant Jesus.[79] As Abraham was prophesied to arise as a plant of righteousness in a corrupt world, so Isaiah prophesied that the Savior would grow up as a tender plant out of dry ground (Isa. 53:1–2). As a new star arose in the east when Abraham was born in a cave, so did it happen with the Savior (Matt. 2:1–11), whose birth, according to early Christian sources, was also in a cave.[80] The terrible slaughter of the infants at Abraham's birth was repeated at the birth of Moses (Ex. 1:15–22; 2:1–10) and again at the birth of the Savior (Matt. 2:16–18).

In fact, according to rabbinic tradition, Abraham's entire life "prefigured the future history of Israel"[81] in such a comprehensive way that "in his biography lives out the future history of Israel."[82] "Everything that Abraham experienced," maintained the Jewish sages, "has also been experienced by his descendants."[83] If Isaiah's writings are valuable for prophesying all of Israel's future (3 Ne. 23:1–3), so Abraham's life is a rich portrait portending that same future, for "whatever happened to him would occur to his descendants."[84] For example, his birth looks ahead also to his latter-day descendant Joseph Smith, whose birth was also prophesied, anciently by the patriarch Joseph (2 Ne. 3:6–19), and later by Joseph Smith's grandfather Asael Smith when he foretold that one of his descendants would "promulgate a work to revolutionize the world of religious faith."[85] And as the powers of darkness seemed poised to persecute the infant Abraham, so it was with Joseph Smith who commented that "the adversary was aware, at a very early period of my life, that I was destined to prove a disturber and an annoyer of his kingdom; else why should the powers of darkness combine against me? Why the opposition and persecution that arose against me, almost in my infancy?"[86]

Purity and Prayer in Seeking God

Despite the opposition, Joseph Smith would go on to seek God in prayer and experience the First Vision. In an 1832 account of that remarkable theophany, the Prophet explained how he gained confidence in the Creator's existence and His mercy by reflecting on His creations:

> I pondered many things in my heart concerning the situation of the world of mankind, the contentions and divisions, the wickedness and the abominations and the darkness . . . and I felt to mourn for my own sins and for the sins of the world. . . . I looked upon the sun, the glorious luminary of the earth, and also the moon rolling in their majesty through the heavens, and also the stars shining in their courses, and the earth also upon which I stood, and the beast of the field and the fowls of heaven and the fish of the waters, and also man walking forth upon the face of the earth. . . . And when I considered . . . these things, my heart exclaimed . . . [that] all these bear testimony and bespeak an omnipotent . . . power, a being who maketh laws. . . . Therefore, I cried unto the Lord for mercy, for there was none else to whom I could go.[87]

As Hugh Nibley has pointed out, "this was exactly the case with young Abraham,"[88] who as a child found there was none else to whom he could go for truth, and began his ardent and unrelenting search for God. It is this theme of seeking that appears so prominently in the opening lines of the Book of Abraham (Abr. 1:1–4) and similarly in numerous ancient texts and traditions. The medieval Jewish sage Maimonides wrote of young Abraham that "when this giant was weaned," he began to ponder "by day and by night, and he would wonder, 'How is it possible that this sphere moves constantly without there being a mover, or one to turn it, for it is impossible that it turns itself?' And he had no teacher or source of knowledge but he was sunk among senseless idol worshippers in Ur of the Chaldeans. . . . But his mind roamed in search of understanding."[89] As Nibley noted, "from infancy he was asking searching questions about God, the cosmos, and the ways of men—embarassing questions."[90]

At just three years of age, as one source has it, the boy already "began to understand the nature of God,"[91] so that the next year he resisted when his grandfather tried to teach him to worship idols.[92] Nor could Abraham's father, despite long and persistent effort, persuade his son to revere the statues. Young Abraham "was alone with God," says Hugh Nibley, "dependent on no man and no tradition, beginning as it were from scratch. . . . Having no human teachers, he must think things out for himself, until he receives light from above."[93] The rabbis report that Abraham's "own father did not teach him, nor did he have a master to teach him. From whom, then, did Abraham learn Torah? It was the Holy One."[94]

And where was Abraham's mother in all of this? What role did she play in the formation of this man who would change the world? Although not mentioned in the Bible or the Book of Abraham, she is referred to in several old sources, even if they disagree on her name.[95] She is credited with saving her infant son's life from the murderous machinations of the king and bringing Abraham safely into the world,[96] and had enough maternal instinct to later try to persuade her son to save his own life—by renouncing his opposition to idolatry. According to a midrash called the Maaseh Avraham Avinu, or "Works of Our Father Abraham," she was an idolator,[97] and her failure to figure in any of the accounts describing young Abraham's search for God indicates her lack of spiritual depth and inability to provide guidance on such matters. Some traditions even tell that it was the son who eventually tried to tutor the mother in spiritual things.[98] In Abraham's own account in the Book of Abraham, he expressly mentions the idolatry of his father but says not a word about his mother. The silence is revealing, both of her failure to provide guidance, and of his own sensitivity in not speaking ill of the woman who had brought him into the world and whom he loved despite her faults.

If young Abraham had no maternal guidance, what he apparently did have was access to the most learned minds and advanced knowledge of his day, the assemblage of scholars and texts located at the royal court where his father occupied a position of power second only to Nimrod himself. Young Abraham was no stranger to Nimrod's court; an ancient Samaritan source even recounts that when Abraham came of age, Nimrod "placed him under his command, and he was among those who stood before him, to wait on him."[99] Maaseh Avraham Avinu recounts that on one occasion "as the king, Nimrod, sat upon the throne of his kingdom, he sent for Abraham to come to him, with his father, Terah. And Abraham passed before the governors and the officers until he reached the royal throne."[100]

As with Moses, who would be raised amid the fabled learning of the Egyptian court, young Abraham was exposed to the best and brightest of his day. "Abraham from his birth had his upbringing among the Chaldeans," reported George Syncellus, "and from them he was taught in their astrology and in all the rest of their wisdom,"[101] in which, says Georgius Cedrenus, he was "thoroughly instructed."[102] The elite education afforded young Abraham—the training of his mind and his exposure to the wisdom of the world—would be important in his development. But he found it devoid of the most important truths for which he was searching, truths long since distorted or expunged and forgotten altogether.

In the spiritual and emotional solitude in which he found himself, young Abraham thought and pondered deeply, sensing that somehow he was not alone. The copious compiler of Jewish legends Louis Ginzberg noted that "in all the sources stress is laid upon the fact that Abraham came to know God through his own reasoning about the universe and its ruler who must necessarily exist."[103] The legends describe how the young man carefully observed the earth and the heavens, the sun, moon, and stars, and "wondered in his heart: Who created heaven and earth and me?"[104] According to Byzantine tradition, young Abraham "was an astronomer extremely well trained by his father."[105] It is known that the people of Abraham's day studied the heavens carefully as astrologers[106] and even worshipped the stars and heavenly bodies.[107]

But as the child Abraham thoughtfully gazed at those same stars, he came to see that these creations bore witness to the majesty of their Creator,[108] a truth to be declared by one of his posterity: "The heavens declare the glory of God; and the firmament shows his handiwork" (NKJV Ps. 19:1).[109]

Hence, as related by Maimonides, by his diligence in seeking the Almighty, Abraham finally "achieved the true way and understood. . . . He knew that there is one God who moves the spheres, who created everything, and there is none beside Him. He knew that the whole world was in error."[110] A thousand years before the erudite Aristotle would posit the Prime Mover of the universe, the boy Abraham discovered the truth on his own.[111]

But not quite on his own, for as he drew near to the Creator, he sensed the Creator drawing near to him. "God inspired Abraham," declared Elder Wilford Woodruff, "and his eyes were opened so that he saw and understood something of the dealings of the Lord with the children of men. He understood that there was a God in heaven, a living and true God, and that no man should worship any other god but Him."[112]

And as Abraham came to understand the reality of the Creator, he came to understand something also about the Creator's most prominent trait. According to a medieval Jewish source, "When Abraham our father arrived, . . . he looked and saw, investigated and understood the great secret of the blessed God and how He had created the world through the *hesed*." Abraham "too then held fast to this quality," so "just as God had created the world through *hesed*, so did Abraham know his Creator through *hesed*."[113] Young Abraham discovered, in other words, what Joseph Smith would discover by reflecting on the majesty of God's creations: not only the reality of the Creator, but the reality of his merciful love that had prompted such creation. Abraham's experience constitutes a timeless lesson, insisted Moses Maimonides, for "only through knowledge of God's handiwork" can one fulfill the commandments "to love and stand in awe of God."[114] The continuing relevance of Abraham's experience is insisted upon by a modern rabbi, who wrote that "Abraham's divine discoveries and ongoing relationship with the Creator serve as a model for us, his spiritual progeny."[115] Latter-day Saints immediately think of the revelation inviting their own contemplation of the Creator's handiwork, for "any man who hath seen any or the least of these"—the earth, sun, moon, and stars—"hath seen God moving in his majesty and power" (D&C 88:47).

Following the divine lead, Abraham himself practiced *hesed*, which in the human realm means not only loving-kindness and mercy but also righteous conduct.[116] Hence, as a modern scholar expressed: "Yahweh [Jehovah] was the God of Abraham; Abraham was his servant. Theirs was a very distinct relationship which imposed upon them certain rights and duties—a relationship of mutual reciprocity expressed by *hesed*."[117] It is the same principle that Moroni would express in his dialogue with the Lord: "I know that this love which thou hast had for the children of men is charity; wherefore, except men shall have charity they cannot inherit that place which thou hast prepared in the mansions of thy Father" (Ether 12:34). This principle of righteous loving-kindness, or charity, would become the governing principle of Abraham's life, for which he is still remembered among his Jewish descendants as the embodiment of *hesed*, "for the decisive factor in Abraham's personality was the unceasing urge to help others."[118] It is also a decisive factor demonstrating Abrahamic descent, for according to the Talmud, "Performing deeds of loving-kindness is a distinguishing characteristic of the descendants of Abraham."[119] The other side of the coin, according to Maimonides, is that cruelty and impudence are not qualities of "the seed of Abraham, our father."[120]

By understanding God and His love, Abraham came also to understand that mankind was in grave error. According to Jubilees, "the child began to realize the errors of the earth—that everyone was going astray after the statues and after impurity. . . . When he was two weeks of years [=14 years], he separated from his father in order not to worship idols with him. He began to pray to the creator of all that he would save him from the errors of mankind and that it might not fall to his share to go astray after impurity and wickedness."[121] In that same year, according to George Syncellus, "Abraham discovered the God of the universe, and worshipped him."[122]

Young Abraham's choice to conform his will to that of the Almighty is remembered in Jewish tradition as "present[ing] God with a gift that even He in all His infinite power, could not fashion for Himself. For even God cannot guarantee that man's mind and heart would choose truth over evil, light over darkness, spirit over flesh."[123] It is the great lesson of mortality, as explained by President Boyd K. Packer: "Obedience to God can be the very highest expression of independence. Just think of giving to him the one thing, the one gift, that he would never take. . . . Obedience—that which God will never take by force—he will accept when freely given. And he will then return to you freedom that you can hardly dream of."[124]

Young Abraham's prayer that God would keep him from impurity is an important window into his soul, which purity of heart is further attested in other sources. In the Apocalypse of Abraham, young Abraham determines that "I will set my mind on what is pure."[125] The Church Fathers likewise knew that Abraham was "clean of heart,"[126] or, in the words of the learned Origen, "pure in heart."[127] The Qur'an relates that Abraham "came before his Lord with a pure heart,"[128] while the medieval Muslim historian El-Masudi stated that Abraham was "pure from sin" and thereby "received the strength of God."[129] Without probably ever having heard of the ancient Zion, young Abraham was establishing it anew in his own heart, for as a modern revelation states, "this is Zion—THE PURE IN HEART" (D&C 97:21). He is a model for anyone and everyone aspiring to Zion. According to Brigham Young, "When we conclude to make a Zion we will make it, and this work commences in the heart of each person."[130]

Abraham's heart was also "contrite," as noted in Jewish tradition,[131] an important key to opening the door of revelation and blessing as seen in the first words God ever spoke to Abraham's descendant Nephi: "Blessed art thou Nephi, because of thy faith, for thou hast sought me diligently, with lowliness of heart" (1 Ne. 2:19).[132] Such humility is one of the distinguishing characteristics of "a true disciple of our father Abraham,"[133] according to rabbinic sources. It is also the key to receiving the cleansing power of the Atonement of Christ, who was crucified "for the remission of sins unto the contrite heart" (D&C 21:9).

As young Abraham drew near to the Almighty, the Almighty drew near to him. "When God saw how he yearned to find Him, He revealed Himself unto him and spoke with him," says the Zohar.[134] In the Apocalypse of Abraham, Abraham attests that "the true God . . . has sought me out in the perplexity of my thoughts."[135] An important Ethiopic text relates that in response to the lad's prayer, "there appeared unto him a chariot of fire which blazed." Abraham was terrified and fell to the ground, but was assured by the voice of God, saying, "Fear thou not, stand upright."[136] Only in time would Abraham come to appreciate the significance of the chariot and all that it portended for him, including divine protection (see 2 Kgs. 6:17). But even now there was again a seer on earth, one who had seen beyond the mortal realm.[137]

According to the Zohar, Abraham "loved righteousness; this was Abram's love of God, in which he excelled all his contemporaries, who were obstinate of heart and far from righteousness."[138] Abraham's own heart, according to rabbinic tradition, was like the mighty cedar, which was constantly directed heavenward, straight and true.[139] Indeed, Abraham is honored in Judaism as the supreme example of those who love God and keep his commandments.[140] The Book of Abraham unerringly reveals this same Abraham who in the opening lines of his own record tells how he "sought for the blessings of the fathers, . . . having been myself a follower of righteousness," and "desiring also to be . . . a greater follower of righteousness, . . . and to keep the commandments of God" (Abr. 1:2). Or, as told by Franklin Richards, Abraham "loved righteousness" and "hunger[ed] for more righteousness."[141] In Nibley's words, "it was Abraham's unique merit that he loved righteousness in a hard-hearted and wicked generation, without waiting for others to show him the way."[142]

By following righteousness, Abraham was also following his ancient forefathers, for as Noah is described in Genesis as *zadik*, or righteous,[143] so Abraham's righteousness is emphasized in ancient sources. Turkish tradition records the commitment of young Abraham: "I will . . . live a righteous life."[144] Abraham is remembered in the Qur'an as "Abraham the righteous [Sadiq],"[145] and likewise stands out in Jewish tradition as the example par excellence of the true *zadik*, the righteous man who fears God and serves him.[146] In the Damascus Document produced by the Dead Sea Scrolls Jewish community, Abraham is held up as an example of one who "did not choose his own will," but rather "kept the commandments of God."[147] In the words of a more modern Jewish writer, speaking of Abraham's relationship with God, "It seems that it was in Abraham's nature to be submissive, that he was an innately gentle, humble man."[148]

Abraham's exceptional righteousness and fear of God set an example for his descendants who seek Zion. And whoever possesses the same fear of God that Abraham possessed, says a medieval Jewish text, "will endeavour to improve himself and hasten to beautify his soul" and "purify his soul" in order "to find favour in the eyes of [the Lord]."[149] In other words, whoever fears God as Abraham did will seek Zion as he sought it.

Idolatry and Its Evils

The obstinacy of Abraham's people included ostentatious ceremonies designed to legitimize the idols that were central to the culture. Mesopotamian sources describe the sophisticated rituals and incantations employed by the artisans and priests to bring into being the cult statues, which after proper "opening of the mouth" and the duly impressive dedication rites were actually considered to be born of the gods, having become earthly manifestations of heavenly powers.[150]

Why the elaborate facade? Because in the end these statues provided the ultimate convenience for their owners, allowing—in the words of the Lord concerning the idolatry of our own day—"every man [to walk] . . . in his own way, after the image of his own god" (D&C 1:16). Idolatry was in Abraham's day what it has always been, as articulated by the early Church Father Tertullian—"the chief crime of mankind, the supreme guilt of the world," for "even if every sin retains its own identity and even if each is destined for judgement under its own name, each is still committed under idolatry."[151] According to Abraham's record, mankind had "turned from their righteousness, and from the holy commandments which the Lord their God had given them, unto the worshiping of the gods of the heathen" (Abr. 1:5), or, as mentioned in Jubilees, "statues, images, and unclean things."[152] But this "worship" was of a perverted sort that not only condoned any conduct but even included ritual acts of gross immorality as part of the so-called fertility rites.[153] Thus, the wickedness went beyond the widespread individual acts, having become a part of the customs, culture, norms, and even laws. Not since the generation of the Flood had the earth seen such a depraved, anti-family society. "There appeared to be little justice, certainly no chastity or decency, in the operation of this establishment,"[154] says a modern writer about the flagrantly immoral practices of Abraham's day, practices said to be required by the gods inhabiting the idols. In a world of rampant immorality, Abraham lived the law of chastity.

The great paradox of the statues, then, was that while they purported to be the earthly manifestation of gods, they were in fact tools of the devil, as so emphatically expressed in the Book of Mormon's condemnation of idolatry: "Wo unto those that worship idols, for the devil of all devils delighteth in them" (2 Ne. 9:37). When one scholar describes Abraham's society as one of "crass polytheism and demonology,"[155] it is no exaggeration, for ancient sources tell of people conversing with devils, who demanded not only the sacrifice of virtue but also of the lives of children. It is reported that the people "slaughtered their sons and their daughters to the devils, and they poured out innocent blood."[156]

Standing for Truth

Young Abraham is said to have "despised the idols and held in abomination the graven images,"[157] boldly raising his voice against idolatry.[158] According to Jubilees, Abraham admonished his father,

> What help and advantage do we get from these idols before which you worship and prostrate yourself? For there is no spirit in them because they are dumb. They are an error of the mind. Do not worship them. Worship the God of heaven. . . . He created everything . . . and all life (comes) from his presence. Why do you worship those things which have no spirit in them?

For they are made by hands and you carry them on your shoulders. You receive no help from them, but instead they are a great shame for those who make them and an error of mind for those who worship them. Do not worship them.[159]

Terah acknowledged the truth of these words, but stated that if he didn't go along with the idolatrous practices of the people, "they will kill me. . . . Be quiet, my son, so that they do not kill you."[160] In another version of the story told in the Apocalypse of Abraham, perhaps referring to another occasion, Abraham recounts that when he told Terah that his idols were a sham, "he became angry with me, because I had spoken harsh words against his gods."[161] According to the Qur'an, Abraham pled with Terah to "not worship Satan . . . lest a chastisement from the Most Gracious befall thee," at which Terah angrily retorted, "Dost thou dislike my gods, O Abraham? Indeed, if thou desist not, I shall most certainly cause thee to be stoned to death! Now begone from me for good!" To which Abraham replied, "Peace be upon thee! I shall ask my Sustainer to forgive thee; for, behold, He has always been kind unto me."[162]

The irony of such threats to young Abraham is that he had already proven himself extremely valuable to his society. Jubilees tells that during planting, before the seed could be plowed under, it would be eaten by the ravens, who thus "reduced [the people] to poverty." Abraham accompanied the planters and continually ran at the ravens before they could land, shouting and ordering them to return whence they came. He persisted tirelessly, and was so successful that "his reputation grew large throughout the entire land of the Chaldeans" as the following harvest produced plenty. The next year, he invented a device to be used during plowing that would insert the seed into the ground and cover it up. Abraham's invention was widely used, solving the problem of the birds and bringing fame to the youthful Abraham.[163]

Hence it was no small matter when he began, despite the warnings of his father, to publicly oppose idolatry. The courageous lad "protested in public and in private against the errors of the time,"[164] raising his voice both loud and long as he insisted that the idols "are not gods that can [offer] deliverance."[165] "He alone, of those everywhere suffering from the error of idols, recognized the true God and preached the Creator of all things."[166]

His listeners countered: "Would you turn us away from the faith of our fathers and introduce us to another religion?" To which Abraham replied: "Your ancestors . . . adhered to a vain faith. I am summoning you to the right path."[167] He spoke with fervor but not arrogance, and preached righteousness without being self-righteous. Demonstrating the contrast between the helpless idols and the true God of heaven, the young man explained that "the Sustainer of all the worlds . . . has created me and is the One who guides me, . . . who gives me to eat and drink, and when I fall ill . . . restores me to health, and who . . . in the resurrection will bring me back to life—and who, I hope, will forgive me my faults on Judgment Day!"[168] (The words are remarkably similar to those later used by Abraham's descendant King Benjamin; see Mosiah 4:19, 21.) Hence "Abraham offered a new vision of man's purpose and destiny. Not wallowing in pleasure or the arrogance of power, but clinging to God, to find Him and to please Him—these were man's primary purpose."[169] But, as Abraham lamented, his listeners "utterly refused to hearken to [his] voice" (Abr. 1:5).

Object Lesson

An ancient and widespread legend tells of bold action taken by the young Abraham. The story is not found in the Bible, but it is the most oft-repeated Abrahamic narrative in the Qur'an,[170] is found in numerous ancient Jewish sources,[171] and was repeated by Brigham Young, John Taylor, and Wilford Woodruff.[172] As recounted by Jewish sources, it began when the young Abraham found himself alone in a room full of idols. But one important source, the Maaseh Avraham Avinu, specifies that this was not just any occasion and not just any room full of idols. The event was a major religious festival called by King Nimrod himself and was centered at Nimrod's pagan temple. Abraham had been urged to attend by his father but declined to go and was instructed to stay behind to guard the idols. "And the king's idols were also there," says the Maaseh.[173]

When Abraham was all alone, he acted boldly and decisively. Some sources report that "the Spirit of God came upon [him]."[174] As recounted by the Maaseh Avraham Avinu, "He took an axe in his hand, and as he saw the idols of the king sitting, he said, 'The Eternal, He is God,'" and he "pushed them off their thrones to the ground, and he smote them mightily. With the large ones he began, and with the small ones he finished. He lopped off this one's hands, he cut off this one's head and blinded this one's eyes, and he broke that one's legs" until "all of them were broken." Then, placing "the axe in the hand of the largest idol," Abraham left.[175]

When his father and the king returned and discovered the wreckage, they were wroth. "The king commanded that Abraham be brought before him. And they brought him. The king and his ministers said to him, 'Why did you shatter our gods?' He said to them, 'I didn't break them, no. Rather, the large one of them smashed them. Don't you see that the axe is in his hand? And if you won't believe it, ask him and he will tell.' And as [the king] heard his words, he became angry to the point of killing him."[176]

"Abram Found Guilty of Destroying Idols." Had there been a newspaper at the time, it might have carried this shocking headline, as one chronicle imaginatively reconstructs.[177] Abraham's actions posed a challenge to the whole society steeped in idolatry. "The whole world stood on one side and [Abraham] on the other,"[178] said the rabbis. Or in Nibley's words, "it was Abraham against the whole society,"[179] including the king himself. And "with all the world going in one direction, he steadily pursues his course in the opposite direction."[180]

But if Abraham was against the whole world, it was only because he was truly for the whole world, for "even when they preach repentance and thunder words of warning, the prophets bring nothing but good news . . . [and] glad tidings of great joy."[181] In a world that had strayed as far away from Zion as possible, one pure lad was courageously seeking to reestablish it, and setting a pattern for his posterity. "It is the mark of a descendant of Abraham that he is able to swim against the tide, to stand up . . . for what he believes and, even though he be in the minority, not be corrupted by the pressures of the environment."[182] Abraham's action "points to the fact that it is not enough to merely serve as an example of goodness. Sometimes it is necessary to fight actively to eradicate evil."[183]

A FACSIMILE FROM THE BOOK OF ABRAHAM
NO. 1

Explanation

Fig. 1.   The Angel of the Lord.

Fig. 2.   Abraham fastened upon an altar.

Fig. 3.   The idolatrous priest of Elkenah attempting to offer up Abraham as a sacrifice.

Fig. 4.   The altar for sacrifice by the idolatrous priests, standing before the gods of Elkenah, Libnah, Mahmackrah,
Korash, and Pharaoh.

Fig. 5.   The idolatrous god of Elkenah.

Fig. 6.   The idolatrous god of Libnah.

Fig. 7.   The idolatrous god of Mahmackrah.

Fig. 8.   The idolatrous god of Korash.

Fig. 9.   The idolatrous god of Pharaoh.

Fig. 10. Abraham in Egypt.

Fig. 11. Designed to represent the pillars of heaven, as understood by the Egyptians.

Fig. 12. Raukeeyang, signifying expanse, or the firmament over our heads; but in this case, in relation to this subject,
the Egyptians meant it to signify Shaumau, to be high, or the heavens, answering to the Hebrew word,
Shaumahyeem.

CHAPTER 2

The Beginnings of a New Zion:
Divine Intervention, Marriage, and Seeking a New Home

Fear not . . . ; let earth and hell combine against you,
for if ye are built upon my rock, they cannot prevail.
—DOCTRINE AND COVENANTS 6:34

Consigned to Death

Since the days of Abraham, in times of grave danger for the House of Israel, it is the God of Abraham who comes to their rescue as both God and His people remember Abraham and the covenant made to him. When the Israelites groaned under the heavy burden of Egyptian bondage, "God heard their groaning, and . . . remembered his covenant with Abraham, with Isaac, and with Jacob" (Ex. 2:24), whereupon he announced himself to Moses and his colleagues as "the God of Abraham, Isaac, and Jacob" (Ex. 3:6, 15–16). Later when Israel was about to be destroyed in the wilderness for worshiping the golden calf, Moses persuaded God to mercy by imploring Him to remember Abraham, Isaac, and Jacob (see Ex. 32:13). "In each of these dangerous times," notes a prominent scholar, "the memory of Abraham induces a turn of mind and opens a possibility for overcoming a dire crisis."[1]

Likewise at the commencement of the New Testament story, with Israel under Roman oppression, God's impending intervention in sending His Son is hailed by Mary and Zechariah praising God for rescuing Israel in remembrance of His covenant to Abraham (Luke 1:46–55, 68–79). A similar phenomenon is seen repeatedly in the Book of Mormon. Limhi's people in bondage are counseled to "put your trust in God, in that God who was the God of Abraham, the God of Isaac, and the God of Jacob" (Mosiah 7:19), while the three different reports of God delivering Alma's people from bondage all emphasize that it was done only by the power of the God of Abraham, Isaac, and Jacob (Mosiah 23:23; Alma 29:11; 36:2). Later when the Nephite nation is delivered from their enemies, they declared: "May the God of Abraham, and the God of Isaac, and the God of Jacob, protect this people in righteousness" (3 Ne. 4:30). And when Moroni seeks to convince latter-day readers about the power of the Almighty, he promises to show them "a God of miracles, even the God of Abraham, and the God of Isaac, and the God of Jacob" (Morm. 9:11).

What all these passages consistently presuppose is some kind of miraculous deliverance of Abraham himself, momentous enough to inspire his future descendants to trust in that same God for their own deliverance in the face of otherwise impossible odds. No such event in Abraham's life appears in Genesis, but it was the opinion of no less an authority than Nachmanides, the learned medieval rabbi who wrote an extensive commentary on the Torah, that Genesis had in fact once contained just such an account, but that "Scripture no longer mentions this miracle."[2] Fortunately, with the restoration of the gospel came the restoration of scripture—the Book of Abraham—narrating that singular miracle, which is similarly described in numerous other ancient sources.

The story begins with young Abraham on a collision course with the world around him. He was opposing the practices not merely of a few wicked individuals but of a whole society whose "hearts were set to evil" (Abr. 1:6) and who would tolerate no questioning of their evil ways. The result was a tumult not unlike what Joseph Smith would excite, part of what Hugh Nibley calls the "astonishing parallels"[3] between the two even as boys:

> The youthful Abraham, like the youthful Joseph Smith, seems to have been in trouble with his society, and . . . caused a great stir and annoyance. . . . When we read of an . . . innocuous young man exciting general uproar throughout the length of Mesopotamia or causing a mighty monarch to spend sleepless nights, we smile and brush the thing aside as the stuff of legend. . . . Such things, we say, just don't happen in real life. Only oddly enough, there is an exception—in the case of real prophets, they do happen, as modern history attests. What would students say 3,500 years from now to the proposition that thousands of years before there lived a naive, uneducated, and guileless country boy in a small village somewhere in the woods beyond what were known as the Allegheny Mountains who by a few tactless and unbelievably artless remarks created the greatest excitement in the large seaboard cities of the continent, was hotly denounced in thousands of pulpits throughout the civilized world, and was

given front-page coverage in the major newspapers of the capitals of Europe? Could a less plausible story be imagined?[4]

Jewish tradition remembers that "when Abraham attacked the doctrines of his fellow-men who adhered to erroneous views, he was denounced and scorned,"[5] "reviled and cursed," but responded only with silence.[6] Nevertheless, "they rose against him, looted his property, imprisoned him."[7] According to ancient Jewish tradition, Abraham was incarcerated several times for lengthy periods, perhaps years, in cities in the region of present-day eastern Turkey.[8] From the crucible of tribulation can come greatness, and Abraham is the parade example. He "learned compassion by being an outcast himself,"[9] observes Hugh Nibley. Several sources report miraculous protection during the difficult trial: when Abraham was deprived of food and water by direct order of the King, the Lord provided the needed sustenance.[10] Abraham used the occasion to teach the astonished jailer about the power of the true God, and the jailer believed.[11]

The incredible persecution heaped upon young Abraham foreshadowed the same fate awaiting Joseph Smith, who would marvel at the "bitter persecution and reviling" he was called to pass through while yet in his youth (JS—H 1:23), and who also would endure imprisonment and privation (see D&C 121–123). Both were warned at an early age by God of the tribulation that awaited them in this life: "In this world," God told young Abraham, "thy life will indeed be precarious, but thy reward awaits thee in the hereafter."[12] The youthful Joseph Smith was similarly told to "be patient in afflictions, for thou shalt have many; but endure them, for, lo, I am with thee, even unto the end of thy days" (D&C 24:8).

Thus did the Almighty predict their many problems, but why did He allow such problems in the lives of these choicest of servants? While the Prophet Joseph languished in Liberty Jail, he received a revelation assuring him that the unjustified maltreatment would "give [him] experience, and . . . be for [his] good" (D&C 122:7). What Brigham Young later said of Joseph Smith seems to apply equally to Abraham: he "could not have been perfected, though he had lived a thousand years, if he had received no persecution."[13] In the words of Jewish scholars, "great though Abraham was, he became greater with each triumphant surmounting of a new trial."[14] As did his future posterity, as understood by Judaism: every trial that he had "remained with us and became a part of us" as God proceeded each time "to chisel a new trait into the eternity of Israel."[15]

The same truths that Abraham preached to the lowly jailor he was no less shy in proclaiming to the king. "Oh Nimrod," declared Abraham in one of apparently many face-to-face dialogues with the monarch, "I ask you to become a true believer."[16] But Nimrod and the others in power remained as hard-hearted as ever, and, inspired by Satan,[17] decided that Abraham was to become the victim of the human sacrifices that he had preached against. Abraham's message was dangerous, striking at the very heart of the royal ideology that served as the foundation of Nimrod's power. No wonder that Nimrod finally "decided that Abraham's presence would be a menace to his throne."[18]

Abraham received no assistance from his father, whose worldly wealth and status depended directly on Nimrod's favor. A midrash tells of a time when the Lord warned Abraham of the evil intent of his smooth-talking relatives and own father: "Thy father and thy brethren speak fair words; do not believe them, for they are all in conspiracy against thee, seeking to slay thee."[19] In Abraham's own words reported in the Book of Abraham, "My fathers . . . hearkened not unto my voice, but endeavored to take away my life" (Abr. 1:5–7; and see v. 30). Jewish tradition tells that it was Terah himself who delivered Abraham into the hands of Nimrod.[20]

The Book of Abraham tells of an "altar which stood by the hill called Potiphar's Hill, at the head of the plain of Olishem," where human sacrifices were offered. "And it came to pass that the priests laid violence upon me, that they might slay me also" (Abr. 1:10, 12). A Turkish source relates that they took him from the place where they had kept him bound "with heavy fetters."[21] Nibley explains that "the setting is typical of the ancient cult-places with their broad 'plain of assembly,' the elevated mound, hill, or tower (hence pyramid and ziggurat), and the altar for sacrificing."[22] Jewish tradition tells of a vast audience assembled: "all the king's servants, princes, lords, governors and judges, and all the inhabitants of the land, about nine hundred thousand" in number, came "to see Abram. And all the women and little ones crowded . . . together . . . ; and there was not a man left that did not come on that day to behold the scene."[23]

One can get some idea of the horrific scene from atop one of the pyramids at Teotihuacan outside Mexico City, where Aztec priests likewise sacrificed human beings in front of multitudes. Why the grandiose display? Because these were not just executions, but carefully staged rites designed by the ruling powers pursuant to an elaborately evil theology. As one scholar has explained about human sacrifice among the Mayas, it "was a public spectacle, a collective experience" that "crowds . . . pressed" to witness, carefully orchestrated to increase the power of the ruling elite.[24]

But in Abraham's case there was something more, something that made this particular sacrifice unique in all of history. Abraham's own illustration of the scene shows a ceremonial ritual setting with himself lying on an altar shaped like a lion, next to which are idols representing different gods, including the gods of Pharaoh, king of Egypt. But standing over the altar is a figure described as the priest of both Pharaoh and of Elkenah,[25] the latter being probably one among that "circle of gods, attested from the earliest inscriptions of the thirtieth century B.C., who were current at the [Egyptian] royal court as well as having their own cult places."[26]

In Abraham's case, the cult place was outside of Egypt, on Asiatic soil in the land of Ur, yet there is still heavy Egyptian influence—calling to mind that in Jewish tradition, Nimrod is repeatedly referred to as a descendant of Canaan[27] (whose sister, as the Book of Abraham relates, founded the first dynasty of Egypt with her son as the first Pharaoh; see Abr. 1:20–27). An early Samaritan source tells that in the days of Abraham, Egypt and Canaan were ruled by the same monarch.[28] And recent archeological findings, as explained in Redford's authoritative *Oxford Encyclopedia of Ancient Egypt,* confirm that during the early second millennium B.C., Egypt exercised great influence in the region of Syria-Palestine.[29]

The remarkable thing for Latter-day Saints is that none of this was known in Joseph Smith's day, and the twentieth-century discovery of Egyptian political and cultural influence during Abraham's day was startling enough to warrant special comment in the 1965 revised edition of the *Cambridge Ancient History.* Recent discoveries in Syria and Palestine, say the authors, leave "the impression of domination by the pharaohs, uneven and interrupted, no doubt, but on the whole vigorous. Its precise nature still eludes us; fifty years ago it was barely suspected. In view of this progressive increase in our knowledge, we shall err less if we exaggerate than if we minimize the hold the Twelfth Dynasty had over Syria and Palestine. For the first time in history, those countries experienced the effects of a considerable expansion on the part of Egypt and were likewise subjected to her cultural influence."[30] It is yet another vindication of the Book of Abraham, explaining what was not apparent in Joseph Smith's day—how it was that a ritual human sacrifice could have been performed under Egyptian auspices in Ur of the Chaldees.

In fact, one of the Twelfth Dynasty pharaohs of that era is famous for his military campaigns abroad, including in Syria-Palestine.[31] That same pharaoh is also on record[32] as an example of the ancient requirement that the king lay down his life for his people in a ceremony to propitiate the gods.[33] It was "the ancient penalty of kingship"[34] for both Egyptian and Mesopotamian kings, a penalty usually paid by means of a substitute sacrifice who was often a foreigner.[35] Abraham was apparently being offered in that same rite as a sacrifice for the king.[36] As Nibley explains, "Abraham is not simply being executed; he is the central figure of an extremely important ritual in which 'the idolatrous god of Pharaoh' figures conspicuously, and the competing powers of heaven and hell come into conflict both in their superhuman and their appointed representatives."[37]

The profound irony was that Pharaoh, like Nimrod[38] (one tradition remembers Pharaoh as being the son of Nimrod[39]), was a pretender to the patriarchal authority reserved for Abraham, and had—as we learn from Abraham himself in the Book of Abraham—established a highly sophisticated but corrupt imitation of the ancient order of Zion (Abr. 1:26–27). Hence the intended sacrifice of Abraham was not only the height of paradox but was, and remains to this day, absolutely unique in all of history: the true patriarchal heir to the authority of Zion was about to be slaughtered as a ritual substitute for his rival who falsely claimed that very authority. Zion's evil counterfeit in all its pomp and ceremony was about to execute the one righteous man whom God had sent to bless the world and reestablish on earth the true Zion. Only in the sacrifice of the Savior do we see a similar phenomenon, of which Abraham on the altar is a striking type.

"Abram, Abram!"

With Abraham lying bound on the altar, his death already seemed a *fait accompli,* for the odds appeared overwhelming. With the vast multitude gazing on, Abraham was apparently given a final opportunity to recant. Jewish tradition tells of Satan appearing in human form and urging Abraham to save himself by bowing down in worship to Nimrod. Abraham refused.[40] Even Abraham's mother urged her son to "bow down to Nimrod and convert to his faith, and you will be saved." Again Abraham refused, whereupon his mother said to him: "May the God whom you serve, save you."[41]

As the solemn sacrificial ceremony proceeded to its climax, the priest of Pharaoh grasped the knife and raised it above Abraham. Meanwhile, according to Jewish tradition, the angels on high were pleading with God to allow them to intervene and save Abraham.[42] But it was Abraham's own prayer that he reported later: "As they lifted up their hands upon me, that they might offer me up and take away my life, behold, I lifted up my voice unto the Lord my God" (Abr. 1:15). According to Jewish tradition, Abraham "raised his eyes heavenward" with a "confidence in God [which] was unshakable."[43] Al-Tabari reports that Abraham also raised his head heavenward.[44]

As told in the Book of Abraham, "the Lord hearkened and heard, and he filled me with the vision of the Almighty, and the angel of his presence stood by me, and immediately unloosed my bands" (Abr. 1:15). Abraham heard a heavenly voice call his name twice—"Abram, Abram!"[45]—while "the Lord broke down the altar of Elkenah, and of the gods of the land, and utterly destroyed them, and smote the priest that he died" (Abr. 1:20). That the angel was visible to the onlookers is attested in Jewish and Muslim traditions,[46] which also tell of a great earthquake[47] and of a cataclysmic fire that consumed many thousands of onlookers.[48] Meanwhile, says a Turkish source, "in Abraham's breast there was the fire of his love for the Lord."[49] Abraham's deliverance was an unprecedented miracle, noted the Pirke de Rabbi Eliezer, and its fame would soon spread to the kings of the earth.[50]

Those present that day who witnessed the miracle and escaped the destruction were, as told in the Book of Abraham, smitten with a severe famine (Abr. 1:29–30). A Turkish account says that "there was famine in all the countries," and "there was no food to be found."[51] It was recompense for the harm that had been designed for Abraham when he had been deprived of sustenance and had then seen the priest lift his hand to inflict the death blow, and it was sent by the Almighty: "God took away the rain from them," reports one Islamic tradition.[52]

When the angel of the presence intervened and called to Abraham, it was with a message from the Lord: "Behold, my name is Jehovah, and I have heard thee, and have come down to deliver thee, and . . . I have come down to visit them, and to destroy him who hath lifted up his hand against thee . . . to take away thy life" (Abr. 1:16–17).

Abraham's vision of the Almighty was remembered by the New Testament character Stephen, who, just before receiving his own vision of the Almighty, attested that "the God of glory appeared to our father Abraham while he was still in Mesopotamia, before he lived in Haran" (NIV Acts 7:2). Stephen's vision came as he was being martyred, on his way to the God of glory. Had Abraham died on the altar in Ur after his vision, he also would surely have gone to God as one of history's courageous martyrs, secure in his eternal reward. But it was far more than Abraham's fate that was at stake that day. "What if . . . ?" is the thought-provoking question posed by a group of historians who analyzed some of history's most pivotal events and how the world would be different if any one of those events had gone differently.[53] But none of those events matches what was hanging in the balance on that fateful day in Ur over three millennia ago when Abraham was strapped to an altar. What the world would have been like had he perished that day will become more evident as his story unfolds, but suffice it to say for now that in God's grand design, Abraham's work had just begun as the divine instrument of blessing and transforming the world.

It was poetic justice, then, that God had not just saved Abraham, but had done so in the most visible and dramatic fashion possible, and in a way that vindicated him in the eyes of all. Abraham had insisted that the idols were devoid of any power to deliver, and now God had delivered Abraham by breaking down the idols—even as Abraham had broken them down before.

Abraham's remarkable deliverance from death is memorialized to this day in a Muslim teaching to "consider and understand the trials given to the prophets," as, for example, "Abraham with Nimrod and with his father." Indeed, God's protection of Abraham remains a living reality for Muslims, who direct their prayers to Him "who [did] succour Abraham against his foes."[54] Judaism similarly declares that "we . . . pray . . . to him who answered Abraham."[55]

But Abraham's deliverance would prove to be not just inspirational but actually a pattern of things to come. Many years hence, the same God who had delivered

Abraham would call him to lay his beloved son Isaac on an altar in a sacrificial rite. Abraham's deliverance further portended what will transpire in the last days, when Abraham's righteous posterity will be vastly outnumbered by enemies bent on their destruction (1 Ne. 14:13–14). Again the earth will quake (Moses 7:61; D&C 88:87), and the Lord will descend with his angels (Jude 1:14–15) to deliver Abraham's righteous seed and destroy their enemies (1 Ne. 22:17; 2 Ne. 30:13). Speaking of the great event, Isaiah foretold that those "diligent for evil shall be wiped out" by the same Lord "who redeemed Abraham" (JPST Isa. 29:20, 22).[56] One apocryphal source even specifies that when the Lord comes "to work vengeance on the nations . . . all their idols will he destroy"[57]—a repeat of Abraham's experience. Abraham's miraculous deliverance on the altar in Ur may well be history's most prophetic similitude of the Second Coming.

Young Abraham had desired to change his world, and God honored that desire by rescuing him in a way that already began some dramatic changes. So marvelous, in fact, was Abraham's deliverance that many of the onlookers, including Nimrod's own officials and ministers, believed in God and bore witness to others of God's power and that Abraham was his servant.[58] In addition, "many followed Abraham home, and brought their children to him, and said, 'Now we see that the God in whom thou trustest, is the only true God; teach our children the truth, that they may serve Him in righteousness.'"[59]

It was but the beginning of tremendous change for the world, for the Lord had designated Abraham as a divine instrument of change: "I [will] . . . take thee away from thy father's house, and from all thy kinsfolk, into a strange land which thou knowest not of; and . . . I will lead thee by my hand"—echoing an ancient Jewish source telling that Abraham was saved from death when God "put forth His right hand and delivered him."[60]

The message from the Lord continued: "And I will take thee, to put upon thee my name, even the Priesthood of thy father, and my power shall be over thee. As it was with Noah so shall it be with thee; but through thy ministry my name shall be known in the earth forever, for I am thy God" (Abr. 1:16, 18–19).

The Lord spoke these words, the Book of Abraham tells, through "the angel of his presence" (Abr. 1:15–16). Who was this angel? Read in isolation, the Book of Abraham passage may seem to indicate that the angel was Jehovah himself: "my name is Jehovah, and I have . . . come down to deliver thee" (Abr. 1:16). Later, however, the Book of Abraham makes it clear that the angel of the presence was not the Lord but indeed one of His angels, as Abraham tells the Lord: "Thou didst send thine angel to deliver me" (Abr. 2:13; and see 3:20).

In the Book of Abraham, the angel remains unnamed, but a passage in the Joseph Smith Translation of Genesis seems to suggest a connection with Enoch, whose priesthood, we are told, not only allowed mortals to be "translated and taken up into heaven" but also to "subdue principalities and powers" and to "break every band" (JST Gen. 14:31–32). So had Abraham's bands been broken as the principalities and powers about to destroy him were subdued by the divine power of God's mighty angel. The angel of the presence is mentioned in Exodus (23:20–21), and is identified as Enoch in Talmudic tradition[61] and, as we shall see, in apocryphal Enoch sources. All this suggests that the angel of the presence who rescued Abraham from the altar was none other than his forefather Enoch, about whom Abraham would later learn by reading Enoch's record. From Zion above had come Enoch to rescue Abraham, the man who had already begun to establish Zion in his own heart. It is an event never to be forgotten: at the very moment of the seeming greatest triumph of the forces arrayed in their sanctimonious might to destroy Zion below, Zion above broke through, triumphant. And so shall it happen again.

Sarai the Princess

If Zion begins in the heart, it culminates in the union of righteous hearts, as when Abraham married the lovely Sarai. All the sources attest that she was a close relative—perhaps a half-sister (the daughter of his father through another wife) (Gen. 20:12),[62] or perhaps a niece[63] or a cousin.[64] The close kinship with Abraham and the quality of her character suggest the possibility of mutual sympathy and support long before their marriage. Had she been in the crowd that day when Abraham had been miraculously rescued? Had her prayers and faith helped sustain him during his trials and tribulations? Had her strength already been part of his success? Had she long prayed for this eternal union? Such questions remain as yet unanswered, although we do have Philo's observation that she was "the darling of his heart," and their love for each other was profound.[65]

The name Sarai, which God would later alter to Sarah, means "princess" or possibly "queen,"[66] suggesting royal blood. Was this perhaps a reflection that her bloodline ran through the royal patriarchal line to which Abraham himself was heir? Or was her father, as an Islamic tradition tells, called Haran and did he rule as the king of Haran[67] (perhaps Abraham's uncle)? Or, as another Islamic tradition relates, was Sarah closely related to Nimrod[68] or to one of his highest officials?[69] (Given Terah's high place at court, some sort of blood relationship with the Nimrod dynasty does not seem impossible.)

Any or several of these are possible. But whatever the biological relationship with royalty, her name was a fitting title for a woman who possessed singular loveliness of both body and soul. Her unequaled physical beauty[70] would turn the heads of the most powerful kings, while she was also "gifted with every excellence"[71] and "great wisdom."[72] It is said that her spiritual attainments matched and in some cases exceeded those of her remarkable husband,[73] she being gifted with profound "intuitive perception" of spiritual realities.[74] A number of sources assert yet another name for her—Iscah, meaning "prophetess" or "seer."[75] And with all her talents, she had a deep "love and compassion . . . for the needy."[76] She was indeed "a Princess in name and in nature."[77]

Abraham had been alone in the world, alone against the world, but now everything had changed. It might be said of Abraham and Sarah what was said of another couple: "These two were alone in the world, and yet they might scarcely be said to feel their loneliness; for they were all the world to each other."[78] Jewish tradition insists that they were perfectly suited for each other.[79]

Genesis gives no direct description of Sarah as a wife, but Jewish tradition insists that she is the one described in the famous Proverbs passage extolling the "virtuous woman" (31:10)[80] (or the woman "of valor,"[81] or the "capable" or "accomplished" woman[82]). Her worth is far above rubies, and her husband safely trusts in her; she is an industrious homemaker, a tireless worker, and generous to the poor; she speaks wisdom and kindness (*hesed*[83]), is cheerful and hopeful about the future, and is clothed with strength and splendor; she is, in short, the ideal wife, deserving of her husband's highest praise. Sarah's example was held up through the generations among her Jewish descendants, in whose homes the Proverbs passage was traditionally recited on the Sabbath eve.[84]

Sarah had her work, and Abraham had his, but it was all part of the same cause. From this point on in Abraham's life, to speak of his mission and accomplishments is necessarily to include Sarah also; for as a modern rabbi has observed, she was not merely a strong personality in her own right, but, as Abraham's spouse, was "an important balancing factor in his life. Abraham and Sarah were not just 'a married couple' but a team, two people working in harmony," as seen in the Genesis portrayal "of the two as one unit" and "as equals"—"as partners, working together for the same goals, walking together along the same path, united in thought, word, and deed."[85] Or, as told by Philo, "Everywhere and always she was at his side, . . . his true partner in life and life's events, resolved to share alike the good and the ill."[86] Theirs was that priceless unity of heart and mind that is ever the hallmark of Zion. Having established Zion in their own hearts, they now began to establish it in their marriage and home, an enduring example for all couples aspiring to build Zion. "When the father of a family wishes to make a Zion in his own house," declared Brigham Young, "he must take the lead in this good work, which . . . is impossible for him to do unless he himself possesses the Spirit of Zion. Before he can produce the work of sanctification in his family, he must sanctify himself, and by this means God can help him to sanctify his family."[87]

Abraham and Sarah were a part of something larger than either of them. They were a family, they were Zion, and they are to be remembered together, according to Isaiah: the righteous are to look not only to their father Abraham but also to their mother Sarah (Isa. 51:1–2).

"Get Thee Out!"

That Abraham and Sarah ever became parents at all is a remarkable story, which begins with the poignant verse in Genesis: "But Sarai was barren; she had no child" (Gen. 11:30). This statement is absent at the corresponding point in the Book of Abraham narrative (see Abr. 2:2),[88] indicating a later insertion by Moses (or a subsequent editor) remarking on what Abraham himself kindly refused to say, that his beloved wife bore him no child. Moreover, the Genesis statement pointing to Sarah as the cause of the problem presupposes the writer's knowledge about later events in Abraham's life which will demonstrate that it was in fact Sarah who was infertile. But the statement is important for the reader, as it introduces a key dimension of the story, whose unfolding will include repeated divine promises of a vast and illustrious posterity.

Even before the receipt of those promises, however, the inability of Abraham and Sarah to conceive a child would have proven a sore trial. As a modern Jewish commentator notes, the Genesis report of Sarai's barrenness is "freighted with irony," for while all the world effortlessly reproduce, the life of this righteous couple was "marked by an emptiness."[89] To this day, infertility can be a unique trial whose depth seems to be fathomed only by those who experience it. Modern women speak of it as "an emotional roller coaster, the worst thing I've ever gone through in my life,"[90] an agony whose "frustrations . . . can indeed seem endless."[91] With each passing month and year comes an ever heightened awareness of, and increased hope for, the great blessing that is yet withheld, eclipsing all other concerns and bringing what can turn into a deep anxiety and longing. With the birth of each new infant around them, the sense of loss becomes ever more acute.

It was in this context of trial, without visible prospects for the future continuation of his line, that Abraham was given yet another trial, as he was divinely commanded to cut himself off from his past: "Get thee out of thy country, and from thy kindred, and from thy father's house, unto a land that I will show thee" (Abr. 2:3; and see Gen. 12:1). It was one of Abraham's great tests, notes the Pirke de Rabbi Eliezer; for "being compelled to pick oneself up and move is one of the most difficult things for a human being to do."[92]

This watershed command—portrayed as clearly unprecedented[93]—is reported in both Genesis (12:1–3) and the Book of Abraham (2:3), the latter indicating that it followed deep reflection on Abraham's part (1:1–2). According to the Zohar, the command came only after the Holy One saw how Abraham "bestirred himself, and . . . yearned for divine communion."[94] As to how the revelation came, there is no indication of any vision or appearance by the Lord, indicating that the command was probably delivered by the Lord's voice alone, the same voice described by Nephi as "a still small voice" that is heard through "feeling" (1 Ne. 17:45). Modern rabbi Levi Meier observes that "what Abram most certainly heard was an inner voice, something inside him. And the inner voice is a silent voice," one that Abraham would hear "on many occasions during his lifetime. . . . For most of us [this voice] is drowned out by so many competing voices. . . . This is why Abram is such an exemplary role model. Because he hears the call and goes."[95] In fact, an ancient midrash recounts that upon hearing the command, "without hesitation Abraham made answer: 'Lo, I stand before Thee; whithersoever Thou desirest, I go.'"[96]

To where? A destination unknown. "Is there a man who travels without knowing to what destination he travels?" asks a midrash.[97] Abraham was asked to leave the known for the unknown, relying, to borrow Nephi's phrase, "wholly upon the merits of him who is mighty to save" (2 Ne. 31:19). Commenting on Abraham's experience, John Taylor stated:

> I fancy I see some of his neighbors coming to him and saying, "Abraham, where are you going?"
>
> "Oh," says he, "I do not know."
>
> "You don't know."
>
> "No."
>
> "Well, who told you to go?"
>
> "The Lord."
>
> "And you do not know where you are going?"
>
> "Oh, no," says he, "I am going to a land that he will show me. . . . I believe in God, and therefore I am starting."[98]

Even so, as a modern Jewish writer observes, "there must have been considerable apprehensiveness among his followers, for their leader could not tell them precisely where he was headed."[99] But Abraham's obedience did not depend on public opinion. Constant obedience would be a hallmark of his life. He always, Philo noted, "made a special practice of obedience to God."[100] Or, in the words of modern writers, "Abram's characteristic was that in simple unhesitating faith he acted at once on every intimation of the divine will,"[101] demonstrating that his "one supreme motive [was] to honor and obey God."[102] It was Abraham's first principle, the foundation of everything else he would accomplish, recalling the teaching of latter-day leaders that "*obedience* is the first law of heaven, the corner-stone upon which all righteousness and progression rest."[103] Abraham stands out in Judaism as "the illuminating example of perfect obedience to the commands of God rendered out of love."[104]

And not just Abraham, but Sarah also. A midrash declares that both "perfectly obeyed the will of God."[105] In Nibley's words, "they kept the law fully, and they kept it together."[106] Their perfect obedience is like that of their descendant Joseph Smith, who stated: "I made this my rule: When the Lord commands, do it."[107]

Abraham's call to leave his homeland prefigured what would happen with many of his descendants, as noted by a number of latter-day leaders. "When the Latter-day Saints received the gospel in the nations afar," noted Lorenzo Snow, "the voice of the Almighty to them was to leave the lands of their fathers, to leave their kindred as Abraham did."[108] Franklin D. Richards further noted that as Abraham had to leave his native land for a place he had never seen, "this is just the same feeling and spirit that took hold of many of us Latter-day Saints in the various nations where we heard this Gospel. We became all at once strangers. Our relations and best friends became our enemies, many of us were turned out and found a gathering place with the saints."[109] Thus did the latter-day fulfillment of Abraham's covenant echo the pattern of his own life.

But God's command to Abraham required more than just a physical journey. The phrase "Get thee out"—or "Go-you-forth"[110] or "Go forth"[111]—translates the Hebrew *lek leka* (or *lech lecha*), an emphatic double imperative rendered by some translations as "Leave . . . and go"[112] or "Get up and get going!"[113] Implicit in the Hebrew phrase is the idea of "separating,"[114] so that the Lord was requiring of Abraham a "clean break with his traditions and previous way of life, . . . his environment, associations, experiences";[115] in other words, a "separation from the world."[116] By this command to Abraham, said a nineteenth-century Torah scholar, "God told him that the purpose of his leaving was to become severed from ideas and a way of life that were corrupt."[117]

Hence God's call to Abraham is a call also to his posterity, a fact that Judaism sought to perpetually remember by titling Abraham's biography, both in the Torah and its commentaries, by the very words of that call: "Lek leka."[118] Early Christianity similarly understood Abraham's call as a call still in force in their day, a call for all to leave their sins and follow Jesus.[119] And as Abraham was commanded to leave the land of idols, so his latter-day posterity are warned of the spiritual idolatry of modern-day Babylon, which, the Lord declares, will soon fall

(D&C 1:16). Therefore, the Lord declares, "Go ye out from . . . Babylon, from the midst of wickedness, which is spiritual Babylon" (D&C 133:14).[120]

To where are we to go? This same passage specifies the destination: "Flee unto Zion" (D&C 133:12).[121] Zion is not made by reforming corrupt and apostate institutions; it is a plant of pure, new growth, beginning with a pure, prayerful lad like the young Abraham, or later like his descendant young Joseph Smith. Abraham, one man, was called to separate himself physically and spiritually from the Babylon of his day in order to go and establish a new community, even Zion. His call was the turning point in human history, a watershed event "setting in motion the greatest chain of events the world has known."[122] It is an event never to be forgotten, as the Lord commanded the righteous through Isaiah: "Look to Abraham your father and to Sarah who bore you; for he was but one when I called him, but I called him and made him many. For the Lord will comfort Zion" (NRSV Isa. 51:2–3).

Thus did the Lord call Abraham and send him forth, as implied in the word *lek*, an important term used in Israelite and other ancient Near Eastern enthronement rituals to send forth one whom the Lord has divinely commissioned, following the pattern of Enoch.[123] Zion would begin again with Abraham, whom the Lord had sent. Indeed, one Jewish writer sees a parallel between Enoch being taken to heaven, and Abraham being commanded to leave his native land: in both cases God takes "His chosen, His loved ones, those who walk with Him," to a place of closer fellowship with God.[124]

Genesis misleadingly reports this command to leave as having been accompanied by promises of blessing, which, as the Book of Abraham makes clear, were actually not given until years later.[125] But even the command itself in its original Hebrew carries the meaning of "Go for yourself,"[126] or, as in the Zohar, "for thine own advantage, to prepare thyself, to perfect thy[self]," and "to know thyself,"[127] or, as Rashi says, "for your own benefit,"[128] for your "own good and . . . happiness"[129]—or, according to a Hasidic source, "to yourself," implying that only by means of this journey would Abraham reach his full potential.[130] The redundancy in Hebrew, *lek leka*, may thus refer to a journey that has both physical and spiritual dimensions. It is a perfect illustration of the principle expressed by Joseph Smith that the Lord "never will . . . give a commandment . . . that is not calculated . . . to promote . . . happiness," for "happiness is the object and design of our existence."[131] How well Abraham understood this is seen in his statement in the Book of Abraham that even though he left Ur pursuant to the divine command—"the Lord had said unto me . . . , Get thee out" (Abr. 2:3)—yet he knew it was for his own happiness and would facilitate his quest for further blessing:

> I, Abraham, saw that it was needful for me to obtain another place of residence; and, finding there was greater happiness and peace and rest for me, I sought for the blessings of the fathers, and the right whereunto I should be ordained to administer the same; having been myself a follower of righteousness, desiring also to be one who possessed great knowledge, and to be a greater follower of righteousness, and to possess a greater knowledge, and to be a father of many nations, a prince of peace, and desiring to receive instructions, and to keep the commandments of God. (Abr. 1:1–2)

No text is more important than this one for understanding Abraham. He was seeking neither fortune or fame, the great objects so feverishly pursued by the world. What he was seeking was righteousness and its rewards: happiness, which never follows wickedness (Alma 41:10); peace, which is a sure reward of righteousness (D&C 59:23); rest, a spiritual condition which comes to the meek and lowly of heart (Alma 37:34); and blessings, which are always predicated on obedience (D&C 130:20–21). He sought, in other words, the kingdom of God, even Zion, with its gospel and its ordinances, and the authority to administer those to others—the very things the Lord had already promised when He said He would lead him by the hand and give him the priesthood and make him a minister (Abr. 1:18–19). "Abraham sought for his appointment to the priesthood," emphasized President Spencer W. Kimball; "he did not wait for God to come to him; he sought diligently through prayer and obedient living to learn the will of God."[132] And Abraham's search, adds President Ezra Taft Benson, is a pattern for modern men to "seek their priesthood blessings just as Abraham sought his."[133]

For Abraham it was a difficult search; as the Lord would later tell him, his contemporaries "have gone astray from my precepts, and have not kept mine ordinances, which I gave unto their fathers" (JST Gen. 17:4). The book of Jubilees likewise laments that in Abraham's day "everyone was going astray."[134] Particularly hard for Abraham was the straying of his own father, who had sought to have Abraham killed. Abraham might easily have refused any further association with this murderous man, but such was not Abraham's nature. In fact, he invited Terah to come with them to a new land, hoping it would open the door to repentance for his father and give him a fresh start. Abraham's forgiving nature is rare in the best of men, but would be replicated again in the person of Joseph Smith, who once explained that "nothing is so much calculated to lead people to forsake sin as to take them by the hand, and watch over them with tenderness."[135] Terah, humbled also because of famine, accepted his son's hand of forgiving friendship, and, as recounted in the Zohar[136] and the Book of Abraham (1:30; 2:4), repented.

By the kindness of the very son he had tried to kill, Terah would be led out of the land in which death now threatened him.

So Abraham bid good-bye to Ur of the Chaldees to begin "the life of a pilgrim,"[137] for *lek leka* can also mean "keep moving!" "Perpetual migration was one of the Ten Trials of Abraham," notes Hugh Nibley.[138] In that age of great migrations, one more family on the move would have seemed nothing unusual. But this journey was truly unique, undertaken at God's command and in further search of Him. It was a journey of faith—"simple, earnest, obedient faith!" Abraham "was willing to give up a certainty for an uncertainty—to leave all that he saw around him, for an unseen possession—to resign what was actually his, for something that was only promised." But "cheerfully and hopefully he set out."[139] Faith would be one of his constants; it "directed him in the whole course of his life."[140]

Thus, as related by British Rabbi J. H. Hertz, "in obedience to the heavenly voice, he leaves the land of his birth and all the glamor and worldly prosperity of his native place; he becomes a pilgrim for life, enduring trials [and] privations," and "all for the sake of humanity, that it might share the blessing of his knowledge of God and righteousness."[141]

And with him every step of the way was Sarah.

> When Abraham made the great venture of faith, renouncing hearth and home for conscience' sake; when he lived a nomad life among strangers, summering and wintering under canvas, enduring trials and afflictions, she was always by his side, lightening the way he travelled, doubling his joys and dividing his sorrows, ordering the peace and comfort of his house, cheering him to face all hardships with constancy of mind.[142]

Together they journeyed, "taking refuge in the Lord," noted the Muslim historian al-Thalabi.[143] They came to a place they called[144] Haran, strategically located at a busy crossroads of three major trade routes that brought a constant flow of travelers and newcomers from Babylon in the south, Ninevah in the east, and Damascus in the west.[145] The land was fruitful and well watered,[146] the flocks abundant (Abr. 2:5), and the people open and receptive. Would this be Abraham's ultimate destination? Was this the land that God had promised to show Abraham? Abraham did not as yet know, according to the medieval Jewish scholar Nachmanides.[147] What Abraham *did* know was that God had promised to lead him by the hand (Abr. 1:18). Arriving at this goodly land, somehow Abraham sensed that here he was to stop and set down roots, and he was determined to make the most of the situation.

According to the Pirke de Rabbi Eliezer, Abraham built a house in a location where all who entered or exited the city would pass by.[148] This would be no exclusive retreat, no hermitage, but an open house, a visitors' center welcoming all comers. The land was already blessed with water, but he would bring spiritual water to this thirsty people. "God brought him first to Haran," wrote the fourth-century Christian scholar Ephrem the Syrian, "like a spring of water into the midst of those who are parched."[149]

Meanwhile, Abraham himself would drink deeply from the living water provided in the scriptures God had given him, the patriarchal records that he had brought from Ur.

Abraham Studying the Patriarchal Records

CHAPTER 3

Reading the Records of Zion:
Abraham and the Patriarchal Records in Haran

Seek not for riches but for wisdom, and behold,
the mysteries of God shall be unfolded unto you,
and then shall you be made rich.
Behold, he that hath eternal life is rich.
—DOCTRINE AND COVENANTS 6:7

Precious Patriarchal Records

"I have found it written in the books of my forefathers."[1] These words from Jubilees, spoken by the dying Abraham to his beloved Isaac, point to the profound effect of the patriarchal records on the life of Abraham, who first read them in Haran. What he read in the records made a deep and indelible impression, changing the course of his life and the course of history. They gave him his bearings, guiding and shaping his life, informing his remarkable ministry, and providing the blueprint of what he would spend the rest of his life building and seeking and becoming. It would be difficult to overstate the importance of those records for understanding the life of Abraham. "Everything I have obtained has been only because I occupied myself with Torah and God's precepts," Abraham is reported to have once said.[2]

The Book of Abraham gives significant but compressed glimpses of what Abraham read in the records, glimpses that are fortunately amplified by other passages of restored scriptures like our Book of Moses and Doctrine and Covenants 107. In addition, we now have a host of ancient writings dealing with Adam and Enoch and their era, many of which sources purport to have been written by those very patriarchs. And although such sources are, says Niblcy, "copies of copies," yet "we cannot escape the impression that they have a real model behind them."[3] This is especially so when we see numerous convergences between latter-day scripture and the newly discovered ancient writings,[4] which often elaborate on matters more concisely mentioned in latter-day scripture. We can thereby form some idea of what Abraham read in those records, providing us with a mental map of what Abraham learned from the records of his fathers. That map is key to understanding Abraham.

Abraham attributed his acquisition of the records to divine providence: "The Lord my God preserved in mine own hands," while still in Ur, "the records of the fathers, even the patriarchs" (Abr. 1:31). Jubilees similarly tells of Abraham having the "books of his fathers"[5] or "forefathers," including the words of Enoch and Noah.[6] A Muslim source relates that when Abraham opened the chest of Adam, he found books written by Adam, Seth, and Enoch[7]—men who our Book of Moses also mentions as record keepers (see 6:5–6; 6:46). An early Christian work called the Book of the Bee further tells that Abraham also received a wooden staff originally owned by Adam, who had cut it from the tree of good and evil.[8]

The tradition that these earliest sacred records were kept in a chest raises the tantalizing possibility that what Abraham had may have been essentially an ark of the covenant like that to be built centuries later by Moses, for that later ark would likewise be a wooden chest housing the sacred records.[9] And as the later ark would serve as God's throne in the portable tabernacle and finally in the temple, so the chest that Abraham had may have served the same function in the temples that tradition credits him with building.

Speaking of the sacred records had by Adam, the Book of Moses mentions that some were written by the finger of God (Moses 6:46). Jewish tradition similarly tells that the original Torah had "been written with the finger of consuming fire,"[10] apparently the same heavenly book given to Adam and subsequently handed down to Abraham,[11] and perhaps including what George Syncellus reports as the heavenly book given to Seth and handed down through the generations.[12] But it is Enoch, builder of the city of Zion, who stands out in apocryphal literature and our Book of Moses as "the greatest transmitter of records,"[13] the preeminent and prolific "scribe of righteousness"[14] whose writings were quoted so heavily in early Jewish and Christian sources and now predominate in our modern collection of apocryphal texts.[15] The patriarchal records that Abraham now gazed upon with wonder were what Mesopotamian tradition called "the Tablets of Destiny, the Tablets of Wisdom, the Law of Earth and Heaven, the Tablets of the Gods, . . . the Mystery of Heaven and Earth. . . . They contain supreme wisdom."[16] They were the records of Zion.

But they were written in a strange language long since extinct, the original "language of the creation."[17] How was Abraham to read them? The Book of Abraham mentions a Urim and Thummim in Abraham's possession that God had given him in Ur (Abr. 3:1), where Abraham had also received the records of the fathers (Abr. 1:31). That the Urim and Thummim was found with the records is suggested by the Jewish tradition insisting that Abraham possessed the same precious shining stone that Noah once had.[18] The scenario fits precisely the pattern of what Joseph Smith received, not only the ancient sacred records written in a dead language, but also the divinely-prepared means to translate them.

Such sacred implements, as seen in the case of Joseph Smith, are reserved for those chosen seers who themselves are divine instruments to bring forth God's word to the world. Jubilees further tells that God sent an angel who tutored Abraham in the lost language so he could decipher the books, and who "explained to him everything he could not understand."[19] One is again reminded of the experience of Joseph Smith, who after being visited by Moroni was divinely tutored in the history of the inhabitants of the ancient Americas.[20] The angel that tutored Abraham was, says Jubilees, the very angel of the presence, a point emphasized by Byzantine chronographers as well.[21] Enoch, the greatest author and compiler of the sacred records that Abraham now held in his hands, had come to teach Abraham all about them.

Even with angelic assistance, the process still called for careful concentration on Abraham's part. Speaking of the Torah that Abraham perused, the Jewish sage Nachmanides stated that Abraham "occupied himself with its study and the reason for its commandments and its secrets."[22] One thinks immediately of Nephi, whose soul delighted in the scriptures and whose heart pondered them continually (2 Ne. 4:15).

What Abraham Learned about Cosmos and Creation, Fall and Atonement

The patriarchal records gave Abraham his bearings on the universe, teaching him about the cosmos and creation. The Book of Abraham tells that the patriarchal records dealt with "the planets, and . . . the stars, as they were made known unto the fathers" (Abr. 1:31), while 1 Enoch contains extensive astronomical material,[23] while 2 Enoch records that God told Enoch "all the things of heaven and earth . . . , the sun and the moon and the stars, their courses and their changes."[24] And in 3 Enoch, Enoch explains "the Holy One . . . has given to every single star a name," for "as it is written, 'He counts the number of the stars and gives each of them a name.'"[25]

The Book of Abraham further tells that from the patriarchal records he obtained "a knowledge of the beginning of the creation" (Abr. 1:31). The apocryphal Enoch literature describes what God revealed to Enoch about the premortal existence,[26] the rebellion and expulsion of Satan,[27] and the creation.[28]

Abraham would have also read what we can read in the Book of Moses about God teaching Enoch that "thy brethren . . . are the workmanship of mine own hands, and I gave unto them their knowledge in the day I created them; and in the Garden of Eden, gave I unto man his agency" (7:32). Similarly, in 2 Enoch the

Lord tells Enoch that "I created man . . . and I gave him his free will; and I pointed out to him the two ways—light and darkness. And I said unto him, 'This is good for you, but that is bad'."[29] Abraham also would have read about the fall of man, as we can read in Enoch's record in the Book of Moses (6:48–49, 53–56).

In his youth, Abraham had correctly deduced the existence of the Creator by observing the majesty of His creations. Now, reading the patriarchal records, Abraham discovered that the Creator was also the Redeemer, who in time would leave his glorious heavenly abode to come to earth as a man and minister in power, and to suffer untold agony for the sins of mankind, only to die and rise again in glory. Abraham may well have had a version of what we can now read in the Testament of Adam about how Adam, while still in the Garden of Eden, learned of the future mission and ministry of the Savior.[30]

Abraham would have read what we can read in restored scripture about how Adam, after being expelled from the garden, obeyed the Lord's commandments by "offer[ing] the firstlings of [his] flocks, for an offering unto the Lord" without understanding why.

> And after many days an angel of the Lord appeared unto Adam, saying: Why dost thou offer sacrifices unto the Lord? And Adam said unto him: I know not, save the Lord commanded me. And then the angel spake, saying: This thing is a similitude of the sacrifice of the Only Begotten of the Father, which is full of grace and truth. Wherefore, thou shalt do all that thou doest in the name of the Son, and thou shalt repent and call upon God in the name of the Son forevermore. (Moses 5:6–8)

A similar account in the Combat of Adam and Eve tells that after Adam had made "an offering on the altar, and had begun to pray, with his hands spread unto God," the voice of the Lord explained what would later happen to the Lord Himself "when I shall be pierced and blood shall flow."[31] The restored writings of Enoch report what the voice of God further taught Adam:

> If thou wilt turn unto me, and hearken unto my voice, and believe, and repent of all thy transgressions, and be baptized, even in water, in the name of mine Only Begotten Son, who is full of grace and truth, which is Jesus Christ, the only name which shall be given under heaven, whereby salvation shall come unto the children of men, ye shall receive the gift of the Holy Ghost, asking all things in his name, and whatsoever ye shall ask, it shall be given you. (Moses 6:52)

When Adam inquired why repentance was necessary, the Lord explained:

> Inasmuch as ye were born into the world by water, and blood, and the spirit, which I have made, and so became of dust a living soul, even so ye must be born again into the kingdom of heaven, of water, and of the Spirit, and be cleansed by blood, even the blood of mine Only Begotten; that ye might be sanctified from all sin, and enjoy the words of eternal life in this world, and eternal life in the world to come, even immortal glory; for by the water ye keep the commandment; by the Spirit ye are justified, and by the blood ye are sanctified; therefore it is given to abide in you; the record of heaven; the Comforter; the peaceable things of immortal glory; the truth of all things; that which quickeneth all things, which maketh alive all things; that which knoweth all things, and hath all power according to wisdom, mercy, truth, justice, and judgment. And now, behold, I say unto you: This is the plan of salvation unto all men, through the blood of mine Only Begotten, who shall come in the meridian of time. (Moses 6:59–62)

Then Adam prayed, apparently asking for these blessings, and "was caught away by the Spirit of the Lord, and was carried down into the water, and was laid under the water, and was brought forth out of the water. And thus he was baptized, and the Spirit of God descended upon him, and thus he was born of the Spirit, and became quickened in the inner man" (Moses 6:64–65).

This may have been the occasion when, as related by Adam in the *Life of Adam and Eve,* while he and Eve were praying, a "messenger of God came to me. And I saw a chariot like the wind and its wheels were fiery. I was carried off into the Paradise of righteousness,[32] and I saw the Lord sitting and his appearance was unbearable flaming fire."[33] If this account was part of the record that Abraham read, he would have reflected on the time when he had seen a fiery chariot, and would now have understood that it represented transport to the realm of Paradise.

What Abraham Learned about Adam's Posterity and Enoch's Zion

But Adam's mission was to continue on earth, where he was commanded to teach the gospel "freely" to all his posterity. He did so faithfully, and many believed (Moses 6:57–58). According to the chronicle of Syncellus, Adam's son Seth was granted an apocalyptic experience like that of Adam: Seth was temporarily taken up into heaven and received a revelation about the "transgression of [mankind], the coming cataclysm [the Flood] and the advent of the

Savior."[34] Further, according to the chronicle of Dionysus, Seth "received a heavenly book of secrets, which was passed down from generation to generation."[35]

Not all of Adam's posterity hearkened to the truths he taught. In fact, "many
. . . believed not" (Moses 7:1), but rebelled, being led by Satan into increasing
wickedness (5:12–13). Abraham probably read what we can read in Enoch literature now extant, that the generation of the Flood "rejected [God's] commandments"[36] and "committed adultery and erred, and all their conduct became
corrupt."[37] They made "molten images" and practiced idolatry, "worship[ing] vain
gods" and delving into "occult powers" as they "practice[d] sorcery."[38] They were
so given to violence and bloodshed that they "delight[ed] in seeing the murder of
their beloved ones," even "the destruction of their children."[39] Nation rose up
against nation and people against people to such an extent that mankind was
engulfed in "wars and bloodshed" (Moses 7:16) and "the whole world was filled
with blood and oppression."[40] In short, it was a cruel age of wickedness and
warfare when "Satan had great dominion among men" (Moses 6:15).

Abraham may well have recognized in such descriptions a distant mirror of his
own day. But he would also have read what is now available in a restored portion of
a lost Book of Enoch (see D&C 107:57) about the society of the righteous, led first
by Adam and in turn each of the patriarchs, noble men who were "preachers of
righteousness, and spake and prophesied, and called upon all men, everywhere, to
repent" (Moses 6:23). These were the men who, in the lineage of the firstborn sons,
were heirs to and received their ordination to that exclusive order of the patriarchal
priesthood given to Adam and passed on to the righteous firstborn, but exercised
only by the senior living patriarch, as when the aged Adam gathered his righteous
posterity and gave them his final blessing (see D&C 107:40–53).

> The Lord appeared unto them, and they rose up and blessed Adam,
> and called him Michael, the prince, the archangel. And the Lord
> administered comfort unto Adam, and said unto him: I have set thee
> to be at the head; a multitude of nations shall come of thee, and thou
> art a prince over them forever. And Adam stood up in the midst of
> the congregation; and, notwithstanding he was bowed down with
> age, being full of the Holy Ghost, predicted whatsoever should befall
> his posterity unto the latest generation. (D&C 107:54–56)[41]

That Adam did gather his posterity to give them his final instruction and
blessing is also recounted in the Conflict of Adam and Eve, which proceeds to tell
that the patriarchal authority was passed on from Adam and held successively by
each of the antediluvian patriarchs as each in turn presided over all of Adam's
posterity, and cared for and taught and nurtured all who would join the society of

the righteous,[42] a happy people who "because of their own purity . . . were named 'Children of God'"[43]—as attested also in the Book of Moses (7:1; 8:13).

As Abraham also discovered, something remarkable happened with the seventh patriarch, Enoch, who, as related in restored scripture, suffered from a speech impediment so severe that nobody expected he could follow the pattern of his patriarchal forefathers in becoming a powerful preacher of righteousness. But it was God Himself who called Enoch to go forth and open his mouth in proclaiming the gospel to mankind (see Moses 6:26–33).[44] As Enoch did so, his words flowed forth with such eloquence and power that "fear came on all them that heard him," and "the people trembled, and could not stand in his presence" (6:39, 47). Those who accepted his message joined the people of God, but not without tribulation, for "their enemies came to battle against them." Despite apparently overwhelming odds, Enoch courageously "led the people of God" and then with unprecedented faith invoked heavenly powers to defeat the earthly powers threatening Zion as "he spake the word of the Lord, and the earth trembled, and the mountains fled, even according to his command; the rivers of water were turned out of their course; and the roar of the lions was heard out of the wilderness; and all nations feared greatly" (7:13).

Under Enoch's continued leadership, the Saints of his day built a city of such peace and love that it "was called the City of Holiness, even Zion" a community of Saints who achieved such unity and righteousness that "the Lord came and dwelt with his people" (Moses 6:18–19). It stood out in the sharpest contrast with the rest of the world, literally a city of light in a dark world, causing all nations to fear because "so great was the glory of the Lord, which was upon his people" (7:17). And it was a city so beloved by God that he finally took it up from this world to a higher realm: "and lo, Zion, in the process of time, was taken up into heaven" (7:21), to a terrestrial paradise[45] or, as indicated in Jubilees, the Garden of Eden.[46] If the Garden of Zion could not come to earth, Enoch's Zion would go to it, and remain there until the last days to then return to earth and join another city of Zion that would be built on earth (Moses 7:62–64).[47] The people of Enoch's city were changed from mortality to a sanctified condition (see 3 Ne. 28:36–40) so that they "should not die at that time," but should serve as "ministering angels"[48] until that future day when they will experience "a change equivalent to death" and then enter into the fullness of God's rest.[49]

What Abraham Learned about the Transformation of Enoch

But Enoch himself received special authority and standing. According to Sirach, Enoch was "taken into the divine presence."[50] As Enoch recounts in 3 Enoch, "When the Holy One . . . took me away from the generation of the Flood, he lifted me on the wings of the wind of *Shekhinah*."[51] For the word *Shekinah* we might read "fire," for in that same source (and elsewhere[52]) the Shekinah is said to have the appearance of brilliant dazzling fire.[53] In fact, another Jewish text tells that "Enoch was carried into the heavens in a fiery chariot."[54] Enoch's fiery transport took him, as he relates in 3 Enoch, "into the great palaces . . . on high," where he beheld the "glorious Throne" of God in the midst of divine beings whose appearance he describes as fiery, flaming, and burning[55]—reminiscent of Joseph Smith's statement that God dwells in "everlasting burnings."[56] In the similar account in 1 Enoch, Enoch describes the divine throne (as the prophet Ezekiel later would in Ezek. 1) as a glorious fiery chariot with wheels: "Its appearance was like the crystals of ice and the wheels thereof were like the shining sun. . . . And the glory of the Great One sat thereon, and his raiment was brighter than the sun, and whiter than any snow . . . and the Lord called me with his own mouth and said to me: 'Come hither, Enoch, and hear my word. . . . Fear not, Enoch, righteous man and scribe of righteousness.'"[57] Surrounding the divine throne, according to 3 Enoch, was a rainbow.[58]

In 2 Enoch, Enoch reports that "I saw the face of the Lord,"[59] who was surrounded by choirs with "their never-ceasing songs, and their unchanging beauty."[60] Enoch continues: "With his own mouth the Lord called to me, Take courage, Enoch, do not be afraid; get up and stand in my presence [or, 'in front of my face'[61]] for ever. And Michael, the Lord's great archangel, raised me up and led me into the Lord's presence." Then, at God's command, Michael oversaw the anointing of Enoch and his being clothed in "glorious garments. . . . And I looked at myself," says Enoch, "and I was like one of the glorious ones, and there was no apparent difference."[62] The Lord called him "beloved Enoch"[63] and, as described in 3 Enoch[64] and in Mesopotamian tradition, ushered him onto a throne of splendor.[65] Mesopotamian tradition also adds that he was presented with a tablet of the gods and handed a royal scepter of cedar,[66] which is "the sign of rulership as well as of priestly . . . activities, [and] a symbol of the Tree of Life."[67]

Then, continues Enoch in 3 Enoch, "the Holy One . . . made [for] me a garment of glory," "a robe of honour on which were fixed all kinds of beauty, splendour, brilliance and majesty [or 'luster of every kind'[68]]"[69]—probably the royal garment of divine splendor mentioned in rabbinic texts which is described as having a purple hue.[70] Then, says Enoch, the Lord "made [for] me a royal crown"[71] whose "brilliance shown into the four quarters of the heaven . . . and into the four quarters of the world,"[72] and "he put it on my head. And he called me THE LESSER YHWH [JEHOVAH] in the presence of all His heavenly household; as it is written (Ex. xxiii.21): 'For my name is in him.'"[73] At that point, Enoch saw that his own person was changed so that he had the appearance of fire.[74]

Mesopotamian tradition further tells that Enoch in turn brought several men from the earth "into his presence and he honoured them"[75]—apparently a reference to some of Enoch's colleagues who had been translated with him.

Furthermore, according to 3 Enoch, "the Holy One, blessed be He, put His hand upon me and blessed me,"[76] and "appointed me to attend the throne of glory,"[77] and "placed me (there) to attend the Throne of Glory day after day."[78] Similarly in the Book of Moses, Enoch tells the Lord that "thou hast . . . given unto me a right to thy throne" (7:59; see also verse 31). And as in the same source Enoch refers to himself as "but a lad" (6:31), so in 3 Enoch the angel Metatron, or Enoch, "had seventy names, but the King called him Na'ar, the youth."[79] According to Joseph Smith, "this Enoch God reserved unto himself" to be "a ministering angel, to minister to those who would be heirs of salvation."[80] Enoch became the very angel of the presence or "the Prince of the Presence," or "the great prince of the throne of God," the prince on whom the Lord placed his name and who was appointed as the special "representative and vice-regent of the Holy One."[81] Enoch was appointed as ruler over all of the heavenly hosts except several of the highest princes,[82] the chief prince being Michael,[83] who is Adam (D&C 107:54).

Abraham now knew, if he didn't before, the identity of the angel of the presence who had rescued him from death on the altar in Ur, even the same angel who was now helping Abraham to read and understand the very books formerly written by that angel. Enoch, the renowned builder of ancient Zion, had been sent to help Abraham reestablish Zion.

What Abraham Learned about Enoch's Heavenly Vision and Earthly Heritage

Abraham would further have read how Enoch was "granted access to all manner of heavenly mysteries regarding the governance of the cosmos and the progression of terrestrial history."[84] From his privileged station of being "high and lifted up," Enoch saw "all the nations of the earth . . . before him" (Moses 7:23–24), and was even taken on a tour to the ends of the earth, to the north, west, south, and east.[85] He then saw future history unfold before his eyes, as we can now read in the Book of Moses (7:23–69) and the apocryphal Enoch literature.[86] For at least some of this vision it is Michael who acts as Enoch's guide and tutor.[87] Enoch saw the fate of the wicked ones perishing in the Flood, that they would "suffer" and be "shut . . . up [in] a prison" (Moses 7:37–38),[88] while the heavens wept over them (7:28–31) and Enoch himself wept (7:41, 44).[89] These passages apparently had a profound effect on Abraham, who, as would later be said of the sons of King Mosiah, "could not bear that any human soul should perish" (Mosiah 28:3).

Enoch also heard mother earth "mourn" and lament the wickedness of her children (Moses 7:48–49) against whom she "made accusation,"[90] and he began to pray for mercy for the earth and for his posterity (7:50). The Lord "could not withhold; and he covenanted with Enoch, and sware unto him with an oath" and "sent forth an unalterable decree" to preserve and protect his posterity, adding:

"Blessed is he through whose seed Messiah shall come; for he saith—I am Messiah, the King of Zion" (7:51–53).

Enoch saw the Flood and Noah being saved on the ark (Moses 7:42–43),[91] and he saw "generation upon generation" (7:23–24) as he heard the earth groan from Noah down through the future history of the kingdoms of Israel and Judah.[92] He also "saw the day of the coming of the Son of Man, even in the flesh; and his soul rejoiced, saying: The Righteous in lifted up, and the Lamb is slain from the foundation of the world" (7:47).

The scene continued to unfold until Enoch beheld the last days and was told that "another generation will arise, the last of many. . . . And I will raise up for that generation someone who will reveal to them the books in your handwriting and those of your fathers."[93] The modern-day translator of this passage in 2 Enoch comments that "the context requires the introduction of an authoritative teacher along with the restitution of the books of Enoch, to provide for the needs of the faithful in the end-time."[94] It appears, in other words, that Enoch saw the raising up of Joseph Smith, through whose instrumentality God would restore lost writings of Enoch. Enoch further beheld "righteousness" come "down out of heaven" and "truth" come "forth out of the earth, to bear testimony of [the] Only Begotten" (Moses 7:62). He saw, in other words, the restoration of divine authority and the coming forth of the Book of Mormon,[95] and then saw "righteousness and truth . . . sweep the earth as with a flood, to gather out [the] elect from the four quarters of the earth" to build "Zion, a New Jerusalem," in preparation for the glorious coming of the Lord and his descent with Enoch's city of Zion (7:62–65). As Enoch tells in 3 Enoch, "the Holy One . . . will reveal his Great Arm . . . to the nations of the world,"[96] and "at once Israel shall be saved from among the gentiles and the Messiah shall appear to them and bring them up to Jerusalem with great joy. Moreover, the kingdom of Israel, gathered from the four quarters of the world, shall eat with the Messiah."[97] Through that turbulent time of massive destruction and change, as Enoch wrote, the Lord "will preserve the elect, and kindness shall be upon them."[98]

Kindness was in fact one of the Lord's unchanging qualities, as Abraham read in a passage recording that Enoch told the Lord, "Thou art merciful and kind forever" (Moses 7:30). Abraham would also have read that kindness is one of the traits of God's people, "the righteous," they "who suffer every kind of tribulation in this life,"[99] and "who carry out righteous judgment, and who give bread to the hungry, and who cover the naked with clothing, and who lift up the fallen, and who help the injured and the orphans."[100] For such, the Lord told Enoch, is prepared a glorious paradise.[101] These passages appear to have exercised a profound influence on Abraham, for they offer a perfect description of the future course of his life. And surely he could not have failed to recognize the prophecy of his own life when Enoch had foretold that one of his descendants "shall be chosen as a plant of righteous judgement; and his posterity shall come forth as a plant of eternal righteousness."[102]

Abraham also learned that his future ministry required the authority originally possessed by Enoch, whose firstborn son, Methuselah, "was not taken, that the covenants of the Lord might be fulfilled" (Moses 8:2). Abraham would have read of Noah's ministry to the hardened generation of the Flood (8:18–25) and of his clearly inviting them to believe in Jesus Christ, to repent of their sins, to be baptized in his name, and to receive the Holy Ghost (8:24). Abraham would have further read of God's covenant with Noah following the Flood. The sign of the covenant was the rainbow, as we read in Genesis 9:12–17, but the covenant encompassed far more than God's promise never again to flood the earth with water. We learn in the Joseph Smith Translation of Genesis that the covenant to Noah was actually a renewal of the covenant to Enoch, as God told Noah: "And the bow shall be in the cloud; and I will look upon it, that I may remember the everlasting covenant, which I made unto thy father Enoch; that, when men should keep all my commandments, Zion should again come on the earth, the city of Enoch which I have caught up unto myself." And "when thy posterity shall embrace the truth, and look upward, then shall Zion look downward, and all the heavens shall shake with gladness, and the earth shall tremble with joy; and the general assembly of the church of the first-born shall come down out of heaven, and possess the earth, and shall have place until the end come" (JST Gen. 9:21–23).

Abraham would also have read how the patriarchal authority continued to pass down in orderly succession from Noah to his son Shem, and down through the patriarchal line, providing Abraham with, as he tells in the Book of Abraham, a "chronology running back from myself to the beginning of the creation" (1:28). In that genealogy he discovered that he himself was in the chosen patriarchal line with the right to be ordained to the patriarchal priesthood. In his own words, he was "a rightful heir" holding "the right belonging to the fathers," even "the right of the firstborn, or the first man, who is Adam" (Abr. 1:2–3), he who exercised "the first patriarchal reign," even as it would later be exercised by Noah (1:26). It was Abraham's right, in other words, to be ordained to the patriarchal priesthood to establish and preside over Zion for the benefit of all mankind.

All he needed was the gospel ordinances and his ordination. The question was, from whom? Generations of his patriarchal forefathers had been unworthy to receive their ordination, having turned to idolatry. But if Abraham was to build Zion, he would need to receive the power and authority to do so.

Abraham Giving Thanks to God

CHAPTER 4

Seeking to Build Zion:
Ordination, Covenant, and Journey to the Promised Land

Seek to bring forth and establish the cause of Zion.
—DOCTRINE AND COVENANTS 6:6

Ordinances and Ordination in Haran

For Abraham, the scriptures were a constant source of spiritual nourishment and refreshment, as will be seen later by his repeated reference to them in teaching his posterity. The scriptures "exalted and blessed him in his early years, and gave him hope in his latter years."[1] Even so, in those same scriptures Abraham learned that they by themselves were insufficient, that he needed the constant and immediate revelation that can come only from the Holy Ghost and the ordinances. "The circumstances of Abraham were different than those of Enoch and Noah," explained John Taylor, "and if Abraham had the history of their times, as he unquestionably had, . . . he would know that the revelations they received were not applicable to his case, but he needed revelation from God for his own guidance and direction."[2]

Indeed, the patriarchal records themselves clearly taught that God could not be fully found except through the ordinances He had established, ordinances that brought direct revelation through the gift of the Holy Ghost. Joseph Smith stated that there is "no salvation between the two lids of the Bible without a legal administrator."[3] Hence "reading the experience of others, or the revelation given to *them,* can never give us a comprehensive view of our condition and true relation to God. Knowledge of these things can only be obtained by experience through the ordinances of God"[4] offered by "an administrator legally authorized from God."[5]

By Abraham's day, his people had for many generations been without any such legal administrator and the blessings that flow therefrom: the gospel, the priesthood, the ordinances, the Church—in a word, Zion. "It was time," says Nibley, "for God to speak with Abraham face to face, restore the covenants, and organize the church."[6]

The Book of Abraham never tells who Abraham's legal administrator was, but does recount that by the time Abraham left Haran, he had received the gospel ordinances and priesthood, as God speaks to him and refers to "this Gospel," "this ministry and Priesthood," and "thy Priesthood."[7] A midrash says that Abraham kept the ordinances "and therefore became great."[8] Abraham's conversation with God took place face to face, a privilege granted only after Abraham had learned that the God whom he sought was the premortal Jesus Christ, and only after receiving His ordinances and being cleansed by His blood, thus becoming His son (see Moses 6:59, 68), and only after continuing to seek this Jesus "earnestly" (Abr. 2:12) through prayer (2:6). Neither Abraham's seeking the Lord nor the Lord's appearing to Abraham in Haran is reported in Genesis, but both are mentioned not only in the Book of Abraham but also in the Zohar: "When the Holy One observed his great yearning and pursuit after divine knowledge, he appeared unto him."[9]

That the gospel was preached to Abraham was mentioned by the Apostle Paul (Gal. 3:8), while Joseph Smith emphasized that it was preached to Abraham "in the name of Christ" and with the same ordinances of baptism and receipt of the Holy Ghost that always accompany the true gospel.[10] The Talmud insists that the Fathers—the foremost among whom was Abraham—"were not admitted to the covenant except by . . . baptism, and propitiation by blood."[11] By "Abraham's immersion" in water, says rabbinic tradition, "he becomes, in effect, reborn, changed, a new person."[12] Early Judaism in fact looked to Abraham as "the prototype of the proselytes" because he "receive[d] the Spirit" and became a model of "the reception and indwelling of the Spirit,"[13] and thereafter "was possessed by the Holy Spirit at all times."[14] An important Ethiopic source recounts that "Abraham was baptized with baptism, even as our Lord saith in the Book of the Covenant, 'He gave to Abraham the baptism of life and the right hand.'"[15] In an early illustrated Christian manuscript of the Septuagint version of Genesis, in the picture of God commanding Abraham to leave Haran, Abraham sees a right hand being extended to him from above through a multicolored, rainbow-like arc, through which several rays of the sun are breaking forth.[16]

The picture is reminiscent of what the Pirke de Rabbi Eliezer says about the divine oath sworn to Noah when God gave him the sign of the rainbow: "He put forth His right hand, and swore to Noah."[17] Abraham was receiving the ordinances that Noah had once received, pursuant to what the Lord had promised Abraham at Ur through the angel of the presence, that "I will lead thee by my hand. . . . As it was with Noah, so shall it be with thee" (Abr. 1:18–19). There were additional ordinances that Abraham would yet seek and receive, but he clearly had the beginning, including the first principles and ordinances of the gospel. Abraham was, as described by Epiphanius in the fourth century, "a follower of the gospel."[18]

Abraham also received the patriarchal priesthood and robes, or, as Jewish sources attest, God granted to Abraham "to rule as king over the whole world"[19] and "conferred upon him the power of bestowing blessings"[20] along with the "high-priestly raiment in which God had clothed Adam," raiment reserved for "the first-born males [who] officiated as priests."[21] Abraham's patriarchal priesthood, according to Joseph Smith, included the authority to organize the church and administer the gospel and its ordinances to others.[22]

From whom did Abraham receive his ordination to the patriarchal priesthood? Who was worthy to give him that ordination? Certainly not his idolatrous father: "Abraham . . . was . . . worthy of a blessing," stated an early Church Father, "but . . . Terah could not bless."[23] Nor apparently could Terah's father, for as Abraham reports in the Book of Abraham, his "fathers" had "turned from their righteousness . . . unto the worshiping of the gods of the heathen" (Abr. 1:5; see also 1:7, 30; 2:5). In fact, the book of Jubilees reports that the three immediate generations of Abraham's patriarchal forefathers—his father (Terah), grandfather (Nahor), and great-grandfather (Serug)—were all idolaters.[24] Terah repented for a short while, but had returned to his idolatry by the time Abraham left Haran,[25] apparently close to the time that Abraham received the gospel ordinances and his patriarchal ordination.[26]

And who of Abraham's patriarchal ancestors was even alive when he left Haran? Such information can be calculated based on chronological data in Genesis providing the life span for each patriarch before Abraham and telling how old each was at the birth of his firstborn son, the next patriarch (see Gen. 11:10–26).

The difficulty comes in deciding which version of Genesis to use, for there are vast differences between the ancient versions on this chronological point. According to the chronology of the Masoretic (standard Hebrew) text, from which the King James was translated, the time from the Flood to Abraham's birth was 292 years. This number differs radically from that found in most other ancient sources, which preserve a chronology more than three times as long—about a thousand years, as found, for example, in the Seputagint, the Samaritan Pentateuch, Josephus, Armenian apocryphal sources,[27] and a New Testament apocryphal source.[28] The Masoretic chronology is further remarkable in that every one of Abraham's patriarchal forefathers back through Shem is alive at Abraham's birth, and only two (Nahor and Peleg) have died by the time he is sixty-two (when he leaves Haran), while several forefathers, including even Shem, actually outlive

Abraham.[29] Only in this Masoretic chronology is Shem alive at the birth of Abraham. In the other chronologies, Shem is long since dead, and by the time Abraham is sixty-two, the only one of his patriarchal ancestors still alive is his father. (See Appendix for details and further comparison of chronologies.)

Why is the Masoretic chronology so much shorter? Some scholars have suggested that it was deliberately altered for the very purpose of portraying Shem as contemporary with Abraham, so that the rabbis could identify Shem with Melchizedek and therefore "remove the mystery surrounding" this man to whom their ancestor Abraham paid tithes and from whom he received the priesthood.[30] By thus "being identified with Shem," Melchizedek "was brought firmly inside the Jewish fold, and thus no priesthood was admitted outside Judaism."[31] The identification of Shem with Melchizedek is unknown in early sources like Josephus[32] and the Genesis Apocryphon;[33] is refuted by various early Christian and Muslim sources telling that Melchizedek was not one of the patriarchs,[34] and telling who his parents were;[35] and appears impossible according to latter-day scripture.[36]

What all this suggests is that the Masoretic chronology was in fact deliberately shortened.[37] Using the other chronologies narrows down who it was that could have ordained Abraham to the patriarchal priesthood just before he left Haran. Only Terah was alive, but he had returned to his idolatry. Nor does it seem likely he ever had received the ordination himself. And since priesthood and keys can be transferred to mortals only by beings with tabernacles of flesh and bone,[38] this leaves just one individual in the entire patriarchal line who could have given Abraham his patriarchal ordination, the only worthy patriarchal forefather still alive, he who had never died but had been translated: Enoch.[39] That "Enoch . . . came . . . to confer with Abraham"[40] was in fact the opinion of a Flemish author cited in the early 1700s by the learned French abbey Dom Augustin Calmet.[41] Enoch's initiating Abraham into the ordinances and giving him the priesthood may well have been the occasion alluded to by Clement of Alexandria when he wrote that "the region of God is hard to attain" but was "seen by Abraham afar off," who was "forthwith initiated by the angel."[42] Jewish kabbalistic tradition directly attests that Abraham's rabbi, or teacher, was none other than the angel Enoch.[43] Enoch's extending the right hand to Abraham in the ordinances would further fit the context of the rainbowlike arc through which the right hand is being extended to Abraham on this occasion, as depicted in the early Christian illustration of the event; for, as we shall see in a later appearance of Enoch to Abraham, surrounding the person of Enoch was a rainbow.

That Enoch would be sent to restore authority on the occasion of the Lord's appearing to Abraham seems very much like what happened in the Kirtland Temple in 1836, when angels restored lost authority, and the Lord also personally appeared to talk about the blessings that would flow to tens of thousands because of the authority bestowed that day (see D&C 110:1–16, especially verses 9–10). Once again, Abraham's life foreshadowed that of Joseph Smith.[44]

If Enoch was indeed the one who ordained Abraham to the patriarchal priesthood and gave him the ordinances of "the baptism of life and the right hand,"[45] then the word of the Lord spoken years earlier to Abraham on the altar by the angel of the presence, Enoch, takes on added meaning: "I will lead thee by my hand, and I will take thee, to put upon thee my name, even the Priesthood of thy father" (Abr. 1:18). It seems that it was Enoch himself who now literally extended his hand to Abraham in the ordinances and to confer the patriarchal priesthood authority. Zion above had descended to pass on its authority so that Zion might again be established below. In fact, this event may well have been a key part of the Lord's purpose in translating Enoch, so he could return on this very occasion and transfer the long-lost authority and ordinances to Abraham for the reestablishment of Zion on earth.[46]

"The Souls We Had Won"

Abraham lost no time in seeking to reestablish Zion, for by the time he left Haran, he did so, as he comments in the Book of Abraham, with "the souls that we had won in Haran" (Abr. 2:15).[47] How had they been won? Abraham had lived in Haran for a number of years,[48] and from the moment he arrived there, says Jewish tradition, he attracted attention by his exemplary and magnanimous manner of life. "The people of the land of Haran saw that Abram was good and upright with God and men, and that the Lord his God was with him."[49] Similarly in the Qur'an, Abraham is repeatedly referred to as "the upright"[50] and is called "a man of truth"[51] or "very truthful."[52] Indeed, in Islamic tradition, "one of his most prominent and distinctive qualities was that he was truthful *par excellence.*"[53]

He was also a missionary *par excellence*, freely imparting both spiritual and physical sustenance, with which in both regards he was blessed abundantly. In the Book of Abraham he specifically speaks of the "many flocks in Haran," and, upon finally leaving the place, mentions "all our substance that we had gathered" (Abr. 2:5, 15). The hand of the Lord prospered him in his temporal affairs, which included raising livestock. He probably engaged in mercantile activity with merchants and caravaneers with whom he would have come in nearly constant contact, since his own journeys and residences seem to have been along the important trade routes.[54]

Abraham "was an immensely wealthy man who surely had business dealings of all varieties," providing him "as much opportunity as the next man for sharp dealing, even dishonesty."[55] But "he never drove a hard bargain"[56] and he "took no advantage of others' weakness," for "all men received their due at his hand"[57] even though many with whom he dealt "were scoundrels—mean and inhospitable," their "one guiding principle [being] the maximizing of profits."[58] His life was in stark contrast, his example such that many wanted to learn more of his principles and religion. "Word of his teaching traveled beyond the borders of the city, and spiritual pilgrims from elsewhere in Mesopotamia had no trouble finding Abram if they wished to go sit with him and learn."[59]

For Abraham, the temporal blessings God placed in his hands were opportunities to extend blessings to others. "He was the father of guests," reported al-Thalabi; "he would not eat the morning meal or evening meal without a guest."[60] The Midrash says that "Abraham our father used to bring them into his house and give them food and drink and be friendly to them . . . and convert them" in a joint effort with Sarah: "Abraham used to convert the men and Sarai the women."[61] Hence does Abraham write about the souls "we" had won. Sarah was "an equal partner with her husband" in this endeavor, and though she was biologically barren, her success in winning souls to God's kingdom was already making her the mother of many.[62]

The people of Haran "readily yielded to the influence of Abraham's humane spirit and his piety. Many of them obeyed his precepts,"[63] and "he taught them the instruction of the Lord and his ways"[64] in this "large-scale missionary effort."[65] His teaching was as eloquent as his example, for the Lord had blessed him with the gift of mighty teaching, says the Qur'an: the Lord made Abraham "a prophet; and . . . bestowed upon [him] gifts of . . . grace, and granted [him] a lofty power to convey the truth unto others."[66] He was "an eloquent speaker," says Islamic tradition,[67] and according to Jewish tradition, "call[ed] out in a mighty voice to all the world."[68] "He led them to righteousness by speaking persuasively. . . . Even the guilty he led to righteousness,"[69] as their hearts were changed and they felt to declare that "the Lord, He is God in the heavens above and the earth below, and you are Abraham, His prophet."[70] Thus was Abraham fulfilling his baptismal covenant to stand as a witness of God "at all times and in all things, and in all places" (Mosiah 18:9), doing what his latter-day descendants would likewise be commanded to do—"open their mouths" (D&C 60:2) and "declare my gospel with the sound of rejoicing, as with the voice of a trump" (29:4).

Abraham's voice was mighty because of the Almighty, by whose inspiration Abraham spoke. Philo of Alexandria reported that the Spirit came on Abraham, making him persuasive in his speech and granting understanding to his hearers[71]—reminding us of Nephi's words that "when a man speaketh by the power of the Holy Ghost the power of the Holy Ghost carrieth it into the hearts of the children of men" (2 Ne. 33:1). Abraham is the great example of the Lord's mandate to Latter-day Saints to teach by the Spirit (D&C 42:14), as exemplified also by the first Latter-day Saint, the Prophet Joseph Smith, who was "supernaturally blessed to teach, to speak, and to counsel" with convincing power.[72]

The converts that Abraham made in Haran, as Jewish tradition reports, "remained with [him] in his house and they adhered to him"[73] and "became God-fearing and good,"[74] being called "the people of the God of Abraham."[75] Altogether they constituted a "great crowd."[76] The Book of Jasher puts the number at seventy-two men,[77] most of whom presumably would be heads of families. If so, the total number would have been at least several hundred. The number would continue to grow with Abraham's travels and missionary labors; no less an authority than Maimonides says that Abraham's converts came to be numbered into the thousands and tens of thousands.[78] If this seems exaggerated, one need only remember the remarkably rapid growth of the Church restored by Joseph Smith, who, like his forefather Abraham, was also a missionary *par excellence*.

And as Joseph Smith organized the Church and delegated authority in the work of building Zion, so did Abraham. The situation would have been similar also to that of Alma, who, "having authority from God," established "the church of God, or the church of Christ," and "ordained priests . . . to teach [the church members] concerning the things pertaining to the kingdom of God, . . . command[ing] them that there should be no contention one with another, but that they should look forward with one eye, having one faith and one baptism, having their hearts knit together in unity and in love one towards another" (Mosiah 18:17–18, 21). According to Hugh Nibley, "Abraham founded his Zion, and those who wished to follow became the followers of Abraham. By special rites and ordinances they were adopted into the family. . . . So he founde[d] the church with the ordinances of the temple,"[79] even though there were yet higher ordinances he would still seek—not unlike the Latter-day Saints doing temple work in Kirtland even though there were additional ordinances yet to be revealed.

Such were the fervent efforts to build the kingdom of God by the man who, as he himself said, had left Ur seeking "peace, happiness, and *rest*"—not by looking forward to retirement, or by building his dream house away from humanity, but by living among them and serving them tirelessly. The "rest" that Abraham sought was not a life of affluent ease. He was striving to "enter into the rest of the Lord,"[80] obtainable only by serving Him with all of one's heart, might, mind, and strength.

Call and Covenant

So it was that Abraham qualified for the momentous call that now came from God Himself, who personally appeared to Abraham and declared: "Arise, . . . for I have purposed to take thee out of Haran, and to make of thee a minister to bear my name in a strange land which I will give unto thy seed after thee for an everlasting possession" (Abr. 2:6). For fourteen years, says the book of Jubilees, had Abraham resided in Haran,[81] having obediently left behind his native Ur and extended family. Now, after that long time of building life and relationships anew, of establishing himself and his family in this goodly location, he was asked to

uproot everything yet again and take to the road toward a strange land. "The challenge now thrust on him . . . was to journey to a distant land . . . in a very
different place . . . among a different people . . . speaking a different language and
practicing a different religion."[82] It was a daunting task at best.

But the divine reassurance of Him who was sending him seemed more than
adequate as the Creator identified Himself, speaking of His creations:

> I am the Lord thy God; I dwell in heaven; the earth is my foot-
> stool; I stretch my hand over the sea, and it obeys my voice; I
> cause the wind and the fire to be my chariot; I say to the moun-
> tains—Depart hence—and behold, they are taken away by a
> whirlwind, in an instant, suddenly. My name is Jehovah, and I
> know the end from the beginning. (Abr. 2:7–8)

Early in life, Abraham had sought God as the Creator, and God now identified
Himself to Abraham using what appears to be an allusion to the Creation, when the
Lord had stretched His hand over the turbulent primeval waters to bring them
under His dominion.[83] The same imagery may also look ahead to the time when the
Lord would, through Moses, stretch forth His hand over the sea for the salvation of
Abraham's chosen seed as they fled the Egyptian chariots.[84]

In addition, Abraham had probably read in the patriarchal writings how
Christ had foretold that in His mortal ministry He would "walk on the waves of
the sea" and would "motion to the waves and they will stand still."[85] Abraham
may well have recognized in the imagery a reference to when, as we can read in the
Gospels, during a storm on the sea, the Savior "rebuked the wind, and said unto
the sea, Peace, be still. And the wind ceased, and there was a great calm" (Mark
4:39; and see Matt. 8:26; Luke 8:24). Early Christians also associated the chariot
with that event, and used both the chariot and the sea as important symbols associated with Christ and His ordinance of baptism. Cyril of Jerusalem, for example,
spoke of Christ walking on the water as "the charioteer of the sea" and as the
"charioteer and creator of the waters."[86] Other writers apparently compared the
waters of baptism to the chariot or the throne of God,[87] while Gregory of Nyssa
observed that by receiving the Holy Spirit after baptism, "our mind is taken up in
the chariot of fire and carried through the air to the glories of Heaven."[88]

In light of such symbolism, it seems more than coincidental that it was just
after Abraham's baptism and receipt of the Holy Spirit that he heard the Lord
speak of His chariot and of the sea. Early Christians further spoke of Elijah's fiery
chariot (in which he, like Enoch, was taken to heaven) as a type of baptism, and a
type of Christ's ascent to heaven after His Resurrection,[89] an event of which
Abraham had also read in the patriarchal records. Indeed, Moses reportedly

referred to God as "the Rider of the Heavens" in a passage alluded to by an ancient kabbalistic book attributed to none other than Abraham.[90]

After identifying Himself to Abraham, the Lord proceeded to pronounce promise after promise of blessing and glory, all centered in his family and future posterity:

> My hand shall be over thee. And I will make of thee a great nation, and I will bless thee above measure, and make thy name great among all nations, and thou shalt be a blessing unto thy seed after thee, that in their hands they shall bear this ministry and Priesthood unto all nations; and I will bless them through thy name; for as many as receive this Gospel shall be called after thy name, and shall be accounted thy seed, and shall rise up and bless thee, as their father; and I will bless them that bless thee, and curse them that curse thee; and in thee (that is, in thy Priesthood) and in thy seed (that is, thy Priesthood), for I give unto thee a promise that this right shall continue in thee, and in thy seed after thee (that is to say, the literal seed, or the seed of the body) shall all the families of the earth be blessed, even with the blessings of the Gospel, which are the blessings of salvation, even of life eternal. (Abr. 2:8–11)

Only a brief summary of these breathtaking promises has survived in our traditional Genesis text (Gen. 12:2–3), which mentions nothing about the gospel or priesthood that Abraham had just received and which he and his posterity would offer to the nations as a blessing. But the Apostle Paul seems to have understood the larger picture as portrayed in the Book of Abraham, for he wrote, as summarized by one scholar, that God spoke "his word of blessing to all nations through Abraham, but Abraham could only be that channel of blessing by hearing, believing and obeying," and in turn "the nations could only appropriate that blessing by imitating his faith."[91]

But even the terse Genesis account of God's call and blessing of Abraham emphasizes the contrast between him and the rebellious generation in which he lived, as well as his pivotal role in God's plan for the human race and the rest of human history. The covenant granted to Abraham makes him, in the words of one scholar, "the most pivotal and strategic man in the course of world history."[92] Or, as expressed by the rabbis, through the Abrahamic covenant "the order of the world was established."[93] Indeed, to try to compress the scope and significance of what God promised to Abraham into the single word "covenant" is illusory, for as one scholar emphasizes, there is simply no English word that adequately covers the concept of the covenant in Judaism.[94]

As Abraham had heard, this covenant would be the defining factor throughout the rest of human history. But already its effects were in process, for, as Abraham had just been told, all those accepting the gospel would henceforth be accounted his seed—a process that Joseph Smith described as including literal physiological changes.[95] Childless though Abraham remained, yet the converts he had already made were accounted his seed! To this day, converts to Judaism "are considered to be born anew, children of Abraham and Sarah,"[96] and are even given new names, men the name of Abraham, women the name of Sarah.[97] Indeed, Judaism expressly teaches that "Sarah was an equal and indispensable partner of Abraham in the covenant and in the propagation of the faith,"[98] and that "there can be no covenant without Sarah."[99]

Already at Haran, what we see, to use the words of a modern writer, is "this one man, Abraham, . . . in the process of becoming a people."[100] And we see also the promise that must have brought untold joy to the heart of both Abraham and Sarah, still childless—the promise of literal posterity, the promise that will "run as a leitmotif through the Abraham [story]."[101] It must have seemed as rain after a long drought, the divine word that both Abraham and Sarah would surely have interpreted as assurance that their long trial of infertility was about to end, that they were about to be blessed with the great desire of their hearts. Abraham's blessing and glory centered in family and posterity. He was to become the new father of the human race, possessing, as he himself mentions, the right of the first-born, even Adam (Abr. 1:3), and being promised that his posterity would do as Adam's once did (D&C 107:54): rise up and bless him as their father.

Why was this covenant with its lavish blessings given to Abraham? He himself tells that he had sought the Lord through righteousness (Abr. 1:2; 2:12), part of the concept of *hesed*. Another part is Jehovah's "loyalty" and "love" in "accept[ing] . . . Abraham and his descendants into the covenant" and "fulfilling the conditions thereof."[102] This dual dimension of *hesed* is captured perfectly by what Nephi said of Abraham: the Lord "leadeth away the righteous into precious lands," and "loveth those who will have him to be their God. Behold, he loved our fathers, and he covenanted with them, yea, even Abraham, Isaac, and Jacob; and he remembered the covenants which he had made" (1 Ne. 17:38–40). Judaism further recognizes that the spread of love and mercy, or *hesed*, is "the very purpose of the covenant of Abraham."[103] In fact, the Talmud speaks of "bestowers of lovingkindness, sons of bestowers of lovingkindess, who hold fast to the covenant of Abraham our father."[104]

And why, the rabbis ask, did God's pronouncement of blessings include the promise to curse those that cursed Abraham? Because when Abraham had been reviled and cursed for teaching righteousness, he had not responded in kind, but had kept silent; therefore, God would step in and curse those who cursed him.[105]

The principle would be expressed by Moroni: "Judgment is mine, saith the Lord, and vengeance is mine also" (Morm. 8:20).

Seeking Enoch's Zion

Abraham tells that, at the close of God's conversation delivering the covenant in Haran, "after the Lord had withdrawn from speaking to me, and withdrawn his face from me, I said in my heart: Thy servant has sought thee earnestly; now I have found thee; thou didst send thine angel to deliver me from the gods of Elkenah, and I will do well to hearken unto thy voice, therefore let thy servant rise up and depart in peace" (Abr. 2:12–13). Great were the blessings that Abraham had sought and found, but his seeking was not over. According to the New Testament letter to the Hebrews,

> By faith Abraham, when he was called to go out into a place which he should after receive for an inheritance, obeyed; and he went out, not knowing whither he went. By faith he sojourned in the land of promise, as in a strange country, dwelling in tabernacles [or "tents"[106]] . . . : for he looked for a city which hath foundations, whose builder and maker is God. (Hebrews 11:8–10)

Bible scholars have pointed out the similarity in description between this city and the one mentioned in certain Jewish and Christian apocryphal texts.[107] In the book of Revelation, when the Apostle John sees "that great city, the holy Jerusalem, descending out of heaven from God," he sees that it has twelve foundations adorned with precious stones (Rev. 21:10, 14, 19). It is the same city mentioned in 4 Ezra when the prophet Ezra sees in vision "an established city, and a place of huge foundations,"[108] and hears the Lord explain that "in the last days"[109] "Zion will come and be made manifest to everybody, prepared and built."[110]

According to a popular view, this city was attainable by Abraham only after death, for "entrance into the heavenly city is not experienced on this side of the grave." In this view, Abraham "did not focus [his] faith on the present and the earthly, but on the future and the heavenly."[111] Not so, say the Joseph Smith sources, which disclose that the heavenly city Abraham had in mind had once been an actual earthly city that had been translated, even as Abraham had discovered in the patriarchal records. And it was not just the people that were taken, said Joseph Smith, but also the very "city which they occupied, and the foundations on which it stood, with a large piece of earth immediately connected with the foundations and the city."[112] Hence, according to Bruce R. McConkie, in looking for the "city which hath foundations," Abraham "sought for the city of Enoch which God had before taken."[113]

But how could he seek it if it was gone from the earth? Latter-day scripture also describes an order of priesthood available in Abraham's day that could actually give mortals access to that translated city. Different than the patriarchal order (D&C 107:40–57); it was called "the Holy Priesthood, after the Order of the Son of God," and later the "Melchizedek Priesthood" (D&C 107:3–4), and was generally available to all who believed in God (JST Gen. 14:29: "unto as many as believed on his name") and worked righteousness (see Alma 13:10–11). And according to the Joseph Smith Translation of Genesis, that same order of priesthood gave men "power, by faith," to perform mighty miracles, and was described as the "the order of the covenant which God made with Enoch," for "men having this faith, coming up unto this order of God, were translated and taken up into heaven" (JST Gen. 14:27, 32). It was this order of priesthood that Abraham was seeking when he left Haran. He was seeking, in other words, to be translated to the city of Enoch.

Abraham's quest for the city of Zion may well be alluded to in ancient sources. The Qur'an records this prayer by Abraham: "O Lord, . . . join me with the righteous. . . . Include me with the heirs of the paradise of bliss."[114] Rabbinic tradition reports the suggestive statement that Abraham longed to have "wings like a dove" that he might "fly away, and be at rest."[115] And an early Christian illustration of God commanding Abraham to leave Haran shows a right hand being extended to Abraham through a multicolored rainbowlike arc[116] —an event echoing God's putting forth his right hand to Noah when the rainbow was given as the sign of the covenant.[117] What covenant? Not only the promise not to flood the earth, but also, as disclosed in the Joseph Smith Translation of Genesis, the promise to eventually bring Enoch's Zion back to the earth (JST Gen. 9:21–23). What makes this scene with Abraham particularly poignant is the fact that, as we have seen, the right hand that was extended to him at Haran was most likely that of Enoch himself, acting as messenger of the Almighty. The illustration of Enoch's right hand being extended to Abraham may well be symbolic of Abraham seeking Enoch's Zion.

But if Abraham were to achieve his quest of being translated, how could his posterity bless all the nations of the earth? In the same way as happened with Enoch, whose son, as Abraham had read, "was not taken, that the covenants of the Lord might be fulfilled, which he made to Enoch" (Moses 8:2). And if Abraham was seeking the order of priesthood that gave access to the city of Enoch, why hadn't Enoch himself simply ordained Abraham to this order at the same time Enoch ordained him to the patriarchal order? Apparently for the same reason that the Lord appeared in the Kirtland Temple and then sent other messengers: once He delegates authority, such authority is to be obtained only from those to whom it has been delegated.[118]

Hence Enoch, the only living patriarch with the patriarchal priesthood, had been sent to ordain Abraham to that priesthood. But since the Melchizedek Priesthood was available through a mortal whom Abraham would later meet—the man Melchizedek—Abraham must be patient and continue to seek it, and thereby obtain Enoch's translated city of Zion.

Thus Abram—whose very name can mean "the father is high" or "the father lifts himself on high"[119]—left Haran to seek residence with his forefather Enoch, who was already "high and lifted up" (Moses 7:24). Might Abram himself possibly have thought that his own name prophetically portended his own destiny, that he was to join his forefather Enoch in that beautiful terrestrial world that was high and lifted up? And if Abraham had read his ancestor's prophecy about a descendant who would "set his dwelling on high,"[120] did he possibly interpret this to mean that he would be translated to the city of Enoch?

Devout Prayer and Divine Protection on the Journey into Canaan

As we have seen, it was Abraham's fate to live in the age of the great sacral kingships that claimed not only rule by divine right but also global dominion. Abraham's own writings hold the key to understand those audacious claims as but an imitation of Adam's patriarchal priesthood authority, to which Abraham himself was the rightful heir. What most occupied those ancient pretenders can be seen to this day in the various inscriptions scattered throughout the world's great museums. Written in first person, they declare in lofty words the daring military conquests and ostentatious building projects of those mighty monarchs. In sharp contrast, the restored writings of the true holder of that royal patriarchal authority attest to an entirely different agenda. Also written in first person, Abraham's record declares that with that authority he sought to neither conquer nor to build monuments, but to obediently travel forth to build the kingdom of God.

Thus with the patriarchal authority received from Enoch, Abraham obeyed the divine command to leave the goodly land of Haran for a "strange land" (Abr. 2:6; Heb. 11:9—"a strange country"), a destination he had never seen. Commenting on Abraham's situation, Joseph Smith stated that "the word spoken to Noah was not sufficient for Abraham," and "it was not required of Abraham to seek an inheritance in a strange country upon the word spoken to Noah, but for himself [Abraham] obtained the promises at the hand of the Lord."[121] Orson Hyde similarly observed that "Abraham might have searched all former records and revelations, but here was a duty he never could have learned therefrom—Depart . . . ! . . . Hence the circumstances required new revelation, and God gave it by commanding this great man . . . to go forth into a country where he never had been."[122]

In Abraham's words in the Book of Abraham, "I, Abraham, departed as the Lord had said unto me . . . and I, Abraham, was sixty and two years old when I departed out of Haran" (Abr. 2:14). This number contradicts that given in Genesis,[123] but happens to correspond precisely with Abraham's age as given in the chronicle of George Syncellus, the ardent chronographer from Byzantium.[124]

Abraham's parents did not go, his mother having died in Haran,[125] and his father having returned to his idolatry and choosing to remain behind (Abr. 2:5). Abraham took his wife and his nephew Lot,[126] and the large community of Saints, numbering at least into the hundreds, that had joined him. He led by inspiration: "Abraham was guided in all his family affairs by the Lord," said Joseph Smith, and "was told where to go, and when to stop."[127] President Spencer W. Kimball added that it was "Abraham's faithfulness in all things [that] qualified him to receive revelation for his family."[128]

And having received that revelation, Abraham led his family and his people by love, beginning with Abraham's love for the Author of the commandment he was now following. "Not only did Abraham listen to God's command," says a rabbinic text about Abraham's leaving Haran, "though it entailed hardship and inconvenience, but he did so joyfully and not grudgingly."[129]

Abraham's love encompassed also those whom he led, beginning most ardently with his own wife. Speaking of Abraham taking Sarah out of Haran, the Zohar comments that "it was by persuasion and not by compulsion [that] he induced Sara to go with him."[130] Abraham's priesthood leadership was the model of what the Lord commands concerning latter-day priesthood leadership: never by "compulsion" but "only by persuasion" and the similar attributes of gentleness, meekness, kindness, and love unfeigned—qualifications for the constant companionship of the Holy Ghost and the presence of God (D&C 121:37, 41–42, 45–46).

And if Abraham so qualified, so did his beloved Sarah, whose faith at least matched that of Abraham. He had heard the command to leave directly from God, she only from Abraham.[131] Yet she went without argument and with full purpose of heart, qualifying for the continuous presence and protection of the Almighty. And what of the multitude of his converts following him on this journey? One writer supposes that they must have been apprehensive inasmuch as their leader could not tell them exactly where they were headed.[132] In reality, they had faith in their prophet and leader, who was leading by the Spirit. In the words of W. F. P. Noble, "Following the leadings of divine Providence with the one supreme motive to honor and obey God, he carried with him the presence of the Lord."[133]

As did Sarah. Jewish tradition tells of a visible "cloud of holiness"[134] that hovered over her tent as "God's testimony to what went on within."[135] Sarah constantly "brought . . . holiness into her home," which was imbued with the divine presence,[136] a light that spread over the rest of the camp as well. The Jewish sage Nachmanides held that "the Divine Presence rested upon [their] tents."[137] It was perhaps this visible divine protection to which Abraham alluded when he wrote, as recorded in the Book of Abraham, "we . . . came forth in the way to the land of Canaan, and dwelt in tents as we came on our way; therefore, eternity was our covering and our rock and our salvation" (Abr. 2:15–16). For both Abraham and Sarah, this "was a journey that transformed them both."[138]

The glory hovering over Abraham's caravan was an indisputable manifestation that Zion was again upon the earth, even as divine glory had once visibly rested on Enoch's city of Zion (Moses 7:17). But if the phenomenon reflected the past, it also foreshadowed the future, for according to Exodus, the Israelites under Moses were accompanied by "a pillar of cloud by day" and "a pillar of fire by night" (JPST Exodus 13:21), as they were led by the Lord's angel on whom he had placed his name (Ex. 23:20–21), namely Enoch[139] (raising the possibility that Enoch was also leading Abraham and his followers in their journey). As remembered in rabbinic tradition, the Israelites were "surrounded . . . with the Clouds of Glory" which "protect[ed] them," covering them like a "canopy" or a "pavilion."[140] Thus the children of the Patriarchs, in the words of Nachmanides, "returned to the eminence of their forefathers who had God's mystery upon their tents, and who were themselves the . . . bearers of His *Shekhinah* [Divine Presence]."[141]

All this seems to be echoed in the Jewish festival Sukkot, or Feast of Tabernacles, which according to tradition is intended to symbolize the protective clouds of glory that covered the Israelites in their march. On the first day of Sukkot, the invited heavenly guest is none other than the patriarch Abraham.[142]

For Latter-day Saints, however, the most important foreshadowings of Abraham's experience have yet to be fulfilled. Similar glory will rest on Abraham's latter-day seed. Isaiah prophesied of the time when the Lord would "create upon every dwelling place of mount Zion, and upon her assemblies, a cloud and smoke by day, and the shining of a flaming fire by night" (Isa. 4:5),[143] which sounds like the Lord's invitation to latter-day Zion to "arise and shine forth, that thy light may be a standard for the nations" (D&C 115:5). It is yet another example of the events of latter-day Zion being foreshadowed by Abraham, who "is one of those key figures," says Hugh Nibley, "in whom all the events of the past are brought into focus as by a burning glass and whose actions are in turn projected into the future as an ever-expanding image."[144]

Abraham's fateful journey from Haran southward left an indelible imprint still visible in the Middle East, for "virtually every country through which Abraham passed en route to Canaan has its own holy site and legend associated with him."[145] Various routes for his travels have been suggested,[146] but it appears likely he passed through the city of Aleppo, which contains the "Mosque of Abraham" and since ancient times has claimed the honor of being on Abraham's route.[147] Continuing south, the journey would have taken them through the Syrian desert undoubtedly into Damascus.[148] At least two ancient historians[149] reported that Abraham had reigned there as king, while Josephus added that the name of Abraham "is still even now famous in Damascus,"[150] near to which was a village called "Abram's abode."[151] It may be the same village that still today claims to have once been home to Abraham, located near Damascus in a secluded hilly area considered one of the Middle East's more remarkable survivals, being the only place where ancient Aramaic has survived as a living language.[152]

But the very terseness of Abraham's own description of their route to Canaan seems to leave open the possibility of other settlements visited but not mentioned. Maimonides' description of the journey seems to suggest a course that (not unlike the missionary journeys of Abraham's descendant the Apostle Paul) may have meandered as they were led by the Spirit to perform their missionary labors. Abraham and his company "were walking and calling and gathering the people from town to town and from country to country," insists Maimonides.[153] As the Lord would later lead Abraham's descendant Lehi into "the more fertile parts of the wilderness" (1 Ne. 16:16), so it seems that the Lord led Abraham to the most fertile fields of souls ready to harvest.

The Book of Abraham adds a stop on the itinerary southward not mentioned by Genesis: the land of Jershon (Abr. 2:16–17), which some have identified as the ancient city known to us as Jerash, located in present-day Jordan. In Jershon, Abraham "built an altar . . . and made an offering unto the Lord, and prayed" (Abr. 2:17). That prayer and the accompanying sacrifice would have been offered, as he had learned to do from the patriarchal records (Moses 5:8; 6:52), in the name of Jesus Christ. And this particular prayer included a petition for mercy on behalf of his father, who had nearly succeeded in having Abraham killed, and who, after repenting and following Abraham to Haran, had "turned again unto his idolatry" and had chosen not to continue the journey with Abraham. It could have been cause for Abraham to reject and forget his father, but Abraham was a man of mercy and forgiveness. "I, Abraham, . . . prayed that the famine might be turned away from my father's house, that they might not perish" (Abr. 2:17). Nor did Abraham wish his father to perish spiritually; the Qur'an reports that Abraham implored the Lord to "forgive my father—for, verily, he is among those who have gone astray."[154]

From Jershon, Abraham would probably have headed west and crossed the Jordan River to arrive at Shechem in the land of Canaan. It was a delightful land, described by a nearly contemporaneous account thus: "Figs were in it, and grapes. It had more wine than water. Plentiful was its honey, abundant its olives. Every kind of fruit was on its trees. Barley was there, and emmer. There was no limit to any kind of cattle."[155]

But there was also danger in this lush land. Here he built another altar and prayed, as reported by an Armenian apocryphal source, holding "his hands on high."[156] In Abraham's own words, "I offered sacrifice . . . and called on the Lord devoutly, because we had already come into the land of this idolatrous nation" (Abr. 2:18). The idolatry was as rank as that which he opposed in Ur, and included human sacrifice and ritual prostitution. It was to the heart of such spiritual darkness that God sent his messenger of light, for, as a modern Jewish writer relates, "as God directed Abram's steps steadily to the south, far from keeping him away from the centers of Canaanite deviancy, their temples and high places, He guided him straight for strategically located cultic sites."[157] Shechem was in fact located at the crossroads of two intersecting trade routes, making it "well suited to maximize the potential number of spiritually starved Canaanites Abram might teach."[158]

But not without some peril. A passage from the Testament of Levi discloses that travelers through Shechem were often murdered and their wives ravished, and that in fact Abraham and Sarah had been in just such danger from the residents. "But the Lord prevented them," even though they "grossly mistreated" one of Abraham's group.[159] Abraham did not respond in kind.

Profound prayer brought profound revelation, as told in Genesis and in first person in the Book of Abraham: "And the Lord appeared unto me in answer to my prayers, and said unto me: Unto thy seed will I give this land" (Abr. 2:19; cf. Gen. 12:7). The momentous event is still commemorated at a site revered by Druze Arabs as the place where God covenanted with Abraham. Here barren women of all religions make pilgrimage, praying for a child.[160]

Commenting on Abraham's experience, nineteenth-century clergyman Christopher Wordsworth, nephew of the famous poet, observed that it was "at Sichem [Shechem], the centre of Canaan, in the beautiful valley between Mount Ebal on the north, and Mount Gerizim on the south," where "the Lord appeared unto Abraham for the first time in Canaan. And afterwards . . . to Sichem, JESUS CHRIST, the Incarnate Word of God, the Lord JEHOVAH in [the] flesh, the true Seed of Abraham, came, and sat at the well, in the weariness and weakness of humanity, and first revealed Himself as the Messiah, and declared, that He would give to all the living water of the Holy Spirit. . . . Thus Christ at Sichem explained and fulfilled the promise given to Abraham there."[161]

God's promise to Abraham of posterity is still commemorated by Druze Arabs at a site to which barren women of all religions make pilgrimage, praying for a child[162]—as undoubtedly did Sarah herself, whose expectation of children was vibrant and sustaining. As recounted by a modern Jewish mother, "Sarah left home, just as Abraham did, with the expectation that if they had the courage to follow God's way and if they kept their pact, staying in an obedient, loving relationship, they would be showered with blessings.... Knowing that she would have a child to love and fill with a dramatically new vision... gave her identity, meaning, and focus. It kept her going" during the long years and even decades when, despite her faith and obedience, somehow she did not get pregnant. "She never cut off her conversation with God; she prayed continually for a child of her own," and "God took pleasure in hearing her voice," as did a host of people in need of spiritual and temporal sustenance. "She became a teacher and spiritual guide, teaching women about God and God's covenant. She was a hostess extraordinaire, whose capacious tent was a place where travelers on their own journeys could feel temporarily at home and could become refreshed." And she "was graced with an abundant spiritual presence," a visible sign of God's approval of her life and mission.[163]

Each new renewal of God's promise must have brought renewed hope and joy to both Abraham and Sarah. It was the word of the Lord: Abraham would be blessed with posterity. What else could this mean but that Sarah would have a child? The question and its answer were simply taken for granted as they both, with childlike faith, continued to look forward to the event that would change their lives and fulfill the great promises.

The verse in the Book of Abraham relating God's appearance in the land of the Canaanites is one of but four short verses chronicling Abraham's journey to and through the land of promise, and all four verses mention prayer (Abr. 2:17–20).[164] Abraham personifies the oft-repeated latter-day commandment to "pray always."[165] In fact, according to Maimonides, no matter what Abraham was doing, his heart and mind were always with God[166]—a striking example of his descendant Amulek's exhortation that "when you do not cry unto the Lord, let your hearts be full, drawn out in prayer unto him continually" (Alma 34:27). Well did a nineteenth-century cleric observe that Abraham "was a man of prayer, and therefore he was a man of power."[167] President Spencer W. Kimball counseled that "like Abraham, we must seek to qualify for such revelation by setting our lives in order and by becoming acquainted with the Lord through frequent and regular conversations with him."[168]

But Abraham's altar in Canaan served a larger purpose than prayer. He built it, insisted nineteenth-century clergyman David Breed, to openly "acknowledge his God" before all men. "Such was the character of his religion wherever he dwelt, and to the end of his days. . . . His principles were manifest to prince and to people." Of God, Abraham was not ashamed; he lived his religion openly. So likewise, counseled Breed, "let it be manifest that you are the friend of God, and the follower of Jesus."[169]

But Abraham's purpose was larger still, according to Ephrem the Syrian, who maintained that Abraham built his altar in the land of the Canaanites "so that he might teach the worship of holiness in their land."[170] What worship? The same performed by Adam, Noah, Enoch, and all the Saints since the beginning: the worship of the Father in the name of His Only Begotten Son, He whose blood would be shed even as the sacrificial animal on the altar. Abraham preached Christ and Him crucified, and offered the ordinances Adam himself had followed, beginning with baptism in water for the remission of sins. Commenting on the Lord's promise to Abraham in Haran that "thou shalt be a blessing," the Genesis Rabbah explains that the Hebrew word for "blessing," *berachah*, is associated with the Hebrew word for "pool of water," *beraychah*; and "just as a pool of water purifies those who are impure [or, according to another translation, "just as a pool of water removes the cultic uncleanness of an unclean person"[171]] so you, Abraham, shall bring near to God those who are afar and shall purify them to their Father in Heaven."[172] If we had the full record, we would read of Abraham testifying of the Son of God and leading his converts into the waters of baptism. And, says a midrash, "how great is his reward who leads his fellowman back in penitence to the Almighty!"[173]

The Power of the Pure Love of Christ

Journeying still southward, Abraham came to a mountain between Bethel and Ai, where, as Genesis records, he "pitched his tent" (Gen. 12:8; see also Abr. 2:20). Ancient Jewish tradition remembers that he actually first pitched Sarah's tent and only then his own, a reflection of his constant consideration for his wife.[174] Throughout his life, says Midrash Rabbah, Abraham "acted lovingly toward Sarah," for which God blessed Abraham in all things.[175] It is an example of the Lord's commandment to Abraham's latter-day posterity that each husband shall "love thy wife with all thy heart" (D&C 42:22).

Having set up camp, Abraham lost no time in building yet another altar, at which he prayed (Gen. 12:8; see also Abr. 2:20). His prayer is mentioned also in the ancient book of Jubilees, which describes the beauty and bounty of the place: Abraham "saw that the land was spacious and most excellent and that everything was growing on it: vines, fig trees, pomegranates, oak trees, holm trees, terebinths, olive trees, cedars, cypresses, incense trees, and all kinds of wild trees; and there was water on the mountains. Then he blessed the Lord who had led him from Ur of the Chaldeans and brought him to this mountain."[176]

But if the inhabitants had the bounties of the earth, it was Abraham who had the bread of life, which he offered freely. Each altar that Abraham built as he went along also served, according to Jewish tradition, as "a center for his activities as a missionary,"[177] in which he was assisted by Sarah. She taught the women, while Abraham taught the men.[178] It was a perfect place to do so, for Bethel, like many of the other locations Abraham stopped at, was located at a major crossroads, offering expanded opportunities to preach the gospel.

And as before, Abraham's altar provided an effective opportunity to preach of the Savior's mission and Atonement so poignantly foreshadowed by animal sacrifice.

The Book of Mormon specifically affirms that Abraham, like all other prophets, testified of Christ (Hel. 8:16–19, 22).[179] It was the same gospel that Noah had taught, following the pattern of his forefathers: "Believe and repent of your sins and be baptized in the name of Jesus Christ, the Son of God, even as our fathers, and ye shall receive the Holy Ghost, that ye may have all things made manifest" (Moses 8:24). Abraham was living the law of the gospel, and inviting others to do so. His observance of God's laws even included keeping the Sabbath day, says Jewish tradition.[180]

He also taught the plan of salvation to a world that had long since lost the knowledge of it. Ancient sources tell that "no one among them believed in the Last day and the Resurrection,"[181] for "the whole world . . . believed that the souls of men were perishable," but "Abraham came and preached the doctrine of immortality and transmigration."[182] He taught, in other words, the unchanging truths of God's majestic plan of happiness for His spirit children who are afforded the opportunity to come to earth and take bodies of flesh and blood in order to qualify, through obedience, for glory later in the Resurrection.

In all this, Abraham was building Zion as it had once been built by Enoch, who had gone "forth in the land, among the people . . . testifying" (Moses 6:37). So it was with Abraham, who, as reported by Maimonides, went forth "walking and calling and gathering the people from town to town and from country to country."[183] According to John Taylor, "Abraham was raised up as a special agent in the hand of the Almighty to disseminate correct principles among the people, and as a medium through which God would communicate intelligence and blessings to the human family."[184]

Abraham not only preached to his fellow men but also ministered to them. Wherever he traveled, the legends tell, people would come and ask him to pray for them, and his prayers on their behalf were answered.[185] He also exercised his priesthood power to heal[186] and bless others. Latter-day revelation even provides the name of one such beneficiary, a man named Esaias, who "lived in the days of Abraham, and was blessed by him" (D&C 84:13).

And as "no one can assist in this work except he shall be humble and full of love" (D&C 12:8), no one was more qualified than Abraham to invite souls to Christ. Jewish tradition insists that Abraham was the epitome of the love of God,[187] and that "Abraham summoned mankind to believe in God out of his own great love for Him,"[188] and "served Him out of love"[189] by "showing loving-kindness" (hesed) to mankind and thus "doing the same work" as God[190]—a pattern that would be followed by Joseph Smith, who "because of his love for his fellowmen, never missed an opportunity to preach the gospel."[191]

The rabbis compared Abraham to a vial of fragrant myrrh "closed with a tight-fitting lid and lying in a corner, so that its fragrance was not disseminated." Hence

God commanded Abraham to travel and spread the sweet odor.[192] The metaphor could not be more apt, for if Nimrod had compelled worship, Abraham's approach was precisely the opposite. Not by control or compulsion would Abraham change the world or win the hearts of mankind, but rather by the principles of righteousness and love upon which the rights of the priesthood are always based (see D&C 121:41–42).

The mighty power of love that drew mankind to Abraham would be manifest in the life of Joseph Smith, who said of himself: "Sectarian priests cry out concerning me, and ask, 'Why is it this babbler gains so many followers, and retains them?' I answer, It is because I possess the principle of love. All I can offer the world is a good heart and a good hand."[193] Abraham also "was charitable with all his heart and soul,"[194] and it is even said that the divine attribute of love "was incarnate in Abraham."[195]

When we see such fruit we know the tree, for as Mormon would explain, pure love results from a process available to all: faith, repentance, and baptism, followed by "the visitation of the Holy Ghost, which Comforter filleth with hope and perfect love" (Moro. 8:26). This love is "charity," or "the pure love of Christ," and it remains and grows by "pray[ing] unto the Father with all the energy of heart" and proving oneself a "true follower" of Christ (7:47–48). Abraham's possession of that pure and perfect love bespeaks his own obedience to the ordinances, his own fervent prayers unto the Father in the name of Christ, and his own course in proving himself a true follower of Jesus Christ.

In Abraham's case, being a true follower of Christ meant also foreshadowing Him, for as with the Savior, Abraham's loving service was rendered by one with supreme authority. In Abraham's ordination to the patriarchal authority, he had succeeded Adam and Noah in his own royal patriarchal reign, heir to the right that kings like Pharaoh falsely claimed and earnestly sought to imitate as they amassed their wealth and built their kingdoms of glory. In contrast, Abraham occupied himself in selfless service by building not his own kingdom but the kingdom of God with an eye single to the glory of God. Only in the life of the Son of God would there be such paradox, when He as the Heavenly King would descend from His throne on high (see Mosiah 3:5) to serve and suffer because of His profound love for His fellow beings (see Ether 12:33).

It was that pure love of Christ that Abraham offered to the world of his day to heal hearts and unite the human family. "It is Abraham the missionary," says Nibley, "who makes brothers of all the world, who abolishes the differences between the nations and the races."[196] As expressed by the rabbis, Abraham "won people over" by his love and teachings.[197] "Charity . . . slept," and "Abraham woke [it] up." Also, "the nations of the world slept, and did not come under the wings of the Shekhinah. Who woke them up so that they might come? Abraham,"[198] as he "began to make proselytes and bring them under the wings of the Shekhinah,"[199] for "he carried with him the presence of the Lord."[200]

In Judaism and ancient Israel, the Shekhinah was the "majestic presence or manifestation of God which has descended to 'dwell' among men," most importantly and conspicuously "on Mount Zion . . . and in the Temple,"[201] for "it is upon [the Cherubim] and upon the Ark [of the Covenant] that the Shekhinah rests."[202] The one day a year when it was symbolically visible to man was on the Day of Atonement, when the High Priest on behalf of all Israel would enter the Holy of Holies and create a cloud of incense symbolizing the Shekhinah, and then sprinkle sacrificial blood on the top of the Ark, the very throne of the Lord. Only then could Israel, if they had repented, be forgiven.[203] In calling all to the Shekhinah, Abraham was inviting all to come unto Christ—to His gospel, His Atonement, His throne, and His temple, all in the loving arms of Zion.

What all this seems to suggest is that Abraham was traveling with a portable temple, like the later tabernacle carried by the Israelites in their sojourn through the wilderness (see Ex. 25–27). We have already seen that divine glory rested upon Abraham's camp, even as such glory would rest upon the Israelite tabernacle (Ex. 40:34). And as that tabernacle would house the Ark, the sacred wooden chest (see Ex. 25:10–22) containing the tablets (1 Kgs. 8:9) written upon by the finger of God (Ex. 31:18), so did Abraham possess, as we have seen, the wooden chest of Adam that likewise contained ancient patriarchal records written by the finger of God. Jewish tradition insists that Abraham observed all the temple ordinances, including the all-important temple ritual of the Day of Atonement.[204] And ancient sources emphasize Abraham's careful and exacting obedience in performing such ordinances.[205]

Abraham's mission of inviting all to Christ was to last a lifetime and beyond, for the great blessing to Abraham's posterity, as pronounced at Haran, was that they also were to bless others by bearing the gospel to all nations (Abr. 2:9, 11). Abraham's own travels to accomplish this would be anything but easy—"the hardships were many and severe which he encountered,"[206] according to Jewish tradition. But, as noted by nineteenth-century pastor Samuel Crothers, "for the sake of being instruments in the hand of God," Abraham "and his sons continued all their lives to labor as faithful Missionaries, from one kingdom to another . . . , foregoing the comforts of a fixed and fortified habitation, cheerfully encountering the dangers and hardships. . . . Abraham was not only the Father of the Faithful, but he was the . . . father of Missionaries."[207]

Jewish sources attest, for example, the missionary activity of both Isaac and Jacob in emulation of Abraham.[208] Abraham was not just the father of converts but also of those who would convert others, those who would establish Zion. As John Taylor stated, "Abraham's posterity were to stand as messengers of God, as legates of the skies, commissioned of the great Jehovah to proclaim His word to fallen man . . . and bring them to Zion."[209]

Abraham's missionary example is especially relevant for latter-day Zion. According to President Spencer W. Kimball, "just as the Lord called his servant Abraham to serve as a missionary . . . , so is he calling the Saints today. . . . Like Abraham, we must declare the gospel to the world, not stopping with a vocal declaration, but living the gospel so others can see the truth."[210]

A FACSIMILE FROM THE BOOK OF ABRAHAM
NO. 3

Explanation

Fig. 1.   Abraham sitting upon Pharaoh's throne, by the politeness of the king, with a crown upon his head, representing the Priesthood, as emblematical of the grand Presidency in Heaven; with the scepter of justice and judgment in his hand.

Fig. 2.   King Pharaoh, whose name is given in the characters above his head.

Fig. 3.   Signifies Abraham in Egypt as given also in Figure 10 of Facsimile No. 1.

Fig. 4.   Prince of Pharaoh, King of Egypt, as written above the hand.

Fig. 5.   Shulem, one of the king's principal waiters, as represented by the characters above his hand.

Fig. 6.   Olimlah, a slave belonging to the prince.

Abraham is reasoning upon the principles of Astronomy, in the king's court.

CHAPTER 5

Showing Forth the Power and Knowledge of Zion:
Abraham in Egypt

Teach ye diligently and my grace shall attend you, that you may instructed more
perfectly in . . . things both in heaven and in the earth, and under the earth; things
which have been, things which are, things which must shortly come to pass; things
which are at home, things which are abroad; the wars and perplexities of the nations,
and the judgments which are on the land; and a knowledge also of countries and of
kingdoms—that ye may be prepared in all things when I shall send you again.
—DOCTRINE AND COVENANTS 88:78–80

A Mighty Cedar

Some three years[1] after Abraham and his followers arrived in the promised land, it was struck by famine. A modern writer has observed that for a person of Abraham's day, "'famine' had the same resonance of terror as 'cancer' or 'AIDS' today. A modern American can find a twenty-four-hour supermarket packed with food within a ten-minute drive, so he has difficulty imagining the dread evoked in other times and places at the prospect of death by starvation."[2]

What made matters worse for Abraham was the fact that the last time he had seen famine years earlier, it had come in the wake of the society's failed attempt to execute him, and therefore appeared to be a vindication of his righteousness and God's protection of him—that same God at whose command Abraham had now come to this land of promise. And in giving that command, God had announced Himself to Abraham as the Controller of the world, at whose word the sea is calmed and mountains removed "in an instant, suddenly" (Abr. 2:7).

Surely, then, it would be a small thing for God to simply reverse or remove this famine. One of the patterns of Abraham's life was devout prayer for relief in the face of difficulty, and there is no reason to believe that he did otherwise in this instance. But the famine continued in all its severity, blighting crops and fruit, killing animals, and finally threatening the lives of Abraham and his community. The heavens, from which God had spoken so often to His friend Abraham, now seemed bolted shut, allowing neither rain nor explanatory revelation. How could Abraham explain this to his followers, who had exercised faith in him as their inspired leader? Had God forgotten them after they had obediently come to this promised land? Why weren't Abraham's prayers answered? And what about God's promise to bless Abraham and make his name great? The unfolding events seemed to be doing just the opposite.

But we read no words of complaint or questioning. The very purpose of the famine, according to Rashi, was "to test him whether he would have qualms about God's promises."[3] Other Jewish sources note that "after having unquestioningly complied with God's command, Abraham should have been pelted with garlands, honored and revered. . . . Instead, his journey to [the promised land appeared to be] a fiasco. Abraham should have protested. But no! Abraham did not question or complain."[4] He "murmured not,"[5] and "neither protested nor assailed God's justice."[6]

For Abraham, it was yet another disappointment, another challenge in a life that seemed to be one trial after another. "The trials of Abraham" is how the learned Rabbi Eliezer wrote of the life of the Patriarch,[7] which is exactly how one might write of the life of Joseph Smith. And for both men, it seems that God was polishing his finest gemstones. "I am like a huge, rough stone rolling down from a high mountain," said the Prophet Joseph, "and the only polishing I get is when some corner gets rubbed off by coming in contact with something else, striking with accelerated force . . . —all hell knocking off a corner here and a corner there. Thus I will become a smooth and polished shaft in the quiver of the Almighty."[8] So it was with Abraham: rabbinic legend claims that among the stones that David used in his sling to slay Goliath, on the first stone was written the name of Abraham.[9]

Abraham met his trials with patience. "In every test to which the Lord subjected him," says Jubilees, "he had been found faithful, and he was not impatient, nor was he slow to act, for he was faithful and loved the Lord."[10] It was this love that sustained him; rabbinic sources tell that all of his many trials he "received with love"[11] and "stood firm in them all,"[12] thereby "demonstrating the extent of [his] love of God."[13] In fact, "Abraham showed his love for God by responding to his tests with deeds of loving-kindness," thereby "utiliz[ing] each test as a tool for spiritual and personal growth."[14] Abraham is the great example of the path to sainthood available to anyone who becomes "full of love" and, in a childlike manner, becomes "submissive, meek, humble, patient" and "willing to submit to all things which the Lord seeth fit to inflict upon him, even as a child doth submit to his father" (Mosiah 3:19).

And with that love came vision, as Nibley points out. "What keeps him going? He has a vision of something else. He knows something else besides the regular routines of this world."[15] What did he know? John Taylor observed that although Abraham "was tried in almost every possible way," yet he continued faithful, and, "inspired by the Spirit of the living God, in possession of the principles of revelation, holding the keys of the everlasting Priesthood, which unlocked the mysteries of the kingdom of God," Abraham "looked forward and backward, and felt that" he was "part of the great program which God had designed to accomplish in regard to the earth."[16]

His vision and commitment were shared by Sarah. No murmuring word escaped her tongue when she could have easily complained of having left the goodly land of Haran for this famine-stricken place.[17] Such silence in the record speaks loudly, as she above anyone else had cause—even the right—to protest, for if Abraham had been told to come here by the Lord, she had been told only by Abraham. She might easily have complained also of the fact that, despite Abraham's report of God's promise of posterity, she yet continued childless. But her love for her husband was too great, her commitment to her covenants too strong, her faith in the Almighty too unyielding, to allow her to criticize or complain. In the words of the learned Muslim scholar al-Tabari, Sarah "was one of the best human beings that ever existed. She would not disobey Abraham in any way, for which God honored her."[18]

In good times and bad, Sarah constantly lived the law of Zion, faithfully maintaining that unity of heart that is always Zion's crowning virtue. "From Sarah," says a Jewish source, people "learn strength and constancy no matter what the odds."[19] Together, Abraham and Sarah are, in the words of Erastus Snow, "models of noble character, purity of purpose," and "superior integrity to God," whom they "hesitated not to obey . . . at all hazards even to the sacrifice of that which was nearest and dearest unto them."[20]

But having obeyed, they now faced the agonizing reality that there was simply not enough food in the famine-stricken land, making it impossible for them to remain. Nor could they return to Haran or Ur, which were also afflicted by famine and from out of which God had ordered them. Only one possibility loomed: Egypt, "the gift of the Nile," where crops depended not on the vagaries of rainfall but on the annual flooding of the Nile. And so, Abraham tells in his autobiography, "I . . . concluded to go down into Egypt" (Abr. 2:21).

"Concluded," he says, implying that this was a deliberate decision he alone had arrived at, and probably not without some difficulty. For this was the land of Pharaoh, whose evil priest had once raised the knife to sacrifice Abraham in a pagan rite (Abr. 1:7–20); Pharaoh, the powerful monarch who falsely claimed Abraham's true patriarchal authority, and whose kingdom was but an idolatrous imitation of the true order of Zion on earth (Abr. 1:26–27). All this must have given Abraham pause as he contemplated journeying to Egypt; and, consistent with his practice, he must have made this a matter of fervent prayer.

Yet we read of no divine disclosure on this occasion. Apparently, Abraham was left to work this out on his own. The Zohar tells that "God purposely refrained from telling Abram to go down to Egypt, and allowed him to go of his own accord."[21] But the experience was necessary and part of the Lord's plan for Abraham, for if he "had not gone down into Egypt and been tested there, his portion would not have been in the Lord."[22] In fact, the Pirke de Rabbi Eliezer expressly reports that getting Abraham into Egypt was God's purpose in sending the famine.[23] If the famine in Ur had been sent to vindicate Abraham, this one was sent to bless him, although such blessings are difficult to recognize at the moment. The famine became, in Abraham's own description, "very grievous" (Abr. 2:21), making it impossible for Abraham and his people to remain. Sometimes even with His most faithful Saints, for their own good the Lord guides them by means of circumstances without disclosing His plan.

The trip to Egypt may have taken weeks, as they made their way slowly by the inland route through the Negev desert, probably via the Way of the Wells. Along the way, there were apparently settlements where some provisions might be bought. A group of Semites traveling to Egypt during this era was not unusual, as seen in the famous Beni Hasan mural showing just such a group around the time of Abraham.[24]

Arriving at the border, at the famed Wall of the Ruler, which consisted of a series of fortresses, Abraham's group camped and prepared to pass through customs on the morrow. The border of Egypt, land of plenty, would have been a welcome sight for people fleeing from a famine-stricken land.

Only now did the Lord again speak to His servant Abraham, but what was said must have seemed perplexing: "Behold, Sarai, thy wife, is a very fair woman to look upon; therefore it shall come to pass, when the Egyptians shall see her, they will say—She is his wife; and they will kill you, but they will save her alive; therefore see that ye do on this wise: Let her say unto the Egyptians, she is thy sister, and thy soul shall live" (Abr. 2:22–24).

In the Genesis Apocryphon version of the story, the divine warning comes in the form of a dream that Abraham has and recounts to Sarah on the very night of his entry into Egypt.

> And I, Abram, had a dream in the night of my entering into the land of Egypt and I saw in my dream [that there wa]s a cedar, and a date-palm (which was) [very beautif]ul; and some men came intending to cut down and uproot the cedar, but leave the date-palm by itself. Now the date-palm remonstrated and said,

"Do not cut down the cedar, for we are both from one family" [or, "the two of us grow fr[om] but a [sin]gle root"25]. So the cedar was spared with the help of the date-palm, and [it was] not [cut down]. (That) night I awoke from my sleep and said to Sarai my wife, "I have had a dream; [and I] am frightened by this dream." She said to me, "Tell me your dream that I may know (it too)." So I began to tell her this dream; [and I made known] to [her the meaning of this] dream, [and] s[aid], "[ ] who will seek to kill me and to spare you. [N]ow this is all the favor [that you must do for me]; whe[rev]er [we shall be, say] about me, 'He is my brother.' Then I shall live with your help and my life will be saved because of [you. [ ] they will seek] to [ta]ke you away from me and to kill me." And Sarai wept at my words that night. [ ], and Pharaoh Zo[an . . . so that] Sarai [no longer wished] to go toward [Egypt], lest any[one] should see her.26

It is yet another window into the soul of Sarah that although she wept, and even expressed her desire not to proceed to Egypt, yet we read not a word of contention or criticism on her part. Always she was Sarah the faithful, the loyal, the loving wife. And the comparison of these particular trees, the palm and the cedar, with Sarah and Abraham is a powerful statement about their character, for according to the Psalms, "the righteous flourish like the palm tree, and grow like a cedar in Lebanon" (NRSV Ps. 92:12). The Midrash, commenting on the story of Abraham in Egypt, explains how the righteous are like cedars and palms: "Just as a palm tree and a cedar produce neither crooked curves nor growths,"27 so "the righteous have [no] crookedness" of character. Just "as the shadow of the palm and the cedar is cast afar, so is the reward of the righteous far away in the future world." And just "as the heart of the palm and the cedar is directed upward, so are the hearts of the righteous directed toward the Holy One."28

Abraham's dream reflects the high demand for the precious cedar, the *cedrus libani*, or cedar of Lebanon, which was the most sought-after wood in the ancient Near East.29 Adorned with bluish-green needles, the branches grow straight out as the tree develops into its distinctive and majestic pyramidal shape,30 attaining magnificent heights upwards of a hundred feet. The finely-grained, reddish-colored wood is not only fragrant but strong, straight, and extremely durable, as well as resistant to rot and insects, making it anciently the coveted wood of choice for everything from furniture to coffins, and on a larger scale for ships and large and important buildings. With good reason does the modern flag of Lebanon bear the image of its famous tree, which from earliest times constituted an important trade item and figured prominently in the rise of the ancient Near East. The original great

cedar forests covering mountainous Lebanon and surrounding regions were extensively exploited by the successive dominant powers to float their imperial navies and
erect their great edifices—everything from Solomon's temple to Pharaoh's palace.[31]
But Pharaoh had to import the cedars, for while Egypt was nearly self-sufficient in
natural resources, the major exception was timber from Lebanon and Syria.[32]

It is with some irony, then, that the Lord would later, speaking through
Ezekiel, compare Pharaoh himself to "a cedar of Lebanon . . . of great height" and
"beautiful in its greatness." The tree described by Ezekiel is also a most unusual
tree, whose roots penetrated down to the "abundant water" of "the deep" and
whose top "towered high above the trees of the field" and ascended even "among
the clouds," and "in [whose] shade all great nations lived" (NRSV Ezek. 31:1–10).
According to one scholar, "while at first it seems to be a tree from Lebanon that is
being depicted, the description soon broadens out beyond earthly proportions and
sketches the picture of the great world tree," that mythological cosmic tree offering
shelter and protection for all life on earth.[33]

But as the Ezekiel passage and the Book of Abraham both show, Pharaoh's claim
to such grandeur was merely pretense, as Abraham well knew: "Abraham, possessed
of the authentic records, knew Pharaoh's secret—that his authority was stolen and
his glory simulated."[34] Nor did the other powerful monarchs of the ancient Near
East possess the true patriarchal authority to preside over the human race, even
though they would compare their rule to the qualities of a cedar, expressing the hope
that their reign would be as benevolent and sheltering as the majestic tree.[35]

Such royal symbolism associated with the cedar was very ancient,[36] going back
to the earliest traditions of ancient Near Eastern royalty in imitation of the deity,
who as he sat on his throne was said to be holding a scepter of cedar, "a derivative
of the Tree of Life [and] indicative of his royal status in heaven and on earth." [37]
Hence when the seventh antediluvian king in Mesopotamian tradition, Enoch, had
been taken up and enthroned by the gods, he was handed a scepter of cedar.[38]
Enoch's patriarchal authority was now held by Abraham, who was the mighty
cosmic cedar that Pharaoh only pretended to be. Commenting on Abraham's experience in Egypt, the Zohar expressly compares him to "a cedar [that] is pre-eminent
and all sit under him. The world is supported upon one righteous one, as it is
written, 'the righteous is the foundation of the world.'"[39] Abraham's patriarchal
authority was to establish what the Lord in latter-day scripture has called "Zion, . . .
a defense, and . . . a refuge from the storm" (D&C 115:6). Zion itself is the great
cosmic cedar offering refuge and protection to all mankind.

The Wisdom of Heaven and Earth

Ironically, to preserve his own life, the righteous Abraham was now being
commanded to violate one of his fundamental principles, that of perfect honesty

in his dealings with his fellow men, by asking Sarah to represent herself as his sister. Or was it a violation? If Jubilees is correct, which seems to be vindicated by a later statement in Genesis, Sarah was in fact his sister, the daughter of his father but through a different wife.[40] Or, as other traditions hold, if she was his niece or cousin, she still could, according to ancient custom, properly be called his sister.[41] The word sister could also be used, in both Hebrew and Egyptian, as a term of endearment, meaning "sweetheart" or "wife."[42] The Zohar mentions yet another dimension: "Abraham always called her 'sister' because he was attached to her inseparably" in a spiritual bond that the world did not understand[43]—apparently a reference to eternal marriage. In sum, as Augustine stated, when Abraham called his wife his sister, "he told no lie."[44]

But in the context that the Lord was commanding, it would also result in a deception, masking her relationship as his wife. Earlier in his life, according to the Qur'an, Abraham had prayed, "O Lord, . . . let me be honest in all I say to others."[45] The Zohar insists that Abraham's "words were always truth."[46] Among all who knew him, Abraham had built a reputation for uncompromising integrity. Now he was being asked by God not only to veer from that course, but to involve his wife in the duplicity, which would further require the complicity of his followers, those who honored him as their righteous prophet and patriarch. Jasher reports that Abraham asked not only Sarah but also all those who accompanied them to say that Sarah was his sister.[47]

But it was the Lord's command, reminding us of His command to young Nephi, who hesitated before complying and taking the life of Laban (1 Ne. 4:7–18). "Whatever God requires is right," said Joseph Smith, "no matter what it is, although we may not see the reason thereof till long after the events transpire."[48]

In the short term, however, some commandments can be confusing, and Abraham was so troubled on this occasion that he apparently arose in the night and built an altar and offered sacrifice.[49] To offer up one of his remaining animals after suffering through famine conditions was a sacrifice indeed, but Abraham was equal to the task. Sacrifice was, says Hugh Nibley, "the theme of Abraham's life," which has everything to do with us. "We will be called upon to make some sacrifices; indeed, to please God we must be willing to sacrifice all the way, taking Abraham for our model."[50]

Abraham then, according to his own account in the Book of Abraham, consulted the Urim and Thummim, apparently trying to see if they should continue on into Egypt.[51] What he saw instead was a close-up view of the stars, even as he heard the voice of the Creator begin to explain His creations and their organization in relation to "the throne of God" (Abr. 3:9–10). Jewish legend echoes this event in reporting that Abraham possessed a stone through which he gazed at the heavens,[52] a kind of super-telescope about which he is reported to have said: "I have looked through my crystal to see the stars."[53]

But as further related in the Book of Abraham, somehow the scene changed and Abraham now found himself face to face with the Creator who, as Abraham tells, "said unto me: My son, my son (and his hand was stretched out), behold I will show you all these. And he put his hand upon mine eyes, and I saw those things which his hands had made, which were many; and they multiplied before mine eyes, and I could not see the end thereof" (Abr. 3:12).

We are reminded of the statement of Galileo, the first human to peer at the heavens through a telescope, which, although rudely primitive by today's standards, revealed a multitude of stars that left him in utter amazement: "You will behold through the telescope," Galileo recorded, "a host of other stars, which escape the unassisted sight, so numerous as to be almost beyond belief."[54]

Galileo's view, of course, was nothing compared to what Abraham was now being shown. Having earlier in life discovered the Creator by his starry creations, Abraham now has the privilege of learning about those creations from their Creator, who allows Abraham to see His handiwork and even see the great stars nearest God's own residence. Abraham is that "certain unique man"[55] spoken of in the Orphic hymn "whose insights pierced the mysteries of the stars and the heavenly sphere."[56] John Taylor insisted that Abraham knew more about the cosmos "than all the combined wisdom of the world today"[57]—a statement that is surely still no exaggeration despite the incredible modern advancements in astronomy.

Abraham further tells that "it was in the night time when the Lord spake these words unto me: I will multiply thee, and thy seed after thee, like unto these; and if thou canst count the number of sands, so shall be the number of thy seeds." (Abr. 3:14). This incident, not reported in Genesis, is the first time that the Lord compares Abraham's future posterity to the stars. No metaphor could have been more meaningful or moving to Abraham, whose early years had been spent with stargazers and star worshippers, and whose very discovery of the Creator had come by reflecting on the starry heavens. Now the Creator, who has just personally shown to Abraham something of the vastness of those heavens with their seeming infinitude of stars—numbers too great for mortal man to begin to fathom (Moses 1:37)—makes the breathtaking announcement that the vastness of Abraham's posterity would match that of the stars. Abraham does not recount what his feelings were upon hearing this, but to use the word "overwhelming" may well be an understatement. Such matters are simply beyond the ken of mortals without divine revelation. We can read and reflect, but fully fathoming Abraham's experience must necessarily await our own qualification for those same blessings.

Abraham continues his account by relating that "the Lord said unto me: Abraham, I show these things unto thee before ye go into Egypt, that ye may declare all these words" (Abr. 3:15). Abraham now understood that he must continue on into Egypt, even if he didn't understand why the Lord had directed that Sarah say she was his sister.

As the Lord continued the lesson, He compared the stars to the spirits, symbolism apparently also known to Abraham's forefathers.[58] The Lord then showed Abraham the host of premortal spirits, including "many of the noble and great ones" who "were good" and were chosen, before they were born (Abr. 3:22–23) to be "rulers in the Church of God" (D&C 138:55). The Lord then said, "Abraham, thou art one of them; thou wast chosen before thou wast born" (Abr. 3:23). The passage is reminiscent of the Qur'anic verse in which God tells Abraham that "I have appointed you a leader of mankind,"[59] and reminiscent of a Jewish kabbalistic source that states, "When Abraham our father understood, . . . probed, thought, and was successful, the blessed Holy One revealed himself to him, declaring to him, 'Before I formed you in the womb, I knew you, and before you emerged from the womb, I sanctified you. I have made you a prophet for the nations.'"[60]

According to the Book of Abraham, he was further shown the presentation of the great plan for God's children in order to "prove them . . . to see if they will do all things whatsoever the Lord their God shall command them," so that those "who keep their second estate shall have glory added upon their heads forever and ever" (Abr. 3:25–26). Among all of the vast multitudes of God's children that Abraham saw, he alone was now being honored with this vision of the premortal life and this precious truth that the primary purpose of mortality was to test the obedience of God's children. Is it coincidence that this foundational purpose of mortality as a test of obedience would be revealed to this consummately obedient mortal?

Abraham saw Satan's rebellion and expulsion, followed by the Creation, in which Abraham and other great and noble spirits participated (Abr. 3:24–28; 4:1ff). Similarly Jewish tradition held that God "called him His partner in creation,"[61] and that Abraham wrote down what God had revealed to him about the Creation in a work called the Book of Creation, or Sefer Yetzirah[62]—echoing the fact that Abraham's record known as the Book of Abraham contains not only a Creation account but also Facsimile 2, an astronomical document of deep significance.[63]

Abraham had now been taught firsthand what he had only read about in the writings of Enoch, namely "a knowledge of the beginning of the creation, and also of the planets, and of the stars" (Abr. 1:31).[64] It was all part of Abraham's continuing quest to "acquire ever more and more knowledge from above."[65] As we have seen, part of this quest was through the miraculous means God had provided him, the Urim and Thummim. Talmudic tradition similarly reports that "God blessed Abraham . . . and delivered to him a rare stone in which he could read a man's destiny," and that Abraham "used [this] rare crystal" and "studied [it] with great care."[66]

But Abraham also sought knowledge directly through prayer: "Teach me, show me," Abraham prayed on one occasion,[67] while on another occasion he implored: "My Lord, grant me wisdom."[68] Abraham asked and received revelation upon revelation teaching him about history, astronomy, theology, and science.[69] He also ardently searched the scriptures[70] as well as the wisdom of the world.

Jewish tradition remembers Abraham as one who "possessed great genius,"[71] including "the wisdom of a Just Man [and] the fiery language of a prophet or high priest. He spoke every tongue and mastered every art,"[73] and "was the greatest scientist of his day."[73] He gained such wisdom that his advice and knowledge were widely sought out,[74] and he became admired "as a man of extreme sagacity, gifted not only with high intelligence but with power to convince his hearers on any subject which he undertook to teach."[75] Referencing fragments of a second century B.C. Jewish history a modern scholar notes, "it is the figure of Abraham who spreads [astronomical] learning" from his native land "to Phoenicia and then to Egypt."[76] And among both Jewish and non-Jewish authors of the ancient world, Abraham was "widely regarded as a great sage."[77] In Sufi tradition, Abraham personifies knowledge, one of the essential divine attributes.[78] According to Nibley, if we were to make a list of the greatest minds of the last forty centuries, "Abraham must surely make a strong bid for number one."[79]

Abraham personifies the Lord's command to Latter-day Saints to "seek to bring forth and establish the cause of Zion; seek not for riches, but for wisdom, and behold, the mysteries of God shall be unfolded unto you" (D&C 6:6–7). Abraham further exemplifies the Lord's latter-day command to prepare for missionary service by seeking learning "by study and also by faith" (D&C 88:118), about not only "the gospel" and "the kingdom of God" but also "things both in heaven and in the earth, and under the earth; things which have been, things which are, things which must shortly come to pass; things which are at home, things which are abroad; the wars and the perplexities of the nations, and the judgments which are on the land; and a knowledge also of countries and kingdoms" (D&C 88:78–79). Accordingly, "we follow the example of Adam and Abraham," notes Hugh Nibley, "ever seeking *more* light and knowledge."[80] Indeed, "it is the merit of the seed of Abraham… that above all people they treasure the things of the mind."[81]

Sarah's Great Trial

Knowing that he should proceed on his journey, Abraham entered the "the land of the sons of Ham"[82]—Egypt, long fabled for its wisdom and learning,[83] having been originally founded by a righteous king who was blessed by Noah "with the blessings of the earth, and . . . of wisdom, but cursed . . . as pertaining to the Priesthood." That original pharaoh even sought "earnestly to imitate" the ancient "order established by the fathers," the order of Zion, but later pharaohs would falsely claim the patriarchal right of rulership that Abraham possessed (Abr. 1:26–27). Abraham was entering the kingdom of the imitators of Zion.

As he passed through "customs" at one of the fortresses along the Egyptian frontier, perhaps the station called the Way of Horus,[84] Abraham heeded the warning about Sarah and apparently sought to shelter her from Egyptian eyes. A very widespread tradition recounts that he had hidden her inside a locked chest or trunk, and when the customs official insisted that Abraham pay tax on the contents of the chest, he agreed. The problem was that the official kept insisting on increasing the tax, accusing Abraham of concealing ever more valuable goods, and Abraham repeatedly agreed to pay the higher amount. The official finally became so suspicious that he demanded that the chest be opened. Sarah arose in all her loveliness, by far the most beautiful woman ever to enter the kingdom.[85]

But according to the Genesis Apocryphon, it was not the border incident that got them in trouble, for they were able to enter Egypt and live there undisturbed. In which city did he live? During the twelfth Egyptian dynasty, Abraham would likely have resided in or near Memphis in lower Egypt in the north, an alternate or secondary capital that was much closer than the major capital of Thebes far up the Nile in upper Egypt. Whichever city it was, we are told that he lived there for some five years[86] before things took an unexpected and dangerous turn. The Genesis Apocryphon describes a scene in which Abraham is "instructing three visitors from the Egyptian royal court in 'wisdom and truth.'"[87] In that instruction, as Abraham relates, "I read in front of them the [book] of the words of Enoch."[88] Abraham was reading to them, in other words, from the records of Zion. He was preaching the gospel as God had revealed it through His holy prophets.

But when the visitors saw Sarah, they were smitten with her beauty, and returned to report to Pharaoh, who—as king and god, omnipotent and unquestioned in his realm—immediately sent retainers to bring her to the palace. Such a practice was not unusual, to judge from a papyrus, that tells of a pharaoh who, acting on the advice of his princes, sent soldiers to seize a beautiful woman and exile her husband.[89]

Abraham reports in the Genesis Apocryphon that Pharaoh "was amazed at all her beauty, and took her for himself as a wife. He wanted to kill me, but Sarai said to the king: He is my brother. . . . I, Abram, was spared on her account and I was not killed."[90] Then, continues Abraham,

> I wept bitterly—I, Abram, and Lot, my nephew, with me—on the night when Sarai was taken away from me by force. That night I prayed, I entreated, and I asked for mercy; in (my) sorrow

I said, as my tears ran down (my cheeks), "Blessed (are) you, O God Most High, my Lord, for all ages! For you are Lord and Master over all, and have power to mete out justice to all the kings of the earth. Now I lodge my complaint with you, my Lord, against the Pharaoh Zoan, the king of Egypt, because my wife has been taken away from me by force. Mete out justice to him for me and show forth your great hand against him and against all his house. May he not be able to defile my wife tonight—that it may be known about you, my Lord, that you are the Lord of all the kings of the earth." And I wept and talked to no one.[91]

"Would he have wept so for his own life," asks Nibley, "which he had so often been willing to risk?"[92] Abraham proved time and again that he would gladly risk his life in the cause of truth and to protect his fellow beings, for whom he bore such love that he is remembered in Jewish tradition as the very personification of empathetic loving-kindness,[93] "the spring whence flowed compassion to the world."[94] Now, however, to obey God, Abraham was forced to stand by silently and without protest as Egyptian emissaries took his beloved wife to Pharaoh's harem. This severe test "required the greatest faith yet" in the Patriarch's life.[95] Even so, explains the Zohar, Abraham "firmly trusted in God that He would allow no harm to come to Sarai, as it is written, 'the righteous are bold as a lion.'"[96]

But Abraham was not the only one being tested. According to the fourth-century Christian scholar Ephrem the Syrian, God placed Sarah in this situation "because it was her trial," for he "willed that she should be examined and tested in a woman's task just as Abraham had been in a man's task. . . . It was right that both of them be tried."[97] And as Hugh Nibley has pointed out, Sarah's trial can be described as the "the test of the lion couch," for the royal bed, like the royal altar on which Abraham had once lain, was a lion couch.[98]

The trial placed Sarah in jeopardy of her very life, for if she "honored both Abraham's request (by feigning maidenhood) and her marital vows (by refusing Pharaoh's advances), she faced certain death. The alternative was simply to accept her new role with its dazzling wealth and influence,"[99] for the "pomp and luxury" and utter "magnificence" of the royal palace ever "impressed on native and foreigner the glittering majesty of the Pharaoh of Egypt."[100] Indeed, this was the very era when "the cult of the pharaoh, the godking, was given monumental expression of a grandeur unsurpassed in the ancient Near East."[101] And what mighty Pharaoh intended with Sarah, according to Nachmanides, was nothing less than to marry her and install her as the new queen of Egypt.[102] As Nibley notes, "there was nothing in the world to keep her from exchanging her hard life with

Abraham for a life of unlimited ease and influence as Pharaoh's favorite except her loyalty to her husband. . . . Abraham is abiding by the law of God; the whole question now is, Will Sarah abide by the law of her husband? And she proved that she would, even if necessary at the risk of her life."[103] In the words of Ephrem the Syrian, she "did not exchange her sojourning husband for the king."[104] Not even the dazzling wealth and power of Egypt's royal throne could persuade her to forsake her covenants and loyalty to God and her husband.

But it was not only Sarah's life that was at stake but also the future of the entire chosen race to be born through her. Ironically, her test involved the virtue she had so zealously protected ever since coming to the licentious land of Egypt, where from the start she had "guarded herself against immorality."[105] Now, despite the severity of the trial, she "did not grumble against God,"[106] but rather prayed mightily to Him. Great is the prayer of a righteous woman, and greater still the power of united prayer[107] as Abraham was praying with at least equal fervor outside the palace.[108]

God heard and answered. Genesis reports that "the LORD plagued Pharaoh and his house with great plagues" (Gen. 12:17), or, as other translations have it, "mighty plagues" (JPST Gen. 12:17) or "terrible plagues" (GTC Gen. 12:17), so that, as told in the Genesis Apocryphon, Pharaoh "was unable to approach her."[109] The severe plagues included not only a violent and virulent disease but also, as Josephus mentions, civil strife that threatened Pharaoh's power.[110] The mighty kingdom of Egypt seemed to be suddenly unraveling at the seams. Meanwhile, Jewish tradition tells that God sent an angel to protect and comfort Sarah,[111] even as had happened with Abraham years before in his hour of great need. Rabbinic tradition mentions that the night that Sarah was taken to the palace was Passover night, thereby foreshadowing the time when again Pharaoh's house would be plagued for the benefit of Sarah's descendants.[112]

Pharaoh had questioned not only Sarah but also Lot about Abraham's relationship with Sarah, and Lot had loyally held to the same story.[113] As soon as Pharaoh believed that Abraham was merely Sarah's brother, Abraham became the recipient of royal favor. "Pharaoh pledged himself to make Abraham great and powerful, to do for him whatever she wished. He sent much gold and silver to Abraham, and diamonds and pearls, sheep and oxen, and men slaves and women slaves, and he assigned a residence to him within the precincts of the royal palace."[114] A nearly contemporary account of what it was like to be favored by Pharaoh describes the "splendid things" showered upon the one favored, including royal linen, myrrh, a host of servants in a sumptuous house with exquisite woodwork and a garden, and meals furnished by the palace cooks.[115]

Abraham's attitude toward such gifts may be readily deduced from his flat refusal years later to accept anything from another wicked monarch, the fawning king of Sodom. Pharaoh's gifts to Abraham, coming from the abducter of his wife, would surely have been immediately refused were it not for the unique position Abraham and Sarah found themselves in due to God's strange command. With Sarah in the palace, Abraham could hardly have afforded to incur Pharaoh's displeasure with possible consequences for Sarah. More importantly, such a refusal on Abraham's part might have raised suspicions about Abraham's real relationship with Sarah in a manner inconsistent with God's commandment. These were gifts that Abraham was required to accept, although as Jewish tradition insists, "the blessings really came from God. Pharaoh was merely the instrument through whom God bestowed blessings on Abraham."[116]

Abraham's sole concern, meanwhile, was the welfare and protection of his beloved Sarah. Viewed in retrospect, however, his residence in the royal palace may well have proven of great benefit. He was there for two years,[117] associating with the most learned men of the realm and learning the Egyptian language and lore so well that he would use them as a vehicle to write for his posterity what we now have as the precious Book of Abraham.

Not only Pharaoh but all his household were afflicted with "punishments and plagues," which only "increased and intensified" over the next two years. Nor could the royal magicians or physicians or healers, so famed for their curative powers, help the ailing king, for when they tried, they themselves became afflicted.[118] All of Egypt would have been alarmed at this crisis of their king, on whose welfare was thought to rest the welfare of the entire realm and even the continuation of the cosmic order.[119]

The solution came when it was Pharaoh's turn to have a dream, which showed Abraham laying his hands on the monarch's head and healing him.[120] Abraham's healing of Pharaoh is likewise attested in Samaritan[121] and Turkish[122] tradition.

So only this foreigner could cure the mighty Pharaoh! In one of the great turnabouts of history, the life of Pharaoh and all that theoretically depended on him were literally in Abraham's hands.

Abraham on Pharaoh's Throne

As the story continues in the Genesis Apocryphon, Abraham relates that Pharaoh's messenger "came to me and asked me to come and pray for the king, and lay my hands upon him so that he would recover."[123] Abraham would have been fully justified in refusing this nearly incredible request to save the man who had forcibly taken Sarah and had been ready to kill Abraham. Had not Pharaoh brought this trouble on himself? Indeed, was it not divine punishment for his arrogant crimes against the Lord's anointed? And given Pharaoh's rapidly declining health, Abraham could easily have opted to wait out the king's imminent demise, and then simply taken Sarah and left Egypt a vindicated man.

But Abraham was of different stuff. As the rabbis said, he lived the whole law before it had been revealed.[124] And part of the divine law as it would be revealed through the mortal Messiah would be the command to "love your enemies, bless them that curse you, do good to them that hate you, and pray for them which despitefully use you, and persecute you" (Matt. 5:44). Widely known by most Christians as the most difficult part of Christ's gospel, it was practiced perfectly by Abraham, who could not refuse his archenemy's request to bless and heal him.

When Pharaoh's messenger had requested Abraham's help, Lot divulged that Sarah was really Abraham's wife and would have to be restored to him before he could help. Summoning Abraham to his side, the ailing Pharaoh chided Abraham and pled with him. "What have you done to me . . . ? . . . Here is your wife; take her away! . . . But now pray for me and for my household that this evil spirit may be banished from us."[125] Thus, observes Nibley, "the roles of victim and victor are almost ludicrously reversed," showing that for "all [his] pride and power," Pharaoh is merely the pretender to Abraham's patriarchal authority.[126]

Using that authority, Abraham complied with Pharaoh's request: "I prayed that [he might be] cured,"[127] says Abraham in the Genesis Apocryphon. As recorded in the Asatir, an important Samaritan source, Abraham begged for mercy for the king "and prayed for the loosening of the bonds," saying, "O, Lord! God of heaven and earth, all merciful, be merciful."[128] Then, says Abraham in the Genesis Apocryphon, "I . . . laid my hands upon his [hea]d. The plague was removed from him; the evil [spirit] was banished [from him] and he recovered."[129] Islamic legend likewise remembers that Abraham cured Pharaoh.[130] "The wonderful thing about Abraham," says Nibley, "is that he always does the right thing, whether anybody else does or not."[131]

Not only was Pharaoh healed, but also all his household, explains the Asatir.[132] Then, continues the Genesis Apocryphon, "the king got up" and proceeded to give Abraham "many gifts"[133] beyond the lavish riches and flocks he had already bestowed on Abraham (see Gen. 12:16).[134] To Sarah the king gave "much [silver and go]ld and many clothes of fine linen and purple and . . . also Hagar,"[135] a beautiful girl[136] who was one of the king's many daughters, as a servant.[137] The unfolding of events was, in the words of Church Father Chrysostom, "marvelous and surprising," for "a woman dazzling in her beauty is closeted with an Egyptian . . . king and tyrant, of such frenzy and incontinent disposition, and yet she leaves his presence untouched, with her peerless chastity intact."[138]

Then, according to a medieval Turkish historian, Pharaoh "seated Abraham on a throne."[139] The event is pictured in Facsimile 3 of the Book of Abraham, showing that the throne was Pharaoh's own, the splendidly magnificent throne of Egypt, where Abraham is sitting "by the politeness of the king."

Appropriately, it was probably the lion throne,[140] emphasizing Abraham's remarkable rise years earlier from the Egyptian lion-altar of death to the most exalted seat of Egypt—reflecting, says Hugh Nibley, the broad outlines of the royal ritual enacted throughout the ancient Near East at the New Year's drama, an "indispensable element" of which was "the temporary humiliation of the true king while a rival and substitute displaces him on the throne." And as in the New Year's drama where "the true king is always vindicated in the end," so it is with Abraham when Pharaoh ends up "acknowledging that superior power and priesthood of his rival."[141]

The scene is the ultimate vindication of Abraham and his patriarchal authority to establish Zion on earth. In a momentous event unique in history, Pharaoh—pretender to that authority, and ruler of the mighty kingdom that was but an imitation of the order of Zion—willingly steps down from his throne to defer to Abraham. No wonder that "to the ancients," says scholar Ben Zion Wacholder, "the encounter between Pharaoh and the traveler from Ur of the Chaldees seemed as a crucial event in the history of mankind."[142]

Abraham's rise from the altar of death to the exalted throne of Egypt foreshadowed his own destiny when he would inherit his heavenly throne, the throne mentioned in the Testament of Isaac[143] and in latter-day revelation.[144] And as with Abraham, so also with his faithful posterity, who will likewise inherit thrones (D&C 132:19) prepared for them by Christ, who would descend below all things in order to rise above all and sit on His exalted throne forever.

As Abraham sat on Pharaoh's throne, according to Facsimile No. 3 of the Book of Abraham, he reasoned upon the principles of astronomy. Josephus tells that Abraham conversed "with the most learned of the Egyptians, whence his virtue and reputation became still more conspicuous." He "introduced them to arithmetic and transmitted to them the laws of astronomy."[145] Jewish tradition adds that the court members even brought their children to be instructed, and that Abraham began his preaching with the words: "Blessed be God who created the sun, the moon, and the planets."[146] Such language would have established common ground with his listeners and been particularly appropriate in context, for the lion throne on which he was sitting symbolized Pharaoh's role as heir to the Creator god.[147]

That Abraham would be qualified to enlighten Pharaoh's court on astronomy is as much a miracle as was his healing of Pharaoh, for of all the accomplishments of ancient Egypt, none was more significant or renowned than its advancements in astronomy,[148] a science central to sacred Egyptian ritual and architecture.[149] In fact, the first of Pharaoh's many titles used by his courtiers was "Lord of the Sky."[150] The title reflected the fact that the king's highest eternal aspirations were linked to the stars, among which he desired one day to take his place with his predecessors who had already been transformed into "the imperishable stars, that is, . . . the circumpolar stars that never set in the northern sky."[151]

And here the imagery of the cedar converges with that of the stars, for while Pharaoh is frequently depicted with upraised arms supporting the star-studded heavens,[152] other texts describe the sky as "a huge tree overshadowing the earth, the stars being the fruits or leaves which hang from its branches. When 'the gods perch on its boughs,' they are evidently identified with the stars."[153]

With what amazement Pharaoh and his court must have listened to Abraham as he explained things no other mortal could about the starry heavens, things he had learned directly from the Creator. According to Eupolemus, Abraham explained astronomy and other sciences to them and "taught them much," but "attributed the discovery of them to Enoch."[154] The historian Artapanus, writing centuries before Josephus, is even more specific in painting Abraham as the "mentor of the Egyptian pharaoh,"[155] personally teaching him astronomy.[156]

Abraham was teaching the knowledge of Enoch, of Zion, to Egypt's mighty monarch and his learned court. The picture that emerges is of Abraham as a "pivotal contributor to the origins of culture and learning" as he "play[s] a critical part in the generation and transmission of Near Eastern learning."[157] And in all his teaching, "his narratives brought people close to God."[158] Abraham's grand purpose was not scholarly interchange or demonstration of knowledge, but to bring his fellow beings to their Creator.

Thus while Abraham taught the Egyptians, as suggested by Elder Mark E. Petersen, he utilized this opportunity "as a means of proclaiming the name of Christ."[159] A Turkish source tells that Abraham "taught the faith and true religion," and adds that the king was "converted."[160] As told by a Samaritan source, "Pharaoh believed in the truth of the faith of Abraham," for Pharaoh "knew that his prayer before the idols had not cured him from the plague which he had, but that only the prayer of Abraham to his God had cured him. And at that time he commanded the destruction of the houses wherein the idols were, and the breaking of the idols and the destruction of all the pillars."[161]

If this tradition is accurate or even close, the ensuing effect would have crescendoed throughout the vast kingdom of Egypt in a manner similar to the widespread conversions experienced among the Lamanites after the conversion of King Lamoni and his father (see Alma 17–26). The extent of Abraham's missionary success even in his lifetime may be vastly greater than that for which he is normally given credit. Abraham's sojourn in Egypt, says Jewish tradition, "was of great service to the inhabitants of the country, because he demonstrated to the wise men of the land how empty and vain their views were."[163]

And as Abraham sat high on Pharaoh's throne teaching the knowledge of Zion and the cosmos, he was drawing from his store of revealed knowledge that, according to John Taylor speaking in 1880, exceeded "all the combined wisdom of the world today." Surely it is no different today, except that Abraham's latter-day seed are fast approaching the day when, as John Taylor foretold on another occasion, "Zion will be as far ahead of the outside world in everything pertaining to learning of every kind as we are today in regard to religious matters."[164] It is all part of what Isaiah foretold:

> And it shall come to pass in the last days, that the mountain of the LORD's house shall be established in the top of the mountains, and shall be exalted above the hills; and all nations shall flow unto it. And many people shall go and say, Come ye, and let us go up to the mountain of the LORD, to the house of the God of Jacob; and he will teach us of his ways, and we will walk in his paths: for out of Zion shall go forth the law, and the word of the LORD from Jerusalem (Isa. 2:2–3).

Abraham and Melchizedek

CHAPTER 6

Melchizedek and His Zion:
The Rescue of Lot and the Meeting with Melchizedek

For whoso is faithful unto the obtaining these . . . priesthoods . . . and the magnifying their calling, are sanctified by the Spirit unto the renewing of their bodies. They become the . . . seed of Abraham, and the church and kingdom, and the elect of God.
—DOCTRINE AND COVENANTS 84:33–34

Offering Peace and Mercy to Mankind

Escorted out of Pharaoh's kingdom with highest honors, Abraham went, says Genesis, "up out of Egypt" (13:1). The words indicate, according to the Zohar, not only his travel route but also that through his experience in Egypt he had "ascended spiritually."[1] He had also been blessed in temporal matters, returning to the promised land "very rich," says Genesis, "in livestock, in silver, and in gold" (NRSV Gen. 13:2). Apparently, some of his followers chose to remain behind in Egypt "on account of the prosperity of the land."[2] But upon Abraham the blessing of prosperity rested as a divine gift. He "prospered exceedingly," explained Joseph Smith, "because he and his family obeyed the counsel of the Lord."[3] His coming out of Egypt prefigured the experience of his descendants when the Israelites came out of Egypt "with great wealth"[4] and when the Lord Himself came out of Egypt as a boy (Matt. 2:19–21; Hosea 11:1).

But wealth was not what Abraham sought, and while the pharaohs were busy amassing their royal fortunes and building impressive monuments to themselves that still awe travelers today, Abraham would continue to build Zion. "His object," says Nibley, was "not to conquer or impress, but to bless all with whom he [came] into contact, ultimately shedding the blessing that God gave to him on the whole human race."[5] According to Ephrem the Syrian, God brought Abraham "once again to the land of the Canaanites who were sitting and dwelling in darkness. He shone over them like a light."[6] The statement reminds us of the Isaiah passage about the Savior: "the people that walked in darkness have seen a great light" (Isa. 9:2; Matt. 4:16; see also John 1:4–5).

The journey northward was probably broken up by a series of frequent stops, due to the magnitude of the baggage and possessions they had.[7] When they finally arrived at their former campsite near Bethel where he had built an altar, he rebuilt it and, as he relates in the Genesis Apocryphon, "I . . . laid on it a sacrifice, and an offering to the Most High God. And there I called on the name of the Lord of worlds and praised the Name of God and blessed God, and I gave thanks before God for all the riches and favours which He had bestowed upon me. For He had dealt kindly towards me and had led me back in peace into this land."[8] Abraham's constant gratitude for his blessings stands in sharp contrast to the tendency of most mortals. "The crime of ingratitude," noted President Joseph Fielding Smith, "is one of the most prevalent and . . . one of the greatest with which mankind is afflicted. The more the Lord blesses us the less we love him."[9]

But the peace was soon interrupted when a quarrel broke out between Abraham's shepherds and those of Lot. "The patriarch had been a father to him—a friend kinder than many fathers," notes one writer.[10] Even so, according to Ephrem, Abraham "did not consider himself a head or master" over Lot, but rather "a brother and . . . friend,"[11] and, in the words of President Spencer W. Kimball, "he sought peace among his brethren."[12] Said Abraham, "Let there be no strife, I pray thee, between me and thee, and between my herdmen and thy herdmen; for we be brethren" (Gen. 13:8).

As told by Ephrem, Abraham's "humility and meekness" won the day as he "speedily eliminated" the contention. "He called Lot in love, and made him an heir like himself."[13] Although God had given the land to Abraham, he in turn gave to Lot the first choice of the land, evoking the admiration of many commentators. "See Abraham's magnanimity!"[14] "See the extraordinary degree of his humility; see the height of his wisdom."[15] By his "self-denying and peace-loving" conduct,[16] he averted contention with a loved one. "Virtue humbles itself, whereas wickedness becomes arrogant."[17]

Nineteenth-century cleric Ashton Oxenden observed that the incident demonstrates "how little Abraham was influenced by worldly motives. He was rich, but he cared little for his riches."[18] According to another such cleric, W. F. P. Noble,

> The uncle generously bestows on the nephew a share of his own property; more than that, as if he was the younger and also the weaker of the two—as if the land of Canaan had been promised to the other rather than to him—as if he had been the party who

had received rather than conferred favors—in determining their respective positions, Abraham leaves the choice to Lot. . . . What self-denial, self-control, self-sacrifice . . . ! What liberal and magnanimous generosity his! What a model of a Christian this man! . . . He seeks not his own.[19]

The language echoes the words of two of Abraham's descendants, Paul and Moroni, who both said of charity—or the pure love of Christ—that it "seeketh not her own" (1 Cor. 13:5; Moro. 7:45). And still another cleric of the nineteenth century, Henry Blunt, marveled:

Abram . . . proceeds with almost un[paralleled] tenderness and humility to address his younger and far less amiable kinsman, "Is not the whole of the land before thee? separate thyself, I pray thee, from me; if thou wilt take the left hand, then I will go to the right; or if thou depart to the right, then I will go to the left." What forbearance, what generosity, what true nobility of mind was here! Abram . . . does not . . . claim, as he might have done, from the expressed promise of the Almighty, the whole for himself: he does not, as all must allow he would have been fully justified in doing, even claim for himself the priority of choice; he waives every right . . . in favour of one far younger and less deserving, humbly contenting himself with the portion which Lot should leave him. Well did our Lord declare, "Blessed are the peace-makers, for they shall be called the children of God."[20]

And if, as Nibley points out, Abraham "seemed to be generous to the point of lacking common sense,"[21] it was only because of his uncommon insight into life. By Abraham's action, said Philo, "he considered that he would thereby get peace, the greatest of gains."[22] It was the peace of Zion that Abraham sought, that same unity of heart and mind that once existed in Enoch's Zion (Moses 7:18). On this principle would Abraham's Zion be built, and on this same principle is the latter-day Zion to be built. Abraham's treatment of Lot teaches us, notes President Kimball, that "once we have found peace within ourselves, we must share it by being long-suffering, gentle, and meek and by having the pure love of Christ for all we meet."[23]

Lot chose the luscious land near Sodom and went his way, knowing that he would still be within Abraham's protective sphere. For Abraham had told him, according to Jewish tradition, that he would remain close enough to come to his aid if necessary.[24]

The years of daily association with his uncle Abraham had wrought a profound effect on Lot. "Everyone who walks with the righteous acquires some of their good ways and deeds," says Rabbi Eliezer, as happened with Lot, "who walked with our father Abraham, and learned of his good deeds and ways." Hence when Lot came to Sodom, he followed Abraham's example of magnanimously offering hospitality and preaching the gospel.[25] Indeed, Lot was one of the Lord's messengers, says the Qur'an, sent to preach to the cities of the plain.[26] One early Islamic source expressly mentions that Abraham "sent Lot as a prophet to the cities" of the plain.[27]

But the people of Sodom refused to listen, for they were "arrogant because of the bounty the Holy One had bestowed upon them,"[28] and as "wealthy men of prosperity" they "did not trust in . . . their Creator, but . . . in the multitude of their wealth"[29]—the same indictment the prophet Nephi would make of his people (see Hel. 6–8), whose errors were a remarkable repeat of the sins of Sodom, and brought a similar fate (see 3 Ne. 9:3). The Sodomites had grown proud, inhospitable, morally perverse, cruel, and corrupt in every way. Even their laws and judges were corrupt.[30] "Overweeningly proud of their numbers and extent of their wealth," they "showed themselves insolent to men and impious to the Divinity."[31] "They were savage and very sinful,"[32] notorious not only for their inhospitality[33] but also for their terrible vices (NRSV 3 Maccabees 2:5), cruelty, and murder.[34] They "distorted every fundamental rule by which relationship is made possible and sustained."[35] In sum, "the Sodomites represent . . . the negation of the value most characteristic of Abraham: *hesed*, or kindness."[36]

When Lot warned them plainly about their abominations, they taunted: "If you are telling us the truth bring down on us the punishment of God."[37] In the ensuing years, when Lot would visit Abraham, Lot "complained to him of the iniquity of the people. But Abraham urged him to patience,"[38] and practiced it himself. "The neighbors of Abraham were cruel, covetous, and licentious. . . , but Abraham never ceased to be on friendly terms with them. He ever manifested toward them an amicable disposition, treated them with . . . noticeable courtesy and did them signal favors."[39] They that are well need no physician, the Savior would say as he likewise ministered among sinners (Matt. 9:12).

Lot's parting had been hard for Abraham, who loved him. "It grieved me," says Abraham in the Genesis Apocryphon, "that my nephew Lot had departed from me."[40] In the midst of that grief, God came to comfort His friend Abraham, appearing to him in a vision at night and directing him to climb the highest mountain in the region, Ramat Hazor, and "raise your eyes and look to the East, to the West, to the South and to the North. Look at all this land, which I am giving you and your descendants for ever."[41] It is a remarkable reality that God's greatest land grant to Abraham came as a reward for Abraham's magnanimity with the land God had already given him.

The Zohar adds that as Abraham surveyed the land of promise, God actually "raised him high above the land of Israel and made him see how it is bound up with the four cardinal points."[42] As Abraham gazed at the earth, he heard God promise that "all the land which thou seest, to thee will I give it, and to thy seed for ever. And I will make thy seed as the dust of the earth: so that if a man can number the dust of the earth, then shall thy seed also be numbered" (Gen. 13:15–16). God's promise was not only sure but literal, "not mere rhetoric," insists a rabbinic text.[43] Another such text explains that this blessing came "because God saw how Abraham loved the commandments."[44] Which commandments? There was none that Abraham did not keep, but the one he had just kept with unusual valor was the one in force since the beginning, the commandment to "love one another," as God had told Enoch (Moses 7:33).

Abraham's experience of being lifted above the earth repeated that of Enoch, who, as Abraham had read, had been lifted up and shown the four cardinal directions of the earth. In fact, the Joseph Smith Translation adds that God commanded Abraham to "remember the covenant which I make with thee; for it shall be an everlasting covenant; and thou shalt remember the days of Enoch thy father" (JST Gen. 13:14).

The Genesis Apocryphon tells that God commanded Abraham to actually walk around the perimeter of the entire land that God was giving him, and Abraham did so[45]—a lengthy journey that must have taken weeks. It was apparently a legal formality denoting acquisition of the land.[46] That this event comes right after Abraham's stay in Egypt is noteworthy, for it echoes what the pharaohs did at the Sed festival in ritually walking around the perimeter of a field simulating the land of Egypt granted to Pharaoh by the creator god.[47] Abraham, as the true heir, now receives his land, itself but a microcosm of the larger world that Abraham and his seed were to bless.

What he saw on his journey was that the land was occupied, as Genesis reports, by the Canaanites and Perizzites, with their idolatrous ways. "They dwelt at ease and in tranquility," according to Jewish tradition, "with none to challenge their peace, and yet could not harm Abraham."[48] God was fulfilling his promise that his hand would be over Abraham (Abr. 2:8), not only to bless him but to allow him to be a blessing to others.

And to maximize his opportunity to spread that blessing, after Lot parted, Abraham moved to Hebron, a city of such strategic importance that King David would later choose it as his capital. Located on a height that at one point overlooks the cities of the plain, Hebron happened to be at the juncture where an important trade route branched off into three roads.[49] Bustling with travelers, it was an opportune location for Abraham to reach out to as many of his fellow men as possible, as he proceeded to establish a society sharply in contrast to that of nearby

Sodom. "In the most inhospitable of worlds," says Nibley, "Abraham was the most hospitable of men."[50] And always at his side was Sarah, his partner in extending hospitality. She worked along with him (see Gen. 18:6), and "during her lifetime, the doors to her house were always hospitably open," and the lamp was always lit.[51] Having been abundantly blessed by God, Abraham and Sarah proceeded to show their gratitude by using their resources to bless others, an illustration of the principle taught by President Harold B. Lee: "There is only one way to thank your Heavenly Father, and that is by faithfulness in what He has given you in the way of time, means, and talent in service to those less fortunate than you."[52]

At Hebron, Abraham made himself accessible to the many who sought him out. According to one rabbinic source, "He was like a king of the entire civilized world. He possessed great genius; all the kings of the east and the west would come to seek his advice."[53] But Abraham's door was equally open to the lowly and needy, as he "welcomed everyone—rich and poor, kings and rulers, the crippled and the helpless, friends and strangers, neighbors and passersby—(all) on equal terms."[54] His life is a supreme illustration of the truth expressed by President David O. McKay, that "the noblest aim in life is to make other lives better and happier."[55]

Thus were Abraham and Sarah, biologically childless still, merciful parents to all in need. How many had come to consider Abraham as a father and provider, and Sarah as a mother and friend! It is said that "Abraham cultivated the friendship of the common people,"[56] and would even go in search of poor wayfarers needing assistance.[57] The lesson is remembered to this day in Judaism: "if the poor do not come to your house, you are obligated to seek them and bring them into your home, for this is what Abraham did."[58] Or, as seen in light of the Savior's teachings, Abraham had already been privileged several times to speak face to face with the Savior, but now visited Him daily as he lovingly reached out to the least of his brethren (see Matt. 25:40), seeking to bless them temporally and spiritually. "Who was greater than Abraham," asks the Zohar, "whose kindness extended to all creatures?"[59]

The Zohar tells that near Abraham's residence at Hebron was a spring and pool of water that he used for "those who required immediate immersion," for he sought to make "known the true faith to the whole world."[60] Anglo-Saxon tradition even seems to indicate that Abraham had a temple here.[61] Through his love of his fellow beings, his sharing of the gospel and his administering in temple ordinances, Abraham was reaching out to all within his power. Abraham was, says a modern rabbi, "both Friend of God and Friend of Man,"[62] or, according to Hugh Nibley, Abraham "was 'the Friend of God' because he was the friend of man."[63]

Abraham was practicing charity, or in Judaism *hesed*, and only those who follow his example can be included in his covenant, according to Jewish tradition.[64]

Compassion is the one sure test of true Abrahamic descent, insists the Talmud: "When someone has mercy on God's creatures, we can be certain that he is descended from our father Abraham."[65] In the New Testament, such Abrahamic acts of love and service are called simply "pure religion" (James 1:27).[66]

His action is a model for Latter-day Saints, who are urged by President Gordon B. Hinckley: "May we bless humanity with an outreach to all, lifting those who are downtrodden and oppressed, feeding and clothing the hungry and the needy, extending love and neighborliness to those about us."[67] "Let us open our hearts, let us reach down and lift up, let us open our purses, let us show a greater love for our fellowmen."[68]

Waging War and Meeting a Prince of Peace

Unfortunately, as Winston Churchill observed, "The story of the human race is war."[69] It was the story also of Abraham's day, one of the most warlike generations ever,[70] echoing Enoch's time (see Moses 7:16) and foreshadowing the latter-days (see D&C 45:66–71). If the Abraham story mentions war rarely, it is only because the Lord led him out of harm's way and preserved him in relatively peaceful venues. But the time did come when the ravages of war touched even the great Abraham.

Just miles from where he resided in Hebron came the combined military forces of a coalition of kings "ravaging and laying waste."[71] They killed many and took some captives, among them Lot and his family. As recounted in the Genesis Apocryphon, one of Lot's shepherds who had escaped "came to Abram . . . and told him that Lot . . . and all his flocks had been captured, but that he was not dead, and that the kings had taken the road of the Great Valley towards their territory, taking prisoners, ravaging, smiting, killing and proceeding as far as the city of Damascus. Abram wept for Lot."[72] Josephus adds that Abraham "was moved" also "with compassion for his friends and neighbors, the Sodomites,"[73] many of whom had likewise been taken captive. Abraham's compassion for these people is a remarkable commentary on his character: he did not shun the wicked but befriended them in the hope of helping them.

Only such compassion could move Abraham to now take up arms. Like his descendant Captain Moroni, Abraham was a man of "perfect understanding" who "did not delight in bloodshed" but "did joy in the liberty and the freedom of his country, and his brethren from bondage and slavery" (Alma 48:11). Indeed, Abraham's ardent desire from the beginning was to become "a prince of peace" (Abr. 1:2). But now, as related in the Genesis Apocryphon, "Abram braced himself, stood up and chose from among his servants those fit for war: three hundred and eighteen,"[74] men from his Zion community. As a modern writer comments, "A man of peace, the battle was not of his seeking."[75]

And yet "he did not trust in these, for they were but a small fraction of the kings' forces, but in God, the champion and defender of the just."[76] They were going in the strength of the Lord, and Abraham urged no one to come who was fearful[77] or had committed any trespass against God.[78] "If your hearts are turned toward Heaven," he declared, "you will go forth and the Almighty will make your enemies like herbage."[79] The speech was similar to what ancient Israel's high priest would later make to soldiers before going to war.[80] It was the same faith that Abraham's Nephite descendants would manifest when they trusted that if they kept God's commandments, he would prosper and protect them (Alma 48:14). Abraham actually hoped to accomplish the rescue mission without the shedding of blood, taking gold and silver to ransom the captives,[81] but he was prepared to engage in battle if need be. With these few hundred men, and joined by a few faithful friends, Abraham hurriedly set out northward "in pursuit."[82]

What the sources do not state, but what latter-day revelation makes clear, is that God had actually commanded Abraham to undertake this expedition. "This is the law I gave unto . . . Abraham, and all mine ancient prophets and apostles . . . that they should not go out unto battle against any nation, kindred, tongue, or people, save I, the Lord, commanded them. . . . And I the Lord, would fight their battles" (D&C 98:32–33, 37).

When Abraham arrived, he discovered what he had already suspected, that he was vastly outnumbered and would not be able to ransom the captives with money. And although he knew that the Almighty was with him, he immediately began to deploy his limited resources in the most strategic manner possible. Using the cover of night to conceal the smallness of his forces,[83] he divided up his men and fanned out in preparation for a sudden surprise attack[84] from all four sides.[85]

But ancient sources also tell of miraculous happenings that evening. Not only was Abraham's way illuminated by planetary light,[86] but as he began the battle, he became aware of divine assistance extended to him in a miraculous way: "he saw the Shekhinah, attended by celestial hosts, lighting up his path,"[87] so that, despite outward appearances, he understood that they who were with them were more than those against them.[88] What must have seemed by objective standards an absurd attack soon proved to be a miraculous rout as, according to the Genesis Apocryphon, Abraham's vastly outnumbered army courageously gave battle to the kings' soldiers, killing some and chasing the others until "all [were] fleeing before him. . . . He retrieved from them all that they had captured, all that they had looted and all their own goods. He also saved Lot . . . and all his flocks and brought back all the captives."[89] He led them back home, and also, says the Zohar, back to repentance. [90]

It was truly the sword of the Lord and of Abraham,[91] for the Holy One fought with him and slew his enemies.[92] The royal armies that Abraham opposed would surely have had their chariots, judging from other battles around the same time and place of which we have record.[93] But Abraham's strength that night came from him who had once told Abraham, "I cause the wind and the fire to be my chariot"—even the invincible Lord of creation (Abr. 2:7). Abraham's small army availed him only because God helped him. Conversely, God helped him in battle only after he had mustered his armed men and prepared himself militarily. God helps those who take all measures necessary to help themselves"[94] as seen in the life of Abraham's righteous descendant Mormon, a man of God who took up the sword to defend his people, qualifying for the Lord's deliverance by first making use of the means the Lord had provided.[95]

Abraham's victory was miraculous also for the fact that he lost not a single one of his men,[96] not unlike the later miraculous preservation of his two thousand young Lamanite descendants serving under Helaman (see Alma 57:25). And Abraham's victory was actually won before the clash of swords began, for, according to a midrash, his victory came not by strength of "weapons and armor but rather with prayer and supplication."[97] For which he gratefully knelt again and gave thanks to the Almighty: "Sovereign of all the worlds! Not by the power of my hand, nor by the power of my right hand have I done all these things, but by the power of Thy right hand with which Thou dost shield me in this world and in the world to come."[98] "Had Your glory not fought alongside me and aided me, how could one man have prevailed against such an overwhelming force. They fell into my hands only because You helped me."[99] Thus it was that Abraham, contrary to human nature, "became more humble, not more proud, in victory."[100]

Abraham's miraculous victory echoed that of his forefather Enoch, whom the Lord had strengthened with miraculous power as Enoch led the people of Zion to defend themselves in battle (Moses 7:13–17). According to Jewish tradition, Abraham's victory also foreshadowed the future, even the redemption of his descendants in Egypt on Passover night, as well as the still-future redemption of Israel: "At the End of Days, the Messiah will deal just such a stunning, total defeat to his adversaries."[101]

Christians recognize the Messiah as Jesus Christ, seed of Abraham, whose final victory, according to early Christian tradition in England, began on the cross and was foreshadowed by Abraham's remarkable victory against the kings of the earth. "Of all men living," says the Saxon Genesis concerning Abraham, "never did anyone conduct with a small troop against so great a force a more worthy warfare"—which thing was a type, insists the Venerable Bede, of the ultimate Victory that would rescue us all: "Therefore well did Abram conquer his enemies . . . and set his brother free, since he prefigured the one to be born from his own seed, who through suffering on the cross summoned the world from death."[102] Such prefiguring of Jesus was only possible because, as told by the early Church Fathers, "Jesus was . . . the strength of Abraham in this encounter."[103]

As Abraham journeyed home with the ransomed captives and their property, according to ancient Jewish tradition, relieved and grateful peoples and their kings came to hail the conquering hero and express their gratitude and allegiance. They made a cedar throne for Abraham, bowing to him as their king and even their god.[104] Suddenly, here was an unexpected opportunity laid at Abraham's feet to extend his influence over the land that God had already given him and to create political alliances and a dominion that could possibly continue to grow into a scope commensurate with his mandate to bless all nations.

Even from a purely defensive posture, the opportunity seemed uncannily timely, for according to a number of ancient sources, the coalition's original intent had been first to take Lot and then Abraham, whose success in his missionary efforts had been extensive in turning many from their idolatry.[105] The success may have been significant enough to threaten the very order of things, including tribute based on the economy of idolatry. Accordingly, for Abraham to now accept this offer of kingship would put him in a position to counter any further attack by the coalition, thereby securing the land that God had given him.

And wasn't Abraham already the planet's rightful monarch, holding the same royal patriarchal authority over all the human race as held earlier by Adam and Noah in their "patriarchal reign" (Abr. 1:26)? Might this unusual offer even be God's vindication of that right, allowing Abraham the opportunity to seize what was rightfully his and secure the land God had given him by accepting political power? It was the kind of rare opportunity that ambitious souls throughout history have craved, as seen in the careers of conquerors like Alexander and Napoleon and Genghis Khan. Commenting on the opportunity presented to Abraham, a modern rabbi has observed that "grateful nations often seek to confer kingship and even deification upon victorious military leaders. It takes great strength of character for a military leader to spurn the power and the adulation that is his for the taking."[106] Only rarely does history produce such strength, with the greatest example being the first—Abraham.

Responding to the cheering crowds, he simply "warded them off, and said, 'The universe has its King, and it has its God!' He declined all honors,"[107] urging that "if I am pleasing to you and you desire to deal kindly with me, then love one another and deal peacefully together. Open the doors of your houses to the poor, the stranger and the wayfarer, and believe in the Lord God, the Creator of heaven and earth, and serve him with all your heart."[108]

Abraham's royal patriarchal authority and its exercise was governed solely upon the priesthood principles of righteousness and humility, not upon the accolades of men. Indeed, it was precisely because Abraham did not set his heart upon the things of this world, nor aspire to the honors of men, that he had such power in the priesthood (see D&C 121:34–36) as he presided over Zion. And the door to that Zion could not be opened by heaping praise on Abraham, but only by obeying the eternal gospel that he taught concerning faith in Christ, repentance of sins, baptism, and the Holy Ghost. It was yet another occasion to bring men to Christ. Abraham's goal was not to change the map but to change hearts. He would conquer not by the sword but only by love.

But the king of Sodom had unfinished business. He came forward and asked for the return of his subjects that Abraham had rescued, while recognizing Abraham's right to the war booty. "Give me the people," said the king, "you take the property."[109] In fact, by rights of war, Abraham now owned not only the goods but also the people, and he could have kept them as slaves, sold them, or demanded a ransom from the king of Sodom.[110] "He might have done so," notes one writer. "Many would have done so."[111] But Abraham had made a prior covenant with the Lord not to enrich himself in the rescue operation. "The king of Sodom knew nothing of Abraham's covenant with the Lord," observed President Kimball. "Abraham could have made himself rich by receiving of the king's [offer]. But he had made an oath which he would not violate. Oh, that all of God's children could be so true!"[112]

Abraham returned both the people and the goods, renouncing his right to everything. He "would have nothing to do with an offer of reward from the king of Sodom. . . . Abraham's reward would come not from the kings of this world but from Yahweh [Jehovah], 'the LORD, the Creator of heaven and earth.'"[113] Indeed, "Abraham's motives had been pure from the very beginning" of the enterprise,[114] and he was not about to compromise his principles now. "Here is a pattern to copy."[115]

Another monarch stepping forth to greet Abraham was Melchizedek, who, according to Genesis, brought forth bread and wine and blessed Abraham, who in turn paid tithes to Melchizedek.[116] Genesis gives no hint as to who this mysterious Melchizedek was, who appears suddenly and then will not be mentioned again. Some of the mystery is removed by other sources, which tell that the reason his genealogy isn't given in Genesis is because he was not one of the patriarchs.[117] But it is latter-day scripture as restored through Joseph Smith that gives us the most information about the remarkable Melchizedek. He was "a man of faith, who wrought righteousness; and when a child he feared God, and stopped the mouths of lions, and quenched the violence of fire," and qualified for and received his ordination to the Holy Priesthood after the Order of the Son of God (JST Gen. 14:26). Later, as told in the Brass Plates, Melchizedek ruled as a king over the land of Salem.

> And his people had waxed strong in iniquity and abominations;
> yea, they had all gone astray; they were full of all manner of

wickedness; but Melchizedek, having exercised mighty faith, . . . did preach repentance unto his people. And behold, they did repent; and Melchizedek did establish peace in the land in his days; therefore he was called the prince of peace, for he was the king of Salem [literally "peace" in Hebrew]; and he did reign under his father. Now there were many before him, and also there were many afterwards, but none were greater (Alma 13:17–19).

Faith, righteousness, miracles, preaching repentance, establishing peace— such were Abraham's accomplishments also. If, as the proverb goes, it takes a prophet to understand a prophet, then Abraham and Melchizedek had found in each other a truly resonant soul. It was one of the most important meetings in history, a summit of two spiritual giants establishing the order of the kingdom of God.

Abraham and His Friend Melchizedek

Details of Abraham's encounter with Melchizedek are supplied in extra-biblical sources. Philo relates that Melchizedek and Abraham were already close friends, and that Melchizedek rejoiced in Abraham's victory as if it had been Melchizedek's own.[118] According to the Conflict of Adam and Eve, Melchizedek "welcomed [Abraham] with joy. And Abraham, when he saw Melchizedek, made haste and bowed . . . and kissed him on his face."[119]

Then, says the Book of the Bee, "Melchizedek embraced him and blessed him."[120] The Genesis Apocryphon tells that the bread and wine were but a part of the "food and drink" that Melchizedek provided.[121] Josephus adds that it was a veritable "feast" in which Melchizedek "hospitably entertained Abraham's army, providing abundantly for all their needs."[122] But the bread and wine apparently had more than nutritional value, for the Joseph Smith translation adds that Melchizedek actually "brake bread and blest it; and he blest the wine" (JST Gen. 14:17), a clear echo of which is found in the messianic or eschatological banquet celebrated at Qumran,[123] and indicating, according to Milton R. Hunter, that the meal Melchizedek provided may have actually been the ordinance of the sacrament.[124] For the Church Fathers, Melchizedek's meal was at least a type; according to the third-century bishop and martyr Cyprian of Carthage, "in the priest Melchizedek we see prefigured the sacrament of the sacrifice of . . . our Lord Jesus Christ, who offered . . . that very same thing which Melchizedek had offered, that is, bread and wine, to wit, His body and blood."[125]

As with so much of Abraham's life, then, this event held prophetic significance for the future, adumbrating in this case Christ's very Atonement and the sacramental ordinance that would ever after commemorate it, along with the great future messianic banquet where Christ will "drink of the fruit of the vine . . . on the earth . . . with . . . Abraham" and all the righteous (D&C 27:5, 10).

The rabbis taught that Melchizedek instructed Abraham in the laws of the priesthood and transmitted the priesthood to him.[126] Joseph Smith stated that Melchizedek taught Abraham about the priesthood and the coming of the Son of Man,[127] and ordained him to the priesthood[128] after the order of the Son of God (D&C 107:2–3), even "the last law, or a fulness of the law or priesthood, which constituted him a king and priest after the order of Melchizedek."[129] Abraham's ordination and the accompanying ordinances showed "in what manner to look forward to [the] Son for redemption" (Alma 13:2). Jewish tradition adds that Abraham was also instructed by God Himself on that occasion. [130]

In other words, as indicated in the Book of Abraham, Abraham received the remaining temple ordinances from Melchizedek.[131] When Melchizedek "brings out" bread and wine, according to Claus Westermann, the Genesis text implies that he brings it out "from his city and temple."[132] A midrash identifies Salem with a temple,[133] while Josephus expressly states that Melchizedek had a temple.[134] Pseudo-Eupolemus tells that Abraham was actually ushered into a temple in Melchizedek's city.[135] Jewish tradition tells of "a secret sign" that God "communicated to Abraham, the secret of the mystery of the Redeemer."[136] Early Christian sources state that Melchizedek taught Abraham about "the holy mysteries"[137] and even "made him to participate in the Holy Mysteries . . . of redemption."[138] These mysteries, or ordinances of the Holy Priesthood after the Order of the Son of God, were—says a Book of Mormon passage speaking of Melchizedek—"given after this manner, that thereby the people might look forward on the Son of God, it being a type of his order, or it being his order, and this that they might look forward to him for a remission of their sins" (Alma 13:16). Abraham is a prototype, notes Nibley, for "every follower of Abraham must receive the signs and tokens."[139]

Latter-day revelation adds that the power of the Melchizedek Priesthood includes "the privilege of receiving the mysteries of the kingdom of heaven, to have the heavens opened," and "to commune with the general assembly and church of the Firstborn" (D&C 107:19), which is the "church of Enoch" (D&C 76:67). Well did one modern writer observe that on this occasion, "mysteries, revelations, and visions of truth flooded over Abraham's soul. He it was who looked for a city with foundations whose Builder and Maker is God. . . . In spirit was [Abram] not now reveling in th[at] city?"[140]

Abraham's relationship with Melchizedek was not confined to this one incident. The Genesis account of Abraham paying tithes seems to evidence, says one scholar, "a tradition about a city and a sanctuary to which tithes were brought in early times."[141] According to the Joseph Smith Translation of the passage, Melchizedek received tithes from Abraham not just of the war booty, but "of all that he had, of all the riches which he possessed, which God had given him more than that which he had need," inasmuch as Melchizedek was "the high priest, and the keeper of the storehouse of God; him whom God had appointed to receive tithes for the poor" (JST Gen. 14:37–39). The passage shows not only that Abraham willingly lived the law of consecration, but also that the tithes he paid to Melchizedek—of all of Abraham's substantial wealth—could hardly have been paid in this single encounter while returning from a hurried military rescue operation.

But this particular occasion must have been fraught with joy for Abraham as he now received what he had so long sought: the priesthood after the order of the Son of God, that order of priesthood that in times past allowed mortals to be translated to Enoch's city of Zion. And what joy must have been Abraham's to learn that Melchizedek was seeking that very blessing of translation. According to the Joseph Smith Translation, Melchizedek and his people of Salem "sought for the city of Enoch, which God had before taken, separating it from the earth, having reserved it unto the latter days, or the end of the world" (JST Gen. 14:34). At that final event, at "the burning" that shall then take place, says a latter-day revelation, "he that is tithed shall not be burned" (D&C 64:23–24). He that is tithed, in other words, shall qualify to see the Son of God when He comes in glory. The paradigm for these blessings is Abraham, who, not long after paying his tithing to Melchizedek, would avoid the great burning sent on a wicked and miserly people residing just miles away. And soon thereafter Abraham would be privileged to see and converse with the Son of God face to face.

Abraham was also blessed temporally. In the Joseph Smith Translation telling of Abraham's payment of tithing on everything he possessed, this verse immediately follows:

> And in came to pass that God blessed Abram, and gave unto him riches, and honor, and lands for an everlasting possession; according to the covenant which he had made, and according to the blessing wherewith Melchizedek had blessed him (JST Gen. 14:40).

Jewish tradition adds that God "did not withhold a single blessing from him. He blessed him with wisdom and understanding, knowledge and discernment, wealth and prosperity; gave him possession of heaven and earth, and made him [master] of the world."[142] Why did the Lord bless Abraham, as Genesis will later say, "in all things" (Gen. 24:1)? As a reward, says the Midrash, for Abraham's paying tithing to Melchizedek.[143] As with so many other principles of righteousness, Abraham remains the great exemplar of the blessings of tithing, the blessings of Zion. "By this principle," declared Joseph F. Smith, "it shall be known who is for the kingdom of God and who is against it. By this principle it shall be seen whose hearts are set on doing the will of God and keeping his commandments, thereby sanctifying the land of Zion unto God, and who are opposed to this principle and have cut themselves off from the blessings of Zion."[144]

"Blessing" is in fact what this episode of Abraham and Melchizedek is all about, says the Zohar: the passage "teaches that . . . the righteous bring blessings to the world, and for their sake are all its inhabitants blessed."[145]

Salem the Great and Melchizedek the Great

By his tithing, Abraham was sanctifying the land of Zion, not only the land where he resided but also Melchizedek's Salem, referred to in a Samaritan source as "Salem the great."[146] Where was that great city? It has been assumed by many that Salem was Jerusalem, based on a reading of the Psalms passage stating: "In Judah God is known: his name is great in Israel. In Salem also is his tabernacle, and his dwelling place in Zion" (Ps. 76:1–2). But as Fred Horton has pointed out, the same passage if read as a chiasm would show just the opposite: that Zion is a city in Judah, while Salem is a city in Israel (north of Judah).

Horton explains why the rabbis would have wished to identify Salem with Jerusalem: "Since Melchizedek was the first priest of God [in the Bible], it would be natural to think of his place of priesthood as being Jerusalem, the one legitimate seat of sacrificial worship."[147] However, continues Horton, identifying Salem with Jerusalem contradicts a very early identification of Salem as being near the city of Shechem, located some twenty-five miles north of Jerusalem at the foot of Mount Gerizim.[148] Most significantly, the one ancient source mentioning Abraham entering Melchizedek's temple locates that temple and Melchizedek's city at the foot of Mount Gerizim.[149] A number of modern scholars have identified Melchizedek's Salem as being near Shechem.[150]

In the end, however, the important thing about Salem is not where it was but where it went. One source says that Melchizedek built his city on a place called Zion,[151] while a Jewish midrash makes the intriguing claim that "Salem is the celestial Jerusalem."[152] In fact, we know from Joseph Smith's translation of Genesis that Melchizedek and his city of Salem were eventually taken up to join the translated city of Enoch's Zion, the very city they had been seeking (JST Gen. 14:34). And assuming that Salem was translated in the same manner as was Enoch's city—people, buildings, and all—then part of what ascended with Melchizedek had actually been built with Abraham's substantial tithes. Abraham had thereby literally helped build what became a part of the Zion above. And thus was enacted, in Abraham's day and with his preparation, the great event of pre-Flood times, the spectacular ascension of the earthly city of Zion to heavenly realms. Exactly when Salem was translated, how long after the momentous meeting between Abraham and Melchizedek, we are not told.

As for Melchizedek, he would be gone but not forgotten, for his name would become the name of the very order of the priesthood that he bore, even the Holy Priesthood after the Order of the Son of God. The change was made by "the church, in ancient days" (perhaps by Abraham himself[153]) "out of respect or reverence to the name of the Supreme Being, to avoid the too frequent repetition of his name," and "because Melchizedek was such a great high priest" (D&C 107:4).

So great, in fact, that the early Christians recognized in him a foreshadowing of someone even greater. As the name "Melchizedek" means "King of Righteousness," so is Christ the true King of Righteousness. And as the name "Salem," where Melchizedek reigned, means "peace," so Christ is the true King of Peace. Hence in traditional Christianity, as Jerome would say, "Melchizedek represents to us Christ, and the Church of Christ."[154] The symbolism is even richer in restored Christianity: the Joseph Smith Translation tells not only that Melchizedek was of the order of the Son of God, and not only that his people sought and obtained the heavenly city of Enoch, but that Melchizedek himself "was called the king of heaven by his people" and "was called the Prince of peace" (JST Gen. 14:33, 36). Both titles point to Christ, who, as foreshadowed by Melchizedek, leads His people to heaven, where He reigns in peace forever.

Melchizedek's title "prince of peace" also has a distinct echo of Abraham, who from the time he had left Ur was seeking to be "a prince of peace" (Abr. 1:2). It was yet another irony of Abraham's life that his dear friend Melchizedek, epitomizing what Abraham sought to be, would be taken to the heavenly city that Abraham sought—and thereby leave Abraham behind. Abraham had indeed "looked for a city which hath foundations" but as yet had found it not, confessing that he was but a stranger and pilgrim on the earth (Heb. 11:10, 13). But Abraham now had all the authority of Melchizedek, who, having thus ordained and blessed the man appointed by God to bless the world, was ready to lead his city in ascending to the city of Enoch. It was likely the most important ordination and blessing Melchizedek ever gave, his spiritual magnum opus, his great and final act before leaving this world for a higher realm.

No wonder ancient rabbinic tradition, commenting on the blessing Melchizedek gave to Abraham, insists that "when they heard this, heaven and earth and all Creation rejoiced and were glad."[155] For the kingdom of God was now fully established in the person of Abraham, who held all the priesthood and authority of his predecessors. When such a thing would be repeated in the person of Joseph Smith, it would again be a cause, as the Prophet Joseph would write, for heaven and earth and all creation to rejoice and be glad (D&C 128:23).

As for Abraham, having been "faithful unto the obtaining of [God's] priesthoods" available to him and "the magnifying [his] calling," he would yet experience, along with his wife, what latter-day revelation calls being "sanctified by the

Spirit unto the renewing of their bodies" (D&C 84:33). As we shall see, it was that very renewal that would make possible their having posterity, the very reason that Abraham remained behind when Melchizedek ascended. And for those among Abraham's posterity who follow his example of obtaining and magnifying the Melchizedek priesthood, the same blessing of renewal is promised, whereupon they become in the ultimate sense "the seed of Abraham, and the church and kingdom, and the elect of God." Only then do they qualify to receive all the blessings of Abraham, meaning all that God the Father has (D&C 84:33–38).

Abraham's Ascension to Heaven

CHAPTER 7

A Vision of the Future Zion:
The Ascension of Abraham

I, the Lord, am merciful and gracious unto those who fear me, and delight to honor those who serve me in righteousness and in truth unto the end. Great shall be their reward and eternal shall be their glory. And to them will I reveal all mysteries, yea, all the hidden mysteries of my kingdom from days of old, and for ages to come, will I make known unto them the good pleasure of my will concerning all things pertaining to my kingdom. Yea, even the wonders of eternity shall they know, and things to come will I show them, even the things of many generations. And their wisdom shall be great, and their understanding reach to heaven.
—DOCTRINE AND COVENANTS 76:5–9

Crisis in a Covenant Ceremony

According to John Taylor, the Melchizedek Priesthood conferred upon Abraham "would be the means of introducing him into the presence of God" and "some of the greatest and most sublime truths that ever were made known to man."[1] On another occasion John Taylor declared that Abraham "gazed upon his posterity as they should exist through the various ages of time"[2]—a statement remarkable for the fact that when made, no known source described any such thing in the life of Abraham. Since John Taylor's day, a number of ancient sources have emerged that describe in striking detail an occasion when Abraham was indeed introduced into the presence of God in heaven, who taught him and showed him his posterity as they would exist through the ages. The event is not recorded in Genesis, but corresponds to the occasion that Genesis does describe immediately following Abraham's encounter with Melchizedek.

"After these things," says Genesis, "the word of the LORD came unto Abram in a vision" (Gen. 15:1). A rabbinic commentary notes that "the word of the Lord came to Abraham after he had returned all the possessions of Sodom and Gomorrah."[3] In other words, says a modern rabbi, Abraham qualified for his special relationship with God because of his exemplary relationship with his fellow beings.[4]

More immediately, however, according to another rabbinic source, the revelation came only after Abraham "had occupied himself in studying the words" of scripture[5] with "deep meditation and reflection."[6] This phenomenon of revelation following scripture study and meditation would be repeated over and over among Abraham's righteous posterity, as with, for example, his descendants Joseph Smith, after reading and reflecting on the promise of James (JS—H 1:11–17), and Joseph F. Smith, after perusing and pondering the epistle of Peter (D&C 138:1–11).

What God told Abraham, according to Genesis, was: "Fear not, Abram, I am a shield to you; your reward shall be very great." (JPST Gen. 15:1). Once again, Abraham exemplifies what is possible for all, for as the rabbis commented, God "is a shield to all them that take refuge in him."[7]

Jewish sources further point out that, ironically, God's instruction to Abraham to "fear not" is addressed "only to a person who truly fears God," showing that "only one who truly fears God can be without fear of man. The courage and strength of character needed to face the trials and tribulations of our world can come only from a deep and abiding faith in God and his goodness."[8]

A similar paradox governs the law of rewards, as seen in what God told Abraham: *"Your reward shall be very great"* means "Because you spurned the reward of mortal man a great reward is in store for you from Me." The lesson is clear, says a modern rabbi. "He who looks to man for his rewards in life denies himself the far greater rewards, spiritual and material, that can come only from God and that are bestowed only upon those who are not consumed with the desire for reward from their fellowman."[9] Or, in the parlance of latter-day revelation, one can receive the fulness of the Lord's blessings only by serving with "an eye single to the glory of God" (D&C 4:5).

Coming as it does immediately following Abraham's reception of the Melchizedek priesthood and temple ordinances, the timing of the Lord's statement that He would be Abraham's shield and reward appears particularly significant for Latter-day Saints. President Boyd K. Packer has explained, "Our labors in the temple cover us with a shield and a protection."[10] In addition, Abraham was about to be taught firsthand precisely how the Lord could act as his protection and shield. In latter-day revelation, when the Lord gave the same counsel to Abraham's latter-day seed, "Fear not"—repeated three times! (D&C 6:33–34, 36)—the Lord indicated why they need not fear: "Behold the wounds which pierced my side, and also the prints of the nails in my hands and feet" (D&C 6:37). Abraham was about to see in vision the great event that would inflict those wounds and win victory for the Son of God and all those who follow Him.

The dialogue recorded in Genesis between God and Abraham on this occasion is merely an abridgement, as stated by the Midrash Rabbah.[11] One lost piece of the original is restored by the Joseph Smith Translation, which adds that after God promised to be a shield, He said, "And according to the blessings of my servant, I will give unto thee" (JST Gen. 15:2).[12] In context, this servant must be Melchizedek, who had just blessed Abraham. Similarly, the Combat of Adam expressly names Melchizedek in its more detailed account of what God now told Abraham: "Fear not, great is thy reward with Me; and in like manner as Melchizedek My high priest blessed thee, and made thee partaker with himself of Holy Mysteries, so will I make thee partaker with him of heavenly grace."[13] While this statement could refer in the long run to the final celestial inheritance that both Abraham and Melchizedek would ultimately attain, in a more immediate sense it might well have been interpreted by Abraham to indicate that he might ascend with Melchizedek to the translated city.

But there may have been even more to the opening portion of the dialogue between the Lord and Abraham, which was introduced, according to most rabbinic sources, when Abraham was concerned about something, perhaps over whether he had shed innocent blood, or whether the kings would return with revenge.[14] Pursuant to Abraham's pattern, he would have prayed fervently over such concerns, and as such prayers sometimes brought personal appearances of the Lord, as seen in the Book of Abraham (see Abr. 1:15–16; 2:18–19), so Jewish sources tell that God appeared to Abraham on this occasion.[15] This seems to be the setting for God telling Abraham to not fear.

Abraham's response, according to Genesis, was: "Lord GOD, what will [or 'can'[18]] thou give me, seeing I go childless [or, 'I am going to my end childless'[19]]. . . . Behold, to me thou hast given no seed: and, lo, one born in my house is [or 'expects to be'[20]] mine heir" (Gen. 15:3). The Midrash insists that Abraham's question to God—"What will Thou give me . . . ?"— presupposes that God had instructed Abraham to ask for whatever he desired.[16] If such a thing appears to be merely the stuff of legend, in the case of God's most faithful servants it does happen, as seen in the Book of Mormon when the Savior appeared to His Nephite Twelve in answer to fervent prayer over a pressing problem, and then invited each of them to ask whatever they wished of Him. What three of the Nephite disciples desired and received was to be translated (3 Ne. 27–28).

If the Jewish tradition is correct in telling that Abraham also was offered whatever he desired, it presented him with the opportunity of his lifetime, the chance to attain what he had so long sought—translation to the city of Enoch's Zion. Finally it was his just for the asking. But apparently this opportunity touched a deep chord. Something else, associated with the future of Zion below, was paramount in his thoughts. For despite the great blessings of "riches, and honor, and lands for an everlasting possession" that Abraham had been promised (JST Gen. 14:40), yet one thing weighed so heavily on him that, according to one source, he "wept, and supplicated before the Holy One"[17] and asked the Lord what He would give to Abraham.

Above the riches and popularity of the world, and even above Abraham's long quest for the city of Zion, was his desire for fatherhood, his desire for the posterity that would bless the world. But how is it that Abraham, paragon of faith, queried God about what he already repeatedly promised? Was Abraham perhaps simply reminding God that despite all His gifts, the one not yet given was the one long promised, the gift of posterity? Or was Abraham saying something like, "What good will your gifts be, if I keep on being childless?"[21] Or, "to what purpose are your gifts, when I continue childless?"[22]

Yet even this was no lack of faith in God's prior promises, for as the rabbis explain, Abraham was wondering if he had misunderstood, thinking perhaps those promises of posterity might have "meant to his *family*, or to his *household*, but not to his own son who would come out of himself."[23] And so, according to Jubilees, Abraham pled with the Lord: "Give me descendants."[24] It was a poignant plea for what had already been long promised but never fulfilled, a direct and childlike petition by the great and humble man whose heart longed for posterity.

The Lord answered by specifying that one born from his own body would be his heir, and that Abraham's seed would indeed inherit the land.

"How," Abraham asked, "wilt thou give me this land for an everlasting inheritance?"

The Lord answered, "Though thou wast dead, yet am I not able to give it to thee?" (JST Gen. 15:9–10). Abraham, ever the seeker after further light and knowledge, inquired: "My Lord, show me how Thou givest life to the dead."[25]

In the Genesis version of the story in chapter 15, Abraham is then told to offer sacrifice, and in doing so, hears God tell him about the Egyptian sojourn of his descendants (see Gen. 15:9–16). But as one biblical scholar explains, the account as we have it appears to have been "composed of various fragments" that "have been brought or have grown together."[26] That the original account in fact included much more is indicated by the Joseph Smith Translation, which adds that Abraham saw in vision the days of Christ (JST Gen. 15:12), and by rabbinic tradition relating that Abraham ascended to heaven on this occasion.[27] Similarly, the Samaritan Asatir asserts, "Great was this event: there was none like it."[28]

Since Joseph Smith's day, there has emerged a text that not only affirms Abraham's vision of Christ, but also tells that Abraham was not on earth when he saw the vision. The text is the Apocalypse of Abraham, which appeared for the first time in English in the *Improvement Era*. At the present time, except for the Book of Abraham and Genesis, the Apocalypse of Abraham is undoubtedly our most important ancient Abrahamic text.[29] Besides its parallels with the Book of

Abraham, the Apocalypse describes in detail a heavenly ascent by Abraham in a story that connects snippets of the experience alluded to in a number of other texts from ancient Judaism, Islam, and Christianity.

The story of that ascent begins when the Lord instructs Abraham to prepare himself and everything necessary[30] to make a solemn sacrifice of several kinds of animals and birds—the sacrificial creatures of the future Jerusalem Temple.[31] "And in that sacrifice," the Lord promised, "I will set out for you the secrets of the ages, and tell you hidden things; and you shall see great things, which you have not seen; for you have loved me to seek me out, and I have called you my friend [or 'my beloved'[32]]."[33]

The sacrifice was to be performed strictly according to the Lord's instructions, while Abraham was fasting, and, "in the place which I will show you on a high mountain."[34] After all the preparation, as Abraham stood in the appointed place, he took the sacrificial beasts and "cut them in two and arranged the halves opposite each other; the birds, however, he did not cut in half" (NIV Gen. 15:10). As explained by scholars, what to the modern mind may seem a mysterious ceremony actually was a standard "ritual of covenant-making, which, in a similar form, was well known to many ancient peoples. . . . When the animals are halved and laid opposite each other, and when the partners to the covenant stride through the lane that has been thus formed, they express thereby a curse upon themselves in the event the covenant is broken,"[35] saying, "May the deity chop the covenant-breaker into pieces like these animals!"[36] But "the surprising fact [in the Abraham story], which is also unique in the history of religions, is that God himself enters a communal relationship with Abraham under the forms which among men guarantee the greatest contractual security."[37]

As Abraham arranged the carcasses, the ceremony was unexpectedly interrupted, as Genesis recounts: "Then birds of prey came down on the carcasses, but Abram drove them away" (NIV Gen. 15:10–11). Gerhard von Rad comments that "the swooping down of birds of prey could be understood as an evil omen. Or are they perhaps evil powers who intend at the last moment to thwart the conclusion of the covenant?"[38] In fact, in the Apocalypse of Abraham, the "unclean bird" that swoops down on the carcass is Satan,[39] who attempted to intimidate Abraham.[40] The Genesis report that Abraham drove the birds away, in addition to a literal event, may carry a deeper meaning: he drove them away through repentance[41]—that is to say, Abraham's constancy in keeping the commandments meant that, as Jesus would later say, "the prince of this world cometh, and hath nothing in me" (John 14:30).

As darkness fell, according to Genesis, "a smoking fire pot and a flaming torch" passed between the pieces (NRSV Gen. 15:17)—perhaps signifying, as an early Church Father said, the end of the world and the burning that will take place.[42] It was apparently then, as told in Genesis, that "a trance fell upon Abram"[43] and "a thick and dreadful darkness[44] came over him" (NIV Gen. 15:10–12)—not unlike the "thick darkness" that would surround young Joseph Smith before his momentous revelatory experience (JS—H 1:15). As Abraham tells in the Apocalypse, "I looked this way and that; and behold, there was no sign of anyone,"[45] and "my spirit was amazed, and . . . I became like a stone, and fell face down upon the earth, for there was no longer strength in me to stand up on the earth."[46] This appears to be the occasion reported by Origen, apparently quoting an Abrahamic text, telling that "the angels of righteousness and of iniquity disput[ed] over . . . Abraham, each band wishing to claim him for its own company."[47]

Led by an Angel from on High

At that terrifying moment, Abraham heard the voice of God directing an angel to go and strengthen him. Abraham even heard God call the angel by name: "Iaoel [or "Yahoel"[48]] of the same name."[49] The same name as whom? Of God Himself, who will later in the Apocalypse of Abraham be called by this very name.[50] In fact, the name is a combination of the two divine names from the Hebrew Bible: the Greek form of *Yahweh* (transliterated by the King James translators as "Jehovah," the name of the God of Israel[51]), along with the word *El,* meaning God.[52]

So who was this angel that was privileged to bear the Lord's own name? It was none other than Enoch, whose first of the seventy other names listed in 3 Enoch is Yahoel.[53] The twentieth century's leading authority on the Kabbalah, Gershom Scholem, has similarly shown that the angel who appears to Abraham in the Apocalypse is indeed the same that later Jewish sources call Metatron, or Enoch.[54] It was the same angel who had rescued Abraham from the altar in Ur and had later delivered to him the patriarchal authority and the ordinances, including "the baptism of life and the right hand."[55]

The first thing Enoch does upon arrival is to cast out Satan from Abraham's presence. "Depart from this man!"[56] declares Enoch. "Depart, for you can never lead him astray!"[57] Enoch then extended his right hand to Abraham (an indication that this was no spirit, but rather a translated being of flesh and bones [see D&C 129:4–9], for as yet there were no resurrected beings serving as angels to planet earth). As told by Abraham, the angel "took me by the right hand" and "said to me, Stand up, friend of God, who loves you. . . . I am sent to you to strengthen you and to bless you in the name of God, who loves you. . . . It is for your sake that I have made the journey to earth. . . . Take courage and come; rejoice and be glad of heart; and I will rejoice with you; for eternal honor has been prepared for you by the Eternal One." And "come with me to meet him with all speed," but first "carry through the sacrifice as you have been commanded; for behold, I am appointed to be with you and with the people who are to spring from you."[58] "And with me Michael blesses you forever."[59] "Take courage: come."[60]

As Abraham relates in the Apocalypse, "I got up and looked at him who had taken my right hand and set me on my feet.[61] And his body was like sapphire, and his face like chrysolite, and the hair of his head like snow; and there was a linen band about his head, and it was like a rainbow, and the robes he was wearing were purple, and he had a golden staff in his hand."[62] Not only does his apparel have "strong priestly associations,"[63] but the rainbow surrounding his head seems to be a sign that he is from God's throne, which was surrounded by a rainbow. Medieval Jewish texts associate Enoch (Metatron) with the rainbow,[64] which in restored scripture figures prominently as a sign of the covenant that God had made with Enoch that in the latter days he and his city would return to the earth (JST Gen. 9:21–24). Enoch thus exhibited around his own person the very sign portending his latter-day return to the earth.

Enoch explains that Abraham will be allowed to see "what is in heaven and on earth . . . , and in the fulness of the universe and its circle: you shall see it all."[65] Enoch then takes Abraham to a holy mountain from where he sees hell and its tortures, a sight that leaves Abraham weak[66]—apparently similar to what Moses would experience when he "began to fear exceedingly" and "saw the bitterness of hell" (Moses 1:20). Enoch also introduces Abraham to other men, at which point, according to Nibley, "Abraham . . . receiv[es] instruction at an altar . . . surrounded by men . . . form[ing] a circle around [him]."[67] These men are not otherwise named or described, but they are apparently some of Enoch's colleagues from the translated city of Zion, including perhaps some from Melchizedek's Salem.

Then came "the sign of the Holy Ghost unto Abraham, in the form of a dove,"[68] as Abraham was caught up by the Spirit and accompanied by Enoch to heaven.[69] He had glimpsed God's abode from afar on the night before he had entered Egypt, but now was being taken there following the pattern of his righteous forefathers Enoch, Seth, and Adam.

In heaven, Abraham sees glory like a great fire approaching, and hears the voice of the Lord like "the voice of many waters"[70] or "the sound of rushing waters,"[71] the same description given by Joseph Smith of the Lord's voice in the Kirtland Temple.[72] Then, "clad in the garment of glory, Abraham becomes like 'one of the glorified beings and takes part in the song of praise chanted by them in heaven to God.'"[73] The profound effect of this experience on Abraham may be surmised by the later experience of his descendant Alma who, upon seeing the same scene and hearing those same celestial strains sung at the throne of the Almighty, felt that "my soul did long to be there" (Alma 36:22). Such also was the righteous King Benjamin's greatest desire, that he might one day "join the choirs above in singing the praises of a just God" (Mosiah 2:28). And such was the Prophet Joseph Smith's great desire for himself and all the Latter-day Saints, "that we may mingle our voices with those bright, shining seraphs around thy throne, with acclamations of praise, singing Hosanna to God and the Lamb" (D&C 109:79).

Abraham had spoken face to face with the Lord before, but never in the Lord's own abode. Having received the fulness of the temple ordinances from Melchizedek, Abraham was qualified to be ushered into the presence of the Lord. And so it happened, as Enoch took Abraham to the divine throne, where he saw four fiery winged creatures and behind them "a chariot with fiery wheels. . . . And above the wheels was the throne . . . covered with fire and the fire encircled it round about."[74] It was the same blazing chariot-throne that would be seen by Abraham's descendants Daniel (Dan. 7:9) and Ezekiel (the latter also reporting the presence of four creatures protecting the throne; Ezek. 1:1–25; 10:6–12).[75] Abraham now understood the significance of the chariot of fire that he had once seen and that the Lord had mentioned in Haran: it was an image of the divine throne, as imitated extensively by rulers throughout the ancient Near East[76] and as Abraham himself had probably seen in the courts of Nimrod and Pharaoh.

The Beloved Son Teaches the Beloved Abraham

Having introduced Abraham at the throne of God, Enoch apparently steps away. According to the Sefer Yetzirah—a temple text, says Nibley[77]—Abraham "raised his hand" and the Lord "filled [it] to overflowing,"[78] a scene which may possibly be depicted in figure 7 of Facsimile 2 in the Book of Abraham. Apparently Abraham was then handed a crystalline object allowing him to read the secrets of the universe and of creation,[79] and handed a heavenly book.[81] The Lord identified himself to Abraham as "the one whom you have searched for or who has loved you."[82] Rising from his throne, the Lord "revealed Himself to him, and took him in His bosom"[82] and "kissed him on his head, and He called him, 'Abraham my beloved.'"[83]

It is the title for which Abraham is remembered, the title appearing in the Lord's mention of Abraham as recorded in the writings of Isaiah: "Abraham my beloved friend."[84] Nephi would similarly remember that God "loved . . . Abraham" (1 Ne. 17:40), and to this day among many of Abraham's Muslim descendants he is still spoken of as Abraham the Beloved Friend.

The Sefer Yetzirah further tells that Abraham's experience came after he had "looked, . . . probed, . . . and thought,"[85] or "searched, discerned, delved,"[86] or, as described in the Recognitions of Clement, "was desirous to learn the causes of things, and was intently pondering upon what had been told him." It was then that God "appeared to him . . . and disclosed all things which he desired."[87] Abraham's experience foreshadows that of his admiring descendant Nephi, who similarly pondered prior to his revelatory experience when he also was shown the things that he desired (1 Ne. 10:17; 11:1–3). So also the youthful Joseph Smith reported that prior to his glorious first vision, "I pondered many things in my heart."[88]

What Abraham first learned, says the Recognitions of Clement, concerned "the knowledge of the Divinity,"[89] the importance of which can be judged by Joseph Smith's statement that "It is the first principle of the Gospel to know for a certainty the Character of God, and to know that we may converse with him as one man converses with another."[90] Although Abraham had conversed with God face to face before, this occasion was further divine disclosure along that path to eternal life, which is, as Joseph Smith taught, to know the only wise and true God.[91] And is it a coincidence that the one mortal man who had most frequently visited the Savior on earth in caring for the least of His brethren, now had been brought to greet the Savior and learn yet more about Him at His celestial throne? We also know from Joseph Smith's writings that Abraham ended up with such knowledge of the Godhead that he wrote about each of them and their individual functions and relationship.[92] We might surmise that on this occasion, the Savior introduced Abraham to the Father and the Holy Ghost.

The Savior then showed Abraham "the heavens and all that they contain,"[93] including "the kingdom of the heavens"[94] and the very "streets of heaven"[95] (even as would be seen later by Joseph Smith when he saw Abraham in that kingdom[96]). An Islamic source says that "our Lord removed the veils from the seven spheres of heaven and earth for him," so that "Abraham saw everything from the dust on earth to the high Throne of heaven."[97] Also included in Abraham's view was the panorama of the stars that he had once been shown from the earth. Now from this vantage point he heard the Lord tell him: "Look from on high at the stars which are beneath you and count them for me and tell me their number!"[98] To which Abraham replied, "How can I, for I am but a man."[99] Said the Lord, "So shall be your seed" (GTC Gen. 15:5).[100] As Abraham saw the number of stars multiply beyond human capacity to count, "his heart was filled with joy and gladness."[101]

But it was to the earth[102] and to its future that God now pointed as he began to unfold to Abraham "the secrets of the ages."[103] Years earlier he had seen the early history, beginning with the creation of the world and the events in the Garden of Eden.[104] Now he was shown the rest of history, from his day forward.[105] "From the fire of the divine throne God speaks to Abraham, revealing to him the future of his descendants,"[106] even "the course of Israel's history and the history of the whole world."[107] In the words of John Taylor, Abraham "gazed upon his posterity as they should exist through the various ages of time."[108] He saw, for example, that his posterity would sojourn in Egypt and come out with great possessions (Gen. 15:13–14), and would inherit Abraham's land and build the temple on Mount Zion in Jerusalem.[109]

In the Genesis account, which says nothing of Abraham being in heaven or seeing a vision on this occasion, he is merely told that his posterity will come out of Egypt, and then hears God suddenly change the subject and say: "And thou shalt go to thy fathers in peace; thou shalt be buried in a good old age" (Gen. 15:15). The statement is generally interpreted to be a soothing assurance to Abraham of a peaceful death in the contentment of old age.[110] But in the larger context of the Apocalypse, with Abraham now basking in the glorious divine presence at the very throne of God, to hear that his mortal life will be prolonged is surely no comfort (see Alma 36:22; 3 Ne. 28:1–2). But according to the Joseph Smith translation, the Lord not only mentioned the peaceable nature of Abraham's future passing, but specifically informed Abraham about his future death: "thou shalt die . . ." (JST Gen. 15:18). Death is the common lot of mankind, so why would the Lord bother mentioning this to Abraham?

Abraham had long sought the translated city of Enoch and the order of priesthood giving access to that city. Having finally received that priesthood from Melchizedek, another mortal seeking Enoch's city, Abraham had then been told that he would be a partaker with Melchizedek of heavenly grace. Then Enoch himself had led Abraham into heavenly realms, perhaps leading him to expect that he was to finally receive what he had so long sought: translation to Enoch's city of Zion. In fact, it appears that Abraham could have asked for and received this gift, but chose otherwise: he chose to remain on earth to receive fulfillment of the blessing of a posterity that would bless the earth, bless all nations and build Zion. Abraham would remain on the earth to instruct and train his offspring for the great mission that lay ahead of them and their descendants.

No sooner did God tell His friend Abraham that he would die, than God also showed him how the Savior would overcome death. As related in the Joseph Smith Translation, Abraham "looked forth and saw the days of the coming of the Son of Man" (JST Gen. 15:12)—who, as Abraham was told, would be his own descendant.[111] As Abraham beheld the mortal ministry of the Savior, he saw, according to the Apocalypse of Abraham, "a great crowd, and they worshiped him," but "others insulted this man, and some struck him."[112] From the unique vantage point of standing at the very throne of the premortal Christ—He who would be Abraham's descendant in the flesh and He whose life Abraham was foreshadowing in his own—Abraham saw the amazing depth to which the King of Heaven would descend to minister to mankind and atone for their sins. Abraham saw for himself what his descendant King Benjamin would hear an angel declare:

> The time cometh . . . that with power, the Lord Omnipotent who reigneth, who was, and is from all eternity to all eternity, shall come down from heaven among the children of men, and shall dwell in a tabernacle of clay, and shall go forth amongst men, working mighty miracles. . . . And lo, he shall suffer temptations and pain of body, hunger, thirst, and fatigue, even more

than man can suffer, except it be unto death; for behold, blood cometh from every pore, so great shall be his anguish for the wickedness and the abominations of his people. And he shall be called Jesus Christ, the Son of God (Mosiah 3:5, 7–8).

As Abraham viewed these events, he also heard the Savior explain, as recorded in the Joseph Smith Translation, that "the day cometh, that the Son of Man shall live; but how can he live if he be not dead? he must first be quickened" (JST Gen. 15:11). Thus Abraham saw not only the Savior's crucifixion and death but also His Resurrection; and, as had happened with Enoch (Moses 7:47, 56), Abraham "was glad, and his soul found rest, and he believed in the Lord; and the Lord counted it unto him for righteousness" (JST Gen. 15:12). The early Church Father Ambrose similarly explained of Abraham on this occasion that "he believed that Christ through the incarnation would become his heir."[113] Thus did Abraham see and believe in Jesus Christ and His atoning sacrifice that would bring resurrection to all and celestial victory to the righteous. It was because of that victory and the Victor that Abraham need not fear.

The abbreviated version that survived in the Genesis text says nothing about the Savior, but says simply that Abraham "believed in the LORD," who "counted it to him for righteousness" (Gen. 15:6). Commenting on this verse, a rabbinic source states that "great is belief, since the Lord counted it to Abraham for righteousness."[114] One thinks immediately of the words of the angel to Nephi: "Blessed art thou, Nephi, because thou believest in the Son of the most high God" (1 Ne. 11:6). Abraham's belief is a pattern, according to Chrysostom: "Let us learn, I beseech you, a lesson for ourselves as well as from the patriarch: Let us believe in the words of God and trust in his promise. Let us not apply the yard-stick of our own reasoning but give evidence of deep gratitude."[115]

But another translation of the Genesis verse telling that Abraham "believed" in the Lord points to what it means to believe: because Abraham "put his trust in the LORD, He reckoned it to his merit" (JPST Gen. 15:6). Abraham's lifelong trust in the Almighty was the key determinant of his life, insisted the ancient rabbis: "You find that Abraham inherited both this world and the World to Come only because he put his trust in the Lord,"[116] a trust that impelled him to come before God with "clean hands, and a pure heart."[117] Trust in the Lord figures prominently also in the record of Abraham's Nephite descendants, whose first author, Nephi—an ardent admirer of Abraham—wrote: "O Lord, I have trusted in thee, and I will trust in thee forever. I will not put my trust in the arm of flesh; for I know that cursed is he that putteth his trust in the arm of flesh" (2 Ne. 4:34). And it was Nephi's successor King Benjamin who emphasized that the Atonement was prepared "that thereby salvation might come to him that should put his trust in the Lord" (Mosiah 4:6). In Abraham's case, he is privileged to be shown the future atoning sacrifice by Him who would make it—a supreme illustration showing in whom mankind must put their trust.

God then told Abraham, according to a Samaritan source, that "he was one of those who will in the future inhabit the Garden of Eden."[118] Paradise would indeed be his, not the temporary terrestrial paradise of the city of Enoch, but the eternal celestial paradise of God—which Enoch's city would also eventually enjoy. Abraham's eternal paradise would eventually be on the very land where he was living, the land that God now covenanted to give to him and his posterity forever (Gen. 15:18). Abraham received the promise as recorded in Mandean texts, that after returning to the world as God's special messenger or apostle, he would eventually "be allowed to return to heaven" and be "given his crown, his garment and his throne."[119]

A View of the Last Days

God then "revealed [to him] the end of the times."[120] Abraham saw that "in the last days" his own righteous posterity would be "the people set apart for" the Lord, but would be "put to the test" in that "ungodly age" of great "plagues" and "misfortunes,"[121] and would be "humiliated" and "mocked" and "ruled over"[122] and threatened with destruction.[123] When Abraham's forefather Enoch had been shown events in the future, he had pled for mercy for his descendants, and the Lord granted Enoch's request by making a covenant (see Moses 7:48–67, especially 50–52). So it apparently happened now with Abraham as he foresaw the distress of his latter-day posterity and, according to Jewish tradition, petitioned God for their benefit,[124] whereupon the Lord made a covenant with Abraham.

In the highly abbreviated Genesis version of the story, the covenant concerns merely the promise of the land (Gen. 15:18–21). But Jewish tradition held that the covenant encompassed more, and that the Lord "promised Abraham to redeem his children"[125] and to "deliver them from the kingdoms,"[126] or, in the words of 4 Ezra, to "never forsake his descendants."[127] The Midrash speaks of "the deep designs which the Holy One, blessed be He, . . . arranged between Himself and His noble companion," namely Abraham.[128] These deep designs were made part of the covenant, by virtue of which the Lord would protect His Latter-day Saints as foretold in the Book of Mormon: "I will show unto them that fight against my word and against my people, who are of the house of Israel, that I am God, and that I covenanted with Abraham that I would remember his seed forever" (2 Ne. 29:14).

The passage is found in the writings of Nephi, who elsewhere uses another word in describing the same event: "And all that fight against *Zion* shall be destroyed" (1 Ne. 22:14, emphasis added). Nephi further describes how that destruction will come, promising that the Lord "will preserve the righteous by his power, . . . even unto the destruction of their enemies by fire" (1 Ne. 22:17; see also verse 22, and 2 Ne. 30:10). Nephi was paraphrasing Isaiah's writings, which in turn, as one scholar has shown, preserved much of the old Enochic heritage.[129] In fact, 1 Enoch tells that at the last day the wicked "shall quiver. And great fear and trembling shall seize them unto the ends of the earth. Mountains and high places will fall down and . . . melt like a honeycomb before the flame. . . . He will preserve the elect" but "destroy the wicked ones."[130]

Abraham had undoubtedly read this Enoch passage, along with the one telling that the Lord's return to the earth would be in fulfillment of His covenant to Enoch (Moses 7:59–60). Now Abraham himself, having received the Lord's promise to protect Abraham's latter-day posterity, was shown that the Lord would maintain them "safe in my keeping,"[131] "protected by me."[132] He would "sound the trumpet from the air, and I will send my Elect One, with a full measure of all my power. And he shall summon my people . . . ; and those who have reviled them and have had dominion over them in the present age will I burn with fire."[133] Abraham saw, in other words, that his Descendant who had once been humiliated by the powers of the earth would in the last days come in glory to rescue others of Abraham's righteous descendants in their hour of grave danger.

Then, as attested by various ancient sources, God showed him "the resurrection of the dead [and] the future judgment"[134] and "the fates of sinners and the righteous."[135] He thus saw not only "the punishment of the evil,"[136] even "the wicked [who] rebelled . . . during their lives,"[137] but also "the reward of the good,"[138] and he "watched as seats were arranged and thrones were set up."[139] A vision of such things is reserved, as the Lord has stated in latter-day revelation, for "those who fear me, and . . . serve me in righteousness and in truth unto the end" (D&C 76:5). It was a vision for which Joseph Smith also qualified (see D&C 76).

As Abraham continued to watch, he saw something else, something that moved him deeply, something of which he had been reminded when he noticed the rainbow surrounding Enoch. What Abraham saw is mentioned in a text attributed to Baruch, a contemporary of Lehi who, like Lehi (1 Ne. 1:12–13), had foreseen in vision the fall of Jerusalem. As Baruch was "grieving over Zion . . . because of the captivity,"[140] God informed him of another city, "not this building that is in your midst now," but one that "is preserved with me" and that in time "will be revealed." And "I showed it to my servant Abraham in the night between the portions of the victims."[141]

It is the same city that 4 Ezra calls Zion: "And Zion will come and be made manifest to all people, prepared and built."[142] Thus Abraham foresaw the glorious descent of Zion, the city he had long sought in the flesh. Having just learned that he would never reside in that city in its terrestrial translated state, Abraham now saw its latter-day glory after it would return to the earth, in remarkable fulfillment of the covenant signified by the rainbow. The vision of that millennial Zion was a sight that Abraham "contemplated with delight" and that "fired" his soul as he saw in advance "the destruction of the powers of darkness, the renovation of the earth, the glory of God, and the salvation of the human family,"[143] including the purification of the Lord's people.[144] Wilford Woodruff stated that Abraham saw that "a reign of righteousness would commence and the honest and meek of the earth would be gathered together to serve the Lord, and upon them would rest power to build up the great Zion of God in the latter days."[145]

For many years Abraham had longed to join the translated city of Zion; now, seeing in vision its latter-day glory, he longed to be there. A latter-day revelation speaks of "Enoch, and his brethren, who were separated from the earth, and were received unto myself—a city reserved until a day of righteousness shall come—a day which was sought for by all holy men, and they found it not because of wickedness and abominations; and confessed that they were strangers and pilgrims on the earth; but obtained a promise that they should find it and see it in their flesh" (D&C 45:11–14). If Abraham had sought the city of Enoch, he had with equal diligence sought to establish Zion and an era of righteousness on earth, but "found it not because of wickedness and abominations." Now he received the promise that he would yet see it in the flesh in the great and last day when he would also join with the city of Enoch.

And as Abraham had rejoiced in the vision of the first coming of Christ, so now he rejoiced in the vision of Christ's Second Coming, when the Son of Man would rescue Abraham's latter-day seed, those inhabitants of the earthly Zion who would then be joined by Enoch's Zion descending from realms above. It was all a part of the covenant to Abraham, who thanks to the Savior's Atonement and Resurrection, would finally in the flesh join the glorious city of Zion on earth.

Having been offered the opportunity to choose what gift he wished from the Lord, notwithstanding Abraham's long quest for the translated city of Zion, he had chosen to remain below in order to become the father of those who would build Zion again on earth. No matter that at least one of his followers—the very steward and administrator of his own house, Eliezer, who had expected to be Abraham's heir[146]—would eventually, according to a rabbinic tradition, be translated.[147] Abraham's role was to live out his life as a mortal model for his posterity who would be charged with carrying on his mission of building the earthly Zion.

And once again in Abraham's life, Zion above—the angel Enoch—had been sent to strengthen Abraham and teach him, this time about the Zion of the future. But this time the translated Enoch had taken Abraham to the Lord Himself, following the pattern of Enoch's own prior ascension and that of earlier patriarchs, a pattern that would come to be reflected in royal ritual of the ancient Near East in which "the king is the Sent One. He has ascended to heaven to receive . . . his commission. Then he is sent out, i.e., he descends again" bearing the "tablets of wisdom," the heavenly book.[148] Thus Abraham, heir to the royal patriarchal authority of Adam, now descends as a Sent One, a special witness of the Greater One whom the Father would send as His Beloved Son, even the King of Zion, He who had welcomed Abraham at the royal throne above.

Abraham's exhilarating experience at the throne of God would be but a foretaste of the eternal glory awaiting him when he would inherit his own throne of glory in the presence of God the Father and His Only Begotten Son. In the meantime, many centuries after Abraham when the Only Begotten Son would descend from His throne to be born in a manger, He would be recognized and honored as the Heavenly King by magi from the East.[149] Who were they, and how did they know how to find and recognize the infant King? "The Magi are said to have called their religion *Kêsh-i-Ibrâhîm,* i.e., creed of Abraham, whom they considered as their prophet and the reformer of their religion. They traced their religious books to Abraham, who was believed to have brought them from heaven."[150] According to this tradition, it was the books brought down by Abraham from the throne of Jesus which guided the magi to the manger to worship the infant King of Heaven.

Abraham Serving His Three Visitors

CHAPTER 8

Visitors from Zion:
Three Holy Men and Their Mission

I will go before your face. I will be on your right hand and on your left, and my Spirit shall be in your hearts, and mine angels round about you, to bear you up.
—DOCTRINE AND COVENANTS 84:88

Looking Forward with an Eye of Faith

From the first divine promise made to Abraham about his posterity, the years of continuing childlessness had turned into decades of delay. And yet, as one scholar observes, still Abraham "believed the promise, although from a human aspect everything spoke against it."[1] Or, as eloquently expressed by the Danish philosopher Soren Kierkegaard,

> By faith Abraham received the promise that in his seed all races of the world would be blessed. Time passed, the possibility was there, Abraham believed; time passed, it became unreasonable, Abraham believed. . . . There is no song of Lamentations by Abraham. He did not mournfully count the days while time passed, he did not look at Sarah with a suspicious glance. . . . Abraham became old, Sarah became a laughingstock in the land, and yet he was God's elect and inheritor of the promise that in his seed all the races of the world would be blessed. . . . What is it to be God's elect? It is to be denied in youth the wishes of youth, so as with great pains to get them fulfilled in old age.[2]

How had Abraham maintained his faith in the long-delayed promises? We have already seen his constant gratitude and praise to God for blessings already bestowed—apparently a key to Abraham's faith. For as one of his faithful latter-day descendants observed, "I have discovered that if I insist on tormenting myself with obvious facts, I cannot hold on to the precious peace that is His Gift. But if I give heartfelt praise to our Father in Heaven while in the midst of my trials, He grants me instant peace, strength, and abiding hope."[3] It is an expression of the principle articulated by Moroni, who explained that God has never worked miracles for men "until after their faith," so that when they finally "saw with their [mortal] eyes" what they had hoped for, it was only after "they had beheld [it] with an eye of faith" (Ether 12:18–19).

So had Abraham looked ahead with an eye of faith, continually leaning upon the divine promises through the years as he offered "myriad prayers," says Josephus, for the fulfillment of those promises.[4] In the words of the Apostle Paul, Abraham "against hope believed in hope, that he might become the father of many nations, according to that which was spoken" (Rom. 4:18). Meanwhile, in selfless exercise of his faith and priesthood, he offered prayers for the welfare of others, including prayers for childless women, and they would conceive.[5]

God had confirmed to Abraham that his heir would be a son issuing from his own body, but nothing had been said about Sarah being the mother. Her faith had been firm as she had interpreted the promises of posterity to Abraham as any reasonable wife would, to mean that she was to be the mother. As the promises had been renewed from heaven time after time, her hope and expectation had been renewed and reinvigorated. But months had turned into years as they endured "the anguish of childlessness."[6] Such an anguishing trial might well have damaged many a marital relationship, but not this one. He "had simply loved her the more tenderly, making the deepening of his love for her entirely clear. Not only had he made no complaints, never even mentioned the word 'barren,' he had refused to allow anyone else to do so either."[7]

But ten years after returning from Egypt, Sarah, having always considered the promises of posterity as applying to her also, apparently began to consider another possibility. For those promises had never actually mentioned her. Was she holding up their fulfillment? Approaching Abraham, she suggested that he marry her maid, Hagar. Sarah had taught Hagar the ways of the Lord, and Hagar had learned well, "walk[ing] in the same path of righteousness as her mistress."[8] Sarah's words to Abraham are reported in Genesis, the very first time Sarah speaks in the Bible: "See how the Lord has prevented me from bearing children. I beg you [or 'please'[9]] now, go and sleep with my maid, and perhaps I will have a son through her."[10]

By those words, according to Jewish tradition, Sarah "took the blame for childlessness upon herself rather than seeking to blame her husband,"[11] and thereby demonstrated her "spiritual strength: she was not jealous of her handmaid, but acted with the purest of motives" and even with the prompting of the Holy Spirit.[12] Modern rabbi Amos Miller comments:

> The secret of the wonderful marital relationship between Abraham and Sarah was that when things went wrong neither sought to blame the other or to find fault with the other. If fault was to be found, each found it within himself. This remains the secret of a happy marriage to this day.[13]

Abraham and Sarah were living the law that the Lord would give to their latter-day descendants seeking to build Zion: "See that ye love one another. . . . Cease to find fault one with another. . . . And above all things, clothe yourselves with the bond of charity, as with a mantle, which is the bond of perfectness and peace" (D&C 88:123–25).

Sarah's language also implies, according to the nineteenth-century rabbi Samson Raphael Hirsch, that Abraham was reluctant to do what his wife was suggesting. "Sarah wants to do it only for his sake, but she knows that he would not do it for his own sake; hence she says . . . 'perhaps I [will have a son through her].' If Abraham would not want to do it for his own sake, then let him do it for the sake of his wife because she wants it so badly."[14] Such was the mutual love and loyalty of this couple, each putting the other first even in the matters that touched their hearts most deeply. Their relationship illustrates the truth taught by President Gordon B. Hinckley that "if you will make your first concern the comfort, the well-being, and the happiness of your companion, sublimating any personal concern to that loftier goal, you will be happy, and your marriage will go on throughout eternity."[15]

Modern revelation adds that Sarah gave Hagar to Abraham "because this was the law" (D&C 132:34), a statement confirmed by Bible scholars who note the obligation of an infertile wife after ten years to bring her husband a second wife to bear children.[16] But it was also one of the great acts of Sarah's life, noted Erastus Snow, done out of "love and integrity to her husband" so "that he might not be childless because she was childless."[17] It was the ultimate sacrifice, a decision made, no doubt, after much soul searching and prayer. Sarah was by no means giving up, nor did this mark a loss of hope; both Rashi and Nachmanides held that Sarah still harbored the expectation that God would yet bless her some day to conceive, but that for now, as throughout her life, Sarah was acting in righteousness and under divine guidance in the matter.[18] She was acting out of love, and "did not render herself distant" from Abraham,[19] but kept her heart knit together in love with his. According to a modern Muslim scholar, it was because of this unselfish act of Sarah that God would eventually reward her with a son of her own.[20]

But up to now the yearning of her heart was not forthcoming, having grown more elusive with each passing year. Indeed, as difficult as Abraham's long trial of childlessness had been to him, "Sarah must have been the one most deeply hurt by her barrenness."[21] And yet, at this time of profound personal grief, out of the greatness of her loving heart poured forth only soothing words of hope for Abraham, as reported by Philo:

> Do not let the trouble of my barrenness extend to you, or [your] kind feeling to me to keep you from becoming what you can become, a father, for I shall have no jealousy of another woman. . . . And if our prayers for the birth of children are answered the offspring will be yours in full parenthood, but surely mine also by adoption. But to avoid any suspicion of jealousy on my part, take if you will my handmaiden . . . , proved and tested by me for many years from the day when she was first brought to my house, an Egyptian by birth, but a Hebrew by her rule of life.[22]

Philo further reports that Sarah's words instilled in Abraham "increased admiration for the wifely love, which never grew old and was ever showing itself anew, and her careful forethought for the future."[23] Even still, Abraham accepted Sarah's proposal only after receiving revelation on the matter,[24] whereupon Sarah magnanimously declared to Hagar, "Happy art thou to be united to so holy a man."[25] Abraham married Hagar, who immediately became pregnant—even though, in the poignant words of modern writers, "as Hagar's belly swelled with child, Sarah's womb remained empty."[26]

Hagar, although remembered as a woman of righteousness and faith,[27] began to "despise" (NIV Gen. 16:4) Sarah and treat her with "contempt" (NRSV Gen. 16:4) and "disdain."[28] Her unbearable insolence included claiming that Sarah's infertile condition proved her spiritual inferiority.[29]

Sarah's reaction is reported by Genesis, which tells that she went to Abraham and said: "I am being wronged; you must do something about it. It was I who gave my slave-girl [or 'maid' (JPST)] into your arms, but since she has known that she is pregnant, she has despised me" (REB Gen. 16:5). Genesis then reports the following words by Sarah, words which the English reader would automatically suppose were part of what Sarah said to Abraham: "The LORD decide [or, 'Let the LORD judge' (GTC)[30]] between you and me" (JPST Gen. 16:5). These adversarial words color the immediately prior sentence, making Sarah's entire communication to Abraham appear angry and divisive.

But it was Judaism's greatest grammarian and all-time Torah authority, Rashi, who pointed out that the Hebrew word "between you" in this passage is written with a feminine indicator for the person being addressed, showing—according to Rashi and other Jewish sources—that Sarah's statement about the Lord judging was addressed not to Abraham but to Hagar.[31] Other Jewish sources agree that Sarah was invoking the Lord not against Abraham, but against anyone who would try to cause dissension between her and Abraham.[32] Sarah's commitment to build Zion by being of one heart with her husband was of highest priority, even when she felt wronged.

By Abraham's supportive response to Sarah—"Your maid is in your hands; deal with her as you think right" (JPST Gen. 16:6)—he was apparently hoping that his soft answer would turn away Sarah's wrath.[33] In any event, Abraham's reaction to Sarah shows that "he willingly accepts any corrections that come from her."[34]

As Genesis tells, the pregnant Hagar fled. But an angel appeared to her by a spring of water in the wilderness, and instructed her to return to Sarah. That her child would play an important role in God's plan is evident from the blessing the angel then pronounced upon Hagar, in the name of the Lord: "I will so greatly multiply your offspring that they cannot be counted for multitude" (NRSV Gen. 16:10). The angel even designated the name of the son she was carrying in her womb: he would be called Ishmael, meaning "God has heard." For, as the angel explained, the Lord had heeded Hagar in her distress.

The angel further assured Hagar that the freedom she had sought would in fact be enjoyed by her son. The closest an English translation can come to what the angel then said about Ishmael is that he would be "a wild donkey of a man" (NJB Gen. 16:12), a phrase that can strike the modern ear as pejorative. But the Hebrew word is not the term for a domesticated donkey, but rather for a particular species that lives wild in the desert and, according to biblical scholar Gordon Wenham, "looks more like a horse than a donkey, and is used in the Old Testament as a figure of an individualistic lifestyle untrammeled by social convention."[35] As explained by some of Judaism's most prominent authorities, the angel's description of Ishmael carries no negative sense whatsoever, but means "a free man among men," enjoying the freedom of the desert.[36] And according to Samson Raphael Hirsch, the angel's words in naming Ishmael and then prophesying about his freedom constituted instruction to Hagar in the "basic ideal" she must seek to instill in her son, and which alone would truly make him free: an awareness of that Divine Providence—memorialized by the name *Ishmael,* "God has heard"—that watches over the deeds of men and assists them in their suffering.[37] In short, Ishmael was, according to the words of the angel, destined to be a great man.

Hagar returned and bore Ishmael, giving Abraham a son at long last. It was part of the divine plan, for as latter-day revelation explains, "from Hagar sprang many people. This, therefore, was fulfilling, among other things, the promises" (D&C 132:34). Islamic texts tell of the tenderness of the relationship between Abraham and Ishmael, while Jewish tradition reports that Abraham loved him.[38]

Meanwhile, the faithful Sarah remained barren. What trials God requires of His most faithful!

"Live in My Presence, Be Perfect"

Thirteen years had passed, years of faith, of prayer, of service, of sacrifice, of missionary and temple work, of building Zion—and of believing. "By all objective criteria God's promise to Abraham seemed impossible of fulfillment, yet Abraham continued to believe that the promise would be kept."[39] As did Sarah. But by now they had come to understand the promises differently, for Sarah had entered menopause, and had finally given up the idea that the promises of posterity to Abraham would include her as a mother. It was the ultimate disappointment for her after so many years of longing expectation, selfless service, and looking forward in faith. But even now there was no word of complaint.

Then, suddenly, unexpectedly, the Lord appeared to Abraham. The last time Abraham had seen the Lord was in heaven, when Abraham had been taken up to the divine throne and had been shown the future Zion as his descendants would build it. Now the Lord descended to earth, to Abraham's abode, and spoke of their relationship, as Genesis reports: "I am God Almighty,"[40] the Lord began. "Walk with me and be blameless"[41]—or, as in other translations, "Walk in my ways and be blameless" (JPST Gen. 17:1), or "Walk in my presence and be blameless,"[42] or "Live in my presence, be perfect" (NJB Gen. 17:1).[43]

A rabbinic text recounts that upon hearing these words, Abraham was troubled as he mentally reviewed what he might have done amiss.[44] Rabbi Amos Miller comments that "the righteous man never feels secure in his righteousness. He is always on guard against some shortcoming in himself and strives to improve himself. It is this sensitivity to any imperfection that makes him truly righteous."[45] Similarly, Latter-day Saints are warned that because "there is a possibility that man may fall from grace and depart from the living God," the church is commanded to "take heed and pray always, lest they fall into temptation; yea, and even let those who are sanctified take heed also" (D&C 20:32–34).

In Abraham's case, in fact, it was his very goodness that had prompted the revelation, according to Jewish tradition. When the Holy One saw Abraham "walking in perfection and integrity of heart,"[46] He revealed Himself to him and commanded Abraham to attain "a perfect love,"[47] recalling Joseph Smith's statement that we are liable to fall until we have perfect love, which comes "when we have a testimony that our names are sealed in the Lamb's book of life."[48] It was this attainment that God wanted for Abraham, who was also extended an invitation to enter the same fellowship once granted to Enoch and his people. While still in mortality, they had "walked with God" (Gen. 5:22, 24),[49] not only Enoch but "all his people" (Moses 7:69), such that "the Lord came and dwelt with his people, and they dwelt in righteousness" (Moses 7:16). Having read these passages in the patriarchal records, Abraham would have recognized this new commandment as an invitation to build and perfect the earthly Zion to the point where once again the Lord could dwell with His people on earth. If it was not in the Lord's plan to translate Abraham's Zion, yet it could still be perfected to the point that Zion's King could dwell there.

According to Lorenzo Snow, the Lord's command to Abraham to be perfect reveals something important about both God and Abraham. It reveals that God is a God of blessing, who desired Abraham to prepare himself for yet further blessings: "The Lord appeared to Abraham and made him very great promises," but "before he was prepared to receive them a certain requirement was made of him, that he should become perfect before the Lord."[50] The command further reveals something about Abraham, who for all his greatness and valor, was yet mortal, subject to weakness and temptation, and needing perfecting: "If we could read in detail the life of Abraham or the lives of other great and holy men, we would doubtless find that their efforts to be righteous were not always crowned with success. . . . But . . . they constantly sought to overcome, to win the prize, and thus prepare themselves for a fulness of glory."[51]

It is a pattern, continues Lorenzo Snow, for Latter-day Saints, upon whom "the Lord proposes to confer the highest blessings . . . ; but, like Abraham, we must prepare ourselves for them. . . . We also are required to arrive at a state of perfection before the Lord," a process that "requires time" and "much patience and discipline of the mind and heart."[52]

Such striving for perfection is in fact the only road to Zion, for as Hugh Nibley emphasizes, "Zion is perfect, flawless, and complete—not a structure in the process of building. We work for the building up of the kingdom of God on earth and the establishment of Zion. The first step makes the second possible."[53] Hence as the Lord once commanded Abraham to be perfect, so the Lord likewise commanded the Jews (Matt. 5:48), the Nephites (3 Ne. 12:48), and the Latter-day Saints: "continue in patience until ye are perfected" (D&C 67:13).

Abraham's own course in carrying out the commandment to be perfect is revealed in Epiphanius' assessment of Abraham: he was "perfection itself in godliness."[54] Abraham constitutes the pattern for the process urged by Moroni in his farewell passage in the Book of Mormon: "Come unto Christ, and be perfected in him, and deny yourselves of all ungodliness" (Moro. 10:32).

New Parents of a Covenant Community

The Lord's command to Abraham was immediately followed by a promise: "And I will make my covenant between me and thee, and I will multiply thee exceedingly" (Gen. 17:2). At this, "Abraham fell on his face" (Gen. 17:3) and, adds the Joseph Smith Translation, "called upon the name of the Lord" (JST Gen. 17:3). The Lord then proceeded to explain that the new community to come through Abraham's loins would be a covenant community, founded on ordinances revealed from heaven. As recounted in the Joseph Smith Translation:

> And God talked with him, saying, My people have gone astray from my precepts, and have not kept mine ordinances, which I gave unto their fathers; and they have not observed mine anointing, and the burial, or baptism wherewith I commanded them; but have turned from the commandment, and taken unto themselves the washing of children, and the blood of sprinkling; and have said that the blood of the righteous Abel was shed for sins; and have not known wherein they are accountable before me. But as for thee, behold, I will make my covenant with thee, and thou shalt be a father of many nations. And this covenant I make, that thy children may be known among all nations. Neither shall thy name any more be called Abram, but thy name shall be called Abraham; for, a father of many nations have I made thee. And I will make thee exceedingly fruitful, and I will make nations of thee, and kings shall come of thee, and of thy seed. And I will establish a covenant of circumcision with thee, and it shall be my covenant between me and thee, and thy seed after thee, in their generations; that thou mayest know for ever that children are not accountable before me until they are eight years old. And thou shalt observe to keep all my covenants wherein I covenanted with thy fathers; and thou shalt keep the commandments which I have given thee with mine own mouth, and I will be a God unto thee and thy seed after thee. (JST Gen. 17:4–12)

For Abraham personally, the commandment and God's explanation of it pointed him not only back to his forefathers but also forward to his exceedingly numerous posterity, now memorialized by the momentous change in his very name. As related in other translations, "Your name," declared the Almighty, "will no longer be Abram, *Exalted Father*, but Abraham, *Father of a Multitude*,[55] for I will make you the father of a multitude[56] [or 'host'[57] or 'throng' (FBM Gen. 17:5)] of nations" (GNTCBS Gen. 17:5). The rabbis pointed out that the additional letter added to Abraham's name, the *he* (pronounced "hey") is one of the letters from the personal name of the God of Israel, Jehovah (*Yahweh*),[58] a fact perhaps symbolizing that God was sharing part of His glory and divine nature with Abraham.

As noted by a seventeenth-century clergyman, God's covenant to Abraham of a multitudinous posterity was thereby "sealed" in his very name.[59] Becoming a father of many nations was one of the blessings that Abraham had long sought (Abr. 1:2), probably indicating that it was a blessing promised earlier to Abraham's patriarchal forebears. In fact, God's promise to Enoch—as recorded in the Book of Moses (Moses 7:51–52)—that his seed would inhabit all nations until the end of time may well have been the promise Abraham was seeking.

In Abraham's case, however, this promise seemed particularly to point to Abraham's mission: not to ascend to Enoch's Zion as Abram, or "exalted father," but to be the founder of the multitudinous Zion to be built anew on earth—as Abraham, "father of a multitude." Abraham is the new father of the human family, receiving the same promise once given to Adam, as Abraham had read in the patriarchal records, that "a multitude of nations shall come of thee" (D&C 107:55). It is the same concept reflected in the rabbinic tradition that by this name-change Abraham was given authority over all nations on earth.[60] From one—Abraham—would come many, a covenant community, even Zion, as Isaiah said (Isa. 51:2–3).

And the mother of this community would, after her decades of waiting and faith and faithfulness, be Sarah, as the Lord proceeded to explain: "As for Sarai your wife, you are no longer to call her Sarai; her name will be Sarah. I will bless her and will surely give you a son by her. I will bless her so that she will be the mother of nations; kings of peoples will come from her" (NIV Gen. 17:15–16). Sarai's new status was thereby reflected in her new name, Sarah, which connoted royalty[61] and "denoted that henceforth she would be 'a princess for all mankind.'"[62] Her inclusion in the covenant was neither incidental nor an afterthought, but an essential part of God's blessing to Abraham, who was now being crowned, according to Jewish tradition, through the merit of his wife Sarah.[63] Abraham and Sarah were to "share a spiritual role which [would] reach out unto the nations of the world. He was to become . . . 'the father of a multitude of nations' and she 'a princess to the entire world.' Abraham could not be 'a father of multitudes' if Sarah were not crowned as a 'mother' of this multitude."[64]

But this bestowal of her new name may have also been a divine affirmation of the mothering role she had already played for decades. For during her long agonizing wait to become a biological mother, Sarah had been a mother indeed to those around her as she had reached out in righteousness and compassion to those needing her assistance, spiritually and temporally. Sarah is the great example of what Sister Sheri L. Dew taught when, speaking to Latter-day Saint women, she explained:

> Are we not all mothers? . . . For reasons known to the Lord, some women are required to wait to have children. This delay is

not easy for any righteous woman. But the Lord's timetable for each of us does not negate our nature. Some of us, then, must simply find other ways to mother. And all around us are those who need to be loved and led. . . . As daughters of our Heavenly Father, and as daughters of Eve, we are all mothers and we have always been mothers. And we each have the responsibility to love and help lead.[65]

It is forever noteworthy that Sarah became a biological mother of multitudes only after her valiant mothering of multitudes to whom she reached out in maternal love and caring.

And now, having been designated by God as the biological mother of the chosen heir and given a name indicating "a princess to all the nations of the world,"[66] her husband was blessed through her.[67] In the words of Rabbi Joseph Soloveitchik, they "attained together, and only together, covenantal sanctity, being elected by God to be the founders" of God's people and community,[68] for "there is no covenant without Sarah. . . . The covenant was entrusted to the two, man and woman."[69] As pointed out by Rabbi Adin Steinsaltz, of the few people in the Bible who undergo a change of name, the only woman to be granted the privilege was Sarah. Hence the dual change of name of both Abraham and Sarah "hints at a change of essence in both Abraham and Sarah's being, in their whole way of life."

It is a profound transformation which involved them both equally, which had a double dimension, Abraham and Sarah together. One striking indication of this duality is the recurrent mention of the two as one unit—'Abraham and Sarah'—which is not found elsewhere in the Bible. . . . They are depicted as a team, as a couple, and invariably as equals. . . . Abraham and Sarah saw themselves (and are thus seen by future generations) not as a couple raising a family, but as a people building a society, realizing an ideal: parents of a nation.[70]

They were, in other words, the parents and founders of Zion, whose inhabitants forever after would be commanded to their forefather and foremother.

Some time had elapsed since Abraham and Sarah had relinquished the joyful expectation that their marital partnership would include participating in the greatest of God's promises to Abraham—that he would have posterity. Now, to suddenly learn that their original expectation was correct overwhelmed Abraham with emotion, and he "fell on his face and rejoiced"[71] or laughed for joy.[72] "It was a laugh of joy and faith," notes a modern Jewish writer.[73] Abraham laughed, explained Barhebraeus, "because he rejoiced in the tidings."[74] A midrash explains that "he rejoiced and was happy at heart that the Almighty had promised to perform this great miracle for him."[75] Hence his falling to the ground was out of joyful worship, not doubt or disbelief. "Against hope [he] believed in hope," wrote the Apostle Paul, and "staggered not at the promise of God through unbelief," but "was strong in faith, giving glory to God." For "being fully persuaded that, what [God] had promised, he was able to perform," he "considered not his own body now dead, . . . neither yet the deadness of Sara's womb" (Rom. 4:18–21). Abraham's joyful laughter was forever memorialized in the name that God now appointed for the newborn: Isaac, meaning "he laughs" or "he rejoices."[76]

Rabbinic tradition commenting on this event speaks of Abraham as a kind of heavenly chariot surrounded by clouds of glory,[77] while Philo's commentary on what God told Abraham on this occasion asserts that the Lord "carried him off and brought him up from earth to heaven . . . to Himself, showing Himself clearly."[78] Such a sequence of revelatory events, beginning with God's appearance on earth and ending in heaven, is not unknown in scripture.[79] God's revelation was a continual unfolding of Himself and His ways to His friend, making Abraham's life a perfect illustration of Joseph Smith's statement that "when we understand the character of God, and how to come to him, he begins to unfold the heavens to us, and to tell us all about it. When we are ready to come to him, he is ready to come to us."[80]

In contrast to Abraham, the world in which he lived had gone far astray, denying not only the Atonement of Christ but also the resulting innocence of little children. And as Christ's atoning blood was foreshadowed in the blood of animal sacrifice, so now it would be foreshadowed in the blood of circumcision that God was now commanding. It was "a sign and a seal of God,"[81] says an Armenian apocryphal source, or in the words of a modern author, a covenant "written into the very organ of male regeneration."[82] And so would it be for Abraham's male posterity for many generations on the eighth day of life—a perpetual reminder that "little children are alive in Christ"[83] and not accountable until the age of eight years. For if circumcision was already extensively practiced in Abraham's day, it was only adult circumcision; the circumcision of infants was something new.[84] Beginning with Abraham, infants in Zion would bear the mark in their own bodies of the future shedding of Christ's blood that had already made them "alive in Christ."

Only with the advent of Christ, and the shedding of His blood that was foreshadowed by circumcision, would the law of circumcision be fulfilled and the requirement cease.[85] But the underlying spiritual reality represented by the circumcision would continue, the reality spoken by the Book of Mormon prophet Jacob, who foretold woe not for the uncircumcised of body, but for the uncircumcised of heart (2 Ne. 9:33). Said the the early Church Father Ambrose: "Bodily circumcision is a sign of spiritual circumcision. Therefore the sign remained until the truth arrived. The Lord Jesus arrived, [who] circumcises the whole person in truth, not a minor bodily member in sign. He abolished the sign; he installed the truth."[86]

Abraham was already living the truth; he would now bear the sign, though advanced in years. One might ask, though, if this had been God's plan for him all along, why did God wait until Abraham was so old? A rabbinic text answers that it was in order to demonstrate, by Abraham's own willingness to undergo this surgery, that it is never too late to convert.[87] But perhaps also that the forefather of the Savior might bear in his own flesh, aged though it had become, a sign of the blood to be shed by Jesus. Abraham's blood had not been shed on the altar in Ur when the angel of the presence had protected him from the raised knife. Now, God was asking for Abraham to voluntarily shed a little of his own blood, foreshadowing the voluntary and supreme sacrifice of the greatest of his offspring, the Lord Jesus Christ. And Abraham, true to the charge, and in perfect emulation of his Savior, "hastened to perform God's precept with eagerness and joy, not for reward nor through fear of punishment, but out of love."[88] It is a striking similitude of the Savior's acceptance of the burden asked of Him, who responded to the Father, "Thy will be done, and the glory be thine forever" (Moses 4:2), and then followed through by "lov[ing] the world, even unto the laying down of [his] life for the world" (Ether 12:33).

The pain of surgery and its aftermath were, as recounted in Jewish tradition, one of the trials of Abraham—he "felt the pain"[89]—but his concern, as always, was for others, beginning with those who were circumcised on the same day—"part of the trial lay precisely in putting so many loved ones to such pain."[90] His thoughts reached out also to potential converts whom this new requirement might dissuade from accepting the gospel. Inquiring of the Lord on this point, Abraham was told not to worry, that the Lord was in charge and was the Protector of him and the world.[91]

As soon as he had received the command, Abraham proceeded to circumcise himself and all eligible males "on that very day."[92] Not later in the day, but immediately, as seen in the Jubilees narrative, in which no sooner does the Lord finish speaking with Abraham than "Abraham did as the Lord told him" in having all eligible males circumcised, including himself.[93] Jewish tradition recounts that Abraham "did not hesitate, and thought neither of reward nor pain, but obeyed" with "eagerness and joy." As for the other eligible males in his household, he persuaded them "with kindly words," explaining how fortunate they all were to be singled out by God and invited to keep this new commandment so as to enjoy a greater measure of the Divine Presence.[94]

This unquestioningly immediate obedience, particularly in this situation, stands out as one of the signal events of his model life. Having assumed for decades that the promise of posterity was to be fulfilled through Sarah, he had, as we have seen, finally abandoned that hopeful assumption, only to learn now that she indeed would become a mother. One would think that he would go to her first. But intimacy to make the promise possible would now have to wait until the Lord's new command of circumcision was fulfilled, thereby necessitating weeks of further delay before he healed sufficiently to beget a son. His prompt obedience on this occasion was later extolled among his descendants at Qumran as an example of the dedication expected of the members of the chosen community,[95] and is remembered to this day in Judaism, in which circumcision is always performed on the eighth day of life for each male infant, and preferably in the morning, "thus emulating Abraham in his eagerness to undertake a divine command."[96] His example remains a supreme illustration of the first and foundational law of Zion: obedience. "Instead of . . . procrastinating his obedience," emphasized President Spencer W. Kimball, "Abraham went out and complied 'in the selfsame day.'"[97]

Which day? According to the Pirke de Rabbi Eliezer, Abraham's blood was shed on the very day that would be commemorated by Abraham's Israelite descendants as the Day of Atonement,[98] which in turn would foreshadow the sacrifice of the Savior.

The Three Visitors

"The recuperation period for adult circumcision is long and painful," notes a modern Jewish author, "not least if the patient is ninety-nine years old and underwent surgery without anesthetic."[99] It was during this tender recovery period, just three days after his circumcision,[100] and while Abraham was yet "in great pain,"[101] says Jewish tradition, that Abraham was visited by three men.[102] Genesis reports the incident in elaborate detail, beginning with the statement that "The Lord appeared to him by the terebinths of Mamre" (JPST Gen. 18:1).

Why a terebinth, asks a midrash? Because Abraham's Israelite descendants are like the terebinth tree, which, although it can appear dried up and dead, yet can be revived with water. So also Israel, though they might long languish in apparent spiritual death, yet "when they will repent and the time of redemption will come, they will bloom and become radiant once again."[103] So latter-day Zion is destined to radiantly "shine forth" and become "fair as the sun, and clear as the moon" (D&C 109:73; 105:31; 5:14).

But the details of God's appearance to Abraham are not immediately clear in Genesis, for the statement that God appeared to Abraham is followed immediately by the account of Abraham's startling discovery of three men who suddenly appear before him, beginning with the detail that Abraham "was sitting at the entrance of the tent as the day grew hot" (JPST Gen. 18:2). It was the hottest part of a very hot day, say the rabbis, with the sun beating down mercilessly.[104] As one writer recounts, "Abraham sits in his tent door enjoying its grateful shade, and looking out on the plain of Mamre, from which the sun's fiery beams have driven men, birds and panting beasts to such shelter as rocks and trees and tents afford."[105]

Abraham, however, was not focused on himself and his discomfort, compounded by his recent circumcision, but was worrying for travelers who might need assistance on a day like that. "Notwithstanding the intense heat and his own sickness he still sat there to invite any stray passer-by."[106] When no one came, he sent his servant to go in search of anyone needing help, even though Abraham had planted trees for the benefit of travelers—rest stops along the way. When the servant returned without success, Abraham determined to go himself.[107]

It was then, says rabbinic tradition, that Abraham discovered the three travelers. "Looking up," says Genesis, "he saw three men standing near him" (JPST Gen. 18:2). Their appearance, according to a rabbinic text, was sudden, as though they had fallen out of heaven.[108] Rashi says that when Abraham caught sight of them, they appeared to be holding back, as if they did not want to approach and trouble him.[109]

Abraham might easily have remained seated, and simply directed a servant or subordinate to attend to these travelers. Or, says one writer, "he may wait their approach, leaving them to solicit his hospitality. Not he—Abraham rises."[110] A modern Jewish commentator notes that "excuses are always at hand and come readily to mind for the one who seeks them, but the true disciple of Abraham does not look for excuses."[111] Abraham arose and, despite the scorching heat, and "although he was in great pain from his wound, ran forward to meet them," according to the Zohar.[112] Genesis tells that upon reaching them he "bowed himself toward the ground" (Gen. 18:2).

Who were these three men to whom Abraham ran? As the story unfolds in Genesis, one of them is named as the Lord Himself. But according to biblical scholar Claus Westermann, the text cannot intend to really mean what it says here; it must mean simply that the messenger speaking had been sent by the Lord.[113]

So it is also in the Joseph Smith Translation, which expressly identifies the three visitors as "angels of the Lord" (JST Gen. 18:13, and repeatedly thereafter), an identification also made by Jubilees[114] and most rabbinic texts,[115] one of which calls the three men "ministering angels."[116] The Joseph Smith Translation reports the angels as saying that the Lord had told them: "I will send you, and ye shall go down now" (JST Gen. 18:20), and further describes them as "holy men . . . sent forth after the order of God" (18:23).

The last time the phrase "order of God" was used in the Joseph Smith Translation was in association with the translated city of Enoch: "And men having this faith, coming up unto this order of God, were translated and taken up into heaven" (JST Gen. 14:32). The term "holy men" is found in a revelation to Joseph

Smith (D&C 49:8), where it means, according to Joseph Fielding Smith, translated beings.[117] That the visitors to Abraham will actually eat is further indication of their translated status, for spirits (whether premortal or postmortal) could not have eaten, nor were there any resurrected beings at that time on this earth. And since, as Joseph Smith explained, "there are no angels who minister to this earth but those who do belong or have belonged to it" (D&C 130:5),[118] if Abraham's visitors were not mortal, they were necessarily translated beings.

But did Abraham recognize them as messengers of God? Most commentators presume that he did not, but the Joseph Smith Translation adds an intriguing detail as Abraham first addresses them: he calls them "My brethren" (JST Gen. 18:3). Nowhere else in the Abraham story does he use this form of address. But even without the benefit of the Joseph Smith Translation, the medieval Jewish sage Nachmanides held that when the three angels came to Abraham, he recognized them[119]—a view held also in early Anglo-Saxon tradition.[120] Likewise according to modern Jewish scholar Benno Jacob, Abraham's recognition of his visitors is indicated by both his words and his actions: nowhere else does Abraham call himself the servant of men, as he refers to himself in Genesis when he first greets them, humbly calling himself "your servant" (JPST Gen. 18:3). And as magnanimous and generous as Abraham was, he entertained enough guests that "he cannot possibly have received every passer-by in th[e] exuberant manner" in which he was about to entertain these guests. "Yet, he recognizes the messengers of God."[121] Modern scholar Gordon Wenham holds that Abraham's gestures of running and bowing to the three men "express both the warmth of Abraham's welcome and his deep respect for his visitors. Elsewhere in Genesis people run to greet long-lost relatives, and they bow down to the high and mighty."[122] And according to Van Seters, Abraham's "obeisance to the visitors [is] in a manner befitting only a king or deity. This is certainly more than a show of politeness."[123]

If Abraham did recognize these men, who were they? As we saw previously in an early Syriac source, Abraham had once exhibited similar enthusiasm when he bowed in greeting before Melchizedek,[124] who, according to Philo, was Abraham's close friend.[125] It is Philo also who adds a potentially significant detail to the Genesis report about these angels a few verses later. The verses concern one of the three visitors, reported in the traditional Genesis text to be the Lord (Gen. 18:17–19), but the angel of the Lord in the Joseph Smith translation (JST Gen. 18:17–18). Where the visitor says that he would not hide what he would do from "Abraham," Philo adds that the words spoken were actually "Abraham my friend."[126] If these were the words of the angel rather than God, the angel must have already been a friend of Abraham—suggesting the intriguing possibility that one of these holy men, these translated beings, might well have been Abraham's friend Melchizedek, who now resided in Enoch's translated city of Zion.

Abraham pleaded with the three angels not to pass by their[127] "servant," and he pressed them to stop and refresh themselves. "Let a little water, I pray you, be fetched, and wash your feet, and rest yourselves under the tree: and I will fetch a morsel of bread, and comfort ye your hearts" (Gen. 18:4–5).[128] Abraham then sprang into action and set in motion a "flurry of activity."[129] "It is worth noting," says biblical scholar Claus Westermann, "that no one is in a hurry elsewhere in the patriarchal stories; here it is haste in the service of others."[130] Commenting on Abraham's actions, a Jewish midrash notes that "the righteous act with speed."[131]

Abraham quickly enlisted Sarah's and the servants' help in preparing a lavish feast. "And Abraham hastened into the tent unto Sarah, and said, Make ready quickly three measures of fine meal, knead it, and make cakes upon the hearth. And Abraham ran unto the herd, and fetcht a calf tender and good, and gave it unto a young man" who "hasted to dress it" (Gen. 18:6–7). The young man, according to Jewish tradition, was none other than Ishmael, whom Abraham was training in the ways of righteousness and service, not just by preaching to him but involving him.[132]

When the meal was ready, Abraham set before his guests the tender veal along with curds[133] and milk, and then "waited on them under the tree as they ate" (JPST Gen. 18:8). As a modern commentator notes, from first to last the meal is "rich fare," as Abraham "specifies the use of . . . the finest and choicest of wheat flour," then "selects the calf for the main dish, a rare delicacy and a sign of princely hospitality among pastoralists," and even includes milk, which "was highly esteemed in the ancient Near East and was offered to the gods."[134] In the words of another scholar, "the 'little water' and 'morsel of bread' turn out to be a sumptuous feast" for the visitors.[135] The Talmud remarks that "such is the way of the righteous; they promise little, but perform much."[136] And personally waiting on these guests was Abraham himself, who "is completely at their service."[137] An early Jewish source notes that "our father Abraham was the greatest in the world, yet he served the angels"[138]—a telling example of what Jesus would teach, that the greatest among His disciples would be their servant (Matt. 23:11).

Abraham had understated not only what he would do for the meal but also for the washing of the visitors' feet. The bringing of water to allow a visitor to wash his feet was appreciated hospitality for ancient Near Eastern travelers, whose sandaled feet were constantly dusty.[139] But some early sources insist that more than hospitality was involved on this occasion. The Zohar states that the washing of the visitors' feet was done for the purpose of ritual purity.[140] And according to the Testament of Abraham—which, like the Joseph Smith Translation, calls Abraham's three visitors "holy men"[141]—it was Abraham himself who washed their feet.[142]

So said also the Church Fathers,[143] who saw in Abraham's act a foreshadowing of the Savior washing the feet of the Apostles[144] and an example, says Origen, of the New Testament's cleansing the dust off the feet as a testimony in the day of judgment,[145] which latter-day revelation similarly identifies as one of the purposes of the washing or cleansing of feet.[146] Judgment was indeed imminent for Sodom and Gomorrah, the final destination of these three angels.

That the angels' feet were washed by Abraham also indicates that it may well have been the priesthood ordinance described by Joseph Smith as "calculated to unite our hearts, that we may be one in feeling and sentiment, and that our faith may be strong, so that Satan cannot overthrow us, nor have any power over us here."[147] Apparently, these visitors from Enoch's Zion, where all were "of one heart" (Moses 7:18), were participating in an ordinance designed to unite hearts and strengthen faith in the momentous blessing they were about to pronounce.

By the Mutual Faith of Abraham and Sarah

The angels then asked Abraham where Sarah was—a question to which, as would soon become apparent, they already knew the answer. So why ask? The medieval Jewish scholar Rashi repeated a Talmudic tradition reporting that "the ministering angels knew, indeed, where our mother Sarah was, but they asked this question in order to call attention to her modesty and so to endear her all the more to her husband."[148] Another rabbinic source observes:

> Sarah was to be found in her tent. The verse in Psalms, "All glorious is the king's daughter within the palace" (45:14) means that it is the glory of a woman to be within her own home, as is exemplified by Sarah who was to be found in her tent. [149]

But the question regarding Sarah's whereabouts was asked in a voice that she also could hear, apparently intentionally so; for what the angel is about to announce, he wants her to hear. According to the Joseph Smith Translation, one of the angels "blessed Abraham" (JST Gen. 18:9) and said, as recorded in Genesis: "I will return to you next year, and your wife Sarah shall have a son!" (JPST Gen. 18:10). Why did the angel not say, as would be customary for the culture and times, that *Abraham* would have a son through Sarah? Perhaps out of the Lord's tender regard for Sarah, who had waited so long and sacrificed so much, having never murmured against God or her husband.

As the angel spoke, Sarah was standing just out of sight behind the tent door and heard every word. Before reporting her reaction, Genesis provides an explanatory preamble. "Abraham and Sarah were old, well advanced in age; and Sarah had passed the age of childbearing" (NKJV Gen. 18:11), or, as another translation has it, she "had stopped having the periods of women" (JPST Gen. 18:11). In the words of the medieval Jewish grammarian David Kimhi, "old age now weighed heavily upon them."[150] No wonder that despite Sarah's faith and faithfulness, and in the face of her biological reality, as an Islamic source observes, "by then her heart had lost hope of giving birth to a son."[151]

Genesis continues: "Therefore Sarah laughed within herself, saying, 'After I have grown old, shall I have pleasure, my lord being old also?'" (NKJV Gen. 18:11–12).[152] Sarah has been sharply criticized for her behavior, beginning with her apparent eavesdropping. But as Martin Luther pointed out, the very reason that she stood near the tent door where she could hear was that she was waiting to see whether Abraham had any further instructions for her, she having already personally assisted in preparing the elaborate meal.[153] She has been further criticized for what she said to herself, but Luther points out that the very fact that it was simply to herself, and not for the hearing of others, is likewise to her credit.[154]

And at whose words was she laughing? The traditional Genesis text, as translated by the King James, says it was the Lord Himself ("Lord") who overheard Sarah's response and asked Abraham why Sarah laughed. Not so in the Joseph Smith Translation, which makes it absolutely clear that it was not the Lord but merely one of the three men. Nor had Sarah personally interacted with these men, probably according to custom.[155] "She did not know," explains Nachmanides, "that they were the angels of the Supreme One."[156] It was at the words of an apparent human being, a traveler she knew nothing about, that she silently chuckled to herself.

And her spontaneous reaction reveals, as pointed out by some of Judaism's greatest scholars, that she had not yet been apprised of God's promise, made to Abraham shortly before, that she herself would bear a son.[157] Perhaps Abraham had decided that it was better to let Sarah discover it as it unfolded, or more likely, he been directed not to disclose it. Might God have even promised Abraham that he and Sarah would be visited by three messengers who would come to bestow this very blessing on Sarah and deliver the good news to her? If so, this might also explain how it was that Abraham recognized the three messengers but did not mention their identity to Sarah.[158]

What remains clear is that Sarah was caught completely off guard by the seemingly random statement of this unknown traveler, and this was the context for her silent laughter. The episode does not impugn in the least Sarah's faith in the Almighty. Indeed, her unfailing faith in the Lord and His purposes makes her as much a model for her daughters as Abraham is for his sons, according to the Apostle Peter, who had nothing but adulation for the great Matriarch. It is to this very incident and to Sarah's very words that Peter points as an example of a model wife: "Sarah was submissive to Abraham," noted Peter, and "called him lord." And, adds Peter to the women reading his letter, "you are her daughters, so long as you do good works."[159]

Sarah's laughter had been inaudible, but one of the visitors immediately asked Abraham, in a voice that Sarah could hear: "Why did Sarah laugh, saying, 'Shall I surely bear a child, since I am old?'" (NKJV Gen. 18:13). As pointed out by a commentator, "the speaker knows that Sarah has laughed, though he has neither seen nor heard her."[160] The visitor's disclosure of what no mortal could have heard is thereby a disclosure of his own identity as a powerful messenger of God.

But the question he asked raises further questions for the readers of this account. He knew Sarah had laughed, and he knew that she knew it, so why point it out? Was it perhaps to demonstrate to her his own divine power so as to increase Sarah's faith in the blessing he had come to bestow? Perhaps it was, as Ephrem the Syrian maintained, "a sign specifically to her who had not asked for a sign."[161]

But why did the visitor misquote, or not completely quote, Sarah, who had also said that Abraham was old? Because, answered the rabbis, "God . . . loves peace and hates controversy. If [the visitor] had told Abraham that Sarah considered him too old to have children, it might have resulted in strife between them. God wanted to maintain their love and peace."[162] Hence, "for the sake of peace, he merely omitted her remark about Abraham."[163] Nothing was more important to the Almighty and His messengers than maintaining between Sarah and Abraham that peace and unity that are the foundation of Zion, the place from which the visitors had come.

Even so, Sarah was startled at the visitor's words, and when she "discovers to her surprise . . . that her secret thoughts and emotions have been exposed," she "bursts forth from the tent"[164] to exclaim, "I did not laugh." To which the visitor replies, "Yes, you did laugh."[165] A casual reading of this story in Genesis may leave the impression that the visitor is simply insisting on being right and decides to argue the point and have the last word. But a different impression comes in light of the identity of these visitors as hailing from the city of Enoch, that pristine place pulsating with perfect love (Moses 7:18). This is a visitor not prone to argue and who has no reason to insist on being right or having the last word. Why then does he correct Sarah? Perhaps again to convince her of his divine authority and yet again increase her faith in the priesthood blessing he has come to give Abraham.

The angel then added, as reported in Genesis: "Is anything too hard for the LORD?"[166] But perhaps this translation, as one modern scholar insists, "misses . . . the marvellous element of [the Lord's] promise and the power it contains over human weakness and limitations."[167] Other translations render the angel's words as: "Is anything too difficult for the LORD?"[168] "Is anything impossible for the LORD?" (REB Gen. 18:14). "Is anything beyond the LORD?"[169] "Is anything too marvelous for the LORD to do?"[170] "Is anything too wondrous for the LORD?" (JPST Gen. 18:14). "Is anything too wonderful for the LORD?" (NRSV Genesis 18:14).[171]

The words refer not only to the miracle for Abraham and Sarah, according to the Zohar, but also to that future day when the Lord will miraculously bring to pass the resurrection of the dead, the great renewal.[172] But the words also refer, according to Christian scripture, to the birth of Him who would make the Resurrection possible. Many centuries after the angel spoke to Sarah, another angel would speak to another beautiful Hebrew woman, Mary, about the miraculous birth of her son, and would then mention the imminent birth of John to her relative Elizabeth, an old and barren woman. "For with God," the angel would declare to Mary, "nothing shall be impossible" (Luke 1:37)—an intentional allusion, say scholars, to Mary's ancestor Sarah and her miraculous birth.[173]

And if Mary's faith would be bolstered by the allusion to her ancestor Sarah, Sarah's faith was bolstered by the Son to be miraculously born to Mary. In fact, it was Sarah's faith in the Son of God, her future Descendant through the son she would soon bear, that effectuated the miracle allowing Sarah to become a mother. "Neither at any time," says Moroni, "hath any wrought miracles until after their faith; wherefore they first believed in the Son of God" (Ether 12:18). Sarah's belief in Jesus opened the door for her to become the mother of Isaac, and hence foremother of Jesus.

Accordingly, as stated in the New Testament, the blessing of Isaac came on the strength not only of Abraham's faith—"who against hope believed in hope" (Rom. 4:18)—but also of Sarah's, who "through faith . . . herself received strength to conceive seed, and was delivered of a child when she was past age, because she judged him faithful who had promised" (Heb. 11:11).[174] And as faith opens spiritual vistas of new vision, so Sarah's prophetic powers were such that as Jewish tradition remembers, she was also known as a seer; "she foresaw Israel's history, and prayed to God to assist them in their tribulations."[175] Meanwhile, in her long wait, she showed her faith by her works in "her unabated zeal in gathering converts," for which God rewarded her with the desire of her heart.[176]

It was the mutual faith of Abraham and Sarah in the Lord Jesus Christ that qualified them to become parents of Israel (see Heb. 11:12; and Rom. 4:16–22). Indeed, the blessing left that momentous day by the three visitors from Zion was effective for both Abraham and Sarah: Jewish tradition remembers that Abraham was healed from his circumcision.[177] Moreover, according to the Zohar, the blessing left upon them actually looked forward to the day of resurrection, when they would be restored to their pristine youth.[178] Only then, as latter-day revelation makes clear, would they ultimately realize the promise of posterity as innumerable as the stars in heaven and the sand on the seashore (D&C 132:19–37).

The blessing left on Abraham and Sarah was thus an affirmation of their eternal marriage covenant, which is of more than historical interest to Latter-day Saints who enter into that same covenant with the same promises. For as George Q.

Cannon, member of the First Presidency, reminded the Latter-day Saints in general conference,

> God has . . . promised us that we shall sit upon thrones, that we shall have crowns, and that we shall have a posterity as numerous as the stars in heaven, as countless as the sand upon the sea shore; for, said He, "I seal upon you the blessings of kingdoms, of thrones, of principalities, of powers, and of dominions. I seal upon you the blessings of Abraham, of Isaac, and of Jacob. I seal upon you the promise that you shall come forth in the morning of the first resurrection clothed with glory, immortality and eternal lives." These are the promises that are made to the Latter-day Saints.... The Lord promised unto Abraham that as the stars of heaven were innumerable in multitude, and as the sand on the sea shore was countless, so his seed should be. That same promise has been sealed upon your heads, ye Latter-day Saints who have been faithful.[179]

Pleading for Sodom and the World

Having left their blessing on Abraham and Sarah, the three angels "rose up from thence" (Gen. 18:16)—from, as noted by the Jewish scholar Sforno, "the house where they had experienced kind hospitality."[180] Abraham is remembered in Jewish tradition as the one who was beloved not only by God, but by humans and angels.[181] The three angels then "looked toward Sodom" (Gen. 18:16). That poignant look emphasizes the distinctiveness of Abraham's Zion, for as Samson Raphael Hirsch observes, "Sodom offered the most striking contrast to the pure, pristine environment which the three men were just preparing to leave."[182]

At this point the Genesis narrative tells of a remarkable dialogue between Abraham and God, beginning with God's soliloquy that He will not hide what He will do from Abraham. But the Joseph Smith Translation makes it clear that the dialogue is still between Abraham and one of the angels: "And the *angel of the* Lord said, Shall I hide from Abraham that thing which *the Lord will* do *for him* . . ." (JST Gen. 18:17; changes from King James in italics).

The Genesis verse continues, telling why Abraham will be taken into confidence:

> Seeing that Abraham shall surely become a great and mighty nation, and all the nations of the earth shall be blessed in him? For I know him, that he will command his children and his household after him, and they shall keep the way of the LORD, to do justice and judgment [or "righteousness and justice,"[183] or

"what is just and right"[184]; that the LORD may bring upon
Abraham that which he has spoken of him (Gen. 18:18–19).

Even though it is the angel speaking, he does so with authority from the One
who sent him, making this an illustration, as Jewish tradition insists, of the principle announced by the prophet Amos that "the Lord GOD will do nothing, but
he revealeth his secret unto his servants the prophets" (Amos 3:7).[185]

And what was the "way of the Lord" that Abraham would teach to his
posterity? It meant nothing less, says Jewish tradition, than to emulate the qualities of the Almighty himself: "As He is righteous, so you be righteous; as He is
compassionate, so you be compassionate."[186] In short, "'the way of the Lord' is the
exercise of love," says a midrash,[187] and doing "justice and righteousness" includes
"being kind and sympathetic" by doing acts such as "consoling the bereaved and
visiting the sick, all in emulation of Abraham[188] and in fulfillment of his precious
legacy.

This declaration about Abraham teaching his children to keep the way of the
Lord became an important part of the Abrahamic heritage in Judaism, which
deemed it a religious duty of the father to provide proper education for his children.[189] And according to J. H. Hertz, "The last injunction of the true Jewish
father to his children is that they walk 'in the way of the LORD' and live lives of
probity and goodness," a duty that gave rise to the practice of the so-called "ethical
will" in medieval European Jewry whereby the departing father would leave his
last exhortation to his children.[190] Only Latter-day Saints know the ancient roots
of such a practice: it was Abraham himself who wrote the Book of Abraham
expressly "for the benefit of my posterity that shall come after me" (Abr. 1:31).

Abraham's efforts to teach and bless his posterity would be an important part
of his legacy, an enduring example for that posterity to do the same. "Abraham's
desire to do God's will in all things," stated President Spencer W. Kimball, "led
him to preside over his family in righteousness. Despite all his other responsibili-
ties, he knew that if he failed to teach and exemplify the gospel to his children he
would have failed to fulfill the most important stewardship he had received. . . .
Fathers and mothers, your foremost responsibility is your family."[191]

Having determined to confide in Abraham, the angel proceeded to explain that
part of their mission was to destroy Sodom and Gomorrah (JST Gen. 18:19–23),[192]
and the three angels then walked away toward their destination. Having rejoiced in
what the Qur'an calls the "glad tidings"[193] brought to him—namely the priesthood
blessing just delivered concerning the son to be born to Sarah—Abraham is
suddenly grieved for the inhabitants of the cities about to be destroyed. He could
easily have been safe and satisfied with the great blessing he had been promised, but
felt so deeply pained for the fate of his fellow men—whom he had befriended and

even rescued—that he could not help but talk this over with God. Following the path of the three angels who had gone on ahead, Abraham "drew near to Sodom," apparently reaching the height near Hebron where he could see Sodom and all the valley below, and, as the Joseph Smith Translation makes clear, began praying to Him who had sent the angels (JST Gen. 18:25).[194]

Then, according to Rashi[195] (and seemingly the Joseph Smith Genesis Translation[196]), God actually appeared to Abraham—a remarkable fact considering what was on Abraham's mind. For Abraham was about to question the Almighty and even negotiate with him over the fate of the Sodomites, to whom he had been a friend. Abraham was much exercised, and God not only paid attention, but went to the trouble of coming to earth to hear his friend Abraham in person. "Our heavenly father is more liberal in his views," stated Joseph Smith, "and boundless in his mercies and blessings, than we are ready to believe or receive. . . . He will be inquired of by his children."[197] Nowhere is this better illustrated than in this incident with Abraham, surely "the most remarkable instance of human intervention" on record.[198] According to the Qur'an, Abraham was "most tender-hearted," and "began to plead . . . for Lot's people"[199] with such intensity that could have easily jeopardized Abraham's own status with the Lord. A rabbinical source states that "none prayed with such fervor as Abraham" on this occasion.[200] As noted by J. H. Hertz, "Abraham proves true to his new name and embraces in his sympathy all the children of men. Even the wicked inhabitants of Sodom were his brothers, and his heart overflows with sorrow over their doom."[201]

Far from being angry at Abraham's pleading, the Lord allowed Himself to be interrogated. In fact, He listened patiently to Abraham and "heard him out"[202] and answered his questions. Abraham realized, notes a modern rabbi, "that praying is a dialogue. It is talking with God."[203]

But what a strange dialogue this! "Wilt thou," began Abraham, "also destroy the righteous with the wicked?" Surely, Abraham insisted, God would not destroy the place if fifty righteous souls were there. "That be far from thee to do after this manner, to slay the righteous with the wicked: and that the righteous should be as the wicked, that be far from thee: Shall not the Judge of all the earth do right?" (Gen. 18:23–25).

As a modern scholar notes, "the tone of Abraham's pleading shows decisiveness and courage," and emphasizes "the inconceivability of God's doing anything uncharacteristic of perfect justice."[204] One thinks immediately of another prayer by another giant of faith, the brother of Jared, who just centuries earlier had told the Lord: "Thou art a God of truth, and canst not lie" (Ether 3:12).

According to the Midrash Rabbah, Abraham reminded God of His oath made at the time of Noah: "Thou hast sworn not to bring a deluge upon the world.

Wouldst Thou evade Thine oath! Not a deluge of water wilt Thou bring but a deluge of fire? Then Thou hast not been true to Thine oath. . . . If Thou desirest the world to endure, there can be no absolute justice. . . . Unless Thou forgoest a little, the world cannot endure."[205]

God responded that he would not destroy the place if fifty righteous could be found. But Abraham persisted. What if there were lacking just five of the fifty? Again God agreed.

And, continued Abraham, what if forty righteous souls could be found? Once again God relented.

And so it continued, with Abraham aggressively lowering the number and God agreeing, as they went down to thirty, and twenty, and finally to ten (Gen. 18:23–33), whereupon, as the Joseph Smith Translation tells, the Lord "ceased speaking with Abraham" (JST Gen. 18:40).

Who else but Abraham would have done such a thing, risking his own standing and the great blessings he had finally now been promised as he bargained with God over the fate of the Sodomites? Abraham did so, says a rabbinic source, "hoping that perhaps they would repent."[206] Hugh Nibley wrote of Abraham:

> His passion for fair play breaks all the records in his pleading for the wicked cities of Sodom and Gomorrah, to whom he owed nothing but trouble. He knew all about their awful wickedness, but still, Josephus observes, "he felt sorry for them. . . . " He appealed directly to the Lord's sense of fairness: "Wilt thou also destroy the righteous with the wicked?" (Gen. 18:23.) The impressive thing is the way in which Abraham is willing to abase himself to get the best possible terms for the wicked cities, risking sorely offending the Deity by questioning his justice: ". . . far [be it] from thee to slay the righteous with the wicked: . . . Shall not the Judge of all the earth do right?" (Gen. 18:25.) . . . It was not an easy thing to do—especially for the most degenerate society on earth. It can be matched only by Mormon's great love for a people whom he describes as utterly and hopelessly corrupt, or by the charity of Enoch, Abraham's great predecessor, . . . who "refused to be comforted" until God promised to have compassion on the earth.[207]

"O the purity of Abraham!" declared Ephrem the Syrian about the Patriarch's entirely selfless motives.[208] W. F. P Noble observed:

The tenderness of Abraham's heart is as remarkable as [his] purity. . . . Sodom was a sink of iniquity. Abraham could not but know that, and could not but hold the habits of its people in unutterable abhorrence. Yet see how he mourns its doom, regarding its sinners with such pity as filled the eyes of Jesus, and drew from his heart this lamentable cry, "O Jerusalem, Jerusalem, how often would I have gathered thy children as a hen gathereth her chickens under her wings, and ye would not!" . . . Sodom awakens all [of Abraham's] pity. Considerations of its enormous guilt are swallowed up in the contemplation of its impending doom. Truest, tenderest type of his own illustrious Son, with the spirit that dropped in the tears and flowed in the blood of Jesus, [Abraham] casts himself between God's anger and the guilty city. He asks, he pleads, he prays for mercy. . . . Compassion, pity, love for sinners, than these there is no surer mark and test of true religion. May they be found in us as in Jesus Christ!—as in Abraham![209]

If they are not found in us, the Talmud says, then are we not of Abraham: "Whoever is merciful to his fellow-men is certainly of the children of our father Abraham, and whosoever is not merciful to his fellow-men is certainly not of the children of our father Abraham."[210] According to Joseph Smith, "the nearer we get to our heavenly Father, the more we are disposed to look with compassion on perishing souls; we feel that we want to take them upon our shoulders, and cast their sins behind our backs."[211]

Jewish tradition tells that "the intercession of His saints is mighty with God."[212] So it was with Abraham, for "when the Holy One . . . saw how he pleaded . . . , He praised him"[213] and declared: "I love him."[214] He loved him enough to be questioned by him about the fate of fellow mortals in this scene that, according to one scholar, seems not so much a dialogue between a mortal and the Almighty, but rather a deliberation "of the heavenly council"[215] over the fate of mankind. God was deliberating with his friend Abraham even as had happened earlier at the Creation in the grand council in the heavens. In fact, one Jewish text even insists that the very reason God had apprised Abraham of Sodom's fate was so that Abraham would plead on behalf of its wicked inhabitants.[216] Hence the event provides a window not only into the soul of Abraham but also of God himself.

Abraham's example invites his Latter-day Saint descendants to do the same for today's world, according to modern prophets. President Gordon B. Hinckley declared:

I heard President Lee say once to a congregation in Europe that
"we of this relatively small Church could become the few who
would save the world from destruction, as occurred when
Abraham bargained with the Lord concerning the cities of the
plains." Tremendous is our responsibility and great and
marvelous is our opportunity as sons and daughters of God.[217]

In Abraham's case, however, not even his mighty intercession could save
Sodom and its sister cities, for ten righteous souls were not to be found there.
Sodom's fate was sealed, and its destruction could not be averted.[218] Not only were
their deeds vile, but they had disbelieved God's prophets "and reject[ed] the good
counsel which Lot had brought them from their Lord."[219] More specifically, "the
Holy One . . . gave them the opportunity of repenting," and had for decades
"made the mountains to tremble and brought terrors upon them in order that they
might reform, yet they did not."[220] So will it also be at the end when, as latter-day
revelation foretells, the Lord will lament that He has called upon the inhabitants
of the earth to repent not only by the mouth of His servants, but also by the voice
of thunderings, lightnings, tempests, earthquakes, and other forms of warning, but
all to no avail (D&C 43:25).

The angels proceeded and removed Lot and his family out of Sodom, which
the Lord then "overthrew in his anger, and in his wrath" (Deut. 29:23). He rained
down fire and brimstone, or "sulfurous fire" (JPST Gen. 19:24), from the sky, "for
the angels called upon the name of the Lord for brimstone and fire from the Lord
out of heaven" (JST Gen. 19:31). It was altogether as catastrophic, one modern
writer notes, as "atomic destruction,"[221] effected probably "by a great earthquake,
perhaps accompanied by lightning, and the ignition of natural gases and asphalt
seepages common to the region."[222] Whatever the exact means used, the Lord
"annihilated those cities and the entire Plain, and all the inhabitants of the cities
and the vegetation of the ground" (JPST Gen. 19:24–25). What had been the
most lush and fertile of all places was violently "overthrown as in a moment"
(Lam. 4:6), suddenly transformed into an utterly harsh and hostile landscape. So it
remains to this day, at the southern end of the Dead Sea, one of the most inhospitable and lifeless places on the planet.[223]

But even more than a dramatic historical event, the fiery destruction of the
wicked cities is a sobering type of things to come. "God . . . sent fire from heaven
upon them, and it is still unextinguished in its burning," is the ominous warning
found in an Armenian apocryphal text.[224] Jubilees asserts that the destruction of
the wicked at the final judgment will be "exactly as it was on Sodom,"[225] a
comparison likewise later made by the Savior as He explained to His Jewish audience about His Second Coming (Luke 17:28–30).[226]

Hence, according to 3 Maccabees, the Lord made the inhabitants of Sodom "an example to those who should come afterward" (NRSV 3 Macc. 2:5; see also Jude 1:7). The imminence of that future destruction is indicated by the statement made by President Gordon B. Hinckley that "all of the sins of Sodom and Gomorrah haunt our society."[227] And if the final fiery destruction of the wicked is foreshadowed by Sodom, then Abraham—unscathed though just miles away—surely foreshadows those of his righteous posterity who follow his example in paying a faithful tithe (as he had done with Melchizedek), for as stated in modern day revelation, those that are tithed shall not be burned at the Lord's coming (D&C 64:23).

In an early Christian writing, the Apostle Peter tells that even in Abraham's day what happened at Sodom might well have been the beginning of worldwide destruction, inasmuch as "the scourge was hanging over the whole earth." How was it averted? According to Peter, by the intervention of Abraham, who "by reason of his friendship with God, who was well pleased with him, obtained from God that the whole world should not equally perish."[228] Similarly, a Jewish source indicates that Abraham had earnestly pled that God "should not destroy the world."[229] The man holding the keys to establish Zion over the whole earth had pled for mercy for the whole human race, and obtained a reprieve. Mankind would be offered the opportunity to repent through the preaching of the gospel by Abraham and his posterity.

In fact, that posterity was the very subject of what the angel had said the Lord would do *for Abraham*. To be sure, Genesis never follows through to tell us what the angel knew the Lord would do for Abraham, nor does it relate the fulfillment of the angel's promise to return to Abraham. Such return is however recorded in Jubilees, wherein the angels later tell:

> We went to meet Abraham . . . , and we appeared to him as we had told Sarah that we would return to her. . . . And we returned . . . and found Sarah with child before our eyes, and we blessed him and told him everything that had been decreed concerning him—that he should not die till he was the father of [yet more] sons . . . and that he should see them before he died, but that it was through Isaac that his true descent would be traced . . . and one of Isaac's sons would become a holy seed, and not be reckoned with the Gentiles: he would become the Most High's portion, and all his descendants settled in that land which belongs to God, so as to be the Lord's special possession, chosen out of all nations, and to be a kingdom of priests and a holy nation. And we went our way and repeated to Sarah all we had told him; and they were both overjoyed.[230]

Such was the joy brought by the blessing of the messengers from the heavenly Zion for the benefit of the earthly Zion and the establishment of the future Zion—through the posterity of the son about to be born pursuant to that blessing. Once again, Zion above had been sent to open the way for Zion below.

A FACSIMILE FROM THE BOOK OF ABRAHAM
NO. 2

Explanation

Fig. 1. Kolob, signifying the first creation, nearest to the celestial, or the residence of God. First in government, the last pertaining to the measurement of time. The measurement according to celestial time, which celestial time signifies one day to a cubit. One day in Kolob is equal to a thousand years according to the measurement of this earth, which is called by the Egyptians Jah-oh-eh.

Fig. 2. Stands next to Kolob, called by the Egyptians Oliblish, which is the next grand governing creation near to the celestial or the place where God resides; holding the key of power also, pertaining to other planets; as revealed from God to Abraham, as he offered sacrifice upon an altar, which he had built unto the Lord.

Fig. 3. Is made to represent God, sitting upon his throne, clothed with power and authority; with a crown of eternal light upon his head; representing also the grand Key-words of the Holy Priesthood, as revealed to Adam in the Garden of Eden, as also to Seth, Noah, Melchizedek, Abraham, and all to whom the Priesthood was revealed.

Fig. 4. Answers to the Hebrew word Raukeeyang, signifying expanse, or the firmament of the heavens; also a numerical figure, in Egyptian signifying one thousand; answering to the measuring of the time of Oliblish, which is equal with Kolob in its revolution and in its measuring of time.

Fig. 5. Is called in Egyptian Enish-go-on-dosh; this is one of the governing planets also, and is said by the Egyptians to be the Sun, and to borrow its light from Kolob through the medium of Kae-e-vanrash, which is the grand Key, or, in other words, the governing power, which governs fiteeen other fixed planets or stars, as also Floeese or the Moon, the Earth and the Sun in their annual revolutions. This planet receives its power through the medium of Kli-flos-is-es, or Hah-ko-kau-beam, the stars represented by numbers 22 and 23, receiving light from the revolutions of Kolob.

Fig. 6. Represents this earth in its four quarters.

Fig. 7. Represents God sitting upon his throne, revealing through the heavens the grand Key-words of the Priesthood; as, also, the sign of the Holy Ghost unto Abraham, in the form of a dove.

Fig. 8. Contains writings that cannot be revealed unto the world; but is to be had in the Holy Temple of God.

Fig. 9. Ought not to be revealed at the present time.

Fig. 10. Also.

Fig. 11. Also. If the world can find out these numbers, so let it be. Amen.

Fig. 12—21 will be given in the own due time of the Lord.

The above translation is given as far as we have any right to give at the present time.

CHAPTER 9

Building Cities of Zion and Temples of God: Abraham, Ishmael and Isaac for All Mankind

Build a house . . . for boarding, a house that strangers may come from afar to lodge therein. . . . And build a house to my name, for the Most High to dwell therein. . . . that I may reveal mine ordinances therein unto my people.
—DOCTRINE AND COVENANTS 124:22–23, 27, 40

Dealing with the King of Gerar

The morning after the great destruction, according to Genesis, "Abraham hurried back to the spot" where he had stood and pleaded for Sodom, and "as he looked down toward Sodom and Gomorrah and the whole area of the Plain, he could see only smoke over the land rising like the fumes from a kiln."[1] Then, adds the Joseph Smith Translation, "God spake unto Abraham, saying, I have remembered Lot, and sent him out of the midst of the overthrow, that thy brother might not be destroyed. . . . And Abraham was comforted" (JST Gen. 19:35–36).

Lot had not been mentioned when Abraham had negotiated with God over the fate of Sodom. In fact, the Lord had gone beyond what he had agreed to by not only rescuing Lot and his family, but also by now comforting Abraham. Such was the friendship between the Almighty and Abraham, and such was Abraham's friendship with his fellow men. It is also "the first of several instances in the O[ld] T[estament] when a person or entire group is preserved through the protective power of a righteous individual."[2]

Abraham was comforted with respect to Lot, but judging from the depth of his pleading for the Sodomites just the day before, there would have been anguish in his heart at this moment when he gazed on the smoke of their destruction written in the sky. For although God spoke to Abraham to reassure him about Lot, no word is reported in reply by Abraham as he stares in silence, overcome at the destruction of his neighbors whom he loved. Like his descendant Mormon (an admirer of Abraham[3]) viewing the fallen Nephites, Abraham's soul would have been "rent with anguish, because of the slain" who had "rejected that Jesus, who stood with open arms" (Morm. 6:16–17). Those same open arms had welcomed Abraham at the throne, and would have welcomed Abraham's neighbors into the gospel if they had only been willing to repent.

If the region had had a newspaper, the headline might well have been, as two modern writers imagine, "Sodom and Gomorrah Wiped Out in Worst Disaster Since Flood."[4] Even so, the region without Sodom surely was a safer and happier place, improving the moral quality of life for Abraham and his community of Zion. Why then, as Genesis relates without explanation (Gen. 20:1), and with no command of God to do so, does Abraham suddenly move? Tradition tells that the overthrow had dramatically altered traffic patterns in the region, making it impossible for Abraham to offer his customary hospitality.[5] And seeing that travelers stopped coming "and his gold and silver did not diminish, he was grieved and distressed,"[6] exclaiming, "Why should hospitality cease from my house?"[7]

In addition, noted the nineteenth-century Russian rabbi Malbim, Abraham "desired to move about rather than dwell in one place in order to spread the knowledge of and belief in . . . God."[8] Abraham's life illustrates Joseph Smith's statement that "a man filled with the love of God, is not content with blessing his family alone, but ranges through the whole world, anxious to bless the whole human race."[9] This, then, would be yet another occasion in Abraham's life when, as remembered in Jewish tradition, his "preaching was sought by others who thirsted for God's Word, influencing him to move on to other areas . . . to further spread the true faith."[10]

So, instead of simply relaxing and retiring peacefully and graciously amid his substantial wealth, Abraham does exactly the opposite of what most men would do: he moves to a place where he could again use his time, talents, and temporal wealth to bless his fellow men and preach the gospel and continue to build Zion. His motives were not money or comfort, but rather love and service.

Abraham and Sarah moved south to a mountain region[11] not far from Gerar, a powerfully fortified city and one of the biggest settlements in southern Canaan[12]— another apt location to preach the gospel and bless mankind. The king of Gerar was Abimelech, who soon heard of Sarah's dazzling beauty and had her brought to the palace to become his queen (see Gen. 20). When she asserted that she was Abraham's sister, the king legally married her and heaped royal rewards on Abraham,[13] looking forward to consummate the marriage. In the abbreviated Genesis account, it is not clear how long she stayed in the palace, although Nachmanides states that it was many days.[14] Whatever the exact duration, it was long enough for Abimelech to experience a sickness that prevented him from approaching Sarah, and long enough for the women of Abimelech's household to suffer from an inability to conceive,[15] which took effect from the time Sarah entered the palace.

At some point Abimelech had a dream in which he was told he was a dead man because he had stolen another man's wife. Protesting that he had done so innocently, God answered that he knew that and had thus prevented Abimelech from sinning against God. "Therefore I did not let you touch her. Now then, return the man's wife; for he is a prophet"—the first occurrence of this word in the Old Testament—"and he will pray [or "intercede" (JPST Gen. 20:7)] for you and you shall live. But if you do not restore her, know that you shall surely die, you and all that are yours" (NRSV Gen. 20:7).

As Pharaoh had once done, Abimelech called Abraham and restored to him his wife, while bestowing on her a royal robe[16] and on Abraham an abundance of sheep, oxen, slaves, and a sizeable payment of silver. The king then asked for forgiveness and pleaded with Abraham to intervene to save the endangered king and his kingdom. Thus had God arranged it, so that only by Abraham's intercession would God save Abimelech. Rabbinic tradition remembers that when Abimelech asked for forgiveness, Abraham "forgave him with a full heart."[17]

Then, according to Genesis, "Abraham prayed to God; and God healed Abimelech, and also healed his wife and female slaves so that they bore children. For the LORD had closed fast all the wombs of the house of Abimelech because of Sarah, Abraham's wife" (NRSV Gen. 20:17–18). Jewish tradition even insists that Abimelech's wife had previously been unable to bear a child, but Abraham's prayer allowed her to do so.[18] His prayer is remembered in Jewish teaching as an illustration of the principle that "he who prays on his neighbor's behalf, himself being in need of the very thing, is himself answered first."[19]

Thus did another king of this world come to know the superior power of Abraham and his God. So great an impact did the event have on the king that he later approached Abraham to enter into a treaty of perpetual alliance, for, declared the king, "God is with you in all that you do; now therefore swear to me . . ." (NRSV Gen. 21:22–23). The well where the event took place was then called the "Well of the Oath," or Beersheba,[20] and here Abraham would reside. Perhaps the entire encounter with Abimelech was another divinely orchestrated opportunity that opened the doors of the gospel to a kingdom by first convincing the king. And for Abraham's forgiving and praying for Abimelech, the Patriarch is remembered in Jewish tradition as "an exemplar unto all."[21]

The Joy of Isaac

In answer to Abraham's prayer that the curse of barrenness be lifted from Abimelech's house, it was also lifted from his own house.[22] As Genesis reports, "the LORD visited [or 'singled out' (GTC Gen. 21:1), or 'showed favour to' (REB

Gen. 21:1), or 'remembered'[23]] Sarah as he had said, and the LORD did unto Sarah as he had spoken. For Sarah conceived, and bare Abraham a son" (Gen. 21:1–2). Her conception had been just several months following the visit of the three messengers,[24] and had occurred, according to Jewish tradition, on the first day of the New Year, Rosh Hashanah, the day when God remembers all Israel. In synagogues on Rosh Hashanah, the story of God's remembering Sarah is still chanted.[25]

For Sarah, it was the close of an incredibly lengthy ordeal of patience, perseverance, and trusting in the Lord. A rabbinical text states that the Almighty rewarded Sarah as He spoke these words: "You put your trust in Me: by your life! I will remember you."[26] Thirty-seven long years has elapsed[27] since God's promise to Abraham of a glorious posterity, thirty-seven years since Abraham and Sarah had first rejoiced in the expectation of the fulfillment of that promise. Why the decades of waiting and the long trial of faith? The rabbis said that it was to increase Sarah's joy when she was finally blessed with children,[28] and to deepen her and Abraham's dependency on each other and on the Lord.[29] In the words of Hugh Nibley, "It was Abraham and Sarah who restored the state of our primal parents, she as well as he, for in the perfect balance they maintained, he is as dependent on her as she on him." And "when both sides of the equation are reduced, the remainder on both sides is only a great love."[30]

Such love had seen them through the long years of waiting for fulfillment of the divine promises, the long period during which, in the words of Kierkegaard, Abraham "had fought with that cunning power which invents everything, with that alert enemy which never slumbers, with that old man who outlives all things—he had fought with Time and preserved his faith."[31] His aged wife, well past the season of child bearing, now miraculously bore a son in defiance of the laws of nature.

"What was beyond hope by natural processes," noted Church Father John Chrysostom, "came to be, not by human processes but by divine grace."[32] Never in the history of the world, says the Pirke de Rabbi Eliezer, had a ninety-year-old woman given birth.[33] Why did the Lord of life, the Creator of all, so arrange it? Why not grant the son of promise to Sarah during those many years when she could have conceived normally, without divine intervention? The answer would become apparent many centuries later when, as Church Father Ambrose observed: "An aged woman who was sterile brought [Isaac] to birth according to God's promise, so that we may believe that God has power to bring it about that even a virgin may give birth."[34] Sarah's miraculous conception, intentionally arranged by the Almighty as a miracle that had never been seen since the Creation, is surely one of the clearest similitudes of the birth of Him who would fulfill the promise to Abraham and Isaac that in their seed all nations of the earth would be blessed.

But there was yet another miracle, according to Soren Kierkegaard, a miracle not of biology but of faith.

> In an outward respect the marvel consists of the fact that it came to pass according to their expectation, [but] in a deeper sense the miracle of faith consists in the fact that Abraham and Sarah were young enough to wish, and that faith had preserved their wish and therewith their youth. He accepted the fulfillment of the promise, he accepted it by faith, and it came to pass according to the promise and according to his faith. . . . Then there was joy in Abraham's house.[35]

Jewish tradition remembers that Sarah likewise was "overwhelmed with sublime happiness,"[36] while the Joseph Smith Translation of Genesis reports her exclaiming that "God has made me to rejoice; and also all that know me will rejoice with me" (JST Gen. 21:5).[37] The Hebrew word here translated as "rejoice" can also be translated as "laugh," as most translations of Genesis do. "God has brought me laughter," Sarah exclaims, and "everyone who hears will laugh with me." She then adds: "Who would have said to Abraham that Sarah would suckle children?" (JPST Gen. 21:6–7). Why did she say "children" instead of "a child"? Because, according to one Jewish interpretation, she was keenly cognizant that this was the covenant son whom God would multiply into a host of covenant people,[38] a future foreshadowed not only by her words but by her very experience. In a passage clearly alluding to Sarah, the prophet Isaiah described the future of latter-day Israel:

> Sing, O barren one who did not bear; burst into song and shout. . . . Enlarge the site of your tent, and let the curtains of your habitations be stretched out. . . . For you will spread out to the right and to the left, and your descendants will possess the nations. (NRSV Isa. 54:1–3)

It is the latter-day Zion that Isaiah describes, using their foremother Sarah as a prototype. "Isaiah used the story of Sarah's barrenness," explains one scholar, "as a paradigm for Zion and for the future of the people of Israel. For . . . Isaiah the real import of the barren matriarch is not in the past but in the future: what God did for Sarah is evidence of what he will do for his exiled people," so that "the significance of Sarah's story is in its relation to Zion's story."[39]

Like Abraham, then, Sarah foreshadows the future of her posterity as she holds her beloved infant whose features, according to Jewish tradition, were very much like those of Abraham,[40] and whose name memorializes the inexpressible joy of both his parents. His name can also be interpreted, notes the Midrash, as "law went forth to the world, or a gift was made to the world"[41]—a foreshadowing of the latter days when "out of Zion shall go forth the law" (Isa. 2:3) to bless the nations through the seed of Isaac and Abraham.

Sarah's expression of joy would be repeated by her descendant Mary in contemplation of her own miraculous conception of the Son who would bless all nations. "Sarah's *Magnificat*," observed Christopher Wordsworth, "is a prelude" to that of Mary, "whose faith . . . perhaps was excited and quickened by a remembrance of what had been done by God for Sarah, and by His promise to Abraham and to his seed, to which Mary herself refers."[42] Sarah held in her arms, as she well knew, the son of promise, the future blessing of the world. She "feels that she is the mother of 'sons,' mother of an entire nation."[43]

But it was the joyous present that now filled her great soul as she tenderly embraced and—as Genesis specifically points out—nursed her son, thanks to the youthful rejuvenation she had experienced. Sarah's were the feelings that only a new mother can fathom, but even more; for her joy ran as deep as the longing of decades, and as deep as her sorrow at once having to abandon the idea of ever being a mother, thinking she had misunderstood the divine promises to her husband.

And if Sarah had been physically rejuvenated, so was Abraham: "God restored him his youth," reports the Midrash Rabbah.[44] The marvelous event would later be commemorated with coinage showing on one side an old man and a woman, and on the other a young couple.[45] Thus were their bodies renewed by the Spirit, the promise made to all who are faithful in obtaining and magnifying the higher priesthood (D&C 84:33). The promise may include the great renewal beyond the grave when the righteous, in the words of Brigham Young, will be "clothed upon with all the beauty of resurrected saints."[46] A Jewish midrash foretells that "in the world to come every righteous person . . . will be physically rejuvenated and enjoy renewed youth. . . . Should you wonder at this, consider Abraham and Sarah" when God rejuvenated them to have a son. "So too will it be with the righteous in the world to come."[47] Accordingly, "just as Isaac was born to Abraham and Sarah in their old age, so the righteous will be restored to the splendour of their youth in the world to come."[48]

With the renewal of Abraham and Sarah came, in the words of Philo, "a son of their own, a reward for their high excellence, a gift from God the bountiful, surpassing all their hopes."[49] It was the beginning of the real life of Sarah, according to Jewish tradition, the fulfillment of all her faith and dreams.[50] The news of Isaac's birth must have been heralded quickly; as imagined by a modern writer: "Swift runners reached the outmost posts of Abraham's pasture lands with the glad news—Abraham has a son—the Princess has borne Abraham a son!"[51]

In Christian tradition, the birth of Isaac is one of the clearest types of the birth of the Savior: according to Christopher Wordsworth, Isaac's birth is yet "another resemblance to Him . . . whose Birth is the cause of joy to all."[52] As Isaac's birth and name were foretold in advance; as he was conceived only by miraculous means; as his coming into the world brought great joy and rejoicing; and as it made possible the blessing of all mankind—so would be the birth of Isaac's descendant Jesus Christ, the Redeemer of the world, the Beloved Son.

Abraham "exceedingly loved" Isaac, says Josephus.[53] In fact, as a modern commentator notes, "It is doubtful that ever a son was born who was more loved than Isaac. His father and mother . . . , no doubt, rehearsed over and over again all the great promises of God that centered in him."[54] And just as the angel had predicted, Abraham did teach his son to keep the way of the Lord. The Book of Jasher tells that Abraham taught Isaac "the way of the Lord to know the Lord, and the Lord was with him."[55] Or, in the words of President Spencer W. Kimball, "Abraham built a strong spiritual reservoir for his son Isaac, a reservoir that never leaked dry."[56] But the parental instruction of Isaac was as much a joint effort as was the mutual faith that brought about his birth in the first place; Jewish tradition remembers that Sarah "nurtured him . . . , empowering him to become Abraham's covenantal heir."[57]

For his part, Isaac was, according to first-century Jewish sources, not only "a child of great bodily beauty" but also "excellence of soul." And "showing a perfection of virtues beyond his years,"[58] he "won even more the affection and love of his parents" by the practice of "every virtue and . . . zeal for the worship of God."[59] No wonder Abraham "cherished for him a great tenderness," being "devoted to his son with a fondness which no words can express."[60]

Ishmael and His Temple

A few years hence,[61] to celebrate the weaning of Isaac, Abraham put on what Genesis calls "a great feast" (Gen. 21:8) or "a great banquet" (NJB Gen. 21:8). It was a sumptuous spread, a lavish offering open to all and attended by a great multitude, including, as Jasher reports, "all the great people of the land" who "came to eat and drink and rejoice."[62] The event was also a harbinger, says Jewish tradition, of things to come, for "the Holy One . . . will make a great feast for the righteous on the day He shows his love for Isaac's descendants."[63] It is the same feast that Latter-day Saints look forward to as foretold in latter-day revelation (D&C 27:5–14).

The festivities that day for young Isaac were a summit of joy for the aged Abraham, who now had two sons whom he loved profoundly and, as Jewish sources say, equally.[64] As Abraham interacted with both during the celebration, Jubilees reports that he "rejoiced and blessed God because he had seen his sons and had not died childless. And he remembered the words [God] had spoken to him on the day

Lot parted from him. And he rejoiced because the Lord had given him offspring on the earth to possess it, and he blessed and praised the creator of all things."[65] For Abraham it was, to date, the greatest and most fulfilling day of his life.

Then, suddenly, in the midst of the joyous celebration, one brief communication from Sarah turned Abraham's intense joy to intense grief. She had seen Ishmael doing something, which the King James translators rendered as "mocking" (Gen. 21:9). The translation is as inaccurate as it is unfortunate, as shown by noted biblical scholar E. A. Speiser,[66] and is corrected by modern translations which read "playing"[67] or "laughing,"[68] a translation required by the Septuagint, which adds here: "with Isaac her son."[69] Jubilees describes the scene as follows: "Sarah saw Ishmael playing and dancing, and Abraham rejoicing with great joy."[70] Her reaction, as reported in Genesis, was to declare to Abraham: "Cast out that slave-woman and her son, for the son of that slave shall not share in the inheritance with my son Isaac" (JPST Gen. 21:10).

Sarah has received endless criticism through the ages for this seemingly harsh and heartless demand. But one Jewish tradition tells a different story: "God looked into Sarah's heart and saw no hatred for Ishmael there," but saw that she was motivated solely by "her passion to nurture Isaac to his full potential."[71] And not merely motivated, but actually inspired, according to Jewish sages. Her words to Abraham arose not out of impulse or anger, but she was "acting under Divine inspiration," so that, according to the learned Rashi, "Sarah's voice is the voice of prophecy."[72] Sarah well knew of God's promises to Abraham, repeated over decades, about the covenant race that would bless the world, and knew that her son, Isaac, was appointed to be their progenitor. She had even foreseen the history of her covenant descendants,[73] on whose behalf she now acted. And as the instrument of God, what she was proposing would also be for the benefit and blessing of Ishmael and his descendants, whose destiny had already been prophesied to Hagar.

Even so, Sarah's words came as a thunderbolt to Abraham, who, as Genesis tells, was "greatly distressed,"[74] or "troubled . . . very greatly."[75] He was "tormented," says Ephrem the Syrian, for he loved Ishmael just as he loved Isaac.[76] In fact, Jewish tradition remembers that "of all the trials that Abraham had to undergo" up to that time, "none was so hard to bear as this."[77] "How could he drive out people who were part of him, who were dear to him, who were dependent on him and helpless without him?"[78]

That troubled night, as Genesis reports, God told Abraham to implement Sarah's wish (Gen. 21:12–13), but tradition gives a slightly expanded version of the incident: "In that night the Holy One . . . said to him: Abraham! Dost thou not know that Sarah was appointed to thee for a wife from her mother's womb? She is thy companion, and the wife of thy covenant. . . . All that Sarah has spoken she has uttered truthfully,"[79] for she "also is a prophetess."[80] Therefore, "let it not be grievous in thine eyes."[81]

Genesis records that Abraham simply arose the next morning and expelled Hagar and Ishmael into the desert, parsimoniously providing them with only a little bread and a bottle of water[82]—for which Abraham has been severely criticized. But other Jewish sources insist that the highly abbreviated Genesis account fails to communicate the reality that Abraham provisioned them well with necessities for their journey, including gold and silver, and then actually escorted them on their way.[83] Islamic sources, from the descendants of Ishmael who was being "expelled," unanimously remember that Abraham did in fact accompany Hagar and Ishmael well into the desert.[84]

Islamic tradition further describes what transpired when the moment came for Abraham to return. Seeing that Abraham intended to depart, Hagar asked Abraham if God had commanded him to do this. When he answered in the affirmative, this remarkable woman declared her faith in God and God's servant Abraham by courageously stating that she knew that God would take care of them.[85] She was, in the words of a modern Muslim scholar, "willing to do this for God," while for his part, Abraham "is enough of a believer to say, 'I will submerge myself and rely on God.'"[86] It was yet another irony in the life of Abraham, that although he would have instantly given his life for these loved ones, he was now forced to leave them behind in the wilderness in obedience to God, to whom, according to the Qur'an, he prayed fervently for their protection: "Fill the hearts of some among men with love for them."[87] It was a prayer of faith borne of personal experience, recalling the time when as a young man himself, he had been imprisoned without food and water, but miraculously provided for. Hence "Abraham is only providing them an experience that he himself has already lived through."[88] Abraham then expressed his own love for both of his sons: "Praise be to God who has given me Ishmael and Isaac."[89]

Abraham obediently left, although, as Cyril of Alexandria reports, he "took it very hard."[90] Hagar obediently remained, but wept. When the provisions ran out, God sent an angel to protect and provide for them (see Gen. 21:15–19). Genesis recounts that "God was with the lad" (Gen. 21:20), and the Genesis Rabbah adds that the blessing of God rested upon him and all his household.[91] They were prospered,[92] says Jewish tradition, in answer to Abraham's continuing prayer: "Abraham prayed to the Almighty on his son's behalf, and Ishmael's house was filled with every good thing and every blessing."[93] The Qur'an describes Ishmael as one who was "truthful in promise, and he was a messenger, a prophet. And he enjoined on his people prayer and almsgiving, and was one in whom his Lord was well pleased."[94] An early Jewish text likewise pays to Ishmael the ultimate compliment of being one of the righteous.[95]

As Ishmael's descendants remember, Abraham returned to visit Ishmael many times. On one of those occasions, according to the Qur'an, Abraham enlisted

Ishmael's help to build "the Temple," or Ka'ba, a place "to which people might repair again and again, and a sanctuary."[96] The pattern for this Temple was shown to Abraham, says Islamic tradition, by an angel,[97] while the site itself was divinely designated to Abraham by a cloud or wind. Abraham and Ishmael worked together[98] as described by the Qur'an:

> Thus did we command Abraham and Ishmael: "Purify My Temple for those who will walk around it, and those who will abide near it in meditation, and those who will bow down and prostrate themselves in prayer." And, lo, Abraham prayed: "O my Sustainer! Make this a land secure and grant its people fruitful sustenance—such of them as believe in God and the Last Day." . . . And when Abraham and Ishmael were raising the foundations of the Temple, they prayed: "O our Sustainer! Accept Thou this from us. . . . Make us surrender ourselves [or, "make us both submissive"[99]] unto Thee, and make out of our offspring a community that shall surrender itself [or, be "submissive"[100]] unto Thee, and . . . impart unto them revelation as well as wisdom, and cause them to grow in purity.[101]

The temple for Ishmael—built, according to Islam, at Mecca—would share a number of similar motifs with the Jewish Temple at Jerusalem.[102] But it is the temple at Mecca—the holy Ka'ba—which remains to this day the longing of Muslims worldwide, who are expected at least once in their lifetime to make the sacred pilgrimage in which men don white robes, women cover their heads, Satan is cast out, and all walk seven times the circuit around the Ka'ba—all following the pattern, according to Islam, of that set by Abraham and Ishmael in order to attain purity and prepare for the very presence of God.[103] The seven circuits recall the seven ages of the temporal earth (D&C 77:7) in the Lord's "one eternal round" (1 Ne. 10:19).

Islam further tells that God commanded Abraham to summon all mankind to the Ka'ba; and still today when faithful Muslims go there, they do so in response to Abraham's summons as they arrive at the "famous place of prayer, the Place of Abraham, [which] is situated near the Ka'ba."[104] Three different times the pilgrims raise their hands to heaven and say, "Here I am, Lord." Near the Ka'ba they also see the famous black stone with the footprint, believed to be that of Abraham. In their most sacred of all ceremonies, Muslims literally believe themselves to be following the footsteps of their father Abraham.

The seven circuits echo the architectural pattern of the "cosmic city" of the ancient Near East, often constructed with seven circuits or with seven-tiered temple towers made in the "image of the seven cosmic spheres."[105] Seven is also, of course, the number of days of creation, as well as the number of millennial periods of the earth's temporal existence—all of which Abraham had seen in vision. And as to the shape of the circle itself, it is the shape of Facsimile 2, representing what Hugh Nibley called "One Eternal Round."

Muslim tradition holds that in erecting the Ka'ba Abraham was also laying the foundations of a sacred city. "When Abraham offered the [dedicatory] prayer, there was no town existing near the Ka'ba. There existed only the House of God. So Abraham prayed that in that wildest of wildernesses there might grow up a town, and that that town might become a place of security, affording peace to mankind," for "he wished [it] to be the abode of the righteous only."[106] If Ishmael must grow to manhood far removed from Abraham, Abraham could not be content without first establishing his son and laying the foundation for a Zion community with a temple at its center. Abraham would return frequently,[107] for "he longed for his son Ishmael."[108]

Four Gates and a Cosmic City at Beersheba

Even Abraham had his detractors, and back in Beersheba, he found that they seized upon this latest episode in his domestic life to criticize him. "If he were a righteous man," they complained, "would he have thrust away his firstborn son?" Years before, while still childless, his critics had charged, "If he were a righteous man, would he not have begotten children?"[109] Many had been and would be the occasions when, in obeying God, Abraham would risk his reputation for righteousness. It was one of the many ironies of his life, and a sacrifice he was willing to make. It is also an indication of the depth of his testimony, for as explained in the Lectures on Faith, "For a man to lay down his all, his character and reputation, his honor, and applause, his good name among men, his houses, his lands, his brothers and sisters, his wife and children, and even his own life also—counting all things but filth and dross for the excellency of the knowledge of Jesus Christ— requires more than mere belief or supposition that he is doing the will of God; but actual knowledge, realizing that, when these sufferings are ended, he will enter into eternal rest, and be a partaker of the glory of God."[110]

Armed with that knowledge, Abraham proceeded to press forward, inviting all to the Savior and His Zion. At the various locations where Abraham dug wells, he called them by names that would call to mind the reality and goodness of God. "By this he would arouse in [the people] an awareness of the truth by saying, Let us go and draw water from the well of the eternal God! The wells were a public necessity, and in this manner, the people were initiated into a knowledge of the true God."[111]

But the center for his missionary efforts was his own residence, where he planted a lush garden containing vines and figs, pomegranates,[112] and "all kinds of choice fruits."[113] As remembered in Jewish tradition,

He made four gates for it, facing the four sides of the earth, east, west, north, and south, and he planted a vineyard therein. If a traveler came that way, he entered by the gate that faced him, and he sat in the grove, and ate, and drank, until he was satisfied, and then he departed. For the house of Abraham was always open for all passers-by, and they came daily to eat and drink there. If one was hungry, and he came to Abraham, he would give him what he needed, so that he might eat and drink and be satisfied; and if one was naked, and he came to Abraham, he would clothe him with the garments of the poor man's choice, and give him silver and gold, and make known to him the Lord, who had created him and set him on earth. After the wayfarers had eaten, they were in the habit of thanking Abraham for his kind entertainment of them, whereto he would reply: "What, ye give thanks unto me! Rather return thanks to your host, He who alone provides food and drink for all creatures." Then the people would ask, "Where is He?" and Abraham would answer them, and say: "He is the Ruler of heaven and earth. . . . When the people heard such words, they would ask, "How shall we return thanks to God and manifest our gratitude unto Him?" And Abraham would instruct them . . . [in] how to praise and thank God.[114]

And the fame of Abraham the Hebrew spread far and wide, so that from all the corners of the earth men, women, and children, all the lowly and oppressed, the needy and miserable, the suffering and the downtrodden, the hungry and the naked, came to him to seek solace and help. All of them Abraham received with open arms. He fed and clothed them, comforted and consoled them and wiped away their tears. And Sarah, his wife, was sharing in the charitable work of her aged husband. Indefatigably she worked day and night. During the day she assisted her husband and waited upon the travelers, offering them food and drink; and during the night she worked assiduously and industriously, weaving, with her own hands, garments to cover the naked.[115]

Together Abraham and Sarah served in this labor of love to provide "food, drink, and companionship"[116] in this visitors' center designed to lift and bless people and bring them to Christ. It was also "a great school, in which men were taught the true religion, and gratitude to the Almighty God,"[117] and which apparently included a seminary for youth.[118] Abraham's highest priority, of course, was his own son: "Abraham wrote books" about the greatness of God "and taught them to his son Isaac."[119]

Tradition further tells of "an abundant spring of fresh water" at Beersheba,[120] recalling a similar spring at Hebron that Abraham used as a baptismal font. The blessing that Abraham conveyed to humanity was, according the rabbis, associated with a pool, by means of which Abraham cleansed his fellow men and brought them near to God.[121] It was nothing less than the ordinance of baptism for the remission of sins, following faith in the Lord Jesus Christ and repentance of sins.

So trusted and respected was Abraham that people came to him and asked him to settle their disputes. Unlike most judges, however, he did not stop with merely ascertaining a fair resolution between the parties, but "would not let them go until they had made peace with each other," exhorting them to "go in peace and love one another, and the Lord will love you and bless you always."[122] Abraham's peacemaking helps explain why he received such blessings, for, as the Savior would explain, "Blessed are the peacemakers" (Matt. 5:9).

Abraham's kindness was noised abroad far and wide, and guests seeking every manner of blessing visited him "from the ends of the world"[123] and "all parts of the earth," including "all who were unhappy and all who were in despair . . . , and Abraham welcomed them with joy and love."[124] His example would be emulated by a branch of his Nephite descendants, who, in their efforts to qualify to "sit down with Abraham . . . in the kingdom of heaven" (Alma 7:25), used the means that God had given them to liberally bless and comfort their fellow beings.[125] It is the same mission and opportunity devolving on Abraham's latter-day descendants who have received the restored gospel and are charged to bless all nations. "We are a world church with a world message and a world program," explained President Gordon B. Hinckley, "and our whole course is designed to help people, to lift them, to strengthen them."[126]

Judaism also would remember Abraham's example, and even the structure of his welcoming residence. Louis Ginzberg reported in the early twentieth century that Eastern European Jews were still calling a house with many doors a "house with father Abraham's doors."[127]

But Abraham's four gates opening to the four points of the compass were apparently more than hospitable architecture. Years earlier he had viewed the promised land from the heights of Mount Hazor,[128] and then was lifted up for a bird's eye view to apparently see the whole earth along all its four cardinal points.[129] Abraham's very birth had been heralded by a star that swallowed up the four stars at the four corners of heaven. And in Facsimile 2 of the Book of Abraham, Abraham drew four figures standing next to each other "represent[ing]

this earth in its four quarters,"[130] a motif recurring throughout ancient civilizations[131] and used to indicate a ruler's authority over all the earth.[132] The King of
Babylon, for example, bore the title of "The King of the Four Quadrants of the
Earth."[133] Pharaoh was enthroned facing in turn all four directions at his corona-
tion,[134] while at the ceremony celebrating the renewal of his kingship, an arrow
was shot in the four directions, wherupon he made a ritual walk around the field
and consecrated it four times.[135] And in the Egyptian Book of the Dead, "the four
quarters of Ra [are] the extent of the earth."[136] But there may well be even more
than geographic symbolism in Abraham's four quarters of the earth in Facsimile 2,
for the perfectly perpendicular angles of Abraham's design might perhaps represent
the exactness of his obedience to the covenants and commandments he had
received.

And with those commandments that God had given him had come his
appointment to the the cosmic kingship that all those other rulers falsely claimed
and memorialized by constructing "cosmic cities" following a pattern similar to
what Abraham built at Beersheba. Their circular shape was divided into four quadrants representing the four quarters of the world, with a gate at each cardinal
point.[137] The circular shape of these cities reflected the sun's circuit in the
heavens,[138] so that the king claimed to be "ruler of all that which is encircled by
the sun,"[139] again reminiscent of the shape of Abraham's own Facsimile 2.

Where did such concepts originate? The earliest evidence points directly to
Enoch, who in restored scripture is remembered as the great city builder (Moses
7:18–21). As the seventh patriarchal ruler, he was remembered in Mesopotamian
tradition as Enmeduranki, the king of a city whose god was the solar deity.[140]
Additional solar associations are suggested by the number 365, the number of
years that Genesis says Enoch walked with God before being taken (Gen. 5:23), or
the number of years the Book of Moses says Enoch's city was in existence before
God took it (Moses 7:68). In addition, the apocryphal Enoch literature makes
much of the solar calendar.[141] Enoch's city appears to be the pattern copied over
and over by monarchs of the ancient world as they built their cosmic cities.

A Temple in Zion

But the most prominent feature of those cities, and located at the center, was
always a temple,[142] "the largest, tallest, and most impressive building" of the
city.[143] If all this was patterned after Enoch's city, why does scripture not mention
a temple there? The Book of Moses does give an important clue when it relates
that "the Lord came and dwelt with his people" (Moses 7:16), for the single most
important function of an ancient temple was to be "a house for the god, his
dwelling place."[144] But apparently the intent of the Book of Moses is not to
describe the buildings in the city of Zion but rather the spiritual righteousness and

harmony of the people (see Moses 7:18), again reminiscent of the ancient cosmic city whose inhabitants are subject to the cosmic laws reflected in the city's layout.[145]

In the case of Enoch's city, its inhabitants included all those who had accepted Enoch's preaching and had moved to Zion, or, as John Taylor described them, "were gathered together . . . unto a place which they called Zion."[146] And if gathered, then necessarily to build a temple, according to Joseph Smith, for the object of gathering in any age of the world is always to build a temple.[147] Hence Brigham Young said that even though "we have no account of it," Enoch must have had a temple and officiated therein.[148] Since Brother Brigham's day, Enoch texts have emerged that expressly refer to a temple among Enoch and his people, and relate that Enoch taught his sons to go to the temple.[149] Enoch's cosmic city, built around a temple, was indeed the ancient pattern for the many temple cities that would later spring up throughout the ancient Near East.

Central to the theology of those temples was a re-creation of the original paradise, as seen, for example, in the Jerusalem Temple, which was viewed as a paradise where "the primal perfection of Eden is wonderfully preserved."[150] The description calls to mind Enoch's city being translated to the terrestrial paradise where, according to Jubilees, Enoch was "led . . . into the Garden of Eden."[151]

It also calls to mind the lush garden that Abraham planted at Beersheba, described in Jewish tradition as the "paradise at Beersheba"[152] and referred to by Nibley as Abraham's "model Garden of Eden."[153] The Zohar tells that Abraham restored the earth to its paradisiacal condition as the ground again blossomed in loveliness and "all the powers of the earth were restored and displayed themselves."[154] It was an echo of the first Edenic Zion, connected to the powers of heaven: one tradition tells that by planting his grove of trees to serve mankind, Abraham "planted a tree for himself in heaven which would produce the fruits of his reward,"[155] calling to mind Alma's similar metaphor used for all the righteous who plant the seed of God's word (Alma 32:28–43).

Would not Abraham's paradisiacal garden, so carefully laid out to mirror the cosmos, have had its temple? One of the sources cited by the famous medieval alchemist Nicholas Flamel expressly reports that Abraham did have a temple, following the pattern of his forefathers.[156] Having received the remaining temple ordinances from Melchizedek in his temple at Salem, Abraham now passed these on to the community of Saints over whom he presided. According to Elder Bruce R. McConkie, "From the days of Adam to the present, whenever the Lord has had a people on earth, temples and temple ordinances have been a crowning feature of their worship. 'My people are *always* commanded to build' temples, the Lord says, 'for the glory, honor, and endowment' of all the saints. . . . These temples have been costly and elaborate buildings whenever the abilities of the people have permitted such."[157] Abraham's temple at Beersheba would surely have been one of the most costly and elaborate of all, given the vast resources with which God had blessed him.

At least part of his temple structure at Beersheba, an altar, is mentioned by Jubilees, which describes in some detail the many kinds of sacrifices Abraham made thereon as he celebrated the seven-day Festival of Tabernacles that his posterity would later follow.[158] But the rabbis insisted that Abraham observed *all* the Mosaic laws, including those related to temple. Among the rabbinic texts making this assertion[159] is Yoma, the Talmudic tractate describing in detail the all-important temple ritual of the Day of Atonement. Yoma emphasizes that "our father Abraham kept the whole Torah," not just some of the laws and ordinances, but all of them.[160] And his performance thereof was meticulous and exacting, according to ancient sources.[161]

Hence, as Hugh Nibley has pointed out, "the works of Abraham center around the Temple."[162] Abraham was rebuilding the city of Zion on the earth following the ancient pattern of Enoch, even while the pretenders to Abraham's authority were building their imitations. Unlike those ostentatious monarchs, Abraham built no walled city or garrisoned castle or fortress, but an open facility with a door at each point of the compass, inviting all mankind to come and partake of his hospitality and learn of Zion. Most importantly, he built neither a palace nor throne for himself, but rather a temple for the throne of God. Abraham's entire resources were consecrated to the establishment of Zion.

Foreshadowing the Future Descent of Zion

The pattern of Abraham's cosmic city of Beersheba looked not only backward but also forward to the latter days, when, as Abraham had read in the patriarchal records, the Lord would gather His people from the four quarters of the earth to Zion, or the New Jerusalem (Moses 7:62), and would make bare his arm in saving them[163] and then dine with them in Enoch's city that would return to the earth.[164]

If we have no architectural description of Enoch's city as it was taken from the earth, we do have a description of it as it will return: it is said in John's book of Revelation to be "foursquare" with three gates at each point of the compass, for a total of twelve gates—one for each tribe of Israel, Abraham's twelve great-grand-sons by Jacob (Rev. 21:12–16). Similarly in 1 Enoch, Enoch describes heaven as having a similar distribution of twelve gates, three at each compass point.[165] The twelve gates also correspond to Plato's cosmic city divided into twelve parts for twelve tribes.[166] But it is the foursquare structure that remains the critical feature, bespeaking its wholeness and lack of defect, for the square was one of those "ancient symbols that conveyed the notion of divinely wrought perfection."[167]

Both architecturally and spiritually, Zion must be built on the principles of exactness and honor.[168]

Abraham had seen in vision the future descent of Enoch's glorious city of Zion, and the closer we look at what Abraham built at Beersheba, the more it reflects that city, not only as it was first built on earth but also as it will come again when the earth will receive her paradisiacal glory and when, as Brigham Young said, "Zion will extend . . . all over this earth. . . . It will all be Zion."[169]

Abraham's Sacrifice

CHAPTER 10

On Mount Zion:
Abraham's Offering of Isaac

They must needs be chastened and tried, even as Abraham.
—DOCTRINE AND COVENANTS 101:4

God's Request and Abraham's Obedience

The temple site for which Abraham is most remembered, however, is not at Beersheba but a place some forty miles north, the destination of an unexpected journey he was called to make while living at Beersheba. It is the startling story of his supreme sacrifice, the crowning event of his life. And it involves his beloved son Isaac, who according to the earliest sources was about twenty-five at the time.[1] Genesis announces the event as a test for Abraham (Gen. 22:1),[2] but the Zohar insists that Isaac "was also included in the trial."[3]

It began with a surprise conversation initiated by God, apparently at night.[4] Orson Hyde states that "the Spirit of the Lord came upon [Abraham],"[5] while Josephus tells that God actually appeared to him.[6] God addressed him by the name he had given him, the name meaning "Father of a multitude": "Abraham" (Gen. 22:1), or, according to the Septuagint, God called his name twice: "Abraham, Abraham."[7] To which Abraham responded in deep humility, "Here am I, Lord what willest Thou of Thy servant?"[8] According to Genesis, the Lord answered: "Take now thy son, thine only son Isaac, whom thou lovest, and get thee into the land of Moriah; and offer him there for a burnt offering upon one of the mountains which I will tell thee of" (Gen. 22:2).

In the words of a nineteenth-century writer,

> God bids him sacrifice the son for whom he had waited so many
> years, and over whose birth he had so rejoiced: He bids him sacri-
> fice his only son, the one link which there was between himself and

the promise that his posterity should be as the dust of the ground and the stars of heaven in number: He bids him sacrifice Isaac whom he loved, towards whom his heart yearned with infinite tenderness, who had made his home bright and joyous, and to lose whom would be the darkening of all the days he had yet to live. [9]

Josephus insists that this was not a command but a request,[10] a fact not apparent in the King James Translation "Take now thy son . . ." (Gen. 22:2). But this word "now" translates the Hebrew *na,* a particle of entreaty,[11] which translators of the stature of Robert Alter and Everett Fox say should be rendered in this verse as a request: "Take, pray, your son."[12] So also the preeminent medieval Jewish scholar Rashi held that the meaning of this Genesis passage is not a command, but God was saying: "I request of you . . . "[13] Jewish tradition similarly records the Lord as saying "please"[14] or "I have come to ask of thee something."[15] Standing face to face with His beloved friend Abraham, and looking him in the eye, God gently requests the sacrifice of Abraham's own beloved son, and then "keeps silent about his reasons."[16]

Many had been the commands that Abraham had received from the Lord, but never a request. It seemed to leave the door open for questions or discussion about the nearly unbelievable task the Lord had asked for. But the man who had pled with such fervor with the Almighty over the fate of Sodom now offered no dissent or discussion, no hedging or hesitation. He did not "stop to reason or argue with the Almighty," noted Joseph F. Smith, but simply "went . . . without complaining or murmuring" to fulfill what God had asked.[17]

Abraham could well have offered "a justifiable excuse," pointing out that what God had asked contradicted the prior promises, says Yosef Albo, "but he refrained from doing so, suppressing his paternal feelings out of love of God."[18] God had expressly recognized Abraham's love for Isaac in asking for his sacrifice, and it was indeed Abraham's love that was being tested: whom did he love the most, Isaac or God?[19] Such was Abraham's love for and trust in the Almighty that even in the face of this horrendous deed, and even when it had been put to Abraham as a mere request, apparently all he needed to know was what God desired. God's wish was truly Abraham's command, no matter how hard.

Abraham is the focus, but what about Sarah? "Has he told her where he is going? Has he said anything to her about what he is about to do?... The story does not tell us."[20] At least directly, it doesn't. But the lack of any protest makes it clear, as observed by one Latter-day Saint mother and leader, that "out of kindness to her," Abraham did not disclose what he had been asked to do.[21] He simply, as Genesis tells, "rose early in the morning and saddled his donkey"—he did it himself, although he had many servants[22]—"and took his two lads with him, and

Isaac his son, and he split wood for the offering, and rose and went to the place that God had said to him."[23] Before they left that morning, according to rabbinic texts, Abraham and Isaac said their morning prayers, as was always their practice.[24]

With the donkey carrying the wood and provisions, the party of four began the long walk northward and gradually upward to the hill country of Moriah, the destination designated by God. "The severity of the trial," notes Henry Blunt, "was unspeakably increased by the three days' journey."[25] The deed was not to be done upon sudden impulse, but only after due deliberation as he walked beside his beloved son carrying the weight of a terrible secret. "The secret was his alone," says Elie Wiesel; indeed, "he alone knew there was a secret—and he refused to share it."[26] He would keep his beloved son safe from pain or anxiety as long as possible, shouldering the entire overwhelming burden as long as he could.

It might, of course, have been different. God might, as Origen pointed out, have asked Abraham simply to take Isaac to the appointed place, and there asked for the sacrifice. But with Abraham knowing fully why he is going, the painful journey "is prolonged for three days, and during the whole three days the parent's heart is tormented with recurring anxieties, so that the father might consider the son in this whole lengthy period, that he might partake of food with him, that the child might weigh in his father's embraces for so many nights, might cling to his breast, might lie in his bosom. Behold to what an extent the test is heaped up."[27]

And what did Abraham tell Isaac as they walked along for three days together? Surely he had expected some day to impart to his beloved son his final testimony and blessing, but never under circumstances like these! And what was Abraham thinking as he walked along? "Notice the old gentleman," said John Taylor, "tottering along with his son, brooding over the promises of God and the peculiar demand now made upon him."[28] "We cannot conceive of anything that could be more trying and more perplexing than the position in which he was placed."[29]

Indeed, it would have been difficult enough to have even been apprised of Isaac's impending death, but Abraham was asked to do the deed by his own hand. Did God not abhor human sacrifice? Was it not a perversion of that true order of sacrifice intended to signify the future sacrifice of the Beloved Son? Had not Abraham himself courageously opposed human sacrifice in Ur? Had not God rescued Abraham when he was about to be offered up in a sacrificial rite? This new request was the ultimate of ironies. Nor was there anything in all the patriarchal records like it, for among the righteous, "nothing of the kind had ever transpired before as a precedent," noted John Taylor.[30]

And how could the divine promises through Isaac now be fulfilled? For "had not God promised great blessings *through this very son*?"[31] Thus Abraham was asked "to destroy the very thing that God had promised to protect and enhance: his posterity."[32] In the words of John Taylor, "It was not only his parental feelings that were touched,"[33] for "through the spirit of prophecy, [he] had gazed upon his posterity as they should exist through the various ages of time. And among other things he saw the days of Jesus [and] . . . was glad. And after all this, God told him to take the life of his son. What, and thus prevent your posterity from coming upon the earth as you beheld it in vision? Yes, and in one stroke of the knife blast all these glorious, . . . blessed hopes."[34] With Isaac, then, rested the future salvation of the entire world, the future of Zion, as Abraham well knew.

And what of the salvation of those already living in Abraham's Zion? As pointed out by Jewish scholars,

> What would happen to his followers and those who admired him if he slaughtered Isaac and the world learned that Abraham's teachings had been violated in the grossest manner by the teacher himself? His entire lifetime of achievement would have been nullified. He would have been despised, vilified, ridiculed.[35]

Well did one writer observe that what Abraham was asked to do "threatened to empty all the meaning from the story of his life."[36] And yet he also knew, noted President Spencer W. Kimball, "that God would require nothing of him which was not for his ultimate good. How that good could be accomplished he did not understand,"[37] for this sacrifice seemed "so contradictory! . . . It was irreconcilable, impossible!"[38] It was, says Jacques Derrida, simply the "most cruel, impossible, and untenable" thing imaginable.[39] Joseph Smith even indicated that "if God had known any other way whereby he could have touched Abraham's feelings more acutely and more deeply he would have done so."[40] God was putting His beloved friend to the severest test that divine wisdom could design.

No wonder that Abraham went, in the words of Spencer W. Kimball, "with breaking heart"[41] as he walked along with his beloved but condemned son, each step bringing them closer to the slaughter. In the Genesis account the journey is one of silence; we are not privy to Abraham's words, much less his thoughts or feelings that he could share with no one. His alone was the agony.

"On the third day," says Genesis, "Abraham looked up and saw the place far away" (NRSV Gen. 22:4). How did he recognize it? Jewish tradition says he saw a pillar of fire or a cloud of glory resting on the mountain.[42] Then, continues Genesis, "Abraham said to his lads: You stay here with the donkey, I and the lad will go yonder"(FBM Gen. 22:5)[43] and "we will worship, and then we will come back to you" (NRSV Gen. 22:5). Why did Abraham expressly say that he and Isaac would both return? Was he perhaps confused, not really knowing what he was saying? Was he carefully hiding the truth, knowing that he and Isaac would not really be returning? Or, as some of the Jewish sages believed, had the Holy Spirit suddenly prompted Abraham to utter these words, which were actually a prophecy?[44] Or, as another Jewish interpreter thought, did Abraham intend to bring Isaac's bones back with him?[45] Or did Abraham believe that God would resurrect Isaac on the spot, so that Abraham and Isaac would indeed walk back together?[46] Once again we are not privy to Abraham's inner thoughts as we witness his unstinting obedience.

Then "Abraham took the wood of the burnt offering and laid it on his son Isaac" (NRSV Gen. 22:6). The rabbis commented that Isaac's carrying the wood for his own sacrifice "is like one who carries his own cross on his shoulder."[47] Then, taking "the firestone and the cleaver . . . in his own hand," Abraham set out with Isaac, "and the two walked off together"[48]—hand in hand, says one midrash.[49] "Isaac broke the silence"[50] and "said to his father Abraham, 'Father!' And he said, 'Here I am, my son.' He said, 'The fire[stone[51]] and the wood are here, but where is the lamb for a burnt offering?' Abraham said, 'God himself will provide the lamb for a burnt offering, my son.' So the two of them walked on together" (NRSV Gen. 22:7–8).

In the Hebrew text, the words "offering" and "my son" can be read in apposition, making Abraham's answer ambiguous: was he merely addressing his son, or had he told him that he, Isaac, would in fact be the offering? Rashi insisted that Isaac now "understood that he was going to be slaughtered,"[52] yet he went willingly, "with equal heart."[53] In the words of Elie Wiesel, "The two of them [were] alone in the world, encircled by God's unfathomable design. But they were *together*. . . . Together they reached the top of the mountain; together they erected the altar; together they prepared the wood and the fire."[54]

Binding and Submitting

Genesis records no conversation between Abraham and Isaac on Mount Moriah, but at some point Abraham told him, perhaps in the words suggested by Martin Luther: "You, my dearly beloved son, whom God has given me, have been destined for the burnt offering."[55] Josephus records these words by Abraham:

> My child, having asked with myriad prayers from God that you be born to me, when you came into life, there is nothing that I did not take trouble with regard to your upbringing, nor was there anything that I thought would bring me greater happiness than if I should see you grown to manhood and when I died, I should have you as the successor of my realm. But since it was by God's wish that I became your father and again since, as it seems best to Him, I give you up, bear this consecration nobly, for I

concede you to God, who requires now to obtain this honor from us, in return for the fact that He has been a benevolent helper and ally to me. Since you were born out of the course of nature, depart now from life not in a common fashion but sent forth by your own father to God, the father of all, by the rite of sacrifice. I think that He has judged that you are deserving to be removed from life neither by disease nor by war nor by some other of the afflictions that are conditioned by nature to befall humanity, but that He would receive your soul with prayers and sacrificial rites and would keep it near Himself. And you will be a guardian for me and supporter in my old age, wherefore also I especially reared you, by offering me God in place of yourself.[56]

Martin Luther surmised that Abraham must have also spoken to Isaac of the resurrection of the dead and the fulfillment of the promise that in Isaac the world would be blessed: "God has given a command; therefore we must obey Him, and since He is almighty, He can keep His promise even when you are dead and have been reduced to ashes."[57] And Philo reports Abraham telling Isaac that "to God all things are possible, including those that are impossible or insuperable to men."[58]

Isaac replied, according to Josephus, that he did not deserve "to have been born in the first place, if he were . . . to spurn the decision of God and his father and not readily offer himself to the wishes of both, when even if his father alone were choosing this it would have been unjust to disobey."[59] Thus, as a midrash reports, "was Isaac reconciled to his death, in order to obey his Maker's command."[60]

Perhaps Abraham spoke also of the symbolic significance of sacrifice, that since its institution with Adam it represented the Savior's future sacrifice, and that Isaac's sacrifice—as the only human sacrifice that God had ever commanded—would be uniquely symbolic of that of the Savior.

Genesis reports that Abraham "bound Isaac his son" (Gen. 22:9), memorialized in the word Judaism still uses to refer to this event: the Akedah, or "binding" of Isaac.[61] Genesis contains not the slightest hint of any struggle, and several sources relate that Isaac actually asked his father to bind him, lest at the last minute he lose his nerve and spoil the sacrifice. The Targum of Pseudo-Jonathan reports Isaac as saying: "Bind me well that I may not struggle at the anguish of my soul, and that a blemish may not be found in your offering."[62] According to Al-Tabari, Isaac[63] implored his father: "Fasten my bands so that I do not move about, and tie back your garments so that none of my blood splashes on them, lest Sarah see it and be saddened."[64] Jewish tradition further recounts that Isaac urged his father, once he returned home, to break the news gently to Sarah in a way and setting that she would not harm herself out of grief.[65] A modern rabbi notes that "even when his life was in mortal danger, Isaac's main concern was not for his own safety but for his parents."[66] In Judaism, Isaac remains an exemplar of the commandment to love God with all your soul.[67]

In the words of Clement, Isaac "cheerfully yielded himself as a sacrifice."[68] Isaac's greatness is seen in the fact that while Abraham had heard the directive for the sacrifice directly from God, Isaac had heard it only from Abraham, another human being. But Isaac did not question the source, for according to John Taylor, he "knew very well . . . that it was in obedience to a commandment of God; he knew very well that his father had communicated with the Lord and received revelations from him."[69]

They were absolutely united, proceeding, noted Rashi, "with a common mind."[70] In the words of Elie Wiesel, "The sacrifice was to be their joint offering," and "father and son had never before been so close" as "Isaac lay on the altar, silently gazing at his father."[71] Elder Melvin J. Ballard added that Abraham "must have given his son his farewell kiss, his blessing, [and] his love."[72] Islamic tradition similarly reports that Abraham kissed his son good-bye.[73]

And as Abraham, following the pattern of Adam, always performed sacrifice in the name of Jesus Christ (see Moses 5:8; 6:52), so he would have done on this occasion, offering a prayer for acceptance of the sacrifice. But it is an Islamic text from the early 1600s that purports to provide the contents of that unique prayer, beginning with a striking allusion to a prior experience of Abraham. "Most High and Omnipotent Sovereign! May all the Celestial potentates of thy blessed seraphic choirs give praises to thy Holy Name, with their melodious and echoing hymns, for ever and ever!"[74] It is a touching and poignant reminder to God of when Abraham had once been lovingly welcomed at the divine throne, an allusion to the highest moment of fellowship between God and Abraham, and the occasion when God had shown Abraham his future posterity—who God had subsequently promised would come through Isaac.

Later in the prayer, Abraham gratefully acknowledges the Lord's goodness, and implores His grace: "We have hourly tokens of thy great and boundless love towards us. . . . I am now, Lord, upon the point of accomplishing what thou hast commanded me to perform; grant, therefore, I beseech thee . . . , that I may be illuminated with thy grace, so that I may be able perfectly to complete what I have taken in hand to thy honour and glory."[75]

These words are a veritable window into the soul of Abraham, who in his mortal moment of deepest distress was unfailingly grateful for the Lord's unfailing goodness. Like Nephi, Abraham did not know the meaning of all things, but knew that God loved him (see 1 Ne. 11:17). And so, with a perfectly submissive heart, he pled for strength to perform the almost undoable task. It is the consummate demonstration of what the Lord requires of Zion, as he said in a latter-day revelation: "the Lord requireth the heart and a willing mind" (D&C 64:34, and see verse 22).

At this most difficult moment, did Abraham remember when he himself had been on a pagan altar, and had prayed to God for help? In contrast now, Isaac did not, could not, pray for help, for God himself had asked for this sacrifice. But it was more than Isaac laying on the altar; it was Zion itself, for had not the Lord Himself promised that "in Isaac" would the world be blessed and through him the Messiah and Zion be born? Indeed, if the ancient concept of sacrifice "suppose[d] the putting to death of the unique in terms of its being unique, irreplaceable, and most precious,"[76] then this surely was the ultimate sacrifice, as Abraham and Isaac well knew.

And yet, in the words of the Qur'an, Abraham and his son "together . . . submitted to God's will."[77] The word *submitted* is a form of the Arabic word *islam*, or "submission," the word chosen by Muhammad for his new religion, which he insisted was actually a restoration of the religion of Abraham. Abraham's submission is the great paradigm for his Muslim descendants.

How hard was this for Abraham? With this act, said John Taylor, Abraham saw "all his hopes blasted," and among the thoughts "crowding upon his mind" was the expectation of being left "a dry root, helpless, hopeless, tottering on the grave without any heir."[78] Jewish tradition similarly reports that Abraham expected to live "a few days only" after completing the sacrifice,[79] and reports that the agony he underwent caused his hair to turn white on this occasion[80]—a detail captured in Rembrandt's haunting painting of the scene.[81] The painting also shows the tears streaming down Abraham's face, the same tears described in both Jewish[82] and Islamic tradition, the latter of which speaks of the ground becoming soaked with tears.[83]

Meanwhile, "Isaac, seeing his father's hand, with knife in it, fall down against him, did not flinch."[84] But then Isaac saw something else, as reported by the Targum of Pseudo-Jonathan: "The eyes of Abraham were looking at the eyes of Isaac, and the eyes of Isaac were looking at the angels on high. Isaac saw them but Abraham did not see them."[85]

How does one explain Abraham's actions? What made it possible to perform this near-impossible deed? Faith, answers W. F. P. Noble:

> It furnishes the only key to the questions that rise unbidden as we read the story—a fond and doting father, how could Abraham undertake the task? How was he able to contemplate imbruing his hands in the blood of his son? How did his reason withstand the shock? How did his heart not break? How had he the nerve to

disclose the dreadful truth to Isaac, to kiss him, to bind his naked limbs, to draw the knife from its sheath and raise his arm for the blow? How did not the cords of life snap under the strain, and Abraham, spared the horrid sacrifice, fall dead on the altar—a pitiful sight, a father clasping within his lifeless arms the beloved form of his son? It is by the power of faith he stands there, the knife glittering in his hand, his arm raised to strike.[86]

Rabbinic texts tell of the angels weeping and pleading with God to stop the sacrifice.[87] It was then, as Genesis recounts, that "the angel of the LORD"[88] called out of heaven, "Abraham, Abraham" (Gen. 22:11). As related in Jubilees, Abraham was "startled."[89] In Rembrandt's painting, the knife is dropping from Abraham's hand as his eyes look up toward the voice—eyes full of a supernal submission and a profound peace that defies description. The voice continued, as Genesis reports: "for now I know that you fear God, since you have not withheld your son, your only son, from me" (NRSV Gen. 22:11–12).

But Jubilees has a different reading of the verse: not "now I know" but "now I have shown."[90] Shown to whom? To Abraham, for one: the reason for this trial, said President Hugh B. Brown, was that "Abraham needed to learn something about Abraham."[91] And the world needed to learn something *from* Abraham. A few verses later, Jubilees reports God as saying, "I have shown to all that thou art faithful unto Me."[92] The Midrash Rabbah similarly interpreted the Genesis verse to mean not "now I know" but rather "now I have made it known to all,"[93] and added that when the angel called Abraham's name twice, it was both "to him and to future generations."[94]

Hence by this trial, says the medieval Jewish commentator Abrabanel, God "made a demonstration," holding Abraham up "as an example and banner to all."[95] According to the nineteenth-century British reverend Ashton Oxenden, "truly such an act of faith . . . was never seen either before or since."[96] But if the great Abraham could withstand a test unique among mortals, it is unique only in degree, for modern revelation tells that the Latter-day Saints "must needs be . . . tried, even as Abraham, who was commanded to offer up his only son"(D&C 101:4).[97]

Dedication, Vision, and Guarantee of Eternal Life

Genesis does not describe Isaac's rising from the altar, but another Rembrandt depiction of the scene shows Abraham and Isaac with their arms around each other—"embracing," says Elie Wiesel, "with a tenderness that must have moved the Creator and his angels."[98] Al-Tabari reports that Abraham "kissed his son, saying, 'O my son! Today you have been given to me.'"[99] Another Islamic tradition relates that when Abraham went to untie Isaac, he found the bonds had already been miraculously loosed.[100] It was a another echo of what had happened when Abraham himself had been rescued on the altar in Ur.

The rabbis observed that Isaac's rising from the altar was as one rising from the dead: "Then his father unbound him, and Isaac rose, knowing that in this way the dead would come back to life in the future."[101] The New Testament also considers Isaac's experience a kind of resurrection. In offering up Isaac, according to the letter to the Hebrews, Abraham "considered that God is able to raise men even from the dead; from which he also received him back as a type" (NASB Hebrews 11:19).

Looking around, Abraham saw what he had not seen before: a ram caught by its horns in a thicket, a sign, God now explained to Abraham, that his descendants would likewise be "trapped through their sins and entangled by foreign powers," but would in the end be redeemed when God would blow the horn—a ram's horn, according to Israel's prophets—and gather them home.[102] Then, as Genesis tells, "Abraham went and took the ram and offered it up as a burnt offering in place of his son. And Abraham named that site Yahweh-yireh,"[103] meaning "the Lord will (or does) provide,"[104] or "the Lord will (or does) see."[105]

Accordingly, says Genesis, "it is said to this day" that "In the mountain of the LORD it was provided" (REB Gen. 22:14), or "On the mountain Yahweh provides" (NJB), or "On the mount of the LORD it shall be provided" (NRSV). The Hebrew words have a broad range of meaning, and can also be read, "In the mount the Lord was seen,"[106] or "On the mountain Yahweh makes himself seen,"[107] or "In the mountain of the LORD he may be seen,"[108] or "In the mount (where) the Lord is seen,"[109] or "In the mount will the Lord be seen,"[110] or "On the mountain the LORD will see."[111] Or, "On YHWH's mountain (it) is seen" (FBM), or "On the mount of the LORD there is sight,"[112] or "On the mount of the LORD there is vision" (JPST).[113]

What vision? According to the Midrash Rabbah, as Abraham offered up the ram, "the Holy One . . . showed [Abraham] the Temple built, destroyed and rebuilt" and yet again "rebuilt and firmly established in the Messianic era, as in the verse [from Psalms], When the Lord hath built up Zion, when He hath been seen in His glory."[114] Thereby Abraham saw the significance of the place where he was standing: "It is Mount Zion," says Jubilees.[115]

Only then could Abraham have known why, or at least partially why, God had asked him to come all this way to this particular mountain, and why He had capped it with a cloud of glory to indicate the site of the sacrifice. For as has happened throughout history on various occasions, and as yet will happen again, the glory of God rests on Zion visibly. The Targums tell that Abraham proceeded to dedicate the site for the future temple to be built and maintained by his posterity:[116] "Abraham worshipped and prayed there, in that place, and he said,

'Here, before the Lord, shall future generations worship,'"[117] and they would exclaim: "On the Mount of the Holy Temple of the Lord, Abraham offered up his son Isaac." Abraham saw, apparently even in greater detail than what he had seen before, the distress his posterity would undergo, and again prayed for mercy on their behalf, asking the Lord to forgive their sins and deliver them from oppression. And again the Lord promised to do so.[118] "Was ever a father so compassionate as Abraham?" asks a Jewish text.[119]

The Lord spoke a second time from heaven, again through his angel:

> By myself have I sworn, saith the LORD, for because thou hast done this thing, and hast not withheld thy son, thine only son: that in blessing I will bless thee [or 'I will greatly bless you' (GTC Gen. 22:17), or 'I shall bless you abundantly' (REB Gen. 22:17) or 'I will shower blessings on you' (NJB Gen. 22:17)], and in multiplying I will multiply thy seed as the stars of the heaven, and as the sand which is upon the sea shore; and thy seed shall possess the gate of his enemies; and in thy seed shall all the nations of the earth be blessed; because thou hast obeyed my voice. (Gen. 22:16–18)

Only then did the reason for the terrible trial become apparent: It was God's design to bless Abraham. "Whereby a man suffers," said the rabbis, "he is also exalted. Abraham suffered greatly" through various trials, the most severe of which was when he "bound his son upon the altar. . . . Yet thereby was he also exalted."[120]

The New Testament letter by the Savior's brother James states that it was through the offering of Isaac that Abraham's faith became perfect (James 2:21–22), a statement that takes on added significance when read in light of God's command years earlier to Abraham: "Walk with me"[121] and "be perfect."[122] Abraham's three-day walk to Moriah in the depths of agony and loneliness turned out to be his closest walk yet with God, bringing the perfection and exaltation that God desired for him. Thereby, according to James, Abraham "was called the Friend of God" (James 2:23), a statement similar to that found in the Damascus Document of the Dead Sea Scrolls: "Abraham . . . was accounted a friend of God because he kept the commandments of God."[123] That obedience would be memorialized among Abraham's Jewish descendants, who still in the orthodox traditional morning synagogue service read the account of the binding of Isaac not only to "emphasize the theme of covenant and everlasting loyalty" but also "as a reminder of the ancient standards of obedience to God's commandments."[124]

Thus when God now announced the blessings, it was not just by promise but by oath, as emphasized by the letter to the Hebrews: "When God made promise to

Abraham, because he could swear by no greater, he sware by Himself. . . . And so, after [Abraham] had patiently endured, he obtained the promise" (Heb. 6:13, 15). So what did it mean for the Almighty to swear by himself? God was really saying, according to the Midrash, "Even as I live and endure for ever and to all eternity, so will My oath endure for ever and to all eternity."[125] It was the unconditional promise of eternal life, his calling and election made sure, which, says Joseph Smith, comes to a man after "the Lord has thoroughly proved him, and finds that the man is determined to serve him at all hazards."[126] Accordingly, explained Joseph Smith, it was "the power of an endless life . . . which . . . Abraham obtained by the offering of his son Isaac,"[127] an event that "shows that if a man would attain to the keys of the kingdom of an endless life, he must sacrifice all things."[128]

The rabbis stated that at the beginning of the great trial when God had first called Abraham's name and he had answered "Here am I," the real meaning was: "Here am I—ready for priesthood, ready for kingship, and he attained priesthood and kingship."[129] Similarly Joseph Smith stated that by the "oath of God unto our Father Abraham," his children were "secured [to him] by the seal wherewith [Abraham had] been sealed."[130] In the greatest irony of Abraham's life, only by binding Isaac for the sacrifice had Abraham bound him to himself in the eternal bonds of priesthood sealing.

And not just Isaac, but through that same oath Abraham had secured all of his future righteous posterity, who would be as numerous as the stars and the sand. But the difference between stars and sand even served to symbolize the righteousness necessary to claim the blessings of Abraham. "When they do the will of the Holy One," says an ancient Jewish source, "they are as the stars of the heaven, and no kingdom or people can wield dominion over them. But when they flaunt His will, they are as the sand of the sea, trampled by every imperious foot."[131]

Even so, the sand also demonstrates, even more than the stars, the utter vastness of Abraham's posterity. "The sand on the seashore is innumerable to us," commented Orson Pratt, and "if we take a handful, it numbers its tens of thousands of grains." Hence "if Abraham's seed are to become as numerous as the sands on the seashore they will fill a great many worlds. . . . There is to be no end to the increase of the old Patriarch."[132] It is nothing less than, as latter-day revelation indicates, the promise of "eternal lives" (D&C 132:24), even "a fulness and a continuation of the seeds forever and ever" (D&C 132:19), "both in the world and out of the world" (D&C 132:30). The Pirke de Rabbi Eliezer similarly explains that at the end of Abraham's trial on Mount Moriah, God "swore to bless him in this world and in the world to come," saying, "I will surely bless you in this world, and greatly multiply you in the world to come."[133]

All this is of special relevance to latter-day Zion, whose Saints are heirs to the same promise because, says a revelation, they "are of Abraham" (D&C 132:31).

According to Bruce R. McConkie, "When he is married in the temple for time and for all eternity, each worthy member of the Church enters personally into the same covenant the Lord made with Abraham. This is the occasion when the promises of eternal increase are made, and it is then specified that those who keep the covenants made there shall be inheritors of all the blessings of Abraham, Isaac, and Jacob."[134]

In the words of Orson Hyde, "may not we, if faithful to our God and to our covenants, be as Abraham? Shall there be any end to our posterity? May they not be as numerous as the stars in the firmament, and as the sands upon the sea shore?"[135]

Zion and Her Atoning King

Most importantly, as the Apostle Paul emphasized, God's promise to Abraham focused on that one particular Descendant who would bless all nations, even the Savior (Gal. 3:16)—as Abraham himself well knew, having previously seen in vision the Savior's birth and ministry. In fact, Abraham must now have recognized, if he hadn't already, that his own intense trial had been a remarkably detailed fore-shadowing of the great Atonement of Christ. According to the Cave of Treasures, an early Christian work, when "Abraham took up his son as an offering, . . . he at the same time foresaw in this act the crucifixion of Christ."[136]

Nor would some of Abraham's offspring miss the symbolism of this poignantly unique event as simply the clearest and most powerful type of the most important event ever to take place on this planet, the sacrifice of the Son of God. Hence when the Book of Mormon prophet Jacob chose from all of past history an event that would serve as a compelling "similitude of God and his Only Begotten Son," it was the obedience of "Abraham in the wilderness . . . in offering up his son Isaac" (Jacob 4:5).

The same comparison is evident in the New Testament, where the Greek word used by James to describe Abraham's faith being made "perfect" (*teleioun*) when he offered up Isaac (James 2:21–22), is the same word used in the gospel of John when Jesus prays that His disciples may be "perfect" in one (John 17:23), and yet again the same word used by John to describe the crucifixion of Jesus as bringing scripture to "complete fulfillment."[137]

But already John had written that "God so loved the world, that he gave his only begotten Son" (John 3:16), the one passage that best sums up the entire gospel of John.[138] The words carry a distinct and intentional echo of God's ancient directive to Abraham to offer up his beloved son.[139] Moreover, as the first occurrence of any form of the word *love* in the Old Testament is God's mention of Abraham's love for Isaac in Genesis 22, so the first occurrence of love in the New Testament is by a heavenly voice speaking of the love of a Father for His Son: "This is my beloved Son, in whom I am well pleased."[140] And as Abraham had walked up the mountain to perform the sacrifice, he had promised Isaac that God would provide a lamb. What God provided that day was a ram. So where was the lamb? The answer comes only later as recorded in the gospel of John when John the Baptist sees Jesus and announces, "Behold the Lamb of God" (John 1:29). This was the fulfillment of Abraham's prophecy, uttered in the only conversation that Genesis records between Abraham and his posterity.

Hence, according to the second-century theologian and martyr Irenaeus, "Abraham . . . delivered up, as a sacrifice to God, his only-begotten and beloved son, in order that God also might be pleased to offer up for all his seed His own beloved and only-begotten Son, as a sacrifice for our redemption."[141] Or, as portrayed in Armenian apocryphal sources, "Abraham is the type of God the Father, Isaac is Christ, the wood is the wood of the Cross, Abraham's sacrifice is God's sending of his Son."[142] Such redemption would take place very near the site of Abraham's similitude, even as prophetically foretold by generations of ancient Israelites exclaiming, "In the mount will the Lord be seen."[143] Ironically, only when Abraham had obediently undertaken the act whereby he would apparently relinquish the promise of being the Savior's ancestor did he secure the guarantee of that promise.

This guarantee of God's swearing an oath is unprecedented in Genesis, but not in the writings of Abraham's forefathers. When Enoch had prayed for mercy for his posterity, the Lord had covenanted with Enoch and irrevocably sworn with an oath to preserve and protect his posterity—adding that "blessed is he through whose seed Messiah shall come; for he saith—I am Messiah, the King of Zion" (Moses 7:51–53). The Messiah's unnamed blessed ancestor could well be Abraham, who upon completing the similitude of the Messiah's Atonement heard the Lord swear an oath guaranteeing that through Abraham's seed would indeed come the Messiah, the King of Zion.

The word *Zion* is used throughout the Prophetic and Psalms literature and extensively in the rabbinic writings to designate that most important of all Jewish geographic locations, the Temple Mount. Curiously, Jewish and biblical scholars are at a loss to explain the origin of the name,[144] noting that from earliest times "it is transmitted as a proper name" and "undoubtedly comes from pre-Israelite times,"[145] having been "only secondarily transferred" to Jerusalem and its Temple Mount.[146] And a key part of that inherited tradition "depict[s] the city of God in the light of complete happiness and prosperity."[147] In short, the Zion tradition at Jerusalem is now recognized to be far older than Jerusalem itself, pointing back to an ancient golden age. Only with the loss of the Enoch texts did later generations forget the original, the order of Enoch that those at Jerusalem sought to reestablish on the very site dedicated by Abraham for that purpose.

Nor would the Jerusalem effort to reestablish Zion be the last, for as Brigham Young said, it is "the order of Enoch" that "God has established for his people in all ages of the world when he has had a kingdom upon the earth."[148] It would thus be the order of the latter days, as Abraham also foresaw when he beheld in vision the temple as it would stand in the far-distant Messianic era. It was all part of the original oath to Enoch about the latter-day return of his city of Zion, to meet the earthly Zion built by Abraham's posterity—pursuant to the oath sworn to Abraham by God through his angel on Mount Moriah.

Who was that angel? Jubilees specifies that it was the very angel of the presence,[149] who, as seen before, is elsewhere identified as Enoch. Similarly in the Midrash ha-Gadol the angel who called out of heaven is specifically named as Metatron,[150] who is Enoch.[151] This source further tells that Metatron was chosen to relay the message because, as Abraham was about to sacrifice Isaac, "Metatron arose before the Holy One . . . and said before him, 'Lord of the Universe, let not the seed of Abraham perish from the world.'" The Lord then "indicated to Metatron to call him, as it is written 'The angel of the Lord then called to him from heaven.'"[152]

Having once been God's messenger to rescue Abraham from death on the altar in Ur, Enoch again serves as God's messenger to rescue Abraham's son of promise from another altar and to convey the oath encompassing the future building of Zion. In fact, a Turkish source seems to indicate that it was concern for the latter-day Zion that prompted the plea of the angels, who saw "from the Preserved Tablet that the Prophet of the End of Time will come from . . . [the] line" of the son about to sacrificed.[153] For Latter-day Saints, this End-Time prophet is none other than Joseph Smith.

Hence on Mount Moriah, Zion above had interceded for Zion below, and particularly for the benefit of latter-day Zion—but only after Abraham's obedience had foreshadowed the price to be paid for Zion by her King, the Messiah, the Son of God and of Abraham.

Well did the Danish philosopher Kierkegaard title his treatment of Abraham's sacrifice *Fear and Trembling,* for as a later philosopher, Jacques Derrida, would comment about Abraham's sacrifice, "What is it that makes us tremble . . . ? It is the gift of infinite love."[154] To Him whose death was prefigured by the experience of Isaac, Moroni said: "Thou hast loved the world, even unto the laying down of thy life for the world" (Ether 12:33). It was this divine gift of love, freely given to Zion by her suffering King, that was foreshadowed in Abraham's offering of his beloved son.

The Burial of Sarah

CHAPTER 11

Pressing Forward in Zion to the End:
Rejoicing, Weeping, Testifying, and Departing

Wherefore, ye must press forward with a steadfastness in Christ, having a perfect brightness of hope, and a love of God and of all men. Wherefore, if ye shall press forward, feasting upon the word of Christ, and endure to the end, behold, thus saith the Father: Ye shall have eternal life.
—2 NEPHI 31:20

The Loss of Beloved Sarah

At the conclusion of the great trial wherein Abraham nearly sacrificed his son, according to the Qur'an, a heavenly voice pronounced: "Peace be upon Abraham!"[1] The ancient book of Jubilees similarly reports God's last words to Abraham on Mount Moriah as "Go in peace."[2] "Peace is a precious thing," explains the Midrash Rabbah, "since for all the deeds and meritorious acts which our father Abraham accomplished the only reward given to him was peace."[3] It seems but an expression of the truth revealed to Latter-day Saints that while the ultimate reward for righteousness is life eternal, the interim reward in this life is peace (D&C 59:23).

One modern writer imagined, and it may have been so, that as Abraham walked back down the mountain, his face "shone like the face of an angel of God,"[4] a phenomenon that would recur repeatedly among his righteous descendants after the Spirit rested mightily upon them. Back in Beersheba, Abraham lived "joyfully"[5] for many years, "spreading blessings for his fellow men."[6] Another modern writer imagined that upon his return from Moriah, Sarah "noted his hair of silver and his beard as white as washed lamb's wool—but more, a certain whiteness of his soul . . . shining in his face and looking out of eyes grown deep with suffering turned to joy."[7]

Abraham had indeed been transformed, and although God's revelation on Mount Moriah constitutes the last recorded revelation of Abraham's life, yet in a very important sense it was not the end but the beginning of the kind of divine fellowship not seen on the earth since the days of Enoch's Zion. For according to Joseph Smith, when a man obtains his calling and election made sure, as did Abraham on Mount Moriah, "he will have the personage of Jesus Christ to attend him, or appear unto him, from time to time, and even He will manifest the Father unto him, and they will take up their abode with him, and the visions of the heavens will be opened unto him, and the Lord will teach him face to face, and he may have a perfect knowledge of the mysteries of the Kingdom of God."[8]

While this description obviously includes some of Abraham's earlier encounters with God, yet it is clear that he was now closer to God than ever before. It may well be that the greatest revelations of Abraham's long life came during these closing years, revelations of which we currently have no record. In any event, the type of fellowship he now enjoyed with the Almighty seems to have been that enjoyed by Enoch and his city when the Lord came and dwelt with them.[9] And if Enoch had walked with God (Moses 6:69; Gen. 5:22), so now did Abraham, beginning with his walk to Moriah whereby he qualified to do what the Lord had commanded years earlier: to live in His presence. Zion in her glory was again on the earth; again the God of heaven dwelt with men on earth. "Like Enoch," one writer noted of Abraham, "he walked with God" and "lived on terms of fellowship with God such as had not been seen" for many generations.[10]

Thus had Abraham entered into what Book of Mormon writers call the "rest of the Lord" by a lifetime of service that would qualify anyone, it would seem, for a peaceful and reflective retirement. But the exemplary nature of Abraham's very long life—he would live another five decades after the trial on Mount Moriah, to the ripe age of 175 years—extends to the very finish line of mortality, as he demonstrated how his descendants must press forward with hope and faith and endure in their efforts to the end of mortality. The Testament of Abraham, the document relating Abraham's death, attests to his loving service to mankind to the very end of his days. There was no "quiet retirement" period, no waning commitment or diminished service, but a perfect example of what Nephi says about enduring to the end (see 2 Ne. 31:20). Abraham's pattern of persistence to the end is remarkably repeated in the lives of latter-day prophets—descendants of Abraham and heirs to his authority—like that model of selfless endurance, President Gordon B. Hinckley.

Following his years in Beersheba, Abraham moved his family back to Hebron, where, according to Muslim tradition, he was directed to build yet another sanctuary, or temple.[11] At Hebron he experienced the last major recorded trial of his life, the death of Sarah at the age of 127 years, as recounted by Genesis, which also tells the place of her burial. "Of no other woman are the days and years of her life and the place of her burial recorded" in scripture, notes an ancient Jewish text, demonstrating the uniqueness of this woman.[12] "What kind of person was this regal woman, and what constituted the uniqueness of her personality?"[13] Jewish tradition answers in terms of her loyalty and love for her husband, whom she "had followed . . . in all his ways and had joined . . . in life's path and purpose."[14] In her own words once spoken to Abraham, as reported in the Fragmentary Targum, "I forsook my land, and my childhood, and the house of my father, and I went with you in the faith of the heavens."[15]

And what a journey it had been! She was, observes Philo, continually at his side as his dearly beloved "life-long partner," accepting in stride both the good and ill, "show[ing] her wifely love by numberless proofs, by sharing with him the severance from his kinsfolk, by bearing without hesitation the departure from her homeland, the continual and unceasing wanderings on a foreign soil and privation in famine, and by the campaigns in which she accompanied him."[16]

She could have traded it all in for the dazzling wealth and power that the mighty king of Egypt, and later the king of Gerar, had offered her on a silver platter to become their favorite wife and queen of their realm. But she chose to be faithful to her covenants and her husband, whose revelations she believed and to whose counsel she hearkened. She had grown old believing, faithful still in her undying love and service, and when her childbearing capacity had long passed, angels from on high brought a miraculous blessing of renewal, granting her the inexpressible joy of the son she had long awaited.

And such had the Lord arranged her life that the fulfillment of his promises to her of a son pointed ahead with clarity to the greater fulfillment of her Descendant who would also be born by miraculous means, born to bring joy to the world and the blessing of eternal life to her and her husband and their righteous posterity. In the end, it will ever be remembered that she refused the queenship of this world to attain her celestial queenship, and therefore became the paradigm of what the Lord instructed Emma Smith: "Thou shalt lay aside the things of this world, and seek for the things of a better" (D&C 25:10).

The nineteenth-century British clergyman Henry Blunt observed:

> Sarah is . . . the pattern of conjugal fidelity and love: her example is held forth by the apostle [Peter] as the highest model for Christian women, and the title of her "daughters" as her most honourable distinction. The very fact that so few of the incidents of her history are recorded speak strongly in her favour, for there is little in the even tenour of . . . life, when that life is passed in the unobtrusive and noiseless path of devotedness to God, and in

the peaceful round of domestic duties, which can, or ought, to form the subject of the chronicler. The very privacy of the Christian graces, manifested in such a walk and conversation, endears them the more to the few who have the opportunity of intimately knowing their value, and daily and hourly appreciating their loveliness and worth.[17]

"Greatness," observed Elder Neal A. Maxwell, "is not measured by coverage in column inches, either in newspapers or in the scriptures. The story of the women of God . . . is, for now, an untold drama within a drama," to remain so until "the real history of mankind is fully disclosed."[18] Only in time will the faithful daughters—and sons—of Sarah know the fuller story of her quiet selflessness that built Zion in her home and made possible the rest of the Abraham story.

But even in the small part of the story we have, we have seen her reach out with her husband to lovingly welcome the hungry and the needy and provide for their needs; to encourage the discouraged and downtrodden; to preach the gospel and teach the way of the Lord—in short, to be a full partner with Abraham in building Zion. Jewish tradition remembers that "Sarah was perfect. In wisdom, in beauty, in innocence, in accomplishment, in consistency, her life was a tapestry of perfection," being "without blemish, and of complete faith."[19] Of such great faith, in fact, that she, like her husband, had foreseen the history of her descendants, and had petitioned God to aid them in their tribulation.[20] If her spiritual vision at times exceeded even that of Abraham,[21] yet she was always his ardent support, sharing her unique insight but ever faithful in hearkening to his counsel and thereby keeping her covenants and maintaining that precious unity of heart found only in Zion.

No wonder Abraham wept (Gen. 23:2) at the loss of his sweetheart, she whose heart had constantly been knit together with his in love[22] in this Zion marriage. Now "his beloved Sarah was gone,"[23] she with whom he had "toiled, planned, hoped, suffered, [and] rejoiced together during a long life. Now she was silent in death,"[24] and "no one could share his personal pain."[25]

But even in this loss, says Jubilees, "he was found to be faithful (and) patient in spirit" and "was recorded on the heavenly tablets as the friend of the Lord."[26] In fact, Jewish tradition tells of him reaching out and offering consolation to others, for the death of Sarah was a loss not only for Abraham but for the whole country,[27] as the goodness of her life had left "an indelible mark" on the world.[28] It is said that the widows and the numerous children "to whom Sarah had done so much good . . . came to weep for her, and there was a very great mourning for her,"[29] such that Abraham was greeted by throngs of people grieving over her passing.[30] These Abraham comforted, eulogizing Sarah for her unparalleled goodness and kindness, and particularly "prais[ing] her preeminence as a mother."[31]

One midrash maintains that although Genesis omits the actual words of Abraham's eulogy at Sarah's funeral, that eulogy is in fact preserved in chapter 31 of Proverbs which speaks of the "woman of virtue" or "woman of valor."[32] Her memory is constantly kept alive in Jewish homes, where in the traditional service welcoming the weekly Sabbath, parents pronounce the blessing on their daughters that "God should establish you as he did Sarah."[33]

As Abraham did not complain at Sarah's death, neither did he murmur at the irony of having to purchase the burial plot from the then-owner (Gen. 23). Abraham was over-generous in the transaction, paying more than what the land was worth. "He never drove a hard bargain," notes Hugh Nibley, "not even with . . . the generous Ephron the Hittite, who would have given him the burial cave for nothing."[34]

"A stranger in a strange land!" marvels one modern writer. "Owning no foot of earth in a country that had been given to him by the Almighty, [Abraham] must *buy* a burial place for his dead!"[35] As Jewish texts say, "Come and see the humility of Abraham our father!"[36] For "he said nothing about the promise of the land which said that the Lord would give it to him and his descendants after him,"[37] but simply purchased the plot of ground, called the cave of Machpelah. God would later tell Moses, according to the Midrash Rabbah: "I said unto Abraham: 'Arise, walk through the land . . . ; for unto thee will I give it'—[afterwards] he sought to bury Sarah and did not find where, until he purchased a place with money—yet he did not question my ways."[38]

For some four decades in the spirit world, Sarah would await the arrival of her beloved husband, whose body would finally be laid to rest alongside hers in the cave of Machpelah. Over their graves a mosque would eventually be erected, which, in the words of one writer, "stands even unto our day as a monument to that divine injunction—What God hath joined together, let no man put asunder."[39] In fact, the word *Machpelah* itself was understood by early translations to mean "double," referring, according to some rabbinic sources, to the fact that Abraham and Sarah were eventually laid to rest as a couple, as would be Isaac and Jacob and their wives in the same cave.[40] Centuries later, after their descendants had erected the Jerusalem temple, the temple service was not begun until the priestly lookout saw the sun's rays shining on the graves of the patriarchs.[41]

But Jewish kabbalistic sources interpret the word *Machpelah* to mean a doubling of the Hebrew letter *heh,* and thereby a veiled reference to the Lord's own name, *Yahweh,* which contains two such letters.[42] It was the Lord himself who had changed Abram's name by adding the letter *heh,* resulting in "Abraham," or "Father of a Multitude"—the name that God urgently spoke twice to stay Abraham's hand on Mount Moriah and to place upon him the divine seal of his exaltation. In this sense the word *Machpelah* seems particularly fitting to memorialize the temporary resting place of the mortal bodies of Abraham and Sarah, who, because of the Lord's priesthood power that had joined and sealed them as an eternal couple, would be inseparable not only in mortality but also in the future world.

As God is not the god of the dead but of the living, so Abraham and Sarah would rise together in the resurrection, for "the righteous will be joined by their wives in the world to come,"[43] says a midrash. Then shall they become "gods," declares latter-day revelation, enjoying "a fulness and a continuation of the seeds forever and ever" (D&C 132:19–20).[44] And then would the noble Sarah, she who for so many years longed for posterity in mortality, become indeed a mother of a multitude as her posterity would increase like the stars of heaven.

Teaching and Preparing His Posterity

During the ensuing years, fulfillment of the divine promises to Abraham seemed to crescendo. Isaac married the wife that Abraham selected (see Gen. 24), while Abraham himself, knowing that he was yet to have more offspring, married a woman named Keturah, who according to an early Christian source was the daughter of a powerful desert monarch.[45] With Keturah, Abraham fathered six sons (see Gen. 25:1–4). That he took yet a fourth wife is asserted by early Muslim tradition repeated by both al-Tabari and al-Thalabi,[46] a tradition that seems to be substantiated by the Lord's statement in latter-day revelation that Abraham received "concubines, and they bore him children; and it was accounted unto him for righteousness" (D&C 132:37). Keturah would not be a concubine—a secondary wife—for Sarah was no longer alive. So the only way Abraham would end up with more than one concubine is if he married yet a fourth wife while Keturah, the primary wife, was still alive. By this fourth wife, according to Islamic tradition, Abraham fathered five additional sons.[47] Both Jewish[48] and Islamic[49] tradition mention that Abraham also had at least one daughter. Little is said of her except that "Abraham loved her dearly, and taught her all that he had learned, and she was the center of Abraham's household." Later after his passing, she is said to have carried his teachings far and wide.[50]

But Abraham was a father in more than a biological sense. From a variety of ancient sources we know, for example, that he taught his children to love God and keep his commandments;[51] he taught them to love their fellow men and to serve them by acts of loving-kindness;[52] he counseled his family on important matters;[53] he exercised his priesthood in giving blessings to his family;[54] he instructed family members in their individual roles and missions;[55] he transmitted to his family the wisdom he had attained;[56] and he carefully administered to his family the ordinances,[57] including the "signs" and "oaths" encompassing "the mystery of the Redemption,"[58] or temple ordinances. One nineteenth-century rabbi suggested that the secret societies that transmitted the mysteries in the Mediterranean world a millennium after Abraham were transmitting forms of knowledge whose origin had flowed from Abraham.[59] With the latter-day restoration of the gospel through the Prophet Joseph Smith came the restoration of the Abrahamic temple truths and ordinances in their purity.

Abraham also transmitted to his posterity the written records he had made, as he says in the Book of Abraham, "for the benefit of my posterity that shall come after me" (Abr. 1:31). Abraham's writings are not mentioned in the Bible, but are referred to in numerous ancient sources,[60] which indicate that these writings were handed down through the generations and highly prized. As mentioned in the Qur'an, for example, the descendants of Ishmael had "the books . . . of Abraham"[61] or "the scriptures of Abraham."[62]

More evidence of the extent and content of those records is found among Isaac's descendants. "There is a tradition," reports the Talmud, "that the [tractate on idolatry] of our father Abraham contained four hundred chapters."[63] The Talmud further mentions a book of Jasher as being a book of Abraham,[64] and asserts that Abraham is the author of Psalm 89, or at least part of it.[65] Jewish tradition further attributes the Sefer Yetzirah, a text on Creation, to Abraham,[66] and specifically tells that it was one of the books that Abraham's grandson Jacob possessed.[67]

Among Alexandrian scholars in the third century B.C., Abraham was acknowledged as an authoritative author on the subject of astronomy, and scholars in the early centuries A.D. even claimed to quote from his astronomical writings.[68] An early Christian sect had a book they called the *Revelation of Abraham,* and the Zoroastrians purportedly had books written by Abraham.[69]

The Qumran community on the shores of the Dead Sea had what scholars now call the Genesis Apocryphon, most of which is an account of Abraham, and most of that written in first person.[70] And the Apocalypse of Abraham is entirely written in first person,[71] as is the Book of Abraham.

Such records guided Abraham's posterity and strengthened them in times of trial and temptation, as dramatically seen with Joseph in Egypt, who when tempted by Potiphar's wife, received strength to resist when he "remembered the Lord and what his father Jacob would read to him from the words of Abraham—that no one is to commit adultery."[72] For Latter-day Saints, the Book of Abraham is the crown jewel of Abrahamic texts, a remarkably concise work that, as Nibley comments, "answers with astonishing economy the most fundamental and baffling questions of our existence," including questions like "Where did I come from?" "Why am I here?" "How did it all begin and how will it all end?"[73] No wonder Wilford Woodruff referred to it as one of our "rich treasures."[74] The Book of Abraham provides both exhilarating perspective and a proven pattern for Latter-day Saints.

The genius of the Book of Abraham is that interwoven through the description of . . . momentous events is a panorama of mankind's divine origin and potential. As literal spirit offspring of God, we are sent into mortality to be "prove[n] . . . to see if [we] will do all things whatsoever the Lord [our] God shall command [us]" so that we can "have glory added upon [our] heads for ever and ever." Parley Pratt noted that in Abraham's record "we see . . . unfolded our eternal being—our existence before the world was—our high and responsible station in the councils of the Holy One, and our eternal destiny." The Book of Abraham even describes the road to that highest destiny: strictly obeying all God's commandments; diligently seeking righteousness and peace; making and keeping sacred covenants; receiving the priesthood and sacred ordinances; building a family unit; searching the scriptures; keeping journals and records; sharing the gospel; and proving faithful in the face of opposition—all works of Abraham, who is as much a model for Latter-day Saints as he was in ages past for those aspiring to be the people of God.[75]

All this from the tiny Book of Abraham, even though we currently have only the first part of the book![76] How did it end? Judging from the Apocalypse of Abraham, the primary focus of Abraham's writings was to bear testimony of the Son of God and His marvelous works, including His creations, His future mortal ministry, and His Second Coming in glory.[77]

Abraham further transmitted all priesthood authority necessary for his descendants to establish Zion. Abraham undoubtedly ordained Isaac to the patriarchal priesthood authority,[78] and then saw that his grandson Jacob would be Isaac's successor. Abraham explained to his daughter-in-law Rebekah that "all the blessings that the Lord has promised me and my descendants shall be Jacob's and his descendants' always. And by his descendants shall my name be blessed, and the name of my fathers, Shem, and Noah, and Enoch, and Mahalalel, and Enosh, and Seth, and Adam."[79]

Furthermore, said Abraham, his descendants "shall serve to lay the foundations of heaven."[80] The language seems to recall the city of foundations, even the latter-day Zion, to which Abraham was looking ahead. Then summoning Jacob, Abraham proceeded to ordain him to the patriarchal order of the priesthood, pronouncing upon him "all the blessings" of "Adam and Enoch and Noah and Shem."[81]

No wonder that President Spencer W. Kimball recommended Abraham as "a model that will lift and elevate any father in this Church who wishes to become a true patriarch to his family."[82]

Final Days on Earth and Experience in the Spirit World

"Happy are the righteous," says a midrash, who "before they depart this world . . . instruct their children . . . , as did Abraham."[83] Near the end of Abraham's life, following the pattern of the aged Adam who had gathered his righteous posterity to give them his last instructions and a blessing, Abraham gathered all his family in a family reunion. The incident is told in the Book of Jubilees, which relates that Abraham "summoned Ishmael and his twelve children, Isaac and his two children, and the six children of Keturah and their sons," and urged them "to keep the way of the Lord so that they should do what is right and that they should love one another," and "love the God of heaven and hold fast to all his commandments."[84]

Later, speaking to Isaac, Abraham reminded him of his own lifetime of obedience, as Jubilees also relates: "Throughout all the days of my life I have remembered the Lord, and sought with all my heart to do His will, and to walk uprightly in all His ways. . . . For He is the living God. . . . And do thou, my son, observe His commandments and His ordinances."[85] To the very last, Abraham was teaching his posterity to keep the law of the Lord.

But as valuable as is such information from Jubilees, which has come down to us through Jewish channels,[86] we may surmise that Abraham's final instructions were emphatically focused on what Nephi and Moroni emphasized in their final testament and testimony: an invitation to "believe in Christ" (2 Ne. 33:10) and "come unto Christ" (see Moro. 10:30–32). Like Abraham's Nephite descendants, he had spent a lifetime "talk[ing] of Christ, . . . rejoic[ing] in Christ, . . . preach[ing] of Christ, . . . [and] prophesy[ing] of Christ" (2 Ne. 25:26). Abraham had been repeatedly visited and tutored by Christ, who had even welcomed him at the divine throne and shown him the Savior's own future mortal ministry. Later in obedience to the Savior's request, Abraham had acted out the most poignant prophetic similitude ever of the Atonement, learning the depth of the divine love that would make that Atonement possible. Abraham's final testimony of the Son of God would have been uniquely and unforgettably powerful.

And as Abraham testified of the Son of God to the last, so did he serve Him to the last by attending to the least of His brethren. As told in the Testament of Abraham, he continued to welcome and care for the needy and downtrodden, remaining ever the magnanimous friend of mankind, "hospitable and loving to the end of his life."[87] Abraham's long life was but "an exercise in perfect service," and "never was there a selfish consideration."[88]

The Testament of Abraham further relates that as the end drew near, God sent to Abraham an angel who announced he was "from the great city,"[89] come to apprise Abraham of his impending death: "you are about to leave this vain world and depart from the body, and you will come to your own Master among the good."[90] The angel—one of the three who decades earlier had visited Abraham to announce the birth of Isaac—was also instructed to grant to Abraham a last request.[91] Abraham asked that before dying he be allowed to see "all the inhabited world."[92] Having labored all his days to fulfill the divine mandate to bless all nations by establishing Zion over the entire earth, Abraham now wishes to assess what remains to be done.

The angel "took Abraham and sat him on the cherubim-chariot and lifted him up to the heights of heaven and acted as his guide on the cloud."[93] Riding on the chariot, Abraham "soared over the entire inhabited world" and "beheld the world" and all of its inhabitants, the righteous as well as the wicked[94]—it is perhaps for this that he was remembered among the Hebrews as the "Eye of the World."[95] Abraham's experience echoes that of Enoch, who had been "lifted up" and seen "all the inhabitants of the earth" (Moses 7:21–24), and who Abraham now saw as he was taken on a tour of heaven. Enoch, "the teacher of heaven and earth and the scribe of righteousness," was acting as scribe in the Lord's judgment of souls.[96] The picture must have turned Abraham's mind again to the glorious scenes of the latter days.

Rabbinic tradition adds that God then showed Abraham the unspeakably glorious reward that awaited him, even his eternal portion in the celestial paradise.[97] Abraham beheld a place "abundant in light" inhabited by "myriads of radiant angels" in paradisiacal scenes full of exquisite flowers and stately trees watered by serene streams. He inhaled the sweet fragrances, listened to strains of angelic choirs, saw the Tree of Life, and experienced infinite delight. Although informed that all this was but a small part of the paradise that lay in store for him, Abraham longed to remain there and pled with the Lord to take his soul to its rest.[98]

Jubilees relates that Abraham's passing occurred when Isaac and Ishmael and all their families had come to Hebron to be with Abraham to celebrate the Feast of Weeks. "Abraham rejoiced because his two sons had come." As they feasted, Abraham lifted his voice one last time in praise and thanksgiving to his Creator: "I give thanks unto Thee, my God, because thou hast caused me to see this day."[99] "I am now 175 years of age, old and with (my) time completed."[100] "And all of my days were peaceful for me."[101] "The sword of the adversary has not overcome me in all that Thou hast given me and my children all the days of my life. . . . My God, may Thy mercy and Thy peace be upon Thy servant, and upon the seed of his sons, that they may be to Thee a chosen nation and an inheritance from amongst all the nations of the earth from henceforth until all the days of the generations of the earth, unto all the ages."[102]

Calling his grandson Jacob, the chosen patriarchal heir with the mandate and authority to establish Zion over all the earth, Abraham then pronounced his final blessing, invoking the blessings of heaven upon Jacob and his seed forever, and urging Jacob to "keep the commandments of your father Abraham."[103] Young Jacob was tired, and "the two lay together on one bed, and Jacob slept in the bosom of Abraham," who "kissed him seven times, and . . . his heart rejoiced over him." And while Jacob yet slept, Abraham "blessed him with all his heart," asking the Lord that "Thy grace and Thy mercy be . . . upon him and upon his seed. . . . And may Thine eyes be opened upon him and upon his seed, that thou mayst preserve him, and bless him, and . . . sanctify him as a nation for Thine inheritance; and bless him with all Thy blessings . . . , and renew Thy covenant and Thy grace with him and with his seed . . . unto all the generations of the earth." With that, Abraham "blessed the God of gods, and he covered his face and stretched out his feet and slept the sleep of eternity, and was gathered to his fathers."[104]

> During all of this (time) Jacob was lying on his bosom and did not know that Abraham, his grandfather, was dead. And Jacob awoke from his sleep and, behold, Abraham was cold as ice, and he said, "O father, father!" And none spoke. And he knew that he was dead. And he rose up from his bosom and ran and told Rebekah, his mother. And Rebekah went to Isaac in the night and told him. And they went together and Jacob was also with them, and a lamp was in his hand. And when they went, they found Abraham lying dead. And Isaac fell upon his father's face and wept and kissed him. And the sound was heard in Abraham's house and Ishmael, his son, arose and went to Abraham, his father. And he wept for Abraham, his father, he and all of Abraham's house, and they wept bitterly.[105]

The sadness spread quickly, for, according to Jewish tradition, "when the inhabitants of Canaan heard that Abraham was dead, they all came with their kings and princes and all their men to [help] bury Abraham. . . . And all the inhabitants of the land . . . , and all those who had known Abraham, wept . . . , and men and women mourned over him. And all the little children, and all the inhabitants of the land wept on account of Abraham, for Abraham had been good to them all, and . . . had been upright with God and men."[106]

How many untold stories of compassion and kindness by Abraham are covered in that brief report alluding to what the poet Wordsworth called "that best portion of a good man's life, his little, nameless, unremembered acts of kindness and of love."[107] In addition, "all the great ones of the nations of the world" came to pay their respects, lamenting, "Woe to the world that has lost its leader and woe to the ship that has lost its pilot."[108] How profoundly mankind missed their righteous priesthood patriarch, their loving friend and exemplar.

But his greatest eulogy was pronounced some time later by God Himself, who, when he appeared to Isaac, renewed His promises once made to Abraham, thereby making Isaac and his posterity instruments to bless the world—"because," God declared, "Abraham obeyed my voice, and kept my charge, my commandments, my statutes, and my laws" (Gen. 26:5). It was the ultimate lesson in blessing, an eternal guide for Abraham's posterity.

As for Abraham himself, his immortal spirit was, as the Lord had foretold, gathered to his fathers, to that glorious realm where he was, as described by Alma, "received into a state of happiness, which is called paradise, a state of rest, a state of peace, where they . . . rest from all their troubles and from all care, and sorrow," awaiting the resurrection of the dead (Alma 40:12). To this realm of righteous and noble spirits would eventually come the disembodied Son of God and of Abraham, Jesus the Christ, following His atoning death on the cross. His appearance to those who had accepted Him and testified of Him in the flesh is described in the vision of President Joseph F. Smith, who specifically mentions seeing Abraham among that vast multitude of spirits.

> The saints rejoiced in their redemption, and bowed the knee and acknowledged the Son of God as their Redeemer and Deliverer from death and the chains of hell. Their countenances shone, and the radiance from the presence of the Lord rested upon them, and they sang praises unto his holy name. (D&C 138:23–24)

If Jesus only a short time later would, as a resurrected being appearing to the Nephites, take time to invite each person of the large crowd to personally take a moment with Him individually, surely He would have done so now among these His friends and prophets. Of the reunion of the Beloved Son with His beloved friend Abraham we are not told, but the context was poignant. Having once as the premortal Son of God welcomed the mortal Abraham at the heavenly throne, the Savior now again was a spirit, but this time so was Abraham, both soon to rise in the splendor of the resurrection made possible by the Savior's atoning sacrifice as once foreshadowed by Abraham's offering of Isaac. Isaac himself may have been standing next to Abraham to welcome the Savior, whom he had typified both in suffering and rising from death.

But after the greetings there was much to do, as Abraham, who had spent his mortal life preaching the gospel of Christ, now was privileged to participate with Christ as He "organized his forces and appointed messengers, clothed with power and authority, to go forth and carry the light of the gospel to them that were in darkness, even to all the spirits of men; and thus was the gospel preached to the dead" (D&C 138:30). The same event was described in an early Christian writing known as the Shepherd of Hermas, which speaks of "the apostles and teachers who proclaimed the name of the Son of God, who, having fallen asleep in power and faith of the Son of God, even proclaimed to those who had previously fallen asleep."[109] Those messengers represented the Savior, who would not go in person to the wicked, for His mission was to now rise as the first fruits of the resurrection.

But He no sooner left this august assembly of righteous spirits than many of them, certainly Abraham included, followed the Son of God in rising from the dead. "The graves were opened," Matthew reports, "and many bodies of the saints which slept arose, and came out of the graves after his resurrection, and went into the holy city, and appeared unto many" (Matt. 27:52–53). An epistle from Ignatius, one of the early Christian martyrs, likewise recounts that the Savior's "disciples the prophets themselves in the Spirit did wait for Him as their Teacher," and "therefore He whom they rightly waited for, being come, raised them from the dead."[110] In the case of Abraham, a Jewish source foretold that the Messiah himself would "go to the Cave of Machpelah and say to the Fathers: 'Abraham, Isaac, and Jacob, arise! You have slept long enough.'"[111]

They arose to glory, for as explained in latter-day revelation, Abraham, Isaac, and Jacob "have entered into their exaltation, according to the promises," where they "sit upon thrones, and are not angels, but are gods" (D&C 132:37).

Joseph Smith's First Prayer

CHAPTER 12

Abraham's Legacy and the Latter-Day Zion:
Expanding Influence and the Latter-Day Fulfillment

Go ye, therefore, and do the works of Abraham.
—DOCTRINE AND COVENANTS 132:32

Legacy on Earth and Abraham's Bosom in Heaven

Abraham's royal status in heaven was not marked on earth in the manner of his burial. With the acclaim and adulation of a grief-stricken world, one might suppose that Abraham's interment would have followed the manner of contemporary kings with a jewel-encrusted sarcophagus or a massive pyramid or some other impressive monument to forever memorialize the patriarchal leader of mankind. That there was no such marker must be attributed to what Abraham himself had wanted.

Nor did he leave behind any likeness of his own person. We have no statue or bust or painting or golden death mask of the Patriarch like those magnificent representations made of and by his contemporary pharaohs, and even pharaohs far more ancient, who left their faces forever enshrined in stone or paint or gold. Similar endeavors seem to have occupied many monarchs throughout history, who sought to ensure that their royal visage would endure for all time. We can thereby contemplate the countenances of rulers like Ramses II, or Alexander the Great, or Julius Caesar, or even a mighty monarch in the region of Nimrut in present-day Turkey, perhaps the very Nimrod that was Abraham's mortal rival. But of Abraham himself, no such statue exists, or apparently ever did.

The great irony of all this is that Abraham actually held and exercised the divine royal patriarchal authority to which all these kings so ardently aspired. For all their pretension to power and for all their elaborate work in leaving their likeness eternally enshrined for mankind, they were only pretenders to the divine royal authority actually held by Abraham. With the treasures of the earth that God bestowed upon him, and with the multitudinous following he had, and with the popularity in his day of images of stone, Abraham might easily have ordered, or allowed to be made, a royal statue of himself. That he did not reveals something important about his character and what he valued.

And if he left no creed that we know about, one of his like-minded latter-day descendants—President George Albert Smith—did, and in so doing seems to have captured perfectly the essence of Abraham's life as well:

> I would be a friend to the friendless and find joy in ministering to the needs of the poor. I would visit the sick and the afflicted and inspire in them a desire to be healed. I would teach the truth to the understanding and blessing of all mankind. I would seek out the erring one, and try to win him back to a righteous and happy life. I would not seek to force people to live up to my ideals, but rather love them into doing the thing that is right. I would live with the masses and help to solve their problems that their earth life may be happy. I would avoid the publicity of high positions and discourage the flattery of thoughtless friends. I would not knowingly wound the feelings of any, not even one who may have wronged me, but would seek to do him good and make him my friend. I would overcome the tendency to selfishness and jealousy and rejoice in the success of all of the children of our Heavenly Father. I would not be an enemy to any living soul. Knowing that the Redeemer of mankind has offered unto the world the only plan that would fully develop us, and make us really happy here and hereafter; I feel it not only a duty, but a privilege to disseminate this truth.[1]

Or, if Abraham's great motive were to be captured in one sentence, it would be what another like-minded descendant—Nephi—wrote of himself: "The fulness of mine intent is that I may persuade men to come unto the God of Abraham, and the God of Isaac, and the God of Jacob, and be saved" (1 Ne. 6:4).

Because Abraham, Isaac, and Jacob were laid to rest in the same cave, the site would be venerated forever after as the grave of the Patriarchs; the eleventh-century official in charge of maintaining the area was called "The Servant to the Fathers of the World."[2] But it is Abraham's personal legacy of kindness that still echoes in the name Hebron, which in popular etymology is said to derive from the Hebrew word for "friend,"[3] making it the "place of the friend."[4] The Arabic name of the city, el-Khalil, similarly means "the friend," which is memorialized yet again in the name of the mosque covering the cave: Haram el-Khalil, "Sacred Precinct of the Friend."[5] And friendship was practiced there at least into the Middle Ages when the weary and needy could still find food and lodging at a charitably endowed institution called "Abraham's guest-house."[6]

But the tradition of hospitality begun by Abraham was hardly confined to his burial place, for he had taught his posterity well. His oldest son, Ishmael, was "a strenuous observer of all the precepts of his [father], . . . imitat[ing] him in being . . . munificent and compassionate; for he was extremely . . . hospitable, courteously entertaining travelers, charitably and generously succouring the indigent, . . . visiting the sick, and comforting the afflicted."[7]

He in turn transmitted these virtues to his large and noble posterity,[8] who handed them down through the generations that still remember their forefather as they pray, "Liberality belongs to the Prophet of God, Abraham."[9] And it is that liberality that they emulate. Speaking of the history of nomadic hospitality, Raphael Patai notes that it is a continuation of Abraham's own "exceeding hospitality. . . . The hospitality of the Bedouins, the modern-day heirs of Abraham, has often been described. It is a noble trait, exhibited proudly even by the poorest Bedouin, and impressive even in the modified and reduced form in which one encounters it among Arab city folk."[10]

Isaac also "became wise and intelligent, and he loved to give the poor and needy bread and raiment. He made peace between man and his neighbour and he comforted the unhappy and despairing, and he helped them with all his power; he was beloved by all who knew him and he became famous and praised by all."[11] Abraham's heritage was important in Judaism, and figured even in the national survival of ancient Israel: when Pharaoh commanded the Hebrew midwives to kill the baby boys, "the midwives feared God; they did not do as the king of Egypt commanded them, but they let the boys live" (NRSV Exodus 1:17). In doing so, says the midrash, "they modeled their conduct on that of their progenitor, Abraham. They said, 'Abraham, our ancestor, opened an inn where he fed all the wayfarers, men who were uncircumcised; and, as for us, not only have we nothing with which to feed them, but we are even to kill them. No, we will keep them alive!'"[12]

Thus was kept alive also the Abrahamic heritage of kindness. The "followers of Abraham . . . possess three traits: generosity, simplicity, and humility,"[13] says Jewish tradition. And as a recent study observes, the ancient Hebrew practice of hospitality and mercy, of helping "the poor and disadvantaged—the sojourner (outsider), the fatherless, the widowed," was an Abrahamic heritage continued by all three Abrahamic religions, Judaism, Christianity, and Islam, "inspir[ing] countless beings through the centuries to individual acts of lovingkindness and participation in correcting oppression," and "also influenc[ing] many people outside those traditions."[14] Such has been the global spread of kindness inspired by the life of Abraham.

And such has been the almost unbelievable influence of one man, whose effect on the world and whose name and reputation in it eclipse that of the haughty monarchs with whom he once had to deal. So widely revered had he become in the early centuries of the Christian era that the Roman Emperor Alexander Severus—ruler of the dominions once governed by Nimrod and Pharaoh—kept an image representing Abraham among his other gods.[15] It was part of the fulfillment of the Lord's promise to make Abraham's name great among all nations.[16] According to the Reverend W. F. P. Noble,

> Not the mighty Nimrods nor Pharaohs . . . nor any other man, has left such a broad mark on the world. His name is known where the greatest emperors and conquerors were never so much as heard of. There is no quarter of the globe to which it has not been carried, and it is the only one which is venerated alike by Jews and Christians and Mohammedans; for whatever be their differences . . . , all of them . . . claim an equal relationship with this distinguished patriarch, saying, "We have Abraham to our father."[17]

And it is to Abraham their father that they aspire to go, for the highest destiny sought by his righteous posterity is to share in the eternal rewards promised to Abraham. In both Judaism and Christianity from early times, the righteous are finally to be received into the "bosom of Abraham."[18] As an Armenian apocryphal source states: "Those who are worthy rest in his bosom."[19]

Orson Hyde commented about Abraham that "I suppose he has a pretty large bosom and a large heart, large enough to embrace all the faithful from his day down to the end of time, for in him and his seed shall all the families of the earth be blessed."[20] Jews today still pray to be blessed by "the One who blessed our ancestors, Abraham, Isaac, and Jacob."[21] So it is also in Islam, as Muslims throughout the world pray: "O God . . . bless Muhammad and the family of Muhammad as Thou didst bless Abraham and the family of Abraham," and "make us, O Lord, the comrades . . . of Abraham Thy Friend."[22] Muhammad himself, according to Islamic tradition, asked for equality with Abraham and commanded his community to ask for this,"[23] and Islam indeed considers itself "the community of Abraham."[24] In an Islamic funeral rite when the dead person is given instructions on how to answer the questions that will be posed, the person is told to say, among other things, "God is my Lord . . . and Abraham, Thy friend, my Father."[25]

Islamic tradition holds that Abraham sits enthroned in the highest heaven,[26] a tradition showing his "very special position" in Islam.[27] Modern revelation to

Joseph Smith similarly tells that even as Abraham "hath entered into his exaltation and sitteth upon his throne" (D&C 132:29)—the surpassing glory of which is emphasized in Jewish tradition[28]—so will all those who "do the works of Abraham" (D&C 132:32) likewise "inherit thrones" (D&C 132:19). In Nibley's words, "to be exalted means for Latter-day Saints to 'do the works of Abraham.'"[29]

Similarly, according to the Testament of Isaac, the aged Isaac heard the archangel Michael promise: "There has been prepared for you the throne beside your father Abraham. . . . You shall go away to rejoicing which has no end, and to light and bliss which have no limit, and to acclaim and delight without ceasing."[30]

Heritage of Righteousness

The angel also commanded Isaac to "teach your sons your ways and the commandments of your father—all of them which he commanded you . . . so that the faithful may observe them and by them attain to the life eternal, which is forever."[31] This was Abraham's legacy to his posterity: not the substantial property that Genesis says he had divided up among his heirs (25:5–6),[32] but rather the counsel to keep the commandments and to do "righteousness and justice"—the two "precious jewels" that Abraham bequeathed his children, says Jewish tradition.[33] It was a legacy much prized by his posterity, as poignantly remembered by the children of Ishmael. According to the Qur'an, "This very thing did Abraham bequeath unto his children . . . : 'O my children! Behold, God has granted you the purest faith; so do not allow death to overtake you ere you have surrendered yourselves [or 'submitted'[34]] unto Him."[35]

Likewise among the descendants of Isaac, Abraham's true legacy is still remembered as "a spiritual inheritance, . . . a legacy of moral lessons, wisdom, a right way to live."[36] One of Judaism's greatest rabbis, Hillel, taught that the value for Jews of their Abrahamic lineage is to help them "emulate the qualities of Abraham. . . . Deeds are important, not mere birth."[37] Other ancient Jewish sources likewise affirm: "If you are worthy, you are the children of Abraham."[38]

This same Abrahamic legacy was passed on by Abraham's great-grandson Benjamin on his own deathbed:

> You know then, my children, that I am dying. Do the truth, each of you to his neighbor; keep the law of the Lord and his commandments, for I leave you these things instead of an inheritance.[39] Give them, then, to your children for an eternal possession; this is what Abraham, Isaac, and Jacob did. They gave us all these things as an inheritance, saying, "Keep God's commandments until the Lord reveals his salvation to all the nations." And

then you will see Enoch and Seth and Abraham and Isaac and Jacob . . . at the right hand in great joy.[40]

As we approach that "great and dreadful day" (Mal. 4:5; D&C 2:1; 110:14, 16) when all nations will see the Lord's salvation and Abraham at the Lord's right hand, our world seems to become increasingly like Abraham's. As his world was as wicked as Noah's, so shall be ours: "As it was in the days of Noah, so it shall be also at the coming of the Son of Man" (JS—M 1:41). And as Abraham's world becomes ours, his life is not just history but a guide, as it has always been for those aspiring to be the people of God. Isaiah's words are more relevant than ever: "Look to Abraham your father" (NRSV Isa. 51:2).

What do we see when we look to Abraham? We see first a boy in an incredibly wicked world from which Zion had long since fled, a boy who refuses to go along with the evil practices but prayerfully seeks his Creator in purity and humility. We see a marriage of two people building Zion at home, and then reaching out to gather all to Zion. We see answers to prayers but also increasing persecution, for Abraham's life "was a continuous tale of sacrifice and suffering for his cause."[41] And through it all we see a profound faith in the Almighty, a faith carefully culti-vated and richly rewarded, as W. F. P. Noble described in the nineteenth century (decades before the emergence of the Genesis Apocryphon that would compare Abraham to a mighty cedar of Lebanon):

Of Abraham and his whole life . . . , of every journey he under-took, every march he made, every footprint he left . . . —it was true of him as it never was of any other man—'He walked by faith'. . . . But what explains *it*? What fed the faith wherein his great strength lay? Challenging comparison with any, and excelling all . . . , we may apply to him the glowing terms and bold figures of the prophet [Ezekiel]: "He was a cedar in Lebanon, with high stature and fair branches and shadowing shroud . . . , nor was any tree in the Garden of God like unto him for beauty: his root," he adds, explaining how this cedar towered above the loftiest trees, giant monarch of the forest—"his root was by the great waters." And what that root found in streams which, fed by the snows and seaming the sides of Lebanon, hottest summers never dried and coldest winters never froze, the unequaled faith of Abraham found in close and constant communion with God.

Like Enoch, he walked with God. Each important transaction of life was entered on in a pious spirit and hallowed by religious exercises. His tent was a moving temple; his household was a pilgrim church. Wherever he rested, whether by the venerable oak of Mamre, or on the olive slopes of Hebron, or on the lofty, forest-crowned ridge of Bethel, an altar rose, and his prayers went up with its smoke to heaven. Such daily intimate and loving communion did this grand saint maintain with heaven that God calls him his "friend;" and honoring his faith with a higher than earthly title, the Church has crowned him "Father of the Faithful."

He lived on terms of fellowship with God such as had not been seen since the days of Eden. Voices addressed him from the skies, angels paid visits to his tent, and visions of celestial glory hallowed his lowly couch and mingled with his nightly dreams. He was a man of prayer, and therefore he was a man of power.

Setting us an example that we should follow his steps, . . . to revert to language borrowed from the stateliest of Lebanon's cedars—thus was he "fair in his greatness and in the length of his branches, for his root was by the great waters."[42]

Nourished by the Almighty—whose commandments he kept, whose ordinances and priesthood he received, whose scriptures he searched, whose gospel he preached, whose love he shared, whose Zion he built, and of whose Beloved Son he testified—Abraham was not only blessed by God but also chose to be an instrument in carrying those same blessings to all mankind, the blessings of Zion. Zion is what Abraham sought, what he built, and what he qualified for, as Zion above actually partnered with him to protect him, bless him, teach him, empower him, and help in his mission.

As we look to Abraham, we also see him constantly seeking Zion's King, the Savior, through righteousness, prayer, and faith, even as he invites all to Christ and Zion by unwearying missionary labor and abundant kindness and hospitality. We see Abraham living the laws of obedience, sacrifice, the gospel, chastity, and consecration, and constantly doing temple work. "To be sure," wrote the poet Coleridge, "if ever man could, without impropriety, be called, or supposed to be, 'the friend of God,' Abraham was that man."[43] We see, in other words, the epitome of friendship and the pure love of Christ.

No wonder the Lord "revealed unto him," stated John Taylor, "some of the greatest and most sublime truths that ever were made known to man,"[44] and gave him, added Orson Hyde, some of the most sublime "promises that no other man has obtained . . . , the Son of God excepted."[45] In short, we see in Abraham's life a remarkable fellowship with the Almighty and a powerful pattern for obtaining the blessings of Zion. "For what reason," asked Clement, "was our father Abraham blessed? Was it not because he wrought righteousness and truth through faith?"[46]

The pattern is especially important for Latter-day Saints, Abraham's latter-day posterity aspiring to the blessings of their great forefather, whose example they are expressly commanded to emulate: "Do the works of Abraham" is the Lord's latter-day commandment (D&C 132:32). God blessed not only Abraham, explained Erastus Snow, but also "his seed after him . . . on condition that [they] should abide in the truth, follow the teachings and examples of their fathers, and prove themselves worthy."[47]

Or, as stated by Orson Hyde, "if we will do the works of Abraham, we are the children of Abraham."[48] Accordingly, as James Harris observes, "How can we become a Zion people? The same way that Abraham became a Zion man."[49] In the words of Hugh Nibley, "We are commanded to do the works of Abraham and told that there is *no other way for us to go*," for "only by 'doing the works of Abraham' can we hope to establish a better order of things on the earth, that order of Zion" long lost from the earth.[50] For only in Zion does one find charity, that greatest of all things and sine qua non of godliness, which Abraham possessed in full measure and for which he is still remembered in Judaism as the very embodiment.[51]

We further see in Abraham's life remarkable foreshadowings of Zion through the ages, including the King of Zion, whose birth and Atonement are so clearly prefigured in the life of Abraham. We see foreshadowed the great events of the latter-day Zion—from Joseph Smith's life, ministry, and translation of ancient scriptural records, to the gathering of the Latter-day Saints, to the building of temples, to the Lord's glorious Second Coming when He will deliver His people as dramatically and decisively as He once did Abraham from death on a pagan altar in Ur. Abraham's life is truly "a lesson of the future."[52]

And we see Abraham receiving covenants guaranteeing that Zion as it would exist through the ages would be built by his posterity. John Taylor remarked:

> From [Abraham's day] forth, by that lineage the blessings of heaven have flowed to the children of men. . . . Who were Isaac and Jacob? Heirs of the same promise as himself. Who was Joseph, who was sold into Egypt? A descendant of Abraham. Who was Moses, who delivered the people from Egyptian bondage? A descendant of Abraham. Who was Aaron, who was associated with the Aaronic Priesthood, and who presided over it? A descendant of Abraham. Who were the Prophets that we read of in this Bible? They were descendants of Abraham. Who was

Jesus, who as the Son of God, taketh away the sins of the world? A descendant of Abraham according to the flesh. Who were the Twelve Apostles, commissioned to preach the Gospel to all nations? Descendants of Abraham. And who were the [Nephite] Twelve Apostles that lived upon this continent? Descendants of Abraham. Who was Joseph Smith, to whom the Gospel was revealed in these last days? A descendant of Abraham.[53]

Parley Pratt similarly emphasized that from "the lineage of Abraham, Isaac, and Jacob . . . sprang the Prophets, John the Baptist, Jesus, and the Apostles; and from this lineage sprang the great Prophet and restorer in modern times. . . . In this peculiar lineage, and in no other, should all the nations be blessed."[54] Indeed, it was so determined in the premortal councils, said Brigham Young: "Joseph Smith . . . was foreordained to come through the loins of Abraham."[55]

And if descendant, then heir; the Lord declared to Joseph Smith that "Abraham received promises concerning his seed, and of the fruit of his loins— from whose loins ye are" (D&C 132:30). And if Abraham's distinguishing quality was love, so it was with his descendant Joseph Smith, whose love for mankind drew thousands to him.[56] As Abraham the Friend transformed the world by his love, so would Joseph Smith: "Friendship," he declared, "is one of the grand fundamental principles of 'Mormonism'; it is designed to revolutionize and civilize the world, and cause wars and contentions to cease and men to become friends and brothers. Even the wolf and the lamb shall dwell together."[57] Hence President Hinckley's continuing counsel to Latter-day Saints to reach out with "greater love for our fellowmen"[58] by "feeding and clothing the hungry and the needy, extending love and neighborliness to those about us."[59]

And who are the Latter-day Saints? Like their founding prophet Joseph Smith, they also are seed of the great Patriarch, as the Lord has declared: "ye are the children of Israel, and of the seed of Abraham" (D&C 103:17). They in turn are called to go gather out their fellow Abrahamic descendants. "We are now calling upon the Elders to go and gather up Israel," declared President Brigham Young. "Will we go to the Gentile nations to preach the gospel? Yes, and gather out the Israelites, wherever they are mixed among the nations of the earth." And "if any of the Gentiles will believe, we will lay our hands upon them that they may receive the Holy Ghost, and the Lord will make them of the house of Israel."[60]

By this process, all who are gathered are of Abraham's seed, whether actual descendants or by the change that, according to Joseph Smith, is actually physiological.[61] "By obeying this Gospel," explained Elder Parley Pratt, "or by adoption through the Gospel, we are all made joint heirs with Abraham, . . . and we shall, by continuance in well doing, all be blessed in Abraham and his seed. . . . The blessing is broad enough to gather all good, penitent, obedient people under its wings, and to extend to all nations the principles of salvation. We would therefore . . . cordially invite all nations to join . . . this favored lineage."[62]

Abraham's latter-day descendants thereby follow their forefather in inviting all to become heirs of Abraham by accepting the gospel that he himself preached, building the Zion that he foresaw, and qualifying for the blessings he received. And thus, in the words of John Taylor, "will the Zion of our God be built up."[63]

The Abrahamic Drama of Latter-day Zion

If the actors in the Lord's drama are part of Abraham's covenant, so is the drama itself, beginning with fourteen-year-old Joseph Smith's earnest prayer to the Creator, "for there was none else to whom I could go,"[64] as he would explain. Regarding the glorious appearance of the Father and the Son to the boy Joseph Smith that day, one Latter-day Saint scholar wrote: "The entire story of the Restoration as it centers in the opening of the heavens to Joseph Smith is but the fulfilling of the promises God made to Abraham."[65] It is indeed the latter-day fulfillment of what Nephi called "the covenants of the Father of heaven unto Abraham . . . in bringing about his covenants and his gospel unto those who are of the house of Israel" to "bring them again out of captivity" to "be gathered" and "brought out of obscurity and out of darkness" so that they may "know that the Lord is their Savior and their Redeemer, the Mighty One of Israel" (1 Ne. 22:9–12).

Such fulfillment was foreseen with great joy by Abraham and others. Joseph Smith explained that the latter-day Zion "interested the people of God in every age," who have "sung and written and prophesied of this our day," but "we are the favored people that God has made choice of to bring about the Latter-day glory . . . ; a work that is destined to bring about the destruction of the powers of darkness, the renovation of the earth, the glory of God, and the salvation of the human family."[66]

Already half of this human family—including Christians, Muslims, and Jews—look to Abraham as their spiritual, and in many cases literal, forefather, in partial fulfillment of the remarkable promises made to him about his posterity, and in a way that prepares many of them to receive the pristine truths of the restored gospel and ordinances that Abraham once had. John Lord wrote in the nineteenth century:

> Abraham appears to us, after the lapse of nearly four thousand years, as the most august character in history . . . As a religious thinker, inspired to restore faith in the world and the worship of the One God, it would be difficult to find a man more favored or more successful. He is the spiritual father equally of Jews, Christians, and Mohammedans, in their warfare with idolatry. In

this sense, he is the spiritual progenitor of all those nations, tribes, and peoples who now acknowledge, or who may hereafter acknowledge, a personal God, supreme and eternal in the universe which He created.[67]

But it is for what yet lies ahead that another nineteenth-century writer, W. F. P. Noble, saw the extent of Abraham's influence, in a statement reminiscent of that of the Prophet Joseph. Abraham is, said Noble, "in some respects the most remark-able man, the greatest character, in history," for "to his descendants God committed those great truths which . . . are destined to overturn Satan's empire throughout the whole bounds of earth, and establish on its ruins the reign of holy and universal peace, restoring Eden to a defiled and distracted world, and . . . to humanity the image of its God."[68]

To effectuate the great Abrahamic latter-day work of the rolling forth of the restored kingdom of God, "the heavenly Priesthood," said the Prophet Joseph, will not be "idle spectators," but will actually "unite with the earthly"[69]—even as happened in Abraham's day. President Joseph F. Smith similarly taught:

> We move and have our being in the presence of heavenly messen-gers. . . . We are not separate from them. . . . We are closely related to our kindred, to our ancestors, to our friends and associ-ates and co-laborers who have preceded us into the spirit world. We cannot forget them; we do not cease to love them; we always hold them in our hearts, in memory, and thus we are associated and united to them by ties that we cannot break. . . . Those who have been faithful, who have gone beyond and are still engaged in the work for the salvation of the souls of men, . . . can see us better than we can see them. . . . We live in their presence, they see us, they are solicitous for our welfare, they love us now more than ever.[70]

Abraham's continuing concern for his posterity is reflected in a Talmudic tradition telling that at the destruction of the Jerusalem Temple, Abraham "wept bitterly" over his posterity, wondering if because of their iniquities "there was no hope for them." Then came a divine voice saying that "as the olive-tree produces its best only at the very end, so Israel will flourish at the end of time."[71]

Now at this season of latter-day flourishing, Abraham is joyfully involved, a fact of which we have brief but telling glimpses. That Joseph Smith had visited with Abraham and was familiar with him was attested by John Taylor.[72] And when President Wilford Woodruff addressed the Saints assembled at the dedication of the Salt Lake Temple, he stated that "if the veil could be taken from our eyes . . . , we would see . . . every prophet and apostle that ever prophesied of the great work of God. . . . These patriarchs and prophets, who have wished for this day, rejoice . . . far more than we do, because they know what lies before [us] in the great work of God."[73]

They know, for example, that God's covenantal protection of Abraham's righteous posterity will more than equal any challenge they face. They also know the details of how, as Nephi wrote, the Lord "will show unto them that fight against [His] word and against [His] people" that He is God and that He "covenanted with Abraham that [He] would remember his seed forever" (2 Ne. 29:14). For as the Lord has promised his Latter-day Saints, "the redemption of Zion must needs come by power. . . . For ye are the children of Israel" (D&C 103:15, 17).

And speaking of the preservation of the house of Israel at the great and terrible day, Isaiah foretold that those "diligent for evil shall be wiped out" by the same Lord "who redeemed Abraham" (JPST Isa. 29:20, 22).[74] Another ancient Jewish text states that "the God of Israel . . . keeps watch for the redemption, and for the time of salvation which has been preserved for Israel. . . . When will he descend . . . to the seed of Abraham, his beloved?"[75]

According to the apocryphal Enoch writings, Abraham and the rest of the righteous in heaven will actually petition the Lord to stretch forth His mighty arm and deliver Abraham's seed in their hour of dire distress.[76] It will not be the first time, says Jewish tradition, for "Abraham's intervention on behalf of his children."[77]

Meanwhile, as Enoch once foresaw, "the heavens shall shake, and also the earth" (Moses 7:61). And as Enoch had heard the earth complain to its Creator about the wickedness of mankind (Moses 7:48), so at the last day, according to a Jewish midrash, shall it happen again: "The heavens and the earth will be agitated and afraid and shaken" and will complain to their Creator about "the wicked" who "provoke you, and you will destroy. . . . What will happen to us? For you did not create us except for the sake of the sons of Adam." The Lord will reply, "I did not create you except for the sake of Abraham and Sarah," whereupon "the heavens and the earth and all the orders of creation will be glad and will rejoice."[78]

Then will the righteous dead be resurrected, as foreshadowed by Isaac's rise from the altar, and will come forth renewed to the beauty and bloom of youth, as Abraham had been shown in a vision of the future. And then will the Son of God come in glory to bless all nations and deliver Abraham's righteous seed as decisively as He once delivered Abraham from the altar of death in Ur, and according to the pattern of the fiery destruction of Sodom and Gomorrah. As foretold by the prophet Isaiah, "the Lord will come with fire, and with his chariots like a whirlwind, to render his anger with fury, and his rebuke with flames of fire" (Isa. 66:15).

The Lord's riding a fiery chariot recalls his own language when he once told Abraham that "I dwell in heaven; the earth is my footstool; I stretch my hand over the sea, and it obeys my voice; I cause the wind and the fire to be my chariot; I say to the mountains—Depart hence—and behold, they are taken away by a whirlwind, in an instant, suddenly" (Abr. 2:7). But it is a text from New Testament times that most fully uses this imagery to describe the Lord's Second Coming. The text is an apocryphal record reporting the speech that got Stephen arrested. Stephen's subsequent defense, as reported in the New Testament itself, mentions Abraham's call and his leaving Haran (Acts 7:2–4), while the apocryphal speech contains much of the very imagery reported in the Book of Abraham that the Lord used when he appeared to Abraham in Haran—imagery that includes the chariot, the wind, the sea, the mountains, and the earth as God's footstool:

> Stephen, a learned man of the tribe of Benjamin, stood on a high place and addressed the assembly. . . . Blessed is he who has not doubted concerning Jesus. Born of a pure virgin he filled the world with light. . . . Woe to the unbelievers when he shall come as judge, with angels, a fiery chariot, a mighty wind: the stars shall fall, the heavens open, the books be brought forward. The . . . angels who are set over every soul shall unveil the deeds of men. The sea shall move and give up what is in it. The mountains fall, all the surface of the earth becomes smooth. Great winged thrones are set. The Lord, and Christ, and the Holy Spirit take their seats. The Father bids Jesus sit on his right hand.[79]

Regarding the Lord's chariot, an intriguing passage in the midrash makes the startling assertion that the Patriarchs themselves—Abraham, Isaac, and Jacob—"are the Chariot of God."[80] How so? Perhaps because, as the Lord states in latter-day revelation, he will descend in glory with Abraham, Isaac, and Jacob, as well as the other righteous (D&C 133:55).[81] One ancient source states that among the hosts of righteous descending with the Lord, the "great Abraham himself will come."[82]

And according to a rabbinic midrash, Abraham will be honored by the Messiah, who upon setting foot on the earth to sit on His throne, will nevertheless wait to be seated, for first He "will treat with respect Abraham, Isaac and Jacob, Moses and . . . all the . . . prophets, and he will not [yet] sit upon the throne on account of their honour." They in turn will give Him honor and praise, and standing before Him will call Him "our true Messiah,"[83] saying, "even though we came before you, you are greater than we because of all the suffering you have endured for the iniquities of our children."[84]

Thus as the Savior had once stood at His own throne to welcome His friend Abraham, so apparently will the Savior again stand to welcome Abraham and all his righteous posterity, who will then "shine as the brightness of the firmament" in fulfillment of the covenant made to Abraham.[85] For if the world at first was created for the sake of Abraham and his righteous seed, so the new creation in the form of the renewed earth will, according to a midrash, again be for the sake of Abraham and his righteous seed,[86] who will come forth in the resurrection in the splendor of their youth as surely as the Lord once renewed their mother Sarah to bear Abraham's son of promise.[87] And in that future day, as prophesied by John Taylor, "Abraham will . . . realize the fulfillment of the promises made to him and will stand in his proper place and position as . . . father . . . of his seed in the grand jubilee in this earth."[88]

Inaugurating that blessed era of the "new heaven and . . . new earth" will be the great Messianic banquet, depicted in scripture as the marriage supper of the Lamb, to which the hungry and thirsty are invited to come and partake "freely,"[89] "without money and without price" (Isa. 55:1).[90] Then, as the Savior Himself foretold, "many will come from the east and the west, and will take their places at the feast with Abraham" (NIV Matthew 8:11)[91] and other righteous leaders. Why is Abraham named first? Perhaps to honor him for the bounteous hospitality he provided when he invited all from the east, west, north, and south to come and partake of the abundant feast of food and spiritual succor that he freely offered to mankind, thus fulfilling the Lord's promise that He "shall come to recompense unto every man according to his work, and measure to every man according to the measure which he has measured to his fellow man" (D&C 1:10). According to Al-Tabari, Abraham's glory hereafter "is more splendid and tremendous than anyone can describe."[92]

No wonder that as we look forward to the marvelous events ahead, we are commanded also to look back—back to Abraham and Sarah, whose lives foreshadowed Zion and its latter-day redemption. Indeed, Isaiah specifically links the Second Coming and the joyful new era of bliss with Abraham and Zion:

> Listen to me, you that pursue righteousness, you that seek the LORD. Look to the rock from which you were hewn, and to the quarry from which you were dug. Look to Abraham your father and to Sarah who bore you; for he was but one when I called him, but I blessed him and made him many. For the LORD will comfort Zion; he will comfort all her waste places, and will make her wilderness like Eden, her desert like the garden of the LORD; joy and gladness will be found in her, thanksgiving and the voice of song. Listen to me, my people, and give heed to me, my nation; for a teaching[93] will go out from me, and my justice[94] for

a light to the peoples. I will bring near my deliverance[95] swiftly, my salvation has gone out[96] and my arms shall rule the peoples;[97] the coastlands[98] wait for me, and for my arm they hope. Lift up your eyes to the heavens, and look at the earth beneath; for the heavens will vanish like smoke, the earth will wear out like a garment, and those who live on it will die like gnats; but my salvation will be forever (NRSV Isa. 51:1–6).

Look to Abraham—and learn how to come unto Christ and build the latter-day Zion in preparation for the Savior's Second Coming.

Look to Abraham—and discover the powerful and pure love of Christ that latter-day Zion must acquire.

Look to Abraham—and see how the Lord will comfort and deliver Zion when He descends with His hosts of righteous Saints, including His beloved friend Abraham, to fulfill the covenant made to him.

Descending also shall be Enoch's Zion to join the Zion below in bringing unprecedented glory to this planet, for then shall all the earth become Zion,[99] a restoration and extension of the Edenic paradise that will truly be the "bosom of Abraham" for all who have been sanctified through the Lord Jesus Christ, the eternal King of Zion.

Jewish tradition records that when the Almighty was contemplating what blessing to bestow on Abraham, God reasoned thus:

> After seeing the way Abraham conducted himself, God said to him, "Abraham, what blessing can I bestow upon you? That you should be perfectly righteous or that your wife should be righteous? You are righteous and Sarah, your wife, is righteous. What blessing then can I bestow upon you? Only that all the children that are destined to issue from you, may be like you.[100]

Since Abraham's true seed are only those who do the works of Abraham, it is that seed that not only inherits the blessings of Abraham but constitutes the greatest blessing that God gave the Patriarch. "God's blessing to Abraham," observes a modern rabbi, "is still the most meaningful blessing that one can offer to any worthy individual; that his children may continue in his footsteps and seek to emulate his noble acts and deeds."[101] In the end, we become a part of Abraham's greatest blessing as we qualify for his blessings by doing the works of Abraham.

Speaking in general conference, Elder Franklin D. Richards declared that it is our goal to "enter into the fulfillment of the promises made to the fathers, even the blessings of Abraham, Isaac and Jacob. We want to live so as to inherit and receive them in their fullness; so that when the time comes that Abraham, our father, shall come upon the earth to receive that inheritance that has been promised him, they who are the children of Abraham will be blessed with faithful Abraham."[102] In the words of another writer, "if men will learn of Abraham and follow his example then may they too go forth abroad and look toward Heaven, and in their ears may be heard a voice saying, 'So shall thy seed be.'"[103]

The life of Abraham powerfully beckons us to the Savior, to His Zion, and to His richest blessings here and hereafter. Well might we ask ourselves the question posed by a Jewish text: "When shall my deeds be like those of Abraham?"[104] A modern prophet has suggested the answer: "Now is the time to follow Abraham's example."[105]

Notes

Notes to Foreword
1. So writes Middle East historian Cyrus Gordon.

Notes to Preface
1. Scherman and Zlotowitz, *Bereishis: Genesis* 1(a):402.
2. Parley P. Pratt, "Editorial Remarks," *Millennial Star* 3/4 (August 1842): 70.
3. James Carroll, "The Story of Abraham," in Rosenberg, *Genesis: As It Is Written*, 71.
4. Kenney, *Wilford Woodruff's Journal* 2:155.
5. Nibley, *Abraham in Egypt*, 30.

Notes to Introduction
1. It was the "cause of Zion" that Latter-day Saints from the beginning were commanded to establish and bring forth (D&C 6:6; see 11:6; 12:6; and 14:6), and it was this same cause that, according to the revelation given at the organization of the Church, had been "move[d] . . . in mighty power for good" by the Prophet Joseph Smith (D&C 21:7). Severe opposition soon followed, and the Lord revealed to his fledgling flock the Book of Moses, showing that their cause of Zion was actually a continuation of a glorious enterprise that had once been fully established on earth and then taken to heaven. Smith, *History of the Church*, 1:98.
2. Galbraith and Smith, *Scriptural Teachings of the Prophet Joseph Smith*, 183.
3. See Doctrine and Covenants 97:21 and 105:5. According to Hugh Nibley, "Zion is perfect, flawless, and complete—not a structure in the process of building. We work for the building up of the kingdom of God on earth and the establishment of Zion. The first step makes the second possible. Zion has been on the earth before in its perfection, . . . and we have the joyful promise that at some future time it will again descend to earth." Nibley, *Approaching Zion,* 25.
4. In all of the so-called pseudepigraphical Enoch literature that has emerged, and with all the parallels between this literature and the Enoch material restored through Joseph Smith, yet only the Joseph Smith material mentions that Enoch's city was translated with him. Mesopotamian tradition does mention an association between Enoch (or his equivalent in Mesopotamian literature, the seventh predeluvian king named Enmeduranki) and the city of Sippar. See VanderKam, *Enoch: A Man for All Generations,* 13, and 6–14; VanderKam, *Enoch and the Growth of an Apocalyptic Tradition*, 43–45; Kvanig, *Roots of Apocalyptic,* 172–90. As will be seen later, this last source may allude to the fact that other people were translated with Enoch.
5. See Moses 7:16, 18, 21, 69; and Doctrine and Covenants 82:14.
6. "Zion should come again on the earth, the city of Enoch." JST, Gen. 9:21. See also Moses 7:60–64.
7. See, for example, Doctrine and Covenants 1:4: "in these last days."
8. Galbraith and Smith, *Scriptural Teachings of the Prophet Joseph Smith,* 261–62.
9. Nibley, *Enoch the Prophet,* 255.
10. Except to briefly expand on the story centering around him, such as the angels' destruction of Sodom in Genesis chapter 19, and the journey of Abraham's servant to obtain a wife for Isaac in chapter 24.
11. Unless otherwise indicated, all references to the Bible are to the standard LDS edition of the King James Version. References to other Latter-day Saint scriptures are also to standard LDS editions.
12. Isaiah 41:8, in Gileadi, *The Literary Message of Isaiah,* 351. The King James has "Abraham my friend," but the Hebrew word derives from the verb *ahav,* "to love" (see Brown, Driver, and Briggs, *Hebrew and English Lexicon,* 12–13; and Botterweck and Ringgren, *Theological Dictionary of the Old Testament,* 1:99–118), and "implies a more intimate relationship than . . . the usual word for 'my friend/companion,'" so that God literally calls Abraham "him whom I loved" (North, *The Second Isaiah,* 97) or "my beloved" or "my beloved friend," as the passage is translated in some versions both ancient and modern. The Septuagint has the Greek equivalent of "whom I have loved," while Aquila has the Greek equivalent of "my beloved" (Watts, *Isaiah 34–66,* 99); Westermann reads "whom I loved" (*Isaiah 40–66,* 67), and the *Emphasized Bible* reads "my loving one" (Vaughan, *Twenty-Six Translations* 2:2478). Jewish tradition remembers Abraham as "more beloved of [God] than any man" (Ginzberg, *Legends of the Jews,* 1:320).
13. Subsequent biblical passages similarly emphasize the unique role of Abraham, whose covenant is fulfilled in the conception and birth of Christ (see Luke 1:55 and preceding verses), the true seed of Abraham (Gal. 3:16). When Christ in turn teaches of heaven, he identifies it in terms of his illustrious forefather, calling it "Abraham's bosom" (Luke 16:22). And it is the covenant of Abraham that is fulfilled in the preaching of the gospel by the Jewish Christians to all the gentile world (see Gal. 3:14).
14. The "fathers" in these verses are the forbears of not only the Latter-day Saints (verse 12) but also the ancient patriarch Joseph (verse 7), great-grandson of Abraham.
15. Ludlow, *Encyclopedia of Mormonism,* 2:765.
16. Significant additions to the Abraham story include: Abraham remembering the covenant to his forefather Enoch (JST, Gen. 13:13); Melchizedek and his city (JST, Gen. 14:25–40); Abraham seeing the days of the Son of Man (JST, Gen. 15:8–12); the meaning of the covenant of circumcision (JST, Gen. 17:3–12); and the identity of Abraham's three visitors (JST, Gen. 18:19–23). Most of the other changes are found in the story of Lot (JST, Gen. 19:10–14, 30–31, 37); the story of Abimelech (JST, Gen. 20:4–5, 17); and the story of Abraham's servant finding a wife for Isaac (JST, Gen. 24:16).
17. For a history of discovery, translation, and publication of the Book of Abraham, see Ludlow, *Encyclopedia of Mormonism,*

1:132–38.

18. After helping to set the type for the March 1842 printing of one of the original installments of the Book of Abraham, Wilford Woodruff recorded in his journal: "The truths of the book of Abraham are truly edifying great & glorious which are among the rich treasures that are revealed unto us in the last days." Kenney, *Wilford Woodruff's Journal* 2:159.

19. In 1840. Earlier English translations had been published in England in 1750 and 1829. See Noah, *Book of Yashar,* introductory page (unnumbered); and Alcuinus, *Book of Jasher.*

20. Galbraith and Smith, *Scriptural Teachings of the Prophet Joseph Smith,* 293, quoting the article titled "Persecution of the Prophets" in *Times and Seasons,* September 1, 1842.

21. Brigham Young in *Journal of Discourses,* 9:290 and 11:118 (both as President of the Church); John Taylor in *Journal of Discourses,* 14:359 and 22:307 (the latter as President of the Church); Wilford Woodruff in *Journal of Discourses,* 11:244.

22. Stuy, *Collected Discourses,* 3:140–41.

23. "The Book of the Revelation of Abraham," *Improvement Era,* August 1898, 705–706. See also Nibley, *Abraham in Egypt,* 11.

24. See JST, Genesis 15:9–12, and chapter 29 of the Apocalypse of Abraham. See below in chapter 7.

25. *Journal of Discourses,* 17:245.

26. Ibid., 22:318.

27. See Apocalypse of Abraham, 22–29, in Charlesworth, *Old Testament Pseudepigrapha,* 1:700–704.

28. Charles, *Apocrypha and Pseudepigrapha.*

29. Samuel Sandmel, in "Foreword for Jews," to Charlesworth, *Old Testament Pseudepigrapha,* 1:xi, xiii.

30. Nibley, *Enoch the Prophet,* 95.

31. Bloom, *The American Religion,* 101.

32. Bloom, *The American Religion,* 82–84.

33. Galbraith and Smith, *Scriptural Teachings of the Prophet Joseph Smith,* 301.

34. "None ever were perfect but Jesus," explained the Prophet Joseph. Smith, *History of the Church,* 4:272–73.

35. Noble, *Great Men of God,* 57.

36. Jasher 26:34, in Noah, *Book of Yashar,* 77.

37. Panarion 1.4.1,1, in Williams, *Panarion of Epiphanius,* 18.

38. Jubilees 23:10, in Charlesworth, *Old Testament Pseudepigrapha,* 2:100.

39. Judean Antiquities 1.256, in Feldman, *Josephus,* 100.

40. Brinner, *Lives of the Prophets,* 160.

41. On Abraham 46, in *Philo VI,* 135.

42. John C. Cavadini, "Exegetical Transformations: The Sacrifice of Isaac in Philo, Origen, and Ambrose," in Blowers, *In Dominico Eloquio,* 35–36, as summarized by Cavadini.

43. Chavel, *Ramban,* 292, on Genesis 24:1.

44. Spencer W. Kimball, "The Example of Abraham," *Ensign,* June 1975, 7.

45. Maimonides, Mishneh Torah, Hilchot De'ot 1:7, in Maimonides, *Mishneh Torah: Hilchot De'ot and Hilchot Talmud Torah,* 30.

46. Nibley, *Abraham in Egypt,* 651–52.

47. Soloveitchik, *Man of Faith,* 68.

48. Nibley, *Abraham's Creation Drama,* 1.

49. See Scherman and Zlotowitz, *Bereishis: Genesis,* 1:821.

50. See *Encyclopaedia Judaica,* 14:868; and Ginzberg, *Legends of the Jews,* 1:203.

51. Visotzky, *Midrash on Proverbs,* 83.

52. Matthews, *Armenian Commentary on Genesis,* 100.

53. *Journal of Discourses,* 24:337.

Notes to Chapter 1

1. Midrash Aleph Beth 1.10, in Sawyer, *Midrash Aleph Beth,* 94.

2. Genesis Rabbah 12:9, in Freedman, *Midrash Rabbah, Genesis,* 1:94–95.

3. See Midrash Aleph Beth 14:3, in Sawyer, *Midrash Aleph Beth,* 238.

4. Sawyer, *Midrash Aleph Beth,* 247.

5. See Genesis Rabbah 43:7, in Freedman, *Midrash Rabbah, Genesis,* 1:357; Midrash Aleph Beth 14:4, in Sawyer, *Midrash Aleph Beth,* 238, and Sawyer's commentary on 247–48.

6. Levy, *A Faithful Heart,* 13, citing and explaining Genesis Rabbah 12:9.

7. Psalms 89:3, translation in Cohen and Mendes-Flohr, *Contemporary Jewish Religious Thought,* 299.

8. Cohen and Mendes-Flohr, *Contemporary Jewish Religious Thought,* 299. See also Green, *Devotion and Commandment,* 86 n. 88, speaking of God's creating the world because of his *hesed,* and citing among other sources Genesis Rabbah 12:15 and Rashi on Genesis 1:1.

9. On the dual dimension of divine *hesed* as embracing both love and covenantal loyalty, see Glueck, *Hesed in the Bible,* 73; and Botterweck and Ringgren, *Theological Dictionary of the Old Testament,* 5:54–64.

10. Kasher, *Encyclopedia of Biblical Interpretation,* 1:9, paragraph 28, citing Midrash Haneelam B'reshith Zohar Hadash.

11. Galbraith and Smith, *Scriptural Teachings of the Prophet Joseph Smith,* 411.

12. Ibid., 393–95.

13. Sarna, *Genesis*, 3.

14. See, for example, Levenson, *Sinai and Zion*, 128–37, including: "some in Israel saw in Zion the cosmic mountain which is also the primal paradise called the Garden of Eden. . . . The equation of the Temple Mount and paradise . . . [has its] roots in the mythopoetic mind of the ancient Near East." See also Callendar, *Adam in Myth and History*, 50–54, discussing relevant Israelite and Mesopotamian traditions; and Martha Himmelfarb, "The Temple and the Garden of Eden in Ezekiel, the Book of the Watchers, and the Wisdom of Ben Sira," in Scott and Simpson-Housley, *Sacred Places*, 63–78.

15. Levenson, *Sinai and Zion*, 133.

16. See Wenham, *Genesis 1–15*, li.

17. See Westermann, *Genesis 1–11*, 547–548; and Ginzberg, *Legends of the Jews*, 1:179–81.

18. von Rad, *Genesis*, 152–53.

19. Recognitions of Clement 1.32, in *Ante-Nicene Fathers*, 8:86.

20. See, for example, Helaman 6:31; Mormon 5:18.

21. Jubilees 11:2–5, in VanderKam, *Book of Jubilees*, 64–65 (parentheses omitted and brackets added).

22. Yadin, *Art of Warfare*, 1:39, 75.

23. Nibley, *Approaching Zion*, 322, 489.

24. Quoted in Bowker, *Targums and Rabbinic Literature*, 187. The description is of conditions in the days of Serug but sets the stage for Abraham. And see the context in the translation of the entire Book of the Rolls 119a, in Gibson, *Apocrypha Arabica*, 35.

25. See Doctrine and Covenants 107:40–57 and discussion below in chapter 2.

26. Pirke de Rabbi Eliezer 24, in Friedlander, *Pirke de Rabbi Eliezer*, 174.

27. As the scholars state: "Abraham and his seed are to be chosen as the race through which God would bring 'truth and righteousness' into the world." Black, *1 Enoch*, 290, translation on 86. "The sentence . . . describes the election of Abra(ha)m, the ancestor of the chosen people." VanderKam, *Enoch: A Man for All Generations*, 68. "Abraham and his seed chosen as the race in and through which God would reveal his righteous judgments—'the plant of righteous judgment.'" Charles, *Book of Enoch*, 272 n. 5. See also Charlesworth, *Old Testament Pseudepigrapha*, 1:74 n. 93j (noting that Ethiopian commentators also insisted that it referred to Abraham).

28. 1 Enoch 93:5, in Black, *1 Enoch*, 86.

29. 1QapGen [1Q20 in Vermes] 14, in Vermes, *Complete Dead Sea Scrolls*, 452. Noah has just been told that he himself is a great cedar. Later Abraham also will be compared to a great cedar.

30. Pseudo Philo 4.11, in Jacobson, *Liber Antiquitatum Biblicarum*, 1:95.

31. *Journal of Discourses*, 14:358.

32. Meyers, *The Oxford Encyclopedia of Archaeology*, 5:288.

33. Moorey, *Ur "of the Chaldees,"* 9. Moorey also notes disagreement on the historical existence of the person of Abraham.

34. Nachmanides on Genesis 11:28, in Chavel, *Ramban*, 1:157–58.

35. Westermann, *Genesis 12–36*, 139.

36. See "Abraham's Ur: Is the Pope Going to the Wrong Place?" *Biblical Archeology Review* 26.1 (January/February 2000): 16ff. "Abraham's Ur: Did Woolley Excavate the Wrong Place?" *Biblical Archeology Review* 26.1 (January/February 2000): 20ff. Alan R. Millard, "Where Was Abraham's Ur? The Case for the Babylonian City," *Biblical Archeology Review* 27.3 (May/June 2001): 52ff.

37. So asserts Westermann, *Genesis 12–36*, 139–40; and Nibley, *Abraham in Egypt*, 234–38.

38. See, for example, Gordon and Rendsburg, *The Bible and the Ancient Near East*, 113; Westermann, *Genesis 12–36*, 139–40; and Segal, *Edessa*, 1–3.

39. The claim is also made by Syrian village of Berzeh, in a hilly region to the north of Damascus. Ball, *Syria*, 67.

40. Segal, *Edessa*, 1.

41. Ibid.; Budge, *Cave of Treasures*, 153.

42. Segal, *Edessa*, 1.

43. See Graves and Patai, *Hebrew Myths*, 132; Westermann, *Genesis 1–11*, 564; and Segal, *Edessa*, 1.

44. See Pauls and Facaros, *Turkey*, 346–47.

45. See ibid.

46. Granzotto, *Christopher Columbus*, 19.

47. Ten generations from Noah to Abraham are also given in Genesis 11:10–26 in Masoretic [traditional Hebrew] and Samaritan texts, as well as rabbinic tradition. See Ginzberg, *Legends of the Jews*, 1:185.

48. Another generation—Arphaxad's son Cainan—is recorded in the Septuagint genealogy list of Genesis, in Jubilees 8:1, and in Luke 3:36.

49. Ginzberg, *Legends of the Jews*, 1:185.

50. He "claimed to rule the world as God's successor on earth." Nibley, *Teachings of the Pearl of Great Price*, Lecture 23, 10.

51. See Genesis 10:8–12. "In the Hebrew Bible, Nimrod is the name of a Mesopotamian hero known to have been a famous hunter as well as the founder of major Mesopotamian cities and of the first state in post-diluvian primaeval times." Toorn, Becking, and Horst, *Dictionaries of Deities and Demons*, 627. See also Ether 2:1, where his status is indicated by the fact that there was a Valley of Nimrod, "being called after the mighty hunter."

52. Toorn, Becking, and Horst, *Dictionaries of Deities and Demons*, 629.

53. Ibid., 627.

54. Ibid., 629, quoting Augustine, *City of God,* 16.4.

55. By Noah's grandson Canaan (some sources say Ham). See Kasher, *Encyclopedia of Biblical Interpretation,* 2:69–75; and Ginzberg, *Legends of the Jews,* 1:177; 5:199, nn. 78–79. For detailed histories of the handing down of Adam's garment, see John Tvedtnes, "Priestly Clothing in Bible Times," and Stephen D. Ricks, "The Garment of Adam in Jewish, Muslim, and Christian Tradition," both in Parry, *Temples of the Ancient World,* 649–739.

56. Klinghoffer, *Discovery of God,* 23.

57. Research by Kerry Shirts, "Facsimile No. 1 and Opposition of Priesthoods: Nimrod's Garment of Authority vs. Abraham's Garment of Authority."

58. Al-Rabghuzi, *Stories of the Prophets,* 2:93.

59. Assuming the probable location of Ur in what is now southeastern Turkey, in what was the ancient Hittite kingdom, as seen in Bryce, *The Kingdom of the Hittites.*

60. Bryce, *The Kingdom of the Hittites,* 87.

61. See Jasher 7:29–48, in Noah, *Book of Yashar,* 16–18; Ginzberg, *Legends of the Jews,* 1:177–78; Culi, Magriso, and Argueti, *Torah Anthology,* 1:429–30; Graves and Patai, *Hebrew Myths,* 125–29.

62. Rappaport, *Ancient Israel,* 1:235.

63. See Kasher, *Encyclopedia of Biblical Interpretation,* 2:79; and Klinghoffer, *Discovery of God,* 12.

64. Jasher 7:51, in Noah, *Book of Yashar,* 19. See also Baring-Gould, *Legends of the Patriarchs,* 149.

65. F. M. Bareham, quoted in Kimball, *Faith Precedes the Miracle,* 323.

66. Davidson, *Moses Maimonides,* 237.

67. Rappaport, *Ancient Israel,* 1:235.

68. Pitron 5:16–26, in Gaster, *Asatir,* 223–25.

69. Al-Rabghuzi, *Stories of the Prophets,* 2:93.

70. Ginzberg, *Legends of the Jews,* 1:187. The legend is found in many sources. See, for example, Culi, Magriso, and Argueti, *Torah Anthology,* 1:429–31; Bialik and Ravnitzky, *Book of Legends,* 31; Graves and Patai, *Hebrew Myths,* 134–39; Jasher 8.1–36, in Noah, *Book of Yashar,* 19–21; and Chronicles of Jerahmeel 34.1–3, in Gaster, *Chronicles of Jerahmeel,* 73–74.

71. Klinghoffer, *Discovery of God,* 14. This is the title of the second chapter, beginning with Abraham's confrontation with Nimrod.

72. Ginzberg, *Legends of the Jews,* 1:188. quoting Maaseh Auraham Avinu 1:39–43.

73. Budge, *Book of the Mysteries,* 33. According to Budge's translation, at the appearance of the light, "Very many things (or persons) fell down" (parenthesis in original).

74. *Journal of Discourses,* 22:304.

75. Scherman and Zlotowitz, *Bereishis: Genesis,* 1(a):359.

76. Sarna, *Genesis,* 86; Speiser, *Genesis,* 124; Wenham, *Genesis 1–15,* 252; and Westermann, *Genesis 12–36,* 133.

77. Inman, *Ancient Faiths,* 1:191.

78. Jasher 7:51, in Noah, *Book of Yashar,* 19. A different explanation is given in Jubilees: Abram was named after his mother's father who had died earlier. Jubilees 11:15, in VanderKam, *Book of Jubilees,* 67. Obviously, these explanations are not necessarily mutually exclusive.

79. The Book of the Bee 36, in Budge, *Book of the Bee,* 80.

80. See Budge, *Cave of Treasures,* 211; and The Book of the Bee 36-39, in Budge, *Book of the Bee,* 80, 85.

81. Neusner, *Genesis and Judaism,* 136.

82. Neusner, *Confronting Creation,* 168.

83. Miller, *Abraham Friend of God,* 3.

84. Soloveitchik, *Man of Faith,* 68.

85. Smith, *Essentials in Church History,* 25.

86. Joseph Smith—History 1:20. This parallel was pointed out by Nibley in *Abraham in Egypt,* 202–203.

87. History [1828], in Jessee, *Papers of Joseph Smith,* 5–6 (spelling and punctuation standardized).

88. Nibley, *Abraham in Egypt,* 202.

89. Zornberg, *Genesis,* 80, quoting Maimonides's Mishneh Torah, Hilkhot Avodah Zarah 1:3.

90. Nibley, *Abraham's Creation Drama,* 3.

91. Culi, Magriso, and Argueti, *Torah Anthology,* 1:432.

92. Ginzberg, *Legends of the Jews,* 5:216–17 n. 48.

93. Hugh Nibley, "The Unknown Abraham: A New Look at the Pearl of Great Price, Part 7," *Improvement Era,* January 1969, 30.

94. Bialik and Ravnitzky, *Book of Legends,* 31, quoting Genesis Rabbah 61:1 (footnote 8 on page 31 is in error, citing 61:16).

95. She is called Amathlai in the Babylonian Talmud (Baba Bathra 91a, in Epstein, *Babylonian Talmud*); Athrai in Pirke de Rabbi Eliezer 26 (Friedlander, *Pirke de Rabbi Eliezer,* 189); but Edna in the name-conscious book of Jubilees (Jubilees 11:14–15, in VanderKam, *Book of Jubilees,* 66–67).

96. Ginzberg, *Legends of the Jews,* 1:188–89.

97. Levy, *A Faithful Heart,* 8.

98. Ginzberg, *Legends of the Jews,* 1:190–91.

99. Pitron 5:26, in Gaster, *Asatir,* 225.

100. *Maaseh Avraham Avinu* 3:1–8, in Levy, *A Faithful Heart,* 23 (spelling "Terah" instead of "Terach").

101. Tvedtnes, Hauglid, and Gee, *Traditions about the Early Life of Abraham,* 225; translation from the *Chronographia* 1:183.

102. Tvedtnes, Hauglid, and Gee, *Traditions about the Early Life of Abraham,* 270.

103. Ginzberg, *Legends of the Jews,* 5:217–18 n. 49.

104. Bialik and Ravnitzky, *Book of Legends,* 31.

105. George the Monk, quoted in William Adler, "Abraham and the Burning of the Temple of Idols: Jubilees' Traditions in Christian Chronography," *Jewish Quarterly Review* 77:2–3 (October 1986–January 1987): 100.

106. Ginzberg, *Legends of the Jews,* 1:186.

107. Davidson, *Moses Maimonides,* 237.

108. Ginzberg, *Legends of the Jews,* 1:189; Culi, Magriso, and Argueti, *Torah Anthology,* 1:431–32; Bialik and Ravnitzky, *Book of Legends,* 31; and Chronicles of Jerahmeel 34.3–4, in Gaster, *Chronicles of Jerahmeel,* 73–74.

109. Similarly, Alma told Korihor that "all things denote there is a God; yea, even the earth, and all things that are upon the face of it, yea, and its motion, yea, and also all the planets which move in their regular form do witness that there is a Supreme Creator." Alma 30:44. And a revelation to Joseph Smith speaks of the earth, sun, moon, and stars, and says that "any man who hath seen any or the least of these hath seen God moving in his majesty and power." Doctrine and Covenants 88:47.

110. Zornberg, *Genesis,* 80, quoting Maimonides's Mishneh Torah, Hilkhot Avodah Zarah 1:3.

111. As pointed out in Davidson, *Moses Maimonides,* 261, 357.

112. *Journal of Discourses,* 11:244.

113. Green, *Devotion and Commandment,* 43–44, translating a passage from the Sha'are[y] Orah.

114. As summarized by Davidson in *Moses Maimonides,* 261.

115. Levy, *A Faithful Heart,* 15.

116. Glueck, *Hesed in the Bible,* 63.

117. Ibid., 71.

118. Scherman and Zlotowitz, *Bereishis: Genesis,* 1(a):371.

119. Yevamot 79a, quoted in Miller, *Abraham Friend of God,* 107.

120. Davidson, *Moses Maimonides,* 254.

121. Jubilees 11:16–17, in VanderKam, *Book of Jubilees,* 67 (brackets in original).

122. Quoted in William Adler, "Abraham and the Burning of the Temple of Idols: Jubilees' Traditions in Christian Chronography," *Jewish Quarterly Review* 77:2–3 (October 1986–January 1987): 98. The Chronography of Bar Hebraeus has Abraham as fifteen years old when "he entreated God." Budge, *Chronography of Gregory Abu'l-Faraj,* 1:10.

123. Scherman and Zlotowitz, *Bereishis: Genesis,* 1(a):376.

124. Boyd K. Packer, "Obedience," talk given at Brigham Young University, December 1971.

125. Apocalypse of Abraham 6:4, in Sparks, *Apocryphal Old Testament,* 373.

126. Caesarius of Arles, Sermon 83.5, in Oden, *Ancient Christian Commentary,* 2:62.

127. Genesis Homily 4, in Origen: *Homilies,* 106.

128. Qur'an 37:83–84, in Cragg, *Qur'an,* 120 (omitting parenthesis, which are omitted in other translations).

129. *El-Masudi's Historical Encyclopedia* 4.83. The passage states that Abraham received the strength of God and thereby was kept pure from sin. Both components obviously are involved in the process. Similarly the Zohar, commenting on the Abraham story, states that "whoever makes an effort to purify himself receives assistance from above." Zohar, Lech Lecha 77b, in Sperling and Simon, *Zohar,* 1:262.

130. *Journal of Discourses,* 9:283.

131. Kasher, *Encyclopedia of Biblical Interpretation,* 3:18.

132. Later in life, during a great spiritual struggle, Nephi would beg the Lord to shut the gates of hell before him, because "my heart is broken and my spirit is contrite." 2 Nephi 4:32.

133. Kasher, *Encyclopedia of Biblical Interpretation,* 3:18.

134. Ibid., 2:106–107.

135. Apocalypse of Abraham 7:11, in Charlesworth, *Old Testament Pseudepigrapha,* 1:692.

136. Budge, *The Queen of Sheba,* 10.

137. The Bahir, an ancient kabbalistic text, mentions the mysteries of the chariot with regard to visionary experiences. Commenting on the passage, translator Aryeh Kaplan notes that "the Chariot experience is . . . said to be a 'vision' *(Tzefiyah),* which is related to the word for 'seers,' *Tzofim.*" Kaplan, *Bahir,* 133.

138. Zohar, Lech Lecha 76a–76b, in Sperling and Simon, *Zohar,* 1:261.

139. Genesis Rabbah 41:1, in Freedman, *Midrash Rabbah, Genesis,* 1:332.

140. Urbach, *The Sages,* 406.

141. Stuy, *Collected Discourses,* 3:141.

142. Nibley, *Abraham in Egypt,* 201.

143. Genesis 6:9, translated "just" in the King James Version, but "righteous" in most modern translations; see, for example, NRSV; JPST; NIV; REB; and GTC. Regarding the significance of the word *zadik,* von Rad notes that "we have no satisfactory English word for th[is] theologically significant [Hebrew] word" (*Genesis,* 120). According to Sarna, *zadik* "describes one whose conduct is found to be beyond reproach by the divine Judge" (*Genesis,* 50).

144. Al-Rabghuzi, *Stories of the Prophets,* 2:95–96, quoting or paraphrasing Qur'an 6:79.

145. Eisenman, *Dead Sea Scrolls and the First Christians,* 33–34, translating Qur'an 2:135; 3:66.

146. Mach, *Der Zaddik,* 24, makes a similar assessment of Abraham.

147. The Damascus Covenant 3:2, in Vermes, *Complete Dead Sea Scrolls,* 129.

148. Meier, *Ancient Secrets,* 25.

149. Rabbi Joseph, *Sha'are Orah,* 342.

150. Christopher Walker and Michael B. Dick, "The Induction of the Cult Image in Ancient Mesopotamia," in Dick, *Born in Heaven,* 55–121.

151. Tertullian, Idolatry 1.1, in Waszink and Van Winden, *Tertullianus De Idololatria,* 23.

152. Jubilees 11:4, in VanderKam, *Book of Jubilees,* 65.

153. See Nibley's discussion of Abraham's statement in Abraham 1:11 that the three virgins "were offered up because of their virtue; they would not bow down to worship gods of wood or of stone, therefore they were killed upon this altar." Hugh Nibley, "The Unknown Abraham: A New Look at the Pearl of Great Price, Part 7, Continued," *Improvement Era,* February 1969, 65–67.

154. Simonhoff, *And Abraham Journeyed,* 37 (comma added for clarity after "decency"). In Simonhoff's historical novel, he attempts to reconstruct scenes of the atrocious moral condition and circumstances of Abraham's day. Simonhoff's work is more than the product of a fertile imagination; he had done his homework in studying ancient Near Eastern sources. Simonhoff was a noted historian and author, a leader in B'nai B'rith, and a participant in the Palestine Resolution, a catalyst in bringing about the creation of the state of Israel.

155. M. H. Segal, *Jewish Quarterly Review* 52 (1961): 45; cited in Hugh Nibley, "The Unknown Abraham: A New Look at the Pearl of Great Price, Part 7," *Improvement Era,* January 1969, 31.

156. Budge, *Queen of Sheba,* 9. See also Budge, *Cave of Treasures,* 139–40.

157. Pirke de Rabbi Eliezer 26, in Friedlander, *Pirke de Rabbi Eliezer,* 188.

158. See Ginzberg, *Legends of the Jews,* 1:193–98; Culi, Magriso, and Argueti, *Torah Anthology,* 1:434–436; and Rappaport, *Ancient Israel,* 1:237–45.

159. Jubilees 12:2–5, in VanderKam, *Book of Jubilees,* 69–70.

160. Jubilees 12:7, in VanderKam, *Book of Jubilees,* 69–70.

161. Apocalypse of Abraham 4:6, in Charlesworth, *Old Testament Pseudepigrapha,* 1:690.

162. Qur'an 19:44–47, in Asad, *Qur'an,* 462.

163. Jubilees 11:11–24, in VanderKam, *Book of Jubilees,* 66–69.

164. Hugh Nibley, "The Unknown Abraham: A New Look at the Pearl of Great Price, Part 7," *Improvement Era,* January 1969, 31.

165. Budge, *Queen of Sheba,* 9.

166. Georgius Cedrenus, translation in Tvedtnes, Hauglid, and Gee, *Traditions about the Early Life of Abraham,* 269.

167. Al-Rabghuzi, *Stories of the Prophets,* 2:99.

168. Qur'an 26:77–82, in Asad, *Qur'an,* 565–66. The words "in the Resurrection" are in brackets in the original translation.

169. Soloveitchik, *Man of Faith,* 79.

170. See Reuven Firestone, "Abraham," in McAuliffe, *Encyclopaedia of the Qur'an,* 1:6, citing Qur'an 6:74–84; 19:41–50; 21:51–73; 26:69–86; 29:16–27; 37:83–98; 43:26–27; and 60:4.

171. See, for example, Ginzberg, *Legends of the Jews,* 1:197–98; Rappaport, *Ancient Israel,* 1:238–47; Jasher 11:15–27, in Noah, *Book of Yashar,* 19; and Chronicles of Jerahmeel 34.4–11, in Gaster, *Chronicles of Jerahmeel,* 74–76.

172. As reported in the *Journal of Discourses*: Brigham Young, in 11:118 (as President of the Church); John Taylor, in 14:359 and 22:307 (the latter as President of the Church); and Wilford Woodruff, in 11:244.

173. Levy, *A Faithful Heart,* 49–50.

174. Graves and Patai, *Hebrew Myths,* 140–41.

175. Maaseh Avraham Avinu 5:20–36, in Levy, *A Faithful Heart,* 51.

176. Maaseh Avraham Avinu 5:37–65, in Levy, *A Faithful Heart,* 52–53.

177. Eldad and Aumann, *Chronicles,* 1:1:1.

178. Plaut, Bamberger, and Hallo, *The Torah,* 107, citing Genesis Rabbah 42:8.

179. Hugh Nibley, "The Unknown Abraham: A New Look at the Pearl of Great Price, Part 7," *Improvement Era,* January 1969, 31.

180. Hugh Nibley, "A New Look at the Pearl of Great Price, Part 9, Continued: Setting the Stage: The World of Abraham," *Improvement Era,* November 1969, 122.

181. Nibley, *World and the Prophets,* 259.

182. Miller, *Abraham Friend of God,* 79–80.

183. Levy, *A Faithful Heart,* 56.

Notes to Chapter 2

1. Hendel, *Remembering Abraham,* 32.

2. Nachmanides on Genesis 11:28, in Chavel, *Ramban,* 1:159.

3. Nibley, *Abraham's Creation Drama,* 3.

4. Hugh Nibley, "The Unknown Abraham: A New Look at the Pearl of Great Price, Part 7, Continued," *Improvement Era,* April 1969, 67.

5. Faier, *Malbim*, 2:6, the original says "Avraham."

6. Kasher, *Encyclopedia of Biblical Interpretation*, 2:117.

7. Rabbi Joseph, *Sha'are Orah*, 277.

8. See Nachmanides on Genesis 11:28, in Chavel, *Ramban*, 1:157; Pirke de Rabbi Eliezer 26, in Friedlander, *Pirke de Rabbi Eliezer*, 188; Klinghoffer, *Discovery of God*, 21; and Ginzberg, *Legends of the Jews*, 1:198.

9. Nibley, *Abraham in Egypt*, 205.

10. See Ginzberg, *Legends of the Jews*, 1:198; Culi, Magriso, and Argueti, *Torah Anthology*, 1:436–37.

11. Baring-Gould, *Legends of the Patriarchs*, 158.

12. Kasher, *Encyclopedia of Biblical Interpretation*, 2:108.

13. *Journal of Discourses*, 2:7.

14. Scherman and Zlotowitz, *Bereishis: Genesis*, 1(a):387.

15. Ibid., 1(a):390.

16. Al-Rabghuzi, *Stories of the Prophets*, 2:105.

17. Satan appeared to Nimrod and instructed him on how to take Abraham's life. Baring-Gould, *Legends of the Patriarchs*, 159.

18. Knappert, *Islamic Legends*, 1:74.

19. Kasher, *Encyclopedia of Biblical Interpretation*, 2:111, quoting Midrash Hagadol.

20. Miller, *Abraham Friend of God*, 8, citing Genesis Rabbah.

21. Al-Rabghuzi, *Stories of the Prophets*, 2:101.

22. Hugh Nibley, "The Unknown Abraham: A New Look at the Pearl of Great Price, Part 7, Continued," *Improvement Era*, March 1969, 79.

23. Jasher 12:7–8, in Noah, *Book of Yashar*, 32.

24. "The victim met his end at the top of a pyramid. . . . Sacrifice represented the recycling of sacred energy, the blood that was shed bringing divine power into the immediate world to make the crops grow and bring prosperity to the community at large. Of course the whole procedure also bestowed enormous power on the small number who organized it all, who mediated between the humans and the gods, in other words, . . . kings. The drama of human sacrifice was but one element in the display of their religious and political authority, which were indivisible." Drew, *Lost Chronicles of the Maya Kings*, 314, describing the human sacrificial rites of the Mayas.

25. See facsimile 1 in the Book of Abraham.

26. Hornung, *Conceptions of God in Ancient Egypt*, 72.

27. See Ginzberg, *Legends of the Jews*, 1:187, 191.

28. Pitron 5:9–15, in Gaster, *Asatir*, 219–23.

29. Redford, *Oxford Encyclopedia of Ancient Egypt*, 3:337–38.

30. Posener, Bottero, and Kenyon, *Cambridge Ancient History: Syria and Palestine*, 20–21.

31. The Twelfth Dynasty's Senwosret (or "Senusret" or "Sesostris") III, who the classical writers designate as Sesostris. See Redford, *Oxford Encyclopedia of Ancient Egypt*, 3:268; and Clayton, *Chronicles of the Pharaohs*, 85–86.

32. See Wainwright, *Sky-Religion in Ancient Egypt*, 39, 47–51. Senwosret III and Senwosret I may have been combined into one account by the ancient classical writers. See Redford, *Oxford Encyclopedia of Ancient Egypt*, 3:268.

33. Wainwright, *Sky-Religion in Ancient Egypt*, 26–27, 32, 38, 47–53, 60, 64–66, among others. The entire study explores this very phenomenon.

34. Ibid., 38.

35. Ibid., 60. We now have what we did not in Joseph Smith's day: actual archeological and documentary evidence for human sacrifice in ancient Egypt. Ritner, *Mechanics of Ancient Egyptian Magical Practice*, 162-163, mentions archeological evidence. Documentary evidence has been found by Egyptologists at Brigham Young University.

36. Nibley, *Abraham in Egypt*, 80–82.

37. Hugh Nibley, "Facsimile No. 1, A Unique Document: A New Look at the Pearl of Great Price, Part 6, Continued," *Improvement Era*, December 1968, 33.

38. On the possibility that Nimrod was actually Pharaoh, see Nibley's discussion in *Abraham in Egypt*, 227–28. However, the fact that the name Nimrod is so prevalent as a place name in the region of Turkey where Abraham was probably born may suggest that the Nimrod and the Pharaoh of the Abrahamic traditions were not the same individuals, even though they may have been allied politically.

39. Targum of Pseudo-Jonathan on 16:5, in Bowker, *Targums and Rabbinic Literature*, 204.

40. Gorion, *Mimekor Yisrael*, 1:45.

41. Maaseh Avraham Avinu 6:41–63, in Levy, *A Faithful Heart*, 60–61.

42. Gorion, *Mimekor Yisrael* 1:45.

43. Ginzberg, *Legends of the Jews*, 1:201.

44. Brinner, *History of al-Tabari*, 59.

45. As written in the original Book of Abraham manuscripts of Abraham 1:16.

46. See Ginzberg, *Legends of the Jews*, 1:200–201; 5:213; and Al-Rabghuzi, *Stories of the Prophets*, 2:104–105.

47. See Al-Rabghuzi, *Stories of the Prophets*, 2:104; and Pseudo Philo 6.17, in Jacobson, *Liber Antiquitatum Biblicarum*, 1:100.

48. Pseudo-Philo tells that 83,500 people perished in the earthquake when "burning fire leaped forth out of the furnace" into

which Abraham was thrown. Pseudo Philo 6.17, in Jacobson, *Liber Antiquitatum Biblicarum*, 1:100.

49. Al-Rabghuzi, *Stories of the Prophets*, 2:104.

50. Pirke de Rabbi Eliezer 52, in Friedlander, *Pirke de Rabbi Eliezer*, 420.

51. Al-Rabghuzi, *Stories of the Prophets*, 2:99.

52. al-Kisa'i, *Tales of the Prophets*, 145.

53. See Cowley, *What If?*; and Cowley, *What If? 2*.

54. Padwick, *Muslim Devotions*, 169–70.

55. Urbach, *The Sages*, 117.

56. Compare King James translation: "all that watch for iniquity are cut off" by the Lord "who redeemed Abraham."

57. Testament of Moses 10:7, in Charlesworth, *Old Testament Pseudepigrapha*, 1:932.

58. Gorion, *Mimekor Yisrael*, 1:45–46.

59. Baring-Gould, *Legends of the Patriarchs*, 160.

60. Pirke de Rabbi Eliezer 26, in Friedlander, *Pirke de Rabbi Eliezer*, 188.

61. Sanhedrin 38b, in Epstein, *Babylonian Talmud*; and see discussion in Barker, *The Great Angel*, 78–79, 90–94. The angel of the presence is mentioned in Doctrine and Covenants 133:53, without being expressly named. In the larger context, it may be significant that in the following verses, which specify prominent past prophets who "shall be in the presence of the Lamb," it is Enoch who is mentioned first. Verses 54–55. (It should also be noted that verses 54–55 cannot syntactically be read as a continuation of those whom the Lord carried [verse 53] because of the ending of verse 55, which tells that Enoch and others mentioned "shall be in the presence of the Lamb.")

62. Similarly, when Jubilees speaks of the relationship between Abraham and Sarah, she is said to be "the daughter of his father." Jubilees 12:9, in VanderKam, *Book of Jubilees*, 70.

63. A rabbinic tradition espoused by Rashi equates Sarah with "Iscah," mentioned in Genesis 11:29 as the daughter of Haran, apparently the same Haran mentioned two verses previously as Abraham's brother. See Ginzberg, *Legends of the Jews*, 1:203; 5:215; and Tuchman and Rapoport, *Passions of the Matriarchs*, 3.

64. According to Islamic scholars al-Tabari (Brinner, *History of al-Tabari*, 61) and al-Thalabi (Brinner, *Lives of the Prophets*, 135), Sarai was the daughter of Abraham's paternal uncle, Haran the Elder.

65. On Abraham 42, in *Philo VI*, 121.

66. Sarna, *Genesis*, 87; Wenham, *Genesis 1–15*, 273. See also Westermann, *Genesis 12–36*, 138.

67. See al-Kisa'i, *Tales of the Prophets*, 150.

68. See Knappert, *Islamic Legends*, 1:75.

69. Al-Rabghuzi, *Stories of the Prophets*, 2:106.

70. See Ginzberg, *Legends of the Jews*, 1:222; and the description of her in 1QapGen 20.1–8, in Martinez and Tigchelaar, *Dead Sea Scrolls Study Edition*, 1:41.

71. On Abraham 42, in *Philo VI*, 121.

72. 1QapGen 20.7, in Martinez and Tigchelaar, *Dead Sea Scrolls Study Edition*, 1:41.

73. See *Encyclopaedia Judaica*, 14:868; and Ginzberg, *Legends of the Jews*, 1:203.

74. Tuchman and Rapoport, *Passions of the Matriarchs*, 73.

75. Ginzberg, *Legends of the Jews*, 5:214–15, nn. 38, 44, citing Talmudic passages, Josephus, and Christian writers.

76. Levner, *Legends of Israel*, 82.

77. Strachan, *Hebrew Ideals*, 1:111; and see Tuchman and Rapoport, *Passions of the Matriarchs*, 4.

78. Strickland, *Tales from English History*, 201.

79. See Kasher, *Encyclopedia of Biblical Interpretation*, 3:104.

80. See Munk, *Wisdom in the Hebrew Alphabet*, 34.

81. Proverbs 31:10, in Cohen, *Proverbs*, 211.

82. Proverbs 31:10, in Cohen, *Proverbs*, 211; NRSV and JPST; and Munk, *Wisdom in the Hebrew Alphabet*, 34, respectively.

83. Glueck, *Hesed in the Bible*, 65: "She opens her mouth with wisdom and the teaching of kindness [*torot hesed*] is on her tongue" (translation of Proverbs 31:26).

84. Cohen, *Proverbs*, 211.

85. Steinsaltz, *Biblical Images*, 21, 24.

86. On Abraham 42, in *Philo VI*, 121.

87. *Journal of Discourses*, 9:283.

88. Comparing the Book of Abraham narrative with the Genesis narrative shows that the latter rearranged and reduced the former.

89. Zornberg, *Genesis*, 73.

90. "Desperately Seeking Baby," *U.S. News and World Report*, October 5, 1987, 63.

91. Becky Foster Still, "Married, No Children: Infertility: A Special Kind of Loss," *Focus on the Family*, April 1989, 2.

92. Pirke de Rabbi Eliezer 26, translation in Miller, *Abraham Friend of God*, 11.

93. Botterweck and Ringgren, *Theological Dictionary of the Old Testament*, 1:9.

94. Kasher, *Encyclopedia of Biblical Interpretation*, 2:113, quoting Zohar 1, 76.

95. Meier, *Ancient Secrets*, 20.

96. Kasher, *Encyclopedia of Biblical Interpretation,* 2:112, quoting Midrash Hagadol.
97. Midrash Tanhuma, quoted in Zornberg, *Genesis,* 76.
98. *Journal of Discourses,* 14:359.
99. Klinghoffer, *Discovery of God,* 53.
100. On Abraham 35, in *Philo VI,* 95.
101. Strachan, *Hebrew Ideals,* 1:30.
102. I. W. Wiley, in Noble, *Great Men of God,* 19.
103. McConkie, *Mormon Doctrine,* 539. Similarly, Joseph F. Smith: "Obedience is the first law of heaven." *Journal of Discourses,* 16:247–48.
104. Kittel and Friedrich, *Theological Dictionary of the New Testament,* 1:8.
105. Sawyer, *Midrash Aleph Beth,* 247. The words quoted are from Sawyer's explanation of the Midrash Aleph Beth.
106. Nibley, *Abraham in Egypt,* 373.
107. Smith, *History of the Church,* 2:170.
108. *Journal of Discourses,* 20:189.
109. Stuy, *Collected Discourses,* 3:141.
110. Fox, *Five Books of Moses,* 55.
111. Genesis 12:1, in JPST; Speiser, *Genesis,* 85; and in Vawter, *On Genesis,* 174.
112. Genesis 12:1, in Mitchell, *Genesis,* 22.
113. Nibley, *Approaching Zion,* 270.
114. Sarna, *Genesis,* 88.
115. Dreifuss and Riemer, *Abraham,* 8.
116. Martin Buber, cited in Hugh Nibley, "A New Look at the Pearl of Great Price, Part 9: Setting the Stage: The World of Abraham," *Improvement Era,* November 1969, 120.
117. Faier, *Malbim,* 2:1.
118. As emphasized by Nibley in *Approaching Zion,* 270.
119. Oden, *Ancient Christian Commentary,* 2:1.
120. The command is repeated in verses 4 and 7.
121. Zion as the destination is repeated in verses 4 and 9.
122. James Carroll, "The Story of Abraham," in Rosenberg, *Genesis: As It Is Written,* 71.
123. Widengren, *Ascension of the Apostle,* 33–37.
124. Liebes, *Studies in Jewish Myth,* 57–58.
125. Compare Genesis 12:1–4 with Abraham 2:3 and 2:6–11.
126. "Go for thyself," Genesis 12:1, in Young, *Young's Literal Translation,* 7 (Old Testament); and in Kasher, *Encyclopedia of Biblical Interpretation,* 2:107. "Go away for yourself," Genesis 12:1, in Munk, *Call of the Torah,* 1:253.
127. Zohar, Lech Lecha 77b–78a, in Sperling and Simon, *Zohar,* 1:263–64.
128. Rashi on Genesis 12:1, in Rashi, *Commentary,* 101.
129. Munk, *Call of the Torah,* 1:254, citing Rashi.
130. Zornberg, *Genesis,* 87.
131. Galbraith and Smith, *Scriptural Teachings of the Prophet Joseph Smith,* 287–88.
132. Spencer W. Kimball, "The Example of Abraham," *Ensign,* June 1975, 7.
133. Ezra Taft Benson, "What I Hope You Will Teach Your Children about the Temple," *Ensign,*http://www.mormons.org/basic/temples/benson_what.htm. August 1985, 8.
134. Jubilees 11:16, in VanderKam, *Book of Jubilees,* 67.
135. Galbraith and Smith, *Scriptural Teachings of the Prophet Joseph Smith,* 269.
136 Kasher, *Encyclopedia of Biblical Interpretation,* 2:104, citing Zohar 1, 74b.
137. Breed, *Abraham,* 122.
138. Nibley, *Abraham's Creation Drama,* 3.
139. Oxenden, *Portraits from the Bible,* 43–44.
140. Noble, *Great Men of God,* 18.
141. Hertz, *Pentateuch and Haftorahs,* 45–46 (standardizing to American English spelling and capitalization).
142. Strachan, *Hebrew Ideals,* 1:111.
143. Brinner, *Lives of the Prophets,* 135.
144. That *they* called it so is mentioned exclusively in the Book of Abraham.
145 See *Encyclopaedia Judaica,* 7:1328–1330; and Kasher, *Encyclopedia of Biblical Interpretation,* 2:104–105.
146. Baring-Gould, *Legends of the Patriarchs,* 162.
147. Chavel, *Ramban,* 1:167.
148. Pirke de Rabbi Eliezer 25, in Friedlander, *Pirke de Rabbi Eliezer,* 184.
149. Matthews, *Armenian Commentary on Genesis,* 81.

Notes to Chapter 3

1. Jubilees 21:10, in Sparks, *Apocryphal Old Testament,* 68.

2. Kasher, *Encyclopedia of Biblical Interpretation,* 3:162, quoting Genesis Rabbah 56:11.
3. Nibley, *Temple and Cosmos*, 203–204, referring to the entire body of so-called apocryphal literature.
4. For example, a number of such convergences in the Enoch literature were pointed out by Hugh Nibley in *Enoch the Prophet.* Other convergences are given below.
5. Jubilees 12:27, in Charles, *Apocrypha and Pseudepigrapha,* 2:32.
6. Jubilees 21:10, in Charles, *Apocrypha and Pseudepigrapha,* 2:44.
7. Holbrook, *Studies on the Book of Enoch,* 8.
8. The Book of the Bee 30, in Budge, *Book of the Bee,* 50.
9. *Encyclopaedia Judaica,* 3:460.
10. Widengren, *Ascension of the Apostle,* 44.
11. Ginzberg, *Legends of the Jews,* 1:154–57; 5:117–18 n. 110.
12. Syncellus, Chronicle 9.22–25, quoted in Adler, *Time Immemorial,* 138 n. 32.
13. Nibley, *Enoch the Prophet,* 133.
14. 1 Enoch 12:4, in Charlesworth, *Old Testament Pseudepigrapha,* 1:19; and VanderKam, *Enoch: A Man for All Generations,* especially 157 (quoting Testament of Abraham 11:3, Rescension B) and 116 (quoting Jubilees 4:23 about Enoch being taken to the Garden of Eden to write down all the judgment and condemnation of mankind). See also Toorn, Becking, and Horst, *Dictionaries of Deities and Demons,* 301–304.
15. See VanderKam, *Enoch: A Man for All Generations*; and Charlesworth, *Old Testament Pseudepigrapha,* 1:5–316. In Nibley's words, Enoch is "the colossus who bestrides the apocrypha as no other." *Enoch the Prophet,* 19.
16. Widengren, *Ascension of the Apostle,* 11.
17. Jubilees 12:26, in VanderKam, *Book of Jubilees,* 73.
18. Schwartz, *Tree of Souls,* 85-86. See also Ginzberg, *Legends of the Jews* 1:292.
19. Jubilees 12:27, in Sparks, *Apocryphal Old Testament,* 49.
20. Smith, *History of Joseph Smith by His Mother,* 82-83.
21. Both Syncellus and Cedrenus point out that as stated in The Little Genesis (Jubilees), the angel that taught Abraham the lost language was the same angel who spoke to Moses. Adler, *Time Immemorial,* 218 (quotes from Syncellus and Cedrenus).
22. Chavel, *Ramban,* 1:331. Ramban notes that most of the rabbis thought that Abraham had learned the Torah by the Holy Spirit.
23. 1 Enoch 72–82, in Charlesworth, *Old Testament Pseudepigrapha,* 1:50–61.
24. 2 Enoch [J] 23:1, in Charlesworth, *Old Testament Pseudepigrapha,* 1:140.
25. 3 Enoch 46:2, in Charlesworth, *Old Testament Pseudepigrapha,* 1:299 (quoting Psalms 147:4). So also the Lord will tell Moses, as recorded in the Book of Moses, that "the heavens . . . are many, and . . . cannot be numbered unto man; but they are numbered unto me, for they are mine." Moses 1:37.
26. 2 Enoch [J] 23:4–5 speaks of "all the souls of men, whatever of them are not yet born, and their places, prepared for eternity. For all the souls are prepared for eternity, before the composition of the earth." This passage, notes the translator, "implies the pre-existence . . . of all souls." Charlesworth, *Old Testament Pseudepigrapha,* 1:140–41. See also 3 Enoch 43, in Odeberg, *3 Enoch,* part 2, 132–35, and see Odeberg's extensive notes on the unborn spirits. See also the same chapter of 3 Enoch in Charlesworth, *Old Testament Pseudepigrapha,* 1:293–94, and translator's comment on 294 n. 43c, that "the pre-existence of the soul is implied throughout the chapter."
27. In 2 Enoch [J] 29:4–5, God says: "But one from the order of the archangels deviated, together with the division that was under his authority. He thought up the impossible idea, that he might place his throne higher than the clouds which are above the earth, and that he might become equal to my power. And I hurled him from the height, together with his angels." Charlesworth, *Old Testament Pseudepigrapha,* 1:148.
28. 2 Enoch [J] 24–30, in Charlesworth, *Old Testament Pseudepigrapha,* 1:142–52.
29. 2 Enoch [J] 30:10, 15, in Charlesworth, *Old Testament Pseudepigrapha,* 1:152.
30. Adam said to Seth, his son, "You have heard, my son, that God is going to come into the world after a long time, (he will be) conceived of a virgin and put on a body, be born like a human being, and grow up as a child. He will perform signs and wonders on the earth, will walk on the waves of the sea. He will rebuke the winds and they will be silenced. He will motion to the waves and they will stand still. He will open the eyes of the blind and cleanse the lepers. He will cause the deaf to hear, and the mute to speak. He will straighten the hunchbacked, strengthen the paralyzed, find the lost, drive out evil spirits, and cast out demons.

"He spoke to me about this in Paradise when I picked some of the fruit in which death was hiding. 'Adam, Adam, do not fear. You wanted to be a god; I will make you a god, not right now, but after a space of many years. I am consigning you to death. . . . But after a short time there will be mercy on you because you were created in my image, and I will not leave you to waste away in Sheol. For your sake I will be born of the Virgin Mary. For your sake I will taste death and enter the house of the dead. . . . And after three days, while I am in the tomb, I will raise up the body I received from you. And I will make you a god just like you wanted. And I will receive favor from God, and I will restore to you and to your posterity that which is the justice of heaven." (Testament of Adam 3:1–4, in Charlesworth, *Old Testament Pseudepigrapha,* 1:994)
31. Combat of Adam and Eve with Satan 1:69, in Malan, *Conflict of Adam and Eve with Satan,* 84–85.

32. The phrase "Paradise of righteousness" is "found almost exclusively in Enochic literature." Reeves, *Heralds of That Good Realm*, 203 n. 56.

33. Life of Adam and Eve [Vita] 25:2–3, in Charlesworth, *Old Testament Pseudepigrapha*, 2:266, 268.

34. Syncellus, Chronicle 9.22–25, quoted in Adler, *Time Immemorial*, 138 n. 32.

35. Paraphrased in Adler, *Time Immemorial*, 138 n. 32.

36. 2 Enoch 34, in Charlesworth, *Old Testament Pseudepigrapha*, 1:158.

37. 1 Enoch 8:2, in Charlesworth, *Old Testament Pseudepigrapha*, 1:16. They practiced fornication. Jubilees 7:21, in VanderKam, *Book of Jubilees*, 47. They were "steeped in licentiousness." Leviticus Rabbah 12:5, in Freedman, *Midrash Rabbah, Leviticus*, 160. They were "steeped in whoredom." Leviticus Rabbah 23:9, in Freedman, *Midrash Rabbah, Leviticus*, 298.

38. 1 Enoch 65:6, in Charlesworth, *Old Testament Pseudepigrapha*, 1:45.

39. 1 Enoch 12:6, in Charlesworth, *Old Testament Pseudepigrapha*, 1:19.

40. 1 Enoch 9:9, in Charlesworth, *Old Testament Pseudepigrapha*, 1:17. It was a "cruel" generation. Sibylline Oracles 1.177, in Charlesworth, *Old Testament Pseudepigrapha*, 1:339. "They forgot to be merciful to their fellow men, therefore the Holy One, blessed be He, made His mercy forget them." Genesis Rabbah 33:5, in Freedman, *Midrash Rabbah, Genesis*, 1:265.

41. As Joseph Smith explained, "Our father Adam, Michael, . . . is the father of the human family, and presides over the spirits of all men." Galbraith and Smith, *Scriptural Teachings of the Prophet Joseph Smith*, 179.

42. See Combat of Adam and Eve with Satan 2.8 through 3.6, in Malan, *Conflict of Adam and Eve with Satan*, 114–51.

43. Combat of Adam and Eve with Satan 2.11, in Malan, *Conflict of Adam and Eve with Satan*, 118.

44. With limited exception, Enoch preached to all. See Moses 7:12.

45. Galbraith and Smith, *Scriptural Teachings of the Prophet Joseph Smith*, 194. For the translated Enoch's association with the Garden of Eden, see Toorn, Becking, and Horst, *Dictionaries of Deities and Demons*, 302.

46. Jubilees 4:23, speaking of Enoch: "He was taken from human society, and we led him into the Garden of Eden for (his) greatness and honor." VanderKam, *Book of Jubilees*, 28.

47. The Conflict of Adam and Eve tells of Enoch that "God transported him . . . to the land of life, to the mansions of the righteous and of the chosen, the abode of Paradise of joy." Combat of Adam and Eve with Satan 2.22, in Malan, *Conflict of Adam and Eve with Satan*, 141.

48. Galbraith and Smith, *Scriptural Teachings of the Prophet Joseph Smith*, 194–95.

49. Ibid., 217.

50. Toorn, Becking, and Horst, *Dictionaries of Deities and Demons*, 302, translating the Hebrew of Sirach at 49:14.

51. 3 Enoch 7:1, in Odeberg, *3 Enoch*, part 2, 22.

52. See, for example, Lachower and Tishby, *Wisdom of the Zohar*, 1:398 (part of the section on Shekinah in 371–422); and *Encyclopaedia Judaica*, 14:1349–1354.

53. 3 Enoch 22:7 ("splendour"), 13 ("brilliance of the Glory," "fire"); 22B:7 ("affrighted by the splendour of the Shekina, and . . . dazzled by the shining beauty"); 28:2 ("the brilliance"), in Odeberg, *3 Enoch*, part 2, 74–76, 78, 98. In the text, I have respelled "Shekina" to "Shekhinah."

54. Ginzberg, *Legends of the Jews*, 1:129, citing Yashar Bereshit 11a–13a.

55. 3 Enoch 7:1–4, in Odeberg, *3 Enoch*, part 2, 22.

56. Galbraith and Smith, *Scriptural Teachings of the Prophet Joseph Smith*, 392, 406, 414, and 420.

57. 1 Enoch 14:18, 20, 24; and 15:1, in Black, *1 Enoch*, 33–34.

58. 3 Enoch 22C:4, in Odeberg, *3 Enoch*, part 2, 80; and in Charlesworth, *Old Testament Pseudepigrapha*, 1:306. A rainbow surrounding the divine throne is also attested by Ezekiel 1:28 and Revelation 4:3.

59. 2 Enoch [J] 22:1, in Charlesworth, *Old Testament Pseudepigrapha*, 1:137. The chapter numbering differs from earlier translations: compare chapter 9 of translation in Sparks, *Apocryphal Old Testament*, 336–38.

60. 2 Enoch 22:2–3, in one text. Morfill and Charles, *Secrets of Enoch*, 27 (see translations of both texts).

61. 2 Enoch [J] 22:5, in Charlesworth, *Old Testament Pseudepigrapha*, 1:138.

62. 2 Enoch 9:15–19, in Sparks, *Apocryphal Old Testament*, 337–38. On Enoch's transformation into the glorious angel of the presence, or Metatron, see Wolfson, *Through a Speculum that Shines*, 223–25.

63. 2 Enoch 24:2, in one text. Morfill and Charles, *Secrets of Enoch*, 31, note on verse 2. See also the translation of the same verse in Charlesworth, *Old Testament Pseudepigrapha*, 1:24.

64. 3 Enoch 10:1–6, in Odeberg, *3 Enoch*, part 2, 27–30; and in Charlesworth, *Old Testament Pseudepigrapha*, 1:263–64.

65. The gods honored him and set him "on a large throne of gold." Kvanig, *Roots of Apocalyptic*, 185.

66. The occasion is when the Gods honored Enoch (called "Enmeduranki," the seventh king) in heaven. See VanderKam, *Enoch: A Man for All Generations* 8; Kvanig, *Roots of Apocalyptic*, 184–89; and Haldar, *Associations of Cult Prophets*, 1–3. Also, as Kvanig and Haldar show, Enmeduranki returns to earth and instructs priests in these same rites, which are passed down.

67. Widengren, *Ascension of the Apostle*, 9.

68. 3 Enoch 12:2, in Charlesworth, *Old Testament Pseudepigrapha*, 1:265.

69. 3 Enoch 12:1–2, in Odeberg, *3 Enoch*, part 2, 32.

70. Scholem, *Jewish Gnosticism, Merkabah Mysticism*, 131. Scholem insists that the esoteric tradition about the garment of glory (described in texts like 3 Enoch) has direct affinities with the royal purple garment described in rabbinic tradition, for "the garment of purple which Israel received came 'from the splendor of His glory.'"

71. 3 Enoch 12:3, in Odeberg, *3 Enoch*, part 2, 32.

72. 3 Enoch 12:4, in Charlesworth, *Old Testament Pseudepigrapha*, 1:265.

73. 3 Enoch 12:4–5, in Odeberg, *3 Enoch*, part 2, 33.

74. 3 Enoch 15:1, in Odeberg, *3 Enoch*, part 2, 39.

75. Lambert's translation from a tablet from Ninevah, quoted in Kvanig, *Roots of Apocalyptic*, 185. This source specifies that there were eleven such men from the cities of Nippur, Sippar, and Babylon.

76. 3 Enoch 9:1, in Odeberg, *3 Enoch*, part 2, 25.

77. 3 Enoch 8:1, in Odeberg, *3 Enoch*, part 2, 23.

78. 3 Enoch 7:1, in Odeberg, *3 Enoch*, part 2, 23. Milik mentions "the special connection of Metatron with the divine throne" in 3 Enoch and related sources. Milik, *Books of Enoch*, 130.

79. Barker, *The Great Angel*, 80, referring to 3 Enoch 4:10. See Odeberg, *3 Enoch*, part 2, 13.

80. Galbraith and Smith, *Scriptural Teachings of the Prophet Joseph Smith*, 194. Joseph Smith further states that Enoch appeared to Jude.

81. 3 Enoch 12:1–5, in Odeberg, *3 Enoch*, part 2, 32–33; part 1, 36–37, 81; and Milik, *Books of Enoch*, 130. And see discussions in Fossum, *The Name of God*, 297–301; and Dan, *"Unique Cherub" Circle*, 227–29. For a broader discussion of the angel of the presence in Jubilees and related literature, see James C. VanderKam, "The Angel of the Presence in the Book of Jubilees," *Dead Sea Discoveries: A Journal of Current Research on the Scrolls and Related Literature* (Leiden: Brill, 2000) 7:3, 378–93. The placing of the Lord's name on his angel is mentioned with regard to the angel sent before the camp of Israel. Exodus 23:20–21; and see 14:19. This is the same angel that would later be mentioned in Exodus (Ex. 23:20–21) and identified as Enoch in Talmudic tradition. Sanhedrin 38b, in Epstein, *Babylonian Talmud*; and see discussion in Barker, *The Great Angel*, 78–79, 90–94. The angel of the presence is mentioned in Doctrine and Covenants 133:53, without being expressly named. In the larger context, it may be significant that in the following verses, which specify prominent past prophets who "shall be in the presence of the Lamb," it is Enoch who is mentioned first. Verses 54–55. (It should also be noted that verses 54–55 cannot be read as a continuation of those whom the Lord carried [verse 53] because of the ending of verse 55, which tells that Enoch and others mentioned "shall be in the presence of the Lamb."

82. 3 Enoch 10:3, in Odeberg, *3 Enoch*, part 2, 29.

83. In fact, one of the first things the translated Enoch does in the apocryphal Enoch literature is to expressly affirm Michael's preeminent position among the angels as "Michael, the Great Prince," in charge of the highest heaven. 3 Enoch 17:1–3, in Odeberg, *3 Enoch*, part 2, 45–46; and in Charlesworth, *Old Testament Pseudepigrapha*, 1:269. Similarly in 1 Enoch, the translated Enoch refers to Michael as the "chief" of the angels. 1 Enoch 24:6, in Charlesworth, *Old Testament Pseudepigrapha*, 1:26. The same picture of Michael as the chief archangel prevails throughout the Enoch and related literature. Toorn, Becking, and Horst, *Dictionaries of Deities and Demons*, 569–72. It is within this hierarchy that Enoch would function in his special role as scribal attendant to the divine throne and angel of the presence. For example, Milik quotes the follow passage attributed to Theodosius, archbishop of Alexandria: "'Enoch the righteous man' explains why he rejoices in the festival of Michael: 'I am rejoicing because it is I who write with my own hands in the register of sins . . . the wickedness, and the good deeds which are committed in the whole world. And the holy Archangel Michael taketh them into the presence of God, and presenteth unto Him the good deeds, and for the bad deeds he maketh supplication unto Him, and he forgiveth those who belong to my race. For this reason I rejoice this day'." Milik, *Books of Enoch*, 105. See also below in the Abraham story when Enoch brings the blessing of Michael as well.

84. This summary is by John C. Reeves, in Schiffman and VanderKam, *Encyclopedia of the Dead Sea Scrolls*, 1:249.

85. 1 Enoch 34–36, in Black, *1 Enoch*, 42.

86. See, for example 1 Enoch 83–90, and the convenient summary of the content of Enoch's "Dream-Visions" in Black, *1 Enoch*, 19–20, and the text in 71–83; and 3 Enoch 45 in Charlesworth, *Old Testament Pseudepigrapha*, 1:296–99.

87. 1 Enoch 25 in Charlesworth, *Old Testament Pseudepigrapha*, 1:26; and see Toorn, Becking, and Horst, *Dictionaries of Deities and Demons*, 570.

88. Compare 1 Enoch 10:13: "they shall be dragged off to the fiery abyss in torment, and in a place of incarceration they shall be imprisoned." Black, *1 Enoch*, 31.

89. Compare1 Enoch 90:41: "I wept with a great weeping, and my tears could not stop, till I had no more endurance left, but flowed down on account of what I had seen." Charlesworth, *Old Testament Pseudepigrapha*, 1:71.

90. 1 Enoch 7:6, in Black, *1 Enoch*, 28.

91. Compare 1 Enoch 89:1–9, in Black, *1 Enoch*, 74–75.

92. 1 Enoch 89:10-90:19, in Black, *1 Enoch*, 75–81.

93. 2 Enoch [J] 35:2, in Charlesworth, *Old Testament Pseudepigrapha*, 1:158.

94. Note by F. I. Andersen, in Charlesworth, *Old Testament Pseudepigrapha*, 1:159.

95. Commenting on this passage, President Ezra Taft Benson stated: "The Lord promised . . . that righteousness would come from heaven and truth out of the earth. We have seen the marvelous fulfillment of that prophecy in our generation. The Book of Mormon has come forth out of the earth, filled with truth, serving as the very 'keystone of our religion.' God has also sent down righteousness from heaven. The Father Himself appeared with His Son to the Prophet Joseph Smith. The angel Moroni, John the Baptist, Peter, James, and numerous other angels were directed by heaven to restore the necessary powers to the kingdom. Further, the Prophet Joseph Smith received revelation after revelation from the heavens during those first critical years of the Church's growth." Ezra Taft Benson, "The Book of Mormon—Keystone of Our Religion," *Ensign*, November 1986, 79–80.

96. 3 Enoch 48A:9, in Odeberg, *3 Enoch*, part 2, 158.

97. 3 Enoch 48A:10, in Charlesworth, *Old Testament Pseudepigrapha*, 1:302.

98. 1 Enoch 1:8, in Charlesworth, *Old Testament Pseudepigrapha,* 1:13.

99. 2 Enoch [A] 9:1, in Charlesworth, *Old Testament Pseudepigrapha,* 1:117.

100. 2 Enoch [J] 9:1, in Charlesworth, *Old Testament Pseudepigrapha,* 1:116, 118.

101. See Enoch [J] 8, in Charlesworth, *Old Testament Pseudepigrapha,* 1:114–16.

102. 1 Enoch 93:5, in Black, *1 Enoch,* 86. In context, the prophecy unquestionably refers to Abraham. See note 25 in chapter 1 on this prophecy.

Notes to Chapter 4

1. Kasher, *Encyclopedia of Biblical Interpretation,* 2:135, speaking of the Torah (in standard rabbinic tradition, Abraham kept the Torah even before it was revealed).

2. *Journal of Discourses,* 14:358.

3. Ehat and Cook, *Words of Joseph Smith,* 235. Joseph Smith similarly stated that "salvation cannot come without revelation." Galbraith and Smith, *Scriptural Teachings of the Prophet Joseph Smith,* 182.

4. Galbraith and Smith, *Scriptural Teachings of the Prophet Joseph Smith,* 365 (emphasis in original).

5. Ibid., 310.

6. Nibley, *Approaching Zion,* 382.

7. See Abraham 2:6–11, especially verse 9 ("this ministry and Priesthood"), verse 10 ("this Gospel"), and verse 11 ("thy Priesthood" and "the Gospel").

8. Kasher, *Encyclopedia of Biblical Interpretation,* 3:33, quoting Midrash T'hillim.

9. Zohar, Lech Lecha 78a, in Manhar, *Zohar,* 338.

10. Galbraith and Smith, *Scriptural Teachings of the Prophet Joseph Smith,* 73.

11. Kerithoth 9a, translation in Taylor, *The Teaching of the Twelve Apostles,* 56, and see translation in Kerithoth 9a, Epstein, *Babylonian Talmud:* "immersion."

12. Levy, *A Faithful Heart,* 21.

13. Borgen, *Early Christianity and Hellenistic Judaism,* 262–63, explaining Philo, Virt. 212–19.

14. Schwartz, *Tree of Souls,* 18.

15. Budge, *Book of the Mysteries,* 147.

16. Weitzmann and Kessler, *The Cotton Genesis,* 72 (and see plates 2 and 166): "The arc consists of an enormous quarter circle comprising concentric rings of dark blue, light blue, light magenta, green, and dark blue separated from one another by gold lines. Six gold rays emanate from the magenta band; the Hand issues from the light blue ring."

17. Pirke de Rabbi Eliezer 23, in Friedlander, *Pirke de Rabbi Eliezer,* 172.

18. Panarion 1.4.1,1, in Williams, *Panarion of Epiphanius,* 18.

19. Ginzberg, *Legends of the Jews,* 1:178.

20. Ibid., 5:266 n. 316.

21. Ibid., 1:332.

22. For example, on August 27, 1843, Joseph Smith stated that "Abraham's Patriarchal power is the greatest yet experienced in this church." Ehat and Cook, *Words of Joseph Smith,* 245. See 245–47 and 303–305 for additional statements by the Prophet Joseph, and comments thereon, concerning the power and scope of Abraham's patriarchal priesthood.

23. Ephrem, quoted in Malan, *Conflict of Adam and Eve with Satan,* 237.

24. See Jubilees 11:1–16, in VanderKam, *Book of Jubilees,* 64–67; and Ginzberg, *Legends of the Jews,* 1:186, citing Jubilees. Also on Nahor, see Ginzberg, *Legends of the Jews,* 5:216–17 n. 48. Pseudo-Philo, however, claims that Serug and his sons did not go along with the idolatry. Pseudo Philo 4:16, in Jacobson, *Liber Antiquitatum Biblicarum,* 1:96; also noted by Ginzberg in *Legends of the Jews,* 5:208 n. 5.

25. At the age of sixty-two, according to the book of Abraham 1:30; 2:5, contradicting Genesis, which gives his age as seventy-five. The book of Abraham number is strikingly corroborated by the Byzantine monk Syncellus; see quotes and discussion in Adler, *Time Immemorial,* 189–91.

26. In making the covenant with Abraham just before he departs, the Lord speaks of "*this* ministry and Priesthood" and "*this* Gospel." Abraham 2:9–10 (emphasis added).

27. Stone, *Armenian Apocrypha,* 83, 94, 120: the exact number varies between the sources as 942 or 944.

28. James, *Apocryphal New Testament,* 145: the Acts of Pilate has 1,137 years from the Flood to Abraham.

29. See Horton, *The Melchizedek Tradition,* 115–16.

30. Ibid., 114–24.

31. Bowker, *Targums and Rabbinic Literature,* 198.

32. See Judean Antiquities 1.179–80, in Feldman, *Josephus,* 68.

33. See 1QapGen 22.14–17, in Martinez and Tigchelaar, *Dead Sea Scrolls Study Edition,* 1:47–49.

34. According to the Kitab alMajal, "Moses did not make mention of him [Melchizedek] in his book because he was genealogising (only) the patriarchs." Bowker, *Targums and Rabbinic Literature,* 197 n. *e*.

35. See generally: Milik, *Books of Enoch,* 115; Bowker, *Targums and Rabbinic Literature,* 197 n. *e* (quoting Kitab alMajal); Book of the Bee 21, in Budge, *Book of the Bee,* 33–34; Budge, *Cave of Treasures,* 152–53; and Combat of Adam and Eve with Satan 3.16, in Malan, *Conflict of Adam and Eve with Satan,* 164. The sources differ on who Melchizedek's father was. For example, as noted in Bowker, the Book of the Rolls (Kitab alMajal) makes Melchizedek the son of the patriarch Salah. Likewise Milik notes that in the

account of Pseudo-Athanasius, Melchizedek was said to be a grandson of Salah.

36. For several reasons. First, Genesis 11:10–11 tells Shem's life span in the same manner as it tells the life spans of the subsequent patriarchs, implying that Shem died (a passage left unchanged in the Joseph Smith Translation), while JST Genesis 14 tells that Melchizedek was translated. Second, a latter-day revelation in Doctrine and Covenants 84:14 states that "Abraham received the [Melchizedek] priesthood from Melchizedek, who received it through the lineage of his fathers, even till Noah, and from Noah till Enoch," which seems to require at least two generations between Melchizedek and Noah. And third, in Joseph F. Smith's vision of the redemption of the dead, he saw among the host of righteous post-mortal spirits Shem (D&C 138:41), who would not have been there had he been translated. The revelation does not mention seeing Elijah or Enoch or Moses, who, like Melchizedek, had been translated.

37. Note also Speiser's comment on the chronology of the Masoretic Text: "The statistics cited by [the Masoretic Text] do not commend themselves as the product of a dependable tradition. On this point, M[asoretic] T[ext], Sam[aritan Pentateuch], and LXX [Septuagint] have each their own detailed answers. One can see at a glance that M[asoretic] T[ext] is transparently schematic." Speiser, *Genesis,* 80.

38. See, for example, McConkie, *Doctrinal New Testament Commentary,* 1:400.

39. Enoch's giving the ordinances to Abraham just prior to his departing Haran would also help explain Jubilees' confusion over the giving of the covenant to Abraham in Haran: Jubilees claims that it was by the mouth of the angel of the presence, whereas the book of Abraham expressly affirms that it came from the mouth of the Lord himself in a personal appearance. Jubilees may be preserving, in garbled form, a tradition that the angel of the presence was in fact involved, not as voice for the covenant but as the Lord's agent in giving Abraham the ordinances and patriarchal ordination. See Jubilees 12:19–24, in VanderKam, *Book of Jubilees,* 72–73.

40. Baring-Gould, *Legends of the Patriarchs,* 205, citing Augustin Calmet.

41. Calmet, *An Historical . . . Dictionary,* 3:372 (and see 2:177), citing a work by Henry Hulse, *Enoch Redivivus* (Amsterdam, 1706), stating that Melchizedek must have been Enoch who returned to confer with Abraham.

42. Clement of Alexandria, The Stromata, or Miscellanies 5.11, in *Ante-Nicene Fathers,* 2:462.

43. "The masters of the Kabbalah, of blessed memory, say that Abraham's Rabbi, *i.e.,* teacher, was the angel Zadkiel." Harris, *Hebraic Literature,* 47, quoting Rabbi Menachem's commentary on the Pentateuch at Exodus 3:5. "Zadkiel," or "Sidquiel," is one of the names of Metatron/Enoch. Odeberg, *3 Enoch,* part 2, 174, number 5 within the note.

44. It also seems possible that Enoch may be the angel who came under the title of Elias to Joseph Smith in the Kirtland Temple (in which case all three messengers were translated beings).

45. Budge, *Book of the Mysteries,* 147.

46. Similarly, Elder Bruce R. McConkie observed that the purpose of the translation of Moses and Elijah was so they could return with tangible bodies of flesh and bones to confer priesthood keys on Peter, James, and John on the Mount of Transfiguration. See McConkie, *Doctrinal New Testament Commentary,* 1:400; and McConkie, *Mormon Doctrine,* 805.

47. Compare NRSV Genesis 12:5. Most modern translations similarly read here the "persons" that were "acquired."

48. Jubilees says fourteen. Jubilees 12:15, in VanderKam, *Book of Jubilees,* 71. Jasher says three years. Jasher 13:3, in Noah, *Book of Yashar,* 36.

49. Jasher 13:2, in Noah, *Book of Yashar,* 36.

50. Reuven Firestone, "Abraham," in McAuliffe, *Encyclopaedia of the Qur'an,* 1:5, translating the term *ḥanīf* in Qur'an 2:135; 3:67, 95; 4:125; 6:79, 161; and 16:120, 123.

51. Qur'an 19:41, in Asad, *Qur'an,* 460, omitting a bracketed word.

52. Reuven Firestone, "Abraham," in McAuliffe, *Encyclopaedia of the Qur'an,* 1:5, translating Qur'an 19:41.

53. *Holy Qur'an* 4:1589.

54. This is one factor, among others, that has led some scholars, including William F. Albright, to surmise that he must have been a caravaneer. (See discussion in Klinghoffer, *Discovery of God,* 35, which rejects the theory.) But it seems that such activity with its extended absences would have been inconsistent with the leadership burden he carried of presiding over the community of saints whom he led. Caravaneering would also seem at odds with his constant need to offer hospitality to travelers passing through his own neighborhood. In addition, had he been a caravaneer, he may well have already traveled the trade route southward into Canaan, in which case the Lord would not have spoken to him of the "strange land" to which He was sending him (Abr. 2:6). Nor do any of the legends make him out to be a caravaneer.

55. Scherman and Zlotowitz, *Bereishis: Genesis,* 1(a):385.

56. Nibley, *Abraham's Creation Drama,* 2.

57. Breed, *Abraham,* 72.

58. Nibley, *Approaching Zion,* 321.

59. Klinghoffer, *Discovery of God,* 51.

60. Brinner, *Lives of the Prophets,* 165.

61. Midrash Rabbah on the Song of Songs 1:3:3, in Freedman, *Midrash Rabbah: Song of Songs,* 39. See also Ginzberg, *Legends of the Jews,* 1:203.

62. Tuchman and Rapoport, *Passions of the Matriarchs,* 5.

63. Ginzberg, *Legends of the Jews,* 1:205, citing Yashar.

64. Jasher 13:2, in Noah, *Book of Yashar,* 36.

65. Munk, *Call of the Torah,* 1:262.

66. Qur'an 19:49–50, in Asad, *Qur'an*, 462. The brackets are mine; the passage actually speaks not only of Abraham but also of Isaac and Jacob. For clarity, I have unbracketed the words "unto others," which are bracketed in the original.

67. Knappert, *Islamic Legends*, 1:73.

68. Klinghoffer, *Discovery of God*, 31, quoting Maimonides.

69. Levy, *A Faithful Heart*, 54, quoting Zohar.

70. Maaseh Avraham Avinu 4:102-105, in Levy, *A Faithful Heart*, 38.

71. As pointed out in Wedderburn, *Baptism and Resurrection*, 282, citing Philo's *Virt.* 217.

72. Madsen, *Joseph Smith*, 96.

73. Jasher 13:2, in Noah, *Book of Yashar*, 36.

74. Ginzberg, *Legends of the Jews*, 1:205, citing Yashar.

75. Zohar, Lech Lecha 79a–79b, in Sperling and Simon, *Zohar*, 1:268.

76. Ibid.

77. Jasher 13:21, in Noah, *Book of Yashar*, 38.

78. Soloveitchik, *Man of Faith*, 83, citing Maimonides.

79. Nibley, *Teachings of the Pearl of Great Price*, Lecture 24, 10–11.

80. See Alma 12:36; 13:12; 13:16–17; 60:13; and Moroni 7:3.

81. Jubilees 12:15, VanderKam, *Jubilees*, 71.

82. Klinghoffer, *Discovery of God*, 51–52.

83. Commenting on the statement in Isaiah 23:11 that the Lord "stretched his hand over the sea," John Watts notes that "the sea . . . is often pictured as Yahweh's original archenemy. It is also seen as the one who first fell to Yahweh's expression of his cosmic dominion of all things." Watts, *Isaiah 1–33*, 307. Many biblical passages associate the power of chaos with the sea at the beginning of creation, and allude to Yahweh's victory over that power and His exercise of dominion over the sea. See Toorn, Becking, and Horst, *Dictionaries of Deities and Demons*, 740–42. See also Day, *God's Conflict with the Dragon*.

84. Commenting on the statement in Isaiah 23:11 that the Lord "stretched his hand over the sea," Hans Wildberger notes the allusion to the Exodus story, where Moses stretches out his hand over the sea (Ex. 14:26), and where Yahweh is said to have brought Israel out of Egypt with an outstretched arm (Deut. 4:34). *Isaiah 13–27*, 430.

85. Testament of Adam 3:1, in Charlesworth, *Old Testament Pseudepigrapha*, 1:994.

86. Daniélou, *Primitive Christian Symbols*, 78.

87. Daniélou, *Primitive Christian Symbols*, 78–83, citing, among other sources, Tertullian, Gregory of Nyssa, and the Odes of Solomon.

88. Daniélou, *Primitive Christian Symbols*, 78–79. Daniélou discusses other early Christian authors and texts that speak to the subject, including the very early Odes of Solomon.

89. Daniélou, *Primitive Christian Symbols*, 71–88.

90. The passage is Deuteronomy 33:26, alluded to in the Sefer Yetzirah. See Kaplan, *Sefer Yetzirah*, 206.

91. Wedderburn, *Baptism and Resurrection*, 349.

92. Adams, *Ancient Records and the Bible*, 187.

93. Montefiore and Loewe, *A Rabbinic Anthology*, 245, quoting introduction to Lamentations Rabbah.

94. Akenson, *Surpassing Wonder*, 91.

95. The "Holy Ghost . . . is more powerful in expanding the mind, enlightening the understanding, and storing the intellect with present knowledge, than one who is of the literal seed of Abraham, than one that is a Gentile, though it may not have half as much visible effect upon the body; for as the Holy Ghost falls upon one of the literal seed of Abraham, it is calm and serene; and his whole soul and body are only exercised by the pure spirit of intelligence; while the effect of the Holy Ghost upon a Gentile, is to purge out the old blood, and make him actually of the seed of Abraham. That man that has none of the blood of Abraham (naturally) must have a new creation by the Holy Ghost. In such a case, there may be more of a powerful effect upon the body, and visible to the eye, than upon an Israelite, while the Israelite at first might be far before the Gentile in pure intelligence." Galbraith and Smith, *Scriptural Teachings of the Prophet Joseph Smith*, 170–71.

96. Unterman, *Dictionary of Jewish Lore*, 160; see also *Encyclopaedia Judaica*, 2:116.

97. See Unterman, *Dictionary of Jewish Lore*, 160.

98. Soloveitchik, *Man of Faith*, 83.

99. Ibid., 85.

100. Feiler, *Walking the Bible*, 81. Feiler's observation is made in the later context of Abraham and Isaac in Gerar.

101. Westermann, *Genesis 12–36*, 279. The original quote reads: "The promise of a son runs as a leitmotif through the Abraham cycle."

102. Glueck, *Hesed in the Bible*, 73–74; and see Botterweck and Ringgren, *Theological Dictionary of the Old Testament*, 5:60–62.

103. Warren Zev Harvey, "Grace or Loving-Kindness," in Cohen and Mendes-Flohr, *Contemporary Jewish Religious Thought*, 302.

104. Kethuboth 8b, in Epstein, *Babylonian Talmud*.

105. Kasher, *Encyclopedia of Biblical Interpretation*, 2:117.

106. Hebrews 11:9, in most modern translations, including NRSV.

107. See, for example, Young, *Jerusalem in the New Testament*, 117–64, especially 117, 134–38; and Buchanan, *To the Hebrews*, 191–94.

108. 4 Ezra 10:27, in Stone, *Fourth Ezra*, 326.

109. 4 Ezra 13:20, in Stone, *Fourth Ezra,* 388.

110. 4 Ezra 13:36, in Stone, *Fourth Ezra,* 393; and see Stone's commentary on 327.

111. Young, *Jerusalem in the New Testament,* 137.

112. Young, *History of the Organization of the Seventies,* 14.

113. McConkie, *Mormon Doctrine,* 805, quoting JST, Genesis 14:34 (which refers to what Melchizedek and his people were seeking). Notably, the same chapter of Hebrews had already mentioned Enoch's being "translated that he should not see death," Enoch having "pleased God" by faith, as required of all those who would please God, for "he that cometh to God must believe that he is, and that he is a rewarder of them that diligently seek him," (Heb. 11:5–6). Abraham's diligence in seeking God is mentioned in the book of Abraham at the very point of his departure from Haran when he will, as Hebrews says, go looking for the city with foundations (Abr. 2:12). It is the same city, as scholars point out, that is also referred to in the next chapter of Hebrews: "But ye are come unto mount Sion [Zion], and unto the city of the living God, the heavenly Jerusalem, and to an innumerable company of angels, to the general assembly and church of the firstborn" (Heb. 12:22–23). See Buchanan, *To the Hebrews,* 192; and Hermann Strathmann, in Kittel and Friedrich, *Theological Dictionary of the New Testament,* 6:531. When similar language is used in latter-day scripture, it describes the people of Enoch. Those attaining celestial glory are said to "come unto Mount Zion, and unto the city of the living God, the heavenly place, the holiest of all. These are they who have come to an innumerable company of angels, to the general assembly and church of Enoch, and of the Firstborn" (D&C 76:66–67). Clearly Abraham was seeking Enoch's city of Zion.

114. Qur'an 26:83–85, in Cragg, *Qur'an,* 118.

115. Genesis Rabbah 39:8, in Harris, *Hebraic Literature,* 240, stating explicitly, "This is spoken of Abraham."

116. Weitzmann and Kessler, *The Cotton Genesis,* 72, and Plates 2 and 166.

117. Pirke de Rabbi Eliezer 23, in Friedlander, *Pirke de Rabbi Eliezer,* 172.

118. See also the example of what happened on the Mount of Transfiguration, when not only the Savior but also Moses and Elias transferred keys to Peter, James, and John. Since the Savior holds all the keys, why did he need Moses and Elijah to transfer their keys? Because of the principle of delegation. See: Galbraith and Smith, *Scriptural Teachings of the Prophet Joseph Smith,* 179; McConkie, *Doctrinal New Testament Commentary,* 1:400; McConkie, *Mormon Doctrine,* 805.

119. Inman, *Ancient Faiths* 1:191.

120. Pseudo Philo 4.11, in Jacobson, *Liber Antiquitatum Biblicarum,* 1:95.

121. Dean C. Jessee, ed., *The Personal Writings of Joseph Smith* (Salt Lake City: Deseret Book, 1984), Jessee, *Personal Writings of Joseph Smith,* 298, letter to Silas Smith, September 26, 1833 (capitalization normalized, and comma added after "Noah").

122. *Journal of Discourses,* 15:101. This passage seems to conflate the commands to leave Ur and Haran.

123. Seventy-five years old as reported in Genesis 12:4.

124. See quotes and discussion in Adler, *Time Immemorial,* 189–91. Jasher gives Abraham age at his departure from Haran as fifty. Jasher 13:5, in Noah, *Book of Yashar,* 37.

125. Pirke de Rabbi Eliezer 26, in Friedlander, *Pirke de Rabbi Eliezer,* 189.

126. Abraham 2:14, and see v. 4 ("Lot, my brother's son"). So also Jubilees 12:30 and Genesis Apocryphon 20.22, 33; 22.3. See VanderKam, *Book of Jubilees,* 74; and Martinez and Tigchelaar, *Dead Sea Scrolls Study Edition,* 1:43, 47.

127. Galbraith and Smith, *Scriptural Teachings of the Prophet Joseph Smith,* 281–82.

128. Spencer W. Kimball, "The Example of Abraham," *Ensign,* June 1975, 4.

129. Miller, *Abraham Friend of God,* 18, quoting Midrash Tehillim 112.

130. Zohar, Lech Lecha 79a, in Manhar, *Zohar,* 341.

131. See Tuchman and Rapoport, *Passions of the Matriarchs,* 11, quoting Midrash Rabbah.

132. Klinghoffer, *Discovery of God,* 53.

133. Noble, *Great Men of God,* 19.

134. Munk, *Wisdom in the Hebrew Alphabet,* 27; and *Encyclopaedia Judaica,* 14:868, citing Genesis Rabbah 60:16.

135. Scherman and Zlotowitz, *Bereishis: Genesis,* 1(a):834.

136. Ibid., 1(a):834.

137. Chavel, *Ramban,* 2:4 n. 5: it rested upon "the tents of the patriarchs."

138. Ochs, *Sarah Laughed,* 111.

139. See Sanhedrin 38b, in Epstein, *Babylonian Talmud*; and see discussion in Barker, *The Great Angel,* 78–79, 90–94.

140. Kasher, *Encyclopedia of Biblical Interpretation,* 8:123, 125.

141. Ramban's Introduction to the Book of Exodus, quoted in Munk, *Wisdom in the Hebrew Alphabet,* 27. For consistency, I have changed the spelling of "Shechinah" to "Shekhinah."

142. Steinsaltz, *Guide to Jewish Prayer,* 169–170.

143. See also Isaiah 35:10; 52:7–12; and rabbinic comments thereon in Kasher, *Encyclopedia of Biblical Interpretation,* 8:123, 125. The latter-day Zion will yet "stand like a castle of light" in a dark world. Georg Fohrer, in Kittel and Friedrich, *Theological Dictionary of the New Testament,* 7:313, citing Isaiah 60:2ff.

144. Hugh Nibley, "Facsimile No. 1, by the Figures—A New Look at the Pearl of Great Price, Part 8, Continued," *Improvement Era,* October 1969, 88.

145. Marcus, *View from Nebo,* 30.

146. One of the most plausible was suggested several decades ago by someone who actually made the trip and published his results in *National Geographic.* See Kenneth MacLeish, "Abraham, the Friend of God," *National Geographic* 139:6 (December

1966), 739–789, and see map on 746.

147. Ball, *Syria,* 130.

148. See Klinghoffer, *Discovery of God,* 53.

149. Nicholas of Damascus, cited by Josephus, and Pompeis Trogus, cited in Feldman's comments on the Josephus passage. Judean Antiquities 1.159–60, in Feldman, *Josephus,* 59–60. See also Chronicles of Jerahmeel XXXV.2, in Gaster, *Chronicles of Jerahmeel,* 77.

150. Judean Antiquities 1.159–60, in Feldman, *Josephus,* 59–60. See also Ginzberg, *Legends of the Jews* 5:216, n. 46.

151. *Josephus IV,* 81.

152. Ball, *Syria,* 66–67.

153. Klinghoffer, *Discovery of God,* 36, quoting Maimonides, Mishneh Torah, Hilchot Avodat Kochavim 1:3.

154. Qur'an 26:86, in Asad, *Qur'an,* 566.

155. Pritchard, *Ancient Near Eastern Texts,* 19 (omitting parentheses).

156. Stone, *Armenian Apocrypha,* 95–96.

157. Klinghoffer, *Discovery of God,* 57.

158. Ibid., 61.

159. Testament of Levi 6:8–11, in Charlesworth, *Old Testament Pseudepigrapha,* 1:790.

160. Marcus, *View from Nebo,* 30.

161. Wordsworth, *Holy Bible,* 1:66.

162. Marcus, *View from Nebo,* 30.

163. Ochs, *Sarah Laughed,* 112.

164. In the first two chapters of the Book of Abraham, Abraham prays six times. Abraham 1:15; 2:6, 17, 18–19, 20.

165. Doctrine and Covenants 10:5; 19:38; 20:33; 31:12; 32:4; 61:39; 88:126; 90:24; and 93:49.

166. Davidson, *Moses Maimonides,* 385.

167. Noble, *Great Men of God,* 67.

168. Spencer W. Kimball, "The Example of Abraham," *Ensign,* June 1975, 5.

169. Breed, *Abraham,* 36–38.

170. Matthews, *Armenian Commentary on Genesis,* 79. Ephrem does not mention the location of the altar, but refers to the first altar that Abraham built in the promised land. The first such altar mentioned in the book of Abraham was at Jershon.

171. See Genesis Rabbah 39:11, in Neusner, *Genesis Rabbah,* 2:70.

172. Miller, *Abraham Friend of God,* 15, quoting Genesis Rabbah 39:11.

173. Kasher, *Encyclopedia of Biblical Interpretation,* 2:164, quoting Midrash Haneelam Lech, 25.

174. Genesis Rabbah 39:15, in Freedman, *Midrash Rabbah, Genesis,* 1:325.

175. Genesis Rabbah 59:4, in Freedman, *Midrash Rabbah, Genesis,* 2:518.

176. Jubilees 13:6–7, in VanderKam, *Book of Jubilees,* 75–76.

177. Ginzberg, *Legends of the Jews,* 1:219.

178. Ginzberg, *Legends of the Jews,* 1:203.

179. Abraham is called a prophet in Genesis 20:7 and in the Qur'an 19:49–50 (in Asad, *Qur'an,* 462).

180. Klinghoffer, *Discovery of God,* 150.

181. Book of the Rolls 119a, in Gibson, *Apocrypha Arabica,* 35.

182. Harris, *Hebraic Literature,* 47, quoting Nishmath Chayin, chap. 29.

183. Klinghoffer, *Discovery of God,* 36, quoting Maimonides, Mishneh Torah.

184. *Journal of Discourses,* 17:207.

185. Levner, *Legends of Israel,* 61.

186. See Ginzberg, *Legends of the Jews,* 1:292.

187. Zornberg, *Genesis,* 88, citing Rambam

188. Chavel, *Encyclopedia of Torah Thoughts,* 31.

189. Ginzberg, *Legends of the Jews,* 5:382 n. 4.

190. Ibid., n. 274.

191. Joseph B. Wirthlin, "The Example of Joseph Smith," in *The Prophet and His Work,* 92.

192. Genesis Rabbah 39:2, in Freedman, *Midrash Rabbah, Genesis,* 1:313.

193. Galbraith and Smith, *Scriptural Teachings of the Prophet Joseph Smith,* 350.

194. Culi, Magriso, and Argueti, *Torah Anthology,* 2:166.

195. Ginsburg, *Essenes,* 122 (in *The Kabbalah*).

196. Hugh Nibley, "A New Look at the Pearl of Great Price, Part 9: Setting the Stage: The World of Abraham," *Improvement Era,* January 1970, 57.

197. Buxbaum, *Life and Teachings of Hillel,* 126.

198. Montefiore and Loewe, *A Rabbinic Anthology,* 563–64, quoting Midrash on Psalms 110:1. For uniformity of spelling, I have changed the spelling of "Shechinah" in this passage to "Shekhinah."

199. Kasher, *Encyclopedia of Biblical Interpretation,* 2:125, quoting Genesis Rabbah 39 and other midrashim. For uniformity of spelling, I have changed the spelling of "Shechinah" in this passage to "Shekhinah."

200. Noble, *Great Men of God,* 19.
201. Singer, *Jewish Encyclopedia,* 11:258.
202. Patai, *Man and Temple,* 91, citing various rabbinic texts.
203. For descriptions of the elaborate ritual of the Day of Atonement, the greatest and most important of all the ancient Jewish rituals, see Leviticus 16; Levine, *Leviticus,* 99–110; and *Encyclopaedia Judaica,* 5:1376–1387.
204. See *Encyclopaedia Judaica,* 2:115; and Yoma 28b, in Epstein, *Babylonian Talmud.*
205. See Jubilees 21:5–20, in VanderKam, *Book of Jubilees,* 121–26; and Aramaic Testament of Levi, Bodleian c, lines 12–13, in Hollander and de Jonge, *Testaments of the Twelve Patriarchs,* 463.
206. Ginzberg, *Legends of the Jews,* 1:217.
207. Crothers, *Abraham the First Missionary,* 25.
208. Ginzberg, *Legends of the Jews,* 1:316; 2:3.
209. *Journal of Discourses,* 24:125–26.
210. Spencer W. Kimball, "The Example of Abraham," *Ensign,* June 1975, 6.

Notes to Chapter 5

1. See Jubilees 12:28 through 13:11, in VanderKam, *Book of Jubilees,* 74–77 for chronology. The book of Abraham does not mention how long Abraham stayed in each place as he traveled through the promised land before entering Egypt, although the Genesis Apocryphon apparently asserts that he lived in one location, at Hebron (not mentioned in Abraham's pre-Egyptian itinerary in Genesis or the book of Abraham) for two years. 1QapGen 19.9–10, in Martinez and Tigchelaar, *Dead Sea Scrolls Study Edition,* 1:39.
2. Klinghoffer, *Discovery of God,* 62 (reading "imagining" for "imaging").
3. Zornberg, *Genesis,* 93.
4. Scherman and Zlotowitz, *Bereishis: Genesis,* 1(a):391.
5. Baring-Gould, *Legends of the Patriarchs,* 164.
6. Kasher, *Encyclopedia of Biblical Interpretation,* 2:126.
7. Pirke de Rabbi Eliezer 26–32, in Friedlander, *Pirke de Rabbi Eliezer,* 187–238.
8. Galbraith and Smith, *Scriptural Teachings of the Prophet Joseph Smith,* 339.
9. Staalduine-Sulman, *Targum of Samuel,* 374.
10. Jubilees 17:18, in Sparks, *Apocryphal Old Testament,* 60. This statement in Jubilees directly precedes the account of the binding of Isaac.
11. Rabbi Joseph, *Sha'are Orah,* 342.
12. Pirke de Rabbi Eliezer 26, in Friedlander, *Pirke de Rabbi Eliezer,* 187.
13. Soloveitchik, *Man of Faith,* 68, citing Av. 5:4.
14. Levy, *A Faithful Heart,* xiv, 13.
15. Nibley, *Teachings of the Pearl of Great Price,* Lecture 23, 7.
16. *Journal of Discourses,* 17:207. I have normalized the spelling of the word *programme.*
17. See *Encyclopaedia Judaica,* 14:868; and Ginzberg, *Legends of the Jews,* 1:203.
18. Brinner, *History of al-Tabari,* 62.
19. Scherman and Zlotowitz, *Bereishis: Genesis,* 1(a):826.
20. *Journal of Discourses,* 23:228.
21. Zohar, Lech Lecha 82a, in Sperling and Simon, *Zohar,* 1:273.
22. Zohar, Lech Lecha 83a, in Sperling and Simon, *Zohar,* 1:276.
23. Pirke de Rabbi Eliezer 26, in Friedlander, *Pirke de Rabbi Eliezer,* 189.
24. See Klinghoffer, *Discovery of God,* 67.
25. Wise, Abegg, and Cook, *Dead Sea Scrolls,* 79.
26. 1QapGen 19.14–23, in Fitzmeyer, *Genesis Apocryphon,* 60–61, omitting Zoan as anachronistic. Except for the brackets in bold, all others are in the original and indicate words or parts of words that are difficult to read.
27. Genesis Rabbah 41:1:1, in Neusner, *Genesis Rabbah* 2:87.
28. Genesis Rabbah 41:1, in Freedman, *Midrash Rabbah, Genesis,* 1:332.
29. Meiggs, *Trees and Timber,* 50.
30. Older trees gradually lose their pyramidal shape as the branches become widespread.
31. See, generally, Meiggs, *Trees and Timber,* 49–87, especially 55–56; Freedman, *Anchor Bible Dictionary,* 2:805; Buttrick, *Interpreter's Dictionary of the Bible,* 1:545–46; *Encyclopaedia Judaica,* 5:268; Achtemeier, *Harper's Bible Dictionary,* 159; Myers, *Eerdmans Bible Dictionary,* 197; *New Encyclopædia Britannica* 3:5; 20:453; 28:904, 907; Malek, *In the Shadow of the Pyramids,* 37; and Eisenberg, *The Ecology of Eden,* 116.
32. Malek, *In the Shadow of the Pyramids,* 84.
33. Zimmerli, *Ezekiel 2,* 147.
34. Nibley, *Abraham in Egypt,* 372.
35. Farbridge, *Studies in Biblical and Semitic Symbolism,* 33.
36. See E. Douglas Clark, "Cedars and Stars: Enduring Symbols of Cosmic Kingship in Abraham's Encounter with Pharaoh," in Gee and Hauglid, *Astronomy, Papyri, and Covenant.*

37. James, *Tree of Life*, 101.

38. Kvanig, *Roots of Apocalyptic*, 185. As discussed above, Enmeduranki is the Mesopotamian version of Enoch.

39. Zohar, Lech Lecha 82a, in Sperling and Simon, *Zohar*, 1:274. The quote is from Proverbs 10:25.

40. See Jubilees 12:9, in VanderKam, *Book of Jubilees*, 70; and Genesis 20:12.

41. So states the Midrash Hagadol, in Kasher, *Encyclopedia of Biblical Interpretation*, 2:130.

42. Sarna, *Genesis*, 94.

43. Zohar 111b–112a, in Sperling and Simon, *Zohar*, 1:352–53.

44. City of God 16.19, quoted in Oden, *Ancient Christian Commentary*, 2:8.

45. Qur'an 26:84, in Cragg, *Qur'an*, 118.

46. Kasher, *Encyclopedia of Biblical Interpretation*, 3:94.

47. Jasher 15:6, in Noah, *Book of Yashar*, 41.

48. Galbraith and Smith, *Scriptural Teachings of the Prophet Joseph Smith*, 287.

49. See the explanation to figure 2 of Facsimile 2 of Book of Abraham, combined with the ensuing revelation that occurred "in the night time." Abraham 3:14.

50. Nibley, *Approaching Zion*, 426, 262.

51. The Book of Abraham doesn't mention why Abraham was consulting the Urim and Thummim, but does place the incident immediately after he asked Sarah to say she was his sister. Abraham 3:1.

52. Schwartz, *Tree of Souls*, 332, and see Baba Bathra 16b, in Epstein, *Babylonian Talmud*: "Abraham possessed a power of reading the stars for which he was much sought after. . . . Abraham had a precious stone hung around his neck . . . "

53. Gutwirth, *Kabbalah and Jewish Mysticism*, 98.

54. Bolles, *Galileo's Commandment*, 101.

55. Orphica, Long Version, in Charlesworth, *Old Testament Pseudepigrapha* 2:799.

56. Gruen, *Heritage and Hellenism*, 250, paraphrasing the Orphic Hymn, which states that "no one has seen the ruler of mortal men, except a certain unique man, an offshoot from far back of the race of the Chaldeans. For he was knowledgeable about the path of the Star, and how the movement of the Sphere goes around the earth." Orphica, Long Version, in Charlesworth, *Old Testament Pseudepigrapha* 2:799. For the identification of this "certain unique man" with Abraham, see Gruen, *Heritage and Hellenism*, 250, n. 16.

57. *Journal of Discourses* 21:245. I have normalized the spelling of "to-day."

58. Such symbolism appears to be at least as ancient as the Egyptian hieroglyphics. "As a light shining in the darkness, the star is a symbol of the spirit. . . . As far back as in the days of Egyptian hieroglyphics it signified 'rising upwards towards the point of origin.'" Cirlot, *Dictionary of Symbols*, 309. That such tradition may have originated with the antediluvian patriarchs (Abraham's forefathers) is seen from Abraham's own writings, which mention not only the forefathers' knowledge of the stars, but also that the first pharaohs sought earnestly to imitate the ancient patriarchal order of things. Abraham 1:26, 31. See discussion in E. Douglas Clark, "Cedars and Stars: Enduring Symbols of Cosmic Kingship in Abraham's Encounter with Pharaoh," in Gee and Hauglid, *Astronomy, Papyrus, and Covenant*.

59. Qur'an 2:124, in Dawood, *Koran*, 345.

60. Sefer Yetzirah (Saadia version) 8:8, in Kaplan, *Sefer Yetzirah*, 293.

61. Culi, Magriso, and Argueti, *Torah Anthology*, 2:21.

62. Speaking of the authorship of the Sefer Yetzirah, Aryeh Kaplan explained: "As early as the 10th century, Saadia Gaon writes that, 'the ancients say that Abraham wrote it.' This opinion is supported by almost all of the early commentators. Such ancient Kabbalistic texts as the Zohar and Raziel also attribute Sefer Yetzirah to Abraham. A number of very old manuscripts of Sefer Yetzirah likewise begin with a colophon calling it 'the Letters of Abraham our Father, which is called Sefer Yetzirah.'" Kaplan, *Sefer Yetzirah*, xii. As Charles Poncé observes of the Sefer Yetzirah, "The doctrine outlined within it was revealed to the Patriarch Abraham. After he perceived and understood the nature of the revelation, he recorded it." *Kabbalah*, 39.

63. On the astronomical character of Facsimile 2, see Nibley, *Abraham in Egypt*, 42–67, especially 50; and John Gee, "Eyewitness, Hearsay, and Physical Evidence of the Joseph Smith Papyri," in Ricks, Parry, and Hedges, *Disciple as Witness*, 198–99.

64. Compare the extensive cosmological sections of the extant Enoch literature in 1 Enoch, 2 Enoch, and 3 Enoch.

65. Nibley, *Abraham in Egypt*, 652.

66. Gutwirth, *Kabbalah and Jewish Mysticism*, 97.

67. This prayer by Abraham was taught to him by the angel: "Teach me, show me, and make known to your servant what you have promised me." Apocalypse of Abraham 17:21, in Charlesworth, *Old Testament Pseudepigrapha*, 1:697.

68. Qur'an 26:83, in M. M. Ali, *Qur'an*, 716.

69. See, for example, Abraham 3–5; Apocalypse of Abraham, in Charlesworth, *Old Testament Pseudepigrapha*, 1:689–705.

70. See Abraham's references to his forefathers and his citations and explanations of their writings, for example, in 1QapGen 19.25, in Martinez and Tigchelaar, *Dead Sea Scrolls Study Edition*, 1:41; and Jubilees 19:24, 27; 21:10, in Charlesworth, *Old Testament Pseudepigrapha*, 2:93, 95.

71. Culi, Magriso, and Argueti, *Torah Anthology*, 2:15.

72. Wiesel, *Messengers of God*, 92.

73. Faier, *Malbim*, 2:3, x.

74. Ginzberg, *Legends of the Jews*, 1:292; 5:258–60.

75. Josephus, Jewish Antiquities 1.8.2, in *Josephus 4*, 83.
76. The quote uses the word "astrological," meaning in this context astronomical. Stuckenbruck, *Book of the Giants from Qumran*, 36–37, referring to the two fragments from the source commonly called "Pseudo Eupolemus," but the first of which is probably from Eupolemus. See analysis by translator R. Doran in Charlesworth, *Old Testament Pseudepigrapha*, 2:873–78.
77. James E. Bowley, "The Compositions of Abraham," in Reeves, *Tracing the Threads*, 227.
78. Schimmel, *Mystical Dimensions of Islam*, 379.
79. Nibley, *Abraham's Creation Drama*, 2.
80. Nibley, *Approaching Zion*, 263.
81. Nibley, *Approaching Zion*, 282.
82. 1QapGen 19.13, in Martinez and Tigchelaar, *Dead Sea Scrolls Study Edition*, 1:39.
83. See Silverman, *Ancient Egypt*, 90–103.
84. Klinghoffer, *Discovery of God*, 65.
85. See Ginzberg, *Legends of the Jews*, 1:222; Scherman and Zlotowitz, *Bereishis: Genesis*, 1(a):448; and Kasher, *Encyclopedia of Biblical Interpretation*, 2:129–30.
86. 1QapGen xix.23, in Martinez and Tigchelaar, *Dead Sea Scrolls Study Edition* 1:41.
87. Paraphrase by John C. Reeves (internal quote is from 1QapGen 19.25), in Schiffman and VanderKam, *Encyclopedia of the Dead Sea Scrolls*, 1:249.
88. 1QapGen 19.25, in Martinez and Tigchelaar, *Dead Sea Scrolls Study Edition*, 1:41.
89. Hertz, *Pentateuch and Haftorahs*, 47.
90. 1QapGen 20.9–12, in Martinez and Tigchelaar, *Dead Sea Scrolls Study Edition*, 1:41.
91. 1QapGen 20.10–16, in Fitzmeyer, *The Genesis Apocryphon*, 63–65.
92. Nibley, *Abraham in Egypt*, 366.
93. See, for example, Chavel, *Encyclopedia of Torah Thoughts*, 42; and Cohen and Mendes-Flohr, *Contemporary Jewish Religious Thought*, 299–302.
94. Kasher, *Encyclopedia of Biblical Interpretation*, 3:104.
95. Nibley, *Abraham in Egypt*, 362.
96. Zohar, Lech Lecha 82a, in Sperling and Simon, *Zohar*, 1:276, quoting Proverbs 28:1.
97. Matthews, *Armenian Commentary on Genesis*, 79–80.
98. Nibley, *Abraham in Egypt*, 346.
99. E. Douglas Clark, "Abraham," in Ludlow, *Encyclopedia of Mormonism*, 1:8.
100. White, *Ancient Egypt*, 17.
101. Library of Congress, Country Studies: Egypt: The Old Kingdom, Middle Kingdom, and Second Intermediate Period, 2686 to 1552 B.C., online at http://lcweb2.loc.gov/frd/cs/egtoc.html.
102. Tuchman and Rapoport, *Passions of the Matriarchs*, 12.
103. Nibley, *Abraham in Egypt*, 366–67.
104. Matthews, *Armenian Commentary on Genesis*, 80.
105. Freedman, *Midrash Rabbah, Song of Songs*, 134.
106. Matthews, *Armenian Commentary on Genesis*, 79. Original has both occurrences of "God" in brackets.
107. See Doctrine and Covenants 29:6, 33; 42:3; 50:1; and 84:1
108. Ginzberg, *Legends of the Jews*, 1:223; 5:221 n. 73.
109. 1QapGen 20.16–17, in Martinez and Tigchelaar, *Dead Sea Scrolls Study Edition*, 1:43.
110. Judean Antiquities 1.164, in Feldman, *Josephus*, 61.
111. Ginzberg, *Legends of the Jews*, 1:223.
112. Kasher, *Encyclopedia of Biblical Interpretation*, 2:131.
113. Baring-Gould, *Legends of the Patriarchs*, 175.
114. Ginzberg, *Legends of the Jews*, 1:223.
115. Pritchard, *Ancient Near Eastern Texts*, 22.
116. Finkel, *The Torah Revealed*, 33, citing Bava Metzia 59a.
117. 1QapGen 20.18, in Martinez and Tigchelaar, *Dead Sea Scrolls Study Edition*, 1:43.
118. 1QapGen 20.17–21, in Martinez and Tigchelaar, *Dead Sea Scrolls Study Edition*, 1:41–43.
119. Egyptians considered their king "a divine presence on whom the life of the nation depended." Groenewegen-Frankfort, *Arrest and Movement*, 44. By means of royal ritual "the kingship was clearly very closely connected with agriculture and fertility, and the safety and health of the king entailed the safety of Egypt and the health and well-being of its inhabitants." H. W. Fairman, in Hooke, *Myth, Ritual, and Kingship*, 85. "The destiny of the Egyptian people was linked to that of their Pharaoh and his welfare was also theirs." Putnam, *Egyptology*, 44. In fact, "every aspect of life" was considered "a function of the State centered in the divine throne as the pivot of society in a permanent changeless cosmic order of elemental vastness whose powers were unlimited." *Sacral Kingship*, 65.
120. 1QapGen 20.21–22, in Martinez and Tigchelaar, *Dead Sea Scrolls Study Edition*, 1:43.
121. Pitron 6:22–24, in Gaster, *Asatir*, 232–33.
122. Al-Rabghuzi, *Stories of the Prophets*, 2:114.

123. 1QapGen 20.21–22, in Martinez and Tigchelaar, *Dead Sea Scrolls Study Edition*, 1:43.

124. See citations in *Encyclopaedia Judaica*, 2:115.

125. 1QapGen 20.21–28, in Martinez and Tigchelaar, *Dead Sea Scrolls Study Edition*, 1:43.

126. Nibley, *Abraham in Egypt*, 359–60.

127. 1QapGen 20.28, in Martinez and Tigchelaar, *Dead Sea Scrolls Study Edition*, 1:43.

128. Asatir 6:23, in Gaster, *Asatir*, 254 ("earth" is capitalized in the original).

129. 1QapGen 20.29, in Martinez and Tigchelaar, *Dead Sea Scrolls Study Edition*, 1:43.

130. Knappert, *Islamic Legends*, 1:77–78. In this legend, Abraham cures Pharaoh's hand, which had withered when he tried to approach Sarah.

131. Nibley, *Abraham in Egypt*, 203.

132. Asatir 6:24, in Gaster, *Asatir*, 254.

133. 1QapGen 20.29, in Martinez and Tigchelaar, *Dead Sea Scrolls Study Edition*, 1:43.

134. Jubilees speaks of the "extremely large amount of property: sheep, cattle, donkeys, horses, camels, male and female servants, silver, and very (much) gold." Jubilees 13:14, in VanderKam, *Book of Jubilees*, 77.

135. 1QapGen 20.31–32, in Martinez and Tigchelaar, *Dead Sea Scrolls Study Edition*, 1:43.

136. Brinner, *History of al-Tabari*, 65.

137. Ginzberg, *Legends of the Jews*, 1:223.

138. Homilies on Genesis 32.22, in Oden, *Ancient Christian Commentary*, 2:10.

139. Al-Rabghuzi, *Stories of the Prophets*, 2:112. In this source the story parallels what in other sources occurs in Egypt, though said here to take place in Haran. The invitation to Abraham to sit on a throne occurs before Abraham's healing of the king, said to be the successor of Nimrod.

140. Redford, *Oxford Encyclopedia of Ancient Egypt*, 2:165.

141. Nibley, *Abraham in Egypt*, 359–60.

142. Ben Zion Wacholder, "How Long Did Abraham Stay in Egypt?" *Hebrew Union College Annual* 35 (1964):43.

143. An angel tells the aged Isaac that "there has been prepared for you the throne beside your father Abraham." Testament of Isaac 1:7, in Charlesworth, *Old Testament Pseudepigrapha*, 1:905.

144. Abraham, Isaac, and Jacob "have entered into their exaltation . . . and sit upon thrones, and are not angels but are gods." Doctrine and Covenants 132:37.

145. Josephus, Jewish Antiquities 1.8.1–2, in *Josephus 4*, 83.

146. Bet Ha-Midrash, quoted in Nibley, *Teachings of the Pearl of Great Price*, Lecture 23, 11.

147. Redford, *Oxford Encyclopedia of Ancient Egypt*, 2:165.

148. From the earliest times, explained Diodorus of Sicily in the first century B.C., "the positions and arrangements of the stars, as well as their motion, have always been the subject of careful observation among the Egyptians, if anywhere in the world . . . they have observed with utmost keenness the motions, orbits and stoppings of each planet" Barton, *Ancient Astrology*, 24, quoting Diodorus, *World History* 1.81.

149. "It never occurred to the Egyptians to enter upon the search for truth for its own sake. . . . They had much practical acquaintance with astronomy." Breasted, *A History of Egypt*, 100. The royal ideology and its cult had "need to establish the exact periods of time deemed indispensable for the performance of certain rites." Morenz, *Egyptian Religion*, 8. "Remarkable progress was made in astronomy by observation of the sky" in order "to meet the practical requirements of telling the time for temple services to begin, watching the public calendar with celestial time and correctly orienting sacred buildings such as temples and pyramids." Strouhal, *Life of the Ancient Egyptians*, 239–40.

150. Wainwright, *Sky-Religion in Ancient Egypt*, 16–17.

151. Goff, *Symbols of Ancient Egypt*, 20. See also E. Douglas Clark, "Cedars and Stars: Enduring Symbols of Cosmic Kingship in Abraham's Encounter with Pharaoh," in Gee and Hauglid, *Astronomy, Papyri, and Covenant*.

152. Wilkinson, *Reading Egyptian Art*, 127.

153. Müller, *Egyptian Mythology*, 35.

154. Eupolemus, as quoted by Eusebius, in Praeparatio Evangelica 9:17.8, in Charlesworth, *Old Testament Pseudepigrapha*, 2:881.

155. Gruen, *Heritage and Hellenism*, 150–51.

156. The Fragments of Artapanus, Fragment 1, Charlesworth, *Old Testament Pseudepigrapha*, 2:897.

157. Gruen, *Heritage and Hellenism*, 150.

158. Zornberg, *Particulars of Rapture*, 254, citing Rabbenu Bahya.

159. Petersen, *Abraham*, 53.

160. Al-Rabghuzi, *Stories of the Prophets*, 2:114.

161. Pitron 6:24, in Gaster, *Asatir*, 233. The Pitron is the Samaritan commentary on the Asatir.

162. Ginzberg, *Legends of the Jews*, 1:225.

163. *Journal of Discourses*, 21:245.

164. Ibid., 21:100. I have normalized the spelling of "to-day."

Notes to Chapter 6

1. Kasher, *Encyclopedia of Biblical Interpretation*, 2:135, quoting Zohar 1, 82b.

2. The Fragments of Artapanus, Fragment 1, in Charlesworth, *Old Testament Pseudepigrapha*, 2:897.

3. Galbraith and Smith, *Scriptural Teachings of the Prophet Joseph Smith*, 282.

4. As Abraham himself would later be told in JPST Genesis 15:14. See Exodus 12:35–36.

5. Nibley, *Abraham in Egypt*, 652.

6. Matthews, *Armenian Commentary on Genesis*, 81. There is some ambiguity in the context in which Ephrem makes this statement; it may possibly refer to Abraham's sojourn in Canaanite territory before going down into Egypt.

7. Kasher, *Encyclopedia of Biblical Interpretation*, 2:136, citing Shadal.

8. 1QapGen [1Q20 in Vermes] 21, in Vermes, *Complete Dead Sea Scrolls*, 456.

9. *Doctrines of Salvation*, 1:132.

10. Noble, *Great Men of God*, 59.

11. Matthews, *Armenian Commentary on Genesis*, 81–82.

12. Spencer W. Kimball, "The Example of Abraham," *Ensign*, June 1975, 6.

13. Matthews, *Armenian Commentary on Genesis*, 82.

14. Scherman and Zlotowitz, *Bereishis: Genesis*, 1(a):462.

15. Chrysostom, Homilies on Genesis 33.8, quoted in Oden, *Ancient Christian Commentary*, 2:16.

16. Kasher, *Encyclopedia of Biblical Interpretation*, 2:139, citing Rashi.

17. Ambrose, On Abraham 2.6.33, in Oden, *Ancient Christian Commentary*, 2:17.

18. Oxenden, *Portraits from the Bible*, 51.

19. Noble, *Great Men of God*, 59.

20. Blunt, *Twelve Lectures*, 76–77. The first quote within the quote is from Genesis 13:9; the second is from Matthew 5:9. Blunt's insightful remarks also include the following: "When we look around us in the world, who would believe that the same relationship, and therefore the same blessed motive for peace, still exists among its inhabitants? When we see the quarrels and coldnesses, the lawsuits and the strifes, between those who are not only bound by the common tie of Christian fraternity, but by the closest and most indissoluble bonds of affinity and blood, are we not tempted to inquire, can these men indeed be 'brethren?' Can they be all trusting to the same hope of salvation, and expecting, or even desiring, to dwell together in the same heaven? It is impossible: with such divisions of heart and affections, with such bitterness of feeling and expression, the same eternal mansions could not contain them; the very tranquility of heaven itself would be broken up if they were admitted there; heaven would be no heaven" (75–76).

21. Nibley, *Abraham's Creation Drama*, 2.

22. On Abraham 37, in *Philo VI*, 107.

23. Spencer W. Kimball, "The Example of Abraham," *Ensign*, June 1975, 6.

24. Kasher, *Encyclopedia of Biblical Interpretation*, 2:140.

25. Pirke de Rabbi Eliezer 25, in Friedlander, *Pirke de Rabbi Eliezer*, 184.

26. Qur'an 27:54–58; 37:133–38, in Cragg, *Qur'an*, 125.

27. al-Kisa'i, *Tales of the Prophets*, 155.

28. Bialik and Ravnitzky, *Book of Legends*, 36.

29. Pirke de Rabbi Eliezer 25, in Friedlander, *Pirke de Rabbi Eliezer*, 181.

30. See Ezekiel 16:48–50; Ginzberg, *Legends of the Jews*, 1:245–50; and Pirke de Rabbi Eliezer 25, in Friedlander, *Pirke de Rabbi Eliezer*, 181–83.

31. Bowker, *Targums and Rabbinic Literature*, 192.

32. Jubilees 16:5, in VanderKam, *Book of Jubilees*, 95.

33. Goldman, *In the Beginning*, 787.

34. Kasher, *Encyclopedia of Biblical Interpretation*, 2:143, citing Talmudic and other passages.

35. Bowker, *Targums and Rabbinic Literature*, 190.

36. Klinghoffer, *Discovery of God*, 173 (respelling "chesed" as "hesed").

37. Qur'an 29:28–29, in Cragg, *Qur'an*, 124.

38. Baring-Gould, *Legends of the Patriarchs*, 175.

39. Breed, *Abraham*, 67.

40. 1QapGen [1Q20 in Vermes] 21, in Vermes, *Complete Dead Sea Scrolls*, 456.

41. 1QapGen 21.8–10, in Martinez and Tigchelaar, *Dead Sea Scrolls Study Edition*, 1:45.

42. Zohar, Vayeze 155b–156a, in Sperling and Simon, *Zohar*, 2:100.

43. Kasher, *Encyclopedia of Biblical Interpretation*, 2:145, quoting Sifre Debarim 25.

44. Miller, *Abraham Friend of God*, 32, quoting Tanchuma and others.

45. See 1QapGen 21.13–19, in Martinez and Tigchelaar, *Dead Sea Scrolls Study Edition*, 1:45.

46. See Wenham, *Genesis 1–15*, 298; and Hertz, *Pentateuch and Haftorahs*, 49.

47. See Redford, *Oxford Encyclopedia of Ancient Egypt*, 2:244.

48. Kasher, *Encyclopedia of Biblical Interpretation*, 2:139.

49. See *Encyclopaedia Judaica*, 8:226; and Klinghoffer, *Discovery of God*, 154–55.

50. Nibley, *Abraham in Egypt*, 198.

51. *Encyclopaedia Judaica*, 14:868.

52. Williams, *Teachings of Harold B. Lee*, 195.

53. Culi, Magriso, and Argueti, *Torah Anthology*, 2:15.

54. Testament of Abraham (Recension A) 1:2, in Charlesworth, *Old Testament Pseudepigrapha,* 1:882 (parenthesis in original).

55. McKay, *Pathways to Happiness,* 280.

56. Kasher, *Encyclopedia of Biblical Interpretation,* 3:18.

57. Ginzberg, *Legends of the Jews,* 1:241; 5:248 n. 223.

58. Chavel, *Encyclopedia of Torah Thoughts,* 49.

59. Kasher, *Encyclopedia of Biblical Interpretation,* 3:111, quoting Zohar 1, 10b.

60. Zohar, Vayera 102b, in Sperling and Simon, *Zohar,* 1:328–29.

61. See Doane, *The Saxon Genesis,* 329–30.

62. Miller, *Abraham Friend of God,* 3.

63. Nibley, *Abraham in Egypt,* 203–204.

64. See Warren Zev Harvey, "Grace or Loving-Kindness," in Cohen and Mendes-Flohr, *Contemporary Jewish Religious Thought,* 299–302; and Glueck, *Hesed in the Bible,* 63–64.

65. Buxbaum, *Life and Teachings of Hillel,* 74.

66. In the next chapter of James, Abraham will be held up as an example of faith.

67. Gordon B. Hinckley, "Living in the Fulness of Times," *Ensign,* November 2001, 6.

68. Gordon B. Hinckley, "Reaching Down to Lift One Another," *Ensign,* November 2001, 54.

69. Rose, *Churchill,* 261.

70. Jubilees 11:2–5, in VanderKam, *Book of Jubilees,* 64–65, quoted above in chapter 1, and see accompanying discussion.

71. 1QapGen 21.28, in Martinez and Tigchelaar, *Dead Sea Scrolls Study Edition,* 1:47.

72. 1QapGen 22.1–5, in Martinez and Tigchelaar, *Dead Sea Scrolls Study Edition,* 1:47.

73. Josephus, *Jewish Antiquities* 1.10.1, in *Josephus 4,* 87.

74. 1QapGen 22.5–6, in Martinez and Tigchelaar, *Dead Sea Scrolls Study Edition,* 1:47.

75. Noble, *Great Men of God,* 60.

76. On Abraham 40, in *Philo VI,* 115.

77. "He thinned their numbers by reading the section of the heralds, as you read, *What man is there that is fearful . . . or faint-hearted . . .* (Deut. xx, 8)?" Genesis Rabbah 43:2, in Freedman, *Midrash Rabbah, Genesis,* 1:353.

78. Ginzberg, *Legends of the Jews,* 1:231.

79. Kasher, *Encyclopedia of Biblical Interpretation,* 2:158, quoting Yelamdenu.

80. As pointed out in Klinghoffer, *Discovery of God,* 91, citing Tanchuma, Lech L'chah 13.

81. Zohar, Vayera 112b, in Sperling and Simon, *Zohar,* 1:355.

82. 1QapGen 22.7, in Martinez and Tigchelaar, *Dead Sea Scrolls Study Edition,* 1:47.

83. According to the medieval Italian rabbi Sforno, in Kasher, *Encyclopedia of Biblical Interpretation,* 2:159.

84. See Kasher, *Encyclopedia of Biblical Interpretation,* 2:159, note *e* to commentary on verse 15.

85. 1QapGen 22.8, in Martinez and Tigchelaar, *Dead Sea Scrolls Study Edition,* 1:47.

86. Genesis Rabbah 43:3, in Freedman, *Midrash Rabbah, Genesis,* 1:354.

87. Kasher, *Encyclopedia of Biblical Interpretation,* 2:160, quoting Zohar; and see Zohar, Vayera 112b, in Sperling and Simon, *Zohar,* 1:355. I have changed the spelling of "Shechinah" to "Shekhinah."

88. As would happen later with Abraham's descendant Elisha. See 2 Kings 6:16.

89. 1QapGen 22.9–12, in Martinez and Tigchelaar, *Dead Sea Scrolls Study Edition,* 1:47.

90. Kasher, *Encyclopedia of Biblical Interpretation,* 2:161, quoting Zohar 1, 80b.

91. As it would be with Abraham's descendant Gideon. See Judges 7:20.

92. See Zohar, Vayera 112b, in Sperling and Simon, *Zohar,* 1:355.

93. Cotterell, *Chariot,* 7–21.

94. Miller, *Abraham Friend of God,* 50.

95. "Do ye suppose," Mormon wrote to a colleague during wartime, "that the Lord will still deliver us, while we sit upon our thrones and do not make use of the means which the Lord has provided for us?" Alma 60:21.

96. On Abraham 40, in *Philo VI,* 115.

97. Leviticus Rabbah 28, translation in Miller, *Abraham Friend of God,* 37.

98. Pirke de Rabbi Eliezer 27, in Friedlander, *Pirke de Rabbi Eliezer,* 196.

99. Miller, *Abraham Friend of God,* 37–38, quoting Tanchuma.

100. Oden, *Ancient Christian Commentary,* 2:27.

101. Klinghoffer, *Discovery of God,* 93.

102. Andy Orchard, "Conspicuous Heroism: Abraham, Prudentius, and the Old English Verse *Genesis,*" in Carruthers, *Heroes and Heroines,* 52–53.

103. Bowker, *Targums and Rabbinic Literature,* 195. These are Bowker's words summarizing and paraphrasing passages from Barnabas and Clement.

104. See Levner, *Legends of Israel,* 64–65; Ginzberg, *Legends of the Jews,* 1:232; and Baring-Gould, *Legends of the Patriarchs,* 168–69.

105. See Kasher, *Encyclopedia of Biblical Interpretation,* 2:155, quoting several sources, including Pirke de Rabbi Eliezer, Genesis Rabbah, Midrash Hagadol, and Zohar.

106. Miller, *Abraham Friend of God,* 40.

107. Ginzberg, *Legends of the Jews,* 1:232.

108. Levner, *Legends of Israel,* 65.

109. Genesis 14:21, in Westermann, *Genesis 12–36,* 186.

110. Hertz, *Pentateuch and Haftorahs,* 53.

111. Noble, *Great Men of God,* 61.

112. Spencer W. Kimball, "The Example of Abraham," *Ensign,* June 1975, 6.

113. John H. Sailhamer, in Gaebelein, *Expositor's Bible Commentary,* 2:123.

114. Miller, *Abraham Friend of God,* 43.

115. Noble, *Great Men of God,* 61.

116. In Genesis the wording is ambiguous as to whether Abraham gave or received the tithe. That Abraham paid the tithe is attested not only in the Joseph Smith Translation (JST, Gen. 14:37–39) and the Book of Mormon (Alma 13:15), but also in Josephus, the Genesis Apocryphon, and some rabbinic texts. See Feldman, *Josephus,* 68–69 n. 573.

117. Bowker, *Targums and Rabbinic Literature,* 197 n. *e* (quoting Kitab alMajal). See also The Book of the Bee XXI, in Budge, *Book of the Bee,* 33–34; Budge, *Cave of Treasures,* 152–53; Combat of Adam and Eve with Satan 3.16, in Malan, *Conflict of Adam and Eve with Satan,* 164.

118. On Abraham 40, in *Philo VI,* 115, 117.

119. Combat of Adam and Eve with Satan 4:1, in Malan, *Conflict of Adam and Eve with Satan,* 180.

120. The Book of the Bee 21, in Budge, *Book of the Bee,* 36.

121. 1QapGen 22.14–15, in Martinez and Tigchelaar, *Dead Sea Scrolls Study Edition,* 1:47.

122. Josephus, Jewish Antiquities 1.10.2, in *Josephus 4,* 89.

123. See 1Q28a.2.11–22, in Martinez and Tigchelaar, *Dead Sea Scrolls Study Edition,* 1:103; and see Dennis E. Smith's treatment of the symbolism of the meal in his article "Meals" in Schiffman and VanderKam, *Encyclopedia of the Dead Sea Scrolls,* 1:531–32.

124. Hunter, *Gospel Through the Ages,* 238–39.

125. Epistles of Cyprian 62:4, in *Ante-Nicene Fathers,* 5:359.

126. See Kasher, *Encyclopedia of Biblical Interpretation,* 2:162–66; and Ginzberg, *Legends of the Jews,* 1:233.

127. Galbraith and Smith, *Scriptural Teachings of the Prophet Joseph Smith,* 363.

128. See ibid.; and Doctrine and Covenants 84:14.

129. Ehat and Cook, *Words of Joseph Smith,* 246 (spelling and punctuation normalized).

130. Harris, *Hebraic Literature,* 47, quoting Avodath Hakkodesh, part 3, chapter 20.

131. Book of Abraham, Facsimile 2, explanation to figure 3.

132. Westermann, *Genesis 12–36,* 205.

133. Kasher, *Encyclopedia of Biblical Interpretation,* 2:162, citing Midrash T'hillim 76.

134. Josephus, The Jewish War 6.438, in *Josephus 3,* 503. Josephus maintains that Melchizedek and his temple were at the site of Jerusalem.

135. Eupolemus, as quoted by Eusebius, in Praeparatio Evangelica 9:17.5–6. See translations in Charlesworth, *Old Testament Pseudepigrapha,* 2:880; and Buchanan, *To the Hebrews,* 118.

136. Schwartz, *Tree of Souls,* 378.

137. Combat of Adam and Eve with Satan 4:1, in Malan, *Conflict of Adam and Eve with Satan,* 180.

138. Budge, *Cave of Treasures,* 148.

139. Nibley, *Abraham's Creation Drama,* 4.

140. Lunden, *Abraham and the Life of Faith,* 31.

141. H. Jagersma, "The Tithes in the Old Testament," in Albrektson et al., *Remembering All the Way,* 120.

142. Kasher, *Encyclopedia of Biblical Interpretation,* 2:166, citing various midrashim.

143. Genesis Rabbah on Genesis 24:1, quoted in Miller, *Abraham Friend of God,* 42.

144. Widstoe, *Gospel Doctrine,* 225.

145. Kasher, *Encyclopedia of Biblical Interpretation,* 2:164, quoting Zohar 1, 87a.

146. "Shalem the great." Asatir 7:17, in Gaster, *Asatir,* 258.

147. Horton, *The Melchizedek Tradition,* 159.

148. This early identification of Salem with Shechem was made in Jubilees 30:1 and in most of the early translations of Genesis 33:18—the Vulgate, the Syriac versions, and apparently the Septuagint. In fact, there is a village of Salim a few miles east of Nablus (modern site of the former Shechem. Horton, *The Melchizedek Tradition,* 48–50. George Wesley Buchanan points out that Eupolemus's statement (reported by Eusebius) that Melchizedek admitted Abraham into a temple at the foot of Mount Gerizim supports the Septuagint of Genesis 33:18. Buchanan, *To the Hebrews,* 118. H. Jagersma also finds it "unlikely" that the Salem of Genesis 14 and Jerusalem were the same, and notes H. H. Rowley's similar suggestions. H. Jagersma, "The Tithes in the Old Testament," in Albrektson et al., *Remembering All the Way,* 120.

149. Eupolemus, as quoted by Eusebius, in Praeparatio Evangelica 9:17.5–6. See translations in Charlesworth, *Old Testament Pseudepigrapha,* 2:880, and Buchanan, *To the Hebrews,* 118.

150. See H. H. Rowley's convenient list of citations and scholars who have identified Salem with Shechem or Mount Gerizim, including: C. Mackay, H. S. Nyberg, S. Landersdorfer, and A. P. Stanley. Rowley, *Worship in Ancient Israel,* 17–18 n. 4. Similarly, H. Jagersma acknowledges that "Salem was identified with Jerusalem at some stage of the tradition," but finds it "unlikely that this identification existed from the very beginning." H. Jagersma, "The Tithes in the Old Testament," in Albrektson et al.,

Remembering All the Way, 120.

151. Baring-Gould, *Legends of the Patriarchs,* 207, quoting Suidas the Grammarian.

152. Midrash Haneelam Lech, in Kasher, *Encyclopedia of Biblical Interpretation,* 2:164.

153. It is at least as old as the Psalms (110:4), and seems likely to have been handed down by Abraham, the man with firsthand knowledge of the greatness of Melchizedek.

154. Quoted in Wordsworth, *Holy Bible* 1:72, discussing Hebrews 7 and citing a number of Church Fathers.

155. Kasher, *Encyclopedia of Biblical Interpretation,* 2:166, citing various midrashim.

Notes to Chapter 7

1. *Journal of Discourses,* 21:159–60.

2. *Journal of Discourses,* 22:318.

3. Miller, *Abraham Friend of God,* 46, quoting Seder Eliyahu Rabbah.

4. Miller, *Abraham Friend of God,* 46.

5. Kasher, *Encyclopedia of Biblical Interpretation,* 2:173.

6. Ibid., 2:174, citing Radak.

7. Ibid., 8:149.

8. Miller, *Abraham Friend of God,* 48.

9. Ibid., 48.

10. "...both individually and as a people." Packer, *The Holy Temple,* 265.

11. Genesis Rabbah 44:8, in Freedman, *Midrash Rabbah, Genesis,* 1:366.

12. Just two verses previously, the JST had spoken of "the blessing wherewith Melchizedek had blessed him." JST, Genesis 14:40.

13. Combat of Adam and Eve with Satan 4:1, in Malan, *Conflict of Adam and Eve with Satan,* 180 (spelling "Melchizedek" for the original "Melchizedec" in Malan's rendering).

14. See, for example, Kasher, *Encyclopedia of Biblical Interpretation,* 2:175–77; Scherman and Zlotowitz, *Bereishis: Genesis,* 1(a):503–506; and see the Targums.

15. Kasher, *Encyclopedia of Biblical Interpretation,* 2:174–75.

16. Genesis Rabbah 44:8, in Freedman, *Midrash Rabbah, Genesis,* 1:366.

17. Kasher, *Encyclopedia of Biblical Interpretation,* 2:181.

18. JPST; Alter, *Genesis,* 63.

19. Alter, *Genesis,* 63.

20. Targum of Pseudo-Jonathan on Genesis 15:3, in Maher, *Targum Pseudo-Jonathan,* 60.

21. Genesis 15:2, in Vawter, *On Genesis,* 204.

22. Speiser, *Genesis,* 110.

23. Hershon, *Rabbinical Commentary on Genesis,* 83–84, citing Toldoth Yitzkhac.

24. Jubilees 14:2, in VanderKam, *Book of Jubilees,* 83.

25. Qur'an 2.260, in M. M. Ali, *Qur'an,* 114.

26. L. A. Snijders, "Genesis 15. The Covenant with Abram," in Gemser et al., *Studies on the Book of Genesis,* 261, 278.

27. See Bowker, *Targums and Rabbinic Literature,* 202, and discussion below.

28. Asatir 7:23, in Gaster, *Asatir,* 260.

29. Nibley, *Abraham in Egypt,* 11–26.

30. See Apocalypse of Abraham 9:5–10, in Charlesworth, *Old Testament Pseudepigrapha,* 1:693.

31. See Genesis Rabbah 44:14, in Freedman, *Midrash Rabbah, Genesis,* 1:369–70.

32. Apocalypse of Abraham 9:6, in Charlesworth, *Old Testament Pseudepigrapha,* 1:693.

33. Apocalypse of Abraham 9:6, in Sparks, *Apocryphal Old Testament,* 375.

34. Apocalypse of Abraham 9:7–8, in Charlesworth, *Old Testament Pseudepigrapha,* 1:693.

35. von Rad, *Genesis,* 186–87.

36. Gunkel, *Genesis,* 180, citing Jeremiah 34:17–20, and discussing similar practices among ancient peoples.

37. von Rad, *Genesis,* 186–87.

38. von Rad, *Genesis,* 187, omitting von Rad's citation.

39. Called "Azazel." Apocalypse of Abraham 13:3–14, in Charlesworth, *Old Testament Pseudepigrapha,* 1:695.

40. See Graves and Patai, *Hebrew Myths,* 153.

41. See Miller, *Abraham Friend of God,* 57, quoting Genesis Rabbah.

42. Caesarius of Arles, Sermon 82.3, in Oden, *Ancient Christian Commentary,* 2:39.

43. Genesis 15:12, in Speiser, *Genesis,* 111; and in Vawter, *On Genesis,* 208. Most translations here have "a deep sleep."

44. Or "a deep and terrifying darkness" (NRSV Genesis 15:12), or "a deep dark dread" (Speiser, *Genesis,* 111), or "fright and great darkness" (Fox, *Five Books of Moses,* 67), or "a great dark dread" (JPST Genesis 15:12; Alter, *Genesis,* 65), or "a great dark fear" (Wenham, *Genesis 1–15,* 324).

45. Apocalypse of Abraham 10:1, in Sparks, *Apocryphal Old Testament,* 376.

46. Apocalypse of Abraham 10:2, in Charlesworth, *Old Testament Pseudepigrapha,* 1:693.

47. Sparks, *Apocryphal Old Testament,* 16, quoting from Origen's homily 35 on Luke.

48. Hannah, *Michael and Christ,* 53.

49. Apocalypse of Abraham 10:3, in Charlesworth, *Old Testament Pseudepigrapha*, 1:697.

50. Apocalypse of Abraham 17:13, in Charlesworth, *Old Testament Pseudepigrapha*, 1:693.

51. Transliterated as "Jehovah" by the King James translators.

52. See Hannah, *Michael and Christ*, 52.

53. As pointed out by Hannah in his discussion of the angel Yahoel in the Apocalypse of Abraham. Hannah, *Michael and Christ*,

53. For the list of these names, see 3 Enoch 48D.1, in Odeberg, *3 Enoch*, part 2, 172–74, and see note on verse 1, especially on p. 174.

54. Scholem, *Jewish Gnosticism, Merkabah Mysticism*, 41–42. Scholem specifically concludes that the angel in Chapter 10 of the Apocalypse of Abraham is the same angel known in later Jewish tradition as Metatron.

55. Budge, *Book of the Mysteries*, 147.

56. Apocalypse of Abraham 13:12, in Charlesworth, *Old Testament Pseudepigrapha*, 1:695.

57. Graves and Patai, *Hebrew Myths*, 153, citing Apocalypse of Abraham.

58. Apocalypse of Abraham 10:5–8, 15–16, in Sparks, *Apocryphal Old Testament*, 376–77.

59. Apocalypse of Abraham 10:17, in Charlesworth, *Old Testament Pseudepigrapha*, 1:694.

60. Apocalypse of Abraham 10:18, in Sparks, *Apocryphal Old Testament*, 377.

61. This is what Enoch/Metatron would also do later for Rabbi Ishmael ben Elisha, the High Priest, who in 3 Enoch reports that "Metatron the Prince of the Presence, came and restored my spirit and put me upon my feet." 3 Enoch 1:9, in Odeberg, *3 Enoch*, part 2, 4–5.

62. Apocalypse of Abraham 11:1–2, in Sparks, *Apocryphal Old Testament*, 377.

63. "The linen band around his head recalls Aaron's headdress of fine linen (Ex. 28:39); the rainbowlike appearance of this linen band brings together the two central color schemes employed elsewhere in the description of God as high priest, whiteness and the multicolored glow. The purple of Iaoel's robe is one of the colors of the high-priestly garments of Exodus 28. The golden staff, like other aspects of the description, is not only obviously royal, but also priestly; Aaron's rod figures prominently in the story of the confrontation with Pharaoh (Ex. 7:9, 19–20; 8:1, 12), and in the wilderness . . . it sprouts to indicate the choice of Aaron and his descendants as priests (Num. 17:16–26)." Himmelfarb, *Ascent to Heaven*, 62.

64. See Wolfson, *Through a Speculum that Shines*, 334.

65. Apocalypse of Abraham 12:9, in Sparks, *Apocryphal Old Testament*, 378.

66. See Apocalypse of Abraham 15; 16:1, in Charlesworth, *Old Testament Pseudepigrapha*, 1:696.

67. Nibley, *Mormonism and Early Christianity*, 60. Nibley is citing and paraphrasing (in a targumic type manner) Apocalypse of Abraham 12:9.

68. Book of Abraham, Facsimile 2, explanation of figure 7. See following note.

69. They ascended, says the Apocalypse, on the wings of a pigeon and a dove. Apocalypse of Abraham 15, in Sparks, *Apocryphal Old Testament*, 378–80. Facsimile 2 of the book of Abraham shows, according to Nibley, that "the dove that takes one to heaven is the Holy Ghost." Nibley, *Abraham in Egypt*, 56.

70. Apocalypse of Abraham 17:1, in Charlesworth, *Old Testament Pseudepigrapha*, 1:696.

71. Apocalypse of Abraham 17:1, in Sparks, *Apocryphal Old Testament*, 380.

72. Doctrine and Covenants 110:3: "his voice was as the sound of the rushing of great waters."

73. Ginzberg, *Legends of the Jews*, 5:229 n. 114.

74. Apocalypse of Abraham 18:12–13, in Charlesworth, *Old Testament Pseudepigrapha*, 1:698.

75. The four faces seem to be the four main signs of the Zodiac. L'Orange, *Iconography of Cosmic Kingship*, 50.

76. L'Orange, *Iconography of Cosmic Kingship*, 42–79, especially 44–50.

77. Nibley, *Approaching Zion*, 265.

78. Sefer Yetzirah 6:4, in Suarès, *Qabala Trilogy*, 495.

79. Widengren, *Ascension of the Apostle*, 77–80. The tradition quoted, which appears in several sources, does not purport to be the experience of Abraham, but the connections are unusually striking. The protagonist of the Hermetic-Gnostic story meets an old man sitting on a throne of gold, with a crystalline tablet in his hand, and then sees a book called the Secret of Creation and the Knowledge of the First Causes of Things. Similarly, Abraham's experience at the throne, including his being handed something, is recorded in the Sefer Yetzirah, the kabbalistic Book of Creation purporting to contain the secrets of creation, a book said to be authored by Abraham.

80. The medieval Muslim scholar Ibn 'Abd Allāh wrote that Abraham was one of five prophets (including Adam, Seth, Enoch, and Moses) to whom God revealed heavenly books. Adang, *Muslim Writers on Judaism*, 21. This obviously refers to more than just the handing down of the patriarchal records, which came into the hands of far more than five patriarchs. Ibn 'Abd Allāh does not mention when Abraham received the heavenly book(s), but according to the ancient pattern, the heavenly book is presented to the prophet in heaven. Widengren, *Ascension of the Apostle*, 8–21.

81. Apocalypse of Abraham 19:3, in Charlesworth, *Old Testament Pseudepigrapha*, 1:698.

82. Sefer Yetzirah [the Short Version] 6:4, in Kaplan, *Sefer Yetzirah*, 267.

83. Sefer Yetzirah 6:7, in Kaplan, *Sefer Yetzirah*, 255. See also Ginzberg, *Legends of the Jews*, 5:210 n. 13.

84. Isaiah 41:8 in Gileadi, *Literary Message of Isaiah*, 351. The King James has "Abraham my friend," but the Hebrew word derives from the verb *ahav*, "to love" (see Brown, Driver, and Briggs, *Hebrew and English Lexicon*, 12–13; and Botterweck and Ringgren, *Theological Dictionary of the Old Testament*, 1:99–118), and "implies a more intimate relationship than . . . the usual word for 'my friend/companion,'" so that God literally calls Abraham "him whom I loved" (North, *The Second Isaiah*, 97) or "my

beloved" or "my beloved friend," as the passage is in fact translated in some versions both ancient and modern. The Septuagint has the Greek equivalent of "whom I have loved," while Aquila has the Greek equivalent of "my beloved." Watts, *Isaiah 34–66*, 99; Westermann reads "whom I loved," in Westermann, *Isaiah 40–66*, 67; *The Emphasized Bible* reads "my loving one," in Vaughan, *Twenty-Six Translations* 2:2478. Jewish tradition remembers Abraham as "more beloved of [God] than any man." Ginzberg, *Legends of the Jews*, 1:320.

85. Sefer Yetzirah [Long Version] 6:8, in Kaplan, *Sefer Yetzirah*, 281. Of course, this language later came to be interpreted as terms of art in kabbalistic circles.

86. Kasher, *Encyclopedia of Biblical Interpretation*, 2:186, translating Sefer Yetzirah 6:7.

87. Recognitions of Clement 1.33, in *Ante-Nicene Fathers*, 8:86.

88. History [1832], in Jessee, *Papers of Joseph Smith*, 5–6 (spelling corrected).

89. Recognitions of Clement 1.33, in *Ante-Nicene Fathers*, 8:86. The totality of the event as here reported may well conflate revelations received by Abraham on different occasions.

90. Galbraith and Smith, *Scriptural Teachings of the Prophet Joseph Smith*, 390.

91. Ibid., 391.

92. Ibid., 215.

93. Ginzberg, *Legends of the Jews*, 5:229 n. 114.

94. Qur'an 6:76, in Cragg, *Qur'an*, 118; and see M. M. Ali, *Qur'an*, 293.

95. Genesis Rabbah 44:12, in Freedman, *Midrash Rabbah, Genesis*, 1:367.

96. "I beheld the celestial kingdom of God, and the glory thereof. . . . I saw the beautiful streets of that kingdom, which had the appearance of being paved with gold. I saw father Adam and Abraham." Galbraith and Smith, *Scriptural Teachings of the Prophet Joseph Smith*, 126. See also Doctrine and Covenants 76:50–70.

97. Al-Rabghuzi, *Stories of the Prophets*, 2:93.

98. Apocalypse of Abraham 20:3, in Charlesworth, *Old Testament Pseudepigrapha*, 1:699.

99. Apocalypse of Abraham 20:4, in Sparks, *Apocryphal Old Testament*, 383.

100. This incident is reported in Genesis at the first of the chapter (before the sacrifice), when God "took him outside" to see the stars. So most modern translations of Genesis 15:5 do also, including NIV; JPST; GTC; and Speiser, *Genesis*, 110. However, Jewish tradition insists that God actually "lifted him above the vault of heaven." Genesis Rabbah 44:12, in Freedman, *Midrash Rabbah, Genesis*, 1:368. It appears that the Genesis account may be an abbreviated report of the larger incident recounted in the Apocalypse of Abraham.

101. Kasher, *Encyclopedia of Biblical Interpretation*, 2:182.

102. Abraham was shown, according to the Qur'an, "the kingdom of the . . . earth." Qur'an 6:76, in Cragg, *Qur'an*, 118; and see M. M. Ali, *Qur'an*, 293.

103. Apocalypse of Abraham 9:6, in Sparks, *Apocryphal Old Testament*, 375.

104. As seen in our book of Abraham 3–5.

105. One rabbinic tradition held that on this occasion the Lord "revealed to him [history] *until* that day," while according to another tradition the Lord "revealed to him the future *from* that day." Genesis Rabbah 44:22, in Freedman, *Midrash Rabbah, Genesis*, 1:376. In the Apocalypse of Abraham, he seems to see all of history from the premortal existence. However, if Abraham had earlier been shown history up to his day—which may be the case, judging from the portion of the book of Abraham that we have—then the Apocalypse might be combining the revelations from two different occasions into one. Certainly the Apocalypse seems to restate what Abraham says about seeing the host of premortal spirits.

106. Himmelfarb, *Ascent to Heaven*, 65.

107. Ginzberg, *Legends of the Jews*, 1:235. As God had once shown Enoch. Moses 7:24.

108. *Journal of Discourses*, 22:318.

109. Genesis Rabbah 44:21, in Freedman, *Midrash Rabbah, Genesis*, 1:375.

110. See, for example, Speiser, *Genesis*, 113; Westermann, *Genesis 12–36*, 227; and Vawter, *On Genesis*, 212. See also Sarna, *Genesis*, 116, holding that God's statement was an assurance that the misfortunes on Abraham's posterity would not be during his own lifetime.

111. Apocalypse of Abraham 29:9, in Charlesworth, *Old Testament Pseudepigrapha*, 1:703.

112. Apocalypse of Abraham 29:4–6, in Charlesworth, *Old Testament Pseudepigrapha*, 1:703.

113. Oden, *Ancient Christian Commentary*, 2:32.

114. Kasher, *Encyclopedia of Biblical Interpretation*, 2:186.

115. Chrysostom, Homilies on Genesis 36:15, in Oden, *Ancient Christian Commentary*, 2:32.

116. Miller, *Abraham Friend of God*, 53, quoting Melchiltah, B'shallach 6.

117. Kasher, *Encyclopedia of Biblical Interpretation*, 2:185.

118. Pitron 7:22, in Gaster, *Asatir*, 239. The Pitron is the Samaritan commentary on the Asatir.

119. Widengren, *Ascension of the Apostle*, 67.

120. 4 Ezra 3:14, in Stone, *Fourth Ezra*, 58. As Stone (p. 71) comments, "The occasion of the revelation to Abraham was doubtlessly the Covenant Between the Pieces (Genesis 15)."

121. Apocalypse of Abraham 29:8–15, in Sparks, *Apocryphal Old Testament*, 389.

122. Apocalypse of Abraham 31:1–2, in Charlesworth, *Old Testament Pseudepigrapha*, 1:704–705.

123. Apocalypse of Abraham 29:19, in Charlesworth, *Old Testament Pseudepigrapha*, 1:704.

124. Ginzberg, *Legends of the Jews*, 1:235.

125. Kasher, *Encyclopedia of Biblical Interpretation*, 2:201.

126. Targum Pseudo-Jonathan on Genesis 15:18, in Maher, *Targum Pseudo-Jonathan*, 61.

127. 4 Ezra 3:15, in Stone, *Fourth Ezra*, 59.

128. Genesis Rabbah 84:13, in Freedman, *Midrash Rabbah, Genesis*, 2:779.

129. Barker, *The Older Testament*. The thesis of Barker's fascinating book is essentially that 1 Enoch and other so-called pseudepigraphical writings provide important keys to Israel's pre-exilic religion, but that the biblical texts were edited during the Second Temple times in an effort to remove all traces of the older tenets. See especially her conclusions on 137 and 279–82.

130. 1 Enoch 1:4–9, in Charlesworth, *Old Testament Pseudepigrapha*, 1:13–14.

131. Apocalypse of Abraham 29:17, in Sparks, *Apocryphal Old Testament*, 390.

132. Apocalypse of Abraham 29:17, in Charlesworth, *Old Testament Pseudepigrapha*, 1:704.

133. Apocalypse of Abraham 31:1–2, in Sparks, *Apocryphal Old Testament*, 390–91.

134. Recognitions of Clement 1.33, in *Ante-Nicene Fathers*, 8:86. Jewish sources similarly remember that God "showed him the Resurrection of the dead." And see Kasher, *Encyclopedia of Biblical Interpretation*, 2:195–6; and Ginzberg, *Legends of the Jews*, 1:236.

135. A number of "pseudepigraphic and midrashic sources all take the scene at Genesis 15:7 as suggesting a vision by Abraham of the fates of sinners and the righteous." Jacobson, *Liber Antiquitatum Biblicarum*, 2:717.

136. Recognitions of Clement 1.33, in *Ante-Nicene Fathers*, 8:86.

137. Fragment Targums on Genesis 15:17, in Klein, *Fragment Targums*, 2:13.

138. Recognitions of Clement 1.33, in *Ante-Nicene Fathers*, 8:86.

139. Fragment Targums on Genesis 15:17, in Klein, *Fragment Targums* 2:13; so also Targum Neofiti on Genesis 15:17, in McNamara, *Targum Neofiti 1*, 96–97.

140. 2 Baruch 6:2, in Charlesworth, *Old Testament Pseudepigrapha*, 1:622.

141. 2 Baruch 4:1–6, in Charlesworth, *Old Testament Pseudepigrapha*, 1:622.

142. 4 Ezra 13:36, in Charlesworth, *Old Testament Pseudepigrapha*, 1:552.

143. Galbraith and Smith, *Scriptural Teachings of the Prophet Joseph Smith*, 262, referring to the experience of many ancient prophets.

144. One of the Dead Scroll fragments mentioning Abraham also mentions a carcass (an alternate reading apparently alluding to the sacrifice described in Genesis 15) and contains the quote: "[For I will give] purified lips to the people." The next column of this fragment then proceeds to mention "the judgment" and speaks of the Lord telling Abraham the same thing reported in Genesis 15:13. 4Q464, "Lives of the Patriarchs," in Wise, Abegg, and Cook, *Dead Sea Scrolls*, 402.

145. *Journal of Discourses*, 17:245.

146. See Targum of Pseudo-Jonathan on Genesis 15:2, in Bowker, *Targums and Rabbinic Literature*, 200.

147. Ginzberg, *Legends of the Jews*, 1:297.

148. Widengren, *Ascension of the Apostle*, 21. Abraham had of course received the fulness of the kingly priesthood ordinances from Melchizedek, but he was also the heir to the royal patriarchal authority. Now he descends as yet a greater special witness of the Lord.

149. For the translation of "magi" in Matthew 2:1, see NIV; NASB; Young, *Young's Literal Translation*, 1 of New Testament ("mages"); and Albright and Mann, *Matthew*, 11, and see accompanying commentary on the magi on 12–15.

150. Haug, *Essays on . . . the Parsis*, 16.

Notes to Chapter 8

1. Rendtorff, *Men of the Old Testament*, 16.

2. Kierkegaard, *Fear and Trembling*, 32.

3. Gretchen Clark, private correspondence to family members, March 20, 2001 (quoted by permission).

4. Judean Antiquities 1.228, in Feldman, *Josephus*, 90, reporting what Abraham told Isaac years later.

5. Genesis Rabbah 39:11, in Freedman, *Midrash Rabbah, Genesis*, 1:320.

6. Kasher, *Encyclopedia of Biblical Interpretation*, 2:214.

7. Mastro, *All the Women of the Bible*, 382.

8. Ginzberg, *Legends of the Jews*, 1:237.

9. Hirsch, *T'rumath Tzvi*, 79. Or "pray," in Fox, *Five Books of Moses*, 68, and Alter, *Genesis*, 66.

10. Genesis 16:2, in Mitchell, *Genesis*, 29.

11. Miller, *Abraham Friend of God*, 69, quoting Tanchuma Buber, Vayera 32.

12. Kasher, *Encyclopedia of Biblical Interpretation*, 2:215.

13. Miller, *Abraham Friend of God*, 69.

14. Hirsch, *T'rumath Tzvi*, 80.

15. Gordon B. Hinckley, "Excerpts from Recent Addresses of President Gordon B. Hinckley," *Ensign*, December 1995, 66.

16. "What Sarah did, then, was . . . in conformance with the family law of the Hurrians, a society whose customs the patriarchs knew intimately and followed often." Speiser, *Genesis*, 121. As emphasized by other commentators, the practice was far more widespread than the Hurrians. See Wenham, *Genesis 16–50*, 7; Sarna, *Genesis*, 119; Westermann, *Genesis 12–36*, 239; and von Rad, *Genesis*, 191.

17. *Journal of Discourses*, 23:228.

18. See Tuchman and Rapoport, *Passions of the Matriarchs*, 14–15.

19. Chavel, *Ramban*, 211.

20. Moyers, *Genesis* 193.

21. Hirsch, *T'rumath Tzvi*, 79.

22. On Abraham 43, in *Philo VI*, 123.

23. On Abraham 43, in *Philo VI*, 123, 125.

24. Doctrine and Covenants 132:34–35: "I, the Lord, commanded it." Jewish sources similarly report that Abraham accepted Sarah's proposal only after being "instructed" to do so "by the holy spirit." Ginzberg, *Legends of the Jews*, 1:237.

25. Genesis Rabbah 45:3, in Freedman, *Midrash Rabbah, Genesis*, 1:381.

26. Tuchman and Rapoport, *Passions of the Matriarchs*, 16.

27. See Kasher, *Encyclopedia of Biblical Interpretation*, 2:219.

28. Genesis 16:4, in Vawter, *On Genesis*, 214.

29. Kasher, *Encyclopedia of Biblical Interpretation*, 2:216–18.

30. Or, as in NRSV, "May the LORD judge . . ."

31. Kasher, *Encyclopedia of Biblical Interpretation*, 2:217–18, quoting Rashi; Rashi on Genesis 16:5, in Rashi, *Commentary*, 135; Scherman and Zlotowitz, *Bereishis: Genesis*, 1(a):544–545; Culi, Magriso, and Argueti, *Torah Anthology*, 2:111.

32. Kasher, *Encyclopedia of Biblical Interpretation*, 2:217.

33. So Wenham, *Genesis 16–50*, 8–9.

34. Didymus the Blind, On Genesis 2:41, in Oden, *Ancient Christian Commentary*, 2:45.

35. Wenham, *Genesis 16–50*, 10–11, spelling out "Old Testament" where original has "OT."

36. For example, Rashi said this phrase (from Genesis 16:12) means "liking the wilderness." Rashi, *Commentary*, 137. Ibn Ezra, the learned Spanish commentator of the twelfth century, interpreted the phrase to mean "free among men." Kasher, *Encyclopedia of Biblical Interpretation*, 2:221. Nineteenth-century scholar Samson Raphael Hirsch translated the phrase as "a free man among men." Hirsch, *T'rumath Tzvi*, 81.

Regarding the rest of what was prophesied of Ishmael in Genesis 16:12, the next phrase is "his hand against everyone, and everyone's hand against him" (JPST). Nahum Sarna has suggested that this is a general prediction regarding Ishmael's descendants with regard to the "unceasing tension that exists between the sedentary and nomadic populations in the Near East." Sarna, *Genesis*, 121. But if this phrase refers personally to Ishmael, then in context it again seems to speak of a desert existence where, in the open spaces, danger could come from any quarter. Accordingly, speaking of the entire verse, modern scholar Gordon Wenham notes that it "describes Ishmael's future destiny, to enjoy a free-roaming bedouinlike existence. The freedom his mother sought will be his one day." Wenham, *Genesis 16–50*, 10–11.

The meaning of the final phrase that the angel tells Hagar—"He shall dwell alongside all his kinsmen" (JPST)—is disputed, but the most likely translation seems to be that Ishmael will dwell "alongside" or "in the face of" or "in the presence of" his brothers or kin. See Speiser, *Genesis*, 117: "in the face of"; Fox, *Five Books of Moses*, 68: "in the presence of."

37. Hirsch, *T'rumath Tzvi*, 81.

38. See Levner, *Legends of Israel*, 87; Bialik and Ravnitzky, *Book of Legends*, 40.

39. Miller, *Abraham Friend of God*, 81.

40. Genesis 17:1, in NIV; NRSV; REB.

41. Genesis 17:1, in Alter, *Genesis*, 72.

42. Genesis 17:1, in Wenham, *Genesis 16–50*, 14; and Vawter, *On Genesis*, 218.

43. So also Westermann: "live always in my presence and be perfect." Westermann, *Genesis 12–36*, 253.

44. See Kasher, *Encyclopedia of Biblical Interpretation*, 2:229; and Miller, *Abraham Friend of God*, 81.

45. Miller, *Abraham Friend of God*, 81.

46. Kasher, *Encyclopedia of Biblical Interpretation*, 2:225.

47. Ibid., 2:228.

48. Galbraith and Smith, *Scriptural Teachings of the Prophet Joseph Smith*, 15.

49. Commenting on the Hebrew of God's command to Abraham to walk with him, Robert Alter notes that although the preposition is different, "the verb is the same used for Enoch's walking with God." Alter, *Genesis*, 72 n. 1. Westermann likewise calls attention to the passages about Enoch and Abraham walking with God, and notes that it is "the same sort of phrase." Westermann, *Genesis 1–11*, 358.

50. *Journal of Discourses*, 20:187–88.

51. Ibid., 20:190–91.

52. Ibid., 20:188.

53. Nibley, *Approaching Zion*, 25.

54. Panarion 1.4.1,1, in Williams, *Panarion of Epiphanius*, 18.

55. See discussions of the name *Abraham* in Sarna, *Genesis*, 124; Speiser, *Genesis*, 124; Wenham, *Genesis 1–15*, 252–53; Wenham, *Genesis 16–50*, 21; and Westermann, *Genesis 12–36*, 133, 261. See also Clements' article on the name Abraham in Botterweck and Ringgren, *Theological Dictionary of the Old Testament*, 1:52–58; Baumgartner and Stamm, *Hebrew and Aramaic Lexicon* 1:9–10.

56. So also translations of Genesis 17:5 in NRSV; JPST; Alter, *Genesis*, 73; and Wenham, *Genesis 16–50*, 14.

57. Genesis 17:5, in Speiser, *Genesis,* 122.

58. Kasher, *Encyclopedia of Biblical Interpretation,* 2:232.

59. Hobbs, *Sermons of Henry King,* 154.

60. Tuchman and Rapoport, *Passions of the Matriarchs,* 23, citing Berachot 13a of the Talmud.

61. Sarna, *Genesis,* 126.

62. *Encyclopaedia Judaica,* 14:868.

63. Tuchman and Rapoport, *Passions of the Matriarchs,* 23.

64. Soloveitchik, *Man of Faith,* 86, parenthetical material with references omitted.

65. Sheri L. Dew, "Are We Not All Mothers?" Talk in the 171st Semiannual General Conference, October 2001, of The Church of Jesus Christ of Latter-Day Saints, Saturday morning session.

66. Kasher, *Encyclopedia of Biblical Interpretation,* 2:247.

67. Ibid., 2:248.

68. Soloveitchik, *Man of Faith,* 86.

69. Tuchman and Rapoport, *Passions of the Matriarchs,* 26–27, quoting Rabbi Joseph Soloveitchik.

70. Steinsaltz, *Biblical Images,* 24, 27.

71. JST, Genesis 17:23, changing 17:17 in the traditional text, which is usually translated "laughed." But the Hebrew verb, as pointed out by E. A. Speiser, has a wide range of meaning that includes "to rejoice over, smile on (a newborn child)." Speiser, *Genesis,* 125 (parenthesis in original). See also the following note.

72. Rashi comments that Abraham laughed in the sense of joy, so that he "believed and rejoiced." Rashi on Genesis 17:17, in Rashi, *Commentary.* 34. Similarly, Targum Onkelos reads here that Abraham "rejoiced." Targum Onkelos, Genesis 17:17, in Aberbach and Grossfeld, *Targum Onkelos,* 104.

73. Klinghoffer, *Discovery of God,* 144.

74. Scholia, section 10, folio 16b, on Genesis 18:17, in Sprengling and Graham, *Barhebraeus' Scholia,* 59.

75. Kasher, *Encyclopedia of Biblical Interpretation,* 2:182.

76. Speiser, *Genesis,* 125; Westermann, *Genesis 12–36,* 269; and Sarna, *Genesis,* 124.

77. Kasher, *Encyclopedia of Biblical Interpretation,* 2:255, quoting Genesis Rabbah and Midrash Hagadol.

78. Questions and Answers on Genesis 3.42, in *Philo Supplement 1,* 232. The second "Himself" is in parenthesis in the original.

79. See the experience of the Nephite disciples in 3 Nephi 27–28.

80. Galbraith and Smith, *Scriptural Teachings of the Prophet Joseph Smith,* 394–95.

81. Stone, *Armenian Apocrypha,* 98, echoing Romans 4:11.

82. Podhoretz, Norman. *The Prophets,* 23.

83. The phrase is Mormon's, writing to his son Moroni about another apostate society that similarly denied the innocence of little children. See Moroni 8:12.

84. Klinghoffer, *Discovery of God,* 144–46.

85. Moroni 8:8: "Listen to the words of Christ, your Redeemer, your Lord and your God. Behold, I came into the world not to call the righteous but sinners to repentance; the whole need no physician, but they that are sick; wherefore, little children are whole, for they are not capable of committing sin; wherefore the curse of Adam is taken from them in me, that it hath no power over them; and the law of circumcision is done away in me."

86. Ambrose, On Abraham 1.4.29, in Oden, *Ancient Christian Commentary,* 2:54.

87. Miller, *Abraham Friend of God,* 77, quoting Tanchuma.

88. Kasher, *Encyclopedia of Biblical Interpretation,* 2:256, citing Midrash Hagadol.

89. Kasher, *Encyclopedia of Biblical Interpretation,* 2:256, citing Genesis Rabbah 47.

90. Klinghoffer, *Discovery of God,* 152.

91. See Genesis Rabbah 46:3, in Freedman, *Midrash Rabbah, Genesis,* 1:390.

92. Genesis 17:23, in JPST, NIV, and GTC.

93. Jubilees 15:22–24, in VanderKam, *Book of Jubilees,* 90–91.

94. Kasher, *Encyclopedia of Biblical Interpretation,* 2:255–56.

95. See Menahem Kister, "Demons, Theology, and Abraham's Covenant," in Kugler and Schuller, *The Dead Sea Scrolls at Fifty,* 178–81 (Kister discusses the Damascus Covenant 16:4–6, a passage telling that Abraham was circumcised on the "day of his knowing," meaning, as Kister, shows, on the very day that Abraham received the commandment).

96. *Encyclopaedia Judaica,* 5:570.

97. Spencer W. Kimball, "The Example of Abraham," *Ensign,* June 1975, 4.

98. Pirke de Rabbi Eliezer 29, in Friedlander, *Pirke de Rabbi Eliezer,* 203–204.

99. Klinghoffer, *Discovery of God,* 154.

100. Baba Mezia 86b, in Epstein, *Babylonian Talmud.*

101. Kasher, *Encyclopedia of Biblical Interpretation,* 2:2.

102. See the Targums of Neofiti, the Fragmentary Targum, and Pseudo Jonathan. Miller, *Mysterious Encounters at Mamre and Jabbok,* 10.

103. Miller, *Abraham Friend of God,* 93–94, quoting Midrash Hagadol.

104. See Ginzberg, *Legends of the Jews,* 1:240.

105. Noble, *Great Men of God*, 57.

106. Kasher, *Encyclopedia of Biblical Interpretation*, 3:5.

107. See Ginzberg, *Legends of the Jews*, 1:240–41; and Kasher, *Encyclopedia of Biblical Interpretation*, 3:4–5, 13.

108. See Kasher, *Encyclopedia of Biblical Interpretation*, 3:6, citing Tol'doth Yitzhak.

109. See Rashi; cited in Miller, *Abraham Friend of God*, 95–96.

110. Noble, *Great Men of God*, 57.

111. Miller, *Abraham Friend of God*, 95.

112. Zohar 1:101a, in Sperling and Simon, *Zohar*, 1:326.

113. "The text [of Genesis 18:13] cannot intend . . . that Yahweh [the Lord] is speaking. . . . The explanation of the use of ['the Lord'] in this passage is that a messenger . . . represents the one who sends him as he delivers his message; hence the one who gives the commission can be named in place of the one commissioned." Westermann, *Genesis 12–36*, 281.

114. Jubilees 16:1–4, in VanderKam, *Book of Jubilees*, 94.

115. Miller, *Mysterious Encounters at Mamre and Jabbok*, 16.

116. Kasher, *Encyclopedia of Biblical Interpretation*, 3:20.

117. See Doxey, *Latter-day Prophets and the Doctrine and Covenants*, 2:141–42.

118. This issue of Abraham's visitors actually eating food so troubled some of the rabbis that they insisted the angels only appeared to eat. Miller, *Mysterious Encounters at Mamre and Jabbok*, 10, 27–29.

119. Chavel, *Ramban*, 1:239.

120. Doane, *The Saxon Genesis*, 168–69.

121. Jacob, *Genesis*, 116–17. For a biographical sketch of Benno Jacob, see *Encyclopaedia Judaica*, 9:1206–1207.

122. Wenham, *Genesis 16–50*, 46, citing Genesis 23:12; 29:13; 33:4; 37:9; and 42:6.

123. Van Seters, *Abraham in History and Tradition*, 212.

124. Combat of Adam and Eve with Satan 4:1, in Malan, *Conflict of Adam and Eve with Satan*, 180.

125. On Abraham 40, in *Philo VI*, 115, 117.

126. On Sobriety 55–56, in *Philo III*, 473. Philo attributes these words, as does Genesis, to the Lord. Similarly, in Genesis 18:13, it is the Lord who is said to speak to Abraham, although in context it is clearly one of the three visitors who is speaking. But this cannot be, says no less an authority than Claus Westermann. Westermann, *Genesis 12–36*, 281.

127. The plural here in Genesis 18:3 is found in the Joseph Smith Translation and also in JPST.

128. See also FBM: "Pray let a little water be fetched, then wash your feet and recline under the tree; let me fetch you a bit of bread, that you may refresh your hearts."

129. Letellier, *Day in Mamre, Night in Sodom*, 82.

130. Westermann, *Genesis 12–36*, 277.

131. Miller, *Abraham Friend of God*, 99, quoting Midrash Aggadah.

132. See Kasher, *Encyclopedia of Biblical Interpretation*, 3:19; and Miller, *Abraham Friend of God*, 101.

133. "Butter" in King James, but "curds" in most modern translations, as in NRSV; JPST; and Speiser, *Genesis*, 128. See Sarna, *Genesis*, 129.

134. Sarna, *Genesis*, 129.

135. Westermann, *Genesis 12–36*, 277.

136. Sarna, *Genesis*, 129, citing Bava Metsia 87a.

137. Westermann, *Genesis 12–36*, 277.

138. Buxbaum, *Life and Teachings of Hillel*, 146, citing Melchita on Exodus 18:12.

139. See Driver, *Genesis*, 192; and Westermann, *Genesis 12–36*, 278.

140. See Miller, *Mysterious Encounters at Mamre and Jabbok*, 18–19; and Zohar, Vayera 102a–102b, in Sperling and Simon, *Zohar*, 1:327–29.

141. JST, Genesis 18:23; and Testament of Abraham (Recension A) 6:5, in Charlesworth, *Old Testament Pseudepigrapha*, 1:885.

142. Testament of Abraham (Recension A) 6:5–6, in Charlesworth, *Old Testament Pseudepigrapha*, 1:885.

143. See Miller, *Mysterious Encounters at Mamre and Jabbok*, 52 (Tertullian), 79 (Gregory of Illeberia), 83 (Jerome), and 85 (Augustine).

144. See Miller, *Mysterious Encounters at Mamre and Jabbok*, 54 (Novation), 66–67 (Origen), 82 (Ambrose), and 93 (summary).

145. See Miller, *Mysterious Encounters at Mamre and Jabbok*, 66 (Origen).

146. See Doctrine and Covenants 24:15 ("casting off the dust . . . and cleansing your feet"); 75:20–21 ("shake off the dust of your feet"); 84:92–94 ("cleanse your feet even with water, pure water"); and 99:4 ("cleanse your feet").

147. Smith, *History of the Church*, 2:309; and see discussion in McConkie, *Mormon Doctrine*, 829–32.

148. Soloveitchik, *Man of Faith*, 84, translating Rashi on Genesis 18:9.

149. Pesikta Zutrati, quoted in Miller, *Abraham Friend of God*, 99.

150. Kasher, *Encyclopedia of Biblical Interpretation*, 3:24.

151. Al-Rabghuzi, *Stories of the Prophets*, 2:133.

152. The King James likewise reads here "lord," as do NASB and FBM. The word is rendered "master" in NIV.

153. Pelikan, *Luther's Works* 4:207.

154. Ibid., 4:208.

155. Skinner, *Commentary on Genesis*, 301.

156. Chavel, *Ramban,* 1:240.

157. See Scherman and Zlotowitz, *Bereishis: Genesis,* 1(a):643; Chavel, *Ramban,* 1:240; Jacob, *Genesis,* 119.

158. If so, the coming of these three messengers after Abraham had obeyed God's command about circumcision would follow the familiar pattern of messengers being sent to Saints who have proved themselves faithful.

159. 1 Peter 3:6, in Lattimore, *The New Testament,* 504.

160. Skinner, *Commentary on Genesis,* 302.

161. Ephrem the Syrian, Commentary on Genesis 15.3, in Oden, *Ancient Christian Commentary,* 2:67.

162. Culi, Magriso, and Argueti, *Torah Anthology,* 2:179.

163. Scherman and Zlotowitz, *Bereishis: Genesis,* 1(a):646; and see Tuchman and Rapoport, *Passions of the Matriarchs,* 33–35.

164. Vawter, *On Genesis,* 227.

165. Genesis 18:15, in Alter, *Genesis,* 79.

166. Genesis 18:14, in NIV; KJV ("any thing").

167. Letellier, *Day in Mamre, Night in Sodom,* 101.

168. Genesis 18:14, in NASB, Wenham, *Genesis 16–50,* 34.

169. Genesis 18:14, in Alter, *Genesis,* 79; Fox, *Five Books of Moses,* 76 (". . . beyond YHWH?").

170. Genesis 18:14, in Vawter, *On Genesis,* 227; Mitchell, *Genesis,* 33 (omitting "to do").

171. So also Letellier, *Day in Mamre, Night in Sodom,* 102: "Could anything be too wonderful for YHWH?" Munk, *Aqaydat Yitzchaq* 1:119: "Is anything too wonderful for G'd?"

172. Kasher, *Encyclopedia of Biblical Interpretation,* 3:28.

173. Fitzmeyer, *Gospel According to Luke 1-9,* 352.

174. See also translations in NASB; NJB; Buchanan, *To the Hebrews,* 177–78; and Lattimore, translator, *The New Testament,* 485. Translating the subject of the verse as Sarah is the traditional view, and followed by most translators, although some translations render Abraham as the subject of the verse. For discussions, see Buchanan, *To the Hebrews,* 190; and Ellingworth, *The Epistle to the Hebrews,* 586–87.

175. Ginzberg, *Legends of the Jews,* 1:203; 5:215.

176. Tuchman and Rapoport, *Passions of the Matriarchs,* 51.

177. Ginzberg, *Legends of the Jews,* 1:241.

178. Kasher, *Encyclopedia of Biblical Interpretation,* 3:28–29, quoting Zohar.

179. Stuy, *Collected Discourses,* 1:233.

180. Kasher, *Encyclopedia of Biblical Interpretation,* 3:28, citing Sforno.

181. Ibid., 3:31–33.

182. Hirsch, *T'rumath Tzvi,* 90.

183. Genesis 18:18, in NRSV; and in Alter, *Genesis,* 80.

184. Genesis 18:18, in JPST; and in Fox, *Five Books of Moses,* 77 ("what is right and just").

185. On its applicability to this event in Abraham's life, see Kasher, *Encyclopedia of Biblical Interpretation,* 3:30.

186. Kasher, *Encyclopedia of Biblical Interpretation,* 3:35–36.

187. Ibid., 3:38, citing Midrash Hagadol.

188. Genesis Rabbah 49: 4, translation in Miller, *Abraham Friend of God,* 107.

189. Patai, *The Jewish Mind,* 509.

190. Hertz, *Pentateuch and Haftorahs,* 64. On the practice of ethical wills, see *Encyclopaedia Judaica,* 6:923.

191. Spencer W. Kimball, "The Example of Abraham," *Ensign,* June 1975, 5.

192. It is the angel who explains this, not the LORD as in the traditional text.

193. So Qur'an 11:74, in A. Y. Ali, *Qur'an,* 534.

194. This JST passage clarifies the scene as portrayed in the traditional text of Genesis 18:22–23, in which Abraham seems to be pleading with one of the three visitors.

195. Genesis 18:22 tells that after the angels went toward Sodom, "Abraham stood yet before the LORD." But as a modern scholar notes, "it is possible that the text here originally read, 'But the Lord stood yet before Abraham.'" Bowker, *Targums and Rabbinic Literature,* 214. Indeed, the grammarian expert Rashi relates that this was one of the textual emendations (of the eighteen such) made by the scribes, and that the sequence of the story requires the reading of "God remained standing before Abraham," but was changed out of reverence. Hence, says Rashi, "the Holy One Blessed be He came to him." Rashi on Genesis 22:2, in Rashi, *Commentary,* 160; Goldman, *In the Beginning,* 786.

196. In the traditional Genesis text of this chapter, one of the three visitors is referred to as the Lord (KJV "LORD," the King James designation of the Hebrew divine name *Yahweh,* or *Jehovah*) (Genesis 18:13). Not so in the Joseph Smith Translation, which changes the reference to make it clear that the three visitors are angels sent by the Lord. However, the Joseph Smith Translation affirms the chapter's opening verse that "the Lord appeared unto him [JST: "Abraham"] in the plains of Mamre." When did the Lord so appear? The only possible context in the text for His appearance in the Joseph Smith Translation of this chapter is in the dialogue with Abraham, when Abraham has begun to pray.

197. Galbraith and Smith, *Scriptural Teachings of the Prophet Joseph Smith,* 289.

198. Blunt, *Twelve Lectures,* 181.

199. Qur'an 11:74–75, in Asad, *Qur'an,* 326.

200. Kasher, *Encyclopedia of Biblical Interpretation,* 3:46, quoting Tan. Y. Vayera.

201. Hertz, *Pentateuch and Haftorahs,* 65.

202. Hobbs, *Sermons of Henry King,* 93.

203. Meier, *Ancient Secrets,* 27.

204. Letellier, *Day in Mamre, Night in Sodom,* 123.

205. Genesis Rabbah 39:6, in Freedman, *Midrash Rabbah, Genesis,* 1:315.

206. Kasher, *Encyclopedia of Biblical Interpretation,* 3:46.

207. Nibley, *Abraham in Egypt,* 204–205.

208. Matthews, *Armenian Commentary on Genesis,* 99.

209. Noble, *Great Men of God,* 61–63.

210. Bezah 32b, in Epstein, *Babylonian Talmud.*

211. Galbraith and Smith, *Scriptural Teachings of the Prophet Joseph Smith,* 270.

212. Baring-Gould, *Legends of the Patriarchs,* 174.

213. Kasher, *Encyclopedia of Biblical Interpretation,* 3:46, quoting Tan. Y. Vayera.

214. Hershon, *Rabbinical Commentary on Genesis,* 103.

215. Seters, *Abraham in History and Tradition,* 212.

216. Miller, *Abraham Friend of God,* 105, quoting Tanchuma.

217. Hinckley, *Teachings of Gordon B. Hinckley,* 137.

218. M. M. Ali, *Qur'an,* 453.

219. Brinner, *History of al-Tabari,* 66.

220. Genesis Rabbah 49:6, in Freedman, *Midrash Rabbah, Genesis,* 1:424.

221. Alfred Corn, "The Story of Lot," in Rosenberg, *Genesis: As It Is Written,* 86.

222. Goldman, *In the Beginning,* 790, quoting J. P. Harland.

223. See Feiler, *Walking the Bible,* 55–57.

224. Stone, *Armenian Apocrypha,* 97. I have removed the original parenthesis around the word "its."

225. Jubilees 16:9, in Sparks, *Apocryphal Old Testament,* 58.

226. See also Psalms 11:6: "Upon the wicked he shall rain snares, fire and brimstone."

227. Gordon B. Hinckley, "Living in the Fulness of Times," *Ensign,* November 2001, 6.

228. Recognitions of Clement 1.32, in *Ante-Nicene Fathers,* 8:86.

229. Kasher, *Encyclopedia of Biblical Interpretation,* 3:46, quoting Tan. Y. Vayera.

230. Jubilees 16:15–19, in Sparks, *Apocryphal Old Testament,* 58 (omitting italics, brackets, and bolding in original).

Notes to Chapter 9

1. Genesis 19:27–28, in Speiser, *Genesis,* 138.

2. Letellier, *Day in Mamre, Night in Sodom,* 136–37.

3. See, for example, Mormon 5:14, 20; 7:10. See also the prominence of Abraham and his covenant in the writings of Mormon's beloved son Moroni, in, for example, Mormon 8:23; 9:11; Ether 13:11; and Moroni 10:31.

4. Eldad and Aumann, *Chronicles,* 1:3:1.

5. Ginzberg, *Legends of the Jews,* 1:257.

6. Levner, *Legends of Israel,* 79.

7. Bowker, *Targums and Rabbinic Literature,* 210.

8. Kasher, *Encyclopedia of Biblical Interpretation,* 3:84.

9. Galbraith and Smith, *Scriptural Teachings of the Prophet Joseph Smith,* 199.

10. Scherman and Zlotowitz, *Bereishis: Genesis,* 1(a):442.

11. So Jubilees 16:10 in VanderKam, *Jubilees,* 96.

12. Klinghoffer, *Discovery of God,* 187.

13. According to Jewish tradition. Ginzberg, *Legends of the Jews,* 1:258.

14. Nachmanides on Genesis 20:17, in Chavel, *Ramban,* 1:267.

15. On this point see Nachmanides reasoned discussion in Chavel, *Ramban,* 1:267.

16. According to Jewish tradition. See Ginzberg, *Legends of the Jews,* 1:260.

17. Kasher, *Encyclopedia of Biblical Interpretation,* 3:98.

18. See Ginzberg, *Legends of the Jews,* 1:261; and Kasher, *Encyclopedia of Biblical Interpretation,* 3:98–99.

19. Kasher, *Encyclopedia of Biblical Interpretation,* 3:102.

20. Kasher, *Encyclopedia of Biblical Interpretation,* 3:126.

21. Ginzberg, *Legends of the Jews,* 1:260.

22. Miller, *Abraham Friend of God,* 143.

23. Kasher, *Encyclopedia of Biblical Interpretation,* 3:100.

24. See Klinghoffer, *Discovery of God,* 202; and Kasher, *Encyclopedia of Biblical Interpretation,* 3:100–104.

25. See Klinghoffer, *Discovery of God,* 202; and Kasher, *Encyclopedia of Biblical Interpretation,* 3:100–104.

26. Kasher, *Encyclopedia of Biblical Interpretation,* 3:102.

27. Abraham was now ninety-nine years old; the promise of chosen posterity was given in Haran when he was sixty-two,

according to the book of Abraham 2:14.

28. See Kasher, *Encyclopedia of Biblical Interpretation,* 2:103.

29. See Ginzberg, *Legends of the Jews,* 5:231 n. 16; Genesis Rabbah 45:4, in Neusner, *Genesis Rabbah* 2:148; and Midrash Rabbah on Song of Songs 2.14.8, in Freedman, *Midrash Rabbah, Song of Songs,* 134.

30. Nibley, *Old Testament and Related Studies,* 98–99.

31. Kierkegaard, *Fear and Trembling,* 33.

32. John Chrysostom, Homily 45 on Genesis, in *Saint John Chrysostom: Homilies on Genesis 18–45,* 481–82. Jewish scholars likewise note that "God's direct providence is central to Isaac's birth." Tuchman and Rapoport, *Passions of the Matriarchs,* 51.

33. Pirke de Rabbi Eliezer 52, in Friedlander, *Pirke de Rabbi Eliezer,* 420–21.

34. Oden, *Ancient Christian Commentary,* 2:91.

35. Kierkegaard, *Fear and Trembling,* 33.

36. Tuchman and Rapoport, *Passions of the Matriarchs,* 55.

37. Compare KJV Genesis 21:6: "God hath made me to laugh, so that all that hear will laugh with me." Both translations are possible with the Hebrew. The Peshitta (Syriac) reads here: "God has made me to rejoice today exceedingly; everyone that hears the news will rejoice exceedingly" (Gen. 21:6, in Lamsa, *Holy Bible from the Ancient Eastern Text,* 26). The Geneva Bible (an important early English translation) reads: "God hathe made me to reioyce: all that heare wil reioyce w me" (Gen. 21:6, in Berry, *Geneva Bible,* 9). The Septuagint (Greek) captures both meanings: "The Lord has made laughter for me, for whoever shall hear shall rejoice with me" (Gen. 21:6, in Brenton, *Septuagint,* 24). Among modern translators, E. A. Speiser captures both meanings: "God has brought me laughter; all who hear of it will rejoice with me" (Gen. 21:6, in Speiser, *Genesis,* 153).

38. Tuchman and Rapoport, *Passions of the Matriarchs,* 56.

39. Callaway, *Sing O Barren One,* 211. See also Motyer, *The Prophecy of Isaiah,* 445, commenting on Isaiah 54:1: "The picture of Sarah, the barren woman who was to bear the miracle child and become the mother of a family more numerous than the stars, provides background."

40. See Genesis Rabbah 53:6, in Freedman, *Midrash Rabbah, Genesis,* 1:466.

41. Kasher, *Encyclopedia of Biblical Interpretation,* 3:105, translating Genesis Rabbah 53:7.

42. Wordsworth, *Holy Bible,* 1:94.

43. Kasher, *Encyclopedia of Biblical Interpretation,* 3:109, citing Hirsch.

44. Ibid., 3:24.

45. Ginzberg, *Legends of the Jews,* 1:206.

46. *Journal of Discourses,* 9:193.

47. Kasher, *Encyclopedia of Biblical Interpretation,* 3:26, quoting Midrash Alef Beth.

48. Sawyer, *Midrash Aleph Beth,* 254, Sawyer's paraphrase of Midrash Aleph Beth 14:32, on p. 243.

49. On Abraham 43, in *Philo VI,* 125.

50. See Tuchman and Rapoport, *Passions of the Matriarchs,* 76.

51. Hayden, *The Love of Abraham and Sarah,* 31.

52. Wordsworth, *Holy Bible,* 1:94.

53. Judean Antiquities 1.222, in Feldman, *Josephus,* 84.

54. Morris, *The Genesis Record,* 367.

55. Jasher 22:40, in Noah, *Book of Yashar,* 62.

56. Spencer W. Kimball, "The Example of Abraham," *Ensign,* June 1975, 5.

57. Tuchman and Rapoport, *Passions of the Matriarchs,* 81–82.

58. On Abraham 32, in *Philo VI,* 85.

59. Judean Antiquities 1.222, in Feldman, *Josephus,* 84–85.

60. On Abraham 32, in *Philo VI,* 85–87.

61. Perhaps two years (Tuchman and Rapoport, *Passions of the Matriarchs,* 56, citing Rashi); perhaps three (Wenham, *Genesis 16–50,* 81, calling attention to 2 Maccabees 7:27).

62. Jasher 21:5, in Noah, *Book of Yashar,* 57.

63. Kasher, *Encyclopedia of Biblical Interpretation,* 3:110, citing Pes. 119b.

64. See Levner, *Legends of Israel,* 87; and Bialik and Ravnitzky, *Book of Legends,* 40.

65. Jubilees 17:2–3, in Sparks, *Apocryphal Old Testament,* 60.

66. Speiser, *Genesis,* 155.

67. As in most modern translations of Genesis 21:9. See Speiser, *Genesis,* 153; JPST; NRSV; Mitchell, *Genesis,* 40; Vawter, *On Genesis,* 247; REB; and Westermann, *Genesis 12–36,* 336.

68. Genesis 21:9 in FBM and GTC.

69. Wenham, *Genesis 16-50,* 77.

70. Jubilees 17:4, in Sparks, *Apocryphal Old Testament,* 60.

71. Tuchman and Rapoport, *Passions of the Matriarchs,* 62, recounting a tradition repeated Rabbi Abraham, son of the famous Rambam.

72. Ibid., 62–64.

73. See Ginzberg, *Legends of the Jews,* 1:203; 5:215.

74. Genesis 21:11, in Vawter, *On Genesis,* 247. And see similar translations in NRSV; JPST; NIV; NASB; NJB; and Speiser,

Genesis, 162.

75. Genesis 21:11, in Mitchell, *Genesis,* 40.

76. Matthews, *Armenian Commentary on Genesis,* 96.

77. Ginzberg, *Legends of the Jews,* 1:264.

78. Scherman and Zlotowitz, *Bereishis: Genesis,* 1(a):396.

79. Pirke de Rabbi Eliezer 30, in Friedlander, *Pirke de Rabbi Eliezer,* 216.

80. Baring-Gould, *Legends of the Patriarchs,* 182.

81. Pirke de Rabbi Eliezer 30, in Friedlander, *Pirke de Rabbi Eliezer,* 216.

82. As it is written in Genesis 21:14, and in all of Jewish tradition. See Ginzberg, *Legends of the Jews,* 1:264; and Kasher, *Encyclopedia of Biblical Interpretation,* 3:115–19.

83. Kasher, *Encyclopedia of Biblical Interpretation,* 3:115, citing several sources including Abrabanel and Sforno.

84. Islam insists that Abraham led them to the future site of Mecca. Knappert, *Islamic Legends,* 1:78. See also Asad, *Qur'an,* 26 n. 102: "According to very ancient Arabian traditions, it was at the site of what later became Mecca that Abraham, in order to placate Sarah, abandoned his Egyptian bondwoman Hagar and their child Ishmael after he had brought them there from Canaan. This is by no means improbable if one bears in mind that for a camel-riding bedouin (and Abraham was certainly one) a journey of twenty or even thirty days has never been anything out of the ordinary. At first glance, the Biblical statement (Genesis xxi, 14) that it was 'in the wilderness of Beersheba' (i.e., in the southernmost tip of Palestine) that Abraham left Hagar and Ishmael would seem to conflict with the Qur'anic account. This seeming contradiction, however, disappears as soon as we remember that to the ancient, town-dwelling Hebrews the term 'wilderness of Beersheba' comprised all the desert regions south of Palestine." While it is certainly possible that they went to the place where Mecca would later arise, the immense distance involved makes this appear remarkable, particularly since both Abraham and Ishmael will travel back and forth several times.

85. Kathir, *Stories of the Prophets,* 88–89.

86. Azizah Y. Al-Hibri, in Moyers, *Genesis,* 196, 199.

87. Qur'an 14:37, in A. Y. Ali, *Qur'an,* 631.

88. Levy, *A Faithful Heart,* xv.

89. Qur'an 14:39, in Cragg, *Qur'an,* 117.

90. Cyril of Alexandria, Glaphyra on Genesis 3:10, Oden, *Ancient Christian Commentary,* 2:99.

91. Genesis Rabbah 53:15, in Freedman, *Midrash Rabbah, Genesis,* 1:474.

92. Kasher, *Encyclopedia of Biblical Interpretation,* 3:119, citing Radak.

93. Kasher, *Encyclopedia of Biblical Interpretation,* 3:120, quoting Pirke de Rabbi Eliezer 30.

94. Qur'an 19:54–55, in M. M. Ali, *Qur'an,* 603.

95. See Mekilta, tractate Pisha, in Lauterbach, *Mekilta de Rabbi Ishmael,* 1:134–35.

96. Qur'an 2:125, in Asad, *Qur'an,* 26.

97. The angel Gabriel. Knappert, *Islamic Legends,* 1:81. Joseph Smith explained that the angel Gabriel is Noah. Galbraith and Smith, *Scriptural Teachings of the Prophet Joseph Smith,* 178.

98. See various traditions of the event summarized and discussed in Firestone, *Journeys in Holy Lands,* 80–93.

99. Qur'an 2:128, in M. M. Ali, *Qur'an,* 56.

100. Ibid.

101. Qur'an 2:125–29, in Asad, *Qur'an,* 26–27, omitting brackets in original.

102. See Rachel Milstein, "The Evolution of a Visual Motif: The Temple and the Ka'ba," in Arazi, Sadan, and Wasserstein, *Compilation and Creation,* 23–48, esp. 45–46.

103. See Denny, *An Introduction to Islam,* 117–23; and Syed Ali Ashraf, "The Inner Meaning of the Islamic Rites: Prayer, Pilgrimage, Fasting, Jihad," in Nasr, *Islamic Spirituality,* 119–25.

104. Reuven Firestone, "Abraham," in McAuliffe, *Encyclopaedia of the Qur'an,* 1:7.

105. L'Orange, *Iconography of Cosmic Kingship,* 10.

106. *Holy Qur'an* 1:179.

107. Asad, *Qur'an,* 26 n. 102.

108. al-Kisa'i, *Tales of the Prophets,* 153.

109. Genesis Rabbah 54:2, in Freedman, *Midrash Rabbah, Genesis,* 1:476.

110. *Lectures on Faith* 6:5.

111. Leibowitz, *Studies in Bereshit,* 259, citing Haketav Vehakabala.

112. See Baring-Gould, *Legends of the Patriarchs,* 187.

113. Soteh 10a (Babylonian Talmud), translation in Harris, *Hebraic Literature,* 44.

114. Ginzberg, *Legends of the Jews,* 1:270–71.

115. Rappoport, *Ancient Israel,* 1:276–77.

116. Kasher, *Encyclopedia of Biblical Interpretation,* 3:127.

117. Baring-Gould, *Legends of the Patriarchs,* 174; and see Ginzberg, *Legends of the Jews,* 1:271.

118. The Bablyonian Talmud states that "Abraham was the head of a seminary for youth." Harris, *Hebraic Literature,* 43, quoting Yoma 28b.

119. Kasher, *Encyclopedia of Biblical Interpretation,* 3:110, quoting Or Haafelah.

120. Baring-Gould, *Legends of the Patriarchs,* 174.

121. Genesis Rabbah 39:11, in Freedman, *Midrash Rabbah, Genesis,* 1:322.

122. Levner, *Legends of Israel,* 83–84.

123. Culi, Magriso, and Argueti, *Torah Anthology,* 2:7.

124. Levner, *Legends of Israel,* 82.

125. Alma 1:30: "In their prosperous circumstances, they did not send away any who were naked, or that were hungry, or that were athirst, or that were sick, or that had not been nourished; and they did not set their hearts upon riches; therefore they were liberal to all, both old and young, both bond and free, both male and female, whether out of the church or in the church, having no respect of persons as to those who stood in need."

126. *The Church of Jesus Christ of Latter-day Saints,* 3.

127. Ginzberg, *Legends of the Jews,* 5:248 n. 223.

128. See 1QapGen 21.9–10, in Martinez and Tigchelaar, *Dead Sea Scrolls Study Edition,* 1:45.

129. See Zohar, Vayeze 155b–156a, in Sperling and Simon, *Zohar,* 2:100.

130. Explanation to figure 6, Facsimile 2, the book of Abraham.

131. See the treatment of the cardinal points in O'Neill, *Night of the Gods,* 157–65.

132. See Nibley, *Abraham in Egypt,* 448.

133. L'Orange, *Iconography of Cosmic Kingship,* 13; and Nibley, *The Ancient State,* 106.

134. See Nibley, *Message of the Joseph Smith Papyri,* 152.

135. See Redford, *Oxford Encyclopedia of Ancient Egypt,* 2:244.

136. See Budge, *Egyptian Book of the Dead,* 171.

137. See L'Orange, *Iconography of Cosmic Kingship,* 9–17; Redford, *Oxford Encyclopedia of Ancient Egypt,* 2:244; and Nibley, *The Ancient State,* 112.

138. See L'Orange, *Iconography of Cosmic Kingship,* 9–17.

139. Nibley, *The Ancient State,* 105, speaking of Pharaoh.

140. See VanderKam, *Enoch: A Man for All Generations,* 13, 6–14; VanderKam, *Enoch and the Growth of an Apocalyptic Tradition,* 43–45; and Kvanig, *Roots of Apocalyptic,* 172–90.

141. See VanderKam, *Enoch: A Man for All Generations,* 17–25.

142. See Frankfort, *Birth of Civilization,* 49–77, examining Mesopotamian cities.

143. Referring specifically, in this instance, to ancient Sumerian cities. Samuel Noah Kramer, "The Temple in Sumerian Literature," in Fox, *Temple in Society,* 1.

144. Menaham Haran, "Temple and Community in Ancient Israel," in Fox, *Temple in Society,* 18, speaking of the Jerusalem Temple.

145. See L'Orange, *Iconography of Cosmic Kingship,* 9.

146. *Journal of Discourses,* 21:89: As "the head of that dispensation," Enoch "sent out missionaries among the people who had become very numerous. . . . Many believed . . . and they were gathered together, as we are, unto a place which they called Zion."

147. See Galbraith and Smith, *Scriptural Teachings of the Prophet Joseph Smith,* 344.

148. *Journal of Discourses,* 18:303: "I will not say but what Enoch had temples and officiated therein, but we have no account of it."

149. "In the morning of the day and in the middle of the day and in the evening of the day it is good to go to the Lord's temple." 2 Enoch [J] 51:4, in Charlesworth, *Old Testament Pseudepigrapha,* 1:178. See also the translator's note on 179 that the reading of "temple" is attested throughout the manuscripts and "must be original." Another Enoch text referring to the temple is 3 Enoch, which as "the principal Hebrew record of Enoch's doings," notes Nibley, "is called the *Hekhalot,* or chambers of the temple, indicating the steps in initiation to which Enoch introduced his people as the guide or teacher of the ordinances." Nibley, *Temple and Cosmos,* 78.

150. Levenson, *Sinai and Zion,* 128–29, 131.

151. Jubilees 4:23, in VanderKam, *Book of Jubilees,* 28.

152. Harris, *Hebraic Literature,* 44, summarizing the description of Abraham's garden provided in the Talmud and the Targums.

153. Hugh Nibley, "A Strange Thing in the Land: The Return of the Book of Enoch, Part 5," *Ensign,* April 1976, 63. The passage, and the one it cites in the November 1969 *Improvement Era* on page 120, mistakenly refer to Hebron as the place where Abraham built the garden; this was later corrected in Nibley, *Abraham in Egypt,* 198.

154. Zohar, Vayera 97b, in Sperling and Simon, *Zohar,* 1:321–22.

155. Chavel, *Encyclopedia of Torah Thoughts,* 44.

156. Patai, *Jewish Alchemists,* 229.

157. McConkie, *Mormon Doctrine,* 780, citing Doctrine and Covenants 124:39–40. See also President Joseph Fielding Smith's statement: "Sacred sanctuaries may have been built by the inspired patriarchs before the flood." *Doctrines of Salvation,* 2:232.

158. See Jubilees 16:20–16:31, in VanderKam, *Book of Jubilees,* 99–102.

159. See citations in *Encyclopaedia Judaica,* 2:115.

160. Yoma 28b, in Epstein, *Babylonian Talmud.*

161. See Jubilees 21:5–20, in VanderKam, *Book of Jubilees,* 121–26; Aramaic Testament of Levi, Bodleian c, lines 12–13, in Hollander and de Jonge, *Testaments of the Twelve Patriarchs,* 463.

162. Nibley, *Abraham in Egypt,* 653. See also Nibley's discussion of Abraham's association with the Temple in Nibley, *Temple and Cosmos,* 77–78.

163. See 3 Enoch 48A:9, in Odeberg, *3 Enoch*, part 2, 158.

164. See 3 Enoch 48A:10, in Charlesworth, *Old Testament Pseudepigrapha*, 1:302.

165. As pointed out by Charles, *A Critical and Exegetical Commentary on the Revelation of St. John*, 2:162, citing 1 Enoch 33–35.

166. See L'Orange, *Iconography of Cosmic Kingship*, 9.

167. Young, *Jerusalem in the New Testament*, 159. Perhaps the foursquare structure of the heavenly city also represents the four corners on which the vault of heaven was thought to rest. Hermann Strathmann, in Kittel and Friedrich, *Theological Dictionary of the New Testament*, 6:532.

168. The book of Revelation includes yet another dimension in its description of the descending heavenly city. Not only are its width and length the same, but also its height, making it an exact cube. Revelation 21:16. It is a remarkable echo of the perfect cubic shape of the Holy of Holies in the Jerusalem temple on Mount Zion. 1 Kings 6:20. This structural similarity is matched, as noted by one scholar, by "a most striking similarity in their essential nature and purpose; for the redemptive-revelational relationship that God established with Israel at Jerusalem's temple comes to its final realization in the new Jerusalem. Thus the holy of holies where God dwelt alone, isolated from his people, is transformed into the Holy City where God dwells with his people." Hence "it is not surprising that John 'saw no temple therein.'" Young, *Jerusalem in the New Testament*, 159–60.

169. *Journal of Discourses*, 9:138.

Notes to Chapter 10

1. Josephus says Isaac was twenty-five or in his twenty-fifth year (Judean Antiquities 1.227). Jubilees says he was twenty-three (Jubilees 17:15). One rabbinic tradition says he was twenty-six or twenty-seven (see Feldman's discussion in *Josephus*, 88–89 n. 702). The rabbinic tradition making Isaac thirty-six or thirty-seven appears to be a later embellishment connecting the sacrifice of Isaac with the death of Sarah, a connection absent in and seemingly contradicted by earlier sources. The King James depiction of Isaac as a "lad" (Gen. 22:5) tends to be misleading to our modern ear. The word "lad" in that verse translates the Hebrew *naar*—the same Hebrew word used in the very same verse to describe Abraham's two servants. The word is used throughout the Old Testament with a wide range of age variation, including soldiers. See Brown, Driver, and Briggs, *Hebrew and English Lexicon*, 654–55. Referring to a number of Jewish texts, Louis Ginzberg notes, "Great emphasis is laid in the sources on the fact that although Isaac, at the time of the 'Akedah, was no longer a lad, but a grown-up man (different views are given as to his exact age . . .), yet he willingly submitted to his father's wish." Ginzberg, *Legends of the Jews*, 5:249 n. 229.

2. Most modern translations translate the Hebrew verb as "tried" or "proved."

3. Zohar 1:119b, in Sperling and Simon, *Zohar*, 1:372.

4. After receiving the command, Abraham "rose up early in the morning." Genesis 22:3. In the Qur'an, Abraham saw it in a dream. Surah 37:102, in Khatib, *Bounteous Koran*, 593.

5. *Journal of Discourses*, 11:152.

6. Judean Antiquities 1.223–24, in Feldman, *Josephus*, 85–87.

7. Septuagint of Genesis 22:1, in Brenton, *Septuagint*, 25.

8. Baring-Gould, *Legends of the Patriarchs*, 189; see Genesis 22:1–2.

9. Goldman, *In the Beginning*, 792, quoting J. H. Blunt.

10. Judean Antiquities 1.223–24, in Feldman, *Josephus*, 85–87.

11. See Brown, Driver, and Briggs, *Hebrew and English Lexicon*, 609.

12. Genesis 22:2, in GTC. Similarly, see other translations of this verse: "Pray take . . . " in FBM; "Take, I pray thee . . . " in Young, *Young's Literal Translation*, 13 of Old Testament; and "Take, I beg of you . . . " in Hirsch, *T'rumath Tzvi*, 105.

13. Rashi on Genesis 22:2, in Rashi, *Commentary*, 199. So also Hershon, *Rabbinical Commentary on Genesis*, 121, including n. 2: "Take, I pray thee . . . "

14. Tuchman and Rapoport, *Passions of the Matriarchs*, 68.

15. Baring-Gould, *Legends of the Patriarchs*, 189; see Genesis 22:1–2.

16. Derrida, *Gift of Death*, 58.

17. Stuy, *Collected Discourses*, 2:279.

18. Yosef Albo in *The Fundamentals of Judaism*, quoted in Leibowitz, *Studies in Bereshit*, 202.

19. Levenson, *Death and Resurrection of the Beloved Son*, 221–22, noting the emphasis in the Genesis text on Abraham's love for Isaac, and noting Jubilees 17:16, 18.

20. Dennis, *Sarah Laughed*, 61.

21. Carol B. Thomas, "Sacrifice: An Eternal Investment," *Ensign*, May 2001, 63.

22. As pointed out in Baring-Gould, *Legends of the Patriarchs*, 190.

23. Genesis 22:3, in Alter, *Genesis*, 104.

24. Kasher, *Encyclopedia of Biblical Interpretation*, 3:136, citing several sources.

25. Blunt, *Twelve Lectures*, 220.

26. Wiesel, *Messengers of God*, 97.

27. Origen, Homilies on Genesis 8.3–4, in Oden, *Ancient Christian Commentary*, 2:103, omitting a question mark because only a portion of the first sentence is quoted.

28. *Journal of Discourses*, 14:360.

29. Ibid., 24:264.

30. Ibid., 14:360.

31. Oxenden, *Portraits from the Bible*, 45.

32. Denny, *An Introduction to Islam*, 21.

33. *Journal of Discourses*, 24:264.

34. *Journal of Discourses*, 22:318.

35. Scherman and Zlotowitz, *Bereishis: Genesis*, 1(a):599.

36. Klinghoffer, *Discovery of God*, 61.

37. Kimball, *Teachings of Spencer W. Kimball*, 59.

38. Kimball, *Faith Precedes the Miracle*, 6.

39. Derrida, *Gift of Death*, 58.

40. As reported by John Taylor in *Journal of Discourses*, 24:264.bn Similarly on another occasion John Taylor reported Joseph Smith's statement that if God "could have invented anything that would have been more keen, acute, and trying than that which he required of Abraham he would have done it." *Journal of Discourses*, 14:360.

41. Kimball, *Faith Precedes the Miracle*, 6.

42. Ginzberg, *Legends of the Jews*, 1:278–79.

43. As faithfully reflected in this translation, the same Hebrew word is used in this verse to designate Abraham's two young men ("lads") and Isaac ("lad"). See also translations in GTC, and Wenham, *Genesis 16–50*, 97.

44. See Ginzberg, *Legends of the Jews*, 1:279; and Rashi on Genesis 22:5, in Rashi, *Commentary*, 202.

45. See Bachya ben Asher, quoted in Levenson, *Death and Resurrection of the Beloved Son*, 131.

46. See Hebrews 11:17–19, and discussion in Levenson, *Death and Resurrection of the Beloved Son*, 130–31. Hebrews clearly says that Abraham was expecting that God would resurrect Isaac and thereby fulfill the promises, but whether Abraham thought this would happen immediately remains unclear.

47. Genesis Rabbah 56:3:1, in Neusner, *Genesis Rabbah*, 2:280.

48. Genesis 22:6, in Speiser, *Genesis*, 161.

49. Midrash Hagadol, in Miller, *Abraham Friend of God*, 167.

50. Genesis 22:7, in Speiser, *Genesis*, 161.

51. Ibid.

52. Rashi on Genesis 22:8, in Rashi, *Commentary*, 203.

53. Leibowitz, *Studies in Bereshit*, 200, quoting Rashi.

54. Wiesel, *Messengers of God*, 96 (emphasis in original).

55. Pelikan, *Luther's Works*, 4:112.

56. Judean Antiquities 1.228–31, in Feldman, *Josephus*, 90–92. Original has brackets around the phrase "out of the course of nature," words supplied by Feldman to fill in a lacuna in the Greek text.

57. Pelikan, *Luther's Works*, 4:112–13.

58. On Abraham 33, in *Philo VI*, 89.

59. Judean Antiquities 1.232, in Feldman, *Josephus*, 92.

60. Kasher, *Encyclopedia of Biblical Interpretation*, 3:163, quoting Midrash Vayyosha.

61. See generally *Encyclopaedia Judaica*, 2:480–87.

62. Bowker, *Targums and Rabbinic Literature*, 225, quoting the Targum of Pseudo-Jonathan on Genesis 22:10. See also Pirke de Rabbi Eliezer 31, in Friedlander, *Pirke de Rabbi Eliezer*, 227; and Jasher 23:61, in Noah, *Book of Yashar*, 62.

63. Al-Tabari's report does refer here to Isaac, not Ishmael.

64. Brinner, *History of al-Tabari*, 91.

65. Kasher, *Encyclopedia of Biblical Interpretation*, 3:144.

66. Miller, *Abraham Friend of God*, 169.

67. Ibid., 172, quoting Sifrei, Devarim 32.

68. Clement, The First Epistle of Clement to the Corinthians 31, in *Ante-Nicene Fathers*, 1:13.

69. *Journal of Discourses*, 18:325.

70. Bowker, *Targums and Rabbinic Literature*, 231, quoting Rashi.

71. Wiesel, *Messengers of God*, 102, 96.

72. *Melvin J. Ballard*, 136.

73. Reuven Firestone, "Abraham," in McAuliffe, *Encyclopaedia of the Qur'an*, 1:10.

74. Rabadan, *Mahometism Fully Explained* 1:166 (some commas omitted, capitalization normalized, and spelling of "seraphick" changed to "seraphic"). This work is an English translation of a text purportedly written in 1603.

75. Ibid. (some commas omitted, capitalization normalized).

76. Derrida, *Gift of Death*, 58.

77. Qur'an 37:103, in Cragg, *Qur'an*, 120. The son is unnamed in the Qur'an; but in context, as well as in most of Muslim tradition, the son was Ishmael.

78. *Journal of Discourses*, 14:361.

79. Ginzberg, *Legends of the Jews*, 1:280.

80. See Brown, Kelch, and van Thiel, *Rembrandt*, 181.

81. I refer here to the 1634 painting hanging in the Hermitage in St. Petersburg, not the other one finished by a student.

82. See Genesis Rabbah 56:8, in Freedman, *Midrash Rabbah, Genesis,* 1:498.

83. See Reuven Firestone, "Abraham," in McAuliffe, *Encyclopaedia of the Qur'an,* 1:10; and see Brinner, *History of al-Tabari,* 91.

84. 4 Maccabees 16:20, in Charlesworth, *Old Testament Pseudepigrapha,* 2:561.

85. Targum of Pseudo-Jonathan on Genesis 22:10, in Maher, *Targum Pseudo-Jonathan,* 79–80.

86. Noble, *Great Men of God,* 65.

87. See Moshe J. Bernstein, "Angels at the Aqedah: A Study in the Development of a Midrashic Motif," in *Dead Sea Discoveries: A Journal of Current Research on the Scrolls and Related Literature* (Leiden: Brill, 2000) 7:3, 278–83; Jasher 23:66–68, in Noah, *Book of Yashar,* 62; and Ginzberg, *Legends of the Jews,* 1:281–82.

88. Genesis 22:11, in King James and most translations.

89. Jubilees 18:10, in VanderKam, *Book of Jubilees,* 106.

90. This reading, which is in the Latin manuscript only and is supported by the later verse in Jubilees referred to in the next note, was adopted by Charles, *Apocrypha and Pseudepigrapha,* 2:40. See discussion in VanderKam, *Book of Jubilees,* 107, note on 18:11.

91. As reported by Truman Madsen in his Book of Mormon class in the fall of 1971 at Brigham Young University. Dr. Madsen had just finished a tour of the Holy Land with President Brown.

92. Jubilees 18:16, in Charles, *Apocrypha and Pseudepigrapha,* 2:40.

93. Genesis Rabbah 56:7, in Freedman, *Midrash Rabbah, Genesis,* 1:497.

94. Genesis Rabbah 56:7, in Freedman, *Midrash Rabbah, Genesis,* 1:496.

95. Leibowitz, *Studies in Bereshit,* 190.

96. Oxenden, *Portraits from the Bible,* 48.

97. See also Doctrine and Covenants 132:51: "I did it, saith the Lord, to prove you all, as I did Abraham, and that I might require an offering at your hand, by covenant and sacrifice."

98. Wiesel, *And the Sea Is Never Full,* 22.

99. Brinner, *History of al-Tabari,* 91.

100. al-Kisa'i, *Tales of the Prophets,* 162.

101. Spiegel, *The Last Trial,* 30, citing Pirke, Yalkut, and MhG. See also Kasher, *Encyclopedia of Biblical Interpretation,* 3:150.

102. Kasher, *Encyclopedia of Biblical Interpretation,* 3:153, citing several sources.

103. Speiser, *Genesis,* 162.

104. See, for example, translations of Genesis 22:14 in NRSV: "So Abraham called that place 'The LORD will provide'"; NIV: "So Abraham called that place The LORD Will Provide'"; REB: "Abraham named that shrine 'The LORD will provide'"; NJB: "Abraham called this place 'Yahweh provides'"; Living Bible: "Abraham named the place 'Jehovah provides'" (*Living Bible,* 17); and Mitchell's translation: "And he named that place YHVH-yireh, *The Lord Provides*" (Mitchell, *Genesis,* 43).

105. Jubilees reads: "Abraham named that place 'The Lord Saw.'" Jubilees 18:13, in VanderKam, *Book of Jubilees,* 107–108. See also, for example, translations of Genesis 22:14 in Septuagint (Greek): "And Abraam called the name of that place, The Lord hath seen" (Brenton, *Septuagint,* 25); Vulgate (Jerome's translation into Latin): "And he called the name of that place, The Lord seeth" (*The Holy Bible: Translated from the Latin Vulgate,* 25); "Avraham called the name of that place: YHWH sees"; Westermann's translation: "And Abraham gave this place the name 'Yahweh sees'" (Westermann, *Genesis 12–36,* 353); and Tyndale's translation: "And Abraham called the name of the place, the Lord will see" (Tyndale, *Tyndale's Old Testament,* 38).

106. Genesis 22:14, in Brenton, *Septuagint,* 25.

107. Genesis 22:14, in Westermann, *Genesis 12–36,* 353. So also the Bible in Basic English: "In the mountain the Lord is seen." Vaughan, *Twenty-Six Translations,* 47.

108. Genesis 22:14, in Wenham, *Genesis 16–50,* 98.

109. Rashi on Genesis 22:14, in Rashi, *Commentary,* 206.

110. Genesis 22:14, in Tyndale, *Tyndale's Old Testament,* 38. So also the Geneva Bible: "In the mount wil the Lord be sene," in Genesis 22:14, in Berry, *Geneva Bible,* 9.

111. Genesis 22:14, in Vawter, *On Genesis,* 253.

112. Genesis 22:14, in Alter, *Genesis,* 106.

113. So also Speiser's translation: "On Yahweh's mountain there is vision." Speiser, *Genesis,* 162.

114. Genesis Rabbah 56:10, in Freedman, *Midrash Rabbah, Genesis,* 1:500–501. The Psalms citation is from verse 102:16.

115. Jubilees 18:13, in Charlesworth, *Old Testament Pseudepigrapha,* 2:91.

116. Even as Abraham's descendant Moroni would dedicate the future temple site at Manti. Lundwall, *Temples of the Most High,* 114–15.

117. Targum Onqelos to Genesis 22:14, in Grossfeld, *Targum Onqelos,* 86, omitting brackets in original.

118. Fragment Targums on Genesis 22:14, in Klein, *Fragment Targums* 2:17; and similarly Targums Pseudo-Jonathan and Neofiti. See also Ginzberg, *Legends of the Jews,* 1:284–85.

119. Kasher, *Encyclopedia of Biblical Interpretation,* 3:42, quoting Midrash T'hillim.

120. Kasher, *Encyclopedia of Biblical Interpretation,* 2:197.

121. Genesis 17:1, in Alter, *Genesis,* 72.

122. Genesis 17:1, in NJB, Westermann, *Genesis 12–36,* 253.

123. The Damascus Covenant 3:2, in Vermes, *Complete Dead Sea Scrolls,* 129.

124. Kosofsky, *Book of Customs,* 25, 302.

125. Kasher, *Encyclopedia of Biblical Interpretation,* 3:160.

126. Galbraith and Smith, *Scriptural Teachings of the Prophet Joseph Smith,* 171.

127. Ehat and Cook, *Words of Joseph Smith,* 245.

128. Galbraith and Smith, *Scriptural Teachings of the Prophet Joseph Smith,* 362.

129. Genesis Rabbah 55:6, in Freedman, *Midrash Rabbah, Genesis,* 1:486.

130. Ehat and Cook, *Words of Joseph Smith,* 241. See also Galbraith and Smith, *Scriptural Teachings of the Prophet Joseph Smith,* 380–82.

131. Kasher, *Encyclopedia of Biblical Interpretation,* 3:161, quoting Or Haafelah.

132. *Journal of Discourses,* 15:320, adding a comma after "handful."

133. Kasher, *Encyclopedia of Biblical Interpretation,* 3:160, quoting Pirke de Rabbi Eliezer 31.

134. McConkie, *New Witness for the Articles of Faith,* 508.

135. *Journal of Discourses,* 11:151.

136. Budge, *Cave of Treasures,* 150, omitting brackets in original.

137. John 19:28, in Brown, *The Gospel According to John (13–21),* 898. See discussion of the word on 908–909. For a discussion of the word as used in the John passages and the James passage, see Delling in Kittel and Friedrich, *Theological Dictionary of the New Testament,* 8:82.

138. So Bruce, *The Gospel of John,* 89.

139. Alford, *The Greek Testament,* 1:719; Brown, *The Gospel According to John (1–12),* 147. Furthermore, notes Raymond E. Brown, "even [John's] mention of 'the world' fits in with this background, for Abraham's generosity in sacrificing his only son was to be beneficial to all the nations of the world."

140. Matthew 3:17, as beautifully pointed out in Morris, *Genesis Record,* 374–76.

141. Irenaeus, *Irenaeus against Heresies* 4.5.4, in *Ante-Nicene Fathers,* 1:467.

142. Stone, *Armenian Apocrypha,* 99.

143. Genesis 22:14, in Tyndale, *Tyndale's Old Testament,* 38. So also the Geneva Bible: "In the mount wil the Lord be sene" (Genesis 22:14, in Berry, *Geneva Bible,* 9).

144. *Encyclopaedia Judaica,* 16:1030: "The origin of the name is uncertain."

145. Kittel and Friedrich, *Theological Dictionary of the New Testament,* 7:294.

146. Kraus, *Psalms 1–59,* 78, 83.

147. Kraus, *Theology of the Psalms,* 83.

148. *Journal of Discourses,* 17:113.

149. Jubilees 18:9–16, in VanderKam, *Book of Jubilees,* 106–107, and VanderKam's note to verse 14; James C. VanderKam, "The Angel of the Presence in the Book of Jubilees," in *Dead Sea Discoveries: A Journal of Current Research on the Scrolls and Related Literature* (Leiden: Brill, 2000) 7:3, 389.

150. Moshe J. Bernstein, "Angels at the Aqedah: A Study in the Development of a Midrashic Motif," in *Dead Sea Discoveries: A Journal of Current Research on the Scrolls and Related Literature* (Leiden: Brill, 2000) 7:3, 282.

151. According to the Targum of Pseudo-Jonathan on Genesis 5:24: "Enoch worshiped in truth before the Lord, and behold he was not with the inhabitants of the earth because he was taken away and he ascended to the firmament at the command of the Lord, and he was called Metatron, the Great Scribe." Maher, *Targum Pseudo-Jonathan,* 36–37, and see n. 10. See also Odeberg, *3 Enoch,* part 1, 20–38, 79–146; and Toorn, Becking, and Horst, *Dictionaries of Deities and Demons,* 301–304.

152. Midrash ha-Gadol, translation in Moshe J. Bernstein, "Angels at the Aqedah: A Study in the Development of a Midrashic Motif," in *Dead Sea Discoveries: A Journal of Current Research on the Scrolls and Related Literature* (Leiden: Brill, 2000) 7:3, 282.

153. Al-Rabghuzi, *Stories of the Prophets,* 2:127. In this source the son is Ishmael, while the angels go unnamed.

154. Derrida, *Gift of Death,* 55.

Notes to Chapter 11

1. Qur'an 37:109, in Asad, *Qur'an,* 688–89.

2. Jubilees 18:16, in VanderKam, *Book of Jubilees,* 109.

3. Numbers Rabbah 11:7, in Freedman, *Midrash Rabbah, Numbers,* 445.

4. Pell, *Story of Abraham,* 49.

5. Jubilees 18:18, in VanderKam, *Book of Jubilees,* 109.

6. Munk, *Aqaydat Yitzchaq,* 1:166.

7. Hayden, *Love of Abraham and Sarah,* 42.

8. Galbraith and Smith, *Scriptural Teachings of the Prophet Joseph Smith,* 172.

9. It was when "the Lord came and dwelt with his people, and they dwelt in righteousness." Moses 7:16.

10. Noble, *Great Men of God,* 67.

11. Hanauer, *Folk-Lore of the Holy Land,* 29.

12. Kasher, *Encyclopedia of Biblical Interpretation,* 3:170.

13. Soloveitchik, *Man of Faith,* 88.

14. Hirsch, *T'rumath Tzvi,* 79.

15. Fragmentary Targum on Genesis 16:5, in Bowker, *Targums and Rabbinic Literature,* 204.

16. On Abraham 42, 44, in *Philo VI,* 121, 125.

17. Blunt, *Twelve Lecture,* (several commas omitted). Blunt was the Rector of Streatham, Surrey; a Fellow of Pembroke College,

Cambridge; and Domestic Chaplain to the Duke of Richmond.

18. Neal A. Maxwell, "The Women of God," *Ensign*, May 1978, 10–11. When that history is disclosed, continues Elder Maxwell, "will it feature the echoes of gunfire or the shaping sound of lullabies? The great armistices made by military men or the peace-making of women in homes and in neighborhoods? Will what happened in cradles and kitchens prove to be more controlling than what happened in congresses? When the surf of the centuries has made the great pyramids so much sand, the everlasting family will still be standing, because it is a celestial institution, formed outside telestial time. The women of God know this."

19. Scherman and Zlotowitz, *Bereishis: Genesis*, 1(a):821.

20. See Ginzberg, *Legends of the Jews*, 5:215 n. 44.

21. See *Encyclopaedia Judaica*, 14:868; and Ginzberg, *Legends of the Jews*, 1:203.

22. The expression is from Mosiah 18:21, describing a group of Abraham and Sarah's Nephite descendants.

23. Soloveitchik, *Man of Faith*, 87–88.

24. Strachan, *Hebrew Ideals*, 1:176.

25. Soloveitchik, *Man of Faith*, 87–88.

26. Jubilees 19:9, in VanderKam, *Book of Jubilees*, 111.

27. See Ginzberg, *Legends of the Jews*, 1:287–88.

28. Munk, *Wisdom in the Hebrew Alphabet*, 114–15.

29. Levner, *Legends of Israel*, 96.

30. Tuchman and Rapoport, *Passions of the Matriarchs*, 78.

31. Tuchman and Rapoport, *Passions of the Matriarchs*, 79.

32. Ibid.

33. Ibid., 81.

34. Nibley, *Abraham's Creation Drama*, 2.

35. Hayden, *Love of Abraham and Sarah*, 46.

36. Leibowitz, *Studies in Bereshit*, 210.

37. Jubilees 19:9, in VanderKam, *Book of Jubilees*, 111.

38. Bereshit Rabbah, quoted in Leibowitz, *Studies in Bereshit*, 211.

39. Mensch, *King Solomon's "First" Temple*, 363.

40. *Encyclopaedia Judaica*, 11:670.

41. Scherman and Zlotowitz, *Bereishis: Genesis*, 1(a):887.

42. See Ouaknin, *Mysteries of the Kabbalah*, 388.

43. Sawyer, *Midrash Aleph Beth*, 276, paraphrasing Midrash Aleph Beth 18:5.

44. Speaking of all the righteous who make and keep the covenant of eternal marriage.

45. See Budge, *Cave of Treasures*, 154. Rabbinic sources are divided over whether Keturah was Hagar, with one tradition insisting that Keturah was not Hagar, so that Abraham in his life married three women. See, for example, Kasher, *Encyclopedia of Biblical Interpretation*, 3:225–27; Ginzberg, *Legends of the Jews*, 5:264–65; and Harris, *Hebraic Literature*, 241. That Keturah was not Hagar seems certain from a latter-day revelation stating that "Abraham received concubines [note the plural], and they bore him children." Doctrine and Covenants 132:37. Rabbinic sources assert that Keturah was descended from Noah's son Japeth, and that Abraham, who would father children by Keturah, would thus have descendants among all three branches of Noah's posterity, for Sarah was descended from Shem, and Hagar from Ham. Graves and Patai, *Hebrew Myths*, 179.

46. See Brinner, *History of al-Tabari*, 129; and Brinner, *Lives of the Prophets*, (al-Thalabi) 164.

47. See Brinner, *History of al-Tabari*, 129; and Brinner, *Lives of the Prophets*, (al-Thalabi) 164.

48. Sanhedrin 57b, in Epstein, *Babylonian Talmud*.

49. Al-Rabghuzi, *Stories of the Prophets*, 2:92.

50. Schwartz, *Tree of Souls*, 345, citing various Talmdic and midrashic passages.

51. See Testament of Isaac 2:27–28, in Charlesworth, *Old Testament Pseudepigrapha*, 1:906; and Testament of Benjamin 10:2–7, in Charlesworth, *Old Testament Pseudepigrapha*, 1:828.

52. See Warren Zev Harvey, "Grace or Loving-Kindness," in Cohen and Mendes-Flohr, *Contemporary Jewish Religious Thought*, 302.

53. As he did with his daughter-in-law Rebekah and the destiny of her sons: Jubilees 19:16–25, in VanderKam, *Book of Jubilees*, 113–14.

54. As when he repeatedly blessed his grandson Jacob: Jubilees 19:26–29; 22:27–30, in VanderKam, *Book of Jubilees*, 115, 133–35. And as he did with Jacob's son Judah: "And Abraham my father's father blessed me to be king over Israel." Testament of Judah 17:5, in Hollander and de Jonge, *Testaments of the Twelve Patriarchs*, 215.

55. As when he instructed Isaac: Jubilees 21:1–26, in VanderKam, *Book of Jubilees*, 120–27. And as later with Jacob: Jubilees 22:10–25, in VanderKam, *Book of Jubilees*, 129–33.

56. As he did with his sons by Keturah: "The ancient children of the East were possessed of a wisdom which they inherited from Abraham, who transmitted it to the sons of the concubines." Zohar Vayera 100b, in Sperling and Simon, *Zohar*, 1:325.

57. As he did with Isaac and the laws of sacrifice: Jubilees 21:5–20, in VanderKam, *Book of Jubilees*, 121–26. According to some sources, Abraham also taught his great-grandson Levi, who, speaking of the laws of sacrifice, attested that: "I saw my father Abraham acting with care," and "he told me [what] to offer up on the altar." Aramaic Testament of Levi, Bodleian c, lines 12–13, in Hollander and de Jonge, *Testaments of the Twelve Patriarchs* 463. "For thus my father Abraham commanded me." Aramaic

Testament of Levi, verse 57 (extant only in Greek), in Hollander and de Jonge, *Testaments of the Twelve Patriarchs,* 465. "Abraham taught me." Testament of Levi 9:12, in Hollander and de Jonge, *Testaments of the Twelve Patriarchs,* 155.

58. Pirke de Rabbi Eliezer 48, in Friedlander, *Pirke de Rabbi Eliezer,* 383–85, including note 8 on page 383.

59. Klinghoffer, *Discovery of God,* 296–97, citing Rabbi Elijah Benmozegh.

60. See, for example, the sources mentioned in James E. Bowley, "The Compositions of Abraham," in Reeves, *Tracing the Threads,* 215–38.

61. Qur'an 53:36–37, in A. Y. Ali, *Qur'an,* 1449.

62. Qur'an 53:36–37, in M. M. Ali, *Qur'an,* 1005.

63. Abodah Zarah 14b, in Epstein, *Babylonian Talmud.*

64. Abodah Zarah 25a, in Epstein, *Babylonian Talmud.* Jasher is "the book of Abraham, Isaac and Jacob."

65. Baba Bathra 15a, in Epstein, *Babylonian Talmud.*

66. See Kaplan, *Sefer Yetzirah.*

67. Schwartz, *Tree of Souls,* 363-364, citing Zohar Hadash, Yitro   37b.

68. James E. Bowley, "The Compositions of Abraham," in Reeves, *Tracing the Threads,* 228–33.

69. See Calmet, *An Historical . . . Dictionary,* 1:25–26; and Haug, *Essays on . . . the Parsis,* 16.

70. 1QapGen, in Martinez and Tigchelaar, *Dead Sea Scrolls Study Edition,* 1:28–49.

71. Apocalypse of Abraham, in Charlesworth, *Old Testament Pseudepigrapha,* 1:681–711.

72. The passage is from Jubilees, and reads further that "there is a death penalty which has been ordained for him in heaven before the most high Lord. The sin will be entered regarding him in the eternal books forever before the Lord. Joseph remembered what he had said and refused to lie with her." Jubilees 39:5–7, in VanderKam, *Book of Jubilees,* 256–57.

73. Nibley, *Abraham's Creation Drama,* 10–13.

74. Kenney, *Wilford Woodruff's Journal,* 2:155.

75. E. Douglas Clark, in Nibley, *Abraham in Egypt,* xxi (foreword).

76. See H. Donl Peterson, "Translation and Publication of the Book of Abraham," in Ludlow, *Encyclopedia of Mormonism,* 1:134.

77. See Apocalypse of Abraham 19–31, in Charlesworth, *Old Testament Pseudepigrapha,* 1:698–705.

78. We have no record of this ordination, but following the ancient pattern, it must have taken place. See Doctrine and Covenants 107:40–53.

79. Jubilees 19:23–24, in Sparks, *Apocryphal Old Testament,* 65.

80. Ibid. In this translation, it might seem that Abraham's forefathers are the ones who will lay the foundations of heaven and make firm the earth, but see VanderKam's translation in VanderKam, *Book of Jubilees,* 114.

81. Jubilees 19:27, in Sparks, *Apocryphal Old Testament,* 65. Although Jacob was not the first-born, yet Abraham expressly blessed him that he would be "first-born son" (verse 28), clearly referring to the "right of the firstborn" mentioned in Abraham 1:3.

82. Spencer W. Kimball, "The Example of Abraham," *Ensign,* June 1975, 4.

83. Miller, *Abraham Friend of God,* 106, quoting Midrash Tannaim, Devarim.

84. Jubilees 20:1–10, in VanderKam, *Book of Jubilees,* 115–19.

85. Jubilees 21:2, 4–5, in Charles, *Apocrypha and Pseudepigrapha* 2:43.

86. See the introductory remarks on "Provenance" by Wintermute, the translator of Charlesworth, *Old Testament Pseudepigrapha,* 2:45.

87. Testament of Abraham (Rescension A) 1:5, in Charlesworth, *Old Testament Pseudepigrapha,* 1:882.

88. Scherman and Zlotowitz, *Bereishis: Genesis,* 1(a):358.

89. Testament of Abraham (Rescension A) 2:6, in Charlesworth, *Old Testament Pseudepigrapha,* 1:882. This angel is named as the archangel Michael. However, since Michael is Adam, and since Adam died, he would not have been an inhabitant of the city of Enoch. Also, in this same source, Abraham says that he recognizes the angel as one of the three angels whose feet he had washed. Once again, this makes it impossible that the angel was Adam, who was a spirit and could not eat.

90. Testament of Abraham (Rescension A) 1:7, in Charlesworth, *Old Testament Pseudepigrapha,* 1:882.

91. Testament of Abraham (Rescension A) 8:7, in Charlesworth, *Old Testament Pseudepigrapha,* 1:886. This happens after Abraham resists death and the angel returns to God for further instruction.

92. Testament of Abraham (Rescension A) 9:6, in Charlesworth, *Old Testament Pseudepigrapha,* 1:887.

93. Testament of Abraham (Rescension A) 10:1, in Sparks, *Apocryphal Old Testament,* 407.

94. Testament of Abraham (Rescension A) 10:1–11, in Charlesworth, *Old Testament Pseudepigrapha,* 1:887.

95. Nibley, *Approaching Zion,* 266.

96. Testament of Abraham (Rescension B) 11:3–10, in Charlesworth, *Old Testament Pseudepigrapha,* 1:900.

97. See Kasher, *Encyclopedia of Biblical Interpretation,* 3:232; and see Culi, Magriso, and Argueti, *Torah Anthology,* 2:441–442.

98. Glenn, *Jewish Tales and Legends,* 102–104.

99. Jubilees 22:1, 7, in Charles, *Apocrypha and Pseudepigrapha* 2:45.

100. Jubilees 22:7, in VanderKam, *Book of Jubilees,* 128.

101. Jubilees 22:7, in Charlesworth, *Old Testament Pseudepigrapha,* 2:97.

102. Jubilees 22:8–9, in Charles, *Apocrypha and Pseudepigrapha* 2:45.

103. Jubilees 22:10–25, in VanderKam, *Book of Jubilees,* 129–34.

104. Jubilees 22:26–30; 23:1, in Charles, *Apocrypha and Pseudepigrapha,* 2:47.

105. Jubilees 23:2–6, in Charlesworth, *Old Testament Pseudepigrapha,* 2:99 (for consistency, I have changed the spelling of

"Rebecca" to "Rebekah").

106. Jasher 26:30, 32–33, in Noah, *Book of Yashar,* 76.

107. William Wordsworth, "Lines Composed a Few Miles above Tintern Abbey, on Revisiting the Banks of the Wye during a Tour. July 13, 1798," in Hutchinson, ed., *Wordsworth.*

108. Baba Bathra 91a, in Epstein, *Babylonian Talmud.* See also Ginzberg, *Legends of the Jews,* 5:267 n. 317.

109. Shepherd of Hermas 9.16.5, in Osiek, *The Shepherd of Hermas,* 232-33.

110. Epistle of Ignatius to the Magnesians, Shorter Version, 9, in *Ante-Nicene Fathers,* 1:62.

111. Schwartz, *Tree of Souls,* 516, citing Beit-ha-Midrash 3:68–78.

Notes to Chapter 12

1. Nibley, *Sharing the Gospel with Others,* 1.

2. *Encyclopaedia Judaica,* 11:673.

3. Ibid., 8:226.

4. Goldman, *In the Beginning,* 782; Reuven Firestone, "Abraham," in McAuliffe, *Encyclopaedia of the Qur'an,* 1:5.

5. Buttrick, *Interpreter's Dictionary of the Bible,* 2:575.

6. Pringle, *Churches of the Crusader Kingdom,* 1:224.

7. Rabadan, *Mahometism Fully Explained,* 1:258–59.

8. Ibid., 1:258–59.

9. Padwick, *Muslim Devotions,* 168.

10. Patai, *Arab Mind,* 84.

11. Levner, *Legends of Israel,* 97–98.

12. Zornberg, *Particulars of Rapture,* 67, quoting Exodus Rabbah 1:15.

13. Birnbaum, *Torah and Haftarot,* 16, citing Avoth 5:22.

14. Spretnak, *States of Grace,* 159, 161.

15. See Calmet, *An Historical . . . Dictionary,* 1:25.

16. As the Lord promised to do. Abraham 2:9.

17. Noble, *Great Men of God,* 42.

18. See generally: Kittel and Friedrich, *Theological Dictionary of the New Testament* 3:825–26; James, *Testament of Abraham,* 72–75; Ginzberg, *Legends of the Jews,* 5:268 n. 318; Fitzmeyer, *Gospel According to Luke (10–24),* 1132; and Meyer, *Mark and Luke,* 477–79. In the Book of Mormon, compare Alma 7:25: "that ye may at last be brought to sit down with Abraham, Isaac, and Jacob . . . in the kingdom of heaven to go no more out."

19. Stone, *Armenian Apocrypha,* 96.

20. *Journal of Discourses,* 17:11.

21. Hoffman, *My People's Prayer Book,* 121.

22. Padwick, *Muslim Devotions,* 167, 169.

23. Ibid., 172.

24. Schimmel, *And Muhammad Is His Messenger,* 162, quoting Qu'ran 6:162.

25. Padwick, *Muslim Devotions,* 278–79.

26. When Muhammad ascended to the highest heaven, he saw his forefather Abraham sitting on a throne, of whom Muhammad commented, "Never have I seen a man more like myself." Williams, *Islam,* 68.

27. Schimmel, *And Muhammad Is His Messenger,* 160. See also 57: "Abraham occupies the highest rank after Muhammad."

28. Ginzberg, *Legends of the Jews,* 2:314; 5:419: Abraham is seen occupying the greatest of the thrones.

29. Nibley, *Abraham in Egypt,* 293.

30. Testament of Isaac 2:7, 14, in Charlesworth, *Old Testament Pseudepigrapha,* 1:905–906.

31. Testament of Isaac 2:27–28, in Charlesworth, *Old Testament Pseudepigrapha,* 1:906.

32. Commenting on the statement that Abraham gave the residual property all to Isaac, the Zohar states that Abraham bequeathed to Isaac "the holy heritage of faith to which Abraham clave." Zohar, Vayera 100b, in Sperling and Simon, *Zohar,* 1:325.

33. Kasher, *Encyclopedia of Biblical Interpretation,* 3:37.

34. Qur'an 2:132, in A. Ali, *Al-Qur'ān,* 27.

35. Qur'an 2:132, in Asad, *Qur'an,* 27.

36. Schram, *Stories within Stories,* 299.

37. Buxbaum, *Life and Teachings of Hillel,* 74–75.

38. Kasher, *Encyclopedia of Biblical Interpretation,* 3:50, citing various sources.

39. Another translation reads here: "For these things, I tell you, are of greater value than anything else I can bequeath to you." Testament of Benjamin 10:4, in Sparks, *Apocryphal Old Testament,* 599.

40. Testament of Benjamin 10:2–7, in Charlesworth, *Old Testament Pseudepigrapha,* 1:828. The tribe of Benjamin is not only the source of this statement and the Revelation of Stephen, but perhaps also the letter to the Hebrews (containing the passage telling that Abraham sought the heavenly city), which seems to have been written by someone who "doubtless came under the influence of the teaching of Stephen." Paul—who Clement thought may have written the original version (in Hebrew) of the letter, and who Origen thought was the author of the letter's thoughts, although the letter itself was written by someone else—was of course

present at Stephen's martyrdom (Acts 7:58), and was also of the tribe of Benjamin (Philip. 3:5; Rom. 11:1). Guthrie and Motyer, *Eerdmans Bible Commentary,* 1191. On Abraham's teaching his posterity to keep the law of the Lord, see also Genesis 18:17–19.

41. Mawadudi, *Towards Understanding the Qur'an,* 111.

42. Noble, *Great Men of God,* 65–67. I have taken the liberty of breaking up Noble's wonderful lengthy passage into paragraphs that are not in the original. I hope he will pardon me.

43. Coleridge, "Table Talk," May 16, 1830, in Goldman, *In the Beginning,* 539–40.

44. *Journal of Discourses,* 21:160.

45. Ibid., 2:78. "Who has lived since that day who has been thus blessed? I will venture to say not one."

46. Clement, The First Epistle of Clement to the Corinthians 31, in *Ante-Nicene Fathers,* 1:13.

47. *Journal of Discourses,* 24:160.

48. Ibid., 11:152, echoing the Savior's statement to His Jewish contemporaries that "if ye were Abraham's children, ye would do the works of Abraham." John 8:39.

49. Harris, *Commentary on the Pearl of Great Price,* 231.

50. Nibley, *Abraham in Egypt,* 651–52.

51. Ginsburg, *Essenes,* 122 (in *The Kabbalah*); and see generally Chavel, *Encyclopedia of Torah Thoughts,* 42–26; Cohen and Mendes-Flohr, *Contemporary Jewish Religious Thought,* 299–302.

52. Soloveitchik, *Man of Faith,* 68.

53. *Journal of Discourses,* 22:304–305.

54. Ibid., 1:261.

55. Ibid., 9:290.

56. Galbraith and Smith, *Scriptural Teachings of the Prophet Joseph Smith,* 350.

57. Ibid., 354–55.

58. Gordon B. Hinckley, "Reaching Down to Lift One Another," *Ensign,* November 2001, 54.

59. Gordon B. Hinckley, "Living in the Fulness of Times," *Ensign,* November 2001, 6.

60. *Journal of Discourses,* 2:268–69.

61. Galbraith and Smith, *Scriptural Teachings of the Prophet Joseph Smith,* 170–71.

62. *Journal of Discourses,* 1:262.

63. Ibid., 19:80.

64. In the 1832 account, the portion in Joseph Smith's own hand, in Jessee, *Papers of Joseph Smith,* 6.

65. McConkie, *His Name Shall Be Joseph,* 197 (capitalizing the word "restoration").

66. Galbraith and Smith, *Scriptural Teachings of the Prophet Joseph Smith,* 261–62.

67. Lord, *Beacon Lights of History,* 27.

68. Noble, *Great Men of God,* 42–43.

69. Galbraith and Smith, *Scriptural Teachings of the Prophet Joseph Smith,* 262.

70. Clark, *Messages of the First Presidency,* 6–7.

71. Menahoth 53b, in Epstein, *Babylonian Talmud.*

72. John Taylor taught that even in the earliest days of the newly restored Church, "the spirit of revelation rested down on God's servant Joseph," who "like Adam, Moses, Abraham, Jesus, Jared, Nephi, Moroni and others, had the heavens unfolded to his view. . . . He was conversant with the parties who officiated as the leading men of those dispensations." *Journal of Discourses,* 20:174–75. Speaking on another occasion about Joseph Smith, John Taylor stated: "The principles which he had, placed him in communication with the Lord, and not only with the Lord, but with the ancient apostles and prophets; such men, for instance, as Abraham, Isaac, Jacob, Noah, Adam, Seth, Enoch, and Jesus and the Father, and the apostles that lived on this continent as well as those who lived on the Asiatic continent. He seemed to be as familiar with these people as we are with one another." *Journal of Discourses,* 21:94.

73. Edmunds, *Through Temple Doors,* 21–22.

74. Compare King James translation: "all that watch for iniquity are cut off" by the Lord "who redeemed Abraham."

75. Deutsch, *The Gnostic Imagination,* 135, quoting Synopse §218.

76. Abraham, Isaac, Jacob, and the rest of the righteous will pray, "Lord of the Universe! How long wilt thou sit upon thy Throne like a mourner in the days of his mourning with thy right hand behind thee and not deliver thy children and reveal thy Kingdom in the world?" 3 Enoch 44:7, in Odeberg, *3 Enoch,* part 2, 139. Odeberg comments on this verse that "The *Right Hand* or the *Right Arm of the Lord* represent the actualization of the kingdom of God on earth, the deliverance of Israel."

77. Urbach, *The Sages,* 540, citing Lamentations Rabbah and referring to Abraham's pleading with God at the destruction of the Jerusalem Temple.

78. Midrash Aleph Beth 14:5, in Sawyer, *Midrash Aleph Beth,* 238.

79. Revelation of Stephen, in James, *Apocryphal New Testament,* 565. There are unmistakable echoes here of every element of the book of Abraham passage: the reference to the Lord dwelling in heaven (the heavens open when he comes as judge), the earth as his footstool (the earth becomes smooth, upon which Christ sits on a throne), the sea obeying his voice (by moving and giving up its dead), the wind and fire as his chariot (a fiery chariot, a mighty wind), and the mountains departing in a whirlwind (he comes in a mighty wind as the mountains disappear). That the Lord as he spoke to Abraham may have been alluding to the Second Coming at the end of time seems further indicated by the Lord's next statement to Abraham: "My name is Jehovah, and *I know the end from the beginning.*" Abraham 2:8, emphasis added.

80. Genesis Rabbah 69:3, in Freedman, *Midrash Rabbah, Genesis,* 2:631. The words "of God" are bracketed in the original.

81. Of those named who will be descending with the Lord, the names of the three Patriarchs occur in the text closest to the name of God—the Lamb.

82. Sibylline Oracles 2:246, in Charlesworth, *Old Testament Pseudepigrapha,* 1:351.

83. Midrash Aleph Beth 12, in Sawyer, *Midrash Aleph Beth,* 229.

84. Schwartz, *Tree of Souls,* 516, citing Pesikta Rabbati 37:1–2.

85. Kasher, *Encyclopedia of Biblical Interpretation,* 3:161, citing Sifre D'barim and Midrash Ha Gadol, and other sources, which are citing Daniel 12:3 as a fulfillment of the promise to Abraham in Genesis 22:17.

86. See Midrash Aleph Beth 14:1–5, 13, in Sawyer, *Midrash Aleph Beth,* 238–39, and see 248–50, 253.

87. See Sawyer, *Midrash Aleph Beth,* 243, 254.

88. *Journal of Discourses,* 18:325.

89. Revelation 19:10; 22:17; 21:1; and see Feeley-Harnick, *The Lord's Table,* 108–111.

90. Speaking in the context of the final Messianic era of peace and redemption. See also 2 Nephi 26:25.

91. The King James translation does not mention eating or the feast, but simply says that many shall come and "sit down with Abraham" and the others "in the kingdom of heaven." Matthew 8:11. However, the meaning of "sit down" is clearly to "sit at table," as translated in Feeley-Harnick, *The Lord's Table,* 110. Similarly NASB has "recline at the table," while NJB has "sit down . . . at the feast;" REB has "sit . . . at the banquet," while NRSV has the verb "eat" and Lattimore has the verb "feast" (*New Testament,* 63). The only other gospel to report the Savior's statement is Luke at 13:29, on which Fitzmeyer comments that those who recline at table in the kingdom "share in the eschatological banquet to be provided by God for his chosen ones." Fitzmeyer provides references from the Old Testament, New Testament, pseudepigrapha, and rabbinic writings, to which should be added Doctrine and Covenants 27:10 (which mentions Abraham's presence at the feast).

92. Brinner, *History of al-Tabari,* 105.

93. Or "the law." NIV Isaiah 51:4. Or "law." Isaiah 51:4, in Watts, *Isaiah 34–66,* 195.

94. Or "my ordinances." Isaiah 51:4, in North, *The Second Isaiah,* 60.

95. Or "my victory." Isaiah 51:5, in REB; and in North, *The Second Isaiah,* 60.

96. Or "is on the way." NIV Isaiah 51:5.

97. Or "my arm shall bring justice to the nations." NIV Isaiah 51:5.

98. Or "islands." NIV Isaiah 51:5.

99. "Zion will extend, eventually, all over this earth. There will be no nook or corner upon the earth but what will be in Zion. It will all be Zion." Brigham Young, in *Journal of Discourses,* 9:138.

100. Miller, *Abraham Friend of God,* 52, quoting Numbers Rabbah 2.

101. Ibid., 52.

102. Stuy, *Collected Discourses,* 5:280.

103. Breed, *Abraham,* 39.

104. Soloveitchik, *Man of Faith,* 68, citing Tanna d'bei Eliyahu Rabbah 25.

105. Spencer W. Kimball, "The Example of Abraham," *Ensign,* June 1975, 4.

Appendix
Chronology of Abraham's Patriarchal Ancestors

Ancient sources vary widely in the chronology between the Flood and Abraham. As to the individual life-spans of the partriarchs during that period, Josephus gives neither the number of years lived after the birth of the first son nor total life span, so their ages when Abraham was sixty-two cannot be calculated. Jubilees has yet another chronological scheme, but is incomplete and, like Josephus, does not give life spans. From the Flood to Abraham's birth, Jubilees is shorter than the Septuagint (LXX) and the Samaritan Pentateuch (Sam), but still nearly twice as long as the Masoretic Text (MT).

Compiled from tables in *Josephus IV*, 73; Wenham, *Genesis 1–15*, 250; Skinner, *Critical and Exegetical Commentary on Genesis*, 233; and Westermann, *Genesis 1–11*, 559 (last column's number 107 should be 207). While Josephus' chronology at first blush appears to be based on the Septuagint, a closer look in light of other sources reveals, according to Feldman, that "there were a number of traditions with regard to chronology, and that Josephus' source for this remains to be recovered." Feldman, *Josephus*, 54.

Name	Masoretic Text				Septuagint				Samaritan Pentateuch				Josephus
	Age at first son	Years lived after	Total life span	Age when Abr is 62. ALIVE?	Age at first son	Years lived after	Total life span	Age when Abr is 62. ALIVE?	Age at first son	Years lived after	Total life span	Age when Abr is 62. ALIVE?	Age at first son
1 Shem	100 (2 years after Flood)	500	600	452 Yes	100 (2 years after Flood)	500	600	[1232] No	100 (2 years after Flood)	500	600	[1102] No	(12 years after Flood)
2 Arpha-xad	35	403	438	352 Yes	135	430	565	[1132] No	135	303	438	[1002] No	135
(Kainan)	—	—	—	—	130	330	460	[997] No	—	—	—	—	—
3 Salah	30	403	433	317 Yes	130	330	460	[867] No	130	303	433	[867] No	130
4 Eber	34	430	464	287 Yes	134	370	504	[737] No	134	270	404	[737] No	134
5 Peleg	30	209	239	[253] No	130	209	339	[603] No	130	109	239	[603] No	130
6 Reu	32	207	239	223 Yes	132	207	339	[473] No	132	107	239	[473] No	130
7 Serug	30	200	230	191 Yes	130	200	330	[341] No	130	100	230	[341] No	132
8 Nahor	29	119	148	[161] No	79	129	208	[211] No	79	69	148	[211] No	120
9 Terah	70	135	205	132 Yes	70	135	205	132 Yes	70	75	145	132 Yes	70
From Flood to Birth of Abr	292				1072				937				993

Abbreviations

FBM   Everett Fox, *The Five Books of Moses*, The Shocken Bible: vol. 1 (New York: Shocken Books, 1995).

GTC   Robert Alter, *Genesis: Translation and Commentary* (New York: Norton, 1996).

JPST   Jewish Publication Society translation of Tanakh (Hebrew Old Testament), in *Tanakh: A New Translation of the Holy Scriptures According to the Traditional Hebrew Text* (Philadelphia: Jewish Publication Society, 1985).

JST   Joseph Smith Translation of the Bible, in Joseph Smith Jr., *The Holy Scriptures*, new corrected ed. (Independence, MO: Herald Publishing House, 1944 [1967 reprint]).

KJV   *King James Version*. Biblical quotations not otherwise indicated are from the King James Version.

NASB   *New American Standard Bible* (Nashville: Holman Bible Publishers, 1981).

NIV   The NIV Study Bible: New International Version (Grand Rapids, MI: Zondervan, 1985).

NJB   *The New Jerusalem Bible* (Garden City, NY: Doubleday, 1985).

NKJV   *Holy Bible: The New King James Version* (Nashville: Thomas Nelson Publishers, 1982).

NRSV   Bruce M. Metzger and Roland E. Murphy, *The New Oxford Annotated Bible: New Revised Standard Version* (New York: Oxford University Press, 1991).

REB   *The Revised English Bible with the Apocrypha* (Oxford and Cambridge: Oxford University and Cambridge University, 1989).

Glossary of Terms, Names, and Sources

1 Enoch

Cited as scripture in the New Testament Epistle of Jude, 1 Enoch is a lengthy record of Enoch telling of the last days, the Son of Man, the resurrection, astronomy, future history, the joy of the righteous, and the sorrow of the wicked. Well known to the early Christians, the book disappeared from view for many centuries, finally to be rediscovered when the Scottish explorer James Bruce brought back copies from Abyssinia (Ethiopia) in 1773. Portions of the book are now known in Greek and Aramaic, but still the only complete version is in Ethiopic (Geez). The first English translation appeared in 1821 in England, but was of limited circulation; the more widely circulated 1838 edition was the one discovered in England by Parley P. Pratt, who was so impressed that he wrote about it and published extracts thereof in the July 1840 *Millenial Star*. *See* Nibley, *Enoch the Prophet*, 91–154 (especially 111–12); VanderKam and Adler, *Jewish Apocalyptic Heritage in Christianity*, 33–101. *Translations* in Black, *1 Enoch*; Charlesworth, *Old Testament Pseudepigrapha*; Sparks, *Apocryphal Old Testament*; Charles, *Apocrypha and Pseudepigrapha*; Charles, *The Book of Enoch*; and Knibb, *The Ethiopic Book of Enoch*.

2 Enoch

Also known as the Book of the Secrets of Enoch, 2 Enoch is available (in a short and longer version) only in manuscripts from Old Slavonic. It tells of Enoch's ascension through the heavens and his return to Earth, when he reported his experiences to family members. The book contains sections on creation, astronomy, prophecies of the future, and the ultimate fate of mankind, and is full of exhortations to righteousness. The last part of the book narrates the history of Enoch's successors before the Flood. The first English translation appeared in 1896 by Morfill and Charles, who marveled that "although the very knowledge that such a book ever existed was lost for probably twelve hundred years, it nevertheless was much used by both Christian and heretic in the early centuries" (Morfill and Charles, *Secrets of Enoch*, xii). *See* Nibley, *Enoch the Prophet*, 115–16; and Collins, *Cosmology and Eschatology*, 36–39. *Translations* in Charlesworth, *Old Testament Pseudepigrapha*; Sparks, *Apocryphal Old Testament*; Charles, *Apocrypha and Pseudepigrapha*; and Morfill and Charles, *Secrets of Enoch*.

3 Enoch

Also called the Book of Enoch by Rabbi Ishmael the High Priest, or the Book of the Palaces, 3 Enoch purports to be an account of the journey of Rabbi Ishmael (of the second century A.D.) through heaven and of his receiving instructions from the angel "Metatron," or Enoch. Enoch explains how he was taken up and transformed, and teaches about the organization and activities of the heavenly world and the cosmos, and about the final state of the souls of the righteous and the wicked. 3 Enoch is in Hebrew and was first translated into English in 1928. *See* Nibley, *Enoch the Prophet*, 118–21 (on what Nibley in 1986 called the "Hebrew–Aramaic Enoch," now commonly called 3 Enoch; what Nibley then designated "III Enoch" [115–16] refers to the Greek fragments of 1 Enoch). *Translations* in Charlesworth, *Old Testament Pseudepigrapha*; and Odeberg, *3 Enoch*.

Apocalypse of Abraham

Surviving only in Old Slavonic, the Apocalypse of Abraham, like the Book of Abraham, is a first-person account of events from the life of Abraham, beginning with his rejection of idolatry as a young man. M. R. James' assessment was that the text "is of considerable antiquity and great interest." The use of "Apocalypse" in the title derives from the story's central event, the revelation Abraham receives when he ascends to heaven and is shown the heavens and the future history of the world, including a scene reminiscent of what is recorded in the Book of Abraham. The parallels were immediately recognized by Latter-day Saints, who published the first English translation in 1898 in the first volume of the *Improvement Era*. *See* James, *Lost Apocrypha of the Old Testament*, 17; Nibley, *Enoch the Prophet*, 159–168; Nibley, *Abraham in Egypt*, 11–67; and Collins, *Cosmology and Eschatology*, 34–36. *Translations* in Charlesworth, *Old Testament Pseudepigrapha*; Sparks, *Apocryphal Old Testament*; and Box and Landsman, *Apocalypse of Abraham*.

Apocrypha

Derived from the Greek word meaning "hidden," the word apocrypha has traditionally been applied to a certain body of biblical texts (about fifteen in number) not found in the traditional Jewish canon but included in the Septuagint and early Christian versions of the Old Testament. These books came to be deemed less authoritative than the official canonical books, and the exact list differed between Catholics and Protestants. When Joseph Smith inquired if the Lord wished him to translate the Apocrypha, the Lord said no, explaining that it contained much truth but also much human fabrication. Accordingly, any reader "enlightened by the Spirit shall obtain benefit therefrom" (D&C 91:1–5). Later and in a larger sense, the term apocryphal is increasingly used to designate any noncanonical biblical text, regarding either the Old or New Testament (as used, for example, in the title *Apocryphal Old Testament*, or the "Genesis Apocryphon"). *See* Freedman, *Anchor Bible Dictionary*, 1:292–97; and Schiffman and VanderKam, *Encyclopedia of the Dead Sea Scrolls*, 1:35–39.

Asatir

Also called the Samaritan Book of the Secrets of Moses, the Asatir is a Samaritan text covering the period from Adam to the death of Moses. The Samaritans believe it to be an authentic book of Moses and esteem it a sacred work. The only English translation (translating also the commentary thereon, called the Pitron), was made in 1927. *See Encyclopaedia Judaica*, 14:754. *Translation* in Gaster, *Asatir.*

Book of Abraham

First published in 1842 in three installments of the *Times and Seasons,* the Book of Abraham was translated by Joseph Smith from papyri accompanying four Egyptian mummies purchased by the Church in 1835. The book is an autobiographical account of the early life of Abraham beginning in the land of Ur and continuing through his travels to the border of Egypt, where the Lord shows him the cosmos, the premortal existence, and the Creation. The narrative portion ends here, but the last of the book's three illustrations, or facsimiles, shows Abraham sitting on Pharaoh's throne by politeness of the king. The book was canonized in 1880 and now forms part of the Pearl of Great Price. After helping to set the type for the first installment of the Book of Abraham, Wilford Woodruff recorded in his journal: "The truths of the Book of Abraham are truly edifying great & glorious which are among the rich treasures that are revealed unto us in the last days" (Kenney, *Wilford Woodruff's Journal* 2:159). The Book of Abraham is now part of the official canon of The Church of Jesus Christ of Latter-day Saints. *See* Ludlow, *Encyclopedia of Mormonism,* 1:132–138. *Translation* in the Pearl of Great Price; and Ludlow, *Encyclopedia of Mormonism,* 5:468–476.

Book of Moses

The first seven and a half chapters of the Joseph Smith Translation of the Bible (which correspond to the first five and a half chapters of Genesis) were accepted into the official canon of The Church of Jesus Christ of Latter-day Saints as the Book of Moses. It includes much material not found in the traditional Genesis text, such as a prologue describing the setting for the revelation to Moses, and a lengthy section detailing the history of the patriarch Enoch, his building of a city of holiness called Zion, and the God's removal of Zion from the earth before the Flood to a heavenly place of safety. *See* Ludlow, *Encyclopedia of Mormonism,* 1:216–17. *Translation* in the Pearl of Great Price; and Ludlow, *Encyclopedia of Mormonism,* 5:455–67.

Cave of Treasures

Attributed to Ephraim the Syrian of the fourth century A.D., the Cave of Treasures is a Syriac history of the world from the Creation to the Crucifixion. It contains parallels to other early Christian works and to Jubilees. The only English translation was made in 1927. *See* Bowker, *Targums and Rabbinic Literature,* 91. *Translation* in Budge, *Cave of Treasures.*

Chronicles of Jerahmeel

Compiled by a fourteenth-century Jewish scholar, the Chronicles is an extensive collection of legends from numerous sources and traditions pieced together into a connected narrative from the Creation to the Maccabean era. *See* Bowker, *Targums and Rabbinic Literature,* 86–87. *Translation* in Gaster, *Chronicles of Jerahmeel.*

Conflict (or Combat) of Adam and Eve with Satan

Known only in Ethiopic, this lengthy work tells the history of the world from Adam to the magi who visited the infant Jesus. The title derives from the conflict that arose when Adam and Eve, after leaving the garden, were met by Satan on several occasions. The text shares affinities with other early Christian chronicles, but it also has unique elements and stories. Among the events narrated is the story of the aged Adam gathering his righteous posterity to confer his last instructions and blessings, an event repeated in turn by each of the subsequent patriarchs. The Conflict of Adam and Eve has significant parallels with Latter-day Saint scripture and theology. The only translation was published in 1882, but it has been reprinted many times. *See* Nibley, *Enoch the Prophet,* 168–78, 207–208. *Translation* in Malan, *Conflict of Adam and Eve with Satan*; this same translation, without the notes, was reprinted in Crane, *Lost Books of the Bible,* and was reprinted in later editions and by different publishers (in some of those later editions, Rutherford Hayes Platt and J. Alden Brett appear as editors).

Ephrem the Syrian

Lauded by later Christians as the "harp of the Holy Spirit" and the "sun of the Syrians," and recognized by Jerome for his "sublime genius," Ephrem lived in the tumultuous fourth century and became a teacher, poet, orator, and defender of the Christian faith. A prolific writer of great renown, he produced not only poetry but commentary, and, in the words of Gregory of Nyssa, "pored over every scripture . . . like no one else." The last ten years of his life were spent in the city that claims to be Abraham's birthplace (called Edessa at the time, now Urfa), and his interest in and love for Abraham shine through in his writings and his life. In the last year of his life, he labored tirelessly on behalf of the hungry and suffering during the severe famine that struck the region as it had done in Abraham's day. His Abrahamic efforts to distribute food and provide medical assistance resulted in his own exhaustion and illness, from which he died. *Translation* of his commentary on Genesis is in Matthews, *Armenian Commentary on Genesis.* A few of his other works are found in English translation in Schaff and Wace, *Nicene and Post-Nicene Fathers, Second Series,* vol. 13, part 2.

Genesis Apocryphon

The scroll now called the Genesis Apocryphon was discovered in 1947 at Qumran as part of the Dead Sea Scrolls, the library of the Essenes who perished during the Roman campaign in about A.D. 68. Written in Aramaic, the scroll had apparently been lying on the cave floor and had partly deteriorated. It was finally translated in 1956. A later translator called it Memoirs of the Patriarchs, for it purports to contain autobiographical writings of the ancient patriarchs Lamech, Noah, and Abraham. The Abraham portion is by far the longest. It apparently began with his early life, but that part of the scroll has deteriorated. The story picks up as they are traveling through Canaan, and it continues on into Egypt, where Abraham is divinely directed (as in the Book of Abraham) to ask Sarah to say that she is Abraham's sister. The story proceeds to tell of Sarah being forcibly taken to the royal palace; of Abraham's fervent prayer on her behalf and God's protection; and of Abraham finally healing Pharaoh by the laying on of hands, thus setting the stage for the Book of Abraham's Facsimile no. 3, where Abraham is sitting on Pharaoh's throne by politeness of the king and is wearing a crown representing the priesthood. The scroll further tells of their leaving Egypt and dwelling in Canaan, with the last portion of the narrative changing to third person. The Genesis Apocryphon is one of the earliest and most important ancient sources on Abraham. The most recent translations include some material not published previously. *See* Schiffman and VanderKam, *Encyclopedia of the Dead Sea Scrolls*, 1:302–304. *Translations* in Martinez and Tigchelaar, *Dead Sea Scrolls Study Edition*; Vermes, *The Complete Dead Sea Scrolls*; Wise, Abegg, and Cook, *Dead Sea Scrolls*; and Fitzmeyer, *Genesis Apocryphon*.

Genesis Rabbah

The Genesis Rabbah is, in the words of its translator Jacob Neusner, "the first complete and systematic commentary to the book of Genesis." Forming the initial part of the Midrash Rabbah, or the rabbinical "great commentary" on the Hebrew scriptures, the Genesis Rabbah was "closed" about A.D. 400, but it contains numerous Jewish stories and legends that had been handed down for generations and that are often paralleled in other ancient sources and traditions. *See* Bowker, *Targums and Rabbinic Literature*, 78–79; Neusner, *Confronting Creation*; and Neusner, *Genesis and Judaism*. *Translations* in Freedman, *Midrash Rabbah, Genesis*; and Neusner, *Genesis Rabbah*.

Jasher, Book of

Called in Hebrew the *Sefer ha-Yashar* ("Book of the Upright" or "Book of the Righteous"), the Book of Jasher as we now have it is thought to have been compiled in the Middle Ages, possibly in the thirteenth century. It is a connected narrative of rabbinic traditions from the creation of Adam to when the Israelites take possession of the promised land under Joshua. Jasher was one of the most popular ethical books of the Middle Ages, and it has been reprinted numerous times since. English translations appeared in England in 1750 and again in 1829, and in America (apparently in a longer version) in New York in 1840. It was one of the few rabbinic or ancient texts available to early Church members of this dispensation; and Joseph Smith, noting Jasher's story of young Abraham being cast into the fire, commented simply that Jasher "has not been disproved as a bad author" (Galbraith and Smith, *Scriptural Teachings of the Prophet Joseph Smith*, 293). The comment could not have been more apropos, for when scrutinized in light of restored scripture and other ancient sources, Jasher turns out to contain a curious mixture of some very ancient material along with much later rabbinic embellishment. The book was reprinted by Latter-day Saints in Salt Lake City in 1887 and a number of times since. That the name Jasher was assigned to the book as we have it may derive from the fact that the Old Testament (in Joshua 10 and 2 Samuel 1) quotes from an ancient book called Jasher, apparently the same book of Jasher that the Talmud identifies with "the book of Abraham, Isaac, and Jacob," who were "upright"—raising the possibility that some of the Abrahamic material in Jasher may have originated with the book mentioned by the Talmud. *See Encyclopaedia Judaica*, 14:1099; and Freedman, *Anchor Bible Dictionary*, 3:646–47. *Translation* in Noah, *Book of Yashar*, reprinting the 1840 edition; this same edition was the one reprinted in Salt Lake City beginning in 1887.

Joseph Smith Translation of the Bible

In June 1830, Joseph Smith received a revelation restoring lost passages of the Bible. It was the beginning of his new translation of the Bible, a work that God commanded him to do and that Joseph considered a "branch of his calling." He had no knowledge of biblical languages (he would later study Hebrew), and he had no ancient biblical manuscripts in his possession; rather, this translation was by made by means of the same divine inspiration through which the Bible had originally been composed. Using an English text of the King James Translation, and assisted by scribes, Joseph Smith dictated the revisions and additions. The first seven and a half chapters were later canonized as the Book of Moses. The Joseph Smith Translation is often abbreviated as JST. *See* Ludlow, *Encyclopedia of Mormonism*, 2:763–69; Matthews, *Joseph Smith's Translation of the Bible*; Nyman and Millet, *The Joseph Smith Translation*; and Matthews, *A Bible! A Bible!*, 89–158. *Translation* in Smith, *The Holy Scriptures . . . An Inspired Revision*, and reprinted many times since; *Joseph Smith's New Translation* (parallel columns comparison of JST and the King James); and Faulring, Jackson and Matthews, *Joseph Smith's New Translation*.

Josephus

Josephus was the most important Jewish historian of the early Roman period. Born in A.D. 37 as Joseph ben Matthias (or Mattathias) into an aristocratic priestly family of Judea, he became distinguished for his knowledge of the Torah and Jewish tradition, and also as a statesman. In the war against Rome, he led the revolutionary forces in Galilee until he surrendered in A.D. 67 to the general Vespasian, whom Josephus predicted would become emperor of Rome. Vespasian was so intrigued that he spared his life, and when the prophecy came to pass two years later, Josephus was rewarded and eventually freed. Historians argue over whether Josephus was a traitor or a realistic patriot who tried to save his country from annihilation by a superior power. He chose to spend the remainder of his life in Rome, where, under patronage from the Flavian emperors, he wrote prolifically. His works include the history of his people (*Jewish Antiquities* or *Judean Antiquities*) in a retelling of the Old Testament that apparently drew on traditions familiar to him and on sources that have long since disappeared. *See* Freedman, *Anchor Bible Dictionary*, 3:981–98; Schiffman and VanderKam, *Encyclopedia of the Dead Sea Scrolls*, 427–31; *Encyclopaedia Judaica*, 10:251–65; Bowker, *Targums and Rabbinic Literature*, 31–32; Stone, *Jewish Writings of the Second Temple Period*, 185–232; Mulder and Sysling, *Mikra*, 455–518;

and Hadas-Lebel, *Flavius Josephus*. **Translations** of his works in Mason, *Flavius Josephus*; Thackeray, *Josephus*; and Whiston, *Josephus* (Whiston's translation continues to be reprinted by various publishers).

Jubilees, Book of
Dated by scholars to the early second century B.C., Jubilees recounts stories covering the time of Genesis through the early part of Exodus, as revealed to Moses under God's direction and by the angel of His presence on Mount Sinai. Like the restored Book of Moses, Jubilees begins the Genesis story with a prologue that tells of Moses on a mountain receiving a revelation about the future of Israel. Jubilees also emphasizes themes like priesthood and the latter days, and has strong affinities with early Enoch texts. Among its stories is an account of fourteen-year-old Abraham praying for divine guidance and for strength to keep himself pure from the idolatrous and immoral world in which he found himself. The only complete extant copy of Jubilees is found in Ethiopic (Geez), but its original was Hebrew, and some fourteen fragmentary Hebrew copies were found at Qumran among the Dead Sea Scrolls. According to scholar George W. E. Nickelsburg, "the Jubilees stories are themselves the crystallization of earlier tradition" (Stone and Theodore A. Bergen, *Biblical Figures outside the Bible*, 171). *See* Freedman, *Anchor Bible Dictionary*, 3:1030–1032; Schiffman and VanderKam, *Encyclopedia of the Dead Sea Scrolls*, and 1:434–38; VanderKam, *Jubilees*. **Translations** in VanderKam, *Jubilees*; Charlesworth, *Old Testament Pseudepigrapha*; Sparks, *Apocryphal Old Testament*; and Charles, *Apocrypha and Pseudepigrapha*.

Kabbalah
The term *Kabbalah* denotes a body of Jewish esoteric and mystical teachings of Judaism, said to have been passed down from Abraham through the ages. Today the Kabbalah is known mostly through medieval texts like the Zohar, the Bahir, and the Sefer Yetzirah. *See* *Encyclopaedia Judaica*, 489–654; Scholem, *Kabbalah*; Scholem, *On the Kabbalah and Its Symbolism*; and Scholem, *Major Trends in Jewish Mysticism*.

Maimonides
Rabbi Moses Ben Maimon, also known by his acronym "Rambam," is considered the most illustrious figure of Judaism in the post-talmudic era, and one of the greatest ever. He was born in A.D. 1135 in Cordoba, Spain, under Muslim rule, but with the fall of Cordoba he fled with his family. He studied in Morocco; toured the Holy Land and prayed at the Temple Mount and Abraham's tomb in Hebron; and settled in Egypt, where he was chief rabbi of the large Jewish community in Cairo and served as physician to the Grand Vizier. He was also a brilliant scientist, philosopher, theologian, and scholar, and was called the "marvel" of his generation, a man "very great in wisdom, learning and rank." He died in 1204, leaving such monumental works as the *Guide for the Perplexed* and the *Mishneh Torah*, which contains valuable traditions about Abraham. *See* *Encyclopaedia Judaica*, 11:754–81; and Shulman, *The Rambam*. **Translation** of *Mishneh Torah*) in Maimonides, *Mishneh Torah*.

Masoretic Text
Usually abbreviated as MT, the Masoretic Text is the standard Hebrew text of what Christians call the Old Testament. Originally, it was written with only consonants (a few of which could indicate long vowels), but the meaning of the words could vary depending on which vowels were read with the consonants. The consonantal text became relatively fixed by about the second century. In the ensuing centuries, the Masoretes, or Jewish scholars guarding transmission of the text, developed vocalization signs indicating the vowels based on the Masoretes' textual tradition (Hebrew *masora*, literally meaning "transmission"). The oldest full copy of the Masoretic Text dates to the tenth century A.D. Other textual traditions existed before the Christian era, most notably those embodied in the Septuagint and the Samaritan Pentateuch. *See* Freedman, *Anchor Bible Dictionary*, 4:592–99; and Mulder and Sysling, *Mikra*, 87–136.

Midrash
The word *midrash* derives from the Hebrew verb *darash*, meaning "to inquire," "to seek" or "to investigate." A midrash is a rabbinic commentary on or interpretation of a biblical text, often alluding to or incorporating older rabbinic opinions or traditions. The most famous, and one of the earliest, of the midrashim is the Midrash Rabbah, or "Great Midrash," including the Genesis Rabbah. *See* Freedman, *Anchor Bible Dictionary*, 4:818–22; *Encyclopaedia Judaica*, 11:1507–1514; and Bowker, *Targums and Rabbinic Literature*, 69–90.

Nachmanides
Nachmanides, or Rabbi Moses ben Nachman (also known by his acronym Ramban), was born in A.D. 1194 in Spain, where he earned renown as a scholar, physician, sage, poet, orator, defender of the faith, and prolific author. Widely recognized for his brilliance and judgment, even the Christian king of Spain took his advice on some important Jewish matters. In 1263 in a public debate against a prominent Jew who had converted to Christianity, the elderly Nachmanides performed so well that the king presented him with three hundred pieces of silver. Later Nachmanides was forced to flee Spain, going to Jerusalem, where he established a school to which hundreds of scholars flocked. There he completed his most important writing, his massive Torah commentary, in which he drew on his extensive knowledge and insight to probe the biblical text. *See* *Encyclopaedia Judaica*, 12:774–82; Shulman, *The Ramban*. **Translation** of commentary on the Torah in Chavel, *Ramban*.

Origen

Widely esteemed the greatest of the ante-Nicene Church Fathers, Origen (Origenes Adamantius) was born of Christian parents about A.D. 185 in Egypt. He received an excellent education from his learned father, who suffered imprisonment and martyrdom in the violent anti-Christian persecution in Alexandria when Origen was just seventeen. Origen desired to follow his father in martyrdom, but was prevented by his mother. The family further suffered confiscation of their assets, and Origen labored to support his mother and six younger brothers, while visiting prisoners and comforting the condemned. Continuing his education, he studied under the great Clement of Alexandria and then succeeded him as teacher. The rest of Origen's life was devoted to learning, preaching, studying, and writing, as he authored a vast amount of material, including commentaries, treatises, and letters. He was the first Church Father to study Hebrew. While living at Caesarea, he fell victim to another violent anti-Christian persecution and was imprisoned and cruelly tortured. He died shortly thereafter. In Origen's writings, he attests to early Christian doctrines later lost or discredited, like the preexistence of souls and the probationary purpose of mortality as a time to prepare to return to God. *See* Freedman, *Anchor Bible Dictionary,* 5:42–48; Schiffman and VanderKam, *Encyclopedia of the Dead Sea Scrolls,* 2:624–25; *Encyclopaedia Judaica,* 12:1467; Crouzel, *Origen;* Trigg, *Origen;* Balthasar, *Origen;* and Nibley, *Abraham in Egypt,* 296.

Philo of Alexandria

Philo Judaeus lived from about 20 B.C. to about A.D. 50 in Alexandria, Egypt, where the Greek-speaking Jewish community outnumbered the Jewish population of Judea. Of priestly descent, he was born into the most prominent Jewish family in Alexandria and one of the wealthiest families of the Roman Empire. He led a Jewish delegation to Rome, where he successfully averted the emperor's anger against Alexandrian Jews who refused to worship the emperor's images. Philo was highly educated both in Greek studies and in Judaism, and he was an avid scholar who used his wealth to devote himself to learning and writing, perhaps as a teacher of advanced studies. The most prolific author of Hellenistic Judaism, he wrote many treatises on various aspects of Judaism, including a biography of Abraham. Philo was heir to a rich literary tradition among Alexandrian Jewry that was already several centuries old. *See* Schiffman and VanderKam, *Encyclopedia of the Dead Sea Scrolls,* 2:663–69; *Encyclopaedia Judaica,* 409–415; Freedman, *Anchor Bible Dictionary,* 5:333–42; Bowker, *Targums and Rabbinic Literature,* 29–30; Stone, *Jewish Writings of the Second Temple Period,* 233–82; Mulder and Sysling, *Mikra,* 421–53; Sandmel, *Philo of Alexandria;* and Goodenough, *Introduction to Philo Judaeus. Translations* in Colson, Whitaker, and Marcus, *Philo;* and Yonge, *The Works of Philo* (first published in 1854–55, and based on an inferior Greek text, this translation has been "updated" but still should be used with caution).

Pirke de Rabbi Eliezer

No rabbi is more quoted in the Talmud than Rabbi Eliezer the Great, a scholar of tremendous erudition who lived in the first and second centuries A.D. and who was eventually excommunicated from Judaism. To him is attributed the Pirke, although the text as we have it appears to date from several centuries later. It is not a midrash but a narrative running from the Creation to the Israelite wilderness sojourn, and also describing aspects of heaven and hell, the fall of the rebellious angels, the life hereafter, and the resurrection of the dead, and the Messianic age. The Pirke, which has affinities with the Enoch literature and preserves traditions from many ancient sources, devotes several chapters to Abraham, focusing particularly on his trials. *See Encyclopaedia Judaica,* 13:558–60; and Bowker, *Targums and Rabbinic Literature,* 85. *Translation* in Friedlander, *Pirke de Rabbi Eliezer.*

Pseudo Philo

The *Biblical Antiquities* (or *Liber Antiquitatum Biblicarum,* sometimes abbreviated as LAB) of Pseudo Philo is a narrative of biblical history from Adam to David, but it contains many stories not found in the Bible. The work has survived only in Latin manuscripts that attributed it to Philo of Alexandria, probably because it often circulated with his writings. Once scholars came to see that its original language had been Hebrew, authorship by Philo was questioned and finally dismissed. Who the actual author or compiler was remains a mystery, although he apparently lived in Palestine around the first century A.D. His work is one of the earliest witnesses to some Abraham traditions appearing in later sources, and it contains some Abraham material not found elsewhere. *See* Freedman, *Anchor Bible Dictionary,* 5:344–45; and Bowker, *Targums and Rabbinic Literature,* 30–31. *Translations* in Jacobson, *Pseudo-Philo's Liber Antiquitatum Biblicarum;* Charlesworth, *Old Testament Pseudepigrapha,* 2:297–377; and James, *Biblical Antiquities of Philo.*

Pseudepigrapha

The name given to a body of writings possessed by early Jewish and Christian communities between about 200 B.C. and A.D. 200. The word *pseudepigrapha* is from the Greek, meaning "writings with false superscriptions," and was applied by scholars because of the presumption that these writings could not have really been written by the purported authors—men like Adam, Enoch, Noah, Abraham, Isaac, Jacob, Isaiah, and others. Many of these texts disappeared for centuries and have only recently reappeared in what Samuel Sandmel has called "the strangest quirk of fate respecting literature that I know of." The pseudepigrapha include numerous stories and legends of Abraham as found, for example, in Jubilees, Pseudo-Philo, the Apocalypse of Abraham, and the Testament of Abraham. *See* Charlesworth, *Old Testament Pseudepigrapha,* 1:ix–xxxiv; Freedman, *Anchor Bible Dictionary,* 5:537–41; Schiffman and VanderKam, *Encyclopedia of the Dead Sea Scrolls,* 1:35–39; and Mulder and Sysling, *Mikra,* 379–419. *Translations* in Charlesworth, *Old Testament Pseudepigrapha* (the most comprehensive collection); Sparks, *Apocryphal Old Testament;* and Charles, *Apocrypha and Pseudepigrapha.*

Qur'an

The sacred book of the religion of Islam, the Qur'an is a record of God's revelations transmitted by the angel Gabriel to the prophet Muhammad, to whom was given the task of restoring the religion of his ancestor Abraham. The Qur'an includes stories of Abraham, who is said to be a model for mankind. In the Qur'anic account of Abraham sacrificing his son, Abraham "submitted" (*aslama*) to the will of God, providing the name of the religion restored by Muhammad: *Islam*, or "Submission," to the will of God. The Qur'an refers to books written by Abraham, and Islamic legends claim to preserve other stories about him. Many Muslims believe that since the Qur'an in its original Arabic is the literal word of God, it cannot in the strict sense be translated, and any attempt to do so yields only a rough approximation. *Translations* in M. M. Ali, *Qur'an*; Asad, *Qur'an*; Cragg, *Qur'an*; A. Y. Ali, *Qur'an*; *Holy Qur'an*; Khatib, *Bounteous Koran*; and A. Ali, *Al-Qur'an*.

Rashi
Rabbi Solomon bar Isaac (or Shlomo ben Yitzchak), commonly referred to by his acronym Rashi, was born in France and educated in Germany in the eleventh century during the tumultuous period of the Crusades when life for Jews was dangerous. He is widely esteemed as the greatest commentator ever on the Pentateuch and Talmud, blending ancient traditions with his own profound insights to shed light on the "plain meaning" of the text. His commentaries are known for their erudition and clarity, and are considered standard works in Judaism; they also influenced Martin Luther and other Christian scholars. Rashi was also a powerful teacher who encouraged biblical and talmudic studies, which his descendants carried on in succeeding centuries. *See* *Encyclopaedia Judaica*, 13:1558–1565; Shereshevsky, *Rashi*; and Liber, *Rashi* (reprinted several times). *Translations* of commentary on the Pentateuch in Rashi, *Commentary*; Doron, *Rashi's Torah Commentary*; and Davis, ed., *The Metsudah Chumash/Rashi*.

Samaritan Pentateuch
The Hebrew text of the Pentateuch (written in Samaritan letters) that was preserved by the Samaritan community is known as the Samaritan Pentateuch, which constitutes the entire canon of Samaritan scripture. Many of its variations from the Masoretic Text are unimportant, but some are substantive, such as the chronology between the Flood and the birth of Abraham. Some of the variations find agreement in the Septuagint and in Qumran Biblical manuscripts as well as some Old Testament quotations in the New Testament. The date of the Samaritan Pentateuch (or the date that it became independent from the Hebrew version that would become the Masoretic Text) depends on the date of the final break between the Jews and the Samaritans, a date thought to be at least in the second century B.C. and perhaps as early as the fourth century B.C. The oldest manuscripts of the Samaritan Pentateuch appear to be from about the twelfth century A.D. *See* Freedman, *Anchor Bible Dictionary*, 5:932–40; and Mulder and Sysling, *Mikra*, 95–96.

Sefer Yetzirah
The Sefer Yetzirah, part of the Kabbalah, is the Jewish mystical "Book of Creation," which in many manuscripts and in ancient tradition is said to have been authored by Abraham, or at least some of it; indeed, some manuscripts are titled "The Letters of Our Father Abraham." It is touted to be the oldest Hebrew book. Abraham's authorship of a book about creation is attested in the Book of Abraham. Most of the Sefer Yetzirah is cryptic and difficult to understand, but one passage tells of God making a covenant with Abraham and embracing him, an event which, when read in light of the Apocalypse of Abraham, appears to refer to Abraham's experience in heaven. According to Nibley, the Sefer Yetzirah is a temple text. There are a number of versions of the Sefer Yetzirah. *See* *Encyclopaedia Judaica*, 10:507–508; Kaplan, *Sefer Yetzirah*, ix–xxvi; and Papus, *Qabalah*, 203–248; Nibley, *Approaching Zion*, 265. *Translations* in Kaplan, *Sefer Yetzirah*; and Suarès, *Qabala Trilogy*.

Septuagint
Abbreviated as LXX, the Septuagint (literally "seventy") is the Greek translation of the Old Testament begun in Alexandria, Egypt, in the third century B.C. It is so called because of the legend that the Pentateuch portion was translated by seventy or seventy-two elders. The Septuagint includes not only the canonical books of the Hebrew Old Testament, but also some additional books known as the Apocrypha. The Septuagint is the earliest written translation of the Old Testament, and often witnesses to a different and earlier version of the Hebrew Bible than found in the Masoretic Text. In the Hebrew Old Testament manuscripts found among the Dead Sea Scrolls, for example, their variations from the Masoretic Text often agree with the Septuagint. The Septuagint was the Bible of the early Christian Church. *See* Freedman, *Anchor Bible Dictionary*, 5:1093–1104; Mulder and Sysling, *Mikra*, 161–88; *Encyclopaedia Judaica*, 4:851–56; 14:1178; and Jobes and Silva, *Invitation to the Septuagint*. Translation in Brenton, *Septuagint*.

Stories (or Lives) of the Prophets
The Stories of the Prophets are Islamic collections of stories about twenty-five prophets or so mentioned in the Qur'an, who are for the most part the same as the biblical patriarchs and prophets. Such collections became very popular and widespread, drawing on Qur'anic material, sayings (*hadith*) of the Prophet Muhammad, and a variety of other material purporting to preserve ancient and important traditions about God's chosen messengers to humanity—traditions with important affinities with early Jewish and Christian sources. Some of the most significant of these many collections include those made by Ibn Ishaq (eighth century), Ibn Kathir (ninth century), Tabari (ninth–tenth century), Tha'labi (tenth–eleventh century), and Al-Rabghuzi (fourteenth century). *Translations* in Brinner, *History of al-Tabari*; Brinner, *Lives of the Prophets*; al Kisa'i, *Tales of the Prophets*; Kathir, *Stories of the Prophets*; Al-Rabghuzi, *Stories of the Prophets*; and Wheeler, *Prophets in the Quran*.

Tabari

Abu Jafar Muhammad ibn Jarir al Tabari, or al-Tabari, A.D. 839–923, was born in Persia some two hundred years after the death of Muhammad. He is said to have memorized the Qur'an by the age of seven, and he was educated in various seats of learning, including Syria and Egypt. He traveled extensively throughout the Islamic world assiduously collecting information and traditions, settling finally in Baghdad, arguably the greatest center of learning in the world at the time. He became one of Islam's greatest teachers, historians, and scholars, founded a law school, and authored a massive work of history that was long accepted as the standard work, as well as a massive commentary on the Qur'an. Tabari's indefatigable labors and exhaustive erudition preserved an incredible amount of Muslim exegesis for the first two and a half centuries of Islam. *Translation* of the Abrahamic portion of his history in Brinner, *History of al-Tabari*. Translations of more of his works are widely available.

Talmud

From a word meaning "study" or "learning," the Talmud is a vast repository of Jewish law and legend handed down for generations and finally written down in the first five centuries A.D. by Jewish sages in both Babylon and Palestine, producing the two collections known as the Babylonian Talmud and the Palestinian (or Jerusalem) Talmud. The larger and more important is the Babylonian Talmud, a library of over thirty volumes that became the most important text in Judaism and the basis of traditional Jewish religious life. The Talmud contains rabbinical discussions, elaborations, commentaries, and speculations on Jewish law, lore, and theology, including numerous ancient traditions and stories about biblical characters like Abraham. *See Encyclopaedia Judaica*, 15:750–79; Bowker, *Targums and Rabbinic Literature*, 64–69; Freedman, *Anchor Bible Dictionary*, 6:310–15; Strack and Stemberger, *Introduction to the Talmud and Midrash*; Neusner, *Invitation to the Talmud*; Safrai, *The Literature of the Sages, First Part*, 303–66; and Cohen and Jacob Neusner, *Everyman's Talmud*. *Translations* in Epstein, *Babylonian Talmud*; Steinsaltz, *Talmud*; and *Talmud Bavli*.

Targums

From the Aramaic word for "translation," targum is an Aramaic translation or paraphrase of an Old Testament text. The targums date from about the last two centuries B.C. to the first three centuries A.D., and were produced to be read in the synagogues when Aramaic was the spoken language of the Jews in Palestine and Babylon. The targums contain varying degrees of Jewish tradition regarding the biblical stories that they translate. *See Encyclopaedia Judaica*, 4:841–51; 15:811; Freedman, *Anchor Bible Dictionary*, 6:320–31; Mulder and Sysling, *Mikra*, 217–54; and Bowker, *Targums and Rabbinic Literature*, 3–28. *Translations* of the targums on Genesis in Maher, *Targum Pseudo-Jonathan*; Klein, *Fragment Targums*; McNamara, *Targum Neofiti 1*; Aberbach and Grossfeld, *Targum Onkelos*; and Grossfeld, *Targum Onqelos*.

Testament of Abraham

The Testament of Abraham narrates events immediately preceding the death of Abraham, who is taken on a final tour of Earth and heaven before leaving mortality. The testament exists in a short and a longer form, and is found in manuscripts in Greek, Romanian, and several other languages. The first English translation appeared in 1887. Apparently containing kernels of ancient tradition, the form in which we now have it seems to have been embellished, as seen in the fact that Michael is portrayed as one of the three angels whose feet Abraham washed—an impossibility in light of restored truths about Michael, spirits, and the resurrection. The assessment of M. R. James was that "all the texts of it have been more or less tampered with." *See* James, *Lost Apocrypha of the Old Testament*, 17; and Nibley, *Abraham in Egypt*, 26–67. *Translations* in Charlesworth, *Old Testament Pseudepigrapha*; Sparks, *Apocryphal Old Testament*; *Ante-Nicene Fathers*, 10:185–201 (showing both versions conveniently collated in parallel columns); Gaster, *Studies and Texts*, 1:92–123 (reprinting the 1887 translation of a Romanian version; Gaster calls this the "Apocalypse of Abraham"); and *Testament of Abraham*.

Testament of Adam

Extant in Syriac, Greek, and several other languages, the Testament of Adam contains, among other things, what Adam told Seth about the Creation and the Fall, including what God promised Adam after he ate the forbidden fruit—that God himself would come to earth in the form of a man to work miracles, die, and be resurrected, thus allowing Adam finally to become a god. *See* James, *Lost Apocrypha of the Old Testament*, 3–4. *Translation* in Charlesworth, *Old Testament Pseudepigrapha* (translation is by Stephen Robinson, an Latter-Day Saint scholar).

Testaments of the Twelve Patriarchs

According to the Testaments of the Twelve Patriarchs, just prior to the death of each of Jacob's twelve sons (Abraham's great-grandsons), each gathered his posterity around him and reflected on his life, imparting his final instructions, exhortations to righteousness, and sometimes prophecies about the future. The testaments purport to be a record of what each of the twelve sons said. According to latter-day restored scripture, the practice of a righteous patriarch gathering his posterity for his final instructions and blessings began with father Adam himself (see D&C 107:40–57). The Testaments of the Twelve Patriarchs are known mostly in Greek and Armenian, but some have also survived in Hebrew, Aramaic, and Slavonic. *See* James, *Lost Apocrypha of the Old Testament*, 19–21. *Translations* in Charlesworth, *Old Testament Pseudepigrapha*; Sparks, *Apocryphal Old Testament*; Charles, *Apocrypha and Pseudepigrapha*; and Hollander and de Jonge, *Testaments of the Twelve Patriarchs*.

Tha'labi

Abu Ishaq Ahmad ibn Muhammad ibn Ibrahim al-Tha'labi, usually known as al-Thal'abi, was born probably sometime after A.D. 950 and died in A.D. 1035. He lived and worked in the city of Nishapur (in present-day Iran), the thriving cultural and educational hub of the eastern provinces of Islam, and center for the study of the Qur'an and Islamic tradition. An assiduous scholar and preacher, he was recognized as a righteous man of incomparable knowledge, "the star of the eminent scholars" and "a vast sea and a deep abyss of learning," according to one contemporary. Among his works are a massive commentary on the Qur'an, as well as his Stories (or Lives) of the Prophets, whose motivation is revealed in Tha'labi's comment that God had revealed to Muhammad information about the lives of prior prophets so that these men might serve "as a model and example." ***Translations*** of his Lives of the Prophets in Brinner, *Lives of the Prophets*. His commentary on the Qur'an remains untranslated into English. On Tha'labi's life, see Saleh, *Formation of the Classical* Tafsir *Tradition*.

Zohar

From a word meaning "splendor," the Zohar is the primary text of the Jewish Kabbalah, the mystical literature. The Zohar was apparently compiled in medieval Spain, but it is attributed to Rabbi Simeon ben Yohai of the second century. That it contains some very ancient traditions seems evident in some of the Abrahamic passages, like the one speaking of cedars and palms in connection with Abraham in Egypt—reminiscent of Abraham's dream in the Genesis Apocryphon about a cedar and a palm. The Zohar is written in the form of a commentary on the Pentateuch, and purports to illuminate the hidden and transcendent meaning of the biblical text. ***See*** *Encyclopaedia Judaica,* 16:1193–1215; 10:532–35; Scholem, *Kabbalah*; Scholem, *Zohar*; and Lachower and Tishby, *Wisdom of the Zohar*. ***Translations*** in Sperling and Simon, *Zohar*; Manhar, *Zohar*; and Matt, *Zohar, Pritzker Edition*.

Bibliography

Aberbach, Moses, and Bernard Grossfield, eds. *Targum Onkelos to Genesis: A Critical Analysis Together with an English Translation of the Text.* Denver: Center for Judaic Studies, University of Denver, 1982.

Achtemeier, Paul J. *Harper's Bible Dictionary.* San Francisco: Harper and Row, 1985.

Adams, J. McKee. *Ancient Records and the Bible: A Survey of Archeological Evidences in Their Bearing on the Integrity of the Historical Narratives of the Old Testament.* Nashville: Broadman Press, 1946.

Adang, Camilla. *Muslim Writers on Judaism and the Hebrew Bible: From Ibn Rabban to Ibn Hazm,* Islamic Philosophy, Theology and Science: Text and Studies, vol. 22. Leiden: Brill, 1996.

Adler, William. *Time Immemorial: Archaic History and Its Sources in Christian Chronography from Julius Africanus to George Syncellus,* Dumbarton Oaks Studies 26. Washington, DC: Dumbarton Oaks Research Library and Collection, 1989.

Akenson, Donald Harman. *Surpassing Wonder: The Invention of the Bible and the Talmuds.* New York: Harcourt Brace, 1998.

Albrektson, B., et al. *Remembering All the Way: A Collection of Old Testament Studies Published on the Occasion of the Fortieth Anniversary of the Oudtestamentisch Werkgezelschap in Nederland,* Oudtestamentische Studiën: Namens Het Oudtestamentisch Werkgezelschap in Nederland, Deel 21. Leiden: Brill, 1981.

Albright, F., and C. S. Mann. *Matthew: Introduction, Translation, and Notes,* The Anchor Bible, vol. 26. Garden City, NY: Doubleday, 1971.

Alcuinus, Flaccus Albinus ed. *The Book of Jasher.* London: Philip Rose/Longman, 1829.

Alford,Henry. *The Greek Testament,* 7th ed. 4 vols. London: Rivingtons, 1874.

Ali, Ahmed. *Al-Qur'an.* Princeton, NJ: Princeton University Press, 1988.

Ali, Maulana Muhammad. *The Holy Qur'an: Arabic Text, English Translation and Commentary,* 7th ed. Chicago: Specialty Promotions Co., 1985.

Ali, A. Yusaf. *The Holy Qur'an: Text, Translation and Commentary.* Brentwood, MD: Amana Corp., 1983.

al-Kisa'i, Muhammad ibn 'Abd Allah. *Tales of the Prophets (Qisas al-anbiya),* Chicago: Great Books of the Islamic World, 1997.

Al-Rabghuzi. *The Stories of the Prophets: Qisas al Anbiya, An Eastern Turkish Version.* 2 vols. Leiden: Brill, 1995.

Alter, Robert. *Genesis: Translation and Commentary.* New York: Norton, 1996.

The Ante-Nicene Fathers: Translations of The Writings of the Fathers down to A.D. 325. 10 vols. Edinburgh: T. and T. Clark; and Grand Rapids, MI: Eerdmans, 1985–1986 [reprint].

Arazi, Albert, Joseph Sadan, and David J. Wasserstein, eds. *Compilation and Creation in Adab and Luga: Studies in Memory of Naphtali Kinberg (1948–1997).* Israel Oriental Studies 19. Eisenbrauns [for Tel-Aviv University], 1999.

Asad, Muhammad. *The Message of the Qur'an.* Gibraltar: Dar Al-Andalus, 1980.

Ball, Warwick. *Syria: A Historical and Architectural Guide.* New York: Interlink Books, 1998.

Ballard, Melvin J. *Crusader for Righteousness.* Salt Lake City: Bookcraft, 1966 [1968 reprint].

Balthasar, Hans Urs Von, ed. *Origen: Spirit and Fire: A Thematic Anthology of His Writings.* Catholic University of America Press, 2001.

Baumgartner, Walter, and Johann Jakob Stamm. *The Hebrew and Aramaic Lexicon of the Old Testament.* 4 vols. Leiden: Brill, 1994–99. 1:9–10.

Baring-Gould, S. *Legends of the Patriarchs and Prophets.* New York: Holt and Williams, 1872.

Barker, Margaret. *The Great Angel: A Study of Israel's Second God.* Louisville, Kentucky: Westminster/John Knox Press, 1992.

———. *The Older Testament: The Survival of Themes from the Ancient Royal Cult in Sectarian Judaism and Early Christianity.* London: SPCK, 1987.

Barton, Tamsyn. *Ancient Astrology.* London: Routledge, 1994.

Berry, Lloyd E., introducer. *The Geneva Bible: A Facsimile of the 1560 Edition.* Madison, Wisconsin: The University of Wisconsin Press, 1969 [1981 reprint].

Bialik, Hayim Nahman, and Yehoshua Hana Ravnitzky, eds. *The Book of Legends, Sefer Ha-Aggadah: Legends from the Talmud and Midrash.* New York: Schocken Books, 1992.

Birnbaum, Philip. *The Torah and Haftarot.* New York: Hebrew Publishing Company, 1983.

Black, Matthew. *The Book of Enoch or 1 Enoch: A New English Edition,* Studia in Veteris Testamenti Pseudepigrapha, volumen septimum. Leiden: Brill, 1985. Other translations of 1 Enoch are cited separately.

Bloom, Harold. *The American Religion: The Emergence of the Post-Christian Nation.* New York: Simon and Schuster, 1992.

Blowers, Paul M., et al., eds. In *Dominico Eloquio—In Lordly Eloquence: Essays on Patristic Exegesis in Honor of Robert Louis Wilken.* Grand Rapids: William B. Eerdmans, 2002.

Blunt, Henry. *Twelve Lectures upon the History of Abraham,* 12th ed. London: J. Hatchard and Son, 1849.

Bolles,Edmund Blair, ed. *Galileo's Commandment: An Anthology of Great Science Writing.* New York: W. H. Freeman, 1997.

Borgen, Peder. *Early Christianity and Hellenistic Judaism.* Edinburgh: T. and T. Clark, 1996.

Botterweck, G. Johannes, and Helmer Ringgren, eds. *Theological Dictionary of the Old Testament.* 12 vols. Grand Rapids, MI: Eerdmans, 1977–2003.

Bowker, John. *The Targums and Rabbinic Literature: An Introduction to Jewish Interpretations of Scripture.* Cambridge: Cambridge University Press, 1979.

Box, G. H. *The Testament of Abraham: Translated from the Greek Text with Introduction and Notes.* London: Society for Promoting

Christian Knowledge, 1927.

Box, G. H., and J. I. Landsman. *The Apocalypse of Abraham*. London: 1918.

Breasted, James Henry. *A History of Egypt: From the Earliest Times to the Persian Conquest*. New York: Charles Scribner's Sons, 1937.

Breed, David R., *Abraham: The Typical Life of Faith*. Chicago: F. H. Revell, 1886.

Brenton, Lancelot C. L. *The Septuagint with Apocrypha: Greek and English*. Grand Rapids, MI: Zondervan Publishing House, reprint of 1851 ed.

Brinner, William M., translator. A*bu Ishaq Ahmad Ibn Muhammad Ibn Ibrahim Al-Tha'labi, Arais Al-Majalis Fi Qisas Al-Anbiya or Lives of the Prophets: As Recounted by Abu Ishaq Ahmad Ibn Muhammad Ibn Ibrahim Al-Tha'labi*, Studies in Arabic Literature, Supplements to the Journal of Arabic Literature, vol. 24. Leiden: Brill Academic Publishers, 2002.

———, translator. *The History of al-Tabari: Volume II, Patriarchs and Prophets*, Bibliotheca Persica, Series in Near Eastern Studies. Albany, NY: State University of New York Press, 1987.

Brown, Christopher, Jan Kelch, and Pieter van Thiel. *Rembrandt: The Master and His Workshop: Paintings*. New Haven, CT: Yale University Press, 1991.

Brown, Francis, S. R. Driver, and Charles A. Briggs. *A Hebrew and English Lexicon of the Old Testament*. Oxford: Clarendon, [1980].

Brown, Raymond E. *The Gospel According to John (i-xii)*, The Anchor Bible, vol.29.Garden City, NY: Doubleday, 1966.

———. *The Gospel According to John (xiii-xxi)*, The Anchor Bible, vol. 29A. Garden City, NY: Doubleday, 1970.

Bruce, F. F. *The Gospel of John: Introduction, Exposition and Notes*. Grand Rapids, MI: Eerdmans, 1983.

Bryce, Trevor. *The Kingdom of the Hittites*. Oxford: Clarendon, 1998.

Buchanan, George Wesley. *To the Hebrews: Translation, Comment and Conclusions*, The Anchor Bible, vol. 36. Garden City, NY: Doubleday, 1972.

Budge, Ernest A. Wallis, ed. *The Book of the Bee*, Anecdota Oxoniensia: Semitic Series, vol. I, part II. Oxford: The Clarendon, 1886.

———, translator. *The Book of the Cave of Treasures: A History of the Patriarchs and the Kings Their Successors from the Creation to the Crucifixion of Christ*. London: The Religious Tract Society, 1927.

———, ed. *The Book of the Mysteries of the Heavens and the Earth and Other Works of Bakhayla Mika'el (Zosimas)*. London: Oxford University Press, 1935.

———. *The Chronography of Gregory Abu'l-Faraj 1225–1286, the Son of Aaron, the Hebrew Physician Commonly Known as Bar Hebraeus*. 2 vols. Amesterdam: APA-Philo Press, 1932 [1976 Reprint].

———, translator. *The Queen of Sheba and Her Only Son Menyelek*. London: Martin Hopkinson, 1922.

———, *The Egyptian Book of the Dead: The Papyrus of Ani in the British Museum*. Mineola, New York: Dover, 1967.

Buttrick, George Arthur, ed. *The Interpreter's Dictionary of the Bible: An Illustrated Encyclopedia*. 5 vols. Nashville: Abingdon, 1985 [1962].

Buxbaum, Yitzhak. *The Life and Teachings of Hillel*. Lanham, Maryland: Rowman and Littlefield, 1994 [2004].

Callaway, Mary Chilton. *Sing O Barren One: A Study in Comparative Midrash*. Columbia University, Ph.D. Dissertation, 1979, University Microfilms International facsimile, 1983.

Callendar, Dexter E. Jr. *Adam in Myth and History: Ancient Israelite Perspectives on the Primal Human*, Harvard Semitic Studies. Winona Lake, IN: Eisenbrauns, 2000.

Calmet, Augustin. A*n Historical, Critical, Geographical, Chronological, and Etymological Dictionary of the Holy Bible, in Three Volumes*. 3 vols. London: J. J. and P. Knapton et al., 1732.

Carruthers, Leo, ed. *Heroes and Heroines in Medieval English Literature*. Cambridge: D. S. Brewer, 1994.

Charles, R. H. *The Apocrypha and Pseudepigrapha of the Old Testament Pseudepigrapha*. 2 vols. Oxford: Clarendon, 1913 [1979 reprint].

———. *The Book of Enoch*. Oxford: The Clarendon, 1893.

———. *A Critical and Exegetical Commentary on the Revelation of St. John*, The International Critical Commentary. 2 vols. Edinburgh: T. and T. Clark, 1920 [1989 reprint].

Charlesworth, James H., ed.. *The Old Testament Pseudepigrapha*. 2 vols. Garden City, NY: Doubleday, 1983–85.

Chavel, Charles B., translator and annotator. *Encyclopedia of Torah Thoughts*. New York: Shilo Publishing House, 1980.

———, translator and annotator. *Ramban (Nachmanides): Commentary on the Torah*. 5 vols. New York: Shilo Publishing House, 1971.

The Church of Jesus Christ of Latter-day Saints. [Pamphlet]. Salt Lake City: Intellectual Reserve, Inc., 2003.

Cirlot, J. E. *A Dictionary of Symbols*. London: Routledge and Kegan Paul 1971 [Barnes and Noble reprint, 1995].

Clark, James R., ed. *Messages of the First Presidency* vol. 5. Salt Lake City: Bookcraft, 1971.

Clayton, Peter A. *Chronicles of the Pharaohs: The Reign-by-Reign Record of the Rulers and Dynasties of Ancient Egypt*. London: Thames and Hudson, 1994.

Cohen, Abraham, and Jacob Neusner. *Everyman's Talmud: The Major Teachings of the Rabbinic Sages*. New York: Schocken Books, 1995.

Cohen, A. *Proverbs*, Soncino Books of the Bible. London: The Soncino Press, 1946 [1980 reprint].

Cohen, Arthur A., and Paul Mendes-Flohr, eds. *Contemporary Jewish Religious Thought: Original Essays on Critical Concepts, Movements, and Beliefs*. New York: The Free Press, 1987.

Collins, Adela Yarbro. *Cosmology and Eschatology in Jewish and Christian Apocalypticism*, Supplements to the Journal for the Study of Judaism, vol. 50. Leiden: Brill, 1996.

Colson, F. H., G. H. Whitaker, and Ralph Marcus. *Philo*, The Loeb Classical Library. 12 vols. Cambridge, MA: Harvard University Press, n.d.

Cotterell, Arthur. *Chariot: From Chariot to Tank, the Astounding Rise and Fall of the World's First War Machine*. Woodstock: The Overlook Press, 2004.

Cowley, Robert, ed. *What If?: The World's Foremost Historians Imagine What Might Have Been*. New York: Putnam, 1999.

———, ed. *What If? 2: Eminent Historians Imagine What Might Have Been*. New York: Putnam, 2001.

Cragg, Kenneth. *Readings in the Qur'an*. London: Collins, 1988.

Crane, Frank, ed. *Lost Books of the Bible and the Forgotten Books of Eden*. Cleveland, Ohio: World Publishing Company, 1926.

Crothers, Samuel. *Abraham the First Missionary*. Chillicothe, Ohio: Ely and Allen, 1847.

Crouzel, Henri. *Origen*. San Francisco: Harper and Row, 1989.

Culi, Yaakov, Yitzchok Magriso, and Yitzchok Behar Argueti. *The Torah Anthology: MeAm Lo'ez*. 17 vols. New York: Maznaim, 1977–84.

Daniélou, Jean. *Primitive Christian Symbols*. Baltimore, Maryland: Helicon Press, 1964.

Davidson, Herbert A. *Moses Maimonides: The Man and His Works*. Oxford: Oxford University Press, 2005.

Davis, Avram, ed. *The Metsudah Chumash/Rashi*. Hoboken, NJ: Ktav Publishing House, 1997.

Dan, Joseph. *The 'Unique Cherub' Circle: A School of Mystics and Esoterics in Medieval Germany*, Texts and Studies in Medieval and Early Modern Judaism 15. Tübingen: J. C. B. Mohr (Paul Siebeck), 1999.

Dawood, N. J. translator. *The Koran*, 4th rev. ed. Middlesex, England: Penguin Books, 1974.

Day, John. *God's Conflict with the Dragon and the Sea: Echoes of a Canaanite Myth in the Old Testament*. Cambridge: Cambridge University Press, 1985 [1988 reprint].

Dennis, Trevor. *Sarah Laughed*. Nashville: Abingdon, 1994.

Denny, Frederick Mathewson. *An Introduction to Islam*. New York: Macmillan, 1985.

Derrida, Jacques. *The Gift of Death*, Religion and Postmodernism. Chicago: University of Chicago Press, 1996.

Deutsch, Nathaniel. *The Gnostic Imagination: Gnosticism, Mandaeism, and Merkabah Mysticism*, Brill's Series in Jewish Studies, vol. 13. Leiden: Brill, 1995.

Dick, Michael B., ed. *Born in Heaven, Made on Earth: The Making of the Cult Image in the Ancient Near East*. Winona Lake, IN: Eisenbrauns, 1999.

Doane, A. N. *The Saxon Genesis: An Edition of the West Saxon Genesis B and the Old Saxon Vatican Genesis*. Madison, Wisconsin: University of Wisconsin Press, 1991.

Doron, Pinchas. *Rashi's Torah Commentary: Religious, Philosophical, Ethical, and Educational Insights*. Northvale, NJ: Jason Aronson, 2000.

Doxey, Roy W., ed. *Latter-day Prophets and the Doctrine and Covenants*. 4 vols. Salt Lake City: Deseret Book, 1978.

Dreifuss, Gustav, and Judith Riemer. *Abraham: The Man and the Symbol*. Wilmette, Illinois: Chiron, 1995.

Drew, David. *The Lost Chronicles of the Maya Kings*. Berkeley: University of California Press, 1999.

Driver, S. R. *The Book of Genesis*, Westminster Commentaries. London: Methuen, 1904.

Edmunds, John K. *Through Temple Doors*. Salt Lake City: Bookcraft, 1978.

Ehat, Andrew F., and Lyndon W. Cook, eds. *The Words of Joseph Smith: The Contemporary Accounts of the Nauvoo Discourses of the Prophet Joseph Smith*, Religious Studies Monograph Series, vol. 6. Provo, UT: Religious Studies Center, Brigham Young University, 1980.

Eisenberg, Evan. *The Ecology of Eden*. New York: Alfred A. Knopf, 1998.

Eisenman, Robert. *The Dead Sea Scrolls and the First Christians: Essays and Translations*. Shaftesbury, Dorset: Element, 1996.

Eldad, Israel, and Moshe Aumann. *Chronicles: News of the Past*. 3 vols., Jerusalem: Reubeni Foundation, 1968–1972.

El-Masudi's *Historical Encyclopedia Entitled "Meadows of Gold and Mines of Gems,"* vol. 1. London: Oriental Translation Fund, 1841.

Ellingworth, Paul. *The Epistle to the Hebrews: A Commentary on the Greek Text*, The New International Greek Testament Commentary. Grand Rapids, MI: Eerdmans; and Carlisle, England: Patnernoster Press, 1993.

Ellis, Peter F. *The Yahwist: The Bible's First Theologian*. Notre Dame: Fides Publishers, 1968.

Encyclopaedia Judaica. 17 vols. Corrected ed. Jerusalem: Keter Publishing House.

Epstein, I., ed. *Hebrew-English Edition of the Babylonian Talmud*, new ed. 30 vols. London: Soncino Press, 1987–90.

Faier, Zvi, ed. *Malbim: Commentary on the Torah*. 4 vols. Israel: M.P. Press, in conjunction with Hillel Press, 1982.

Farbridge, Maurice H. *Studies in Biblical and Semitic Symbolism*, The Library of Biblical Studies. New York: Ktav Publishing House, 1970.

Faurling, Scott H, Kent P. Jackson, and Robert J. Matthews, *Joseph Smith's New Translation of the Bible*. Salt Lake City: Deseret Book Company, 2004.

Feeley-Harnick, Gillian. *The Lord's Table: Eucharist and Passover in Early Christianity*, Symbol and Culture. Philadelphia: University of Pennsylvania Press, 1981.

Feiler, Bruce. *Walking the Bible: A Journey by Land through the Five Books of Moses*. New York: William Morrow, 2001.

Feldman, Louis H. translator and commentator. *Flavius Josephus: Translation and Commentary, Volume 3, Judean Antiquities 1–4*. Leiden: Brill, 2000.

Finkel, Avraham Yaakov. *The Torah Revealed: Talmudic Masters Unveil the Secrets of the Bible*. San Francisco: Jossey-Bass, 2004.

Firestone, Reuven. *Journeys in Holy Lands: The Evolution of the Abraham-Ishmael Legends in Islamic Exegesis*. Albany: State University of New York Press, 1990.

Fitzmeyer, Joseph A. *The Genesis Apocryphon of Qumran Cave 1: A Commentary*, 2nd ed. rev. Biblica et Orientalia 18A. Rome: Biblical Institute Press, 1971.

Fitzmeyer, Joseph A. *The Gospel According to Luke 1–9*, The Anchor Bible, vol. 28. Garden City, NY: Doubleday, 1981.

Fitzmeyer, Joseph A. *The Gospel According to Luke (10–24)*, The Anchor Bible, vol. 28A. Garden City, NY: Doubleday, 1985 [1986 reprint].

Fossum, Jarl E. *The Name of God and the Angel of the Lord: Samaritan and Jewish Concepts of Intermediation and the Origin of Gnosticism*, Wissenschaftliche Untersuchungen zum Neuen Testament 36. Tübingen: J. C. B. Mohr (Paul Siebeck), 1985.

Fox, Everett. *The Five Books of Moses*, The Shocken Bible: vol. 1. New York: Shocken Books, 1995.

Fox, Michael V., ed. *Temple in Society*. Winona Lake, IN: Eisenbrauns, 1988.

Frankfort, Henri. *The Birth of Civilization in the Near East*. Bloomington: Indiana University Press, 1959.

Freedman, David Noel, ed. *The Anchor Bible Dictionary*. 6 vols. New York: Doubleday, 1992.

Freedman, H., ed. *Midrash Rabbah, Genesis*, 3rd ed. 2 vols. London: Soncino Press, 1983.

———, ed. *Midrash Rabbah, Leviticus*, 3rd ed., vol. 4 London: Soncino Press, 1983.

———, ed. *Midrash Rabbah, Numbers*, 3rd ed. London: Soncino Press, 1983.

———, ed. *Midrash Rabbah, Song of Songs*, 3rd ed. London: Soncino Press, 1983.

Friedlander, Gerald. *Pirke de Rabbi Eliezer*, 4th ed. New York: Sepher-Hermon Press, 1981.

Gaebelein, Frank E. *The Expositor's Bible Commentary*. 7 vols. Grand Rapids, MI: Regency Reference Library, Zondervan, 1992.

Galbraith, Richard C., and Joseph Fielding Smith, eds. *Scriptural Teachings of the Prophet Joseph Smith*. Salt Lake City: Deseret Book, 1993.

Gaster, Moses, ed. *The Asatir: The Samaritan Book of the "Secrets of Moses."* London: Royal Asiatic Society, 1927.

———, ed. *The Chronicles of Jerahmeel; or, The Hebrew Bible Historiale*. New York: Ktav Publishing House, 1971.

———. *Studies and Texts: In Folklore, Magic, Mediaeval Romance, Hebrew Apocrypha and Samaritan Archæology*. 3 vols. New York: Ktav Publishing House, 1971.

Gee, John, and Brian M. Hauglid, eds. *Astronomy, Papyrus, and Covenant*, Studies in the Book of Abraham, No. 3. Provo, UT: Foundation for Ancient Research and Mormon Studies, 2005.

Gemser, B., et al. *Studies on the Book of Genesis*, Oudtestamentische Studiën: Namens Het Oudtestamentisch Werkgezelschap in Nederland, Deel 12. Leiden: Brill, 1958.

Gibson, Margaret Dunlop. *Apocrypha Arabica*, Studia Sinaitica No. 8. London: C. J. Clay and Sons, Cambridge University Press Warehouse, 1901.

Gileadi, Avraham. *The Literary Message of Isaiah*. New York: Hebraeus Press, 1994.

Ginsburg, Christian D. *The Essenes: Their History and Doctrines* and *The Kabbalah: Its Doctrines, Development and Literature*. New York: Macmillan, 1956.

Ginzberg, Louis. *The Legends of the Jews*. 7 vols. Philadelphia: Jewish Publication Society of America, 1912–38.

Glenn, Mendel G. *Jewish Tales and Legends: Supplementary Readings to the Torah*. New York: Hebrew Publishing, 1929.

Goldman, Solomon. *In the Beginning*, The Book of Human Destiny, vol. 2. Philadelphia: Jewish Publication of Society, 1949.

Glueck, Nelson. *Hesed in the Bible*. Cincinnati: Hebrew Union College Press,1967.

Goff, Beatrice L. *Symbols of Ancient Egypt in the Late Period: The Twenty-first Dynasty*, Religion and Society, vol.13. The Hague, Netherlands: Mouton, 1979.

Goodenough, Erwin R. *An Introduction to Philo Judaeus*, 2nd ed. Oxford: Basil Blackwell, 1962.

Gordon, Cyrus H., and Gary A. Rendsburg. *The Bible and the Ancient Near East*, 4th ed. New York: Norton, 1997.

Gorion, Micha Joseph bin. *Mimekor Yisrael: Classical Jewish Folktales*. 2 vols. Bloomington: Indiana University Press, 1976.

Granzotto, Gianni. *Christopher Columbus*. Garden City, NY: Doubleday, 1985.

Graves, Robert, and Raphael Patai, *Hebrew Myths: The Book of Genesis*. New York: McGraw-Hill, 1966.

Green, Arthur. *Devotion and Commandment: The Faith of Abraham in the Hasidic Imagination*. Cincinnati: Hebrew Union College Press, 1989.

Groenewegen-Frankfort, H. A. *Arrest and Movement: An Essay on Space and Time in the Representational Art of the Ancient Near East*. New York: Hacker Art Books, 1978 [1972].

Grossfeld, Bernard. *The Targum Onqelos to Genesis: Translated, with a Critical Introduction and Notes*, The Aramaic Bible, vol. 6. Wilmington, Delaware: Michael Glazier, 1988.

Gruen, Erich S. *Heritage and Hellenism: The Reinvention of Jewish Tradition*, Hellenistic Culture and Society, vol. 30. Berkeley: University of California Press, 1998.

Gunkel, Hermann. *Genesis*. Mercer Library of Biblical Studies. Macon, Georgia: Mercer University Press, 1997.

Guthrie, D., and J. A. Motyer, eds. *The Eerdmans Bible Commentary*, 3rd ed. Grand Rapids, MI: Eerdmans, 1970 [1987 reprint].

Gutwirth, Israel. *The Kabbalah and Jewish Mysticism*. New York: Philosophical Library, 1987.

Hadas-Lebel, Mireille. *Flavius Josephus: Eyewitness to Rome's First-Century Conquest of Judea*. New York: Macmillan, 1993.

Haldar, Alfred. *Associations of Cult Prophets among the Ancient Semites*. Uppsala: Almqvist and Wiksells Boktryckeri AB.

Hanauer, J. E. *Folk-Lore of the Holy Land: Moslem, Christian and Jewish*. London: Duckworth, 1907.

Hannah, Darrell D. *Michael and Christ: Michael Traditions and Angel Christology in Early Christianity*, Wissenschaftliche

Untersuchungen zum Neuen Testament—2 Reihe 109. Tübingen: Mohr Siebeck, 1999.

Harris, James R. *An Historical and Doctrinal Commentary on the Pearl of Great Price.* Orem, UT: Harris House, 1999.

Harris, Maurice H., ed. *Hebraic Literature: Translations from the Talmud, Midrashim and Kabbala.* New York: Tudor, 1939.

Haug, Martin. *Essays on the Sacred Language, Writings, and Religion of the Parsis,* 3rd ed.. London: Kegan Paul, Trench Trubner, ca 1883.

Hayden, Dorothea Hoaglin. *The Love of Abraham and Sarah.* Pasadena, 1935.

Hendel, Ronald. *Remembering Abraham: Culture, Memory, and History in the Hebrew Bible.* Oxford: Oxford University Press, 2005.

Hershon, Paul Isaac. *A Rabbinical Commentary on Genesis.* London: Hodder and Stoughton, 1885.

Hertz, J. H. *The Pentateuch and Haftorahs: Hebrew Text, English Translation and Commentary,* 2nd ed. London: Soncino Press, 1981.

Himmelfarb, Martha. *Ascent to Heaven in Jewish and Christian Apocalypses.* New York: Oxford University Press, 1993.

Hinckley, Gordon B. *Teachings of Gordon B. Hinckley.* Salt Lake City: Deseret Book, 1997.

Hirsch, Samson Raphael. *T'rumath Tzvi: The Pentateuch.* New York: Judaica Press, 1986.

Hobbs, Mary, ed. *The Sermons of Henry King (1592–1669), Bishop of Chichester.* Rutherford, NJ: Farleigh Dickinson University Press, 1992.

Hoffman, Lawrence E., ed., *My People's Prayer Book: Traditional Prayers, Modern Commentaries: Vol. 4—Seder K'riat Hatorah (The Torah Service).* Woodstock, VT: Jewish Lights, 2000.

Holbrook, Isabel R. *Studies on the Book of Enoch,* No. 1. Rockland, MA: n.d.

Hollander, H. W. and M. de Jonge. *The Testaments of the Twelve Patriarchs: A Commentary.* Studia in Veteris Testamenti Pseudepigrapha, vol. 8. Leiden: Brill, 1985.

Holy Bible: The New King James Version. Nashville: Thomas Nelson Publishers, 1982.

The Holy Bible: Translated from the Latin Vulgate. Rockford, IL: TAN Books, 1899 [reprint].

The Holy Qur'an: With English Translation and Commentary. 5 vols. Islamabad: Islam International Publications, 1988.

Hooke, S. H., ed. *Myth, Ritual, and Kingship: Essays on the Theory and Practice of Kingship in the Ancient Near East and in Israel.* Oxford: Clarendon, 1958.

Hornung, Eric. *Conceptions of God in Ancient Egypt.* Ithaca, NY: Cornell University Press, 1982.

Horton, Fred L. Jr. *The Melchizedek Tradition: A Critical Examination of the Sources to the Fifth Century A.D. and in the Epistle to the Hebrews,* Society for the New Testament Studies Monograph Series 30. Cambridge: Cambridge University Press, 1976.

Hunter, Milton R. *The Gospel Through the Ages.* Salt Lake City: Stevens and Wallis, 1945.

Hutchinson, Thomas ed. *Wordsworth: Poetical Works,* new ed. Oxford: Oxford University Press, 1969 [1984 reprint].

Inman, Thomas. *Ancient Faiths Embodied in Ancient Names.* 2 vols. London, 1868.

Jacob, B. (Ernest I. Jacob and Walter Jacob, eds.). *Genesis: The First Book of the Bible.* New York: Ktav Publishing House, 1974.

Jacobson, Howard. *A Commentary on Pseudo-Philo's Liber Antiquitatum Biblicarum: With Latin Text and English Translation,* Arbeiten Zur Geschichte Des Antiken Judentums und Des Urchristentums 31. 2 vols. Leiden: Brill, 1996.

James, E. O. "The Sacred Kingship and the Priesthood," in *The Sacral Kingship: Contributions to the Central Theme of the VIIIth International Congress for the History of Religions Rome, April 1955.* Leiden: Brill, 1959.

James, Montague Rhodes. *The Apocryphal New Testament.* Oxford: Clarendon, 1953, corrected [1966 reprint].

———. *The Biblical Antiquities of Philo,* The Library of Biblical Studies: Translations of Early Documents, Series I: Palestinian Jewish Texts (Pre-Rabbinic). New York: Ktav Publishing House, 1971.

———. *The Lost Apocrypha of the Old Testament: Their Titles and Fragments,* Translations of Early Documents, Series I: Palestinian Jewish Texts (Pre-Rabbinic). London: Society for Promoting Christian Knowledge, 1920.

———. *The Testament of Abraham: The Greek Text Now First Edited with an Introduction and Notes,* Texts and Studies, vol. 2, no. 2.Cambridge: Cambridge University Press, 1892 [1967 reprint by Kraus Reprint].

Jessee, Dean C., ed. *The Papers of Joseph Smith: Volume 1: Autobiographical and Historical Writings.* Salt Lake City: Deseret Book, 1989.

Jobes, Karen H., and Moises Silva. *Invitation to the Septuagint.* Grand Rapids, MI: Baker Book House, 2000.

Joseph Smith's New Translation of the Bible. Independence, Missouri: Herald Publishing House, 1970.

Joseph Smith Translation of the Bible, in Joseph Smith Jr., *The Holy Scriptures,* new corrected ed. Independence, Missouri: Herald Publishing House, 1944 [1967 reprint].

Rabbi Joseph, the son of Abraham Gikatilla. *Sha'are Orah: Gates of Light,* The Sacred Literature Series. San Francisco: HarperCollins, 1994.

Josephus III. The Loeb Classical Library 210. Cambridge, MA: Harvard University Press, 1979.

———. *The Jewish War, Books IV–VII.* The Loeb Classical Library 210. Cambridge, MA: Harvard University Press, 1979.

Josephus IV: Jewish Antiquities, Books 1–4. The Loeb Classical Library 242. Cambridge, MA: Harvard University Press, 1978.

Journal of Discourses. 26 vols. London: Latter-day Saints Book Depot, 1854–1886.

Kaplan, Aryeh, ed. *The Bahir.* York Beach, Maine: Samuel Weiser, 1979 [1989 reprint].

———. *Sefer Yetzirah: The Book of Creation.* York Beach, Maine: Samuel Weiser, 1990.

Kasher, Menahem M. *Encyclopedia of Biblical Interpretation: A Millennial Anthology.* 9 vols. New York: American Biblical Encyclopedia Society, 1953–79.

Kathir, Al-Imam Ibn. *Stories of the Prophets.* Mansoura, Egypt: El Nour, n.d.

Kenney, Scott G., ed. *Wilford Woodruff's Journal: 1833–1893 Typescript.* 9 vols. Midvale, UT: Signature Books, 1983.

Khatib, M. M. translator. *The Bounteous Koran: A Translation of Meaning and Commentary.* Authorized by Al-Azhar, 1984. London: Macmillan, 1986.

Kierkegaard, Søren. *Fear and Trembling and Sickness unto Death.* Princeton, NJ: Princeton University Press, 1968 [1973 printing].

Kimball, Edward L., ed. *The Teachings of Spencer W. Kimball.* Salt Lake City: Bookcraft, 1982.

Kimball, Spencer W. *Faith Precedes the Miracle.* Salt Lake City: Deseret Book, 1975.

Kittel, Gerhard, and Gerhard Friedrich, eds. *Theological Dictionary of the New Testament.* 10 vols. Grand Rapid, MI: Eerdmans, 1964–76.

Klein, Michael L. *The Fragment Targums of the Pentateuch: According to Their Extant Sources*, Analecta Biblica: Investigationes Scientificae in Res Biblicas 76. 2 vols. Rome: Biblical Institute Press, 1980.

Klinghoffer, David. *The Discovery of God: Abraham and the Birth of Monotheism.* New York: Doubleday, 2003.

Knappert, Jan. *Islamic Legends: Histories of the Heroes, Saints and Prophets of Islam*, Religious Texts Translation Series, Nisaba, vol. 15:1–2. 2 vols. Leiden: Brill, 1985.

Knibb, Michael A. in consultation with Edward Ullendorff. *The Ethiopic Book of Enoch: A New Edition in Light of the Aramaic Dead Sea Fragments.* 2 vols. Oxford: Clarendon, 1978 [1982 reprint].

Kosofsky, Scott-Martin. *The Book of Customs: A Complete Handbook for the Jewish Year.* New York: HarperSanFrancisco, 2004.

Kraus, Hans-Joachim. *Psalms 1–59: A Commentary.* Minneapolis: Augsburg Publishing House, 1988, 89.

———. *Theology of the Psalms.* Minneapolis: Augsburg Publishing House, 1988.

Kugler, Robert A., and Eileen M. Schuller. *The Dead Sea Scrolls at Fifty: Proceedings of the 1997 Society of Biblical Literature Qumran Section Meetings*, Society of Biblical Literature: Early Judaism and Its Literature, no. 15. Atlanta: Scholars Press, 1999.

Kvanig, Helge S. *Roots of Apocalyptic: The Mesopotamian Background of the Enoch Figure and of the Son of Man*, Wissenschaftliche Monographien zum Alten und Neuen Testament, vol. 61. Neukirchen-Vluyn: Neukirchener Verlag des Erziehungsvereins GmbH, 1988.

Lachower, Fischel, and Isaiah Tishby. *The Wisdom of the Zohar: An Anthology of Texts.* 3 vols. Oxford: Littman Library, Oxford University Press, 1989.

Lamsa, George M. translator. *Holy Bible from the Ancient Eastern Text: George M. Lamsa's Translations from the Aramaic of the Peshitta.* San Francisco: Harper and Row, 1968.

Lattimore, Richmond translator. *The New Testament.* New York: North Point Press, 1996.

Lauterbach, Jacob Z., ed. *Mekilta de Rabbi Ishmael*, The Schiff Library of Jewish Classics. 3 vols. Philadelphia: Jewish Publication Society of America, 1949.

Lectures on Faith. Salt Lake City: Deseret Book, 1985.

Leibowitz, Nehama. *Studies in Bereshit (Genesis): In the Context of Ancient and Modern Jewish Bible Commentary*, 7th revised ed. Jerusalem: World Zionist Organization, 1985.

Letellier, Robert Ignatius. *Day in Mamre, Night in Sodom: Abraham and Lot in Genesis 18 and 19*, Biblical Interpretation Series, vol. 10. Leiden: Brill, 1995.

Levenson, Jon D. *The Death and Resurrection of the Beloved Son: The Transformation of Child Sacrifice in Judaism and Christianity.* New Haven, CT: Yale University Press, 1993.

———. *Sinai and Zion: An Entry into the Jewish Bible*, New Voices in Biblical Studies. Minneapolis: Winston Press, 1985.

Levine, Baruch. A. *Leviticus*, The JPS Torah Commentary. Philadelphia: Jewish Publication Society, 1989.

Levner, J. B. *The Legends of Israel*, vol. 1. London: James Clarke, 1946.

Levy, Benjamin. *A Faithful Heart: Preparing for the High Holy Days.* A Study Based on the Midrash Maaseh Avraham Avinu. New York: UAHC Press, 2001.

Liebes, Yehuda. *Studies in Jewish Myth and Jewish Messianism*, SUNY Series in Judaica: Hermeneutics, Mysticism, and Religion. Albany, NY: State University of New York Press, 1993.

Liber, Maurice. *Rashi.* Philadelphia: Jewish Publication Society of America, 1906.

The Living Bible Paraphrased: A Thought-for-Thought Translation. Wheaton, Illinois: Tyndale Publishing House, 1971 [1985 reprint].

L'Orange, H. P. *Studies on the Iconography of Cosmic Kingship in the Ancient World*, Instituttet for Sammenlignende Kulturforskning, Serie A: Forelesninger, 23. Oslo: H. Aschehoug, 1953.

Lord, John. *Beacon Lights of History, First Series. Jewish Heroes and Prophets.* New York: Fords, Howard, and Hulbert, 1888.

Ludlow, Daniel H., ed. *Encyclopedia of Mormonism.* 5 vols. New York: Macmillan, 1992.

Lunden, C. E. *Abraham and the Life of Faith.* BTP, n.d.

Lundwall, N. B., ed. *Temples of the Most High.* Salt Lake City: Bookcraft, 1968 [1974 reprint].

Mach, Rudolf. *Der Zaddik in Talmud und Midrasch.* Leiden: Brill, 1957.

Madsen, Truman G. *Joseph Smith the Prophet.* Salt Lake City: Bookcraft, 1989.

Maher, Michael ed. *Targum Pseudo-Jonathan: Genesis*, The Aramaic Bible, vol. 1B. Collegeville, MN: Liturgical Press, 1992.

Maimonides. *Mishneh Torah.* 27 vols. New York: Moznaim, 1989.

———. *Mishneh Torah: Hilchot De'ot and Hilchot Talmud Torah.* New York: Moznaim, 1989.

Malan, S. C., ed. *The Book of Adam and Eve, Also Called the Conflict of Adam and Eve with Satan.* London: Williams and Norgate, 1882. The text is now usually known as the Combat of Adam and Eve with Satan.

Malek, Jaromir. *In the Shadow of the Pyramids: Egypt during the Old Kingdom.* Norman: University of Oklahoma Press, 1986.

Manhar, Nurho de. *Zohar (Bereshith– Genesis): An Expository Translation from Hebrew.* San Diego: Wizards Bookshelf, 1978.

Marcus, Amy Dockser. *The View from Nebo: How Archeology is Rewriting the Bible and Reshaping the Middle East.* Boston: Little, Brown, and Co., 2000.

Martinez, Florentino Garcia, and Eibert J. C. Tigchelaar. *The Dead Sea Scrolls Study Edition.* 2 vols. Leiden: Brill, 1997–1998.

Mason, Steve, ed. *Flavius Josephus: Translation and Commentary.* Projected 10 vols. Leiden: Brill, 2000– .

Mastro, M. L. del. *All the Women of the Bible.* Edison, New Jersey: Castle Books, 2004.

Matt, Daniel C. *The Zohar, Pritzker Edition.* Multi-vol. Stanford, CA: Stanford University Press, 2004–.

Matthews, Edward G., Jr., translator. *The Armenian Commentary on Genesis Attributed to Ephrem the Syrian,* Corpus Scriptorum Christianorum Orientalium, vol. 573, Scriptores Armeniaci, tomus 24. Lovanii: In Aedibus Peeters, 1998.

Matthews, Robert J. *A Bible! A Bible!* Salt Lake City: Bookcraft, 1990.

———. *Joseph Smith's Translation of the Bible: A History and Commentary.* Provo, UT: Brigham Young University Press, 1975.

Mawadudi, Sayyd Abul A'la. *Towards Understanding the Qur'an,* vol. 1. Leicester, United Kingdom: Islamic Foundation, n.d.

McAuliffe, Jane Dammen, ed. *Encyclopaedia of the Qur'an.* 5 vols. Leiden: Brill, 2001–2005.

McConkie, Bruce R. *Doctrinal New Testament Commentary.* 3 vols. Salt Lake City, 1966–73.

———. *Mormon Doctrine,* 2nd ed. Salt Lake City: Bookcraft, 1966 [1970 reprint].

———. *A New Witness for the Articles of Faith.* Salt Lake City: Deseret Book, 1985.

McConkie, Joseph Fielding. *His Name Shall Be Joseph: Ancient Prophecies of the Latter-day Seer.* Salt Lake City: Hawkes Publishing, 1980.

McKay, David O. *Pathways to Happiness.* Salt Lake City: Bookcraft, 1957.

McNamara, Martin. *Targum Neofiti 1: Genesis,* The Aramaic Bible, vol. 1A. Edinburgh: T. and T. Clark, 1992.

Meiggs, Russell. *Trees and Timber in the Ancient Mediterranean World.* Oxford: Clarendon, 1998 [1982].

Meier, Rabbi Levi. *Ancient Secrets: Using the Stories of the Bible to Improve Our Everyday Lives.* Woodstock, VT: Jewish Lights, 1996.

Mensch, E. Cromwell. *King Solomon's "First" Temple.* San Francisco: Ernest Cromwell Mensch, 1947.

Metzger, Bruce M., and Roland E. Murphy. *The New Oxford Annotated Bible: New Revised Standard Version.* New York: Oxford University Press, 1991.

Meyer, Heinrich August Wilhelm. *Critical and Exegetical Handbook of the Gospels of Mark and Luke.* New York: Funk and Wagnalls, 1884.

Meyers, Eric M. *The Oxford Encyclopedia of Archaeology in the Near East.* 5 vols. New York: Oxford University Press, 1997.

Milik, J. T. *The Books of Enoch: Aramaic Fragments of Qumrân Cave 4.* Oxford: Clarendon, 1976.

Miller, Amos W. *Abraham Friend of God: An Ethical Biography of the Founder of the Jewish People.* New York: Johathan David, 1973.

Miller, William T. *Mysterious Encounters at Mamre and Jabbok,* Brown Judaic Studies, No. 50. Chico, CA: Scholars Press, 1984.

Mitchell, Stephen. *Genesis: A New Translation of the Classic Biblical Stories.* New York: HarperCollins, 1996.

Montefiore, C.G., and H. Loewe. *A Rabbinic Anthology.* New York: Schocken Books, 1974.

Moorey, P. R. S. *Ur "of the Chaldees": A Revised and Updated Edition of Sir Leonard Woolley's Excavations at Ur.* Ithaca, NY: Cornell University Press, 1982.

Morenz, Siegfried. *Egyptian Religion.* Ithaca, NY: Cornell University Press, 1973.

Morfill, W. R., and R. H. Charles. *The Book of the Secrets of Enoch.* Oxford: Clarendon, 1896.

Morris, Henry M. *The Genesis Record: A Scientific and Devotional Commentary on the Book of Beginnings.* Grand Rapids, MI: Baker Book House, 1976 [1987 reprint].

Motyer, J. Alec. *The Prophecy of Isaiah: An Introduction and Commentary.* Downers Grove, Illinois: InterVarsity Press, 1993.

Moyers, Bill. *Genesis: A Living Conversation.* New York: Doubleday, 1996.

Mulder, Martin Jan, and Harry Sysling, eds., *Mikra: Text, Translation, Reading and Interpretation of the Hebrew Bible in Ancient Judaism and Early Christianity,* Compendia Rerum Iudaicarum ad Novum Testamentum, Section Two, vol. 1. Assen/Maastricht: Van Gorcum, 1984.

Müller, W. Max. *Egyptian Mythology.* London: George G. Harrap, n.d.

Munk, Rabbi Elie. *The Call of the Torah.* 2 vols. Jerusalem: Feldheim Publishers, 1980.

Munk, Eliyahu, ed. *Aqaydat Yitzchaq: Commentary of Rabbi Yitzchaq Arama on the Torah.* 2 vols. Jerusalem: Rubin Mass, 1986.

Munk, Michael L. *The Wisdom in the Hebrew Alphabet: The Sacred Letters as a Guide to Jewish Deed and Thought,* 2nd ed., ArtScroll Mesorah Series. Brooklyn: Mesorah, 1983 [1990 reprint].

Myers, Allen C. revised ed. *The Eerdmans Bible Dictionary.* Grand Rapids, MI: Eerdmans, 1987.

Nasr, Seyyed Hossein. *Islamic Spirituality: Foundations,* World Spirituality: An Encyclopedic History of the Religious Quest, vol. 19. New York: Crossroad, 1987.

Neusner, Jacob. *Confronting Creation: How Judaism Reads Genesis: An Anthology of Genesis Rabbah.* Columbia, South Carolina: University of South Carolina Press, 1991.

———. *Genesis and Judaism: The Perspective of Genesis Rabbah: An Analytical Anthology,* Brown Judaic Studies, No. 108. Atlanta: Scholars Press, 1985.

———. *Genesis Rabbah: The Judaic Commentary to the Book of Genesis: A New American Translation,* Brown Judaic Studies, No. 105. 3 vols. Atlanta: Scholars Press, 1985.

————. *Invitation to the Talmud*, revised and expanded ed. New York: Harper and Row, 1989.

New American Standard Bible. Nashville: Holman Bible Publishers, 1981.

The New Encyclopædica Britannica. Chicago: Encyclopædia Britannica, 1997.

New International Version, in *The NIV Study Bible: New International Version*. Grand Rapids, MI: Zondervan, 1985.

New Jerusalem Bible, in *The New Jerusalem Bible*. Garden City, NY: Doubleday, 1985.

Nibley, Hugh. *Abraham in Egypt*, 2nd ed., The Collected Works of Hugh Nibley: vol. 14. Salt Lake City: Deseret Book; and Provo, UT: Foundation for Ancient Research and Mormon Studies at Brigham Young University, 2000.

————. *Abraham's Creation Drama* (transcript). Provo, UT: Foundation for Ancient Research and Mormon Studies at Brigham Young University, 1999.

————. *The Ancient State*, The Collected Works of Hugh Nibley: vol. 10. Salt Lake City: Deseret Book, and Provo, UT: Foundation for Ancient Research and Mormon Studies at Brigham Young University, 1991.

————. *Approaching Zion*, The Collected Works of Hugh Nibley, vol. 9. Salt Lake City: Deseret Book, and Provo, UT: Foundation for Ancient Research and Mormon Studies at Brigham Young University, 1989.

————. *Enoch the Prophet*, The Collected Works of Hugh Nibley, vol. 2. Salt Lake City: Deseret Book, and Provo, UT: Foundation for Ancient Research and Mormon Studies at Brigham Young University, 1986.

————. *The Message of the Joseph Smith Papyri: An Egyptian Endowment*. Salt Lake City: Deseret Book, 1975.

————. *Mormonism and Early Christianity*, The Collected Works of Hugh Nibley: vol. 4. Salt Lake City: Deseret Book, and Provo, UT: Foundation for Ancient Research and Mormon Studies, 1987.

————. *Old Testament and Related Studies*, The Collected Works of Hugh Nibley, vol. 1. Salt Lake City: Deseret Book, and Provo, UT: Foundation for Ancient Research and Mormon Studies at Brigham Young University, 1986.

————. *Teachings of the Pearl of Great Price*. Provo, UT: Foundation of Ancient Research and Mormon Studies, 1986.

————. *Temple and Cosmos: Beyond This Ignorant Present*, The Collected Works of Hugh Nibley: vol. 12, Ancient History. Salt Lake City: Deseret Book, and Provo, UT: Foundation for Ancient Research and Mormon Studies at Brigham Young University, 1992.

————. *The World and the Prophets*, 3rd ed., The Collected Works of Hugh Nibley: vol. 3: Mormonism and Early Christianity. Salt Lake City: Deseret Book, and Provo, UT: Foundation for Ancient Research and Mormon Studies, 1987.

Nibley, Preston. *Sharing the Gospel with Others*, ed. Salt Lake City: Deseret News Press, 1948.

Noah, Mordecai Manuel, ed. *The Book of Yashar*. New York: Hermon, 1972.

Noble, W. F. P. *The Great Men of God: Biographies of Patriarchs, Prophets, Kings and Apostles*. New York: Nelson and Phillips, 1876.

North, Christopher R. *The Second Isaiah: Introduction, Translation and Commentary to Chapters 40–55*. Oxford: Clarendon, 1977 [1964].

Nyman, Monte S. and Robert L. Millet, eds. *The Joseph Smith Translation: The Restoration of Plain and Precious Things*, The Religious Studies Monograph Series, vol. 12. Provo, UT: Religious Studies Center, Brigham Young University, 1985.

O'Neill, John. *The Night of the Gods: An Inquiry into Cosmic and Cosmogonic Mythology and Symbolism*, vol. 1. London: Harrison and Sons, 1893.

Ochs, Vanessa L. *Sarah Laughed: Modern Lessons from the Wisdom & Stories of Biblical Women*. New York: McGraw-Hill, 2004.

Odeberg, Hugo. *3 Enoch, or The Hebrew Book of Enoch*. Cambridge: Cambridge University Press, 1928. Other translations of 3 Enoch are cited separately.

Oden, Thomas C., ed. *Ancient Christian Commentary on Scripture: Old Testament*. Multi-vol. Downers Grove, IL: InterVarsity Press, 2001–.

Origen: Homilies on Genesis and Exodus, The Fathers of the Church: A New Translation, vol. 71. Washington, DC: Catholic University of America Press, 1982.

Ouaknin, Marc-Alain. *Mysteries of the Kabbalah*. New York: Abbeville, 2000.

Oxenden, Ashton. *Portraits from the Bible: Old Testament Series*. London: Wertheim, MacIntosh, and Hunt, 1860.

Packer, Boyd K. *The Holy Temple*. Salt Lake City: Bookcraft, 1980.

Padwick, Constance E. *Muslim Devotions: A Study of Prayer-Manuals in Common Use*. Oxford: Oneworld, 1996.

Papus (Gérard Encausse). *The Qabalah: Secret Tradition of the West*, Studies in Hermetic Tradition, vol. 4. New York: Samuel Weiser, 1977.

Parry, Donald W. *Temples of the Ancient World: Ritual and Symbolism*. Salt Lake City: Deseret Book, and Provo, UT: Foundation for Ancient Research and Mormon Studies, 1994.

Patai, Raphael. *The Arab Mind*, revised ed. New York: Charles Scribner's Sons, 1983.

————. *The Jewish Alchemists: A History and Source Book*. Princeton, NJ: Princeton University Press, 1994.

————. *The Jewish Mind*. New York: Charles Scribner's Sons, 1977.

————. *Man and Temple: In Ancient Jewish Myth and Ritual*. London: Thomas Nelson and Sons, 1947.

Pauls, Michael, and Dana Facaros. *Turkey*, Cadogan Guides. London: Cadogan Books, 1986.

Pelikan, Jaroslav., ed. *Luther's Works*. 55 vols. Saint Louis: Concordia, 1958–89.

Pell, Edward Leigh. *The Story of Abraham as Told by Isaac*. Pell's Bible Stories. New York: Fleming H. Revell, 1920.

Petersen, Mark E. *Abraham: Friend of God*. Salt Lake City: Deseret Book, 1979.

Philo III, The Loeb Classical Library. London: William Heinemann, 1988.

Philo VI, The Loeb Classical Library 289. London: William Heinemann, 1966 [1935].

Philo Supplement I, The Loeb Classical Library. Cambridge, MA: Harvard University Press, 1979.

Plaut, W. Gunther, Bernard J. Bamberger, and William W. Hallo. *The Torah: A Modern Commentary*. New York: Union of American Hebrew Congregations, 1981.

Podhoretz, Norman. *The Prophets: Who They Were, What They Are*. New York: Free Press, 2002.

Poncé, Charles. *Kabbalah*. Wheaton, Illinois: Theosophical Publishing House, 1973.

Poncé, Denys. *The Churches of the Crusader Kingdom of Israel*. 2 vols. Cambridge: Cambridge University Press, 1993–98.

Pritchard, James B. *Ancient Near Eastern Texts Relating to the Old Testament*, 3rd ed. with supplement. Princeton: Princeton University Press, 1969.

The Prophet and His Work: Essays from General Authorities on Joseph Smith and the Restoration. Salt Lake City: Deseret Book, 1996.

Poncé, James. *Egyptology: An introduction to the History, Art and Culture of Ancient Egypt*. London: Grange Books, 1995 [1990].

Posener, G., J. Bottéro, and Kathleen Kenyon. *The Cambridge Ancient History: Syria and Palestine, Revised Edition of Volumes 1 and 2 (Volume 1, Chapter 21)*. Cambridge: Cambridge University Press, 1965.

Rabadan, Mahomet. *Mahometism Fully Explained*. 2 vols. London: W. Mears, 1723.

Rad, Gerhard von. *Genesis: A Commentary*, rev. ed., The Old Testament Library. Philadelphia: Westminster Press, 1972.

Rappaport, Angelo S. *Ancient Israel: Myths and Legends, 3 Volumes in 1*. New York: Bonanza Books, 1987.

Rashi. *The Pentateuch and Rashi's Commentary: A Linear Translation into English: Genesis*. Brooklyn: S. S. and R. Publishing Company, 1949.

Redford, Donald B., ed. *The Oxford Encyclopedia of Ancient Egypt*. 3 vols. Oxford: Oxford University Press, 2001.

Reeves, John C. *Heralds of That Good Realm: Syro-Mesopotamian Gnosis and Jewish Traditions*, Nag Hammadi and Manichaean Studies 41. Leiden: Brill, 1996.

———. *Tracing the Threads: Studies in the Vitality of Jewish Pseudepigrapha*, Early Judaism and Its Literature, no. 6. Atlanta: Scholars Press, 1994.

Rendtorff, Rolf. *Men of the Old Testament*. London: SCM Press, 1968.

The Revised English Bible with the Apocrypha. Oxford University Press and Cambridge University Press, 1989.

Ricks, Stephen D., Donald W. Parry, and Andrew H. Hedges. *The Disciple as Witness: Essays on Latter-day Saint Doctrine in Honor of Richard Lloyd Anderson*. Provo, UT: Foundation for Ancient Research and Mormon Studies at Brigham Young University, 2000.

Ritner, Robert Kriech. *The Mechanics of Ancient Egyptian Magical Practice*, Studies in Ancient Oriental Civilizations, no. 54. Chicago: The Oriental Institute of the University of Chicago, 1993.

Rose, Norman. *Churchill: The Unruly Giant*. New York: Free Press, 1994.

Rosenberg, David. *Genesis: As It Is Written: Contemporary Writers on Our First Stories*. New York: HarperSanFrancisco, 1996.

Rowley, H. H. *Worship in Ancient Israel: Its Forms and Meaning*. Philadelphia: Fortress Press, 1967.

Safrai, Shmuel. *The Literature of the Sages, First Part: Oral Tora, Halakha, Mishna, Tosefta, Talmud, External Tractates*, Compendia Rerum Iudaicarum ad Novum Testamentum, Section Two, vol. 3. Assen/Maastricht: Van Gorcum, 1987.

Saint John Chrysostom: Homilies on Genesis 18–45, The Fathers of the Church: A New Translation, vol. 82. Washington, DC: Catholic University of America Press, 1990.

Saleh, Walid A. *The Formation of the Classical Tafsir Tradition: The Qur'an Commentary of al-Tha'labi (d. 427/1035)*, Texts and Studies on the Qur'an, vol. 1. Leiden: Brill, 2004.

Sandmel, Samuel. *Philo of Alexandria: An Introduction*. New York: Oxford University Press, 1979.

Sarna, Nahum M. *Genesis*, The JPS Torah Commentary. Philadelphia: Jewish Publication Society, 1989.

Sawyer, Deborah F. *Midrash Aleph Beth*, South Florida Studies in the History of Judaism, no. 39. Atlanta: Scholars Press, 1993.

Schaff, Philip, and Henry Wace, eds. *Nicene and Post-Nicene Fathers, Second Series*. Grand Rapids, MI: Eerdmans, reprint 1983.

Scherman, Rabbi Nosson, and Rabbi Meir Zlotowitz. *Bereishis: Genesis—A New Translation with a Commentary Anthologized from Talmudic, Midrashic and Rabbinic Sources*, 2nd ed., ArtScroll Tanach Series: A Traditional Commentary on the Books of the Bible. 2 vols., 1(a) and 1(b). Brooklyn, NY: Mesorah, 1986 [2002].

Schiffman, Lawrence A. and James C. VanderKam, eds. 2 vols., *Encyclopedia of the Dead Sea Scrolls*. Oxford: Oxford University Press, 2000.

Schimmel, Annemarie. *And Muhammad Is His Messenger: The Veneration of the Prophet in Islamic Piety*, Studies in Religion. Chapel Hill: University of North Carolina Press, 1985.

———. *Mystical Dimensions of Islam*. Chapel Hill: University of North Carolina Press, 1975.

Scholem, Gershom G. *Jewish Gnosticism, Merkabah Mysticism, and Talmudic Tradition*, 2nd ed. New York: Jewish Theological Seminary of America, 1965.

———. *Kabbalah*. New York: Meridian, 1974.

———. *Major Trends in Jewish Mysticism*. New York: Shocken Books, 1971.

———. *On the Kabbalah and Its Symbolism*. New York: Shocken Books, 1965.

———, ed. *Zohar: The Book of Splendor*. New York: Shocken Books, 1949.

Schram, Peninnah. *Stories within Stories: From the Jewish Oral Tradition*. Northvale, NJ: Jason Aronson, 2000.

Schwartz, Howard. *Tree of Souls: The Mythology of Judaism*. Oxford: Oxford University Press, 2004.

Scott, Jamie, and Paul Simpson-Housley, eds. *Sacred Places and Profane Spaces: Essays in the Geographies of Judaism, Christianity, and Islam*, Contributions to the Study of Religion, no. 30. New York: Greenwood, 1991.

Segal, J. B. *Edessa: "The Blessed City."* Oxford: Clarendon, 1970.

Seters, John Van. *Abraham in History and Tradition*. New Haven, CT: Yale University Press, 1975.

Shereshevsky, Esra. *Rashi: The Man and His World*. New York: Sepher–Hermon Press, 1982.

Shulman, Yaakov David. *The Rambam: The Story of Rabbi Moshe ben Maimon*. CIS, 1994.

———. *The Ramban: The Story of Rabbi Moshe ben Nachman*. CIS, 1993.

Silverman, David P., ed. *Ancient Egypt*. New York: Oxford University Press, 1997.

Simonhoff, Harry. *And Abraham Journeyed*. South Brunswick: Thomas Yoseloff, 1967.

Singer, Isidore, ed. *The Jewish Encyclopedia*. 12 vols. New York: Funk and Wagnalls, 1905.

Skinner, John. *A Critical and Exegetical Commentary on Genesis*, 2nd ed., The International Critical Commentary. Edinburgh: T. and T. Clark, 1930 [1980 reprint].

Smith, Joseph. *History of the Church of Jesus Christ of Latter-day Saints*, 2nd ed. rev. 7 vols. Salt Lake City: Deseret Book, 1932–51.

———. *The Holy Scriptures: Containing the Old and New Testaments, An Inspired Revision of the Authorized Version*, New Corrected Edition. Independence, MO: Herald Publishing House, 1944.

Smith, Joseph Fielding. *Doctrines of Salvation*. 3 vols. Salt Lake City: Bookcraft, 1954–56.

———. *Essentials in Church History*, 27th ed. Salt Lake City: Deseret Book, 1974.

Smith, Lucy Mack. *History of Joseph Smith by His Mother, Lucy Mack Smith*. Salt Lake City: Bookcraft, 1958.

Soloveitchik, Rabbi Joseph B. *Man of Faith in the Modern World: Reflections of the Rav*, vol. 2. Hoboken, NJ: Ktav Publishing House, 1989.

Sparks, H. F. D., ed. *The Apocryphal Old Testament*. Oxford: Clarendon, 1984.

Speiser, E. A. *Genesis*, The Anchor Bible, vol. 1, 3rd ed. Garden City, NY, 1979.

Sperling, Harry, and Maurice Simon, translators, *The Zohar*, 2nd ed. 5 vols. London: Soncino Press, 1984. Other translations of the Zohar are cited separately.

Spiegel, Shalom. *The Last Trial: On the Legends and Lore of the Command to Abraham to Offer Isaac as a Sacrifice: The Akedah*. Philadelphia: Jewish Publication Society of America, 1967.

Sprengling, Martin, and William Creighton Graham. *Barhebraeus' Scholia on The Old Testament: Part I*, The University of Chicago, Oriental Institute Publications, vol. 13. Chicago: University of Chicago Press, 1931.

Spretnak, Charlene, *States of Grace: The Recovery of Meaning in the Postmodern Age*. New York: HarperSanFrancisco, 1991.

Staalduine-Sulman, Eveline van. *The Targum of Samuel*, Studies in the Aramaic Interpretation of Scripture, vol. 1. Leiden: Brill, 2002.

Steinsaltz, Adin. *Biblical Images: Men and Women of the Book*. New York: Basic Books, Publishers, 1984.

———. *A Guide to Jewish Prayer*, Israel Institute for Talmudic Publications. New York: Shocken Books, 2000.

———. *The Talmud: The Steinsaltz Edition*. Multi-vol. New York: Random House.

Stone, Michael E. *Armenian Apocrypha Relating to the Patriarchs and Prophets*. Jerusalem: The Israel Academy of Sciences and Humanities, 1982.

———. *Fourth Ezra: A Commentary on the Book of Fourth Ezra*, Hermeneia—A Critical and Historical Commentary on the Bible. Minneapolis: Fortress Press, 1990.

———., ed. *Jewish Writings of the Second Temple Period: Apocrypha, Pseudepigrapha, Qumran Sectarian Writings, Philo, Josephus*, Compendia Rerum Iudaicarum ad Novum Testamentum, Section Two, vol. 2. Assen: Van Gorcum, 1984.

Stone, Michael E., and Theodore A. Bergen, eds. *Biblical Figures outside the Bible*. Harrisburg, Pennsylvania: Trinity Press International, 1998.

Strachan, James. *Hebrew Ideals from the Story of the Patriarchs: A Study of Old Testament Faith and Life*, two parts in one volume. Edinburgh: T. and T. Clark, 1902.

Strack, H. L., and G. Stemberger. *Introduction to the Talmud and Midrash*, revised ed. Minneapolis: Fortress Press, 1992.

Strickland, Agnes. *Tales from English History*. Philadelphia: Porter and Coates, n.d.

Strouhal, Eugen. *Life of the Ancient Egyptians*. Norman: University of Oklahoma Press, 1992.

Stuckenbruck, Loren T. *The Book of the Giants from Qumran: Texts, Translation, and Commentary*, Texte und Studien zum Antiken Judentum 63. Tübingen: Mohr Siebeck, 1997.

Stuy, Brian H., ed. *Collected Discourses Delivered by President Wilford Woodruff, His Two Counselors, the Twelve Apostles, and Others*. B. H. S. Publishing, 1987–1992.

Suarès, Carlo. *The Qabala Trilogy: The Cipher of Genesis, The Song of Songs, The Sepher Yetsira*. Boston: Shambala, 1985.

Talmud Bavli: The Schottenstein Edition, The Artscroll Talmud. Multi-volume. Brooklyn: Mesorah, n.d.

Tanakh: A New Translation of the Holy Scriptures According to the Traditional Hebrew Text. Philadelphia: Jewish Publication Society, 1985.

Taylor, C. *The Teaching of the Twelve Apostles*. Cambridge: Deighton Bell and Co., 1886.

Thackeray, H. St. J. *Josephus*. The Loeb Classical Library. 9 vols. Cambridge, MA: Harvard University Press.

Toorn, Karel van der, Bob Becking, and Pieter W. van der Horst, eds. *Dictionaries of Deities and Demons in the Bible*, 2nd ed. Leiden: Brill, 1999.

Trigg, Joseph W. *Origen*, The Early Church Fathers. London: Routledge, 1998.

Tuchman, Shera Aranoff and Sandra E. Rapoport. *The Passions of the Matriarchs*. Jersey City, NJ: Ktav Publishing House, 2004.

Tvedtnes, John A., Brian M. Hauglid, and John Gee, eds. *Traditions about the Early Life of Abraham, Studies in the Book of Abraham*. Provo, UT: Foundation for Ancient Research and Mormon Studies, Brigham Young University, 2001.

Tyndale, William. *Tyndale's Old Testament: Being the Pentateuch of 1530, Joshua to 2 Chronicles of 1537, and Jonah*. New Haven,

CT: Yale University Press, 1992.

Unterman, Alan. *Dictionary of Jewish Lore and Legend*. London: Thames and Hudson, 1991.

Urbach, Ephraim E. *The Sages: Their Concepts and Beliefs*. Cambridge, MA: Harvard University Press, 1987.

VanderKam, James C. *The Book of Jubilees*, Corpus Scriptorum Christianorum Orientalium, vol. 511, Scriptores Aethiopici, tomus 88. Lovanii: In Aedibus E. Peeters, 1989.

———. *Enoch: A Man for All Generations*. Columbia, South Carolina: University of South Carolina Press, 1995.

———. *Enoch and the Growth of an Apocalyptic Tradition*, The Catholic Biblical Quarterly Monograph Series 16. Washington, DC: The Catholic Biblical Association of America, 1984.

VanderKam, James C., and William Adler, eds. *The Jewish Apocalyptic Heritage in Christianity*, Compendia Rerum Iudaicarum ad Novum Testamentum, section 3, vol. 4. Assen: Van Gorcum, 1996.

Vaughan, Curtis. *Twenty-six Translations of the Bible*. 3 vols. Atlanta: American Home Libraries, 1967.

Vawter, Bruce. *On Genesis: A New Reading*. Garden City, NY: Doubleday, 1977.

Vermes, Geza. *The Complete Dead Sea Scrolls in English*. New York: Allen Lane, Penguin, 1997.

Visotzky, Burton L., translator. *The Midrash on Proverbs*, Yale Judaica Series, vol. 27. New Haven, CT: Yale University Press, 1992.

Wainwright, G. A. *The Sky-Religion in Ancient Egypt: Its Antiquity and Effects*. Cambridge: Cambridge University Press, 1938.

Waszink, J. H., and J. C. M. Van Winden. *Tertullianus De Idololatria: Critical Text, Translation and Commentary*, Supplements to Vigiliae Christianae: Texts and Studies of Early Christian Life and Language, vol. 1. Leiden: Brill, 1987.

Watts, John D. W. *Isaiah 1–33*, Word Biblical Commentary, vol. 24. Waco, TX: Word Books, 1985.

———. *Word Biblical Commentary, Volume 25: Isaiah 34–66*. Waco, TX: Word Books, 1987.

Wedderburn, A. J. M. *Baptism and Resurrection: Studies in Pauline Theology against Its Graeco-Roman Background*, Wissenschaftliche Untersuchungen zum Neuen Testament 44. Tübingen: J. C. B. Mohr (Paul Siebeck), 1987.

Weitzmann, Kurt, and Herbert L. Kessler. *The Cotton Genesis: British Library Codex Cotton Otho B.VI*, The Illustrations in the Manuscripts of the Septuagint, vol. 1: Genesis. Princeton: Princeton University Press, 1986.

Wenham, Gordon J. *Genesis 1–15*, Word Biblical Commentary, vol. 1. Waco, TX: Word Books, 1987.

———. *Genesis 16–50*, Word Biblical Commentary, vol. 2. Dallas, TX: Word Books, 1994.

Westermann, Claus. *Genesis 1–11: A Commentary*. Minneapolis: Augsburg Publishing House, 1984.

———. *Genesis 12–36: A Commentary*. Minneapolis: Augsburg Publishing House, 1985.

———. *Isaiah 40–66: A Commentary*. The Old Testament Library. Philadelphia: Westminster Press, 1969.

Wheeler, Brannon M. *Prophets in the Quran: An Introduction to the Quran and Muslim Exegesis*. London: Continuum, 2002.

Whiston, William, translator. *Josephus: The Complete Works*. Nashville: Thomas Nelson Publishers, 1998.

White, J. E. Manchi. *Ancient Egypt: Its Culture and History*. New York: Dover, 1970.

Widengren, Geo. *The Ascension of the Apostle and the Heavenly Book (King and Saviour 3)*, Uppsala Universitets Årsskrift 1950:7. Uppsala: A. B. Lundequistka Bokhandeln, 1950.

Widstoe, John A., ed. *Gospel Doctrine: Selections from the Sermons and Writings of Joseph F. Smith*. Salt Lake City: Deseret Book, 1939.

Wiesel, Elie. *And the Sea Is Never Full: Memoirs, 1969–* .New York: Alfred A. Knopf, 1999.

———. *Messengers of God: Biblical Portraits and Legends*. New York: Pocket Books, 1977.

Wildberger, Hans. *Isaiah 13–27*, A Continental Commentary. Minneapolis: Fortress Press, 1997.

Wilkinson, *Reading Egyptian Art: A Hieroglyphic Guide to Ancient Egyptian Painting and Sculpture*. New York: Thames and Hudson, 1992.

Williams, Clyde J., ed. *The Teachings of Harold B. Lee*. Salt Lake City: Bookcraft, 1996.

Williams, Frank transl. *The Panarion of Epiphanius of Salamis: Book I (Sects 1–46)*, Nag Hammadi Studies 35. Leiden: Brill, 1987.

Williams, John Alden. *Islam*, Great Religions of Modern Man. New York: George Braziller.

Wise, Michael, Martin Abegg Jr.,and Edward Cook. *The Dead Sea Scrolls: A New Translation*. New York: HarperSanFrancisco, 1996.

Wolfson, Elliot R. *Through a Speculum that Shines: Vision and Imagination in Medieval Jewish Mysticism*. Princeton, NJ: Princeton University Press, 1994.

Woolley, C. Leonard. *Abraham: Recent Discoveries and Hebrew Origins*. London: Faber and Faber Limited, n.d. [1936].

———. *Ur of the Chaldees: A Record of Seven Years of Excavation*. London: Ernest Benn, 1929.

Wordsworth, Chr[istopher]. *The Holy Bible, in the Authorized Version; with Notes and Introductions*, 3rd ed. 6 vols. London: Rivingtons, Waterloo Place, 1869–1871.

Yadin, Yigael. *The Art of Warfare in Biblical Lands*. 2 vols. New York: McGraw-Hill, 1963.

Yonge, C. D. translator. *The Works of Philo: Complete and Unabridged (New Updated Edition)*. Peabody, Pennsylvania: Hendrickson, 1993.

Young, James Calvin de. *Jerusalem in the New Testament: The Significance of the City in the History of Redemption and in Eschatology*, Vrije Universiteit Te Amsterdam. Kampen: J. H. Kok N. V., 1960.

Young, Joseph Sen. *History of the Organization of the Seventies. Enoch and His City*. Salt Lake City: Deseret News Steam Printing Establishment, 1878; reprint [Roy, UT]: Eborn Books, 1992.

Young, Robert. *Young's Literal Translation of the Holy Bible*, rev.ed. Grand Rapids, MI: Baker Book House, n.d.

Zimmerli, Walther. *Ezekiel 2: A Commentary on the Book of the Prophet Ezekiel Chapters 25–48*, Hermeneia—A Critical and

Historical Commentary on the Bible. Philadelphia: Fortress Press, 1983.
Zornberg, Avivah Gottlieb. *Genesis: The Beginning of Desire*. Philadelphia: Jewish Publication Society, 1995.
———. *The Particulars of Rapture: Reflections on Exodus*. New York: Doubleday, 2001.

Index

List of Illustrations

1. Canonteign, Devon (w/c on paper), Abbott, John White (1764–1851) / © Birmingham Museums and Art Gallery,;/Bridgeman Art Library.

2. *Facsimile 1* Courtesy of The Church Archives, The Church of Jesus Christ of Latter-day Saints.

3. *Old Testament Prophet* © Judith Mehr.

4. *The Prayer of Jacob*, engraving by Gustave Doré, *The Doré Bible Illustrations,* Dover Publications.

5. *Facsimile 3* Courtesy of The Church Archives, The Church of Jesus Christ of Latter-day Saints.

6. *The Meeting of Abraham and Melchizedek, Rubens,* Peter Paul, Sir (Flemish, 1577–1640), Gift of Syma Busiel, © Board of Trustees. National Gallery of Art, Washington.

7. *Abram and the Angel,* Lord Frederic Leighton, from Illustrations for 'Daziel's Bible Gallery,' engraved by the Dalziel Brothers, © Tate, London 2005.

8. Caspar Luiken, *Historiae celebriores Veteris Testamenti Iconibus representatae* (Nuremberg, 1712). Courtesy of the Pitts Theology Library, Candler School of Theology, Emory University.

9. *Facsimile 2* Courtesy of The Church Archives, The Church of Jesus Christ of Latter-day Saints.

10. *The Sacrifice of Abraham,* 1635 (oil on canvas), Rembrandt Harmensz. Van Rijn, (1606–69) / (studio of) / Hermitage, St. Petersburg, Russia, ; / Bridgeman Art Library.

11. *The Burial of Sarah,* engraving by Gustave , *The Doré Bible Illustrations,* Dover Publications.

12. *The First Vision* by Kenneth Riley © Intellectual Reserve, Inc.